# ONE AN

# The Cornish
# in
# New South Wales

## Patricia Lay

Heritage 2000 Plus

Requests and inquiries concerning reproduction and rights should be addressed to the publisher:

*Heritage 2000 Plus*

PO Box 1604, Queanbeyan,
NSW 2620, Australia.

ISBN 0 9588684 9 2

Cover illustrations:
Byng, New South Wales and Bodmin Moor, Cornwall.

Printed by Copy-Qik Print
40 Allara Street, Canberra City. ACT. 2600

# CONTENTS

# ILLUSTRATIONS AND MAPS

# ABBREVIATIONS

| | |
|---|---|
| *ADB* | *Australian Dictionary of Biography* |
| AJCP | Australian Joint Copying Project |
| *AMHSJ* | *Journal and Proceedings of the Australian Methodist Historical Society* |
| *AMM* | *Australian Men of Mark* |
| ANU | Australian National University |
| ANUBLA | Australian National University Archives of Business and Labour |
| AONSW | Archives Office of New South Wales |
| AO REEL | Archives Office of New South Wales microfilm reel |
| *BA* | *Bathurst Advocate* |
| *BFP* | *Bathurst Free Press and Mining Journal* |
| *BGNSW* | *Bailliere's New South Wales gazetteer and road guide* [1866] |
| *BP* | *Bathurst Post* |
| *BT* | *Bathurst Times* |
| CE | Church of England |
| COL. SEC. | Colonial Secretary |
| C.P.S. | Clerk of Petty Sessions |
| *CWD* | *Central Western Daily* |
| GPDNSW | *Greville's official post office directory and gazetteer of New South Wales 1875-1877* |
| *JRAHS* | *Royal Australian Historical Society Journal and Proceedings* |
| J.P. | Justice of the Peace |
| LAH | Library of Australian History |
| *METHODIST* | *The Methodist* |
| MFICHE | microfiche |
| MFM | microfilm |
| MHR | Member of the House of Representatives [Australia] |
| ML | Mitchell Library, Sydney |
| ML MSS | Mitchell Library manuscript |
| MLA | Member of the Legislative Assembly [New South Wales] |
| MLC | Member of the Legislative Council [New South Wales] |
| *MM* | *Maitland Mercury* |
| NLA | National Library of Australia |
| NLA MS | National Library of Australia manuscript |
| *NMH* | *Newcastle Morning Herald and Miner's Advocate* |
| N.S.W. | New South Wales |
| NSWDJI | Index to immigration deposit journals |
| NSWLA | New South Wales Legislative Assembly |
| NSWLC | New South Wales Legislative Council |

| | |
|---|---|
| NSWRGI | New South Wales Registrar-General's microfiche index to births, deaths and marriages 1787-1905. (Baptisms and burials before 1856, births and deaths after 1856.) |
| *RCG* | *Royal Cornwall Gazette* |
| REEL | microfilm reel. Original material is not issued when microfilm is available. |
| *RICJ* | *Journal of the Royal Institution of Cornwall* |
| SAG | Society of Australian Genealogists |
| *SANDS* | *Sands Sydney and N.S.W. directory 1858-1933* |
| SLNSW | State Library of New South Wales |
| *SMH* | *Sydney Morning Herald* |
| *TCJ* | *Australian Town and Country Journal* |
| UCA | Uniting Church Archives and Research Centre |
| V&P | Votes and Proceedings |
| WB | *West Briton* |
| WBBL | *West Briton* extract, in R.M. Barton, *Life in Cornwall in the late nineteenth century,* Barton, Truro, 1972. |
| WBBM | *West Briton* extract, in R.M. Barton, *Life in Cornwall in the mid-nineteenth century,* Barton, Truro, 1971. |
| *1828 census* | M.R. Sainty and K.A. Johnson (eds.), *Census of New South Wales, November 1828,* Library of Australian History, Sydney, 1985. |

# ACKNOWLEDGEMENTS

I am indebted to the Australian National University, Canberra, for providing the opportunity for me to write the MA thesis from which this book is drawn, and to my former supervisor, Dr John Knott, for his encouragement and guidance. I was helped by discussions with Dr Mark Brayshay, Bernard Deacon, Bob Dunstone, Dr Shirley Fitzgerald, Professor L.E. Fredman, Robin Haines, Dr Philip Payton, Dr Richard Reid, Dr John Rowe and Jennifer Sloggett. Dr C. A. Price devised the system of name counts as a means of estimating the percentage of Cornish settlers in New South Wales, and kindly allowed me to include, in Appendix III, his explanation of that method. Dr Richard Reid gave me access to his extensive files and notes on nineteenth century immigration to New South Wales. Dr Gill Burke, Dr Kath Dermody and Dr Anthea Hyslop generously took time to read and comment upon the final draft of the thesis, and the Rev E.G. Clancy, Professor L.E. Fredman, Dr Charles Price and Dr John Rowe kindly read and commented upon some sections. I am grateful to Richard Gendall for permission to quote from his songs and to Ian Glanville for permission to use an illustration from his *St Just's Point* collection.

Other people have helped me in various ways. The late Mrs Joan Northey helped with the name counts of distinctive Cornish names in Sydney, Val Lyon drew the maps and Nell Berriman checked the *Australian Men of Mark* references in the volumes in Newcastle Region Public Library. Jim Gillespie gave advice and practical computing assistance and Lynn Farkas gave advice about indexing. Merle Beaman and Barbara Dietrich helped with word processing advice.

I wish to thank the staff at the Cornish Studies Library, the Royal Institution of Cornwall and Cornwall Record Office. I also wish to thank the staff of the Archives Office of New South Wales, the Menzies and Chifley Libraries at the Australian National University, the Australian National University Archives of Business and Labour, the State Library of New South Wales and the Mitchell Library, the National Library of Australia and the Uniting Church Archives and Research Centre.

I am also grateful to staff at the Bathurst District Historical Society, Bathurst Family History Society, the Clerk of Petty Sessions at Adelong, the Clerk of Petty Sessions at Cobar, Cobar Museum, Glen Innes Historical Society, Molong Historical Society, Newcastle Region Public Library, Orange Historical Society, Singleton Historical Society, the Society of Australian Genealogists, Tumut Public Library and the University of Newcastle Archives.

During my research trips to areas of Cornish settlement in New South Wales, many people generously offered hospitality and assistance, and willingly shared their knowledge of the district. I am particularly grateful to Mr Don and Mrs Nell Berriman, Mr Bill Broadsmith, Mrs Dot Clayworth, Mr Dominic Eagan, Mr Will and Mrs Barbara Hawke, Mrs Phyllis Hohnen, the Jeuken family, the late Mrs Mary Nesbitt, Mrs Mavis Newcombe, Mr and Mrs B.W. Thomas, Mr Roger and Mrs Sue Thomas, the Thirkettle family, Mrs Joy Prisk, Mr Ken and Mrs Trixie Prowse, Mrs Lyn Quince, Mrs Peggy Richards and Mr W. Snelson.

I am greatly indebted to the many Australians with Cornish ancestry who willingly gave information about their Cornish heritage. Their contributions are acknowledged in the bibliography.

My dear friends, Kaye Dunstone and Anne Greenham, provided friendship, support and humour during some very difficult years. I wish to thank my children, Christopher, Stephen and Catherine, for their support, understanding and practical help which have always been forthcoming in spite of their own study and other commitments. I am grateful to my mother, Beryl Crothers McCooey, not only for her unfailing encouragement, but also for my Cornish genes.

## PLATE 1.    Map of New South Wales

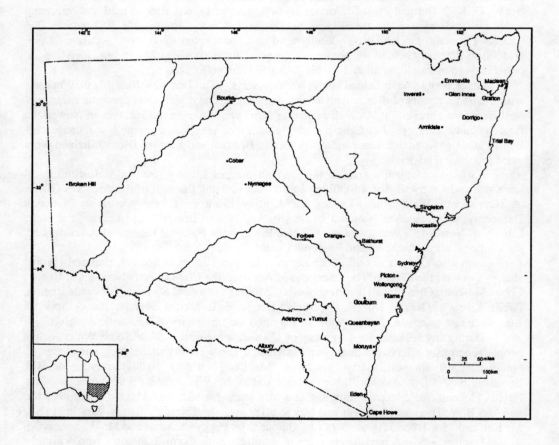

PLATE 2.    Map of New South Wales 1866

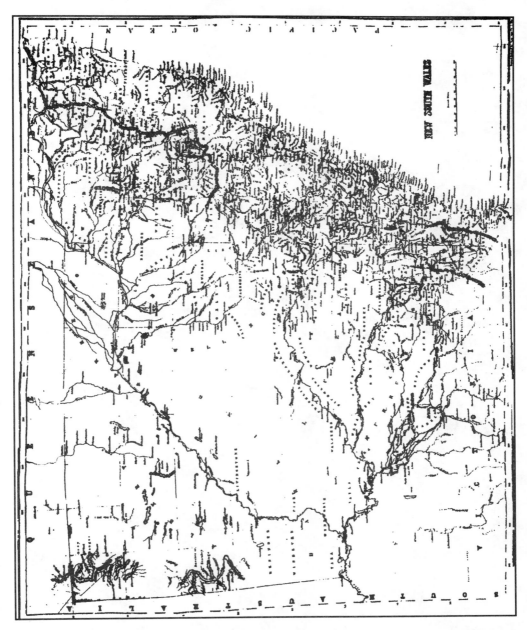

'Map of New South Wales 1866'. (From *The gazetteer of New South Wales 1866*, Sherriff and Downing, Sydney, courtesy of the State Library of New South Wales.)

# INTRODUCTION

Cornish immigrants arriving in nineteenth century New South Wales came from a homeland which, although administratively a county of England, was an ancient land whose people felt a pride in their Celtic heritage and in their difference from their Anglo-Saxon neighbours across the Tamar River. They had far more in common historically, linguistically and culturally, with their Welsh and Breton neighbours to the north and south than with the English to the east. Until Brunel's Royal Albert Bridge spanned the Tamar from Plymouth to Saltash in 1859, bringing the railway age to Cornwall, it had been largely isolated from the remainder of Britain.[1]

No doubt the centuries of isolation contributed to the Cornish characteristic of independence, and also helped the Cornish to retain their language and customs. Elements of the Cornish language survive in Cornish placenames and surnames, and in the distinctive Cornish-English dialect and intonation which even now mark the native of Cornwall as different from English neighbours. In addition, until quite recent times, Cornish Stannary Law was independent of British Law and for centuries tinners had been unaccustomed to recognising any other form of authority than that of their own Stannary Court and Parliament.[2]

Such factors contributed to produce independent, self-sufficient, adaptable and individualistic people (sometimes to the point of eccentricity, a quality which is certainly not denigrated in Cornwall). The Cornish were suspicious of officialdom and of imposed regimentation.[3] They were accustomed to hard work, often in severe climatic or occupational conditions. Many were deeply religious but others retained their superstitious customs. The Wesleys' ministry was very fruitful, influencing large numbers of Cornish who converted to Methodism.[4]

Industrially, Cornwall has long been different from other parts of Britain because of its specialised, limited industries. Cornwall was important as 'the birth-place and cradle of the Industrial Revolution'.[5] Nineteenth century Cornwall was a land dependent on mining, fishing and agriculture for its economic survival. A decline in any of these three affected the others. Although the mining industry produced tremendous technological expertise and practical experience, the early collapse of mining forced the export of personnel and knowledge to all parts of the world during the nineteenth century, as miners and others affected by the decline were forced to emigrate in search of work.

Much has been written on nineteenth century Cornish emigration to the United States of America, Mexico, and to some British colonies.[6] From these studies a pattern has emerged of Cornish emigration, where miners and those in associated trades settled together around

1    A. Bennett, *Cornwall through the mid nineteenth century*, Kingfisher Railway Productions, Southampton, 1987, pp.38-40.

2    J. Rowe, *Cornwall in the age of the Industrial Revolution*, Liverpool University Press, Liverpool, 1953, pp.314-15.

3    *WBBM*, p.7.

4    I. Haile, 'The Wesleys', in *Methodist celebration: a Cornish contribution*, S. Foott, (ed.), Dyllansow Truran, Redruth, 1988, pp.13-19.

5    P.J. Payton, *The Cornish miner in Australia: Cousin Jack Down Under*, Dyllansow Truran, Redruth, 1984, p.7.

6    J. Rowe, *The hardrock men: Cornish immigrants and the North American mining frontier*, Liverpool University Press, Liverpool, 1974. A.L. Rowse, *The Cornish in America*, MacMillan, London, 1969. A.C. Todd. *The Cornish miner in America: mining history of the United States by emigrant Cornish miners - the men called Cousin Jacks*, Barton, Truro, 1967. A.C. Todd, *The search for silver: Cornish miners in Mexico 1824-1927*, Lodenek, Padstow, 1977. G. Dickason, *Cornish immigrants to South Africa: the Cousin Jacks' contribution to the development of mining and commerce 1820-1920*, Balkema, Cape Town, 1978. G.C. Buckley, *Of toffs and toilers: from Cornwall to New Zealand:fragments of past*, Ross, Auckland, 1983.

the mines, working and living in a transplanted Cornish community, which reinforced and emphasised their Cornishness. This same pattern was repeated in New South Wales.

Until now, no comprehensive study has been made of Cornish emigration to New South Wales. There has been a study of Cornish settlement in Australia,[7] in South Australia[8] and also in Victoria.[9] Of course, studies of general and specific aspects of British immigration to Australia have been made[10] and there have been some detailed studies of specific ethnic or geographical groups from the British Isles.[11] Ross Duncan used sample studies to compare and contrast the 'push and pull' factors which influenced inhabitants of Cornwall and Gloucestershire to emigrate to New South Wales under government sponsorship between 1877 and 1886.[12]

Cornish Settlement, (later named Byng) between Orange and Bathurst, inspired several publications.[13] And of course, some local histories mention individual Cornish contributions to the district. Recently there have also been some family histories published by descendants of Cornish immigrants, while many more Australians of Cornish stock have gathered information (as yet unpublished) on their Cornish immigrant ancestors. This book draws on this material, which is a previously untapped source.

Cornish immigrants to New South Wales last century established and maintained recognisable and cohesive groups. There were several factors causing them to do this: their sense of Cornish identity (and their feelings of being different from English and Irish settlers), chain migration and intermarriage within the Cornish community in New South Wales, the shared job skills of farming, mining and trades (and in some cases because of specific recruitment), bonding on the long voyage by sailing ship, and their involvement in certain community activities such as religion, trade unions, lodges and friendly societies, and in politics.

Cornish immigrants to New South Wales fell into three separate groups which often overlapped, because members of the same family frequently used a combination of methods of emigrating, but they followed this pattern of settling together regardless of which of the three methods of emigration they used.

The first group consisted of those who came unassisted. Some of these came before the assisted schemes began, others did not qualify for assistance and so paid their own

7    P.J. Payton, 'Cornish', in *The Australian people: an encyclopaedia of the nation, its people and their origins*, James Jupp, (ed.), Angus and Robertson, North Ryde, 1988.

8    P.J. Payton, 'The Cornish in South Australia: their influence and experience in South Australia from immigration to assimilation 1836-1936', PhD., University of Adelaide, 1978. P.J. Payton, *The Cornish miner in Australia*. P.J. Payton, *The Cornish farmer in Australia or Australian adventure: Cornish colonists and the expansion of Adelaide and the South Australian agricultural frontier*, Dyllansow Truran, Redruth, 1987.

9    A. Colman, 'Colonial Cornish: Cornish immigrants in Victoria, 1865-1880', M.A., University of Melbourne, 1985. R. Hopkins, *Where now Cousin Jack?*, Bendigo Bicentennial Community Committee, Bendigo, Victoria, 1988.

10   F.K. Crowley, 'British migration to Australia 1860-1914', D.Phil., Oxford, 1951. E. Richards, R. Reid and D. Fitzpatrick, (eds.), *Visible immigrants: neglected sources for the history of Australian immigration*, Department of History and Centre for Immigration and Cultural Studies, Research School of Social Sciences, Australian National University, Canberra, 1989. E. Richards, (ed.), *Poor Australian immigrants in the nineteenth century: visible immigrants:two*, Department of Historical Studies and Centre for Immigration and Multicultural Studies, Research School of Social Sciences, Australian National University, Canberra, 1991.

11   For example, F. Chuk *The Somerset years: government-assisted emigrants from Somerset and Bristol who arrived in Port Phillip Victoria 1839-1854*, Pennard Hill Publications, Ballarat, Victoria, 1987. G. Kelly, (ed.), *The lacemakers of Calais*, Australian Society of the Lacemakers of Calais, Queanbeyan, N.S.W., 1990. These were Nottingham lacemakers who were living in Calais immediately prior to their emigration to Australia in 1848.

12   R. Duncan, 'Case Studies in Emigration: Cornwall, Gloucestershire and New South Wales, 1877-1886' in *The Economic History Review*, vol.XVI, 1963-4, pp.272-89.

13   J. Rule, *The Cornish Settlement*, the author, Yagoona, N.S.W., 1978. J. Rule, *The cradle of a nation: the truth about Ophir's gold discovery in 1851*, 2 vols., the author, Yagoona, N.S.W., 1979. Y. McBurney, *Road to Byng*, Educational Material Aid, Strathfield, N.S.W., 1982. (This publication relies almost entirely on quotes from George Hawke's diary, *Colonial experience*.)     M.K. Nesbitt, *James Trevarthen: Cornwall and New South Wales*, the author, Bathurst, N.S.W., 1986.

passages, while others came to New South Wales via other Australian colonies (although sometimes as assisted emigrants to another colony).

The second group consisted of those who were recruited by mining companies, or who came to government posts, or ministers of religion and others who were brought out to engage in a particular occupation. Convicts have not been included, except where known to have been the first link in the emigration chain.

The third group consisted of assisted emigrants who, theoretically, were expected to meet strict health and occupational criteria. Unforunately, detailed statistics are available only for this last group, assisted immigrants. The information provided by almost 4,000 government-assisted immigrants between 1837 and 1877 is used extensively here. The 40 years between 1837 and 1877 were chosen because comprehensive official records about assisted immigrants to New South Wales exist for these years, and because this period coincides with a time of tremendous social and economic upheaval in, and high world-wide emigration from, Cornwall. Also, it precedes the period between 1877 and 1886 used in Ross Duncan's sample study. These individuals could easily become the subject of a separate study, but they were only a proportion of the total Cornish emigration. Although it is impossible to be certain what proportion these assisted immigrants were of the Cornish community in New South Wales, fewer than half of the Cornish in the settlement areas studied were in this category.

Areas of Cornish settlement in New South Wales were identified by noting the residences of relatives already in the colony, as stated by assisted immigrants on arrival. The areas of settlement then selected for more detailed study were Bathurst-Orange, the Hunter Valley, and Sydney, where Cornish settlement began early and continued on a long-term basis. Other areas chosen for less detailed study were Adelong, northern New South Wales, the south coast and Cobar, where Cornish clustering occurred principally in the second half of the century.[14] Although Cobar was not commonly named as their intended place of residence by assisted emigrants, its relevance as an area of Cornish settlement became obvious as research progressed.

The definition of what actually constitutes being Cornish tends to vary.[15] For the purpose of consistency, being Cornish is defined here as having been born in Cornwall. On occasion, reference is also made to persons who were 'genetically Cornish' (although born elsewhere), but in such cases their places of birth are given.

This study investigates the physical, social, religious and occupational backgrounds from which Cornish immigrants originated, and it shows that it is this background which made them different from those belonging to other ethnic groups in New South Wales. The process of the bonding of immigrants, encouraged by experiences shared during the long, sometimes tedious and sometimes terrifying voyage to New South Wales, is also discussed.

Cornish settlement patterns in the colony are examined, with particular reference to occupational influences. The importance of personal factors and the influence of chain migration and intermarriage in the choice of settlement areas, and the links maintained among Cornish families in the colony are also discussed. This includes the extent to which choice was a consideration in occupational and personal influences. The title of the book *One and all: the Cornish in New South Wales* is a reference not only to the Cornish motto 'One and All', but also to the chain migration practised by so many Cornish immigrants – when one came, soon they all came.

---

14 The term 'cluster' is used to describe a recognisably Cornish group living, or living and working, in the same place. These groups varied in size and density, and the term is used where the density was greater than that in the general population of New South Wales. More information on the clusters and their density within the surrounding total population can be found in appendix II and appendix III.

15 At one extreme is the belief that to be Cornish one must be Cornish-born and also descended from generations of ancestors who were natives of Cornwall. At the other extreme is the view of the political party Mebyon Kernow ('Sons of Cornwall') which accepts as Cornish any persons who feel themselves to be Cornish. (C. Thomas, *The importance of being Cornish*, University of Exeter, Exeter, 1973, p.15.)

The religious affiliations of Cornish settlers were relevant to their settlement patterns. Cornish involvement in religious organisations, particularly Methodism, but also in other selected community groups, assisted in their eventual assimilation into the wider colonial community.

Details are given of those Cornish immigrants who achieved some degree of fame or prestige within the wider community and also of those who lived out their lives in relative obscurity, taking advantage of what their adopted country offered and in return contributing their own Cornish culture and background, as well as their skills and labour, to its development.

# CHAPTER ONE

## AN ANTIPODEAN MICROCOSM: CORNISH SETTLEMENT, BATHURST

*So let us all cry 'One and All!!'*
*Across twelve thousand miles of sea,*
*For Cornwall's there,*
*And Cornwall's here,*
*By the tall eucalyptus tree.*[1]

Early in January 1851, the inhabitants of the western New South Wales town of Bathurst marvelled as the first load of copper ore passed through their streets, en route to Sydney. The dray stopped:

> every forty or fifty yards ... surrounded by curious and
> admiring spectators. The bright ingots were handed about,
> examined, and their value freely speculated upon.

It was no coincidence that this valuable load was 'surmounted with a small banner bearing the Cornish coat of arms, with the motto "One and all" inscribed',[2] because the ore had come from a district known as Cornish Settlement west of Bathurst. As its name implies, Cornish Settlement was peopled almost exclusively by those of Cornish birth or descent, an antipodean microcosm of the homeland. The families who had lived there for more than twenty years still considered themselves to be Cornish men and women in an adopted country[3] which did not have 'the home associations with the recollections of my childhood and youth, the home of my kindred'.[4]

Cornish Settlement nestled in a tranquil, sheltered valley sixteen miles east of Blackman's Swamp (Orange), 28 miles west of Bathurst and 2 miles north of the coaching stop at Guyong on the main Bathurst-Wellington road.[5] The secluded valley in 1851 resembled Cornwall in many respects: it was isolated, its community was made up largely of Cornish Methodists, it operated a mixed farming-mining economy, and physically it looked as much like Cornwall as was possible in the Australian landscape.[6] The settlement's narrow lanes were edged with hawthorn hedges, there were avenues of oak, ash and other imported trees, and at the hub of the little community was the Methodist chapel.[7]

The settlement began as an agricultural community in 1829 following the earlier arrival in the Bathurst district of the brothers-in-law William Tom and William Lane and their families.[8] William and Ann Tom moved to the isolated valley in 1829, accompanied by George Hawke, who was tutor to the Tom children. John Glasson followed in 1830,[9] and they were soon joined by others from Cornwall. These pioneers expanded their farming

---

1 'Moonta, Wallaroo, Kadina', words and music by Richard Gendall.
2 *BFP*, 11 January 1851, p.4, c. 2-3.
3 John Glasson, *Letters 1828-1857*, with introduction by his grand-daughter, Mrs O. Phillips, typescript copy held at Bathurst Historical Society, letters 21 March 1834 and 22 May 1848, pp.46 and 96.
4 Ibid, letter 21 March 1834, p.47.
5 Information from Mr B.W. Thomas.
6 Information from Mr Will Hawke.
7 J. Rule, *The Cornish Settlement*, the author, Yagoona, 1978, pp.13-15.
8 J.W. Tom, *Cornish Settlement: reminiscences,1941*, typescript in the possession of Mr B. W. Thomas, pp.1 and 3.
9 John Glasson, *Letters*, p.ii.

interests and earned a reputation for hard work and a sound business sense. 'The Cornish farmers at Bathurst have always wheat to sell when others want to buy.'[10] In 1849 the discovery of copper on farms owned by John Glasson and Richard Lane[11] further emphasised the settlement's similarity with Cornwall, where copper mining and agricultural pursuits were often carried on side by side.

PLATE 3.    Photograph of Byng

The road into Byng (Cornish Settlement).

By 1851, the land owned by the original families (and their later-arriving relatives), spread across the steep-sided valley situated between Sheep Station Creek and Lewis Ponds Creek.    Near their junction stood William and Ann Tom's elegant Georgian home 'Springfield' which had been built at the northern end of Cornish Settlement in 1847 to replace their temporary home.    South of 'Springfield' was John and Annie Glasson's property 'Bookanon' where their new home had been built, also in 1847.    William Bishop, a servant of the Glasson family in Cornwall, who had been sent to New South Wales to help John Glasson, also lived on 'Bookanon'.[12]

'Pendarves', the home of George and Jane Hawke, was built on the other side of Sheep Station Creek in 1850 on land purchased earlier by George Hawke from his friend John Glasson.[13] East of 'Pendarves' on the edge of Sheep Station Creek, was the half-acre of land which John Glasson had given his brother Joseph.    On this, Joseph had built his 'Cottage of Content' where he carried on a thriving business as a tailor.    The business was so

---

10   Ibid, letter 8 January 1834, p.42.
11   Ibid, letters 19 January and 10 September 1849, pp.103 and 108.
12   Information from Mr B.W. Thomas.
13   Information from Mr Will Hawke.

**6**

successful in the growing community that even John Glasson was forced to wait his turn to have a garment made.[14]

PLATE 4.    Map of Cornish Settlement

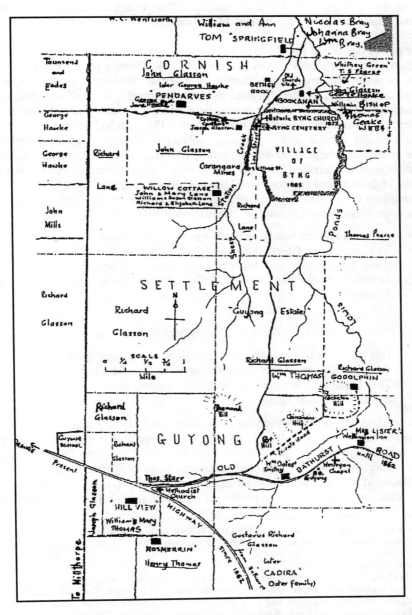

Map of Cornish Settlement and Guyong showing the locations of the Cornish families.    (Courtesy of Mr B.W. Thomas.)

---

14    John Glasson, *Letters*, letters 7 March 1845 and 17 June 1846, pp.68 and 80.

South of 'Pendarves', on a portion of John Glasson's land above Sheep Station Creek was the recently opened Carangara copper mine, and nearby was 'Willow Cottage' occupied since 1846 by John and Mary Lane[15]. The surrounding land was owned by Richard Lane, and further south towards Guyong was Richard Glasson's property 'Godolphin'.[16]

Across the valley from 'Springfield' lived Joanna and Nicholas Bray. Joanna was a sister of William and Richard Lane, and Ann Tom. South of their home lived Thomas Pearse, the son of another Lane sister, Mary, and her husband Geddie Pearse. Later Thomas Geake Webb was to marry one of William and Ann Tom's daughters and take up land near the Bray and Pearse families. His mother, Mary Geake, was a sister of Richard Lane's wife Elizabeth.[17]

The day-to-day life of the families at Cornish Settlement in the 1850s differed little, in any major way, from their earlier lives in Cornwall. J.W. Tom, a grandson of William and Ann Tom, recorded his youthful memories of Cornish Settlement in the 1850s. He remembered that his grandmother, 'assisted by convict women', wove all the cloth required by the household, using wool from the 'Springfield' sheep. She also made cheese and butter and produced bacon and ham from their own animals. The farm had an orchard, and a small mill where convicts ground corn. Although nobody at Cornish Settlement appeared to possess, or even want, large amounts of money, everyone lived a contented, healthy life where dentists were unneccesary,[18] doctor's visits unknown, and deaths occurred only rarely. At the centre of the personal and communal lives of all was their Wesleyan faith.[19]

A grandson of William Tom remembered that 'in my boyhood, I was taught to revere two things, John Wesley, and Cornwall'.[20] He also recalled:

> All our relations and neighbours were Cornish, many being local preachers, Class leaders and Sunday School Teachers, good earnest men and women, some of them, I feel sure believed there was no place in Heaven except for Wesleyans.[21]

Their Wesleyan faith was important in every part of their lives.

> Life at Cornish Settlement in those days was a very quiet one. Our only pleasures were all connected with the Chapel, Tea Meetings, Missionary Meetings, Temperance affairs and an occasional Picnic.[22]

The families at Cornish Settlement grew wheat, and raised sheep, cattle and pigs in their isolated valley. They were largely self-sufficient, even to the extent of weaving their own cloth and growing wine for their own use and for sale. They were 28 miles away from the nearest doctor, who was, in any case, unable to leave because he was a government employee stationed at Bathurst.[23] All four families worked hard, often in co-operation with each other, steadily building up their properties and their assets. During an early drought

---

15  John was a son of Richard Lane (who was a brother of William Lane of Orton Park and a sister of Ann Tom,) and Mary was a sister of John, Richard and Joseph Glasson. (Information from Mr B.W. Thomas.)

16  Information from Mr B.W. Thomas.

17  Information from M.H. McLelland.

18  George Hawke recalled an amusing incident when 'old Bishop' attempted to secure relief from a painful tooth. In an attempt to extract the tooth, he tied it to Hawke's duelling pistol and fired. The tooth remained intact, but was thought to have moved slightly and gave Bishop no further pain for fourteen years. (George Hawke, *Colonial experience: diary of George Hawke of Orange*, typescript, NLA MS 227, pp.9-10.)

19  J.W. Tom, *Reminiscences*, pp.7-8

20  Ibid, p.1.

21  Ibid, p.1.

22  Ibid, p.8.

23  George Hawke, *Colonial experience*, p.9.

William Tom's wheat crops at Cornish Settlement failed, many animals died and others were too emaciated to use as transport, so George Hawke walked to Bathurst and then returned carrying a bag of flour on his back.[24] In 1833, Hawke supervised John Glasson's property, while he took a temporary position as manager on a farm near Sydney.[25] Later, Glasson returned the favour by supervising Hawke's property while he returned to Cornwall to be married.[26]

All four families used convict labour to help them establish their properties in the early days, and apparently treated their assigned servants exceptionally well. George Hawke allowed his convict servants the 'indulgences' of extra provisions usually allowed by other settlers in the colony, but he also paid them at the same rate as free men for any extra work. He could not afford to employ free men, and so when he bought his land from John Glasson, while waiting for his assigned servant, he began to clear the land, working alone. Although he had no woodworking experience, he made himself a Cornish plough and a wooden harrow. He used these with the 'share and cutter and a set of harrow lines which I brought with me in anticipation of requiring them if I became a settler'.[27]

PLATE 5.    Methodist church, Byng.

Methodist church, Byng.

The pioneers kept in contact with those left behind in Cornwall and passed on information concerning other Cornish folk in the colony. John Glasson commented that 'I

24   W.H. Webb, *The life of the late William Tom Senr.,* A.K. Murray and Co., Paddington, N.S.W, 1922, p.8. [Bathurst District Historical Society.]
25   John Glasson, *Letters*, letter 30 September 1833, p.36.
26   George Hawke, *Colonial experience*, p.58.
27   Ibid, pp.52-3.

**9**

am as usual in good health, so also is Bishop and all Cornish friends', and on another occasion, 'Mr Lane and the other Cornish are doing well'.[28] The letters received from Cornwall were of vital interest, being handed from one member of the family to another, and distress was soon evident if they did not appear.[29]

Other members of each of the four families soon joined them from Cornwall, including seven of John Glasson's brothers and sisters. He offered to bring his parents to Cornish Settlement to care for them there, but they chose to stay in Cornwall. The youngest brother, Henry, remained with them in Cornwall and emigrated only after their deaths.[30] John Hawken and his wife Catherine Tom Barrett (a niece of William Tom and Catherine Lane), came in 1838. They had been offered employment at Bathurst with the family. Catherine Hawken's sister and brother-in-law Mary and Walter Bryant, and another sister and brother-in-law Dorothy and William Dale, and Catherine Hawken's brother John Barrett and his wife Johanna also emigrated.[31]

When George Hawke returned from Cornwall in 1838, he brought with him his brother Samuel, sister-in-law Elizabeth and their two children, and his nephew Frederick Hawke aged fifteen.[32] It is most likely that he already knew the Rowe family who travelled with him on the *Florentia* (and whose children he and Jane brought up), although the friendship could have begun during the voyage. Still other relatives of George Hawke emigrated and became involved in the fruitgrowing industry which he initiated after his return in 1838.[33] Also on board *Florentia* was Robert Smith (the brother of John Smith of Molong, who later married William Tom's daughter Mary). The Smiths came from St Keverne, and their lives were to be interwoven with those of the folk at Cornish Settlement in later years. Other Smith connections, the Thomas and Oates families, also came to the district.[34]

Other Cornish people gravitated towards Cornish Settlement. Edmund Harvey and his wife emigrated from Camelford in 1838. They met Mr Lane in Sydney and went with him to Bathurst, renting land (probably from the Lanes) to run the sheep which Edmund had bought from them. Eventually the family settled at the Fish River.[35] John Glasson mentions a Mr Case and family of St Neot, whom he met in Sydney shortly after their arrival aboard *Layton* in 1834, and who had quickly and happily settled at Bathurst. Some of these Cornish immigrants had come with the express purpose of gaining 'colonial experience' with other Cornish folk.[36] Other Cornish families such as the Sloggetts, Shorts, Webbs and Muttons who arrived during the 1820s and 1830s went directly to Bathurst or to the Fish River district.[37]

The four pioneer families, Tom, Lane, Glasson and Hawke had come from a strong Wesleyan background in Cornwall, and their emigration and subsequent settlement in the colony had been affected to varying degrees by the Cornish Wesleyan clergyman, the Rev Walter Lawry and his relatives, the Hassall family and their relatives, the family of the Rev Samuel Marsden, and the merchant John Hosking.[38] Although Lawry, 'the father of

28 John Glasson, *Letters*, letters 21 March and 18 September 1834, pp.46 and 49.
29 Ibid, letter 17 June 1846, p.77.
30 Ibid, p.iii.
31 William and Dorothy Dale's daughter Ellen later married William Lane's son Frederick, and the widowed William Dale later married the widowed daughter of William Lane. The Dales settled in Orange, the Barretts, Bryants and Hawkens settled at Tarana and the Fish River. (Information from Mr Selwyn Hawken.)
32 Information from Mr Will Hawke.
33 *CWD* 28 May 1985, p.4, c.3-4, and 4 June 1985, p.4.
34 Information from Mr B.W. Thomas.
35 Information from Mrs Netta Stoneman.
36 John Glasson, *Letters*, letter 28 August 1850, p.114.
37 Information from descendants of these families.
38 John Glasson, *Letters*, letter April 1828, p.3. George Hawke, *Colonial experience*, p.40. Later, another Hassall son-in-law, the Rev William Walker, became involved with the Lane family. (Information from Mr Peter Hohnen.)

Methodism in Parramatta',[39] had returned to Cornwall before the arrival of the pioneers at Cornish Settlement, he had made two early missionary visits from Parramatta to the Bathurst district.[40]

William Tom was the first Methodist lay preacher to be based permanently west of the Blue Mountains.[41] In the 1830s, 'Parson Tom', as he was known, used Bethel Rock, high above the valley in Cornish Settlement, as a pulpit from which he preached regularly to the pioneer families and their assigned servants, who sat below on the hill sloping away towards John Glasson's property. William Tom was Class leader to a small unofficial group at Cornish Settlement about this time, although the first offical Class group was not approved until the Rev Joseph Orton visited 'Springfield' in 1832.[42] A room at the Toms' first house was used for meetings and services, until the first little chapel was built directly below Bethel Rock in 1842.[43]

Orton had arrived in Sydney in 1831 and visited the Bathurst area in response to requests from 'several friends residing in that district who are very desirous that a missionary be stationed among them and who have promised very liberally to his support'.[44] While there, he met William Lane and was taken to see Lane's new property, 'Orton Park'.[45] Orton visited Cornish Settlement where he baptised two of William and Ann Tom's children, and enjoyed the hospitality of John Glasson and George Hawke.[46]

Although Orton was sympathetic to requests for an official missionary to be appointed to the Bathurst district, he was unable to provide someone immediately. He visited Bathurst again in 1833 and in 1834, conducting prayer meetings, baptisms and services throughout the district. Again he visited the families at Cornish Settlement, stayed overnight at John Glasson's 'bark tenement', and had 'a spirited and profitable conversation with George Hawke' who was 'a good man' with 'a kindred spirit'. Before returning to Sydney, Orton convened a meeting to discuss the building of a chapel and the appointment of a minister to Bathurst. Lane, Tom, Hawke and Glasson were present and 'generous offers of support were made toward the upkeep of an unmarried missionary'. In addition, William Lane offered a donation of £50 and an acre of land as a chapel site. Others gave in 'a manner proportioned to their circumstances' and Orton was quite confident that their efforts in Bathurst would be successful.[47]

The discovery of copper in 1849 brought dramatic change to Cornish Settlement. There had already been finds of copper in 1845 at Copper Hill (Molong), and also near Canowindra, and in 1846 at Rockley, between Bathurst and Oberon.[48] By 1848 mines were operating at Summer Hill and Copper Hill. Captain James Budge Clymo and fifteen miners and their families were brought out aboard *Elphinstone* to Copper Hill in 1848,[49] and miners were recruited from South Australia by Hanbury Clements for his 'Summer Hill' mine at Rockley,[50] while others like William Eade, a copper miner from Germoe who arrived aboard

---

39  R.H. Doust, *After one hundred years: the centenary of Methodism in Bathurst and the west of N.S.W. 1832-1932*, G.W. Brownhill, Bathurst, N.S.W., 1932, p.9.

40  Ibid, pp.8-10.

41  Ibid, p.8.

42  Ibid, p.11.

43  J. Rule, *The Cornish Settlement*, p.13.

44  R.H. Doust, *After one hundred years*, p.12.

45  William Lane was the brother of William Tom's wife Ann, and his wife Catherine was William Tom's sister. The two families had first settled close to each other at Tarana soon after their arrival in the colony, but the Tom family had moved on to Cornish Settlement. Lane named his property in honour of Orton's visit. (Information from Mr B.W. Thomas.)

46  R.H. Doust, *After one hundred years*, pp.13-16.

47  Ibid, pp.18-22.

48  J. Rule, *The Cornish Settlement*, p.38.

49  J.C.L. Fitzatrick, *The good old days of Molong*, Cumberland Argus, Parramatta, N.S.W., 1913, pp.102-104. *SMH* 7 July 1848, p.2, c.1.

50  Hanbury Clements' Station book for 'Summer Hill', photocopy in the possession of Mrs G. Kelly.

*Fairlie* in 1848, were employed there directly on arrival, although Eade had moved to Cornish Settlement by 1854.[51]

John Glasson spoke for all the Cornish settlers when he wished he could visit home and family and friends, but:

> I am afraid the pleasure is very distant for me, unless indeed, I find a rich copper mine on my farm, which after all is not very improbable, I see good specimens of copper in some places on my land, which I can knock out with the toe of my boot, and intend to search more closely in a few weeks time. Mr. R. Lane is very sanguine that he has a fortune on his land close to mine, the lodes coming right into mine.[52]

Soon, Glasson was able to write home with more news of the copper mine.

> I mentioned some time back of copper being found here. Well, we now have 6 miners engaged on tribute.[53] Two on each of Mr Lane's, Mr Hawke's and on my farm, and one as the captain of the pairs. They have taken 'the pitch' for six months from 22 August. They are to give 10/- in the £ to Mr Hawke and to me, and 12/- to Mr Lane. There are several lodes and the miners say they have never seen anywhere such a prospect of ore. They are in great spirits and are confident of getting good wages. They of course, are at all the expenses, only we credit them with provisions until they get the ore ready for market. We intend building a furnace and smelting the ore on the spot to save cartage, and if the miners are not mistaken each of our farms will be worth thousands of pounds. However these are among the uncertainties of this uncertain world.[54]

When he wrote on 28 August 1850, the mining was progressing very satisfactorily:

> I have now six miners employed, all tributors. Mr Lane has eleven. We have an engine house built for a five horse power engine and machinery all the way from Sydney, also a practical smelter to manage the smelting and hope to set to work before I go up the country to shear. We have a good quantity of ore raised. I have, I think, about 100 tons, Mr Lane has about the same amount ... the quality seems rich and <u>if it continues</u> I suppose our fortunes may be made...

His three children entered into the spirit of the enterprise:

---

51   Information from Mrs Pat Eade.
52   John Glasson, *Letters*, letter 19 January 1849, p.103.
53   Tributing was the system used in Cornwall. See appendix IV.
54   John Glasson, *Letters*, letter 10 September 1849, p.108.

> Johnny and Bobby are are very busy in their leisure hours
> digging upon a branch load [sic] near Joe's cottage. They
> have opened a hole about two or three feet deep and got out
> about ¼ ton of rich grey ore. Mary Anne is a shareholder in
> their concern.[55]

It was quite astonishing that these Cornish settlers took up land (out of all which was then available in New South Wales), and then found copper on it so many years later. As the years went on, this small settlement would become even more like a transported piece of Cornwall.

PLATE 6.        View from Methodist church, Byng.

View across the valley from the Methodist church.

The success of the mines brought more people to Cornish Settlement. The 200 people living and working there were too many for the little chapel to accommodate, and rebuilding or extension was planned.[56] The miners and their families lived in huts or hastily constructed cottages close to the mine. In April 1850 two newly built cottages 'connected with the mine of Richard Lane Esq' were destroyed within fifteen minutes when some loose grass used in thatching caught alight from a fire in one of the slab-built chimneys. The two families, one with seven children and the other with four, lost all their belongings, but fortunately there was no loss of life.[57]

---

55    Ibid, letter 28 August 1850, pp.115-16.
56    J. Rule, *The Cornish Settlement*, pp.41-2.
57    *BFP*, 27 April 1850, p.6, c.3.

Although George Hawke was not directly involved as an investor in this mining venture, he managed to profit from it by opening a general store to supply the miners and their families, as there was no other shop within miles. He operated his store for several years, making a good profit from the enterprise.[58]

The smelter employed by Glasson and Lane was Richard Cock, formerly employed at a Sydney smelting works. He claimed 'he was the first that smelted copper ore and bring out fine copper ore in *one operation* in these colonies in 1847'. He provided the plans and specifications for the Cornish Settlement enterprise. It consisted of an engine house with a four horsepower engine and an adjoining shed, a charcoal shed and a building for casting the metal into ingots. There were two blast furnaces, built with an attached platform from which the furnaces were filled with the correct proportions of ore and fuel. A trial firing had been only partly successful, and Cock blamed its failure on inferior charcoal, claiming it had been caused either by poor wood or by inexperienced charcoal burners. He expressed confidence that the process he was using would be 'an example of economy and efficiency combined'.[59] Two smelters, a fireman and five stokers were employed at the furnaces.[60]

The products of the first smelting were the ingots seen in Bathurst, and which were sold in Sydney on 6 February 1851 for £75.15.0 per ton, at 5/- more per ton than the South Australian copper sold at the same time. These valuable ingots were the property of John Glasson, while Richard Lane had a further two tons waiting to be dispatched.[61]

Richard Cock's optimisim was unfounded, and John Glasson wrote to his parents in June 1851:

> You are aware of Mr Lane and I putting up smelting works to avoid the carriage of ore to Sydney. Well, the scheme was a good one; but (what an ugly word) we failed in smelting through the person to whom we entrusted the work not putting up the proper kind of furnace. He erected blast furnaces such as are used to smelt iron ore, whereas draft furnaces should have been constructed ... for two tons of copper in ingots we got two and a half tons of scrap, and the sulphurous ores cannot be smelted at all in such furnaces, and as the ores are in great part of this class we consider our smelting works a failure.

Instead of using their unsatisfactory furnaces again, they had been sending the ore away for smelting. However, Glasson calculated that in spite of paying his £500 share of the smelting works, and the tribute to his miners, he had still made a small profit and hoped for a greater profit from the mine in the future.[62]

In January 1851, when John Glasson's copper was exhibited in Bathurst, Cornish Settlement had expanded from the isolated rural settlement of the 1830s to a busy community of several hundred people. The majority were still Cornish Methodists, and included copper miners and their families, as well as farmers renting land from the larger landholders or gaining 'colonial experience'.[63] Although the pioneer families of Tom, Lane, Glasson and Hawke and their relatives had prospered, their lifestyle had remained largely unchanged, still centred on their family, their work and their Methodist beliefs. The newer arrivals in Cornish Settlement merged into this way of life which was not so different from the one they had left behind.

---

58  George Hawke, *Colonial experience*, pp.82-3.
59  *BFP*, 14 December 1850, p.6, c.1-2.
60  J. Rule, *The Cornish Settlement*, p.44.
61  *SMH*, 14 February 1851, p.2, c.6.
62  John Glasson, *Letters*, letter 10 June 1851, p.196.
63  Information from Mr B.W. Thomas.

The quiet, rural community of Cornish Settlement which had changed because of the discovery of copper in 1849 was about to alter even more dramatically. On 10 February 1851, as they were rejoicing in the high prices received a few days previously for the copper from Cornish Settlement, a certain Edward Hammond Hargraves rode to Mrs Lister's Inn at Guyong to renew his acquaintance with the Lister family. The subsequent expedition with William Lister and his friends James, Henry and William Tom Jr was to produce the goldrush to Ophir, only sixteen miles away. This discovery of payable gold changed the history of the colony, and on a more personal level it involved William Lister and William Tom Jnr in a lifelong battle with Hargraves, as they fought to win official recognition of their part in the discovery.[64] Later in 1851, when the area was inundated by hopeful miners searching for gold, Richard Glasson voiced his concerns.

> The discovery may contribute, perhaps, to my property, but by no means to my happiness. I have so long been accustomed to a tranquil monotonous life, that I dislike the bustle and excitement that prevails.[65]

PLATE 7.     A 'Cornish' lane.

The 'bustle and excitement', which Richard Glasson abhorred, continued unabated almost until the end of the century, when Cornish Settlement became a farming community again, and reverted to its previously tranquil way of life.

For most of the nineteenth century, Cornish Settlement (or Byng as it had become known)[66] remained a recognisably Cornish community and its inhabitants chose to remain within the close-knit group whose lives and surroundings were as similar to Cornwall as was possible in New South Wales. Intermarriage between Cornish families occurred, and chain migration was a common pattern. The occupations of the inhabitants focused on farming and mining, and their personal and community lives centred around the Wesleyan church. Cornish Settlement was a nineteenth century Cornish community transplanted to New South Wales.

Hedges of Cornish vegetation line the lanes at Byng.

---

64   J. Rule, *The cradle of a nation: the truth about Ophir's gold discovery in 1851*, 2 vols., the author, Yagoona, N.S.W., 1979, pp.39-47.

65   *WB*, 31 October 1851, p.5, c.2, (publishing a letter from Richard Glasson of Guyong, dated 26 May 1851).

66   It was named after Admiral Byng.

PLATE 8.      More 'Cornish' lanes.

Cornish lanes at Byng.

# CHAPTER TWO
## THE HOMELAND

*Cornwall, my own dear land,*
*My Kernow,*
*My own dear country.*[1]

In spite of their love for their homeland, the Toms and Lanes, John Glasson and George Hawke chose to emigrate to New South Wales in the hope of a more secure future. Nineteenth century Cornwall was in transition, experiencing periodic booms and busts, and the latter would force thousands more Cornish to follow their example and emigrate. Conditions in the homeland had certainly deteriorated by the 1840s when the early Cornish assisted emigrants began arriving in New South Wales, and they were to worsen as the century continued.

The Cornwall these nineteenth century emigrants left behind still had links with its ancient Celtic origins. Cut off by the natural barrier of the Tamar River, Cornwall had always been physically isolated from the rest of Britain.[2] Although considered by the English as merely another county, nineteenth century Cornwall was actually very different from its English neighbours because of its climate and topography, its industrial and occupational history, and its Celtic heritage, language and religious history.[3] Over hundreds of generations these factors had moulded a distinctly Cornish character, physical appearance and way of life.

Cornwall is dominated by the sea and the winds, battered regularly by wild gales and stormy seas, yet its almost sub-tropical climate can produce plants unknown in other parts of Britain.[4] The tremendous force of the gales which sweep the isolated peninsula is obvious from the trees which grow sideways in unprotected locations, trained by a lifetime of buffeting. There are more sheltered sites in the coves and valleys, and it is here that most farmhouses are built, under the protection of a hill. The higher moorlands are exposed to the worst of the winds and because of this, and their poorer soils, they are used only as pasture for summer grazing, although peat bogs have traditionally provided a source of winter fuel for moorland inhabitants. Nowhere in Cornwall is far from the sea, which fringes the coastline along jagged inlets. The ever-changing sea has influenced both the landscape and the people.[5] Although fishing was a very important part of the economy until this century, and coastal transport was often used in preference to the poor roads, the rugged coastline and the strong tides have always made maritime occupations dangerous.

---

1    'The Story of my Country', words and music by Richard Gendall.
2    This isolation was beginning to change by the mid-nineteenth century. Improved communications and transport drew it inexorably into closer contact with trans-Tamar England, particularly after 1859, when the railway reached Cornwall. (F.E. Halliday, *A history of Cornwall*, first published 1959, Duckworth, London, 1963, p.294.)
3    Even the origins of its name mark Corwall as different. It is commonly believed that its name is a Saxon word derived from the shape of the peninsula ('corn' meaning horn and 'wealas' meaning strangers. (D. Rawe, *Cornish villages*, Hale, London, 1978, p.16.), It is also possible that the name came from the Roman term used about those living west of the Tamar River. (C. Thomas, *The importance of being Cornish*, University of Exeter, Exeter, 1973, p.7.)
4    The climate, though milder than most of Britain, is notoriously unpredictable. (J. Rowe *The hard-rock men: Cornish immigrants and the North American mining frontier*, Liverpool University Press, Liverpool, 1974, p.8.)
5    The north coast is more exposed to the Atlantic than the south coast, and with fewer sheltered inlets it is much wilder. The south coast has a milder climate and sheltered coves and beaches, and several shipping ports.

Cornwall is anchored by a granite spine which runs its whole length, from Dartmoor (in Devon), to the Scilly Isles, occasionally surfacing as high granite moorland.[6] Centuries of weathering have produced the distinctive tors, crowned by heaps of granite called 'clitters', and scattered with large blocks of unquarried granite moorstone. Mineral deposits provided the Cornish with their mining inheritance.[7] The major mineral deposits were tin and copper, but commercial quantities of lead, zinc, iron, wolfram and arsenic also existed.[8] In some areas the granite decomposed to form kaolin or china clay deposits,[9] and high quality slate has been quarried at Delabole in North Cornwall for centuries. The Lizard peninsula is famous for the marble-like serpentine rock once used as building stone but more recently as souvenirs for tourists.[10]

PLATE 9.      Map of Cornwall

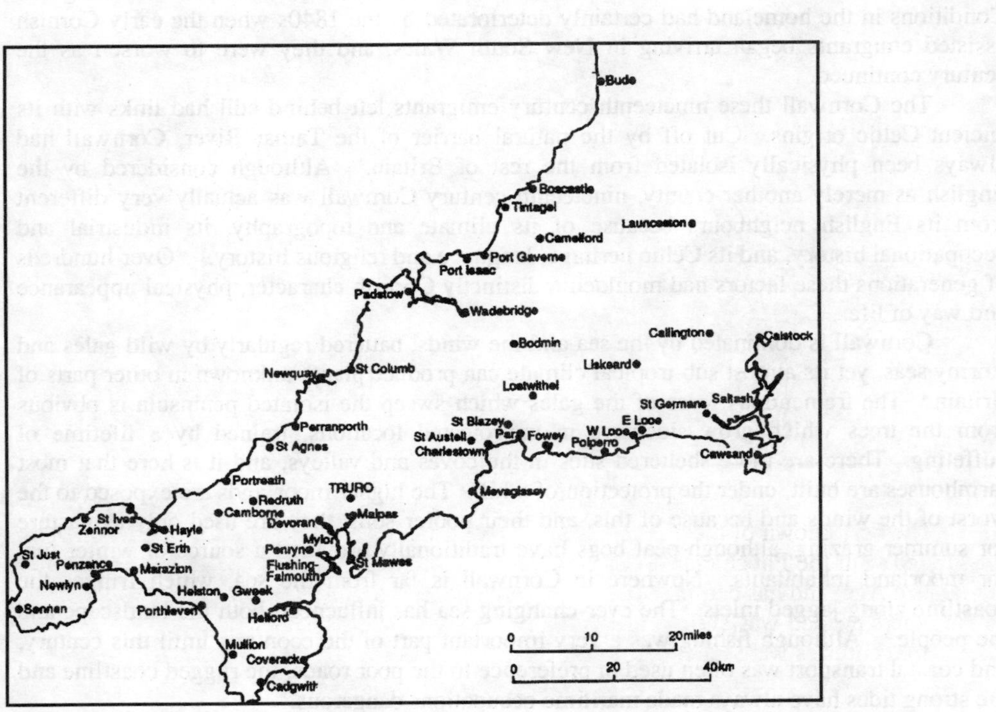

These geographical, geological and climatic factors combined to provide Cornwall with the unique conditions which would suit it for the three industries of fishing, farming and mining, followed in varying combinations by its people almost since settlement of the peninsula began.[11] These three occupations dominated the Cornish economy over many centuries. The old Cornish toast of 'Fish, tin and copper' honours two of them, although

6    At St Austell, Carnmenellis (between St Ives and the Fal estuary), West Penwith, and Bodmin Moor. (D. Kay-
     Robinson, *Devon and Cornwall*, Bartholomew, London, 1977, p.28.)
7    J. Ravensdale, *Cornwall*, National Trust Histories, Willow Books, Collins, London, 1984, p.12.
8    P. Stanier, *Cornwall's mining heritage*, Twelve Heads Press, Truro, 1988, pp.10-11.
9    D. Kay-Robinson, *Devon and Cornwall*, p.29.
10   Ibid., p.30.
11   Ironically, these factors have suited it to the modern tourist industry which brings much needed income to
     Cornwall, while it slowly destroys this unique heritage.

farming which was less exciting and less uncertain (and certainly less dangerous) was equally important.

PLATE 10.     Cornish parish map

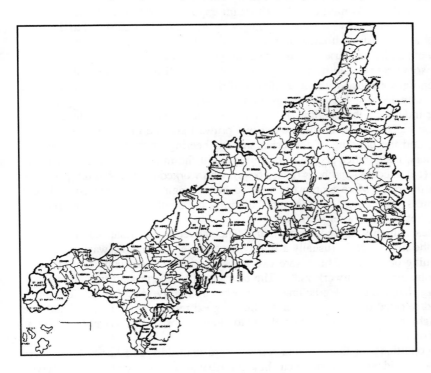

The best known of these three industries was mining.[12]  Legend has it that Cornish tin was traded with the Phoenicians.  Certainly alluvial tin has been obtained in Cornwall since the Bronze Age, and has continued as an industry ever since.[13]  The fact that Cornwall had tin which others needed was an important factor in its difference from its neighbours,[14] and the tinners for centuries were independent, self-reliant people.[15]

12    In 1991, Cornwall faced 'an untimely death blow to a tradition of mining in our county which goes back 2,500 years'.  Matthew Taylor, M.P. for Truro in 'House of Commons debate on the tin mines', in *An Baner Kernewek: The Cornish Banner*, no.64, May 1991, p.6.

13    Until relatively modern times tin was obtained by 'streaming' which referred to the washing of alluvial tin. (J. Ravensdale, *Cornwall*, pp.43-4.)  Mining below ground began in the fifteenth century when tinners were able to locate the lodes where the alluvial tin originated. (R.K. Johns, *Cornish mining heritage*, special publication no.6, Department of Mines and Energy South Australia, Adelaide, 1986, p.6.)  It probably began on the cliffs at St Agnes or St Just, where the lodes could be seen. (H.V. Williams, *Cornwall's old mines*, Tor Mark Press, Truro, n.d., p.7)

14    Tin was brought to the Stannary towns to be tested for purity, stamped and sold, and the duty on it was payable to the Crown. (J. Ravensdale, *Cornwall*, p.45.)  Stannary Law has never been repealed and was invoked as recently as 1978 when St Austell magistrates found they had no jurisdiction in the case of a summons against a Cornishman refusing to pay road tax on his car, and who had displayed a copy of the Stannary seal instead of the tax label on his windscreen. (Dygemysker, 'Cornish Notes' in *An Baner Kernewek*, vol.2 no.4, 1978, p.32.)

15    Because of the importance of tin, tinners were able to bargain for certain entitlements.  In 1201 the Charter of the Stannaries allowed them to prospect on any unenclosed land on payment of one fifteenth of the value of the tin to the landowner.  Tinners were exempt from laws other than those passed by their own parliament and upheld in their own court.  There were four stannaries in Cornwall each with its own court which had both civil and criminal jurisdiction. (J. Ravensdale, *Cornwall*, p.45.)

Industrialisation in mining had begun during the eighteenth century.[16] Mines went deeper because of the availability of gunpowder for blasting and the improvement in engineering technology generally. Early in the nineteenth century, Richard Trevithick's high pressure steam engine allowed mines to go even deeper because they could then be drained satisfactorily, and this in turn began the industrial deep mining of copper. In 1800 Cornwall had 1600 individuals employed in 75 mines, and by 1837 there were 30,000 men, women and children employed in 200 mines, with 170 steam engines operating in these mines to drain water, while still more drove surface machinery.[17] As the mines continued to develop, supporting trades and industries flourished, railways were built to serve the mines and the building industry expanded as houses and other buildings were needed.[18]

Although some copper had been mined in West Cornwall in the eighteenth century, Trevithick's invention coincided with the discovery of rich copper lodes, and steam made the mining of these deep lodes a feasible proposition.[19] Expansion of copper mining in turn encouraged other industries: the building of the huge granite engine houses required for the steam engines, the transportation of the ore out of Cornwall and the importation of coal to fuel the engines, and the building of foundries and engineering works.[20] Apart from the underground miners, many other people were employed at the mine. The surface workers included women (bal maidens) and boys (picky boys), who worked in open buildings sorting and breaking up the ore. More employees worked in the engine house, the count house where mine business was carried out, the store buildings, the smith's shop, and the powder house where supplies of gunpowder were kept.[21]

Mining was a highly skilled occupation. The 'adventurers' financed the mine's activities,[22] and the mine captain (usually a highly experienced ex-miner), was responsible for the actual mining operation. There were two ways in which underground miners could work, either as tributers or as tutworkers.[23] The normal shift underground was eight hours and besides being dangerous and gruelling, the work was highly speculative. The pitch (section) they had selected to work might bring them a good return. On the other hand, the pitch chosen might be disastrous, forcing them to draw 'subsist', an advance on their earnings, to survive.

Working conditions for underground miners were unhealthy and harsh, but miners operated their own accident funds to which they contributed a monthly sum and received payment in the event of injury. Accidents caused by explosions or rockfalls were a fact of life and exhausted men climbing out hundreds of feet at the end of a long shift risked further accidental injuries through falls from ladders.[24] At work they breathed air which was polluted with dust, gunpowder fumes, and the smoke from home-made candles. And there was the contrast between the extremmly hot temperatures in the mine and the often freezing

---

16  Although Cornwall became industrialised early, it was saved from the urbanised fate of South Wales and the Midlands by its lack of coal deposits, making it more practical to ship copper ore to South Wales for smelting.

17  F.E. Halliday, *A history of Cornwall*, pp.281-3.

18  Ibid, pp.285-6.

19  R.K. Johns, *Cornish mining heritage*, p.10.

20  Ibid, p.12.

21  H.V. Williams, *Cornwall's old mines*, p.14.

22  Adventurers were shareholders, but with unlimited liability. They were expected to contribute whatever was the currently required amount towards the mine expenses, but of course shared in any profits. (F.E. Halliday, *A history of Cornwall*, p.255.)

23  Tributers were virtually sub-contractors, working in 'pares' (small groups of men) in an agreed area for an agreed rate for a specified time, usually two months. Tutworkers earned a set rate for a set piece of work, sinking shafts or driving levels. They were quite often boys learning mining work, and older men who had formerly been tributers. Picky boys were youngsters employed on the surface sorting ore, who went on to become tutworkers and tributers as they grew older. (J. Faull, *Cornish heritage: a miner's story*, the author, Adelaide, 1980, pp.9-10.)

24  The man-engine which enabled miners to ride on a platform between levels gave some relief in the few mines where it was installed. The first of these was established near Redruth in 1842, (P. Stanier, *Cornwall's mining heritage*, p.16) but by 1862 there were still only eight in use. (R.K. Johns, *Cornish mining heritage*, p.17.)

temperatures outside which often caused lung complaints.[25]    Cornish miners had to be physically strong, hard-working, self-reliant, adaptable, resourceful and independent just to survive.

As the nineteenth century progressed, the copper industry expanded eastwards to the St Austell area and then yet further eastwards to Caradon Hill in the 1830s and just over the Devon border near Gunnislake in the 1840s.   Mining families moved first from West Cornwall to mid-Cornwall to follow this employment, and still later to East Cornwall.[26]   The industry was still profitable in 1860 but mines in West Cornwall were beginning to fail, although those in the east were still producing well.   Competition from overseas copper was intense and a downward slide for Cornish copper began in the mid 1860s and continued for the remainder of the century.[27]   There was a brief reprieve for the mines where deep tin was found below the copper, and between 1870 and 1872 a brief boom in tin occurred when supplies of overseas tin declined but was followed by a slump in 1873-74 resulted from competition from the new Australian tin mines.[28]  Although some Cornish mines did not immediately take the final step of closing (once closed they are very expensive to re-open), eventually they had no option.[29]

The second of the three major industries was involved with the sea and associated maritime activities.   Fishing and ferrying had been carried on for centuries and fishing ports grew up all along the north and south coasts.   Sheltered estuaries developed into trading ports, and man-made harbours were built along the exposed north coast for vessels servicing quarrying, mining and agricultural interests.[30] Many others relied upon the marine industries for their own livelihoods.   These included boatbuilders, netmakers and tanners, coopers who made the barrels to export pilchards, women and children who processed the fish for sale, ropemakers, ships' chandlers, sailmakers and pilots.[31]

The fishermen's methods of working, like the miners', reflected a sense of independence and fairness.   Small groups of men worked together on a co-operative basis, where all were responsible for the costs of boats, nets and other equipment, and all shared in the profits.[32]   Apart from the independent thinking and behaviour which their work encouraged, another similarity between the life of the miner and the fisherman was that both occupations were physically-demanding, uncertain and often dangerous.[33]

During the nineteenth century the fishing industry continued to be a seasonal and uncertain one.[34]  Pilchards were the most important catch, being found only in Cornish and south-west Devon waters, but their time of arrival and length of stay were variable.   Fish were preserved by smoking, pickling in brine, or drysalting, the two latter methods requiring the use of large amounts of salt.[35]   The major market was in the Catholic Mediterranean countries, but local labourers and miners preserved fish for their own use.[36] Towards the end

---

25    Between 1836 and 1856 in Marazion the death rate of miners was 64.49%, more than double that of males not involved in mining. (A. Bennett, *Cornwall through the mid nineteenth century*, Kingfisher Railway Productions, Southampton, 1987, p.26.)

26    Except in cases of 'short term migration' caused by local economic upheavals, such as those who moved directly from Breage to Liskeard in the late 1840s. (B. Deacon, 'Migration and the mining industry in East Cornwall in the mid-nineteenth century' in *RICJ*, vol.X Part 1, 1986-1987, pp.84-104.)

27    R.K. Johns, *Cornish mining heritage*, p.17.

28    Discussion with Dr John Rowe.

29    H.V. Williams, *Cornwall's old mines*, p.18.

30    A. Kittridge, *Cornwall's maritime heritage*, Twelve Heads Press, Truro, 1989, p.5.

31    Ibid, p.23.

32    C. Berry, *Portrait of Cornwall*, 2nd edition, Hale, London, 1974, p.96.

33    C. Noall, Cornish seines and seiners: a history of the pilchard fishing industry, Barton, Truro, 1972, p.11.

34    The mackerel season lasted from January to June in the Atlantic off the Scilly Isles, and the pilchards came to Cornish waters from July to November or December. (A. Kittridge, *Cornwall's maritime heritage*, pp.6 and 8.)

35    C. Noall, *Cornish seines and seiners*, pp.37-9.

36    J. Rowe, *Cornwall in the age of the Industrial Revolution*, p.273.

of the eighteenth century a heavy tax had been placed on local salt, and an even larger one on the more popular imported French salt. This encouraged the people involved in pilchard exporting, as well as those who depended on fish and potatoes as their staple diet, to turn to smuggling salt to avoid duty.[37]

Cornish fishermen already possessed the skills and equipment needed in smuggling.

> Their intimate knowledge of every inch of the coastline, coupled with an inborn skill in handling fast-sailing luggers, gave them a considerable advantage in out-manoeuvring their "enemies" of the Preventive service.[38]

As well as the illegal importing of salt, wine and other items, Cornish smugglers were also involved in the illegal *export* of tin to avoid the tax payable on it.[39]

By the eighteenth century, smuggling had become a major industry, with whole communities dependent upon it. It differed from smuggling elsewhere, however, as it was organised on a small group basis, and used fishing boats or other small vessels rather than large ones.[40] Although the rugged north coast was a difficult place to land smuggled goods, caves and mine workings in the cliffs made convenient hiding places. On the south coast, Polperro and the coves around the Lizard peninsula were well-known smuggling haunts.[41] Also famous was Prussia Cove in Mounts Bay, the home, in the latter half of the eighteenth century, of the notorious 'King of Prussia', John Carter and his brother Henry.[42] Smuggling survived as a Cornish 'industry' until the mid-nineteenth century.[43]

The third of the major Cornish industries was farming, which had begun with the early attempts of Mesolithic people to raise animals and crops in the transition from a hunting to a pastoral way of life.[44] Since ancient times the countryside had been dotted with hamlets of three or four farmhouses. These hamlets were most likely based on an ancient form of settlement like those in Brittany, Cornwall's Celtic neighbour.[45]

Carew, one of the Cornish gentry, living in the Elizabethan era, noted that even then, farming had been carried on side-by-side with mining, although the balance varied between the two.

> In times past Cornish people gave themselves principally (and in a manner wholly) to the seeking of tin, and neglected husbandry, so as the neighbours of Devon and Somerset shires hired their pastures at a rent and stored them with cattle.

37  Preserving only enough for a family's needs over a winter, used a bushel of salt. (Ibid, pp. 273-5.)
38  C. Noall, *Smuggling in Cornwall*, Barton, Truro, 1971, p.14.
39  It is estimated that up to 75% of tin produced in Cornwall in Elizabethan times was taken out illegally, probably hidden in pilchard boats. (Ibid, pp.10-11.)
40  Ibid, p.11.
41  Ibid, p.12.
42  Although known to be smugglers, the Carters were respected for their integrity. On one occasion the Revenue Officers from nearby Penzance raided the Carters' premises in their absence, confiscated their contraband property and took it to the Customs House store. That night the Customs House was entered but only the property that the Carters regarded as rightfully theirs was removed. (Ibid, p.43.)
43  Ibid, p.13.
44  J. Ravensdale, *Cornwall*, p.13.
45  W.G. Hoskins, *Provincial England: essays in social and economic history*, Macmillan, London, 1964, p.50.

> As for tillage, it came far short of feeding inhabitants'
> mouths ... when the tin works began to fail and the people to
> increase, this double necessity drove them to play the good
> husbands and to provide corn of their own.[46]

By 1894, 601,918 of the 869,878 acres in Cornwall were being used for farming. Most farms were small holdings raising cattle, sheep or pigs. Farmers' wives sold butter and cream, feeding the scalded milk to the pigs. Potatoes were the main crop, and market garden produce and some types of fruit were grown. Grain production had not been an option since the colonies had begun exporting large amounts. Small farms, the hilly terrain, and lack of available fertiliser caused further difficulties.[47]

Problems occurred in all three of Cornwall's major nineteenth century industries. Although corn growing was important in Cornish farming until the agricultural depression of the 1870s, there was a gradual move towards mixed farming from the middle of the nineteenth century.[48] By 1880 the numbers of sheep, cattle and pigs on Cornish farm land was double the average for Britain as a whole. This ability to diversify helped many Cornish farmers survive the agricultural depression of the 1870s,[49] and doubtless assisted Cornish emigrants to diversify and adapt to unfamiliar farming practices in New South Wales.

Cycles of depression in the Cornish farming economy affected the whole community, not only the farmers. When a group of miners went from West Cornwall in May 1849, two of them 'shed tears on leaving and declared that they were being literally starved out of Cornwall by the evil effects of Free Trade'.[50] Although the peak production of copper was not reached until the mid 1850s, the mines in far West Cornwall had begun to decline after 1840.[51] Towards the end of the century, a downturn in the fishing industry occurred when the pilchards stopped coming to Cornwall. With the three traditional industries in decline, the only industries remaining were the slate and granite quarries, the china clay works, and the fledgling tourist industry.

The Cornish were different from their English neighbours not only because of their isolation from the rest of Britain, and the attitudes developed by workers in all three major industries over many generations, but also because of the influence of Methodism, and because of their Celtic heritage. Their Celtic ancestors had arrived from Europe in several waves from about 500BC onwards,[52] bringing with them their language of the Brythonic or British group, linguistically linked to the Welsh and Breton tongues. It survived as a spoken language in Cornwall until about two hundred years ago and is retained in Cornish place names, almost ninety percent of which are of Celtic origin,[53] and in the Cornish accent and dialect.

---

46  R. Carew, *The survey of Cornwall*, first published 1602, F.E. Halliday (ed.), republished Andrew Melrose, 1953, Adams and Dart, London, 1969, p.101.

47  J.J. Daniell, *A compendium of the history and geography of Cornwall*, 3rd edition, Netherton and Worth, Truro, 1894, p.191-195. Cornish soil lacks lime which for generations has been added in the form of sea sand. Farmers have traditionally taken sand and seaweed from the coast to use on their land, but not all arable land was close enough to the sea to benefit from this practice. (C. Berry, *Cornwall*, p.112.)

48  J. Rowe, *Cornwall in the age of the Industrial Revolution*, p.258.

49  Ibid, pp.257-9.

50  *RCG* 25 May 1849.

51  Discussion with Dr John Rowe.

52  They brought with them iron weapons and tools. Their homes were stone or wooden huts gathered in settlements where corn was grown and sheep and cattle raised. They worked surface metals such as tin, copper and iron and engaged in leatherwork, pottery making, and the spinning and weaving of cloth. These Iron-Age Celts built hill forts in strategic positions throughout Cornwall. Many of these, such as Castle an Dinas in St Columb still survive. (S. Daniell, *The story of Cornwall*, Tor Mark Press, Truro, [n.d.], pp.9-13.)

53  T.F.G. Dexter, *Cornish names*, first published 1926, reprinted Barton, Truro, 1968, p. 13.

PLATE 11.    Cornish cross at Altarnun

The name for the parish and village of Altarnun is taken from the Celtic missionary, St Nonna, said to be the mother of St David.

These Celtic or British people were the native population at the time of the Roman invasion of Britain, but those living in the south-west of the country were hardly affected by the centuries of Roman rule.[54]   After the arrival of the Saxons in Britain,[55] the Celtic people were slowly pushed into the peripheral regions of Wales and the south-west peninsula, and retained their Celtic languages, and their own form of Christianity.[56]   Cornish resistance culminated in the final defeat at the Battle of Hingston Down near Callington in 838.[57]

For centuries, English incursions into the Cornish way of life were bitterly resisted.   In 1497 Thomas Flamanc and Michael Joseph led a march to London in protest against taxes being levied in Cornwall to raise funds for the Scottish wars.  This ended disastrously, and Flamanc and Joseph were executed.  Soon after, another unsuccessful rebellion occurred in support of Perkin Warbeck, Pretender to the English throne.[58]   Seventeenth century Cornish support for Bishop Jonathon Trelawney is immortalised in 'Trelawney', the Cornish 'national anthem'.[59]

In 1549 the unsuccessful Prayer Book Rebellion was a reaction against the introduction of compulsory English to replace Latin in churches, forcing the many Cornish people who spoke no English to learn it.[60]  Still the Cornish language did manage to hang on.  In 1584 John Norden (a foreigner observing the Cornish) noted that in West Cornwall most people spoke Cornish amongst themselves but many were 'able to conuers with a Straunger in the Englishe tounge'.  However, he thought it likely that 'in a few yeares the Cornishe Language wilbe by litle and litle abandoned'.[61]  By the nineteenth century the language had gone from general use, but was retained in placenames and surnames, and in many Cornish dialect words which would have been well-known to those emigrating to New South Wales.

54    J. Ravensdale, *Cornwall*, p.29.

55    C.Thomas, *Celtic Britain*, Thames and Hudson, London, 1986, pp.41-2.

56    S. Daniell, *The story of Cornwall*, p.15.

57    F.E. Halliday, *A history of Cornwall*, p.93.

58    D. Kay-Robinson, *Devon and Cornwall*, p.38.   F.E. Halliday, *A history of Cornwall*, pp.165-6.   I.D. Spreadbury, *Famous men and women of Cornish birth*, Kingston, Mevagissey, 1972, p.38.

59    F.E. Halliday, *A history of Cornwall*, pp.247-8.

60    D.R. Rawe, *Cornish villages*, p.18.

61    J. Norden, *Speculi Britanniae Pars: a topographical and historical description of Cornwall, with a map of the county and each Hundred*, first published 1728, facsimile reprint F. Graham, Newcastle upon Tyne, 1966, p.21.

These nineteenth century emigrants came from a strongly Methodist land, which boasted a long history of Christianity. Following the Roman withdrawal from Britain, Cornwall's 'age of the saints' began,[62] bringing holy men and women, Christian Celts from Ireland, Wales and Brittany as missionaries. They came originally to convert the pagan Celts in Cornwall and remained to maintain the Christian heritage against the onslaught of the pagan English. Dozens of place names celebrate their work, and stories about them abound in Cornish folklore. Hundreds of the granite crosses, still existing in Cornwall, date from this time,[63] and also from this period come the legends of Tristan and Iseult, and the tales of King Arthur.[64]

Like their fellow-Celts in Brittany, the Cornish had always needed 'a lively expression of their intrinsic yearning for worship and devotion', but the established church had not completely met their needs after the Reformation. 'The latent spiritual fervour ... became robbed of its outward form of expression, lay for nearly two centuries, not dead, but sleeping'.[65]

John and Charles Wesley first came to Cornwall in 1743, with their message of individual salvation, teaching that all people were equal before God and that they were individually responsible for a personal contact with their Saviour, the Lord Jesus Christ. These beliefs appealed immediately to the Cornish people and the value they had traditionally placed on equality and independence. Wesley himself claimed that Methodists were the only Christian group which expected of its members 'no conformity either in opinions or modes of worship but barely this one thing, to fear God and work righteousness'.[66]

Cornish farm laborers, miners, fishermen and other workers flocked to hear the Wesleys' message and follow their teachings, and chapels sprang up all over Cornwall. Methodism gave the Wesleys' followers self-respect and made the chapel the centre of their community.[67] Self-improvement of Methodists was encouraged, not only moral improvement but intellectual improvement as well.[68] The Cornish temperament with its spiritual nature, welcomed Methodism with enthusiasm, and social and economic conditions in Cornwall fuelled the fervour for the new religion. The Cornish adapted Methodism to suit their own way of life and it contributed to the liberal radicalism which is still politically important in Cornwall,[69] and which came with Cornish emigrants to Australia.

Methodism thrived in Cornwall, but some Cornish retained the superstitious customs which were a legacy from their pagan ancestors. Some of these still survive in celebrations such as the Padstow Obby Oss, and the dozens of holy wells reputed to cure a variety of illnesses from insanity to rickets.[70] Charming warts or other problems was common, and the

---

62   J. Mildren, *Saints of the south west*, Bossiney, Bodmin, 1989, p.8.

63   Cornish crosses are distinctive because of their wheel or round headed design and were used by the saints to mark preaching places which replaced former sites of pagan worship. Other crosses were used to mark pathways across lonely moorland, while some inscribed memorial stones commemorate individuals.

64   S. Daniell, *The story of Cornwall*, p.16. St Piran, the patron saint of Cornwall, is said to have floated from Ireland on a millstone, while St Crantock and St Petroc used their altar stones to cross the water and St Kea used a stone trough. (J. Mildren, *Saints of the south west*, p.20.) St Nonna's portable stone altar gave Altarnon its name.

65   A.K. Hamilton Jenkin, *Cornwall and its people*, first published 1945, paperback edition David & Charles, Newton Abbott, 1988, pp.166-7.

66   I. Haile, 'The Wesleys' in Sarah Foot (ed.), *Methodist celebration: a Cornish contribution*, Dyllansow Truran, Redruth, 1988, p.19.

67   D. Rawe, *Cornish villages*, p.26.

68   C. Thomas, *Methodism and self-improvement in nineteenth century Cornwall*, occasional publication no.9, Cornish Methodist Historical Society, [Redruth?], 1965, p.21.

69   P.J. Payton, *The Cornish miner in Australia: Cousin Jack Down Under*, Dyllansow Truran, Redruth, 1984, p.8.

70   P.O. Leggat and D.V. Leggat, *The healing wells: Cornish cults and customs*, Dyllansow Truran, Redruth, 1987, pp.1-7.

existence of witches and wizards accepted, into the second half of the nineteenth century and miners had their own superstitions.[71]

PLATE 12.     The village of Altarnun

The beautiful moorland village of Altarnun nestles on the edge of Bodmin Moor near Launceston.

Cornwall's basic differences in geography, geology, climate, industrial development, religious, and social history, set it apart from trans-Tamar England. The unique combination of these distinct differences from the rest of Britain produced an identifiable Cornish appearance, character and way of life, which have drawn comments from the Cornish themselves as well as from 'foreigners'.

'The Cornish were - and still are - individualists; to be persuaded rather than pushed - but if pushed, enjoying the battle that ensued'. Their distrust of bureaucracy meant that nineteenth century officials of the English government, (excise officers and tax collectors, police, health inspectors and Poor Law commissioners) were not welcome.[72]  Few Cornish people regarded smuggling as a crime.[73]  Smugglers, not the revenue men, usually had the sympathy of the ordinary people, and even magistrates took a lenient attitude towards them.[74]

John Norden gave his opinion of the 'nature and generall disposition of the people'. He stated:

> The gentlemen, and suche as haue tasted ciuile education,
> are verye kinde, affable, full of humanitie and courteous
> entertaynemente, and in causes of equitie quite stoute ...

71   A.K. Hamilton Jenkin, *Cornwall and its people*, p.261.
72   *WBBM*, p.7.  A. Bennett, *Cornwall through the mid nineteenth century*, pp.6-9.
73   J. Rowe, *Cornwall in the age of the Industrial Revolution*, p.275.
74   S. Baring-Gould, *Book of the west: Cornwall:being an introduction to Devon and Cornwall*, vol.2, Methuen, London, 1899, p.272.

As for the baser sorte of people, that liue by inferior meanes, as *Mechanicks* and *Rustickes*, comprehendinge vnder the latter *Yomen*, *Husbandmen* and *Tyn-workers*; manie of them are of harshe, harde and of no suche civile disposition, verie litigious, muche inclined to lawe-quarrels for small causes ...

And as they are amonge themselues litigious, so seeme they yet to retayne a kinde of conceyled enuye agaynste the Englishe, whome they yet affecte with a desire of reuenge for their fathers sakes, by whome their fathers recuyued the repulse ...

The *Conish-men* are verie stronge, actiue, and for the moste parte personable men, of good constitution of body, and verie valarous.[75]

Richard Carew, a Cornishman writing in the same period also referred to their 'fostering a fresh memory of their expulsion long ago by the English', and observed:

Amongst themselves they agree well, and company lovingly together; to their gentlemen they carry a dutiful regard ... Only it might be wished that divers among them had less spleen to attempt law-suits for petty supposed wrongs, or not so much subtilty and stiffness to prosecute them; so should their purses be heavier and their consciences lighter.[76]

English psychologist Havelock Ellis, who lived amongst the Cornish in the 1890s,[77] identified three predominant types of physical appearance which he related to the neolithic and Celtic inheritance of the Cornish.[78]   He believed that to the Anglo-Saxon, Cornish people in general seemed a dark, lithe race, instinctively courteous and hospitable.  He commented on the strong characteristics of independence, an inborn sense of equality and a powerful democratic instinct, noting that the:

obsequious 'Sir'... as well as the touching of caps, so widespread in England generally, are not prevalent in Cornwall.  The Cornishman, if possible, always addresses you by your name.[79]

He suggested that this democratic instinct was not necessarily politically oriented, rather an inbuilt way of thinking and behaving.  Observing that feudalism never really took hold in Cornwall, he declared that the Cornish were 'distinctly averse to subordination and unquestioning feudalism' but certainly not opposed to 'voluntary communistic co-operation' like that among fishermen and miners.  He believed that the main 'artistic' abilities in the Cornish were the love of music, singing and dancing, and their eloquence of speech as evidenced by the fiery oratory of speakers and preachers.

---

75   J. Norden, *Speculi Britanniae Pars: a topographical and historical description of Cornwall*, pp.21-2.
76   R. Carew, *The survey of Cornwall*, p.139.
77   H. Ellis, 'Men of Cornwall' in *Views and reviews: a selection of uncollected articles 1884-1932*, Harmsworth, London, 1932, pp.100-123.
78   These were a short, lithe and graceful finely boned build, and a larger, more solid build reminiscent of the population of central and western France.  The third was a combination of these two, said to be a dignified, handsome people possessing an unaffected grace and refinement of manner. (H. Ellis, 'Men of Cornwall', p.104.)
79   Ibid, p.105.

Ellis drew parallels between the climate and landscape and the Cornish character, both seen as wild and primitive, and full of contradictions. He warned that neither is as smooth as it appears at first sight:

> When you scratch the gentle surface of the Cornish soul you may, perchance, strike on some unexpected resonant resistance, even with ugly sparks of fire, just as when you penetrate the shallow soil of Cornish land you strike on hard metalliferous strata[80]

PLATE 13.     Cornish fishermen

'Cornish fishermen' in S. Baring-Gould, *A book of the west: Cornwall*, Methuen, London, 1899.

More than half a century later, Claude Berry, a Cornishman, saw these characteristics as still typically Cornish. He, too, likened the granite heart of the land to the core of the Cornish character which is softened by receptivity 'to the legends and superstitions which come to us from the twilight of our past'.[81] He commented on the inherent pride and independence of the Cornish[82] and the courteous and seemingly calm Cornish exterior which belies a mercurial temperament, which can be 'elated by success but as easily depressed by doubts and set-backs',[83] and which, when provoked, can be as intractable and immovable as the granite. Berry also remarked upon the sensitivity of the Cornish who tend to 'smart and quiver at the smallest slight and to brood interminably over a wrong'.[84]

The clannish behaviour of the Cornish was so generally accepted that it was epitomised in their nickname 'Cousin Jack'. But while they are clannish, they are also independent, and historically even Cornish sports such as hurling and wrestling have been individual rather than team activities, the major exception being a nineteenth-century introduction, Rugby.

A.L. Rowse asserted that 'the Cornish are exceedingly individualistic. Coming into a larger society, however, they stick together and are markedly clannish.'[85] Rowse also succinctly described the dry sense of humour as the 'odd-man-out, rather teasing and

80    Ibid, p.121.
81    C. Berry, *Portrait of Cornwall*, p.49.
82    Ibid, p.130.
83    Ibid, p.181.
84    Ibid, p.166.
85    A.L. Rowse, *The Cornish in America*, MacMillan, London, 1969, p.15.

bantering sense of humour of the Cornish' where they 'may be keeping a straight face, but they are really laughing at you; they are keeping it to themselves, but they are laughing *at*, rather than *with*.'[86]

The Cornish character and attitude to life, which had been moulded over many centuries, came with Cornish emigrants to New South Wales. It remained constant in spite of the changes occurring in Cornwall itself during the nineteenth century, and which were already evident at the time the early assisted emigrants began leaving the homeland.

In the 1840s the mining industry in Cornwall was still providing employment for many people, but usually under atrocious working conditions, and for most miners the financial rewards were uncertain. A serious agricultural depression had caused drastic price rises with no increase in wages for farm labourers and miners, few of whom had savings to withstand it. Potato crops were cut by potato blight and grain crops were also affected. There was unrest amongst working people, and protests at the price of grain,[87] such as in May 1847 when protestors at Wadebridge tried to stop the export of corn and to force dealers to accept fair prices.[88]  Many of those affected by the depressed situation in the homeland chose the positive step of migration or emigration in search of better conditions.[89]  This tendency towards emigration from Cornwall was certainly obvious by 1850.

> Emigration has been more largely resorted to in that county,
> than perhaps in any other in England. Out of the population
> of the Penzance Union alone, nearly five per cent. left their
> native land for Australia, or New Zealand, in 1849.[90]

Cornwall's population reached its nineteenth century census peak of 369,390 in 1861, but was about to enter a decline which continued through the century. While the overall population of England and Wales increased at a rate of thirteen percent each ten years, that of Cornwall decreased by two percent in the 1860s and again by nine percent in the 1870s. Emigration continued to drain parishes across Cornwall throughout the century.[91]  A number of mines in West Cornwall had already closed by 1866 when copper prices fell and the level of copper production steadily decreased. Some mines were able to continue by going even deeper to new deposits of tin,[92] but in most cases this was only a temporary respite. Tin and copper mining passed through a series of peaks and troughs before entering a final downturn towards the end of the century. The fishing industry also declined during this period. Agriculture was affected by developments in the mining economy but also by its own peaks and troughs. Migration within Cornwall or to other parts of Britain, or emigration, became the only options to long-term unemployment, but drained Cornwall of a large percentage of its working population.[93]  It was tragic that so many Cornish folk imbued with a deep love for their homeland were forced by the cycles of economic depression to leave it, many of them never to see it again.

---

86   Ibid, p.19.
87   A. Bennett, *Cornwall through the mid nineteenth century*, p.26.
88   J. Rowe, *Cornwall in the age of the Industrial Revolution*,  p.158.
89   F.E. Halliday, *A history of Cornwall*, pp.297-8.
90   Wilkie Collins, *Rambles beyond railways, or notes in Cornwall taken afoot*, first published 1851, Westaway Books Ltd., London, 1948, p.38.
91   For example, between 1841 and 1851 the mining parishes of Breage and Germoe decreased by 27%, and between 1871 and 1881 Perranzabuloe decreased by 22% and St Cleer lost 25% in the same period.  (P.J. Payton, *The Cornish miner in Australia*, p.8.)
92   F.E. Halliday, *A history of Cornwall*, pp.298-9.
93   Although local parish statistics show a decline in some parishes as early as 1841, the major decline occurred between 1861 and 1871. (Discussion with Dr John Rowe.)

The experience of the nineteenth century Cornish 'great migration'[94] from the homeland was influenced by a combination of all the factors which moulded nineteenth century Cornwall itself: its isolation, geography, geology, industries and its early deindustrialisation, its Celtic heritage, and the influence of Methodism. All of these factors made Cornish emigrants different from those of other ethnic groups. Given their independent and adaptable characters, and their marketable occupations, emigration was a logical step and one which, for many, was preferable to remaining in deteriorating conditions in the homeland. This background, and their naturally clannish behaviour, produced an understandable tendency for members of this close ethnic minority group to seek out other Cornish people when they reached their emigrant destination and to cluster together after arrival in the new country.

PLATE 14.     Cornwall

On the edge of Bodmin Moor near Trewint, looking towards the parish of Lewannick, the remains of an ancient settlement are overlaid with evidence of later occupations.

94    P.J. Payton, *The Cornish miner in Australia*, p.12.

# CHAPTER THREE
## NOT ON A MILLSTONE: THE VOYAGE TO NEW SOUTH WALES

*[St] Piran, it is said, floated to Cornwall from Ireland on a millstone.[1]*

It is estimated that between 1830 and 1900 at least 360,000 Cornish people emigrated across the world, a number which almost equalled Cornwall's total population at its census peak in 1861.[2] The most common Cornish emigration pattern was that of miners and tradesmen with related occupations going to mining communities and settling together, with their families, near the mines. However, it was quite a common practice for Cornish miners to 'commute' to the closer destinations of the United States or South Africa, leaving their families in Cornwall.[3] On the other hand, except for single men in the gold rush, who did not always fit the general pattern, nineteenth century Cornish emigrants to New South Wales usually considered their emigration to be a permanent step. They rarely returned to Cornwall because of the distance and the expense involved.

In comparison, though, with the numbers of Cornish who emigrated to North America and South Australia, those who chose New South Wales for permanent settlement were relatively few. Decisions to emigrate were influenced by a variety of 'push-pull' factors: economic conditions in Cornwall and in New South Wales; the availability of employment and land; the presence of family or friends settled in the recipient country; and the regulations controlling free and assisted passages. New South Wales was tainted, for some Cornish, by its convict origins, which reflected on the morality of its population.[4] There was also competition from other Australian colonies. South Australia in particular, with its mining industry and non-conformist background, drew the majority of Cornish settling in Australia.[5] For many, the final decision about their destination was influenced not only by the current conditions in New South Wales and the availability of assisted passages, but also by personal and family considerations. In the case of assisted emigrants, another factor was the pressure by selecting agents who promoted the benefits of emigration to different colonies. In 1841, three of the 26 selecting agents across Britain were located in Cornwall (Duckham in Falmouth, Geake in Launceston and Latimer in Truro) and one (Alger) was in Plymouth. Later, the West Country selection agent J.B. Wilcocks, who was based in Plymouth, employed 49 sub-agents with whom he shared his commission.[6]

Cornish people were among the earliest settlers in New South Wales,[7] but those choosing to emigrate to the colony before the late 1830s needed sufficient capital to establish themselves in the colony. Like the Lanes, the Toms, Glasson and Hawke, they were from the Cornish property-owning classes, and it was not until assisted passages to New South Wales became widely available that the labouring classes were able to contemplate

---

1  J. Mildren, *Saints of the South West*, Bossiney, Bodmin, 1989, p.20.
2  Bernard Deacon, 'The pattern of migration in nineteenth century Cornwall', lecture at the Fifth British Family History Conference, Newquay, Cornwall, 1 April 1990.
3  G. Burke, 'The Cornish diaspora of the nineteenth century', in *International labour migration: historical perspectives*, S. Marks and P. Richardson, (eds.), University of London Institute of Commonwealth Studies, London, 1984, p.60.
4  For example, *WB*, 6 September 1839, p.3, c.2. Latimer's advertisement for emigrants to South Australia compared New South Wales very unfavourably with that colony.
5  P.J. Payton, *The Cornish miner in Australia: Cousin Jack Down Under*, Dyllansow Truran, Redruth, 1984, p.12.
6  Discusion with Dr Mark Brayshay.
7  For example, Cornishmen Phillip Gidley King (later Governor King), and convict farmer James Ruse arrived with the First Fleet in 1788.

emigration.[8] During the period 1837-1877 almost 4000 assisted immigrants arriving in the colony stated their birthplace as Cornwall.[9] Many other Cornish paid their own passage or came via another colony, but it is impossible to calculate the number of non-assisted Cornish accurately, as records of birthplace were not kept on their arrival in the colony. There is a general pattern in each area of settlement, of the Cornish assisted emigrants being outnumbered by those who came to New South Wales by some other means, either directly or via another colony. In this respect they appear to have followed the general trend, where approximately 54% of emigrants were not government assisted.[10]

Theoretically, assisted emigrants had to meet strict criteria relating to their health, strength and usefulness to the colony. Although these criteria were not official requirements for unassisted emigrants, they did need similar attributes, and financial independence as well, to make successful new lives in the colony. In theory all these emigrants were the cream of their generation. In practice, assisted emigrants could be selected only from those who wished to go, and generally both assisted and unassisted emigrants left their homeland only if their prospects in New South Wales seemed to be better than in Cornwall, and if they possessed sufficient initiative.

On the voyage to New South Wales, assisted Cornish emigrants were generally in the minority, and for the first time in their lives they were outnumbered by the English and Irish. This situation caused them to reflect on, and at the same time reinforced, their Cornish identity. Robert Louis Stevenson noted such a tendency amongst Cornish travellers in America.

> There were no emigrants direct from Europe - save ... a knot of Cornish miners who kept grimly to themselves, one reading the New Testament all day long through steel spectacles, the rest discussing privately the secrets of their old-world, mysterious race. Lady Hester Stanhope believed she could make something great of the Cornish; for my part, I can make nothing of them at all. A division of races, older and more original than that of Babel, keeps this close, esoteric family apart from neighbouring Englishmen. Not even a Red Indian seems more foreign in my eyes. This is one of the lessons of travel - that some of the strangest races dwell next door to you at home.[11]

Some Cornish emigrants travelling to Australia were seen as different because of their physical appearance and their clothing. There were:

> some Cornish miners bound for the copper mines of Queensland. Their strongly marked features, coupled with the sombre hoods of the women, and the broad-brimmed straw hats of the children, fluted at the edges, formed a most picturesque sight.[12]

---

8    Cornish convicts are not included in this study because, unlike unassisted and assisted free immigrants, they had little choice in the emigrant destination or in the initial area of settlement after arrival.

9    Information obtained from the author's data base of Cornish assisted arrivals, from AONSW shipping lists.

10   E. Richards, 'Poverty and immigration', in *Poor Australian immigrants in the nineteenth century: visible immigrants:two*, E. Richards, (ed.), Australian National University, Canberra, 1991, p.3.

11   R.L. Stevenson, *Across the plains: with other memories and essays*, Chatto & Windus, London, 1920, p.39.

12   'Outward Bound', *Graphic*, London, vol.v, no.135, 29 June 1872, quoted in D. Charlwood, *The long farewell: the perilous voyages of settlers under sail in the great migrations to Australia*, Penguin, Ringwood, Victoria, 1983, p.93.

An experience common to all nineteenth century emigrants to New South Wales, whether or not they were assisted, was the voyage by sailing ship lasting upwards of 100 days. Apart from the superior quality of food and accommodation afforded emigrants who paid for a cabin passage, the experience of the long journey under sail was common to all classes.

Those who paid their own passage or came under private emigration schemes were of little interest to government officials. By contrast, government-assisted emigrants, and all aspects of their emigration, were subject to strict scrutiny in Britain and in the colony. They were regarded as a form of cargo, whose safe and healthy arrival to swell the labour force produced a payment per head to personnel involved in the emigration process.[13]

Various immigration schemes to New South Wales were adopted during the nineteenth century, giving preference for free or assisted passages to those categories of labour most needed in the colony at a particular time. A constant complaint of the colonists was that, in spite of these criteria and regulations, many of the assisted immigrants were unsuited to rural labour. With regard to single women, colonists complained that they were not sufficiently respectable, or were unused to domestic service.[14]

On arrival in New South Wales, assisted immigrants were required to provide detailed personal information to government officials, including their place of birth. No such information was recorded for those who came to the colony privately. Consequently, statistical data in this chapter are confined to an analysis of the answers given by the 4000 Cornish assisted immigrants who arrived between 1837 and 1877. These answers were provided, on arrival, at an examination by Immigration Board officials. They cannot be regarded as completely factual, because some emigrants gave answers which were different from those given on other official occasions such as marriage or census registrations.

Quite a number of Cornish were shrewd negotiators of the system, using it for their own purposes while managing to remain within the regulations. Alfred Goninan, the St Just-born Newcastle industrialist, summed up the Cornish attitude to officialdom. He recalled with amusement that when traction engines were introduced about 1880 to haul coal from Penzance to the mine seven miles away, a regulation was also introduced, forcing a man to walk ahead with a red flag. But to get round the regulation:

> this flag carrier brought into use a donkey to ease his weary
> feet. I think it was a brainwave, legal or otherwise. Trust a
> Cousin Jack to find a way out of a government regulation.[15]

Other emigrant 'Cousin Jacks' obviously shared this attitude, finding 'a way out of a government regulation' which they considered unnecessary or unfair.[16] Sometimes this must have been with the knowledge and possible collusion of selection agents in Cornwall. One such case was that of Captain James Trevarthen and his family, who came as assisted emigrants aboard *Joseph Somes* in 1852, stating he was a farm labourer. He was not challenged at the examination on arrival, but he, and the Glasson family at Cornish Settlement, were actually using the system quite blatantly, because he was on his way to become the new mine captain at the copper mines at Cornish Settlement, and his employment and journey had been arranged by the Glasson family. John Glasson's brother William was about to emigrate from Breage and on John's instructions, he had organised

---

13    D.Charlwood, *The long farewell*, p.164.
14    R.B. Madgwick, *Immigration into eastern Australia 1788-1851*, first published 1937, Sydney University Press, Sydney, 1969, pp.198-204.
15    *Memoirs of Alfred Goninan (1865-1953)*, L.E. Fredman, (ed.), introduction and typescript unpublished, from the original manuscript in the possession of Mrs Marcovitch, Chatswood.
16    These attempts to 'find a way out of a government regulation' were usually successful, and many were found during my research.

Trevarthen's employment and paid the family's contribution towards their assisted passage.[17] The Glasson family were well-known in Cornwall, and also in New South Wales by this time, because of the Cornish Settlement copper mines, so it is unlikely that this 'way out of a government regulation' was made without officials in Cornwall at least suspecting what was happening. Similar successful attempts to exploit the assisted immigration system occurred in South Australia when Cornish miners accepted assisted passages to South Australia but went immediately to the Victorian gold fields.[18]

Forty two percent of all Cornish assisted immigrants between 1837 and 1877 arrived between 1852 and 1859.[19] The 4000 assisted immigrants, who arrived in New South Wales between 1837 and 1877, did not fit the common Cornish pattern of miners and others settling together in discrete mining communities. They generally stated that they were servants, tradesmen, labourers or agricultural workers. Those few Cornish who admitted they were miners came in several waves, particularly in 1849, 1853 and 1877.[20]

Patterns of Cornish assisted emigration to New South Wales altered (or appeared to alter) between 1837 and 1877, as requirements for assisted emigrants, and the regulations regarding eligibility for assistance, changed. Some immigrants fabricated details about their age, occupation, religion or relatives already in the colony. They chose answers which would secure their assisted passages, or which were most likely to benefit them in their new lives in the colony. Occasionally, such individuals who were ineligible under the government regulations, but had slipped through the selection process, were discovered during the Immigration Board's examination in Sydney. For example, officials were suspicious of Richard Hooper aboard *Plantagenet* in 1857, a Wesleyan aged 43, who claimed he was a labourer. It was noted that he was obviously above the class of farm labourer and that, on being questioned he had admitted to previous employment as a storekeeper's assistant and a farmer, occupations which might not have qualified him for assistance.[21] On another occasion it was discovered that Diana James aboard *Ellenborough* in 1853 was actually Ellen Coad who had come earlier as an assisted immigrant aboard *Julindar* in 1849.[22]

Few Cornish immigrants made complaints to immigration officials about conditions during the voyage. When they did, these generally related to the quality or quantity of rations issued, or to the surgeon's neglect of a family member. One who did complain about the standard of provisions was James Trevarthen who was on his way to Cornish Settlement as the new mine captain. He added that his own family had not suffered unduly, though, because they had brought with them extra supplies of their own.[23] Thomas Toms aboard *Victoria* in 1849 complained that the Surgeon had called his wife Eliza 'a damned humbug and a beggar', and Eliza supported his complaint.[24]

Persons of a respectable nature (or otherwise) were noted, and sometimes their suitability as prospective settlers was commented upon. For example, the five children of stonemason William Knight aboard *Plantaganet* in 1857 were undersized and it was said that the family would find difficulty living on its earnings. Perhaps these children and the tiny Miller sisters aboard *Alfred* in 1837 were victims of malnutrition. Elizabeth and Susannah Miller, aged sixteen and fifteen, who had been living in north Cornwall with their parents,

---

17    Information from Mrs Mary Nesbitt.
18    P.J. Payton, *The Cornish miner in Australia*, pp.23-4.
19    See Table 2.1.
20    The miners in 1849 would have come as a result of the discovery of copper in New South Wales and the alterations in immigration regulations at that time. The 1853 influx would have been a result of the goldrush, and in 1877 many Cornish miners were aboard four emigrant ships which came from New York, while others coming directly from Cornwall were leaving as a result of economic conditions there. It is very likely that miners were amongst earlier Cornish arrivals claiming to be farm labourers.
21    AONSW shipping list, *Plantagenet* 1857, AO reel 2476.
22    AONSW shipping list, *Ellenborough* 1853, AO reel 2464.
23    AONSW shipping list, *Joseph Somes* 1852, AO reel 2463.
24    AONSW shipping list, *Victoria* 1849, AO reel 2460.

were the daughters of a former ropemaker. They apparently had no other family on board, and stated that they had no relatives in the colony. Immigration officials described them as being in good health, but both 'of remarkably diminutive stature'.[25]

In answer to questions about their relatives already resident in the colony, some immigrants who already had relatives settled in New South Wales said that they did not. For example, Jonathon and Mary Mullis who arrived aboard *Lord Stanley* in 1850 both stated they had no relatives in the colony, but Mary's younger brother (Joseph Stephens of Altarnun) had probably been in New South Wales for several years.[26] Perhaps this attitude was often taken because most immigrants did not intend to be dependent on these relatives, or it could be a further example of the Cornish suspicion of officialdom, where they were not prepared to disclose information if they were unsure why it was being requested. However, in some cases, there was an obvious ulterior motive for reticence. The matron[27] responsible for the single women on board had been most impressed during the voyage by the honesty and respectability of Mary Blight, aboard *Fitzjames* in 1857, who had told officials on arrival that she had no relatives in the colony. What she did not mention was that she had relatives in Victoria and had accepted an assisted passage to New South Wales with the intention of joining them there. An enquiry by her sister in Victoria to New South Wales Immigration officials about her whereabouts, prompted a terse memo. She:

> stated she had no relatives in the colony. I see no object in
> appending this information as it is evidently required with
> an intention of removing this girl to the Colony of Victoria.[28]

Although the regulations permitted different assistance to various age groups at different periods, more than three quarters of all Cornish assisted emigrants were under 30 years of age, and more than one quarter under the age of twelve years. Of the 3898 emigrants, 3099 or almost 80% were under 30 years of age. The remainder were between 30 and 70 years of age. See Table 2.2.

The proportions of Cornish people coming in family groups changed over a period of time between 1837 and 1877. For example, as regulations altered in the later periods to permit eligible wives and families of residents in the colony to travel as assisted emigrants, some Cornish families took advantage of the opportunity. They consisted of 24 separate groups totalling 92 people. Although the colony encouraged unmarried female emigrants, apparently very few chose to come from Cornwall. Those young women who did emigrate generally came as part of a family group, or were accompanied by a brother, sister, cousin or other relative. Sometimes teenage children were listed, by immigration officials, as part of the parents' family, while at other times they were recorded separately as single males or females. See Table 2.3.

The male Cornish assisted immigrants claimed a variety of occupations, which fell into three main categories: miners, labourers, and tradesmen. A minority said they were copper miners, tin miners, coal miners or simply miners. The majority claimed to be labourers, (a number defined themselves more specifically as agricultural labourers or farm labourers,) skilled workers or tradesmen. Except for Phillip Hill in 1877[29,] a pilot, no immigrants claimed to be fishermen or to be engaged in other maritime occupations, which might not have qualified for assistance. Many of the 630 women whose occupations were recorded were skilled workers such as milliner, nurse, needlewoman, tailoress, teacher,

---

25  AONSW shipping list *Plantagenet* 1857, and AONSW shipping list, *Alfred* 1837. AO reels 2476, 2654, 1286.

26  P. Lay, 'Clotted cream and chapel: the Mullis family in Cornwall and New South Wales', Dip. FHS., Society of Australian Genealogists, Sydney, 1988, p.9.

27  Matrons were employed to supervise the single women during the voyage. (D. Charlwood, *The long farewell* p.169).

28  AONSW shipping list, *Fitzjames* 1857, reel 2475. AONSW 9/6212, ships' papers, letter dated 27 April 1857 from George Keast in Creswick, Victoria, no.57/1544 15 May 1857.

29  AONSW shipping list *La Hogue* 1877, AO reel 2488.

safety fuse maker. Other women who had no occupation recorded should not be dismissed as having had none. See Tables 2.4 and 2.5.

Many Cornish were practising Methodists, but the answers they gave on arrival do not indicate this. The majority stated they were Church of England, and those stating they belonged to Methodist denominations combined to give a surprisingly low 30%. This discrepancy could be due to the way in which the question was phrased by the official, (for example asking merely if immigrants were Protestant or Catholic) or it could be another example of immigrants' suspicion of bureaucracy, or simply of their supplying the answers they believed would be most likely to benefit them in the colony. See Tables 2.6 and 2.7.

Information provided on the places of birth of assisted immigrants varied.[30] Sometimes officials recorded the immigrant's native place only as Cornwall, and at the other extreme merely the name of a farmhouse or hamlet. The places of birth given by the assisted immigrants, as shown in Appendix VII, are evidence that Cornish assisted immigrants to New South Wales originated in diverse parts of Cornwall, and that there was no strong common mining background obvious in their places of birth. When a parish was recorded, however, it referred to the place of birth, and did not necessarily bear any relation to the place of residence at the time of departure. The birthplaces of the non-Cornish members in a Cornish family sometimes hint at the family's place of residence prior to emigration: 429 people gave birthplaces outside Cornwall, but of these 145 (77 of whom were adults) were from neighbouring Devon.[31] Quite significant numbers came from other places. For example, Durham, Lancashire, Staffordshire, Yorkshire and Warwickshire accounted for 47 (fourteen were adults) and London, Kent, Essex and Middlesex for a further 52 (ten were adults). Wales accounted for 20 (three were adults), Ireland 39 (30 were adults), Scotland three adults, and the United States of America 40 (four were adults) most of whom were from Pennsylvania and arrived in Sydney in 1877.[32]

Evidence of migration within Britain, and prior emigration (to Canada, the United States, Mexico and even one to Victoria, Australia) is shown in the birthplaces of children of assisted immigrants, and in some marriages where one partner is non-Cornish. For example, William Henry Toms, aged three, and his infant brother, John, aboard *Victoria* in 1849, had been born in Yorkshire, but their father had been born in Cornwall and their mother in Devon.[33] Four of the Bawden children, aged between six and seventeen years, who were travelling with their widowed Cornish mother aboard *Ninevah* in 1876, had been born in Mexico, while a five year old, and a ten year old had been born in Cornwall.[34]

The Cornish made varying use, from 1837 onwards, of the different assisted emigration schemes offered.[35] Unlike the Irish,[36] they did not use the Remittance Regulations scheme to any great extent, and between 1853 and 1900 only 654 deposits were made on behalf of persons resident in Cornwall.[37] These individuals were not necessarily of Cornish birth and may have been resident there but born elsewhere. Many of those for whom deposits were paid (by persons already in the colony), defaulted prior to departure, and did

---

30  For details of the immigrants' stated birthplaces, see appendix VII.

31  It is a reasonable assumption that the birthplaces of children in places other than Cornwall indicate residence of the families outside Cornwall.

32  AONSW shipping lists *N. Boynton, Sierra Nevada, Annie H. Smith, Star of the West,* AO reel 2488.

33  AONSW shipping list, *Victoria* 1849, AO reel 2460.

34  AONSW shipping list, *Ninevah* 1876, AO reel 2487.

35  For discussion of these different schemes, see R.B. Madgwick, *Immigration into eastern Australia.* E. Richards, R. Reid and D. Fitzpatrick (eds.), *Visible immigrants: neglected sources for the history of Australian immigration,* Australian National University, Canberra, 1989. E. Richards, (ed.), *Poor Australian immigrants in the nineteenth century: visible immigrants :two,* Australian National University, Canberra, 1991. F.K. Crowley, *British migration to Australia:1860-1914,* D.Phil., Oxford, 1951.

36  Discussion with Dr Richard Reid.

37  P.J. Stemp, (comp.), *Index of depositors for emigrants resident in Cornwall 1853-1900,* compiled from AONSW Immigration deposit journals, computer printout in the author's possession.

not actually emigrate. Most of those who did come from Cornwall using this method arrived during the 1860s and after 1875.

As already stated, a minority of the Cornish who migrated came as assisted passengers directly to New South Wales. Many others came as unassisted emigrants, or as specifically-recruited personnel for mining operations, or via other colonies as assisted and as non-assisted emigrants.[38] Whichever method was used to reach New South Wales, and however much their lives differed after arrival, each emigrant, assisted and unassisted alike, shared the experience of the voyage to New South Wales, and approximately 100 days of prolonged and enforced 'holiday' on the passage. This period of unaccustomed leisure was spent out of paid employment, but on the other hand individuals had no financial responsibility for food, accommodation and medical treatment during the voyage. This was a unique experience for those who had spent their lives up until that time engaged in heavy physical work with few financial rewards and who, as assisted emigrants, were being imported to New South Wales principally for their stated ability to continue such physical labour in the colony.

The *Florentia* carried a mixture of assisted bounty[39] emigrants, full fare paying steerage passengers, and others paying more for intermediate and cabin accommodation. Typically, the Cornish on board were a minority.[40] Of the 26 crew and 85 passengers, only twelve can be identified with certainty as being Cornish. It is difficult to be sure, however, because the shipping lists show places of birth for the bounty passengers only.[41]

The barque, of 452 tons, arrived in Sydney on 3 August 1838. There were no deaths or serious illnesses on the voyage, and only one convalescent passenger on arrival.[42] The master, William Deloitte, had captained six voyages to Sydney aboard *Florentia*. This was his final journey before settling in Sydney as a merchant and shipping agent.[43]

The extremely long and detailed diary of Oswald Bloxsome, one of the English cabin passengers aboard *Florentia*, recounted the experience of a voyage which was common to emigrants to New South Wales during the next 40 years. It recorded the day to day mixture of trivia and drama, boredom and excitement, which filled the lives of the emigrants for three to four months. Although the cabin passengers had more luxury in their accommodation and diet than did the steerage passengers, the experiences of the Cornish steerage passengers aboard *Florentia* were otherwise similar to those of the three cabin passengers whose accounts of the voyage survive.[44]

---

38  More detailed information on individual persons in these unassisted categories will be found in chapters four to eight.

39  Bounty emigrants, selected by agents in Britain, were brought out by New South Wales settlers who were reimbursed by the government after the arrival of the emigrants, providing they met the criteria laid down. A government system operated alongside the bounty system, where emigrants were selected and brought out by arrangements made through government officials. (R.B. Madgwick, *Immigration into eastern Australia*, pp.120-21.)

40  Later assisted emigrants made up the bulk, and sometimes the total, of passengers aboard emigrant ships, but even so the Cornish generally remained a minority group.

41  AONSW shipping list *Florentia* 1838, AO reel 1290.

42  AONSW Col. Sec: *Reports of vessels arrived 1838-December 1839*, AO reel 1266, no. 168, *Florentia*, 3 August 1838.

43  W.S. Deloitte Esq. in 'Minutes of evidence taken before the Committee on Immigration', 17 August 1838, in *NSWLC V&P 1838*, pp.843-5.

44  George Hawke referred briefly to the voyage in his *Colonial experience*, p.64. Diaries of three separate cabin passengers survive. S. Rawson, 'Diary of the voyage aboard *Florentia* 1838', Rawson papers, NLA MS 204/1. O. Bloxsome, 'Journal of a voyage to New South Wales 1838', NLA MS 336. J. Henderson, 'Logbook of *Florentia* 1838', ML B740.

PLATE 15.    Painting of *Florentia*.

'The *Florentia* passing through Tellicherry Roads 1825'. (Courtesy of the National Maritime Museum, Greenwich.)

The ship left Plymouth on 4 April 1838, but after battling rough weather in the English Channel for several days was forced back to Plymouth, and left for the second time on 11 April.  Unlike his fellow passengers in the rough weather in the Bay of Biscay, Oswald Bloxsome was not seasick, and was able to enjoy the food.

> The Dinners are really very good & the variety they manage
> to put on table is extraordinary looking at the miserably
> small apparatus for cooking - we have usually at least 6
> dishes & good substantial ones ... the wine is the worst part
> of the the whole being Marsala/sweetport - two of my
> natural abominations.[45]

*Florentia* carried a cow and calf, pigs, sheep and poultry to provide the cabin passengers with such a varied and extensive diet,[46] but rations issued to the Cornish assisted passengers in the steerage compartment were far more frugal and monotonous.

---

45    O. Bloxsome, 'Journal', 14 April.
46    Ibid, 16 April.

PLATE 16. Scale of victualling for emigrants.

## SCALE OF VICTUALLING IN GOVERNMENT EMIGRANT SHIPS
### FROM
### *England and Ireland to New South Wales.*

### MALE EMIGRANTS.  *April 1839*

| Days | Biscuit lb. | Beef lb. | Pork lb. | Flour lb. | Suet oz. | Raisins oz. | Split Pease pint | Tea oz. | Sugar oz. | Water qts. | Oatmeal | Vinegar | Soap |
|---|---|---|---|---|---|---|---|---|---|---|---|---|---|
| Sunday .... | ¾ | ⅔ | ,, | ¼ | 1 | 2 | ,, | ¼ | 1½ | 3 | 1 Pint Weekly. | ½ Pint Weekly. | 1lb. per Lunar Month. |
| Monday .... | ¾ | ,, | ⅔ | ¼ | ,, | ,, | ⅓ | ¼ | 1½ | 3 | | | |
| Tuesday .... | ¾ | ⅔ | ,, | ¼ | 1 | 2 | ,, | ¼ | 1½ | 3 | | | |
| Wednesday .. | ¾ | ,, | ⅔ | ¼ | ,, | ,, | ⅓ | ¼ | 1½ | 3 | | | |
| Thursday .. | ¾ | ⅔ | ,, | ¼ | 1 | 2 | ,, | ¼ | 1½ | 3 | | | |
| Friday...... | ¾ | ,, | ⅔ | ¼ | ,, | ,, | ⅓ | ¼ | 1½ | 3 | | | |
| Saturday.... | ¾ | ⅔ | ,, | ¼ | 1 | 2 | ,, | ¼ | 1½ | 3 | | | |

### FEMALE EMIGRANTS.

| Days | Biscuit lb. | Beef lb. | Pork lb. | Flour lb. | Suet oz. | Raisins oz. | Split Pease pint | Tea oz. | Sugar oz. | Water qts. | Oatmeal | Vinegar | Soap |
|---|---|---|---|---|---|---|---|---|---|---|---|---|---|
| Sunday .... | ⅔ | ½ | ,, | ¼ | 1 | 2 | ,, | ¼ | 1½ | 3 | ½ Pint Weekly. | ½ Pint Weekly. | 1lb. per Lunar Month. |
| Monday .... | ⅔ | ,, | ½ | ¼ | ,, | ,, | ⅓ | ¼ | 1½ | 3 | | | |
| Tuesday .... | ⅔ | ½ | ,, | ¼ | 1 | 2 | ,, | ¼ | 1½ | 3 | | | |
| Wednesday .. | ⅔ | ,, | ½ | ¼ | ,, | ,, | ⅓ | ¼ | 1½ | 3 | | | |
| Thursday.... | ⅔ | ½ | ,, | ¼ | 1 | 2 | ,, | ¼ | 1½ | 3 | | | |
| Friday...... | ⅔ | ,, | ½ | ¼ | ,, | ,, | ⅓ | ¼ | 1½ | 3 | | | |
| Saturday.... | ⅔ | ½ | ,, | ¼ | 1 | 2 | ,, | ¼ | 1½ | 3 | | | |

And so on in regular succession throughout the Voyage, issuing Beef and Pork on alternate days.

Children of ten years of age and upwards are to be victualled as Adults.

Children under ten years of age, whether male or female, are to have half of Men's Allowance, excepting in the article of Water, of which they are to have full allowance.

There is also to be provided for each one of such Children, 15lbs. of Rice, 3lbs. of Sago, and 4½lbs. of Sugar.

The Medical Comforts are to be as follows :—

| | |
|---|---|
| Preserved Meats and Soups | 160 lbs. |
| Lemon Juice | 648 ,, |
| Sugar to mix with Lemon Juice | 486 ,, |
| Scotch Barley | 64 ,, |
| Tea | 8 ,, |
| Sugar | 48 ,, |
| Vinegar | 8 galls. |
| Oatmeal | 4 bush. |

For every 100 persons.

To the above mentioned Medical Comforts will be added the following, which, in the case of those fitted at Deptford, will be supplied from the Medical Department under the separate name of " Necessaries."

| | |
|---|---|
| Arrow Root | 8 lbs. |
| Sago | 8 ,, |
| Rice | 32 ,, |
| Pearl Barley | 16 ,, |
| Whole Ginger | 4 oz. |

For every 100 persons.

There is also to be on board each Ship, 5 dozen of Port Wine, 12 dozen Pint Cases of Preserved Milk, 24 dozen of Bottled Porter, or a substitution of part of the supply in Cask ... and a quantity of Wine in Cask, not less than two gallons for every person above 10 years of age.

'Scale of victualling in government emigrant ships, 1839.' (CO 384/87, circulars 1817-51, p.337. AJCP reel 5132. Courtesy of the State Library of New South Wales.)

PLATE 17.    Plan of *Florentia*.

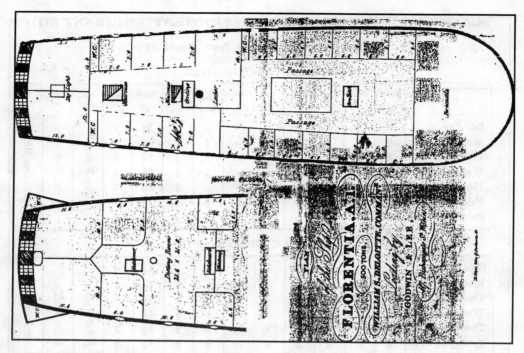

*Florentia.* From Rawson papers, NLA MS 204, folder 3. (Courtesy of the National Library of Australia.)

The ship was off Lisbon on 16 April, and after only seven days had passed within 35 miles of Madeira, hailed as the best run from England that Captain Deloitte had ever made. Already the passengers were feeling the heat and began wearing summer clothing, an awning was erected on deck as shelter from the sun, and the heat was causing the resin in the decks to run.  Saturday evenings were observed regularly as social occasions amongst the cabin passengers and included recitations, singing and 'becoming jovial'.  Sunday church services were conducted by Captain Deloitte on the quarterdeck under the awning.  Flags were attached to the masts and shrouds, benches were set out as seating for the sailors and the steerage and intermediate passengers, with the Cuddy (saloon) passengers seated separately.[47]

On 22 April the north-east Trade Winds arrived and it was hoped they would carry the ship to within five degrees of the equator.  Variable winds and calms were expected on the next section of the voyage, and it could take up to a fortnight to pass through to the south-east Trade Winds.  These would take the *Florentia* to within 400 miles of South America, where they expected to meet north winds for several weeks, then westerly winds for the remainder of the voyage.

As they continued towards their only port of call, the Cape De Verde islands, passengers sighted unfamiliar marine life: Portuguese men-of-war, whales, sharks, porpoises and sea birds.  When the ship reached the islands, passengers bartered clothing with boatloads of natives who came out to the ship selling fresh pineapples, bananas and coconuts.  They went ashore, visited the British consul and wandered through the bazaar while the ship took on fresh water and food including turkeys, fowls and pigs before

---

47    Ibid, 22 April.

continuing the journey. Captain Deloitte brought a monkey on board and two more were taken into the steerage quarters.

The heat became even more oppressive, and meat and poultry killed in the morning was not fit to be eaten the same evening. On 1 May, they lost the Trade Winds and were becalmed in the 'doldrums'. The sheep were shorn because of the heat, and on deck, male passengers bathed to keep cool by having sailors throw buckets of sea water over them. A shark was caught and eaten for the sailors' supper, making a welcome change from salt beef. At last, on 9 May a breeze appeared and the following night the ship crossed the equator. There was:

> some little fun going on between the sailors & steerage
> passengers - the sailors soused every one they could get at
> with buckets of water getting up in the rigging and pouring
> it down upon you - each man had his bucket of water &
> every artifice resorted to, to get at you.[48]

PLATE 18.    Voyage of the *Florentia.*

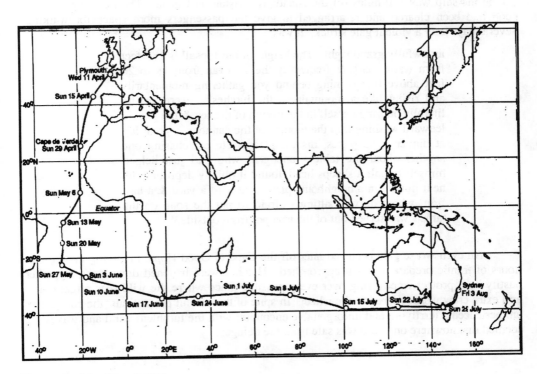

The voyage of the *Florentia* 1838.

---

48    Ibid, 10 May.

The monotony of the next few days was punctuated by the illness and death of a valuable horse being carried as cargo. A trivial quarrel between two passengers escalated to the point where one attempted to throw the other into the sea. Passengers amused themselves by throwing empty bottles overboard, and firing rifles at them. The cow became ill, and there was no milk. Water was rationed to one pint per person daily, for washing, 'ours stunk this morn^g beastly, sometimes in opening a fresh cask the foul air arising from it will actually burn.'[49]

As they approached the coast of South America, a gale struck. It lasted two days and it was so fierce that passengers were often unable to stand upright. On 26 May letters home were written hastily so they could be sent with a ship travelling in the opposite direction. The following day a whale appeared and remained only a few yards away from the ship. One of the cabin passengers shot at it, but missed, prompting Tippett, a shoemaker travelling in the steerage compartment,[50] to bring his old, rusty rifle on deck. This caused consternation amongst the cabin passengers, whose worst fears were realised when the rusty rifle exploded on firing. The whale was unhurt, but Tippett suffered serious injuries to his arm, and in the excitement one of the male cabin passengers fainted from the shock of being almost shot.

The worst of the heat was over, and on 30 May the north-east winds arrived, 'leaving the calms and variables behind' much to Bloxome's relief. The livestock remaining on board consisted of 24 sheep, 21 pigs, 104 fowls, thirteen turkeys, eight geese and fourteen ducks. The calf had pined after the cow's death, so was killed and thrown overboard. An even greater calamity was the news that the cabin passengers were on the last case of claret.[51] On 7 June the ship was 350 miles off the islands of Tristan da Cunha. The hen coops on the poop had been cleared and re-arranged to give the passengers more space for walking. Several days later a violent gale struck. It was:

> an awfully grand sight. The height of our topsail is 18[52] feet
> from water mark & frequently the seas ran from 18 to 20
> feet above that coming behind you gathering momentarily
> and rising like a mountain ... the lurches ... were terrific
> literally burying herself in the trough of the sea & the seas to
> leeward washing into the mouths of the cannons ... great fun
> at dinner - the plates, dishes, glasses etc etc chasing one
> another about the table - one gent who had just helped
> himself to half a sheeps head, found it quietly deposited the
> next minute in a neighbours plate ... at least a yard & a half
> from where he was sitting - afraid to put the soup on the
> table - was served out of the iron pot from outside.[53]

An even worse gale occurred later off the Cape of Good Hope, involving the crew in hours of frantic preparation as it approached. Hatches were battened down,[54] the carpenter hastily built protective covering over every possible place where the wild seas might enter, and extra crew were ordered to the wheel. In spite of the careful precautions, the passengers enxperienced a terrifying and unforgettable encounter with the turbulent wind and waves. It seemed that nowhere on board was safe from the deluge:

---

49 Ibid, 21 May.
50 Ibid, 27 May. His name suggests that he could have been a Cornishman.
51 Ibid, 30 May.
52 This is '18 feet' in the manuscript.
53 O. Bloxsome, 'Journal', 10 June.
54 Presumably with the steerage passengers locked below the hatches as was the custom. (D. Charlewwod, *The long farewell*, pp.6, 116-117.)

as quick as thought there was a general cry to "hold on"
when she gave a terrific lurch to larboard and fairly buried
herself in the waves, the water rushing in at the ports - over
the bulwarks & in every direction - the cuddy door was
forced open & in an instant was knee deep in water the
chairs actually floating about & everything in the greatest
possible confusion - The scene at this time beggars
description, what with the cries & fainting of the women,
the scurry of the men, jumping on the table, anywhere to get
out of the way, the laughter of the sailors, the rushing
backwards & forwards of this immense body of water in the
Cabin - the howling of the wind & sea, altogether formed
such a scene as cannot easily be imagined ... an immense
proportion of the water found its way down ... going down
like a cataract & deluging all the Births [sic] below.[55]

During the next few weeks the weather was reasonable. They passed Madagascar and
organised a lottery to gamble on the time they would reach the island of St Pauls. The
temperature dropped appreciably as they reached latitude 37°S, and complaints began about
the standard of provisions in the cuddy. There was no milk, and the potatoes, the bottled
porter and the cuddy biscuit ran out, forcing them to make do with common sailors biscuit.
The port and sherry were undrinkable, and rumours abounded that rice and yeast supplies
were almost exhausted. There was no oil for the lamps, forcing passengers to make do with
their own candles. It was calculated that food supplies would only just hold out - there were
only twenty fowls, six sheep, five pigs and one old goose left. The following day they were
'250 miles from the westmost point of New Holland'. Soon after, a passenger's
Newfoundland dog went missing, and it was assumed that it had fallen overboard.

On 23 July they had been 61 days at sea without sighting land, but within two days
they were off the coast of South Australia and great excitement prevailed at the thought of
seeing land soon. Soon Cape Howe was sighted, and several of the young cabin passengers
decided to get off the ship and walk to Sydney, buying pannikins and other equipment from
the steerage passengers in preparation, until Captain Deloitte vetoed the scheme.

On 3 August the passengers were delighted when they passed Botany Bay. Soon they
reached Sydney Heads where the pilot boarded and guided them to their destination, 113
days after leaving Plymouth.[56]

George and Jane Hawke travelled as unassisted steerage passengers aboard *Florentia*,
but in the journal written towards the end of his life, he made brief reference only to the
early, abortive section of the voyage, and to the arrival in New South Wales.[57] Although the
surviving detailed descriptions of this voyage were written by English cabin passengers, the
experiences they described were shared by the small group of Cornish aboard *Florentia*, and
by many thousands of Cornish assisted and non-assisted immigrants during the next 40
years. The ships used on the later immigrant voyages to New South Wales were larger,
carried more passengers and a greater proportion of assisted emigrants, and sometimes made
the passage in a shorter time than *Florentia* did. But the experiences of the voyage were
similar, particularly while it was still navigated under sail[58]

Bonding on the long voyage, amongst those who who knew each other before
embarkation and also amongst those who began the voyage as strangers, was often a factor

55   O. Bloxsome, 'Journal', 16 June.
56   Ibid, 3 August.
57   George Hawke, *Colonial experience: diary of George Hawke of Orange*, NLA MS 227, p.64.
58   D. Charlwood, *The long farewell*, p.32.

influencing the choice of settlement area on arrival.[59]  Apparently it was a strong factor amongst the Cornish passengers aboard *Florentia*, because most of them settled in the same area.  They stayed within the colonial Cornish community, and in one particular section of it: the Bathurst-Orange district.

With his considerable experience in conveying emigrants to New South Wales, Captain Deloitte believed that it was 'rather difficult to induce such persons to Emigrate as would come within the terms of the Government Regulations'.  He had found that most emigrants were:

> persons who had a little money, but not enough to pay their
> own expenses, and have had some assistance to enable them
> to join their friends here.  Those friends have often sent
> home for such parties; giving the owner of the vessel a
> guarantee to pay on arrival here the difference between the
> bounty allowed and the actual expense.[60]

The Cornish emigrants he carried aboard *Florentia* were apparently travelling together to a destination they had chosen carefully, and where they had friends or relatives already resident.

Amongst the *Florentia*'s steerage passengers were George Hawke of Cornish Settlement, his bride Jane, and nephew Frederick.  Nine of the fifteen bounty emigrants were Cornish, and consisted of one family group and five single adults.  A Wesleyan, William Rowe of Bodmin aged 34, a house carpenter and joiner, was accompanied by his wife Eleanor also aged 34, and their small children Mary and Rebecca.  The unmarried male bounty immigrants were Edward Nicholls aged 26, a farm overseer of Treglossack, St Keverne, (and believed to be the Edward Nicholls who later married into the Lane family in Cornish Settlement),[61]  John Rogers aged 22 of Manaccan and Robert Smith (brother of John Smith of Molong) aged 25, a farm overseer of St Keverne.  Nicholls and Smith were Church of England and Rogers a Methodist.  The two single women were Ann Wills Tristrain, a dressmaker aged 25 of Truro, and Mary Grace Vercoe aged fifteen, a nursemaid of St Columb.  One was Wesleyan, the other Methodist, and both were under the protection[62] of George Hawke.  Ann Tristrain accompanied the Hawkes to the Bathurst district, and married Samuel Bray, a Cornish tailor and draper of Bathurst, in May the following year.  At the time of her marriage, she was living at Queen Charlotte's Vale, near Cornish Settlement.  A witness to the marriage was John Tom, presumably 'Parson' Tom's son John.[63]

It is likely that George and Jane Hawke already knew the Cornish bounty passengers, and that George had organised a group to travel together as he had done on his first voyage to the colony in 1828.[64]  The Hawkes and the Rowes were certainly close friends in Cornish Settlement, and like George Hawke, an active member of the Wesleyan community.  The Hawkes took Rebecca Rowe in as a daughter following her mother's death.[65]  Robert Smith was a brother of John Smith of 'Gamboola', Molong, who was well acquainted with the families at Cornish Settlement, having made contact with John Glasson almost directly after his arrival in New South Wales in 1836.[66]  Smith, Nicholls and Rogers, who all came from the Lizard Peninsula, doubtless knew each other before embarkation.

---

59  Ibid, p.127.

60  W.S. Deloitte Esq. in 'Minutes of evidence taken before the Committee on Immigration', p.845.

61  Information from Mr Alan Lane.

62  Single women emigrants were placed under the protection of a male family member, or of a married couple. (R.B. Madgwick, *Immigration into eastern Australia*, p.120.)

63  'Wesleyan Chapel Bathurst, marriage register 1839-1844', 9 May 1839. NLA MS 3290. This marriage does not appear in NSWRGI.

64  George Hawke, *Colonial experience*, NLA MS 227, p.24.

65  *BT*, 11 June 1917, p.2, c.4, obituary of Mrs George Hawke.

66  B. Mac. Smith, *Quench not the spirit: merino heritage*, Hawthorn Press, Melbourne, 1972, p.50.

The voyage of the *Florentia* set a pattern which many later emigrants were to follow. Their experiences on the long voyage, and the bonding of the Cornish minority aboard the *Florentia*, and their subsequent settling in the same part of the colony, mirror the experiences of other Cornish emigrants who followed them over the next 40 years. After arrival in the colony, many of these later immigrants also chose to cluster together at Cornish Settlement and in other recognisably Cornish communities in New South Wales.

PLATE 19.     Sydney Heads in sight.

'An Australian emigrant ship – Sydney Heads in sight.' From *The Australian Town and Country Journal*, 15 March 1873, p.337. (Courtesy of the State Library of New South Wales.)

# CHAPTER FOUR

## 'WOOLOOMOOLOO OR OTHER PLACE OF NAME INFINITELY REPETATIVE'

*In 1893 a visitor to Cornwall wrote that "... the Cornish miners have mostly emigrated ..." and that, to find the Cornishman engaged in his traditional pursuit, one had to travel to Australia where "... in some Wooloomooloo or other place of name infinitely repetative, you shall who seek, find him ..."[1]*

The Cornish population in New South Wales after 40 years of settlement was small, less than one percent of the total.[2] Apart from government personnel and convicts, the early Cornish arrivals in the penal colony of New South Wales were those belonging to the landowning classes who could afford to pay for their passages and then to set themselves up on land in the colony. The original Cornish families at Cornish Settlement and the Dangars in the Hunter were such immigrants. The introduction of assisted emigration gave those from the poorer classes in Cornwall the opportunity to emigrate from the late 1830s onwards.[3] While some of these assisted immigrants chose to join relatives in the Bathurst district or the Hunter region, others settled in areas like Sydney, or the coastal districts of Kiama, Eden and Kempsey. After the discovery of copper, gold and tin, Cornish people were also attracted to the mining districts of Adelong, Cobar and New England. Wherever they eventually settled, however, they first had to pass through Sydney.[4]

The Cornish assisted immigrants who began arriving in the late 1830s were coming to a small administrative town perched on the edge of a vast and largely unsettled continent, barely 50 years after its establishment as a penal colony. The rectangular-shaped main settlement covered only a few square miles, bounded by Sydney Cove on the north, by the ridge in the south known as the Surry Hills, the valley below the ridge of Woolloomooloo to the east, and by Darling Harbour to the west.[5] Already Sydney was becoming a busy port, whose merchants engaged in commerce and whaling.[6] They built warehouses and stores at Darling Harbour,[7] and across the water at Pyrmont a waterfront industrial area was developing.[8]

---

1   P.J. Payton, *The Cornish miner in Australia: Cousin Jack Down Under*, Dyllansow Truran, Redruth, 1984, p.31.

2   See Table 3.2.

3   Assisted emigration began early in the 1830s, but it was not until 1837 that Cornish families came in any numbers. For information on the early assisted emigration schemes, see R.B. Madgwick, *Immigration into Eastern Australia 1788-1851*, first published 1937, Sydney University Press, Sydney, 1969.

4   There were a few exceptions, when ships went to other ports like Newcastle, Port Stephens or Moreton Bay.

5   J. Maclehose, *Picture of Sydney and strangers' guide in N.S.W. for 1839*, first published 1839, republished John Ferguson in association with the Royal Australian Historical Society, Sydney, 1977, pp.58-9.

6   M. Kelly and R. Crocker, *Sydney takes shape: a collection of contemporary maps from foundation to Federation*, Doak Press in association with the Macleay Museum, University of Sydney, 1978, p.17.

7   J. Maclehose, *Picture of Sydney*, pp.61-2.

8   M. Kelly and R. Crocker, *Sydney takes shape*, pp.17-18.

Max Kelly has summed up the major developmental problems which dogged Sydney's expansion throughout the century:

> The ambience in which nineteenth century suburban Sydney evolved was free wheeling, desultory and frantic. Profit making dictated the terms. Jobbery was attended by land and property laws decades if not centuries behind the local requirement. Amenity in new suburbia was typically non-existent. The fledgling local government structure was barely able to control the stinks and the slops.[9]

PLATE 20.     Map of Sydney and suburbs 1861

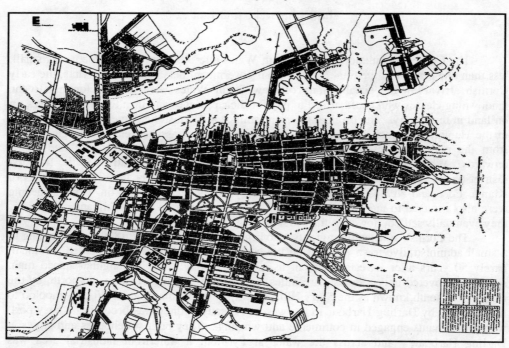

Map of the city of Sydney and suburbs 1861. (From J.W. Waugh, *The stranger's guide to Sydney*, first published 1861, facsimile reprint Library of Australian History, North Sydney, 1978.)

The first suburbs emerged on the outskirts of the town as Sydney's population doubled to 35,000 between 1833 and 1843. Redfern, Alexandria and Chippendale appeared to the south and Woolloomooloo[10] and Darlinghurst to the east. Balmain, Darling Harbour and Pyrmont continued to grow as maritime and mercantile districts.[11]

---

9  M. Kelly (ed.), *Sydney: city of suburbs*, New South Wales University Press in association with the Sydney History Group, Sydney, 1987, introduction, p.2.

10  There has been disagreement about the spelling of this suburb, but Woolloomooloo is commonly accepted. (I. Brodsky, *Sydney's little world of Woolloomooloo*, Old Sydney Free Press, Neutral Bay, N.S.W., 1966, pp.18-20.

11  M. Kelly and R. Crocker, *Sydney takes shape*, pp.19-20.

An outlying settlement already existed at Botany, where market gardeners made use of the fertile soil and abundant water, to supply Sydney with produce.[12] Botany also housed a settlement of fishermen and an embryonic manufacturing industry which expanded later in the century. Separate settlements also existed at Liverpool, and at Parramatta in the other direction,[13] with produce from Parramatta and Lane Cove being sent along the Parramatta River to Sydney by boat.[14]

As Sydney's population continued to increase during the 1840s, the provision of necessary services was already failing to keep pace. A series of articles in the *Sydney Morning Herald* in 1851 examined city localities in turn:

> our Reporter urgently insists that he has never witnessed in the larger towns of England that extent of physical degradation in proportion to numbers, as he has in Sydney.[15]

The newspaper publicised widespread overcrowding, and criticised the unsatisfactory water, sewerage and drainage facilities in most parts of Sydney. The appalling conditions were particularly evident in areas inhabited by mechanics and labourers, who had little choice other than to pay high rents for substandard accommodation.[16]

> the little cabins in which they live, move and have their being in Sydney, are not on the whole near so roomy as those in which we found so much difficulty to pass a hundred days [on the voyage out].[17]

In 1858, W.S. Jevons produced a detailed social survey of Sydney,[18] which supported the findings of the *Sydney Morning Herald* report of 1851. He classified the population into three categories:

> the first includes all who may be termed gentlemen and ladies, including mercantile men, clerks, and other chief employees, professional men, chief shopkeepers, independent gentlemen, etc. The second class includes most mechanics or skilled artisans, shopkeepers, shopmen, etc. The third or remaining class comprises labourers and the indefinable lower orders.[19]

Jevons found that the first class resided either in the town centre or in suburban areas 'chiefly on elevated land' and 'distinctly separated from the lowest class residences'. The second-class residences were generally found in 'intermediate districts at a short distance from the central parts of the town'. They were Woolloomooloo, Surry Hills, Strawberry Hill, Redfern, Chippendale, Glebe, Pyrmont, Balmain, the upper Rocks area, and Newtown, Paddington and Camperdown. The third-class residences were in 'the lowest and least

---

12  F.A. Larcombe, *The history of Botany 1788-1963*, Council of the Municipality of Botany, Botany, N.S.W., 1963, pp.12-13.

13  Although these are now swallowed up in suburban Sydney, originally they were completely separate from Sydney. They are included because of Cornish people who settled along the Parramatta River on small farms or orchards, between Sydney and Parramatta. In the case of Liverpool, settlers such as the Wearne family moved there from Sydney.

14  M. Kelly and R. Crocker, *Sydney takes shape*, pp.19-20.

15  *SMH* 5 April 1851, p.2, c.4.

16  *SMH* 8 February 1851, p.2, c.3. An example is given of a labourer earning an average over the year of 18s weekly, and paying rental expenses (including 1/9 for buying water by the bucket) of 6/6d weekly.)

17  *SMH* 15 February 1851, p.2, c.5.

18  W.S. Jevons, 'A social survey of Sydney 1858', ML B864. Jevons' survey was published as a series of articles in *SMH* between 6 November and 7 December 1929. The section of his manuscript 'Sydney by night, 1858', was not included in the *SMH* articles.

19  *SMH*, 9 November 1929, p.13.

desirable localities', and were often 'of considerable age, showing that the land had been long located'. He named the Rocks, the lower end of Sussex Street, the northern part of Chippendale, and Durands Alley (bordered by George, Pitt, Goulburn and Campbell Streets) as being amongst the worst.

Several years later, a parliamentary inquiry supported these findings, deploring the overcrowded and unsanitary conditions which abounded. The city and suburbs were equally bad, and although the older dilapidated dwellings were strongly criticised, it was reported that new dwellings were being built without proper drainage or ventilation.[20]

There was a dramatic rise in Sydney's population during the 1850s and 1860s, and a resulting overflow into the surrounding suburbs. In 1861 metropolitan Sydney's population of 96,000 was almost double that of 1851.[21] This continued, with a 5% annual growth in the suburban population and a 2.5% annual growth in the city during the 1860s. The already-settled suburbs, (including Surry Hills, Woolloomooloo, Darlinghurst, Paddington, Glebe, Redfern, Waterloo and Alexandria,) experienced consistently high population increases during the decade. Across the harbour, St. Leonards grew by 50%,[22] and Manly began its development as a residential and resort area.[23] Throughout this period, Sydney remained 'a walking man's city', where only those able to afford private transport could live at any distance from their work.[24] From the 1870s, as central Sydney changed from a residential to a business district, the excess population spilled into the closer suburbs, such as Surry Hills.[25]

The population of the suburbs doubled during the 1880s, while that of the city increased by only seven percent.[26] Although suburban growth continued during the building boom of the 1880s, much of it was consolidation of the already-existing suburbs.[27] By the 1890s, Sydney's metropolitan area stretched across an area of 150 square miles, with three quarters of the population of 400,000 living in the suburbs.[28] The tremendous growth in population created further overcrowding, and in 1891 half the residents of Sydney lived in a population density of between 29 and 62 persons to the acre. In Marrickville the ratio was 6.73 per acre, while in Darlington it was 61.88.[29]

Shirley Fitzgerald demonstrated that the health, as well as the living and working conditions of working class people in Sydney worsened over the boom period between 1870 and 1890. Infant mortality was higher in Sydney than in London during the 1880s, and 'young adults died of typhoid at rates far higher than in Britain'. The increasing population continued to outstrip the provision of the necessary amenities, and occupational and social mobility were relatively rare. The economy needed unskilled labourers, and mechanisation devalued traditional skills.[30]

So Cornish immigrants, like others attempting to settle in the city or suburbs of Sydney from the 1840s onward, were likely to be forced into an overcrowded and unhealthy environment which they were powerless to alter. However, just as those who went to the Bathurst district and the Hunter clustered in certain areas, so did those who chose to settle in Sydney. They congregated in certain suburban areas, and in certain streets within the city of

20 'Report on the condition of the working classes of the metropolis', *NSWLA V&P 1859/60*, vol.4, p.1265-1461.
21 M. Kelly and R. Crocker, *Sydney takes shape*, p.27.
22 Ibid, p.29.
23 P. Ashton, 'Inventing Manly', in *Sydney;city of suburbs*, M. Kelly (ed.), New South Wales University Press in association with the Sydney History Group, Sydney, 1987, pp.152-5.
24 G. Aplin, 'The rise of suburban Sydney', in *Sydney;city of suburbs*, M. Kelly (ed.), pp.197-9.
25 M. Kelly, 'Picturesque and pestilential;the Sydney slum observed 1860-90' in *Nineteenth century Sydney: essays in urban history*, Sydney University Press in association with the Sydney History Group, Sydney, 1978, pp.70-2.
26 M. Kelly and R. Crocker, *Sydney takes shape*, p.42.
27 Ibid, p.39.
28 Ibid, p.44.
29 M. Kelly, 'Picturesque and pestilential; the Sydney slum observed 1860-90', pp.68-70.
30 S. Fitzgerald, *Rising damp: Sydney 1870-1890*, Oxford University Press, Melbourne, 1987, pp.7-10.

Sydney.[31] Almost all of their chosen areas of settlement matched those described by Jevons in 1858 as the 'second class areas inhabited by respectable tradesmen and mechanics'.[32]

PLATE 21.     Map of suburban Sydney.

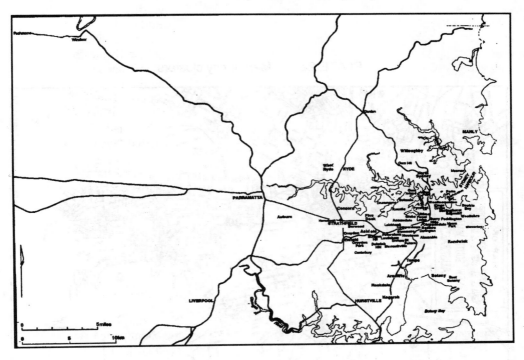

In 1860, John (Hawken) Towzey, originally from Padstow in Cornwall, was living in Sydney and selling window blinds for which he earned £2 per week. He lived in shared accommodation:

> We are living in a house - four of us, all young men at 14/-
> per week Rent and provide ourselves it costs us about 14/6
> to 15/- per week each to live Rent included  if we went to
> lodgings it would cost us 23/- per week. We get a woman to
> cook for us at 6/- per week and keep House clean so we get
> along Jolly.[33]

One quarter of the Cornish in suburban Sydney clustered in three adjoining suburbs: Surry Hills, Woolloomooloo and Darlinghurst.  There were significant groups in other

---

31   It is possible that persons who ensured that their status as natives of Cornwall was recorded on their tombstones or in death notices were more likely to cluster with other Cornish during their lifetimes. However, these are more than balanced by the random Cornish recorded in marriage registers, and by the information from descendants.

32   The 'indefinable lower orders' of Jevons' survey probably were never recorded in *Sands*, so any Cornish in this category may have been missed.

33   John (Hawken) Towzey, letter to his parents in Padstow, Cornwall, 12 May 1860. I am indebted to Mr Robert Jeremy for sending me a copy of this letter.

suburbs in the same part of Sydney: Paddington, Woollahra and Waverley; Balmain, Glebe and Pyrmont; Chippendale, Redfern, Waterloo, Newtown and Darlington; and Botany.[34] Further evidence of this clustering is given in the name counts of New South Wales electoral rolls, which show varying density of Cornish settlement in certain Sydney electorates. See Tables 3.3 and 3.4.

Plate 22 shows the clustering in the city and in some of the surrounding suburbs.[35]

### PLATE 22.    Map of city clusters

Map of the city of Sydney showing Cornish settlement.

Max Kelly used a system of suburban grouping to illustrate population increase between 1881 and 1891.[36]  When the count of the Cornish population is moved into these groupings it continues to show that there was a Cornish preference for certain districts, because almost 70% of the Cornish resident in these divisions lived in Sydney's east, east central, west central and north west divisions.[37]  Almost one quarter were located in the 'east-central' division which included Redfern, Darlington, Waterloo, Botany, North Botany and Alexandria.[38]  See Table 2.9.

---

34  See Table 2.8.

35  Information in Plate 14 was compiled from the Sydney data base.  Each black dot represents a Cornish immigrant known to be at an exact address.  Many others gave merely the suburb and so are not included here.

36  M. Kelly, 'Picturesque and pestilential;the Sydney slum observed 1860-90', p.69.

37  Kelly's groupings were North West, West central, East central, West, South, East, and North Shore.

38  The total numbers of Cornish entries in the data base changed to 553 in this example, as Kelly did not include the inner suburbs which by then were regarded as part of the city.

Within the city of Sydney itself, a preference for certain areas was also evident, and included the following streets: Castlereagh, Clarence, Dixon, Elizabeth, George, Gloucester, Goulburn, Hunter, Kent, King, Liverpool, Macquarie, Market, Pitt, Princes and Sussex.

Movement by Cornish settlers within suburbs or between adjacent suburbs was common, particularly amongst those renting premises. Edmund and Martha Cleave, for example, arrived in 1853 and in 1858 lived at 6 Brown's Terrace, Glebe. In 1861 they were at 37 Chowne Street Pyrmont, in 1873 at 154 John Street Pyrmont, and in 1877 and 1882 at Mill Street Pyrmont. When Edmund died in 1887 their address was 1 Church Street, off Mill Street Pyrmont. Martha had moved, in her old age, to live with her married daughter, and at the time of her death in 1913, her address was Neutral Bay, but 'formerly of Mill Street Pyrmont'.[39] Although the Cleaves had lived in the same part of Sydney throughout their working lives, their daughter's social mobility was evident in her North Shore address.

Others such as Robert and Mary Taylor, who arrived aboard *Andromache* in 1839, established themselves in one place and remained there throughout their lives. The Taylors lived at Wellington Street, Chippendale, where Robert conducted a coachbuilding business.[40] The Hambly, Lobb and Sawle families formed the nucleus of the Cornish community at Botany with market gardening and dairying being their main occupations until the end of the century.[41]

The upwardly-mobile flow from the inner suburbs to the Petersham district began in the late 1870s, and amongst the Cornish involved were successful builders and other businessmen. However, these moves were not confined to any particular occupational group, but were based rather on the Cornish origins they had in common. George Crothers, a builder from Surry Hills, James Bennett a builder from Redfern, and Henry and Joseph Juleff who were ironfounders from Redfern, were amongst those who made such a move. The Juleffs and Bennett moved to the same street, West Street, Petersham. Such stories of metamorphosis, from poor immigrant to successful middle class resident, abound in *Australian Men of Mark*, but none states the facts quite so baldly as does the entry for bootmaker William Harris of Oxford Street, who 'arrived in the colony with only half a crown in his possession, and has worked himself up by indefatigable perseverance. [By the time of the biographical entry in 1888] He has six valuable houses in the city and suburbs'.[42]

Other successful businessmen chose to stay in their original areas of settlement. Typical of these were the Best family, who were builders and in associated trades, and who remained in the Surry Hills district. James Green, a painter of Paddington, settled and remained all his life in that suburb, operating a paint shop. Benjamin Knuckey, a stonemason, for obvious reasons continued to reside near Waverley cemetery.[43] John and Nanny Wills, who came aboard *Hydaspes* in 1853, settled at Ashfield and stayed there, where John was first a carpenter, then a joiner, and eventually a Clerk of Works.[44]

Some Cornish emigrants who had gone originally to the country districts drifted back to the city as part of the increased urbanisation of Sydney in the last quarter of the century. Jonathon and Mary Mullis had come aboard *Lord Stanley* in 1850, going directly to Emu Plains, west of Sydney at the foot of the Blue Mountains. After almost 30 years as farmers in this little rural community, they moved to Redfern where he began permanent employment as a carpenter in the railway workshops.[45] They were typical of others who also chose to move from the country to Cornish areas of settlement in Sydney.

---

39 This information is taken from the Sydney data base, and came from *Sands* and from *SMH* death and funeral notices, and shipping arrivals.
40 Information from Ms Margaret Watts.
41 *AMM*, vol.2 appendix p.9, James Sawle. [*AMM* version in Newcastle Region Library.] Information from Major D.H.V. Lobb.
42 *AMM*, vol.2 appendix p.16. [*AMM* version in Newcastle Region Library.]
43 This information is taken from the Sydney data base, in the author's possession.
44 Information from Miss Grace Thrush.
45 P. Lay, 'Clotted cream and chapel: the Mullis family in Cornwall and New South Wales', Dip. FHS., Society of

Certain Sydney suburbs had a distinct occupational bias, but this was not reflected amongst the occupations of Cornish residents. Max Kelly describes Paddington as 'Sydney's first commuter suburb'. The majority of its residents travelled outside the suburb to work, whereas other suburbs had an 'independent economic life'. Production of food and cheap clothing centred on Surry Hills, Strawberry Hills, Darlington and Chippendale. Newtown and St Peters had industries such as 'tanning, brickmaking, wool washing and soap making'. Balmain was a waterside suburb which developed complementary engineering and timber industries, and many Redfern residents were involved with the railway.[46] Redfern and Waterloo were also suburbs where an extensive bootmaking industry developed.[47]

Cornish settlers with specific occupations were not confined to certain suburbs, however. The occupations amongst the Cornish in Glebe, for instance, varied from clerk to traveller. Even the waterfront suburbs of Pyrmont and Balmain, which did have the expected maritime occupations, also had a variety of others. The other suburbs also contained a cross-section of occupations, which could be explained by clustering according to Cornish ethnicity rather than occupational grouping. See Table 2.10.

Shirley Fitzgerald has classified the occupations of Sydney residents, between 1870 and 1890, into five categories, and for convenience I have adopted her classifications.[48] Forty percent of the Sydney Cornish, whose occupations were known, belonged to the category of tradesmen and skilled workers, 22 percent were in the white collar category, and a further 22 percent were unskilled labourers. Only seven percent belonged to the professional category and nine percent had rural occupations.[49] There was no strong common occupational bias in the places of residence chosen, which supports the view that ethnicity was a major determinant in the Sydney clusters.

Numbers and location in some occupational categories were unexpected. Only thirteen of the 45 Cornish miners resided out of Sydney, but they lived in areas of Cornish settlement like Adelong, Nymagee (near Cobar) and New England. Their marriages, in Sydney, to women who were residents of Sydney suggests that contact between Cornish communities in Sydney and other areas of New South Wales was being maintained. A further fourteen Cornish miners gave no residence, and were generally newly-arrived immigrants supplying the names of relatives in Sydney. The miners claiming to be resident in Sydney stated that they lived in suburbs such as Annandale (1896) and Burwood (1887). These miners may have been engaged in the large-scale tunnelling work for the city's drainage scheme, or may have been unemployed persons who were still identified with their former occupation.[50] The large number of grocers, greengrocers and storekeepers was also unexpected. Such occupations offered independence to unskilled labourers who had managed to amass a small capital, or to skilled men like miner James Smitham, who did not wish to follow that occupation in the colony. An added advantage of such an occupation was that widows and children of these shopkeepers had the financial security of being able to continue alone with the shop, in which they had probably worked in any case. Again, no Cornish occupational bias was evident in particular suburbs. The mix of occupations within the suburban clusters suggests a gathering because of ethnicity rather than occupation alone. See Table 2.11.

On some occasions, assisted immigrants made apparently false statements about their occupations on arrival. For example, Edward (sometimes Edwin) Mount, stated that he was an agricultural labourer when he arrived aboard *Lord Stanley* in 1850. In directories between 1866 and 1886 he was listed as a dyer in Redfern, Glebe and Woolloomooloo. His was not

---

Australian Genealogists, Sydney, 1988, p.28.

46   M. Kelly, *Paddock full of houses: Paddington 1840-1890*, Doak Press, Paddington, N.S.W., 1978, pp.3-4.
47   S. Fitzgerald, *Rising damp*, pp.148-9.
48   I am indebted to Dr Fitzgerald for giving me access to her notes on these classifications.
49   See Table 2.11.
50   Discussion with Dr Shirley Fitzgerald.

an isolated case, and almost 30 years later, in spite of changes in assisted immigration regulations, this practice of telling officials what one thought they wanted to hear was still occurring.[51] Richard H. Bryant of St Ives arrived with his wife and family aboard *St Lawrence* in 1877, claiming to be a shoemaker, aged 42.[52] In 1886, when his daughter Elizabeth was married, she gave her residence as the highly ranked suburb of Petersham and her father's occupation as master mariner.[53]

The occupations of other immigrants may have altered as a response to circumstances, or to take advantage of unexpected opportunities, showing the Cornish ability to adapt easily. For example, James Smitham, a miner aboard *La Hogue* in 1877, was a draper at Pyrmont in 1892, and William Soper, a farm labourer aboard *Lord Stanley* in 1850, had become a partner in a city produce agency by 1863 and a commission agent by 1866.

However, immigrants who were employed throughout their lives as servants were unlikely ever to appear in a directory. One such person, Grace Worden, who was a native of Padstow in Cornwall, died in Sydney in 1911 at the age of 62, 'having lived in the service of the one family for forty two years'.[54]

In Sydney, many of the stated occupations were quite different from those in the Bathurst district and the Hunter region, and such a variation would be expected between city and country areas. However, the types of occupations were similar because the majority of Cornish immigrants demonstrated a preference for the kind of work which allowed them some independence and control over their own lives. Those who were tradesmen preferred trades such as carpenter or stonemason, where they could be self-employed and from which they could progress to the more highly ranked occupations like that of builder. Those who were not tradesmen still showed a preference for occupations like that of storekeeper where they were self-employed or at least had some independence. Many Cornish immigrants were able to move between occupations with apparent ease, showing the flexibility and adaptability which characterised the Cornish.

It cannot be argued that occupation was the sole reason for Cornish clustering in particular suburbs, because many moved between suburbs, and also because many Cornish settlers in Sydney living in the same or nearby suburbs were of quite different occupational mixes. While occupation was an important factor, it was not the only one. There was obviously also a strong element of personal choice, with some immigrants choosing to live in an area because they were close to other Cornish settlers, regardless of their occupations.

Although the Cornish in Sydney comprised only around one percent of the total population there between 1859 and 1898[55] their density was much greater in some areas than others. Long term clustering in Sydney was evident, not only amongst new arrivals, but also amongst those from country areas who came, often after many years, into the Cornish community in Sydney. This in itself demonstrates that contact was being maintained across the geographically scattered colonial clusters.

51  For detailed information on later regulations, see F.K. Crowley, 'British migration to Australia:1860-1914', D.Phil., Oxford, 1951.
52  AONSW shipping list *St Lawrence* 1877, AO reel 2488.
53  Marriage of Elizabeth Bryant and Frederick Thomas, St Peters CE, Cooks River, 14 April 1886. SAG reel 0001. NSWRGI no. 1886, 2745.
54  'Gore Hill Cemetery monumental inscriptions' SAG.
55  See Table 3.1.

# CHAPTER FIVE

## FARMERS, MINERS AND OTHERS.

*There came a day, as well you know,*
*That some took ship and sailed away,*
*And came to plough and till and sow,*
*Far away from where*
*The elm trees grow.*[1]

Cornish immigrants arriving in New South Wales followed the pattern set in other emigrant destinations, of clustering in identifiable Cornish communities. The assisted immigrants who arrived between 1837 and 1877 were only part of the entire Cornish arrivals, but the information they gave Immigration officials about their relatives already living in the colony indicated that groups of Cornish were congregating in certain areas of New South Wales. When assisted immigrants did admit to having relatives already resident in the colony, they generally stated that these persons were living in the Bathurst district, in the Hunter region, in Sydney, in the mining districts of Adelong and New England, and in several coastal areas such as Kiama, Eden and Kempsey. The Cornish settlers making up these resident groups were a mixture of assisted immigrants and unassisted passengers who had come directly from Cornwall, and others who had come via other colonies, or in some cases via the United States. Some of these clusters were called 'Cornish Settlement' or 'Cornish Town' for the very reason that they contained mostly Cornish inhabitants.

One of these, Cornish Settlement between Bathurst and Orange, formed the nucleus for long-term clustering in the Bathurst-Orange district. The gathering of Cornish settlers in the Bathurst district began with a collection of people engaged in agricultural occupations, but they and later arrivals became involved in the copper and gold mining industries which developed in the Bathurst district, heightening its similarity with their homeland, where farming and mining were carried on side by side.

A similar occupational mix of agriculture and mining occurred amongst the Cornish immigrants who clustered in the Hunter region, but here though, the concentration was on coal mining. Another similarity was that Cornish groups in the Hunter formed around the nucleus of an early arriving, landowning Cornish family, the Dangars from St Neot.

Cornish immigrants gathered in other parts of New South Wales as well. Those who engaged in occupations other than farming or mining generally worked in the trades and service industries. Apart from those who concentrated in certain city and suburban areas of Sydney, there were others who formed smaller communities in several localities along the north and south coast of New South Wales, while yet other groups of Cornish were attracted by mining at Adelong, Cobar and New England towards the end of the century. These mining areas produced gold, copper (or sometimes a mixture of both), and tin.

This chapter will examine the settlement patterns of the Cornish who chose to gather in communities in the Bathurst-Orange district[2] and the Hunter region. Chapter Six will

---

1   'Moonta, Wallaroo, Kadina', words and music by Richard Gendall.
2   Hereafter, 'Bathurst' refers to the township of Bathurst and its surrounds, and 'the Bathurst district' to the area around and including the townships of Bathurst, Orange, Molong, Oberon and Hill End.

follow settlement patterns in the smaller or later developing settlement areas of Cobar, Adelong, New England and the coastal districts.

PLATE 23.    Bathurst district map

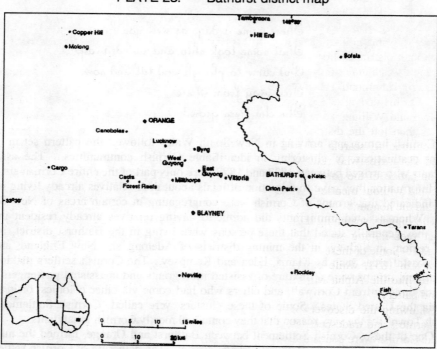

Bathurst was the first inland settlement in Australia.  After the crossing of the Blue Mountains, the barrier west of Sydney, the area beyond them was described by Assistant Surveyor, George Evans, in December 1813.  On his advice a military outpost was established on the present site of Bathurst on the western bank of the Macquarie River.  This site took advantage of the excellent water supply, and the good visibility made possible by the large expanse of open plain.[3]  Later a hamlet of free settlers began across the river at Kelso, separated from the convict establishment by that river.  Free settlement on the Bathurst side of the Macquarie River was not permitted until after 1826, and it was 1833 before town allotments were available in Bathurst itself.  The town remained an outpost for some years, its major function still dependent on the government, but it also became a centre for settlers further out.[4]  A steady stream of settlers came in the early years, despite the ever-present threat of confrontations with aborigines or bushrangers.[5]

By 1841 the Bathurst district had developed a thriving pastoral economy and had a population of 3,599.  Woolgrowing had brought expansion and prosperity which had been slowed, but not halted, by drought in the late 1830s and depression in the early 1840s.  The

3    B. Greaves (ed.), *The story of Bathurst*, 3rd edition, Angus and Robertson, Sydney, 1976, pp.1-4.
4    Ibid, pp.18-19.
5    Ibid, pp.19-23.

only industries in the district were the milling of flour for local use, and wine-making, tanning and cheese-making.[6]

The early Cornish settlers in the Bathurst district took up farming. They did this not necessarily because they were unfamiliar with mining - farming and mining were often carried out side by side in Cornwall - but because there was no major mining industry in New South Wales until the late 1840s.[7] Potential immigrants quickly learnt to emphasise their farming rather than their mining backgrounds.

Commercial mining in the Bathurst district began in the late 1840s when copper was found at Molong, Rockley and Cornish Settlement.[8] This was soon followed by the discovery of payable gold at Ophir near Cornish Settlement in 1851, and the subsequent rush to the Bathurst district by hopeful diggers. Cornish involvement in the discovery of payable gold at Ophir was a major one as William Tom's sons from Cornish Settlement were partners with Edward Hammond Hargraves in this discovery which was to change the colony's history. On his arrival at Guyong, Hargraves had formed a partnership with John Lister, James Tom and William Tom Junior who built a gold cradle according to his instructions. Hargraves then left the district after an agreement was reached that the three young men would continue to search for gold. They soon found payable gold, and immediately contacted Hargraves who returned to Guyong and took the gold to claim the government reward on behalf of the partnership. However, he told officials that he had found the gold himself, and without mentioning his partnership with Lister and the Toms, he claimed the reward and the honour.[9]

The diggers searching for gold in the Bathurst district worked at first with alluvial gold, but reef mining soon began and the expertise of Cornish hard-rock miners was welcomed.[10] Some of these 'Cousin Jacks' experienced in hard-rock mining were already in the colony in 1851, while others came directly to the Bathurst district under contract to companies like the Alpha Mining Company at Hill End, which also imported a Cornish boiler and battery.[11]

Following the discovery of copper and then of gold in the Bathurst district, more miners, farmers and tradespeople came to join those already there. Unlike South Australia, where the Cornish were concentrated in the copper triangle of Wallaroo, Moonta and Kadina, and at Burra and Kapunda,[12] in the Bathurst district copper deposits of varying quantity and quality were scattered intermittently across quite a wide area. Gold often occurred close to the copper deposits, and other minerals such as silver, iron and asbestos existed in sufficient quantities to make their mining and quarrying worthwhile.[13] For example, there was gold at Macquarie Plains (Breewongle), Glanmire, Peel, Sofala, Hill End, Tambaroora, Wellington, Hargraves and Ironbark. There was copper at Cow Flat, gold and copper around Oberon, Rockley, Carcoar, and Orange. There was copper and coal at Molong, and gold and silver at Blayney.[14]

---

6    Ibid, pp.23-4.
7    Ibid, p.24. Many Cornish immigrants were familiar with farming and mining because although tin and copper mining had industrialised much of Cornwall by the nineteenth century, it was a rural area as well. Some Cornish parishes remained totally rural, others were a combination of mining and farming activities. (B. Deacon, 'Migration and the mining industry in East Cornwall in the mid nineteenth century', in *RICJ*, vol.X, part I, 1986-7, pp. 84-5.)
8    See chapter 1.
9    J. Rule, *The Cornish Settlement*, the author, Yagoona, N.S.W., 1978, pp.47-48.
10   This expertise was valued in other parts of Australia as well as in the Bathurst district and in 1861 copper mining companies were attempting to recruit Cornish copper miners to Queensland from the Bathurst district, through advertisements in the Bathurst press. (*BFP*, 8 May 1861, p.3, c.3.)
11   H. Hodge, *The Hill End story*, Book 1, 3rd edition, Hill End Publications, Toorak, Victoria, 1986, p.29.)
12   P.J. Payton, *The Cornish miner in Australia: Cousin Jack Down Under*, Dyllansow Truran, Redruth, 1984, p.1.
13   'Papers relative to geological surveys', *NSWLC V&P*, 1851, vol.2, pp.254-87.
14   A. Middleton and F.B. Maning, *Bathurst and Western District directory and tourist's guide and gazetteer 1886-7*, first published 1886, facsimile reprint LAH, North Sydney, 1978, pp.2-11.

As a consequence, the Cornish spread throughout most parts of the Bathurst district, frequently moving from one community to another before settling permanently in one place, usually as farmers or tradespeople. For example, John Grenfell Pascoe arrived in Adelaide in 1855 and spent several years mining in South Australia and Victoria before coming to the New South Wales goldfields in 1862. In 1873 he took up land at Beneree near Millthorpe, but at the same time he worked locally as a mine captain until he could afford to devote all his time to farming.[15]

Others chose to follow the mining strikes and eventually moved out of the district to other mining areas such as Adelong, Cobar and New England. For example Captain James Trevarthen, mine captain at Carangara mine, turned to carrying and farming briefly, but returned to his first preference, mining, at Currawang mines near Goulburn until his death.[16] William Henry Martin, a miner who arrived in the Bathurst district in 1863, worked there initially and did not deviate from this occupation throughout his life. He followed employment in mines in Queensland and finally in northern New South Wales, where he ended his career as a mine captain.[17]

Despite the importance of mining, agriculture was also significant in these areas. The pattern of mining and farming combined, which immigrants had known in nineteenth century Cornwall, also occurred in the Bathurst district where gold and copper deposits in particular were scattered across the farming area. For the remainder of the nineteenth century the Bathurst district, like Cornish Settlement itself, operated as a mixed mining and farming economy. In 1885 the chief crops were still wheat for grain and hay, oats for hay, and potatoes (which were grown mainly around Millthorpe, near Cornish Settlement).[18]

Cornish Settlement itself was an adopted home which tried as much as possible to look like the Cornish homeland. It maintained a significant place as the main Cornish cluster in the Bathurst district and the majority of its population remained Cornish, or of Cornish descent, throughout the nineteenth century.[19] These Cornish immigrants preferred to stay together in employment, in worship, and in their social relationships, and they encouraged others to join them from Cornwall. Copper mining brought hundreds more people to Cornish Settlement during the 1850s and 1860s, and they lived in tents or in two-roomed slab huts near the mine. Not all the new arrivals were Cornish, however, and the Irish miners camped in a separate area across the creek from the Cornish. They lived in a separate camp because of the continual fighting and ill-feeling which erupted between the Cornish and the Irish.[20] The Chinese miners lived even further away, beyond the Irish camp.[21]

At its height, Cornish Settlement supported a population of about 500. Except for the temporary exodus as copper miners hurried to nearby Ophir in 1851 to join the gold rush, this population remained fairly constant until a decline at the time of the Boer War.[22] The original Cornish Settlement mine proprietors, Lane and Glasson, eventually abandoned their attempts at private mine ownership and in 1853 the Carangarra [sic] Copper Mining Company was established with the sale of 50,000 shares at £10 each. Glasson and Lane, as former owners, were to receive 10% commission on any profits. Copper ore from the mine was included in the Paris Exhibition in 1855, and later both gold and silver were produced in commercial quantities.[23] In the latter part of the century, successful copper smelters were

---

15 Information from Mr Trevor Pascoe.
16 Information from Mrs Mary Nesbitt.
17 Information from Mrs Deborah Shuker.
18 W.S. Campbell, *Extracts from reports on certain agricultural districts of New South Wales*, New South Wales Government Printer, Sydney, 1888, pp.16 and 19.
19 Information from Mr Will Hawke.
20 This Cornish-Irish feuding occurred in other parts of the world, including Upper Michigan, Nevada, and in Cornwall itself, in Camborne in the 1880s. (Discussion with Dr John Rowe.)
21 Information from Mr Will Hawke.
22 Information from Mr Will Hawke.
23 J. Rule, *The Cornish Settlement*, p.50.

built at Byng and Witney Green, and this allowed ore to be processed locally.[24] The Witney Green Gold Mining Company, which operated on the opposite side of the valley from Carangara copper mine,[25] had begun late in the century, after the discovery of gold there by a Cornish miner, Bennett Treloar. He had convinced others of its value, and then inexplicably sold his own shares for £140. He died a 'poor, hard-working miner' who 'did not succeed in reaping the full benefit of his discoveries'.[26]

In 1860 a quarry operated at nearby Guyong, and attempts were being made to establish a National School there.[27] By 1866 Guyong had actually become a more important township than Cornish Settlement, because it was on the main coach road to Sydney.[28] The district around Guyong and Cornish Settlement still relied heavily on its agricultural and pastoral activities, but it also boasted working copper mines at Carangara,[29] Brown's Creek, Icely, and Ophir. As well as its copper ore, Carangara mine produced a black oxide which was sold as a hair restorer and baldness preventative. The company controlling the Icely mine included the Tom brothers, and it was said to be 'one of the richest and most extensive ever discovered in the colony'.[30] In 1875, Guyong was described as an agricultural, pastoral and mining area, with deposits of 'gold, copper, lead, auriferous black sand, and sulphur'. There was also 'asbestos, limestone, freestone and slate'.[31]

At Cornish Settlement, in the Parish of Byng, the proposed village reserve had been divided into building allotments as early as 1854, and its name was changed officially to Byng in 1885 when the village site was proclaimed. However, tradition persisted and the settlement also retained its earlier names of Carangara, Springfield, and Cornish Settlement along with its strong Cornish character.[32]

PLATE 24.  Miner's cottage, Byng

Although the clustering of the inhabitants at Cornish Settlement was mirrored in Cornish groups living in the surrounding districts of Bathurst and Orange, their Cornishness was not so immediately obvious, because they were in the minority. They were outnumbered by English, Irish and other ethnic groups, as they had been on the

24  Information from Mr Will Hawke.
25  J. Rule, *The Cornish Settlement*, p.53.
26  *BP*, 15 March 1898, p.4, c.2-3.
27  *BFP*, 1 December 1860, p.2, c.5.
28  Information from Mr B.W. Thomas.
29  Also written as Carangarra.
30  *BGNSW*, p.154, pp.251-2.
31  *GPDNSW*, pp.323-4.
32  J. Rule, *The Cornish Settlement*, pp.7-8.

voyages to New South Wales, but the original 'little Cornwall' in western New South Wales, Cornish Settlement, had set the district pattern for other Cornish groups.

The pattern continued in five places in particular: Bathurst, Oberon, Orange, Hill End and Molong, where several families had formed a nucleus for later arrivals in each area. They included William and Catherine (nee Tom) Lane whose relatives William and Ann Tom had moved further west to Cornish Settlement.[33]  The Trewren and Bray families in Bathurst, John Smith at Molong, and the Sloggett, Short, Webb and Mutton families near Oberon acted as focal points for later arrivals.  Like Cornish Settlement, all except Hill End had agricultural or pastoral beginnings and after 1848, these places became part of the mining districts as well.[34]  Cornish people in each of these settlements maintained close contact with other Cornish people living in the Bathurst district.  This occurred despite the fact they were scattered across a large area and in smaller groups than the cluster of people at Cornish Settlement.  Possibly because they were so much in the minority though, the Cornish families accepted certain selected (and usually Methodist) families in the district for inclusion in the clannish Cornish group.  These families included Parker, Stanger, Starr, Sweetnam, Spicer, Whalan and Lister, with whom many of the Cornish families intermarried.

PLATE 25.     A Bathurst businessman

The first of the five main cluster areas was Bathurst, and the early Cornish settlers here were farmers and businessmen.  At Kelso, John and Mary Trewren of Gwennap settled on 'Trelispic' in 1834 as farmers and graziers.[35]  He was a member of the Wesleyan Church, and involved in other business and community activities.  Some later-arriving Bathurst farmers were former miners, like William Henry Eade, who arrived in 1848 with his wife Mary and their children.  He worked at Summerhill mine near Rockley and then at Carangara mine at Cornish Settlement, and finally at the copper mine at Cow Flat before moving permanently to their own farm, 'Penrose', at Dunkeld outside Bathurst.[36]

William Trezise with his family outside their store in Bentinck Street, Bathurst.

33    See chapter 1 and appendix VI.
34    See appendix V.
35    Information from Mr Garry Howard.
36    Information from Mrs Pat Eade.

A number of Bathust businessmen were Cornish. William Trezise,[37] and Edmund Webb[38] were storekeepers. Samuel Bray conducted a tailor and draper shop,[39] John Burns was a marble mason[40] and Samuel Paul opened a saddlery business in the early 1850s.[41] William Tremain[42] and Frederick Crago[43] became proprietors of rival flour mills, while Richard Cock (presumably the unsuccessful smelter at Cornish Settlement in 1851) moved into Bathurst to become the proprietor of the Union Steam Mills.[44] These occupations were all jobs where the individual was self-employed, or at least working in an independent fashion.

Cow Flat copper mines, south of Bathurst, which were worked by the Cow Flat Mining Company,[45] attracted Cornish settlers during the 1870s. For example, Ann and George Dennis, James White and William Williams at Cow Flat were given as relatives of immigrants arriving in 1877.[46] Entries in *Greville's official Post Office directory of New South Wales* suggest a Cornish cluster at Cow Flat with names such as Crabbe, Cornish, Eady, Hawkins, Hicks, Hocking, Johns, James, Kissell, Northey, Nicholas, Oats, Pearce, Stevens, Thomas, Tonkin and Youren.[47] See Table 3.5.

The second of the major settlement areas in the Bathurst district was Oberon and the Cornish people there were originally engaged in farming, but later some were involved in mining. From the farming districts of Altarnun and Lewannick on the edge of Bodmin Moor came Joseph Sloggett in 1839 with his brother Thomas and Thomas' wife Catherine (nee Sleep) and their niece Jane Sloggett. Although they stated on their arrival as assisted immigrants that they were wheelwrights, the brothers went directly to the Bathurst district where they took up land near the Fish River and were joined by a third brother, William, in 1848.[48] Another Cornishman Walter Short, from Launceston in the same part of Cornwall, had arrived in the colony in 1829 and soon after arriving had gone to the Bathurst district to join his sister Mary and her husband Richard Mutton, who had arrived in 1826. Descendants of Richard and Mary Mutton believe that they travelled on the same ship as members of the Webb family, so it is possible that they, too, were joining relatives already at the Fish River.[49]

Another brother, Samuel Short, joined them in 1842.[50] William and Ann Webb (nee Mutton) and their three children from across the moor at Bodmin, joined them in 1840 at Mutton Falls near Tarana. In the late 1830s the related families of Barrett, Hawken, Dale and Bryant were encouraged by their aunt, Catherine Lane (nee Tom), to emigrate, and prior to their emigration they had been offered employment and other assistance from William and Catherine Lane at 'Orton Park'.[51]

Also in the Oberon district, Summer Hill mine at Rockley attracted Cornish miners such as William H. Eade, who had only recently arrived in the colony when he 'began a fresh

---

37 Information from Mrs Beryl McCooey.
38 *AMM*, series 1, vol.1, pp.84-6.
39 *BA*, 25 March 1848, p.3, c.4.
40 *AMM*, series 2, vol.2, p.350.
41 Information from Mrs Heather Paul.
42 Information from Miss Nell Tremain.
43 *AMM*, series 1, vol.2 appendix, p.22.
44 *BFP*, 20 October 1855, p.3, c.5.
45 A. Middleton and F.B. Maning, *Bathurst and Western District directory*, p.3.
46 AONSW shipping lists for *Pericles, Ninevah, Kapunda* 1877, AO reel 2488.
47 *GPDNSW*, pp.191-2.
48 Information from Ms Jennifer Sloggett.
49 Information from Joan Edgar.
50 Information from Mr David Short.
51 Information from Mr Selwyn Hawken.

mine' at Summer Hill in 1848.[52]   Obviously there were not enough experienced miners already in New South Wales in the early days of copper mining, and miners from South Australia were recruited to Summer Hill mine in 1848, but apparently not employed under the Cornish tribute system.

> Charles returned from Adelaide last night, Mr Hayley with him, all settled about the mine  John hired some miners at £5 per month.[53]

The third of the major areas of settlment in the Bathurst district was Orange, which received the 'overflow' from Cornish Settlement, and was often the district chosen by those who had come first to Cornish Settlement for 'colonial experience'.[54]  In the Orange district the main Cornish occupations were farming, orcharding and mining, but there was a significant flow between these categories.  Mining was a common Cornish occupation in this district once copper and gold were discovered, and apart from Cornish Settlement, there were mines at Cadia, Lucknow, Icely and Canobolas.  At Cadiangullong (Cadia), there were deposits of gold, iron, and copper.

PLATE 26.       Cadia.

Cadia engine house 1991. (Photographed by Roger Thomas.)

In 1908 the copper mine at Cadia was said to be one of the oldest in Australia.[55]  The Cornish engine house and stack, which housed the engine erected in West Cadia in 1865 still stands, and parts of the engine also remain.[56]

There was quite a lot of movement from farming into orcharding, for example George Hawke's nephew, Frederick Hawke, farmed in the district and then established an orchard near Orange.  George Hawke lived in the Orange district[57] and the brothers Thomas and Sampson Hawke were orchardists at Canobolas on the outskirts of Orange, Sampson being a

---

52   Information from Mrs Pat Eade.

53   H. Clements, 'Station book, Summer Hill', entry for Saturday 26 August 1848. (Photocopy in the possession of Mrs Gillian Kelly.)

54   Information from Mr B.W. Thomas.

55   F.S. Bone, (ed.), *Orange district guide 1908*, facsimile reprint by G. and C. Reynolds, Millthorpe, N.S.W., 1983, p.50.

56   K. Brown, 'Australian Cornish and other beam engines, Part I', in *The Trevithick Society newsletter*, no.47, November 1984, p.4.  I am indebted to Mr Bill Newby for this information.

57   *BT*, 11 June 1917, p.2, c.4.   Rebecca [Rowe] Hawke's obituary, which stated that George Hawke was no relative of George Hawke of 'Pendarves', but had married George Hawke's ward Rebecca Rowe.

pioneer of the cherry industry.[58]  John Hicks came with his family in 1854 and worked first for George Hawke at Cornish Settlement, moving later to his own orchard at Canobolas, as did fellow-Cornishman and shipmate, John Watts.[59]

## PLATE 27. Cadia.

View of Cadia mine 1991. (Photographed by Roger Thomas.)

Cornish settlers moved not only from one type of farming to another, but also from mining to farming.  As in other parts of the Bathurst district, some Cornish immigrants went from one mining village to another before eventually turning to farming.  For example, Richard Hawke arrived in Sydney in 1853 and spent several successful years on the goldfields before buying land near Orange, which he farmed until his death in 1887.  He married Anne Treneman,  of Orange, a daughter of Cornishman Thomas Treneman, (who arrived aboard *Harbinger* in 1849).[60]

## PLATE 28.    Cornish farmers near Orange.

William Selwood and other farmers amongst full bags of wheat during the harvest at Springside near Orange. Selwood owned the machinery and contracted it out at harvest time. (Photograph courtesy of Mrs P. Trevena.)

William H. Selwood arrived in 1860 and worked as a miner at Cadia, Cornish Settlement, and Lucknow until he became a farmer at Springside.[61]  Others came via the

---

58    *CWD*, 4 June 1985, p.4.

59    *CWD*, 16 July 1985, p.4, c.1.

60    *CWD*, 4 June 1985, p.4, c.1.

Cornish clusters in other colonies before settling permanently in Orange. One such person was Peter Floyd who came to Victoria in 1863 and worked as a miner there and in South Australia, Queensland and Cornish Settlement before becoming a farmer at Lucknow until his retirement.[62] Some miners carried on with farming and mining at the same time until they were able to move into full-time farming as John Grenfell Pascoe had done at Beneree. One such person was Captain Josiah Holman, the mine captain at Cadia in 1864. He was at Icely in 1869, but by 1889 he had become a farmer at Cadia, where he died in 1893.[63]

Still others in the Orange district, like James Gartrell, arrived in the colony as miners but eventually chose to enter occupations other than mining or farming. The Gartrell brothers, James, Richard, William and Edwin came via the United States to New South Wales in 1877,[64] to join a relative in Orange. She had lived there since 1848 with her husband William Johns, who had been sent by his mining company first to India and then on to New South Wales.[65] James, a miner, worked first as a stoker at Orange gasworks, but was soon promoted to foreman and in 1888 he was appointed head engineer and manager of the gasworks.[66]

PLATE 29.     Molong mine

'View of the Molong Mine NSW.'  Conrad Martens watercolour 1848.  (NLA PIC T371 NK 229 LOC 811).

---

61   Information from Mrs Phyllis Trevena.
62   *CWD*, 6 November 1984, p.4, c.2.
63   *CWD*, 1 October 1985, p.2, c.4.
64   AONSW Immigration Board's list *Annie H. Smith*, 1877, AO reel 2488.
65   E.G. Clancy, 'More precious than gold': commemorating the 100th anniversary of the Orange circuit of the Methodist church (1860-1960), Central Western Daily, Orange, N.S.W., 1960, chapter 2. [No page numbers.]
66   *CWD*, 22 January 1985, p.4, c.1-2.

The fourth of the main Cornish clusters in the Bathurst district was Molong. Like most of the others, it began with Cornish farmers who were joined by working miners.

John Smith of St Keverne arrived in New South Wales in 1836 bringing a letter of introduction from John Glasson's father in Breage, and immediately contacted John Glasson and George Hawke at Cornish Settlement. Smith first began work on a property owned by the Hassall family near Molong, and doubtless this had been arranged through the 'Cornish connection' with the Hassall and Marsden families through the Wesleyan ministers Carvosso and Lawry. This connection had also been used to advantage earlier by the Toms and Lanes, Hawke and Glasson. John Smith later obtained his own property, 'Gamboola' and his brothers Robert and Francis, and many other relatives including members of the Thomas family of St Keverne, joined him in the colony.[67] He became the Hon. John Smith MLC of LLanarth, Bathurst, and a respected merino breeder.[68] Other Cornish immigrants farmed in the vicinity of Molong, for example, William Rowe, (brother of George Hawke's ward Rebecca Rowe), had married Annie Lister (the sister of the co-discoverer of payable gold) and farmed at Cargo.[69] William H. Couch came via Tasmania in 1859 and farmed at Cargo until his retirement to Molong.[70]

Molong was also a centre for copper miners, first with the mining at Copper Hill, Molong and the arrival of Captain James Budge Clymo and his band of copper miners in 1848[71] and then during later attempts to mine at Copper Hill.[72]

Hill End was the fifth of the major settlements in the Bathurst district. It was primarily a mining town, and the cluster of Cornish there was influenced largely by the occupations of its members. They settled in their own 'Cornishtown', in the area around Hawkin's Hill, a part of Hill End where many of the leases were worked by Cornish miners.[73] A Cornishman, 'Daddy' Nichols, had actually identified as a rich quartz reef an area near Hawkins Hill, which others had seen, but had missed its significance.[74]

The Cornish at Hill End were approximately one-sixth of the town's total population, and many had been brought out under contract in 1856, or had come later to join family members who were already there.[75] Hill End was viewed as a permanent settlement from 1859 onwards, and its population grew steadily but gradually as a 'goldfield of the family unit, rather than one which attracted the single and unattached adventurer'. This settled population quickly established Sunday Schools, a Band of Hope, Sons of Temperance, Oddfellows, Masons, Orangemen, and Reading and Discussion clubs.[76]

Hill End was a stable community like Cornish Settlement. They shared another similarity: sectarian strife was 'always present to some degree, especially between the Cornish and the Irish'.[77]

---

67  Information from Mr B.W. Thomas.
68  See B. Mac Smith, *Quench not the spirit: merino heritage*, Hawthorn Press, Melbourne, 1972.
69  *Methodist*, 20 January 1900, p.4, c.1.
70  Information from Mr David Rutherford.
71  *SMH*, 7 July 1848, p.2, c.1.
72  J.C.L. Fitzpatrick, *The good old days of Molong*, Cumberland Argus, Parramatta, N.S.W., 1913, pp.94-101.
73  Information from Mr Link Van Ummerson.
74  H. Hodge, *The Hill End story*, Book 1, p.29.
75  Ibid, pp.29 and 154. Families known to be Cornish included the Jeffree, Pascoe, Clymo, Trevena, Hawke, Letcher, Tippett, Everett, Uren, Penhall, Nichols, Roberts, Inch, Lobb, Curnow, Plummer, Blewett, Dally, Bartle, Northey, Treglown, Bath, Carkeek, Trestrail and Thomas families.
76  Ibid, p.173.
77  Ibid, p.163.

Battles on a collective basis occurred fairly regularly between the Cornish and Irish miners at Hill End. Sectarianism as well as national rivalry formed the basis of this ceremonial warfare. The 12th of July procession of the Orangemen with white horse, brass band and vulgar parodies on the song 'The Boyne Water' infuriated the Irishmen, as no doubt they were intended to.

The two groups congregated at hotels in different parts of the town, but they:

> converged late in the afternoon, and then it was 'wigs on the green'. It was mostly a matter of plain fisticuffs and little permanent physical damage accrued.[78]

Although Hill End was a stable, family-oriented community, it was not necessarily a healthy environment, and in 1866 one Cornishman, James Letcher, lost his whole family of wife and four children within a period of four months, from fever and other illnesses.[79] As a mining town, it obviously attracted Cornish immigrants whose occupation was mining, but even here, personal influences were important, and others in different occupations joined their mining relatives in the Cornish community there. One such group was the Inch family, who were brewers, but joined their mining relatives, the Jeffrees.[80]

Occupations were an important influence on the places of settlement chosen by the Cornish throughout the Bathurst district. As well as being involved in mining and farming, Cornish tradespeople opened shops and other businesses as saddlers, millers, stonemasons, blacksmiths and builders. In many cases they were taking advantage of the extra trade resulting from the goldfields boost to population. However, whether they were farmers, miners or tradespeople, the Cornish were all part of an inter-related mining and farming community similar to that in Cornwall. Mining of course was an obvious reason for congregating in certain places, but some people who joined the Cornish groups were engaged in the trades and in service industries, like those who gathered in Bathurst. It is clear that personal choice also played an important part in settlement patterns there.

It was certainly common for Cornish family members to travel together in groups to New South Wales, but sometimes groups of miners were brought out together under contract to a certain mine, which obviously produced a cluster at the mine. Captain James Budge Clymo was recruited as mine captain at Copper Hill mine by the Molong Mining Company, arriving aboard *Elphinstone* in 1848, accompanied by his workforce of fifteen miners and their families.[81] John Nankivell came in 1848 aboard *Walmer Castle*, and went directly from Sydney to the Molong mines with his family. It is a reasonable assumption that that he and the other nine familes on board who went to Copper Hill with him were recruited for that purpose, or that they applied for assisted passages with the intention of working at Copper Hill on arrival.[82] James H. Martin came with his family aboard *Tory* in 1853, one of 110 miners recruited through the Australian Agricultural Company for the Cordillera gold mines at Warrah in northern New South Wales, but instead he went on to the Bathurst district where he worked as a gold miner.[83] Icely of 'Coombing Park', himself a Devon man, from

---

78   Ibid, p.140.
79   Ibid, p.174.
80   Information from Mr Harold Jeffree.
81   *SMH*, 7 July 1848, p.2, c.1.
82   A. Williams, *Nankivell-a family affair*, the author, Miram, Victoria, 1990, pp.19-20.
83   P.A. Pemberton, *Pure merinos and others: the 'shipping lists' of the Australian Agricultural Company*, Australian National University Archives of Business and Labour, Canberra, 1986, p.69. Information from Mr Murray Martin.

the area close to the Cornish border,[84] recruited Cornish miners during the 1870s for his copper mine near Blayney.[85]

Recruitment of Cornish farm labourers, servants and tradespeople to specific work in the colony often occurred on an informal or family basis. For example, forty years after his own arrival, John Smith of 'Gamboola' brought his nephew out to manage his property 'Rosemaine'.[86] The Dale, Bryant, Hawken and Barrett families all came after being offered employment by their relatives William and Catherine Lane of 'Orton Park'.[87] The shortage of servants and other workers was complained about in the Bathurst press during the 1850s[88] and Mary Row, who came in 1855 under engagement to Robert Lean, was an example of specific recruitment of domestic servants.[89]

Blacksmiths were needed in all areas, not only at the mines. In 1862, the town of Bathurst alone had twelve blacksmiths.[90] When Cobb and Co. moved its headquarters there in 1862[91] more blacksmiths and wheelwrights were needed, because coaches and equipment were 'made locally from local materials'.[92] However, some tradesmen actually moved into the mining industry in the Bathurst district rather than out of it. For example, John Harris, a blacksmith, came via South Australia to Bathurst to work at the Cobb & Co. coach factory in 1873, but soon after, he became foreman blacksmith at Cow Flat copper mine, moving later to Forest Reefs.[93] Some miners preferred to stick at mining, choosing not to attempt other occupations, while some made short forays into other work but soon returned to mining. Captain Clymo of Copper Hill mine was lessee of a hotel in Molong for a short time in 1850,[94] but was soon back as mine captain at Canobolas copper mine, whose shareholders included Cornishmen Tom, Lane and Hawke.[95]

Clustering in the Bathurst district began in Cornish Settlement and continued in other parts of the district. Examination of directories and electoral rolls shows a concentration of Cornish in the Bathurst district, but in particular the 1899-1900 electoral roll, and *Greville's post office directory of New South Wales* show evidence of distinct clusters in smaller areas within the district. This indicates that even within a large settlement area, the Cornish chose to congregate in more concentrated groups. See Tables 3.5 and 3.6.

Although it was a very important factor, the influence of occupations on clustering was not the only one in the Bathurst district. Obviously there was a strong element of personal choice, and decisions about the areas of settlement chosen by many Cornish were motivated by personal or family reasons. Personal and occupational reasons also encouraged Cornish in the Bathurst district to maintain contact with other Cornish communities in New South Wales, and in other Australian colonies. For example, the intermarriage of the Hambly family of Botany near Sydney with the Tremain family of Bathurst over two generations is evidence of this continuing contact.[96]

84   Thomas Icely was born in Plympton, and his first land grant near Bathurst was named Saltram. (*ADB* 2, p.1.)
85   G. Reynolds, *The Kings colonials: the story of Blayney and district*, the author, Millthorpe, N.S.W., 1982, p.25.
86   Information from Mr B.W. Thomas.
87   Information from Mr Selwyn Hawken.
88   For example, *BFP*, 11 January 1851, p.6, c.1,  7 April 1852, p.2, c.1,  24 September 1853, p.2, c.1,  23 May 1857, p.2, c.6.
89   AONSW shipping list for *Mangerton* 1855, AO reel 2471.
90   B. Greaves (ed.), *The story of Bathurst*, p.151.
91   Ibid, entry for 26 June 1962, p.239.
92   Ibid, pp.150-1.
93   Information from Mr David Rutherford.
94   J.C.L. Fitzpatrick, *The good old days of Molong*, p.93.
95   *BFP*, 22 October 1859, p.2, c.6-7. Information from M.H. McLelland.
96   Information from Mr H. Hambly, Mrs Beryl McCooey and Miss Grace Tremain.

The pattern of clustering which occurred in the Bathurst district was repeated in the Hunter, where Cornish immigrants also chose to concentrate in pockets within the larger settlement area. They did not settle expressly in one area first as they did at Cornish Settlement near Orange, but they did maintain the pattern of settling in groups in the Hunter hinterland districts of Maitland, Singleton and Paterson, and in some of the Newcastle mining townships.

The Cornish were involved in all stages of settlement in the Hunter. They were numbered amongst the earliest convicts and military personnel, and the later miners and tradesmen. They were involved in pastoral and agricultural pursuits, and also in industry.

PLATE 30.      Hunter map

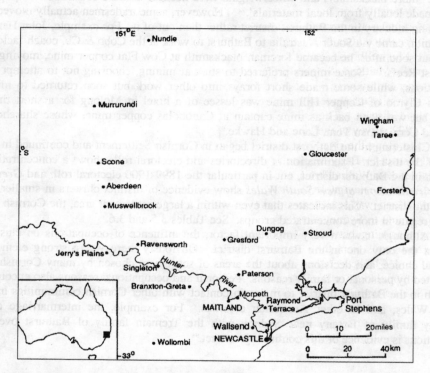

Map of the Hunter region showing areas of Cornish settlement.

Early Cornish influence in the region was evident when the convict settlement at the mouth of the Hunter River was first named King's Town after the Cornish Governor King, and surveyed and laid out by Cornishman Henry Dangar of St Neot. However, the Hunter region consisted of two distinct sections, the mining districts of Newcastle and the largely agricultural Hunter hinterland. The development of Newcastle as a mining district, port, and industrial city was quite distinct from that of the agricultural districts of the Hunter hinterland, and for this reason these two different but inter-related areas are discussed separately.

Apart from Henry Dangar's early exploration of the region, the influence of the Dangar family and their contributions to the Hunter district were considerable, and they formed the nucleus for Cornish clusters in the Hunter hinterland. The family's permanent connection with the region began in 1821 when Henry Dangar was granted 700 acres near Morpeth. In 1825 he was granted another 300 acres, and purchased a further 700 acres near Singleton. This was to become 'Neotsfield', named after his homeland village of St Neot. The prolonged dispute over another 1300 acres was the reason for his return to London to defend his reputation and his property.[97] In 1833 Henry Dangar and his wife Grace moved permanently to 'Neotsfield' which until then had been supervised for them by Henry's brother William who had emigrated in 1825.[98] They were joined by relatives including the Sibley, Rapson and Meyn[99] families, and by other immigrants from St Neot and surrounding parishes, like the Burnetts and the Langsfords. As well as the encouragement he gave to family members who wished to emigrate, Henry Dangar sponsored immigrant families from Devon and Cornwall[100] and employed other assisted emigrants on their arrival.[101]

Following Henry Dangar's survey of the Hunter Valley and the movement of the Newcastle penal settlement to Port Macquarie, agricultural and pastoral expansion of the hinterland escalated after 1825. Settlement spread along the rivers, and towns such as Scone, Singleton, Muswellbrook and Paterson developed. Cornish settlement in the hinterland centred on the Maitland, Singleton and Paterson districts, and in all of these areas, members of the Dangar family were a significant influence.

The first of the three major areas of Cornish settlement in the Hunter hinterland was the Maitland district. The early Europeans in this area were cedar cutters, but Henry Dangar's 1822 survey of the Hunter made settlement possible, and by 1825 much of the rich alluvial land along the river had been allocated.[102] Dangar's first grant of land was in the Maitland district.[103] Early Maitland consisted of two settlements separated by Wallis Creek: West Maitland, or Wallis Plains, and East Maitland. Several miles downstream was Morpeth (Greenhills), at the navigable head of the river.[104] Maitland and Morpeth grew in importance as the hinterland was settled, because there was no acceptable road to Newcastle. A boat service operated to Sydney from 1824, with the first regular steamer service for passengers and freight running between Morpeth and Sydney from 1831 and calling at Newcastle. Produce and goods from the Hunter hinterland and the New England district came through Maitland and Morpeth rather than Newcastle, increasing business opportunity there.[105] Maitland's population (excluding Morpeth) of 2,768 was twice that of Newcastle in 1841, and in 1861 its population of 7,747 was next to Sydney and still more than twice that of Newcastle.[106]

As in the Bathurst district, early Cornish settlers in Maitland were farmers. Amongst them were John Grills, a British army veteran who was granted 40 acres at Maitland in 1829,[107] and Henry Vincent who arrived in 1828. He used the colonial 'Cornish network' of the Rev Walter Lawry and the Hoskings (John Senior in London and John Junior, a Sydney merchant), and received a grant of 640 acres at Mulbring.[108] Members of the Christian

97   E.C. Rowland, 'The life and times of Henry Dangar', in *JRAHS*, vol.XXXIX, 1953, part II, p.57.
98   E.M. Dangar, *The Dangars from St Neot, Cornwall*, John Dangar Christian Reid? Sydney, 1966, p.11.
99   Information from Mrs Peggy Richards.
100  *ADB* 1, p.281. N. Gray, *The promised land: a summary of early settlement in the Shire of Scone*, Scone historical monograph no.3, Scone and Upper Hunter Historical Society, Scone, N.S.W., 1975, p.53.
101  E.C. Rowland, 'The life and times of Henry Dangar', p.63.
102  L.E. Fredman, (ed.), *A History of Maitland*, Council of the City of Maitland, Maitland, N.S.W., 1983, pp.11-13.
103  See appendix VI.
104  *A town to be laid out: Maitland 1829-1979*, Council of the City of Maitland, Maitland, N.S.W., 1979, pp.1-2.
105  L.E. Fredman, (ed.), *A History of Maitland*, pp.14-16.
106  Ibid, p.21.
107  Information from Mrs Joan Grills.
108  W.S. Parkes, J. Comerford, and M. Lake, *Mines, wines and people: a history of Greater Cessnock*, first published 1979, Council of the city of Greater Cessnock, Cessnock, N.S.W., 1989, pp.148-9.

family arrived in 1842, and through their connections with John Eales, an influential Maitland landholder who came from Devon, they settled immediately at Hinton. The Christians owned coal mines near Morpeth, and were in partnership with John Eales in mines near Minmi. They supplied coal to steamships of the Hunter River Navigation Company in the 1840s and by 1854 they also owned three coal-carrying vessels. The family extended its agricultural and pastoral interests throughout New South Wales, Queensland and the Northern Territory between 1858 and 1920. Immediate and extended family, including Bassetts, Cardells and Bulmores, emigrated to join the original settlers.[109]

Other settlers at Morpeth and across the river on the rich alluvial land at Hinton were farmers. John Bunt, a husbandman and innkeeper in Cornwall, became a farmer at Hinton. He had arrived aboard *General Hewitt* in 1848 (stating he was an agricultural labourer), and at the time of his death also owned property at the Manning River.[110] However, some assisted immigrants did not turn to farming. For example, James and Eliza Caddy arrived in Sydney aboard the *Orient* in 1839 and their son Henry was born in Morpeth only twelve days later. Caddy stated on arrival that he was a tailor, but he was a storekeeper in Morpeth until his death in 1866.[111]

The Cornish cluster at Maitland was larger than those at Morpeth and Hinton, and consisted of people of various occupations ranging from woolsorter, schoolmaster, labourer and carrier to trades such as carpenter, wheelwright and baker. There were farmers and several miners, and others who may well have been connected with mining, such as a stationary engine driver and a blacksmith. Apart from the Dangar family's early influence, no particular Cornish family stands out in Maitland as a distinct nucleus for Cornish settlement there, but this occupational mix reflects the background in Maitland as it grew steadily into an important regional centre,[112] and is typical of the Cornish occupational mix in other non-mining clusters. As in Sydney, it indicates that personal choice was a strong factor in Cornish settlement patterns.

The second area of Cornish clustering in the Hunter hinterland was the Singleton district, which was 'Dangar country'. An overland route had been found from Windsor to Patrick's Plains (Singleton) and on to Wallis Plains (Maitland) in 1820, opening up the rich, alluvial land which was equally suited to farming and grazing.[113] The early pattern of settlement was of large pastoral holdings, and later there was diversification into agriculture (mainly grain and tobacco), viticulture and horse breeding.[114]

As had occurred elsewhere, the Singleton cluster was influenced largely by personal factors. The congregating of Cornish settlers in the Singleton district was a result of the Dangar family settling in the region and encouraging others to join them. The occupations of most Cornish immigrants there were agricultural or pastoral, but there were some others such as miller, blacksmith, mason, bricklayer, mining engineer and storekeeper. Blacksmith William Burnett and his wife Melinda, who were both from the Dangars' parish of St Neot, came to Singleton in 1863 and were followed by relatives the Langsfords and the Kents. William Burnett became a prominent citizen of Singleton, involved in Methodism and other community organisations.[115]

Simon Richards was a successful farmer at Goorangoola near Singleton. He was a fine example of Cornish adaptability and typical of the Cornish immigrants who became good citizens and contributed in many ways to the community. He had arrived aboard *Lady*

---

109 Information from Ms Marianne Eastgate.
110 Information from Mrs Vi Rose.
111 Information from Mrs Dianne Minnican.
112 These conclusions are drawn mainly from anecdotal sources.
113 E. Whitelaw, *A history of Singleton*, [Singleton Historical Society?], Singleton, N.S.W., [n.d.], p.1.
114 Ibid, pp.6-8.
115 *Singleton Argus*, 3 February 1916, p.3, c.2.

*Ann* in 1854 as an assisted immigrant, giving his occupation as miner, but had been employed from the ship by a Maitland farmer. Soon after, he became a shoemaker in Maitland, then moved to Singleton. He was one of the first selectors at Goorangoola to take advantage of the Robertson Land Act of 1861, when he selected 320 acres. Eventually his property totalled 7000 acres.[116]

Upstream from Singleton, Cornish people settled near Scone, Muswellbrook, Aberdeen and Murrurundi, and again the Dangars were involved. In 1825 William Dangar's 'Turanville' was the only occupied grant in the Kingdon Ponds valley,[117] and in 1835 William Dangar had moved permanently to 'Turanville', which he developed as a successful racehorse and shorthorn cattle stud. He increased his property to include land in New England, the Liverpool Plains and on the Namoi River. At the same time he helped to manage the business affairs of his brother Henry. He was a benefactor to the Scone district, and 'a good citizen and a good neighbour'.[118] His will directed that £600 be given to charities in the Upper Hunter and a further £600 put in trust for the poor of St Neot.[119]

Unlike the Dangars, two young Cornish immigrants who settled in the Scone district did not live long enough to enjoy success in the new land. Grace Marshall Wilkie, a native of St Columb, died in childbirth at the age of 23, at Murrurundi in 1843, 'leaving three infant sons'.[120] The other was Richard Bodilly, a harnessmaker of Penzance, who had come with his wife aboard *Emigrant* in 1849. In May 1854, aged 33, he was Chief Constable at Scone but died after being accidentally shot in the course of duty. The *Maitland Mercury* questioned the likelihood of his widow being suitably provided for by the Government, even though he had lost his life in the execution of his duty.[121]

Generally though, Cornish immigrants who settled in Scone and Murrurundi were, and remained, farmers or farm labourers, with occasional exceptions like Charles Soady, who had arrived aboard *Earl Dalhousie* in 1877, stating he was a farm labourer. By the time of his marriage in Murrurundi in 1883 he had become a surveyor's assistant.[122] Also, several Dangar relatives operated businesses at Murrurundi. James Sibley, brother of Grace Dangar, owned an inn there, and Jeremiah Brice Rundle, a Dangar cousin, was a storekeeper at Murrurundi and later a partner in the firm of Rundle and Dangar.[123]

Those Cornish who settled at Muswellbrook and Aberdeen were also mainly farmers and farm labourers, with a sprinkling of other occupations such as miner, schoolteacher and blacksmith. An early settler, John Cundy, arrived aboard *Duchess of Northumberland* in 1838 with his family, and they went almost immediately to Aberdeen where he worked at his trade as a blacksmith. By 1849 he was farming at Timor near Murrurundi, then became an innkeeper at the Isis River, taking advantage of the trade caused by the goldrush to Nundle in the early 1850s. After prosecutions for sly grog selling, John and Catherine Cundy returned to Aberdeen, and operated another inn. John Cundy prospered and purchased more property

116 A.J. Greenhalgh, *Times's subjects: the story of Goorangoola, a small community in the Hunter Valley of New South Wales 1839-1939*, the author, Roseville, N.S.W., 1982, pp.89-91, and p.113. Information from Mr Kingsley Richards.

117 N. Gray, *The promised land* p.41.

118 E.M. Dangar, *William Dangar of Turanville*, Scone Historical Society no.1, Scone & Upper Hunter Historical Society, Scone, N.S.W., 1968, p.10.

119 Ibid, p.16.

120 I am indebted to Mrs Nancy Gray, of Scone and Upper Hunter Historical Society, for this information.

121 *MM*, 10 May 1854, p.2, c.3. Several months later, a Cornish newspaper carried the story of Bodilly's injury and stated that he was of Muswell Brook Station, and a son of Mr Bodilly of Penzance. The length of time required for communications to reach Britain is sadly obvious in this case, as the Cornish newspaper at that time was unaware that he had died months before, only several days after the accident. (*RCG*, 18 August 1854, p.5, c.5.)

122 AONSW shipping list for *Earl Dalhousie* 1877, AO reel 2488. *NSWRGI* 1883, No.5286.

123 E.M. Dangar, *The Dangars from St Neot*, p.30.

in Aberdeen, and was joined by a number of relatives from Cornwall. At the time of his death in 1881, he owned a great deal of land in Aberdeen.[124]

The third cluster area in the Hunter hinterland was the Paterson district. A number of Cornish immigrants chose to settle north of Maitland in the Paterson area, and the Dangar influence stretched into this district as well. Sampson and Martha Rapson of Liskeard, encouraged by Sampson's aunt, Grace Dangar, arrived in the colony as assisted immigrants aboard *Tory* in 1849. Henry Dangar arranged work for them with his relatives, the Cory family of Vacy, and in 1855 the Rapsons purchased land near Dungog. This property, 'Mount Pleasant' is still owned by their descendants.[125]

Another assisted immigrant, Jonathon Wilce, who arrived aboard *Orient* in 1839 with his wife Susan, went first to Morpeth and in 1859 purchased their property of 700 acres,[126] near Dungog.[127] Christopher Lean, probably a relative,[128] arrived in the colony about 1839, and after working for some time near Wellington, New South Wales, he purchased his own 1200 acre farm at Dungog.[129] His movement between the Bathurst district and the Hunter illustrates the contact maintained between these communities.

Cornish settlers in the Hunter hinterland worked at farming pursuits, as tradesmen, or in occupations (like storekeeping and innkeeping) which offered independence. There was obviously an element of occupational choice as they settled where their chosen occupations were required. Although their occupations did influence their settlement patterns to varying degrees, personal choice was also a very important influence.

As already stated, the Hunter hinterland developed quite differently from Newcastle. The original settlement at Newcastle was established following the discovery of coal and the subsequent opening of government coal mines. Newcastle's isolation from Sydney was a reason for its early role as a convict settlement, but its position at the mouth of the Hunter River discouraged European settlement of the hinterland. When that settlement did proceed, Maitland became the regional centre in preference to Newcastle.[130] Earlier settlers in the Hunter had been dependent mainly on river transport,[131] until the construction of the Great Northern Railway linking Newcastle with Maitland and northern New South Wales which began in 1858.[132]

Newcastle itself originally developed as a series of discrete coal mining villages: Minmi, Plattsburg, Wallsend, Lambton, New Lambton, Hamilton, Broadmeadow, Adamstown and Merewether,[188] which became twentieth century suburbs of Newcastle.[134] Coal deposits in Newcastle had been seen in the cliffs as early as 1797,[135] and the Australian

---

124 Information from Mrs Enid Farnham and Sr Juliana Googe.

125 Information from Mr Ronald Rapson.

126 *AMM*, series 1, vol. 2 appendix, p.44.

127 *NMH* 22 February 1941, p.4, c.7, 101st birthday of their daughter Frances, at Dungog.

128 His marriage certificate states that his mother was Catherine Wilce. (NSWRGI 1859, No.1822.)

129 *AMM*, series 1, vol. 2 appendix, p.44.

130 J. Sloggett, 'Locating Newcastle', in *Locality;bulletin of the Community History Program*, vol.3, no.5, University of New South Wales, Sydney, October-November 1989, pp.3-5.

131 S. Richards and P. Muller, *Morpeth: a brief history of Australia's oldest river port:where bishops and ships once rode tall*, Kookaburra Educational, Morpeth, N.S.W., 1989, pp.6-9.

132 J. Sloggett, 'Locating Newcastle', p.3.

133 E. McEwen, 'The Newcastle coalmining district of New South Wales 1860-1900', PhD., University of Sydney, 1979, p.7.

134 J. Sloggett, 'Locating Newcastle', p.4. New South Wales coal deposits are saucer-shaped, the edges being closest to the surface at Newcastle, Lithgow and Illawarra, which became the colony's three main coalmining districts. (R. Gollan, *The coalminers of New South Wales: a history of the union 1860-1960*, Melbourne University Press in association with the Australian National University, Melbourne, 1963, pp.3-4.)

135 J. Windross and J.P. Ralston, *Historical records of Newcastle 1797-1897*, first published 1897, facsimile reprint by LAH, North Sydney, 1978, p.43.

Agricultural Company monopoly over coal in the region began in 1828.[136] It continued until 1847, although individuals and other companies began mining on the outskirts of Newcastle before that monopoly ended.[137]

Newcastle developed during the nineteenth century as a port at the mouth of the Hunter River, and also as a coal mining and industrial area. Consequently the Cornish who chose to settle there were tradespeople and miners, rather than the agricultural workers and farmers who preferred the hinterland. As they did elsewhere, those Cornish who chose to go to Newcastle also chose to settle in clusters. These were of varying sizes in several of the mining towns and in some non-mining areas as well. But in Newcastle a further occupational division existed, and this was between the mining and non-mining districts.

An increasing colonial demand for coal meant that Newcastle grew steadily, its boom period lasting from the 1860s to the 1880s. Industries developed to serve the needs of the mines, smelters were built and a steady trade with South Australia in coal and copper ore developed.[138] It seems there was a trade not only in copper and coal, but in mining and other occupations also. In 1881 an advertisement appeared in Newcastle for 50 good copper miners, who were required at the Wallaroo Mines.[139] One unfortunate Cornishman, who had come to Newcastle from South Australia in 1886 was Henry Tonkin, a blacksmith who 'knew nothing of mining'. He had been unemployed for some time when he went to get some coal from the cliffs at the beach and was killed in the resulting rockfall.[140]

The majority of immigrants to the expanding coalmining district came from the industrial areas of northern England and from Wales, with some from Cornwall. This distinct regional background caused their settlements to develop quite differently from other areas of New South Wales, and from the non-mining areas in the Hunter region.[141]

Ellen McEwen's thesis, 'The Newcastle coalmining district of New South Wales 1860-1900', made a clear distinction between the coalmining district and the remainder of Newcastle. She examined the mining towns of Wallsend, Plattsburg, Lambton, New Lambton, Hamilton, Broadmeadow, Adamstown, Junction and Merewether.[142] Her classification of 'English' born coalminers in the mining towns included 6% Cornish, 11% from Staffordshire and 41% from Northumberland and Durham.[143] She attributed the strength of unionism and the popularity of co-operative societies in the coal mining district to the large proportion of Scots and Geordies, who had brought these traditions with them from Britain.[144]

Although Cornish miners' reputation for excellence was built on their expertise as hardrock men, and not as coal miners, there had been nineteenth century migration from Cornwall to the coal mines of Yorkshire and Lancashire.[145] Therefore it is highly likely that many of the Cornish working in the Newcastle pits were miners already experienced in coal mining in the north of England. Such a family, the Rundles from Liskeard, had 'spent about 20 years in the coalmining industry in Co Durham' before emigrating in 1888, but Mr Rundle had died only six weeks after their arrival in Wallsend.[146] In contrast, William

136  J. Sloggett, 'Locating Newcastle', p.3.

137  E. McEwen, 'The Newcastle coalmining district', p.3.

138  J. Sloggett, 'Locating Newcastle', p.4. Contact with the mining areas of South Austrlalia is suggested in the name of Wallaroo State Park north of Newcastle.

139  *NMH*, 25 June 1881, p.5, c.4.

140  *NMH*, 18 September 1893, p.5, c.5.

141  J.M. Sloggett, 'Temperance and class:with particular reference to Newcastle and the South Maitland coalfields, 1860-1928', M.A., University of Newcastle, 1989, pp.53-59.

142  E. McEwen, 'The Newcastle coalmining district', p.5. Mining towns not included in her survey are Newcastle, Stockton, Charlestown, Minmi and West Wallsend.

143  Ibid, p.13, Table 1.6.

144  Ibid, p.89.

145  J. Rowe, *The hard-rock men: Cornish immigrants and the North American mining frontier*, Liverpool University Press, Liverpool, 1974, p.24.

146  *Methodist*, 7 August 1909, p.10, c.1.

Manuell (a copper miner) and his family from St Blazey came directly from Cornwall,[147] aboard *Lady Amherst* in 1849, to the Newcastle coal mines. However, William died three years later, leaving his young family without financial support, and his six year old son, William Henry, was forced to begin as a surface worker at the coal mines.[148]

There is evidence of clusters of Cornish settlers at Hamilton, Adamstown, Junction-Merewether, Plattsburg-Wallsend, and smaller ones at Lambton and New Lambton, Stockton and Minmi. The majority of these people were mining families, but there was a sprinkling of others: a farmer, and several tradesmen such as saddler, carriage builder and blacksmith. It is reasonable to assume that at least some of these men were employed in their trades at the mines.[149] A number of Cornish mining families lived on Hamilton Commonage, which was a tract of Crown Land bordered by the mining towns of Adamstown, Lambton, New Lambton and Hamilton. It was a popular place of residence for miners because of a shortage of accommodation in the townships, and 1050 unofficial 'squattages' had sprung up there by 1887.[150]

Cornish settlers clustered in the non-mining townships of Waratah, Raymond Terrace and Carrington, with a sprinkling at Gloucester, Harrington, Tighe's Hill and Wickham. These people were generally farmers or tradesman, but there was one seaman.[151]

In Newcastle and in the Hunter hinterland, occupations such as mining and the trades and service industries were a factor in the clustering process. As in the Bathurst district, personal choice was also a very strong factor in deciding the place of residence. Also, as in the Bathurst district, certain smaller areas within the larger settlement area developed as higher density Cornish clusters. Evidence of this can be seen in the tables in appendix III.

In both the Bathurst and Hunter districts, early settlement began with members of the Cornish landowning classes taking up land, and encouraging other Cornish immigrants to join them. Cornish settlers clustered in both these areas, but chose to gather in smaller, more specific areas within the larger settlement areas.[152] Occupation was an important factor in this clustering, but personal choice was also a major consideration. Adaptability to a number of different occupations was evident amongst the Cornish settling in the Bathurst district and in the Hunter. Many moved within occupations, and between occupations, as well as moving between Cornish settlements in these regions. However, contact was maintained across the clusters both within and between these major areas, and with other colonial clusters.

---

147 The birthplace of his young children was Cornwall.
148 *Daily Telegraph*, 10 July 1894, p.5, c.6.
149 These conclusions have been drawn from the author's collection of obituaries, marriage records and family information.
150 B.W. Champion, (comp.), *Hunter Valley Register*, register 2, vol 6, Oddments 1884-1890, the author, Newcastle, N.S.W., 1973-9, pp.994-8.
151 These conclusions are drawn from anecdotal sources and from Immigration examinations of arrivals.
152 See Tables 3.5 and 3.6.

# CHAPTER SIX
## SCATTERED CLUSTERS

*They have sold the Motherland*
*That bore and bred them*
*And wandered far away*
*From Cornwall's green.*[1]

In the Hunter region and in the Bathurst district, the mixed farming and mining economy was an important factor in Cornish settlement patterns. However, some Cornish immigrants in these areas were not miners or farmers, but worked in trades, shopkeeping and other businesses which offered independence to the individual. In Sydney, where mining was not a factor, and farming was only of minor importance in Botany and along the Parramatta River, Cornish settlers clustered in certain suburbs of Sydney. Their ethnicity was a major determinant in where they decided to live.

There were smaller mining clusters at Adelong, Cobar and in the New England region. Although mining was obviously an important factor in settlement in these areas, personal choice was as important there as it was in other mining districts. Other smaller clusters formed in the New South Wales coastal areas, and there too, ethnicity and personal choice were major factors.

At Adelong, near Tumut, on the edge of the mountainous south eastern region of New South Wales, the Cornish formed a significant but transitory cluster when quartz mining boomed late in the century. In 1859, less than one percent of the population in the Tumut electorate was Cornish. In 1875 this had increased to just over one percent across the whole electorate, but with a concentration of more than thirteen percent at Adelong. By 1899, the subdivision of Adelong in the electorate of Tumut had reverted to the earlier low Cornish density with around only one percent of Cornish.[2] Births to Cornish parents in Adelong in some years between 1873 and 1888 were as high as nineteen and twenty percent of the total births.[3] Physically Adelong was a total contrast to the Sydney settlement but socially it was similar in one important respect: its population consisted of a mixture of new arrivals and of much earlier Cornish immigrants who had been living for many years in the Australian colonies.

European settlement of the Tumut and Adelong area began soon after an exploratory expedition by Hume and Hovell in 1824,[4] and it was a farming district until the discovery of alluvial gold at Adelong in 1852.[5] Adelong township is situated in a sheltered valley on the western edges of the Great Dividing Range. The early miners worked alluvial gold along Adelong Creek to the north-west of the town, until reef gold was found there in 1857, and the rush to Adelong Reefs began.[6] Gold was also discovered in the nearby Snowy Mountains,

---

1    'Silver Net', words and music by Richard Gendall.
2    See Tables 3.3, 3.4, 3.5 and 3.6.
3    See Table 2.15.
4    *Tumut Centenary Celebrations souvenir: 1824-1924*, first published 1924, republished by Tumut Shire Bicentennial Community Committee and the Tumut Shire Council, Tumut, N.S.W., 1986, p.15.
5    W. Roy Ritchie, *Early Adelong and its gold: a tribute to the work of gold pioneers William Williams and William Ritchie in the discovery and development of Adelong's goldfield*, the author, Adelong, N.S.W., c.1987, p.2.
6    W. Roy Ritchie, *Early Adelong*, p.2.

around Kiandra, bringing hopeful diggers from Bathurst.[7] The extreme cold, together with the ice and snow in these higher regions drove many miners back to their claims at the more temperate Adelong.[8] As well as gold, copper was mined in some parts of the Adelong district.[9]

PLATE 31.   Map of southern New South Wales.

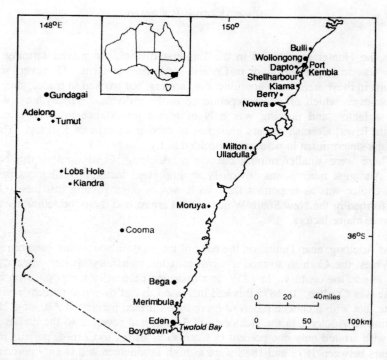

Map of southern New South Wales showing areas where the Cornish settled.

John (Hawken) Towzey who was living in Sydney in May 1860 was 'getting ready for them new <u>Snowy</u> <u>River</u> <u>Diggings</u> in the Spring' because 'People cannot winter there - so much Snow and Rain and Cold'.[10]   A visitor to Kiandra in 1872 observed that even in January, in the height of summer, 'gossipers in the street had their hands deeply buried in their pockets and their coats closely buttoned up'.[11]

In 1872 a speculative boom brought an increasing number of hopeful miners to the Adelong district.[12] Depths of mines increased, with many working deeper than 500 feet. In 1875 one was operating at over 800 feet and this later increased to 1000 feet.[13] Reef mining was at its most productive during the late 1870s and during the 1880s.[14]   At the beginning of

7   *BFP* 28 March 1860, p.3, c.3.
8   R.J. Bird, *Adelong: glimpses at the past*, Stewart Press, Hornsby, N.S.W., 1976, p.14.
9   Information from Mrs Lyn Quince.
10   John (Hawken) Towzey, letter to his parents in Padstow, Cornwall, 12 May 1860. I am indebted to Mr Robert Jeremy for sending me a copy of this letter.
11   *TCJ*, 2 March 1872, p.274, c.2.
12   R.J. Bird, *Adelong*, pp.14-17.
13   W. Roy Ritchie, *Early Adelong*, pp.10-11.
14   Information from Mr Ken Prowse.

PLATE 32. 'Inland towns of New South Wales – Adelong'

1. View of the town.  2. The Falls, Adelong Creek.  3. Bridge of the Adelong Creek.  4. Quartz crushing Works, Adelong Creek.  5.Travelling shearers at Wayside Inn.  6. Business Houses.  (From *The Australian Town and Country Journal*, 28 November 1885, p.1001, courtesy of the State Library of New South Wales.)

the boom in 1872 the town's population was only 600, although many more lived outside the town.[15] In 1876 Adelong, with a relatively small population, was the third largest gold producer in New South Wales, after Hill End and Parkes.[16] In 1878 it had a reputation as 'one of the oldest and most permanent quartz mining districts in the colony'.[17] Gold mining at Adelong continued in one form or another well into the twentieth century.[18] In 1879 Adelong was:

> purely a mining district ... There are about 500 miners amongst us. The yield of gold far exceeds any other mining district in the colony. The claims number about 30 including gold mining leases ... Some of the principal mines reach near 1000 feet in depth; and, until recently, steam power was unknown; but now we have five steam engines on this field.[19]

PLATE 33.     Adelong.

View of Adelong Reefer Battery from Adelong Falls Reserve.

The area just outside Adelong township, where the gold mines were situated, became known as Cornishtown because of the large numbers of Cornish people who settled there.[20] It was similar to other Cornish mining communities across the world, where miners and their families clustered together around the mines. While it was not the 'Little Cornwall' of the South Australian copper triangle, the beauty of the high and desolate landscape must have reminded many moorland Cornish men and women of home.

The intense Cornish participation in Adelong was significant, but comparatively brief. There was some Cornish involvement from the beginning of mining in the 1850s, but the main influx of Cornish miners and their families coincided with the escalation of hardrock mining from 1872 until the late 1880s. In 1874 one fifth of all births in Adelong were to Cornish parents, and in 1880 only slightly fewer. Adelong birth registers began in mid-1872,

15   R.J. Bird, *Adelong*, p.6.
16   L.F. Harper, *The Adeleong goldfield*, Department of Mines, mineral resources no.21, New South Wales Government Printer, Sydney, 1916, p.12.
17   *TCJ*, 16 March 1878, p.503, c.2.
18   R.J. Bird, *Adelong*, p.20.
19   *TCJ*, 11 January 1879, p.86, c.1.
20   W. Roy Ritchie, *Early Adelong*, p.2.

and it was possible to calculate a percentage of births to Cornish parents in Adelong from that time.[21] Table 2.15 shows the percentages of births to Cornish parents each year.

Most of the Cornish fathers in the Adelong birth registers were miners, and a few were in associated trades such as engine drivers and blacksmiths. Parents' places of birth and marriage (as stated on the birth registrations of their Adelong-born children) indicated that many came via the Victorian goldmining areas of Beechworth, El Dorado and Bendigo, while at least one came via California, and others came directly from Cornwall. Many families had only one or two births registered, indicating that they moved on after a relatively short time in Adelong.

PLATE 34.     Cornishtown, Adelong.     Old     workings     at Cornishtown, Adelong.

As would be expected in a mining settlement, most Cornishmen in Adelong were miners, and death registrations, of the few who died there, showed this. More than 70% of the males who died in Adelong between 1856 and 1905 were miners. See Table 2.19.

Marriage registrations also supported the conclusion that the main Cornish occupation was mining, as the bridegrooms were almost exclusively miners. Examination of the stated occupations of each partner and that of their fathers, also showed that little upward mobility occurred as a result of marriage. This is not surprising, given that most of the Cornish population were miners or their families. As shown in Table 2.20, a significant proportion of the grooms obviously came from mining families, but it appears that several were engaged only temporarily in mining, since their fathers worked in occupations unrelated to mining. It is likely that such persons eventually moved from Adelong and returned to their former occupations, another reason for Adelong's atypical (in New South Wales) settlement pattern as a temporary but significant cluster.

Although the major Cornish occupation in Adelong was mining, changes in occupation did occur over time. In cases where families remained at Adelong and produced a number of children whose births were registered, these occupational changes can be followed over a period of many years. One such person moved from work as a miner in 1865 to a farmer between 1873 and 1875, and a grazier between 1879 and 1888. Another, a miner in 1863 and a goldminer in 1873, moved across the related occupations of hay and corn merchant, forager, corn dealer and produce merchant between 1875 and 1888. Those Cornish families who had births registered over a long period and who did establish

---

21    Athough Adelong registers did not begin until mid-1872, Adelong registrations from 1856 had been included in the Tumut register but throughout that period there were only scattered entries for Cornish individuals. It was obvious that the rush (of families at least) did not begin before 1872.

themselves permanently in the district eventually became farmers, or were in other non-mining occupations. An exception was Richard White who, at the time of his death in 1903, had 'lived in Adelong 43 years, chiefly engaged in mining'.[22]

PLATE 35.     Adelong landscape

View of the landscape around Adelong.

Relatively few Cornish people died in Adelong before 1905. This suggests that it was really a temporary settlement from which most people moved before reaching old age. The Cornish deaths which did occur were the untimely results of accidents, or of complications suffered by women in childbirth. See Table 2.16.

There were no deaths recorded in Adelong of Cornish children and young people. This suggests that Adelong was never a permanent, long term settlement. Of course this does not include deaths of children who had been born in Australia to Cornish parents, as they were recorded as deaths of Australians. See Table 2.17.

Almost one fifth of the males and almost one quarter of the females born in Cornwall, who died in Adelong, had lived in at least one other colony before coming to New South Wales. Most of those who had lived in more than one Australian colony (that is other than New South Wales) had been resident in Vicoria, often for many years, before moving to Adelong. This indicated a movement of miners from the Victorian goldfields to Adelong when hardrock mining started up there. See Table 2.18.

Cornish people lived together in Adelong, in their own settlement, near the mines, called 'Cornishtown', during a period which coincided with a boom in hardrock mining there after 1872. They comprised a significant percentage of the population for at least fifteen years before the majority of them moved on, and by 1899 their density in Adelong had decreased to slightly above one percent.[23] Those remaining in Adelong generally turned to farming or to related occupations.

As in Adelong, the Cornish cluster at Cobar in far western New South Wales occurred late in the century and was purely due to mining. The population probably consisted of around twenty percent Cornish in the mid 1870s.[24] Over twenty years later, a name count of the 1899 electoral roll suggested a Cornish component of around three percent across the

22  *Methodist*, 12 September 1903, p.9, c.2.
23  See Table 3.6.
24  See Table 3.5.

whole of the Cobar electorate, but this consisted of a larger pocket in Cobar itself.[25] Both copper and gold were mined at Cobar from 1872 onwards. In 1870 a former Cornish bal maiden,[26] Mrs Sidwell Kruge, recognised as copper some rocks near what was to become Cobar. Her unofficial identification was quickly confirmed,[27] and the subsequent opening of the Cobar Copper Mine was the impetus for closer settlement in the district. At that time the country between the upper Darling and the Lachlan rivers was sparsely populated, with Cobar:

> situated almost in the middle of that blank space on our
> maps between the Lachlan and Darling, a hundred miles
> south of Bourke and a hundred and fifty-two from
> Wilcannia, both Darling River towns, and two hundred and
> fifty miles from Dubbo which we had left a week earlier.[28]

Even in 1886 the coach journey from Sydney to Bourke took nine days. The river journey to South Australia was cheaper and less difficult,[29] but possible only when the rivers were navigable.

John Varcoe acted briefly as the first mine captain until the arrival of Captain Thomas Lean, who came from Moonta in South Australia with a group of Cornish miners in 1871.[30] Lean was born in Devon but had spent his early working life in Cornish mines, and had worked as a mine captain in Victoria and South Australia.[31] Confidence was expressed in his ability and his 'experience and practical knowledge in mining affairs' ensured that he was 'the right man for the right place'.[32] The miners who came with him from South Australia included his son Thomas Lean, and also Edward Tonkin, Peter Andrewartha, Thomas Prisk and Thomas Rogers. Other mines opened quickly. One was the Cornish, Scottish and Australian (the C.S.A. mine), which still operates and which was named for the nationalities of the proprietors, Henry and Richard Nancarrow, George Gibb and John Connelly. By mid-1873 further mines had opened, with the Cobar Copper Mine alone employing 40 miners and labourers, as well as others at the surface.[33] Plans were being made to build a smelter to reduce transport costs,[84] an important consideration with the nearest railway 300 miles away.[35]

In 1875, a visitor noted a potential problem when a number of companies attempted to 'share the hill between them', and amalgamation was suggested as the solution.[86] The result was the formation of the Great Cobar Copper Mining Company Limited in 1876, heralding the 'real development of the Cobar mining industry'.[87] Henry Dangar's son, A.A. Dangar of Singleton, was an important member of the syndicate involved in the formation of the new company.[38]

---

25  See Table 3.6.
26  Bal maiden was the term used in Cornwall for women employed as surface workers at the bal or mine.
27  Information from Mrs Joy Prisk.
28  E.M. La Meslee, *The New Australia*, first published 1883, translated and edited by Russell Ward, Heinemann Educational, Melbourne, 1979, p.130.
29  W. Clelland, *Cobar founding fathers: an illustrated history of the pioneering days in the copper mining district of Cobar, New South Wales*, Western Heritage Series No 7, Macquarie Publications Pty Ltd, Dubbo, N.S.W., 1984, pp.27-9.
30  E.C. Andrews, *Report on the Cobar copper and gold-field*, part I, Department of Mines, mineral resources no.17, New South Wales Government Printer, Sydney, 1913, p.16.
31  W. Clelland, *Founding fathers*, pp.31-3.
32  *TCJ*, 6 July 1872, p.12, c.3.
33  Interview with Mr W. Snelson.
34  *TCJ*, 2 August 1873, p.143, c.3.
35  J.E. Carne, *The copper-mining industry and the distribution of copper ores in New South Wales*, 2nd edition, Department of Mines, mineral resources no.6, New South Wales Government Printer, Sydney, 1908, p.19.
36  *TCJ*, 6 March 1875, p.378, c.3.
37  W. Clelland, *Founding fathers*, p.56.
38  Information from Mr D. Eagan, Curator, Cobar Museum.

The construction of six reverbatory furnaces during 1875 and 1876 allowed smelting of the ore to be carried out locally, and the smelting of lower grade ore became an economic possibility. By 1877 the population of Cobar had increased to about 500, and a further 300 lived in the surrounding district. At this time, Cornishman Captain Dunstan began negotiations to establish a school,[39] and this was achieved in 1878.[40] Some mines first extracted only gold, and copper much later and one, the New Occidental mined gold almost exclusively.[41] Steady production of gold and copper continued during 1878 and 1879, and by 1880 the Great Cobar Mine employed 168 miners, 112 smelters, 167 surface workers, 152 woodcutters and carters and 36 boys:

> The ore was won on contract under the "Cornish" system - by public "setting" or survey every two months. The estimates of the contracts were based on allowing good miners to earn £3 per week. The contracting parties consisted generally of from four to 12 men in each party.[42]

Another traditional Cornish practice, that of contributing towards a fund for the mine doctor, operated at the Great Cobar mine, as it did at Cadia and at Vegetable Creek in New England. Contributions at Cobar were 3/- per month.[43]

However, apart from mining practices, there were few real similarities between Cobar and Cornwall, particularly in the landscape and climate. Surviving the intense heat, dust and constant scarcity of water in the Cobar district was an experience previously unknown to immigrants coming there directly from Cornwall. Even the houses were different. An adaptation to the severe climate of far western New South Wales was the construction of mud houses.[44] Those who went to most other places of Cornish settlement in New South Wales found some similarities between the homeland and the adopted country, and in some cases they were able to increase the likeness by planting hawthorn hedges and other Cornish vegetation. Cobar's seemingly endless flat terrain, the ferocity of its summers, and even the unaccustomed orange colour of its soil, emphasised its status as part of a foreign land.

The settlement which had grown around the mines was disadvantaged by its isolation and the distance from ports, by primitive and difficult conditions, and most of all by the severe lack of water.[45] In spite of the problems, however, the town's population had grown to 2000 in 1880. An evening school was established, and its continued success seemed assured with Captain Dunstan's edict that all boys aged under fourteen who were employed at the Great Cobar Copper mine would lose their jobs unless they attended evening classes three times weekly.[46] A mine had also opened to the south-east of Cobar, at Nymagee, in 1880.[47] As Nymagee grew, tents were being replaced by timber dwellings, and hotels appeared quickly.[48]

As late as 1881, the residents of Cobar continued to suffer from privations caused by lack of water:

39   W. Clelland, *Founding fathers*, p.59.
40   W. Barwood (ed.), *Cobar Public School Centenary 1878-1978*, [Cobar P and C Association?], Cobar, N.S.W., 1978, p.3.
41   E.O Rayner, 'Copper mining at Cobar', in *Australian Natural History*, vol.14, June 1963, p.190.
42   W. Clelland, *Founding fathers*, p.65.
43   Ibid, pp.63-5.
44   *TCJ*, 25 June 1881, p.1227, c.3.
45   Interview with Mr W. Snelson.
46   W. Clelland, *Founding fathers*, p.69.
47   Ibid, p.61.
48   E.M. La Meslee, *The New Australia*, p.122.

> To anyone unacquainted with the climate in this part of the colony, it is difficult to describe how very hot and unpleasant the summer months sometimes are, and how essential a plentiful supply of pure water is to the population. The sun strikes down with an almost tropical strength and the heated atmosphere envelopes the wayfarer, and even the occupant of a house, with a fervid sensation like that from a bath of heated vapour. Then the wind springing up raises clouds of red dust which blinds the eyes, penetrates the thickest clothes, and finds its way everywhere. A dust storm at Cobar is worse than anything of the kind experienced anywhere else in the colony.[49]

In a settlement which existed only because of the mines, it is not surprising that the majority of Cornishmen in Cobar were miners. Almost 70% of the Cornish males who died in Cobar between 1880 and 1907 were miners.[50]

Birth and death register entries indicated that the majority of Cornish people named in these registers between 1880 and 1900 had lived previously either in the Bathurst district or in the Cornish copper triangle in South Australia. There was no evidence that these persons had come via Broken Hill. Causes of death were related to occupation in many instances, with almost half the male deaths caused by phthisis, or other lung complaints such as chronic bronchitis or pneumonia. See Table 2.25.

As in Adelong, no deaths of Cornish-born children or young people were recorded, which indicated that most children of Cornish parents had been born in the Australian colonies. If such children died in Cobar they were registered as Australian deaths. This also suggested that just as with Adelong, the parents were not recently-arrived immigrants but had been resident in other colonies or in other parts of New South Wales before going to Cobar. Deaths were spread across the age groups, with a peak of 35% of male deaths occurring in men aged between 50 and 59. See Table 2.26.

The Cobar Cornish cluster was purely a result of the copper and gold being mined there. The copper was actually identified by a Cornishwoman and Cornishmen from South Australia were amongst the first miners there. Many others later came via the mines in the Bathurst district or from South Australia, but no 'overflow' from Broken Hill was evident.[51] Like those in the other clusters, they maintained contact with other Cornish immigrants. Unlike those in Adelong, however, many of the Cobar Cornish stayed on in the district. Cornish names are still common there and the present residents of Cobar are aware of the Cornish background and contribution to the district.

The Cornish clusters in New England, like those in Cobar and Adelong, occurred late in the century and as a result of mining. Small coastal groups grew individually earlier, but the New England district and the adjoining northern rivers region in the far north of New South Wales were totally different developments. The coastal strip and the tablelands developed separately because of the steep escarpment which divided them. Early European settlement of the vast and inaccessible tablelands (soon called the New England district) was by pastoralists during the 1830s,[52] including Cornishman Henry Dangar, and his relative Edward Gostwyck Cory, who took up prime grazing country near Armidale.[53] The properties, 'Gostwyck' and 'Palmerston' at Uralla, remain in the Dangar family today.[54]

---

49   C. Lynne, 'The industries of New South Wales', quoted in W. Clelland, *Founding fathers*, p.73.
50   See Table 2.24.
51   Information from Mrs Joy Prisk.
52   A.M. Grocott, *Gleanings from Glen Innes*, the author, Glen Innes, N.S.W., 1985, pp.47-8.
53   R.B. Walker, *Old New England: a history of the northern tablelands of New South Wales 1818-1900*, Sydney

PLATE 36.     Map of northern New South Wales.

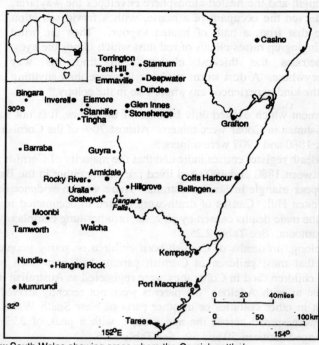

Map of northern New South Wales showing areas where the Cornish settled.

Generally, pastoralists either moved to New England from the Hunter Valley, or came directly from Britain.[55]   One such person was Oswald Bloxsome,[56] who had chronicled the voyage of the *Florentia* to New South Wales in 1838.   Such landowners were rarely resident on their properties, for example in 1848 'Gostwyck' of 89,000 acres, was only one of seven pastoral runs held by Henry Dangar in the unsettled districts,[57] and most of the early New England population were convicts or emancipists.[58]   It was 1846 before a clergyman was resident in Armidale, and a further year before Courts of Petty Sessions were established at Wellingrove, Armidale and Tenterfield.[59]   The gold rush, and later the tin rush, caused a flood of free settlers.   The opportunity to select land after the Robertson Land Act of 1861 encouraged small farmers to come to the district and also enabled miners to move into farming.   While mining boosted the population and the local economy, farming and grazing remained important throughout the nineteenth century.

In the Armidale district in 1852, gold was found near Uralla, at Rocky River, which maintained an average population of about 500 until 1856, when the discovery of the first

University Press, 1966, p.11.
54   P. Newell, and U. White, *New England sketchbook*, Rigby, Adelaide, 1970, pp.40-4.
55   R.B. Walker, *Old New England*, p.21.
56   I. Lobsey, *The Creek: a history of Emmaville and district 1872-1972*, 3rd edition, Emmaville Centenary Celebrations Committee, Emmaville, N.S.W., 1972, p.51.
57   R.B. Walker, *Old New England*, p.11.
58   Ibid, p.26.
59   Ibid, pp.44-5.

deep lead there caused an even bigger rush to the field.[60] Nundle, near Tamworth, although surrounded by land belonging to the Australian Agricultural Company, grew as a result of the discovery of gold nearby in 1852, and became the village for the Peel River diggings. In the mid-1860s it had a population of 500.[61] There is no evidence of any significant Cornish clusters in New England during this period, although information from their descendants suggests that some Cornish immigrants worked temporarily on these early New England goldfields.

Gold was found in other parts of New England,[62] including Hillgrove in 1877. In the same year, further discoveries were made, causing a rush to Hillgrove. By 1890 it had a population of 3,000 and in 1899 there was still a significant group of Cornish people there. See Table 3.6.

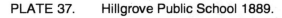

PLATE 37.     Hillgrove Public School 1889.

The public school and master's house at Hillgrove 1889. (From *The Illustrated Sydney News*, 28 November 1889, pp.16-17, courtesy of the State Library of New South Wales.)

Hillgrove had a school, two churches, hotels, banks, a hospital and shops.[63] The average attendance at the well-equipped Hillgrove superior public school was more than 400, and it boasted 'one of the best head teachers, in the person of Mr Henry Tonkin, to be found in the State'. His name, which suggests Cornish ancestry, was said to be 'as familiar as a household word throughout the districts surrounding him, and if his pupils of both sexes do not turn out good and useful Australian men and women, it will not be the fault of their teacher'.[64]

By the 1890s gold mining concentrated on reefs, which were often followed to great depths,[65] and which like those at Adelong, attracted Cornish hardrock miners. Hillgrove was a 'great hole on the New England plateau' which was, 'when first seen, most awe-inspiring'.[66]

Hillgrove provided very demanding conditions for the miners.

---

60   Ibid, pp.48-50.
61   B.T. Dowd, 'The Genesis of Nundle', in *JRAHS*, Vol.XXXI 1945, pp.41-5.
62   I. Wilkinson, *Forgotten country: the story of the Upper Clarence gold fields*, the author, Lismore, N.S.W., 1980, p.1.
63   R.B. Walker, *Old New England*, pp.97-100.
64   T.B. Coe (ed. and comp.), *The Northern districts of New South Wales*, Samuel E. Lees, Sydney, [1907?], Hillgrove section, [no page numbers].
65   R.B. Walker, *Old New England*, p.97.
66   W. Green, 'The old north: story of Hillgrove', *Northern Daily Leader*, 7 October 1936, press cuttings vol.2, p.28. ML Q991.8/N.

PLATE 38.     A promising goldfield - Hillgrove

Scenes from Hillgrove in the *Illustrated Sydney News*, 28 November 1889, pp.16-17.  (Courtesy of the State Library of New South Wales.)

Horses, bullocks, and men dragged loads of ore up the steep slopes, so steep in places that bullocks have been dragged back by their loads. Landslips were common in the treacherous ground ... and after tremendous expenditure of energy in hauling the ore up the gorge slopes, long monotonous journeys had to be undertaken by teamsters over execrable roads to Grafton or Tamworth before their loads could be delivered to steamer or train. Batteries and good tracks came later.[67]

PLATE 39.     Lady Carrington mine.

Mine captain Tom Snow and some of his men at one of the entrances to the workings of the Lady Carrington mine, Hillgrove. (From *The Illustrated Sydney News*, 28 November 1889. Courtesy of the State Library of New South Wales.)

Miners at Hillgrove were faced with a 2,500 feet climb down the steep gully to work, and up again afterwards. 'The path, an acute zig-zag, is cut so steeply that it makes the descent just possible for the pedestrian'.[68]

Such hardrock gold mining was a focus for Cornish clustering in New England late in the century, as was tin mining after 1872. With the discovery of payable tin in New England a tin mining industry developed, and centred on the adjoining tableland towns of Inverell and Glen Innes. Although the presence of tin on the New England tablelands had been noted by the Rev W.B. Clarke in 1853, it was not until 1871 that payable tin near Inverell was discovered by Joseph Wills.[69]

Soon after, Thomas Carlean found tin at Vegetable Creek (later Emmaville), and in 1872 more was located near Beardy's Creek (later Glen Innes).[70] The claims of Carlean and Wills were challenged by James Daw, whose name, like theirs, suggests Cornish ancestry.

He claimed to be the discoverer of tin in New England,[71] and unsuccessfully petitioned the New South Wales Legislative Assembly for official recognition.[72] A second

67    Ibid, p.28.
68    *The Illustrated Sydney News*, 28 November 1889, p.18, c.1.
69    R.B. Walker, 'New England tin, 1871-1900', in *JRAHS*, vol.50, 1964, pp.395-6.
70    Ibid, p.396.
71    *TCJ*, 11 October 1873, p.464, c.3.
72    *NSWLA V&P 1873-74*, vol.4, p.781. I am indebted to Mr Roger Thomas for this information.

petition in 1875 was also unsuccessful.[73] Regardless of who made the discovery, though, within a short time of its publication, tin was the main topic of conversation in New England:

> Everybody here is in tin up to the neck, and tin is the
> metallic subject of conversation for which the old subject -
> the weather - has been quite rolled aside. Everybody carries
> tin now in his hand or pocket; ruby tin, rosin tin, amber tin,
> stream tin, lode tin, or any other type of tin that the granite
> produces ... Squatters, farmers, miners, shepherds, selectors,
> mechanics, tradesmen, publicans, and sinners, are all rolling
> in tin, and hopes of fortune glitter in the distance.[74]

New England produced the majority of tin in New South Wales during the nineteenth century,[75] but it was mainly alluvial, as lode tin did not fulfil early expectations.[76] Few mines went deeper than 100 feet, the Ottery mine at Vegetable Creek being at exception at 300 feet. It was the only significant, long-term lode mine, and it worked continuously between 1882 and 1906, employing 60 men as late as 1898.[77]

The early miners working 'stream' tin, either on the surface or just below it, adapted inexpensive alluvial gold mining techniques.[78]

> At Tingha in 1876 wheelbarrows, wooden windlasses,
> Californian pumps and greenhide buckets were in general
> use; Vegetable Creek at the same time had 16 sluices, 27
> puddling machines, and 89 horses but only three steam
> engines[79]

Most of the tin was being smelted locally by 1887.[80] It was then transported to Grafton or Brisbane for shipment, providing regular work for carters until the railway reached Glen Innes in 1884.[81]

Tin prices varied considerably, and miners moved between the tin and gold fields, particularly between 1873 and 1879, and again between 1890 and 1898.[82] This movement was a likely reason for the apparently low numbers of Cornish in New England in 1875.[83] The tin mining industry brought increased population to New England, and the mining communities provided a local market for agricultural produce. The population of Vegetable Creek in 1880 was estimated at 900 Europeans and 1200 Chinese, and in 1883 it had reached a total of 3,398.[84] The population of Glen Innes quadrupled, and that of Inverell doubled, during the 1870s.[85]

Vegetable Creek (later Emmaville),[86] was the main tin mining town in the Glen Innes district, and within a short time of its establishment it impressed an observer as being a

---

73 J.E. Carne, *The tin-mining industry and the distribution of tin ores in New South Wales*, New South Wales Department of Mines, mineral resources no.14, New South Wales Government Printer, Sydney, 1911, pp.18-20.

74 *Illustrated Sydney News*, 2 August 1872, p.19, c.2.

75 R.B. Walker, 'New England tin, 1871-1900', p.403.

76 For an explanation of the differences between 'stream', 'lode' and 'deep lead' tin, see appendix IV.

77 R.B. Walker, 'New England tin, 1871-1900', pp.405-6.

78 Ibid, p.398.

79 Ibid, p.404.

80 Ibid, p.405.

81 Ibid, p.408.

82 Ibid, p.408.

83 See Table 3.4. Itinerant miners might not have appeared on electoral rolls.

84 I. Lobsey, *The Creek*, p.26.

85 R.B. Walker, 'New England tin, 1871-1900', p.408.

86 The change of name from Vegetable Creek to Emmaville in 1882 (in honour of the wife of the Governor of New South Wales), was imposed on its residents. They refused to alter the name of their hospital, which still

prosperous and stable settlement.[87]    In 1874 alone, it produced 2,400 tons of tin.[88] Vegetable Creek school opened in 1875 with nearly 80 pupils, and a population in the district of about 400, most of whom were 'dependent on the mining industry'.[89]

The town prospered, particularly during the 1880s, and a strong community spirit existed there. A School of Arts and a Progress Association were established and the residents began a system similar to the Cornish 'mine doctor' scheme, in which European residents (Chinese were excluded) contributed to the expenses for a doctor and hospital.[90]

### PLATE 40.    Vegetable Creek

VEGETABLE CREEK TIN MINING COMPANY'S MINE,

'Vegetable Creek Tin Mining Company's mine'. (From *The Australian Town and Country Journal*, 28 March, 1874, p.500, courtesy of the State Library of New South Wales.)

The nearby settlement of Torrington boomed after the discovery of tin lodes there in 1881. It was named after Torrington on the borders of Cornwall and Devon, and honours the large number of miners who came from there:

> 'Cousin Jacks' ... had the expertise, and their techniques
> were followed from the beginning and are still in use
> today.[91]

---

retains the title 'Vegetable Creek Hospital'. (I. Lobsey, *The Creek*, pp.20-1.)

87    *TCJ*, 28 March 1874, p.500, c.1.
88    I. Lobsey, *The Creek*, p.12.
89    Ibid, p.27.
90    R.B. Walker, 'New England tin, 1871-1900', p.407. I. Lobsey, *The Creek*, pp.22-3.
91    C. Alt, (comp.), *Old Torrington: a history of Torrington and district 1881-1981*, 'Back to Torrington Weekend' Committee, Torrington, N.S.W., 1981, pp.9 and 11.

The village began as a collection of bark and corrugated iron buildings occupied by small prospectors. Within two years they had been overtaken by large mining companies, but most of these men stayed on, working for the companies.[92] In 1883 a five head battery and buddles[93] were operating, and as recently as 1920, 500 men were employed at Torrington and sixteen batteries were working in the vicinity.[94] Torrington residents retain a sense of their Cornish identity. Some are descendants of Cornish miners, including George Henry Trewhella (who came to the colony in the 1880s, going first to Sunny Corner near Bathurst), and William and Elizabeth Toy who settled at Bismuth near Torrington at the turn of the century.[95]

Like its neighbour Glen Innes, the farming and grazing district of Inverell was affected by the ebb and flow of mining, but never wholly dependent on it.[96] The discovery of tin did bring increased population and prosperity, though. Gold miners from the worked-out New England fields moved to Inverell, and those 'from Rocky River migrated en masse'.[97] Alluvial gold mining techniques were commonly used in tin mining, as they were in nearby Glen Innes:

> The basic requirements were a small shovel, a wheel-barrow, a cradle for washing the tin and a tent. Small syndicates of miners could pool their resources to buy a horse and dray (to cart the wash dirt) and a California pump. Sluice boxes proved to be the best way of separating the tin from the gravel.[98]

Many of the tin miners who flooded to the Inverell district were Cornish and because of their expertise they were much in demand as mine managers and were addressed as 'Captain', following Cornish custom. Also according to Cornish custom, many mines were called 'wheals'.[99] Some 'Cousin Jacks' had arrived in Australia during the gold rush and moved to New England following the discovery of tin. One of them, Peter Eddy, made a profit of £30,000 within a few years. He invested in land and became 'a pioneer of extensive wheat growing'. Other successful Cornish miners were the Penberthy brothers, tributers at Elsmore, who located valuable deposits.[100] The mining town of Tingha, on Cope's Creek near Inverell, developed on private land around the Britannia mine, and by 1873 it had a school, post office, racecourse, shops and hotels. Within eight years it boasted a population of 2,424, including a large number of Chinese, but by the 1890s the population had fallen to 1,000.[101]

Except for early pioneers like the Dangars, most Cornishmen and women who settled in New England came after 1850 and were first attracted there by the mining. Once there, and after the gold or tin had been fully exploited, many (but not all) grasped the opportunity to move into other occupations. One such person was Charles Michell, formerly an engineer in Redruth, who emigrated about 1858 with his brothers Frederick and William. He went

---

92  Ibid, pp.10.
93  See appendix IV.
94  C. Alt, *Old Torrington*, p.10.
95  Ibid, pp.75 and 95.
96  E. Wiedemann, *World of its own: Inverell's early years 1827-1920*, Devill Publicity, Inverell, N.S.W., 1981, p.85.
97  Ibid, p.79.
98  Ibid, p.80.
99  Telephone conversation with Mrs Elizabeth Wiedemann.
100 E. Wiedemann, *World of its own*, p.82.
101 Ibid, p.87.

gold prospecting at Rocky River near Uralla, where he worked also as a blacksmith. There he and William married sisters Mary Ann and Maria Brown, and Charles and Mary Ann Michell moved to the goldmining district of Bingara where they kept a store, and the Diggers Arms hotel, between 1864 and 1875. By 1880 they were still in the Bingara district, but had taken up land at Barraba, and at the time of Charles Michell's death in 1904 his status had improved to 'grazier'.[102] Another miner Paul Prisk, with his wife Mary, came from Penzance and worked at Nundle as a miner. Later they took up land and settled nearby at Hanging Rock, naming their property 'Wendron'.[103]

On the other hand, William Henry Martin was a miner who preferred to remain in that occupation, ending his career as a highly respected mine captain at Hillgrove. He arrived with his wife and small children aboard the *Severn* in 1863,[104] and worked first as a miner in the Bathurst district. By 1883, he was a mine captain at Stannifer in New England, and at the time of his death in a mine accident in 1899, he was the underground captain at Eleanora mine, Hillgrove.[105] Captain Martin's funeral was 'a demonstration of sympathy and respect, such as has never been equalled in Hillgrove'.[106] Another miner who chose mining as his long-term occupation was William Henry Wesley who came from a humble background as a miner at St Just, rising to become a respected and successful mining entrepreneur at Vegetable Creek.[107]

These Cornish immigrants were typical of those to settle in New England. The main clusters were at Hillgrove, and in the districts of Glen Innes and Inverell. W.H. Martin and Charles Michell were like many others who had moved to New England from other Cornish clusters. Unlike those in Adelong though, many of the Cornish miners in New England took the opportunity to move into other occupations and settled permanently in the district. The occupations they chose were, like those chosen by Cornish immigrants in other areas, farming, storekeeping and hotelkeeping which enabled them to be self-employed and independent.

Small clumps of Cornish settlers gathered along the north and south coasts of New South Wales. Except for the coalmining near Wollongong, there was no major mining industry in the areas of coastal settlement. As in other non-mining areas, the occupations chosen by Cornish immigrants in the coastal settlements were farming, trades and storekeeping. Once again, the most important factor in their clustering was personal choice: they chose to settle together because they were Cornish. That such groups of Cornish men and women congregated even where the central focus of a mine did not exist, gives strong support to the argument that ethnicity was the major determinant in their clustering.

In northern New South Wales the coastal area was separated from New England by a steep escarpment, and settlement in this coastal district grew around the timber and maritime industries, and small farming, particularly dairy farming. The only significant Cornish cluster in this area was at Kempsey. In Kempsey too, the Cornish engaged in occupations which offered independence, but which were not the major reason for the formation of the cluster.

Mr W.T. Dangar, of Bodmin (not a member of the St Neot family), emigrated as a child to Port Macquarie where he served an apprenticeship as a saddler. In 1859 he moved

---

102  Information from Mrs Beryl Michell.
103  Information from Mrs Anne Massey.
104  AONSW shipping lists, *Severn* 1863, AO reel 2481 and AO 9/6283.
105  Information from Mrs Deborah Shuker.
106  *The Hillgrove Guardian*, 24 June 1899, p.3.  I am indebted to Mr Russell Nicholson, Dixson Library, University of New England, for this information.
107  *AMM*, series 1, vol.2, pp.223-5.  For more detail, see appendix VI.

to Kempsey where he was joined by a brother and sister. In later years he operated a sawmill and a butcher shop.[108] Phillip Hill, a pilot, joined his son in Kempsey in 1877.[109] Examination of the Methodist marriage registers showed that Cornish-born persons who married there between 1864 and 1897 included members of the Rowe, Trathen, Teague, Bolt, Burridge, Brenton and Nance families.[110] Examination of stated occupations at marriage produced no evidence of a cluster according to occupation alone.

The river port of Kempsey developed 28 miles upstream from the mouth of the Macleay River, surrounded by rich grazing land, and fertile soil which produced cedar and other valuable timber.[111] Although much of the accessible timber had been removed by 1842, the boatbuilding industry, which had developed alongside timber getting, persisted. Squatting continued,[112] but small farmers also began to settle.[113] After 1861, selectors took up small parcels of land along the Macleay River and its tributaries, and in 1878 it was estimated that almost 7,000 people lived in the Macleay River district, the majority being farmers and graziers.[114]

The fertile soil and valuable native timber of the Macleay were common to the other northern river valleys, and the Bellinger valley was 'one of the finest timber districts in the colony of New South Wales'.[115] The Lean family of Bellingen, who had family connections in the Hunter (at Dungog), were an example of the Cornish movement between communities. George Lean of St Kew had emigrated to join his brothers, Christopher and Robert, there, and after the untimely deaths of George and his wife, their seven children were brought up by Christopher Lean. George's son, William, selected land near Bellingen in 1879 and was soon followed to the district by other members of the family from Dungog.[116]

Like the north coast, the coastal area south of Sydney was settled by Cornish immigrants in small groups, sometimes by miners moving from the southern goldfields to permanent settlements, while others near Wollongong were influenced by the coal mining at Bulli. Cornish settlers lived at Wollongong and Kiama, further south at Moruya, and almost on the Victorian border at Eden. Information supplied by descendants of Cornish immigrants suggested that there was a sprinkling of Cornish residents in the goldmining areas near Braidwood and Araluen, and on the southern tablelands at Yass, Goulburn and Queanbeyan. Although the Currawang Copper Mining Company mine operated near Lake George from 1865,[117] no evidence of long term Cornish settlement there has been found, except for the move there by mine captain, James Trevarthen of Byng,[118] and a small cluster there in 1875. See Table 3.5.

The coal mines in Wollongong attracted some Cornish miners. Albert Cavill, a miner of Truro, who came as an assisted emigrant, with his wife, aboard *Emily* in 1850,[119] spent the remainder of his life as a coalminer at Bulli.[120] Three Tresidder brothers, of Wendron, also settled as miners at Bulli. Andrew arrived about 1878, and his twin brothers and their

108  J.H. Watson, 'Kempsey: early settlement of the Macleay River', in *JRAHS*, vol.VII 1921, part 4, pp.207-210.
109  AONSW Shipping lists *La Hogue* 1877, AO reel 2488.
110  'Methodist marriages Kempsey: 1864-1897', SAG reel 0229.
111  M.H. Neil, *Valley of the Macleay: the history of Kempsey and the Macleay River district*, Wentworth Books, Sydney, 1972, pp.11-13.
112  Ibid, pp.31-2.
113  Ibid, pp.47-8.
114  *TCJ*, 23 November 1878, p.983, c.3.
115  *TCJ*, 13 April 1878, p.695, c.1.
116  N. Braithwaite and H. Beard (eds.), *Pioneering in the Bellinger Valley*, Bellinger Valley Historical Society, Bellingen, N.S.W., 1979, pp.123-5.
117  *Goulburn Evening Post*, 13 April 1977, p.13.
118  Information from Mrs Mary Nesbitt.
119  AONSW shipping list *Emily* 1850, AO reel 2461. He was apparently a relative of the Cavill and Carveth families in Balmain, as he stated that he had an uncle John living at Balmain ferry. See chapter 7.
120  *Illawarra pioneers: pre 1900*, Illawarra Family History Group Inc., Wollongong, N.S.W., 1988, p.33.

families emigrated together in 1880.[121]     Some Cornish settlers in the area engaged in different occupations.  William Guard, a tinner from Marazion, for instance, arrived as an assisted emigrant aboard *Star of India* in 1875.  He lived in Sydney for several years, then worked briefly as a copper miner before settling in Thirroul near Wollongong, as a publican.[122]  Phillip Orchard Tresidder, a blacksmith of Crowan, came via Queensland to become a miner and later a dairy farmer at Corrimal during the 1890s.[123]  This reflects the pattern which occurred in other Cornish settlement areas.  Although occupation was often an important determinant (and one in which choice was also a factor), personal choice played a very important role.

Further south, there were Cornish settlers in the Moruya district.  Once again, ethnicity rather than shared occupations was the major factor.  For instance Peter Williams was a blacksmith of Crowan, who emigrated with his wife Theresa aboard the *Hornet* in 1865.  He worked briefly as an engineer in the gold mining district of Araluen before settling as a blacksmith at Moruya, where it is believed Vulcan Street was named after him.[124] Charles Crapp, a nurseryman at Kiora near Moruya, specialised in fruit trees, and supplied 'most of the coast and quite a long way inland'.[125]  Philip Jeffrey arrived from Cornwall in 1847 and farmed at Bodalla, Kiora and Moruya, and in 1854 he owned almost 4,000 acres near Bodalla, at 'Comerang' which he sold to Thomas Mort in 1856.[126]

On the far south coast, Cornish families settled in the Eden district.  One was the Mitchell family.  Edmund Mitchell, of Kenwyn, arrived aboard *Gloriana* in 1855, and lived first at Pambula before selecting land in the Towamba district.  His father, Edward, joined him in 1857, and the family took up dairy farming, pig-raising and corn growing.[127]

In little pockets along the coast, and inland, there were Cornish settlers, some drawn initially by the gold near Braidwood and Araluen.  Fanny Pascoe from Mawgan-in-Pydar, came aboard the *Andromache* in 1839 with her brother Thomas and his family, married in Sydney the same year, and lived in Richmond before moving to the Braidwood goldfields, at Major's Creek.[128]  Mary Chynoweth, of St Agnes, arrived aboard *Morning Star* in 1864 with five children, to join her husband Richard at Araluen.[129]

Others like Andrew Berriman worked first as miners before moving into other occupations along the south coast.  He came aboard *Gloriana* in 1855 and went first to the goldfields.  He was successful enough to purchase a store near Bateman's Bay, at Mogo, where he spent the remainder of his life.[130]  Other settlers preferred to work at farming or in trades on arrival.  Cornishman William Butson, and his Devonian wife Mary, arrived in 1855 and settled at Ulladulla.[131]  John Hawken, a shipwright of Padstow, came to Australia in 1851 with his wife and two children, and John worked as a shipwright in the Shoalhaven district between 1851 and 1895.[132]

Cornish settlers on the north and south coast formed cells rather than clusters, but members of these smaller groups nevertheless did settle together, and maintained contact with other Cornish groups.  Their occupations were rarely mining-related, though some

---

121  Information from Mr Russ Bell.

122  Information from Ms Pamela Sheldon.

123  Illawarra pioneers, p.176.

124  Information from Miss Mearal Porter.

125  H.J. Gibbney, *Eurobodalla: history of the Moruya district*, LAH in association with the Council of the Shire of Eurobodalla, Sydney, 1980, pp.87 and 181.

126  Ibid, pp.83 and 183.

127  Information from Mrs Lyn Lyon.

128  Information from Mrs Pamala Tancred.

129  AONSW shipping list *Morning Star* 1864, AO reel 2482.

130  Information from Mrs Estelle Neilson.

131  Information from the Rev John Butson.

132  Information from Ms Dorothy Heber.  Some earlier Cornish landholders in the Shoalhaven district were Richard Glanville in the 1830s and his brother John in 1844.  (W.A. Bayley, *Shoalhaven: history of the Shire of Shoalhaven, New South Wales*, Shoalhaven Shire Council, Nowra, N.S.W., 1975, p.29.)

individuals were ex-miners. There was a surprising lack of maritime occupations (although there were some) in the coastal districts. Most were tradesmen, storekeepers or farmers, following the pattern set by non-miners in other settlements. They continued the trend of remaining together because of their Cornishness and not only because of shared maritime, farming, mining or other occupations. These Cornish immigrants, who chose to settle together even when there was no mining focus, and no existing large Cornish cluster, obviously settled together because they wanted to - because they were Cornish.

The occupations of Cornish immigrants influenced where they settled to some degree, and for some their occupations were a very important factor in determining the area of New South Wales they chose as a permanent residence. Of course, there was a certain amount of choice involved even when occupation was a major determinant as it was in the mining communities. Settlement patterns in Sydney and in the New South Wales coastal districts were not the typical Cornish one where immigrants settled in a transplanted Cornish community around a mine, but it was not surprising that such non-mining areas attracted immigrants of other occupations, or miners who wished to move away from that work. Although the occupations of these immigrants were important in influencing their areas of settlement, the occupational mix evident indicated that an extremely important influence was personal choice, and that they settled together because they wanted to, and because they were Cornish. This was even more obvious in the non-mining clusters where there was no mining hub to draw those with mining-related occupations.

In the mining settlements of Cobar, Adelong and New England, the Cornish settlements began as mining clusters, but even there the Cornish chose to settle, because of ethnicity, in specific parts of the mining community which then often became known as Cornishtown. Again, this was a matter of personal choice.

Contact with, and movement between, the Cornish communities in New South Wales and the other colonies was evident and in some cases this had been precipitated by employment prospects, but it was also a decision which was strongly influenced by personal and family factors. There was evidence from some descendants of Cornish immigrants which indicated that very occasionally individuals chose not to settle as part of the Cornish clusters, and that they did not appear to maintain contact with other Cornish people. Sometimes there was a good reason for this desire for anonymity, as in the case of John (Hawken) Towzey of Padstow. He changed his name from Hawken to Towzey on arrival, and kept apart from the Cornish community in an attempt to avoid recognition, after emigrating to escape from the consequences of the loss in Padstow of a boat partly owned by his father.[133] On other occasions, they were merely exercising that option of choice, which for a minority meant settling away from other Cornish, but which for most Cornish immigrants meant choosing to cluster with others from their homeland.

The occupations most often chosen by Cornish immigrants in all areas of settlement were those allowing personal freedom and independence within that work - mining, farming, or trades where they could be self-employed, and shopkeeping and hotelkeeping which offered similar independence. Adaptability, which allowed movement between such occupations was clear amongst the Cornish in all settlement areas.

Although the communities in the Bathurst district and the Hunter region began differently from the other clusters, there was a common thread running through all the Cornish clusters in New South Wales. The Cornish settled together in groups which were often influenced by occupation but in all areas personal choice was a very important factor. Contact was maintained across all these clusters: Bathurst, the Hunter, Sydney, New

---

133 Information from Mr Robert Jeremy.

England, Cobar, Adelong, and the coastal areas. Like their settlement patterns, this contact with their countrymen in other colonial clusters was influenced to some degree by their shared occupations, but also by personal choice and by other personal and family factors.

## PLATE 41. Remains of mining in New England

'The Ottery' arsenic mine near Emmaville. Photographs courtesy of Mr Roger Thomas.

PLATE 42.    Deserted mines in New England

'The Ottery' mine near Emmaville.

An old steam boiler at Curnow's mine near Torrington.

# CHAPTER SEVEN
## 'ALL CORNISH GENTLEMEN ARE COUSINS':
## CHAIN MIGRATION, INTERMARRIAGE AND CORNISHNESS

*This angle which so shutteth them in, hath wrought many inter-changeable matches with each other's stock, and given beginning to the proverb, that all Cornish gentlemen are cousins.*[1]

Shared occupations of Cornish immigrants was an important factor in their settlement patterns, but choice, based on personal considerations, also played a major part. The Cornish in New South Wales preferred to settle as well as to work together, and even to settle together although they had different occupations. This personal choice is shown in their patterns of chain migration as well as in their tendency to intermarry with other Cornish families over several generations. A third factor in their choosing to stay together was the 'Cornishness', which made them identifiably different from other ethnic groups in the colony, and which was also obvious amongst Cornish immigrants in South Australia and in Victoria.[2]

Anne Colman found that Cornish settlers in Victoria were clannish, that they engaged in chain migration, and settled in groups which displayed an identifiable Cornishness, as they did in South Australia.[3] A similar tendency emerged in New South Wales with the early establishment of Cornish Settlement near Orange, and continued in the other Cornish clusters in the colony. Other than the obvious clannishness, the kinds of behaviour which identified them as Cornish were their accent and dialect and their character. Also, the Cornish were noted for their love of music and singing and often for their involvement in the Methodist church. Another facet of this clannishness was the contact and movement maintained between the Cornish colonial clusters, and with Cornwall itself.

Chain migration and intermarriage with other Cornish or 'accepted' families were clear outward signs of their clannish attitude. Evidence of chain migration first appeared in immigrants' arrival statements about relatives already resident in the colony. The Cornish were certainly not the only ethnic group to practise chain migration, but they most certainly did so enthusiastically and often over a period spanning several generations. Information on individual families, in published biographies or supplied by the descendants of immigrants, contained evidence that chain migration occurred to varying degrees in the majority of Cornish families in New South Wales. Only rarely did information from the descendants of Cornish immigrants not include such evidence. This was not necessarily because it did not occur, rather that some family historians had not progressed beyond locating their direct ancestors and so had not yet found wider family relationships. Also, of course, some

---

1   R. Carew, *The survey of Cornwall*, first published 1602, F.E. Halliday, (ed.), republished Andrew Melrose 1953, Adams and Dart, London, 1969, p.136.
2   P.J. Payton, *The Cornish miner in Australia: Cousin Jack Down Under*, Dyllansow Truran, Redruth, 1984. A. Colman, 'Colonial Cornish: Cornish immigrants in Victoria, 1865-1880', M.A., University of Melbourne, 1985.
3   P.J. Payton, *The Cornish miner in Australia*, chapter 3. A. Colman, 'Colonial Cornish', chapter 5.

immigrants did not engage in chain migration if, like John (Hawken) Towzey, they were trying to fade into anonymity in New South Wales.

The Evans and Calloway families of West Cornwall are well-documented examples[4] of Cornish families who used the assisted emigration schemes and practised chain migration extensively. Also, they intermarried with other Cornish families through several generations. Six of the seven surviving children of David and Constance Evans of Madron came to New South Wales as assisted immigrants between 1839 and 1853, and relatives continued to join them until at least 1877. Evan Evans and his wife Sarah Roberts came with their children aboard *Andromache* in 1839. Travelling with them were Evan's brother Thomas Evans and his wife Ann Calloway and their children. Both men were farm servants, and a third unmarried brother, David Evans, accompanied them, claiming he was their servant.[5] A fourth brother Joseph Evans, an agricultural labourer, with his wife Alice Mildren and their children, followed aboard *William Metcalfe* in 1844. A fifth brother, John, and his wife Mary Calloway, came aboard *Bolton* in 1853. A sister Mary Ann Evans, and her husband Thomas Williams and their children, came in the same year aboard *Australia*. The sisters-in-law, Ann Calloway and Mary Calloway were also cousins: both had been baptised in Gulval. One was the daughter of Moses Calloway and Nancy Uren, the other of Philip Calloway and Ann Uren.[6] Joseph and Alice Evans settled in the Corryong district (between Cooma and Albury) amongst other Cornish immigrants who had emigrated via South Australia. The other five Evans siblings settled in Sydney and on the south coast of New South Wales.[7]

The emigration between 1839 and 1853 of these six siblings and their families was, however, far from being the total in this chain of emigration. Other more distant relatives joined them over an extended period. Joseph Williams, a cousin of Thomas Williams of Dapto, arrived aboard *Bermondsey* in 1855. Also aboard *Bermondsey* was a seventeen year old unmarried female, Mary Williams of Ludgvan, who had 'an uncle, Thomas Williams, at Mr Evan Evans', Dapto Illawarra'. Another cousin of Thomas Williams, William Hosking, arrived aboard *Earl Dalhousie* in 1877, and aboard *Trevelyan* in 1877 with his family, was James Uren who was a cousin of James Calloway of Wollongong. Mary Calloway who came aboard *Trafalgar* in 1853 was a sister of Mrs Thomas Evans of Wollongong. In turn, their mother Ann Calloway and brothers James and Moses arrived aboard *Cressy* in 1856. Also aboard the *Trafalgar* with Mary Calloway in 1853 was Elizabeth Palamountain (nee Williams) who was the sister of Alice, the wife of Joseph Evans.[8]

Even friends became part of this particular chain of emigration. William James of St Ives, a stonemason and friend of Evan Evans, arrived aboard *Australia* in 1853, having travelled with Evan's sister Mary Ann Williams and her family. William James also settled near them at Dapto, and built Evan Evans' home 'Penrose' soon after.[9] William James in turn was followed to New South Wales by his own family. He was the cousin of a later emigrant, Edward Kernick, who arrived aboard *Lady Elgin* in 1854.[10] The considerable

---

4    They are well documented in A. Brown's *The Evans family history*, the author, Epping, N.S.W., 1989, which includes initial research by Mrs Fay Cockle of Blaxland, N.S.W. However, because they were unusually forthcoming to immigration officials about their relatives already in the colony, they are also well documented in immigration records. Another who was forthcoming with information about relatives was Amelia Nettle, a married assisted immigrant aboard the *Harbinger* in 1849 and bound for Bathurst. She claimed that not only Ann Lean of Bathurst was a relative, but also that Samuel Lean, Harriet Richards, John Lean and Mary Trewren, also of Bathurst, were her cousins. (AONSW Immigration Board's lists, *Harbinger* 1849, AO reel 2459.) Mostly though, assisted immigrants admitted to only one or two relatives already resident in the colony, if at all.

5    AONSW shipping list *Andromache* 1839, AO reel 1298.

6    A. Brown, *The Evans family history*, pp.25-30.

7    Information from Mr A.J. Brown.

8    AONSW shipping lists *Bermondsey* 1855, *Trevelyan* and *Earl Dalhousie* 1877, *Trafalgar* 1853, *Cressy* 1856, AO reels 2465, 2468, 2473, 2488.

9    A. Brown, *The Evans family history*, p.23.

10   AONSW shipping list *Lady Elgin* 1854, AO reel 2466.

intermarriage which occurred between the Evans and other families is recorded in detail in *The Evans family history*.[11]

PLATE 43.    The Evans family

| FAMILY OF DAVID AND CONSTANCE EVANS OF GULVAL/MADRON/LUDGVAN | | | | |
|---|---|---|---|---|
| 1. Elizabeth 1801- m. 1827 Gulval William EDWARDS | 2. Mary 1803- died in infancy | 3. *Evan Robert 1805-1863 m. 1834 Helston Sarah ROBERTS Emigrated 1839 Settled Dapto and Kiama | 4. *Joseph Barnes 1808-1877 m. 1831 St. Erth Alice MILDREN Emigrated 1844 Settled Corryong | 5. David Lloyd 1810- probably died in infancy |
| 6. *David 1813-1862 Emigrated 1839 m.1854 Sydney Jane JOHNS Settled Sydney | 7. *Thomas 1815- m. 1835 Ludgvan Ann CALLOWAY Emigrated 1839 Settled Wollongong | 8. Elizabeth 1816- died in infancy | 9. *John 1820-1901 m. 1844 Gulval Mary CALLOWAY (cousin of Ann) Emigrated 1853 Settled Milton (South Coast) | 10. *Mary Ann 1823-1896 m. 1843 Gulval Thomas WILLIAMS Emigrated 1853 Settled Shellharbour |

* Emigrated to Australia
Compiled from information provided by Mr A. J. Brown,
from original research by Mrs Fay Cockle of Blaxland, NSW.

Evans and related families. (Compiled from information provided by Mr A.J. Brown.)

There is evidence of some degree of chain migration in almost every Cornish family examined. It occurred amongst the Cornish in all areas of Cornish settlement in New South Wales, and was not restricted by class or occupation. There was also adaptability shown in the variety of family groupings, which changed as wives and children came to join husbands already in the colony, or widows came with adult children or other relatives. For example, aboard the *Harbinger* in 1849 were sisters Mary Ann (Blamey) Treneman and Eliza (Blamey) Northey with husbands, children and step-children. They were accompanied by their widowed mother, Peggy Blamey.[12]   On other occasions, the chain consisted of emigrants generally belonging to the same generation. For instance, in the Bathurst district, John Glasson, who arrived in 1830 and went to Cornish Settlement, brought out seven of his brothers and sisters between 1838 and 1861. Glasson also brought Bishop, an unrelated servant, to join him in the colony.[13]

---

11   A. Brown, *The Evans family history*.
12   AONSW shipping lists, *Harbinger* 1849, AO reel 2459.
13   John's brother Richard Glasson arrived in 1838 with his wife Emma. All their children were born in the colony. A sister, Mary, came with Richard and Emma. She married John Lane and after her death he married Jane Thomas. The next brother, Joseph, arrived in 1841 and married Emma Sweetnam. William Glasson and his wife Susan arrived in 1852, accompanied by his sister Elizabeth who later married Cornishman Thomas Stevens. Finally, Henry and his wife Anne arrived in 1861 accompanied by his sister, Susan, who did not marry. The only sibling to remain in Cornwall married a Mr Treweeke, and some of their children came to New South Wales. (Information from Mr B.W. Thomas.)

A form of chain migration, where individuals emigrated to join apparently unrelated Cornish already in New South Wales, was not uncommon. In the Hunter region there is considerable evidence of extensive, long term chain migration of families, but also of apparently unrelated individuals from similar areas of Cornwall. The history and achievements of the Dangar family in New South Wales are well documented, and provide extensive evidence of long term chain migration. Henry Dangar encouraged his sister and his five brothers, as well as other relatives, to join him in the colony.[14] Close relatives of the Dangars, however, were not the only immigrants to come to New South Wales from the district of St Neot. A total of 76 assisted emigrants arriving between 1837 and 1877 gave their native place as St Neot or one of the surrounding parishes, and it is reasonable to assume that still more were hidden amongst those whose native place was recorded only as Cornwall. Of those whose parish of birth is listed, fifteen were born in St Neot and many more in places close to that parish. Forty had been born in Liskeard, and 21 in the parishes of St Cleer, St Pinnock, Warleggan, Blisland, Braddock, Linkinhorne and Cardinham.[15] It is likely that at least some of these persons were engaging in chain migration, encouraged by the Dangars, through contact maintained between the Cornish in the Hunter and those in the St Neot district.

The chain of migration of other Cornish families in the Hunter is not nearly so well documented as in the Bathurst district, but evidence suggests it was widespread.[16] Some Cornish settlers there came as a result of a family member's much earlier, and temporary, emigration to Australia. One such person was Alfred Goninan of St Just who established the Newcastle engineering firm which bore his name. He emigrated towards the end of the century because of his father's reminiscences about his experiences in Australia during the gold rush, and because his sister was already living in Newcastle. Goninan's father had planned to bring his wife and family to Australia, but his mother had refused to undertake the long journey by sea.[17] In some cases, though, the first link in the chain was a Cornish convict. When Stephen Grose arrived in 1856, he stated that he had no relatives in the colony, and that his parents Richard and Sarah Grose were alive, and both residing in Bodmin. In fact his father Richard was a miner who had been transported more than twenty years earlier for stealing tin. He had arrived in 1835 and had been assigned to the Australian Agricultural Company at Port Stephens. Stephen Grose settled in Newcastle and father and son maintained a close connection.[18]

As in the Bathurst district, most of the families examined in the Hunter region practised chain migration to some extent at least, and the examples above illustrate the variety which occurred there, ranging from the continuing system used by the Dangars which involved not only immediate family but apparently unrelated people from their home district, to the kind chosen by Stephen Grose to join an unacknowledged (to the authorities) convict parent.[19]

---

14   See appendix VI.

15   Data base information taken from AONSW shipping lists, 1837-1877.

16   For example, the Christian family who arrived in 1842 and settled at Morpeth encouraged Bulmore, Bassett and Cardell relatives to join them. (Information from Ms Marianne Eastgate.) William and Melinda Burnett of St Neot, who settled in Singleton, were soon followed to New South Wales by Langsford and Kent relatives. (Information from Mrs Peggy Richards.) John Cundy of Newlyn arrived in the colony in 1838 with his brother William. They were joined in the Hunter by their brother Samuel and family, and sister Elizabeth Googe and her family in 1858. (Information from Mrs Enid Farnham and Sr Juliana Googe.)

17   *Memoirs of Alfred Goninan (1865-1953*, L.E. Fredman, (ed.), introduction and typescript unpublished, from original manuscript in possession of Mrs Marcovitch, Chatswood.

18   Information from Ms Dorothy Heber.

19   A similar occurrence in the Bathurst district was the case of an adult child, William Plummer, a miner, who came with his wife and children to join his parents who had both been transported twenty years earlier, leaving their four children in Cornwall. (Information from Mrs Pat Sheriff.)

The practice of using a variety of combinations in chain migration was not confined to the agricultural and mining districts of Bathurst and the Hunter, however. A comparable variety occurred amongst the Cornish in Sydney, as here too, early arriving immigrants encouraged others to join them. For instance, the first assisted emigrants from the Cavill and Carveth families of St Breock and Egloshayle arrived in 1839.[20] John Cavill, a stonemason, and his wife Mary Ann (nee Carveth) were accompanied by her sister Jane Carveth. The family settled at Balmain and were joined there by John Carveth, a farm labourer, and his wife Mary (nee Carveth, and his cousin), who arrived aboard *Sultana* in 1855. Also in 1855, another John Carveth (he was a brother of Mary Ann Cavill, nee Carveth) arrived aboard *Eliza* with his wife Maria (who was also his cousin, and sister of Mary and John Carveth). Another relative, Syria Cavill, a waterman of Balmain, died there in 1854. The brothers John and William Lightfoot of St Breock, who emigrated in 1855 and 1856 were related through the Carveth family, but they settled in the Hunter, near the Varcoe relatives of John's wife.

Such complicated family migrations were not uncommon amongst Cornish immigrants to New South Wales, but many were discovered only during research by their descendants. These extensive and complicated migrations supported the view that Cornish immigrants settled together from personal choice, and not from any compulsion imposed from outside, or purely because of occupational needs. This argument is strengthened by further evidence of chains of migration which stretched across several generations, as young men and women joined uncles, aunts or parents, or as the reverse occurred, and parents emigrated to join children. The Strongman family used both options. When Caroline Strongman, a general servant aged seventeen, and her brother John, a labourer aged 25, with his wife Mary, arrived in 1874, they had two uncles, Philip and H. Williams living in Dixon Street, Sydney. Caroline's parents, Benjamin and Mary Strongman, aged 59 and 60, came to join her the following year, accompanied by their daughter Ellen Hodge, her husband John, and their small children John and Caroline.[21] On other occasions, those who were seemingly unrelated were actually travelling together to join a common relative. For example, eighteen-year-old Elizabeth Ann Dennis of Chacewater was apparently emigrating alone in 1855, but was actually accompanied by several relatives.[22]

Cornish who used the Remittance Regulations system, paying a deposit to nominate other members of the family to join them, were signalling an intention to settle in Australia.[23] Although this system was not used widely by the Cornish, at least some families did make use of it. One was John Prowse, whose wife, Matilda, travelled aboard *Himalaya* in 1865[24] with their two young daughters, to join him at Adelong.[25] This family combined other

---

20   Apart from details in the AONSW shipping lists, all information on the Carveth, Cavill and Lightfoot families has been provided by Mr Daryl Lightfoot, Mrs J. Harvey and Mr Collin Brewer.

21   AONSW shipping lists *Samuel Plimsoll 1* 1874 and *Jerusalem* 1875, AO reel 2486.

22   She stated on arrival that her cousin, Elizabeth Northey, already lived in Sydney. Further examination of the Immigration Board's list for the *Sultana* revealed that an aunt and two cousins were travelling with her. Susan Northey, a widow aged 44, and her adult sons James and William were joining their daughter and sister, Elizabeth Northey, who was living with Mrs Preddy in Castlereagh Street. An Elizabeth Northey who arrived aboard *Harriet* in 1853, aged seventeen, from Chacewater and with parents of the same names as James', presumably was that sister and cousin. (AONSW shipping lists for *Harriet* 1853 and *Sultana* 1855, AO reels 2464 and 2471, and information from Mr Robert Hay.)

23   During some periods, including most of the 1860s, this scheme was virtually the only one available to assisted emigrants coming to New South Wales. See F.K. Crowley, 'British migration to Australia 1860-1914', D.Phil., Oxford, 1951, p.62.

24   AONSW shipping list *Himalaya* 1865, AO reel 2483. AONSW deposit journals, no.1457, 17 February 1864, AO reel 2671. Matilda Prowse stated that her husband, John, was a miner at 'Long Reefs N.S.W.', presumably Adelong [gold] Reefs.

25   NSWDJI, no.1457 on 17 February 1864, Prouse [sic]. Other Adelong families using the Remittance Regulations scheme were Richard White (NSWDJI, no.2085 on 4 July 1862) and Richard Berryman (NSWDJI, no.2086 also on 4 July 1862). The relatives of these two depositors travelled together aboard *Persia* in 1863. Another member of the family, James Berryman had used the same system the previous year to bring out his bride Jane Peters and his brother Alexander Berryman who travelled together aboard *Abyssinian* in 1862. (NSWDJI, nos.243 and 244 on 30 July 1861. AO reel 2139.)

methods of emigration very successfully, however, and their use of varied methods within one family's chain of migration was typical of many other families who were able to use to best advantage the government regulations which were in operation at a given time. John Prowse and his brothers William and James had arrived in Melbourne in 1857. They had then moved to South Australia where William remained, employed as a wheelwright. Another brother, Richard, arrived in Melbourne in 1864, and immediately joined John and James in Adelong.[26] James had spent some years goldmining in Victoria before moving on to Adelong, where he was an owner of the Prowse and Woodward claim for nine years before selling his share and turning to fruit growing at Adelong.[27]

Even those families engaged in mining usually had some choice, not necessarily of occupation, but certainly of which mining settlement they selected, and many chose mining towns where family members were already resident. Like those in the mining community of Adelong, Cornish immigrants in the other later or short term clusters also practised chain migration widely. On arrival, they too exercised their freedom of choice and settled amongst other Cornish families. This occurred in the non-mining as well as the mining clusters, and was a strong indication that shared occupation was not the major factor. For example on the south coast, relatives of William Chegwidden of Wollongong followed him to New South Wales. A brother, Joseph, came in 1868 and a more distant relative, Frederick Chegwidden, arrived in 1878 with his family and settled in the Cornish cluster at Orange as a farmer.[28] John Stephens/Stevens of Broulee was given as a relative of a succession of Cornish arrivals.[29] Similar patterns emerged on the north coast and in New England, where William Henry Wesley was typical of a number of miners whose families followed them to the colony.[30] Henry Northcott travelled in a Cornish convoy to the colony, married within the Cornish community and moved between clusters.[31]

Where chain migration continued within the same district, or family, over an extended period of time, it is evident that contact was being maintained between the people and places involved. That such contact was continued between New South Wales and Cornwall over a long period of time was obvious in the family of the Wesleyan missionary, the Rev Benjamin Carvosso. He was part of the early Cornish emigration network which also involved the Rev Walter Lawry and the Hosking, Hassall and Marsden families, and which assisted in the emigration of the Tom, Lane, Glasson and Hawke families. He returned to Cornwall with his wife Deborah Banks and their small children in 1830, and died there in 1854,[32] but at least two of his children returned to settle (and marry) in Cornish communities in the colony as adults.[33] This clearly demonstrates the contact maintained between New South Wales and Cornwall over a long period of time.

---

26    Information from Mrs Pam Archer. Irwin Prowse, *From Cornwall to the colonies: a Prowse chronicle*, the author, Merimbula, 1992.

27    *AMM*, series 1, vol.2 appendix, p.48.

28    Information from Mr Rex Chegwidden.

29    They were James Stephens in 1853, Anne Richards in 1855, and Charles and Anne Crapp in 1853. (AONSW shipping lists *Malvina Vidal* 1853, *Australia* 1853, and *Sultana* 1855, AO reels 2464, 2465, 2471.)

30    His widowed mother and his brother and sister came to New South Wales in 1877. (AONSW shipping list *Commonwealth* 1877, AO reel 2488.)    In the same year, his cousin Francis Ivey arrived with his family. (AONSW shipping lists *Samuel Plimsoll* 1877, AO reel 2488.)

31    He had travelled aboard *Amelia Thompson* in 1839, in a group consisting of his sister and brother-in-law Samuel and Jane Short, and John and Catherine Pearn and their children. Members of the group, who were all from the same part of Cornwall, settled in the Maitland district. Northcott married one of the Pearn children, Mary Ann, in 1845. Later, they and the Short family moved north to take up land in the northern rivers district. (Information from Mrs Ann Hodgens.)

32    *ADB* 1, pp.212-13.

33    Baker Banks Carvosso was a schoolteacher at Bathurst in 1862 at the time of his marriage, but had moved to the Cornish community in Sydney at the time of his death, aged 39, in 1866 in William Street, Sydney. His sister, Jane, had joined him in Bathurst in 1860, and later married there. It is possible that Captain D.B. Carvosso, who died in Stanmore aged 70, in 1903, was another of the Rev Benjamin Carvosso's relatives.

Although Cobar was not generally given as a place of residence of their relatives by assisted immigrants, death registers and Methodist marriage records showed that chain migration occurred amongst the Cornish community there. Of the 39 deaths of Cornish people registered in Cobar between 1880 and 1907, on fifteen occasions the informant was an adult child, or a nephew or brother of the deceased,[34] indicating that extended families had settled and then remained in the area. At the other extreme, a female who died in 1884 (aged 60) had only arrived from Cornwall thirteen months before, presumably to join her son who was the informant at her death. In all these cases, it is clear that the immigrants were part of extended family groups living in Cobar.

Movement into Cobar from other Cornish Australian communities was not uncommon. Almost half the Cornishmen and almost a third of the Cornishwomen who died in Cobar between 1880 and 1907 had lived in Australian colonies other than New South Wales.[35] This evidence is supported by the total absence of deaths in Cobar, as in Adelong,[36] of Cornish-born aged under twenty years.[37] Previous residence in South Australia was common. Despite Cobar's relative proximity to Broken Hill, however, there was no evidence to suggest residence there before their arrival in Cobar, rather of direct migration to Cobar from South Australia or from the Bathurst-Orange district.

Many of the places of birth given on Cobar marriage and death registrations were simply 'Cornwall', and unlike Adelong, when the actual place was given it did not suggest a pattern of migration to Cobar of a large group of people from one particular part of Cornwall.[38] The number of different birthplaces indicated a gathering, in Cobar, of persons who may not have known one another in Cornwall. However many came via the Bathurst district in New South Wales or the copper triangle in South Australia and so may well have been acquainted before moving on to Cobar.


On the other hand, many Cornish settlers in Adelong came from the same part of Cornwall. Marriages in Cornwall (of Cornish parents of Adelong-born children) occurred in only a few places, most of which were in the same part of Cornwall.[39] This suggested movement of some persons from the same and nearby parishes, who came directly to Adelong either together or over a period of time. Others went first to the Victorian goldfields and were married there.

Stated places of marriage of parents of Adelong-born children indicated that the Cornish either settled directly in Adelong after migration, or moved there from the Victorian goldfields. Examination of the Adelong birth registers revealed that almost half the births were to parents who had married in Adelong. The next biggest group was those who had married in Cornwall, and then those who had married in Victoria. See Table 2.21.

The stated places of marriage in Victoria were overwhelmingly goldmining areas: Ballarat, Bendigo, Bright, Castlemaine, Chiltern, Daylesford, Dunnolly, El Dorado, Forest Creek, Maldon, Myrtleford, Rutherglen, Sandhurst and Whargunyah. Again, this suggested

---

('Bathurst Wesleyan marriage register', 11 September 1862, UCA. NSWRGI 1862 no.1437, Carvosso-Evenis. *SMH*, 9 July 1866, p.1, c.1, and p.8, c.1. *Times*, 28 November 1863, p.11, c.4, Lean v Lean. Her marriage registration in 'Bathurst Wesleyan marriage register', 16 August, 1865, UCA. *NSWRGI* 1865 no.1579, Carvosso-Allen. *SMH*, 20 April 1903, p.8, c.1.)

34    Death Registers 1880-1907, C.P.S., Cobar.
35    See Table 2.27.
36    See chapter 6.
37    The Australian-born children of Cornish parents appeared as first-generation Australians
38    Places of birth given in death registrations were: Breage, Camborne, Carharrick, Hayle, Helston, Illogan, Lelant, Linkinhorne, Redruth, St Austell, St Blazey, St Cleer, St Erth, Stithians, Tremaine. Places of birth in marriage registrations were Camborne, Charlestown, Helston, Marazion, Menheniot, Penzance, Perranaworthal, Redruth, St Agnes, St Austell, St Erme, Tywardreath.
39    They were: Camborne, Chacewater, Gulval, Hayle Foundry, Helston, Kenwyn, Ludgvan, Paul, Pendeen, Penzance, St Allen, St Day, St Just, Towednack, Wendron.

that most either emigrated directly to Adelong, or came via the Victorian gold fields. In the case of those from Victoria, they married within the Cornish community on the Victorian goldfields prior to moving to the Cornish community at Adelong.

The majority of the fathers of children studied in Adelong were themselves born in Cornwall.[40] The non-Cornish fathers were born in England (including Devon), India, Ireland, Scotland and Victoria. The birthplaces of the Cornish parents also suggest that many of those in Adelong originated in neighbouring areas in Cornwall.[41]

Some Cornish settlers moved from Victorian gold mines to districts in southern New South Wales other than Adelong, with the intention of taking up farming land. T.J.T. Trevaskis, whose father had worked on the gold fields in central Victoria, moved to Lockhart in New South Wales and settled in the Brookdale district, while other Trevaskis families settled further north near Ardlethan.[42]

In all areas where Cornish immigrants clustered in New South Wales, chain migration played an important role in the clustering process, as close relatives, extended family and apparently unrelated persons came to join Cornish men and women already resident in the colony. This process occurred, not only across all the settlement areas, but regardless of class or occupation, and amongst almost every Cornish family examined. It ranged across ages from young to old, and varied considerably in method. Some, like the Evans family, relied principally on the assisted emigration schemes, others used a combination of assisted and unassisted emigration, and also moved to New South Wales through other colonies. Contact was maintained, through chain migration, with these other colonial Cornish clusters and with Cornwall itself. This indicated that chain migration and the consequent settlement of Cornish immigrants in the same area occurred largely because of personal preference, and not only as a result of occupational choices or other outside factors.

The clannish attitude of the Cornish which was demonstrated in their patterns of chain migration also encouraged intermarriage between Cornish families. The families at Cornish Settlement demonstrated this clannish behaviour through intermarriage and in their friendships, and it also occurred amongst the wider Cornish community in the Bathurst district and elsewhere. For example, Mrs Webb (nee Trewren) of Tarana remembered that the friendships which her family particularly valued were with the Stanger, Smith, Paul, Furness, White, Gilmour, Austin, Tremain, Palmer, Golsby, Glasson, Toole and Cousins families.[43] Almost all of these were either Cornish, or married to Cornish people, or from the families 'accepted' by the Cornish group.[44]

The intermarriage which occurred frequently in the Bathurst district is clearly illustrated by the descendants of James and Joanna Lane (parents of Richard, William and Ann [Tom] Lane),[45] and many other Bathurst district Cornish families are known to have

---

40 The births of these children were only noted where a child had at least one parent whose birthplace was given as Cornwall. Sometimes both parents had been born in Cornwall, but on the occasions where only one parent was Cornish, it was generally the father.

41 The birthplaces of the Cornish fathers were Bodmin, Chacewater, Gulval, Gwennap, Helston, Lelant, Ludgvan, Mawgan, Mevagissey, Paul, Pendeen, Penzance, Sancreed, St Agnes, St Allen, St Austell, St Buryan, St Day, St Ives, St Just, St Kew. The birthplaces of the Cornish mothers were Crowan, Gulval, Gwennap, Kenwyn, Madron, Pendeen, Penzance, Redruth, Sancreed, St Allen, St Austell, St Day, St Hilary, St Just, Stithians, Towednack, Truro, Wendron.

42 Information from Mrs A.V. Trevaskis.

43 R.W. Webb, *Concerning my mother*, p.1, typescript, Webb papers, Bathurst District Historical Society.

44 Although Cornish immigrants were clannish, and retained their Cornish identity, they were prepared to accept non-Cornish settlers into their group, and then treated them as part of the group in their friendship and intermarriage patterns.

45 A son, James, remained in Cornwall, but descendants of two of his six children settled in Victoria and married Pearse and Geake relatives. Another daughter married a man named Bray (presumably the parents of James Bray, who accompanied his Tom and Lane relatives to New South Wales in 1823) and came to New South Wales, and yet another daughter married a man named Pearse. Mary Bray married her first cousin Pearse, and

inter-married.[46]    It was not uncommon for intermarriage to continue down several generations, as the Lanes, Toms, Glassons and Geakes demonstrated.    Neither was it uncommon for first cousins to marry: for example, George Hawke married his first cousin Jane Hawke, and their only child married her first cousin, George's nephew William Hawke. In many cases several sisters and brothers in one family married sisters and brothers in another family.[47]    An interesting example of this custom is that of the Nankivell family who went to Molong mines in 1848 and later to South Australia.    Four Nankivell brothers married four non-Cornish sisters, while the fifth brother married his first cousin who had emigrated from Cornwall.[48]    This custom of intermarriage also occurred with the non-Cornish families accepted into the Cornish community.[49]

The pattern of generations of intermarriage with other Cornish families, or with 'accepted' families which occurred regularly in the Bathurst district is not so obvious in the Hunter.    Here the Cornish were integrated, as an ethnic group, more quickly into the wider population - even though individuals retained their love of Cornwall and their sense of Cornish identity.    There were several reasons for this more rapid integration.    First, the Cornish clusters in the Hunter were smaller and more scattered than those in the Bathurst district.    Also, the Dangars and Cooks who encouraged, and formed a nucleus of Cornish settlement there, were not Methodists but strong supporters of the Church of England.    This meant that a further reason for long term Cornish cohesiveness, which existed in the Bathurst district, was lacking in the Hunter.    Another factor was that, in the Newcastle coalmining district, the Cornish were greatly outnumbered by other strong ethnic groups, and although this may have emphasised their Cornishness initially, it made their integration into that wider population more rapid.

Chain migration and intermarriage were external but related signs of Cornish clannishness, and so their statistics tended to overlap.    However, examination of marriage registers provided useful information not only about intermarriage, but also about related factors such as occupational background, and movement between Cornish clusters.    In Sydney, marriage out of the Cornish community appeared, superficially, to be quite common (as might be expected in a large city), but close examination of information found in the

---

after his death in New South Wales she married another first cousin James Lane, son of Richard. A son of her first marriage, Thomas Pearse, married Jane Lane, a daughter of Richard and Elizabeth Lane. A number of Richard Lane's other children also married relatives. John married Mary Glasson and after her death married Cornishwoman Jane Thomas, Mary Rundle Lane married her first cousin John Tom Lane, Thomas Geake Lane married his first cousin Catherine Webb. (Her mother and his mother were (Geake) sisters. Two of Catherine's brothers, Thomas Geake Webb and Edmund Webb married Emma and Selina Tom, daughters of Ann (Lane) and William Tom.) After Catherine's death Thomas Geake Lane married another relative, Jane Pearse. Selina Lane married her first cousin, Charles Wesley Lane. William Geake Lane was the only child to marry a non-Cornish person - Caroline Austin. Jane Lane married Thomas Pearse, the son of her father's niece Mary Pearse (nee Bray) who after being widowed, married James Lane, her first cousin. Catherine Geake Lane married Edward Nicholls, a Cornishman. (M.H. McLelland, *The Lane family*, typescript.)

46    These included the Webb, Trewren, Lane, Glasson, Oates, Hawke, Tom, Smith, Tremain, Trezise, Hambly, Trememan, Trevena, Short, Roberts, Sandry, Penhall, Plummer, Pascoe, Paul, Pryor, Eade, Northey, Nicholls, Mutton, Lean, James, Jeffree, Inch, Hocking, Chegwidden, Rowe, Walkom, Paul, Buttle, Selwood, Nankivell, Dale, Bryant, Barrett, Hawken and Eslick families. (Information from descendants of each of these families.) The Oates family of St Keverne intermarried with the Thomas, Richards, Martin, Hawke and James families, and maintained close friendships with many Cornish families in the Byng-Millthorpe district. These included Hawkes, Glassons, Lanes, Wills, Pascoes, Treweekes, Nicholls, Rowes, Richards, Thomas, Taylors, Goodes and Toms. (Information from Mrs C.A. Oates.)

47    For example, the Webb brothers of Mutton Falls married two Trewren sisters (daughters of John Trewren of Kelso), and Edmund Webb (of Bathurst) and his brother married two of William Tom's daughters.

48    A. Williams, *Nankivell-a family affair*, the author, Miram, Victoria, 1990, pp.29 and 212.

49    For example, Sweetnams married into the Thomas, Kessell and Glasson families, the Whalans married into the Trewren and Hawken families, and the Stangers married into the Trewren and Glasson families. Multiple marriages (not necessarily to other Cornish people) occurred in the Webb, Lane, Glasson, Oates, Tom, Thomas, Tremain, Sloggett, Trevarthen, Smith, Short, Sandry, Penhall, Pascoe, Paul, Northey, Couch, Bradley, Nicholls, Mutton, James, Jeffree, Inch, Hocking, Rowe, Buttle, Eslick, Dale, Nankivell, Hawken and Bryant families. (Information from descendants of these families.)

marriage registers suggested that some apparently non-Cornish spouses may have been Australians of Cornish descent. Although the majority of the Cornish partners chose spouses who had not been born in Cornwall, many of the non-Cornish spouses (or the spouse's father in the case of widows) had a common Cornish surname, or a second Christian name such as Holman. This indicated that they were possibly first or second generation Australians who were, in fact, still part of the Cornish community. Examination of the maiden names (where these were given) of the mothers of the non-Cornish partners, was equally rewarding. Many typically Cornish names occurred there, indicating that these families, although not immediately obvious as Cornish, had remained within the Cornish community. The fact that many of the witnesses to marriages also had typically Cornish names, or names of immigrants known to be Cornish, adds strength to this argument.[50] See Table 2.12.

This practice was not confined to the Cornish living in the city, however. Marriage records in Cobar, like those in Sydney, suggested that some of the seemingly non-Cornish spouses were of Cornish descent. For example, Cornishwoman Lily Leavers married bricklayer Richard James Thomas of Nymagee in 1881. He had been born at Burra Burra in South Australia, and his parents were Joseph Thomas and Mary Ann Mitchell. The following year his brother Joseph, a smelter, also born in Burra Burra, married another Cornishwoman, Elizabeth Downing of Nymagee.[51] The Thomas brothers may well have had Cornish parents, and certainly came from the Cornish community in South Australia.

Examination of the Methodist and Church of England marriage registers for Adelong, and the few marriages where place of birth was recorded in the Clerk of Petty Sessions registers, produced the marriages of 37 Cornish men and women. Comparison with the much larger number of Sydney marriages was difficult, but the pattern of intermarriage was similar to, although more pronounced than, Sydney, with most Cornishwomen choosing Cornish men, and many Cornishmen marrying out. The men had little choice, because of the imbalance in numbers of Cornish male and female immigrants. See Table 2.22.

In the mining communities of Cobar and Adelong, it is obvious that marriage partners were very likely to share a common occupational background, but in the more diverse community of Sydney such backgrounds might be quite different. However, in her study of Sydney between 1870 and 1890, Shirley Fitzgerald argued that upward social mobility was the exception rather than the rule. She used a sample study of marriage records to demonstrate that the majority of marriages were between persons of similar social rank. In the case of the majority of women who had no occupation recorded, the rank of their fathers was compared with that of their spouses.[52] A similar conclusion was drawn from a sample of Cornish marriages in Sydney. Most women married men whose occupations were similar in rank to their own or to that of their fathers.[53] It followed the general trend, identified by Shirley Fitzgerald, that marriages usually occurred between partners of similar occupational ranking.[54] See Table 2.13.

In mining communities occupational backgrounds were similar, but in Sydney (where theoretically a wider choice was available), the Cornish continued the pattern of marrying persons of similar social rank to their own. They often chose partners who were Cornish or who were members of the Cornish community.

---

50   These names are not only the distinctive Cornish names from Dr Price's list. They also include surnames such as Williams and Thomas which are very common Cornish names, but may also belong to ethnic groups other than Cornish.

51   'Cobar-Nymagee Wesleyan marriage register 1881-85', UCA. NSWRGI nos.1881 3299 and 1882 3788.

52   S. Fitzgerald, *Rising damp: Sydney 1870-1890*, Oxford University Press, Melbourne, 1987, chapter 6.

53   In this sample only the male Cornish spouses were included because the majority of the females had no occupation given. The examples were selected at random by marking the margin with a cross without reading the contents of the line.

54   One interesting example was the marriage of Hugh Kent, a Cornish bachelor aged 32, who gave his occupation as 'gentleman', and Cornishwoman Anne Martin, a widow aged 28, who gave her occupation as 'lady'. The occupation of both fathers was stated as 'miner' - obviously two who 'struck it rich'! (Wesleyan marriage register Fort Street, Sydney, 29 March 1873. SAG reel 0034. NSWRGI 1873 No.314.)

Evidence of movement and contact between Cornish clusters and with Cornwall itself, was found in marriage records. For instance, in some Sydney marriages, one spouse was not a permanent resident of Sydney, but of another Cornish cluster like Bathurst or New England. In other cases, although they were being married in Sydney, both spouses lived in other areas of Cornish concentration such as Charters Towers in Queensland, Adelong, or the Bathurst district. This indicated that contact was being maintained between those communities and the Cornish community in Sydney. On several occasions, close connections with the homeland were clear also, for the bride had recently arrived from Cornwall. For example, on 31 May 1862 at St James, Sydney, Cornish miner James Berryman, of Adelong, married Jane Peters who had arrived as an assisted immigrant aboard *Abyssinian* several days earlier,[55] and towards whose passage he had paid a deposit the previous year.[56]

Intermarriage between Cornish families was an outward sign of their clannish attitude and it is evident that such intermarriage was a common occurrence amongst all Cornish occupational and class levels in the colony. Intermarriage between cousins, or the marriages of sisters and brothers from one family, and sisters and brothers from another family was not uncommon, and sometimes continued through several generations of the same families. Evidence suggested that some seemingly non-Cornish spouses were actually Australians of Cornish descent whose families had remained within the Cornish community. Although clannish Cornish immigrants preferred to remain together, they did not necessarily exclude others from joining their group. That they were prepared to accept non-Cornish families into their clannish friendship and marriage groups is obvious in the friendship and marriage groups uncovered by descendants of these immigrants. This willingness to accept others into the Cornish group, while maintaining its distinctive Cornish character, was another example of the adaptability which characterised the Cornish and which assisted in their eventual assimilation.

Chain migration and intermarriage were widely practised throughout the New South Wales Cornish clusters and provided evidence of movement and contact between these communities in New South Wales and other colonies.[57] Although they were not exclusively Cornish practices, they were outward indications of the existence of Cornish clannishness. Another indication of this clannishness was their 'Cornishness', a combination of culture and ethnicity which caused the Cornish to be seen by themselves and by others as different. In some places, such as Hill End and Adelong, the area where they clustered was named Cornishtown, not by the Cornish themselves, but by those outside their clannish group.[58]

Nineteenth century acceptance of the inherent differences between Cornwall and England was demonstrated in the Rev John Dunmore Lang's scheme to establish a border between New England, (including the area known by immigrant Scots as New Caledonia)[59] and a new, separate colony on the northern rivers, to be called New Cornwall. Lang had encouraged the separation movement in 1856, advocating a new colony in the north, and in 1860 he supported the formation of a new colony in the northern rivers district between 30° and the Queensland border.[60] He proposed that this separate colony be named 'New

55 AONSW shipping list of *Abyssinian*, AO reel 2139. CE marriage register Sydney, SAG reel 0065. NSWRGI 1862, no.416.

56 AONSW Immigration deposit journals, no.296-244, 30 July 1861, AO reel 2670.

57 When spouses' places of residence varied from the place of marriage they were often from mining towns in Queensland, Victoria and across the Cornish clusters in New South Wales.

58 In spite of the Cornish population in Cobar however, the local 'Cornishtown' there was not named because the occupants were exclusively Cornish. It was named after a Londoner, Henry Cornish, who subdivided the land into building blocks. (Interview with Mr W. Snelson.) Recent family research by Ms B. Cornish suggests that Henry Cornish was actually of Cornish descent, although not born in Cornwall.

59 P. Newell and U. White, *New England sketchbook*, Rigby, Adelaide, 1970, p.36.

60 R.B. Walker, *Old New England: a history of the northern tablelands of New South Wales 1818-1900*, Sydney University Press, Sydney, 1966, p.156. C.D. Rowley, 'Clarence River Separatism in 1860: a problem of communications', in *Historical Studies Australia and New Zealand*, Melbourne University Press, Melbourne,

Cornwall',[61] and suggested that the capital should be at Grafton.[62] Some areas of northern New South Wales were certainly reminiscent of the homeland, for example at Hillgrove, 'clusters of curiously weathered granite tors are of frequent occurrence',[63] reminding Cornish goldminers of the Cornish moorland.

In other parts of New South Wales, Cornish place names were evidence of the nostalgia felt by Cornish Australians. Although the Cornish were integrated into the wider community more quickly in the Hunter than in the Bathurst district, individuals retained their love of Cornwall and their pride in being Cornish. This was shown in local names such as 'Neotsfield', Kingdon Ponds, Fal Brook and Foy Brook.

> Cornish place names, scattered through the Hunter Valley,
> mark Henry Dangar's surveys and record his deep affection
> for his birthplace.[64]

Cornish names were used as placenames and names of streets in Sydney. Several examples are Padstow, Trelawney Street in Paddington and St Neot Avenue in Potts Point (where Henry Dangar lived in retirement). Examination of the Sydney data base records, where residential addresses were given, uncovered house names with a Cornish flavour. Many of them hinted at a Cornish birthplace: Trebartha, Penlee, Penhall, Tresco, Penbeagle, Penharwood, Penryn, Portreath Villa, Scorrier, Linkinhorne, Treleigh, Trevell, Mount Bay [sic], St. Just, Lanreath, Newlyn.

Although the practice of using placenames in New South Wales as a reminder of the homeland was not exclusive to Cornish immigrants, it was another outward sign of their clannishness. It is clear that many Cornish immigrants felt nostalgia for their homeland and kept their memories alive by giving their residences, in their adopted home, Cornish names. Length of time lived in Cornwall, or length of time lived in New South Wales since emigrating, made little difference to the strenth and longevity of the deep feelings many immigrants retained for the homeland. It is also clear that those outside the Cornish community recognised their clannish groups as being different. This is seen in the naming of the proposed colony of New Cornwall, and in the naming (by others) of the areas where the Cornish lived as Cornishtown or Cornish Settlement.

Cornish men and women exhibited clannishness not only by remaining within the colonial Cornish community but also by maintaining their links with Cornwall through letters and through the newspapers. They returned to visit if they could, and ate the pasties, saffron buns, and clotted cream they had been accustomed to at home. Alfred Goninan, when beginning his engineering works in Newcastle at the end of the century, found that being Cornish was useful in his contacts with the Dangar family. Goninan himself exhibited a pride in his Cornish identity, made many return visits to Cornwall, and referred fondly in his memoirs to pasties and other Cornish delicacies.[65] However, much of the evidence that Cornish Australians retained a love of their homeland, and maintained contact with family and friends left behind, comes from their reminiscences or obituaries, or from information provided by their descendants. William Burnett of Singleton, who 'retained his Cornish sympathies to the end', had the newspaper sent regularly from Cornwall throughout his life.[66] Philip Coleman Williams, who emigrated from Bodmin in 1853, subscribed regularly to the

October 1941, p.225-244.

61 E.J. Tapp, 'The colonial origins of the New England New State Movement', in *JRAHS*, vol.49, part 3, November 1963, p.216.

62 Rev John Dunmore Lang Papers, vol.I, chapter X, ML A2221, CY869.

63 J. Plummer, *Australian mining notes*, vol.2, p.14. ML Q338.2/P.

64 *ADB* 1, p.282.

65 *Memoirs of Alfred Goninan* (1865-1953), L.E. Fredman, (ed.), introduction and typescript unpublished, from original manuscript in possession of Mrs Marcovitch, Chatswood.

66 William Burnett's obituary, *Singleton Argus*, 3 February 1916, p.3, c.2.

Bodmin newsapaper until his death in 1911, and always made a point of contacting newly-arrived Cornish emigrants, whether or not he knew them.[67]

The custom of placing a notice in a Sydney newspaper advising of the death of a parent or other relative in Cornwall, or of requesting Cornish papers to copy a Cornish-Australian death notice, showed that links had been maintained with the homeland over a long period of time. Such evidence exists of James Harry's strong sense of Cornish identity.

> HARRY. December 23, [1907] at his residence, Newlyn House, Macpherson-street, Waverley, James Harry, monumental mason, native of Truro, Cornwall, England, aged 59 years, a resident of Waverley for 30 years, dearly beloved husband of Emily Harry. Deeply regretted. Cornwall and Yorkshire papers please copy.[68]

Although he had spent over half of his total life, and most of his adult life, in Waverley, James Harry lived in a house with a Cornish name, and obviously maintained close contact with his homeland and with members of the Cornish community in Yorkshire. The notices advising of his funeral arrangements gave additional information: the names and marital status of his children (one of whom was the wife of Alderman William C. Tipper) and that he was a member of the Master Monumental Masons' Association, and a member of the Ancient Order of Foresters.[69] His tombstone recorded the fact that he was 'of Cornwall'.[70] The most intriguing aspect of his Cornishness is that, apparently, he was not actually born in Cornwall. The shipping list for the *Star of India* in 1876 gave his occupation as miner and his birthplace (and his mother's residence) as Yorkshire, his wife Emily's (maiden name Lobb) birthplace as Cornwall, and that of their three small children as Yorkshire.[71] Obviously James Harry still considered himself to be a Cornishman, and a native of Truro, although he had been born (presumably of Truronian mining parents) in Yorkshire and had lived in Cornwall only briefly, if ever. His story clearly illustrates the strength of feeling for their homeland amongst many Cornish people and their descendants, which may persist through many generations. When James Harry's wife, Emily, died in 1924, aged 82, (still resident at 'Newlyn', MacPherson Street, Waverley), newspaper notices of her funeral arrangements indicated that her cousins, Mr and Mrs John Lobb, lived in the same street, also in a house with a Cornish name, 'Penlee'.[72]

A similar example is the long biographical entry in *Australian Men of Mark* for James Martin Spargo Esquire, of Baker's Swamp near Wellington in the Bathurst district. It noted that he was 'a Cornishman, born in the land of "Tre, Pol, and Pen"', and continued with considerable detail about Cornwall. It is only after careful reading that it is obvious that he was merely an infant when he left his native land, yet 50 years later he still considered himself a Cornishman.[73]

---

67  Information from Mr G.W.F. Williams.

68  *SMH*, 24 December 1907, p.6, c.1..

69  *SMH*, 24 December 1907, p.10, c.1..

70  Waverley Cemetery Transcript held at SAG, transcribers' manuscript sheets (unchecked) of General Select Section 9. At the time of research these transcripts were not publicly available because the work of checking and indexing had not been completed. I am indebted to Ms Heather Garnsey at SAG for permission to use the original transcripts. Harry's burial in the general section of the cemetery suggested a non-conformist religious background. This was confirmed by the shipping list of his arrival, when he stated that he was Wesleyan. Note that the inscription does **not** claim that he was 'a native of Cornwall' which was the usual phrase appearing on Cornish gravestones in New South Wales.

71  AONSW shipping list *Star of India* 1876, AO reel 2487.

72  *SMH*, 25 October 1924, p.9, c.2, and p.10, c.1.

73  *AMM*, series 2, vol.2, pp.239-241.

In the New South Wales mining communities, Cornish mining terms were used frequently. In Cornwall and in South Australia,[74] responsibility was often assumed by mine captains for the aspects of the lives of mine employees and their families not directly connected with their work, and this also occurred in New South Wales. For example, in New England, mine captain William Knuckey was instrumental in the opening of the school at Torrington in 1883.[75] In Cobar also, a mine captain initiated the move to open a school there.[76]

The Cornish love of music and singing in Victoria was well known[77] and it occurred in New South Wales also, along with other pastimes brought with immigrants from Cornwall. Their love of music was shown in their strong membership of church choirs. The Cornish Settlement Vocal Harmonic Society, for instance, performed at the opening of the new chapel at Orange in 1863.[78] In the gold mining district of Nundle in 1871 the congregations, which contained 'many Cornishmen with good singing voices', were renowned for their singing.[79] Brass bands were very popular with the miners at Hill End.[80] Mr A. Gartrell was a long-time member of the Bathurst Brass Band,[81] and the funeral procession of Captain William H. Martin, of Hillgrove (but formerly of the Bathurst district), was led by a brass band.[82] And then there was simply the singing of Cornish songs. William Thomas, who emigrated in 1849 aged fourteen, was remembered by a grandchild who visited him in Sydney for his 'great love ... for Cornwall', and his enthusiastic singing of 'the old Cornish songs'.[83] The Cornish love of music and singing, although apparent amongst all the Cornish clusters, was particularly noted about those who settled in Cobar. There were eight brass bands in the district. The Jeffery family at Cobar epitomised the musical Cornish family, one son played the piano, one the trombone and another the cornet.[84]

In South Australia, Cornish wrestling was 'another aspect of Cornish cultural influence which manifested itself quite early in the life of the colony'.[85] It was also to be found practised amongst the Cornish in New South Wales. One of the practitioners of the sport was William Oates of St Keverne, who came to the colony in 1853, and worked as a blacksmith and wheelwright at Guyong and Orange. An exceptionally strong man, he 'engaged in the sport of Wrestling, as did his brother Samuel'.[86]

In 1861 the *Bathurst Free Press* gave advance notice of Cornish wrestling to be held at Rockley when it advertised:

74  P.J. Payton, *The Cornish miner in Australia*, p.87.

75  The population in the school's catchment area was about 500, most of whom were tin miners. (C. Alt, *Old Torrington: a history of Torrington and district 1881-1981*, Back to Torrington Centenary Weekend Committee, Glen Innes, 1981, pp.39-40.)

76  See chapter 5.

77  A. Colman, 'Colonial Cornish', pp.133-4.

78  E.G. Clancy, *'More precious than gold': commemorating the 100th anniversary of the Orange Circuit of the Methodist Church 1860-1960*, Central Western Daily, Orange, N.S.W., 1960, chapter 2, [no page numbers].

79  E.G. Clancy, 'The Ranters' Church', typescript, pp.443-4. [UCA.]

80  H. Hodge, *The Hill End story*, Book 1, 3rd edition, Hill End Publications, Toorak, Victoria, 1986, p.139.

81  J.G. Wilson, *Official history of the Municipal Jubilee of Bathurst 1812-1912*, [no publisher], Sydney, 1913, p.51.

82  *The Hillgrove Guardian*, 24 June 1899, p.3.

83  B.W. Thomas, *The Thomas family of Guyong: 1849-1929: William Thomas (1805-1881) and the Thomas family of Guyong N.S.W.*, the author, Wahroonga, N.S.W., 1974, pp.79-80.

84  Interview with Mr W. Snelson, 12 May 1991.

85  P.J. Payton, *The Cornish miner in Australia*, p.69.

86  C.A. Oates, *A gathering of the Oates: to celebrate the centenary of 'Rosewick', Millthorpe*, the author, Millthorpe, N.S.W., 1977, p.6.

BOXING-DAY! BOXING-DAY!

GRAND WRESTLING! MINERS' ARMS, ROCKLEY

THE GAME to be played in Cornish style with the nakedfist.

FIRST PRIZE - One superior Cabbage-tree Hat

SECOND PRIZE - One superior Panama Hat.

Sixteen standards to be made, then play off.

No entrance fee.

In order to give fair play to each individual, one umpire will be from Cornwall, one from Devon, and the other an Australian.[87]

As well as such obvious signs of Cornishness, there were other, more subtle signs. A.L. Rowse declares 'for there is such a thing as a Cornish temperament'.[88] This Cornish temperament has been commented upon by Cornish and non-Cornish alike,[89] and some common Cornish characteristics were present in many Cornish immigrants in New South Wales. They included independence and initiative, adaptablility, stubbornness and determination and a natural dignity.[90] Some Cornish people exhibited a combination of total trust (sometimes wrongly seen by others as naivete) and stubborn determination, which turned to feelings of fury and betrayal if that trust was abused. Newcastle industrialist, Alfred Goninan, of St Just, is a good example of a Cornish immigrant who displayed this misplaced trust. His financial advisors recommended that he borrow a large amount of money to extend his company's buildings. He did so, but borrowed personally rather than through his company, and as a result he lost almost everything.[91]

Some of those in the Bathurst district exhibited stubborn determination very clearly when they were certain they were in the right, but being unfairly treated. William Tom Junior's refusal to accept the decision giving Hargraves full credit, and a substantial reward, for the discovery of payable gold at Ophir in 1851 is an example. He believed that Hargraves had knowingly defrauded him, and with the help of his family he pursued Hargraves through the press, regularly putting his case over a period of many years.[92] When a parliamentary select committee did not fully endorse his claims, Tom fought on and

---

87   *BFP*, supplement to 7 December 1861, p.2, c.4. I am indebted to Mr Theo Barker and Mrs Helen Jeuken for this information.
88   A.L. Rowse, *The Cornish in America*, Macmillan, London, 1969, p.15.
89   See chapter 2.
90   William Burnett of Singleton had 'a strong personality and decided opinions', (*Singleton Argus*, 3 February 1916, p.3, c.2). His wife Melinda was 'a woman of strong character and deep convictions', (*Weekly Advocate*, 31 May 1890, p.91). Martha Rapson of Dungog was remembered for her Cornish 'straightforward statements' when expressing her opinions, and for her independent and determined nature, (L. Smith, *The Rapson family, Williams River Valley*, typescript, Newcastle Region Public Library, pp.2-3. Information from Mr Ronald Rapson.) In Adelong, Richard White's qualities of 'inflexible will, foresight, sound judgement and loyalty' were acknowledged. (*Methodist*, 12 September 1903, p.9, c.2.)
91   *Memoirs of Alfred Goninan (1865-1953)*, L.E. Fredman, (ed.), introduction and typescript unpublished, from original manuscript in possession of Mrs Marcovitch, Chatswood.
92   For example, *BFP*, 1 January 1853, p.1, c.1, and p.2, c.1-3. *BFP*, 8 May 1861, p.2, c.5. *BP*, 15 January 1892, p.4, c.3-4. *Methodist*, 2 June 1894, p.8, c.1. *BP*, 14 December 1895, p.4, c.2-3.

pursued Hargraves practically to the grave, until a second select committee in 1892 granted the Tom brothers and Lister credit as the co-discoverers of payable gold in Australia.[93]

John Smith of 'Gamboola' also became involved in a battle of honour, when he was accused of stealing an iron pot which he believed he had purchased from a neighbour. He brought two court cases against his persecutor but lost them both, so he placed a full page advertisement on the front page of the *Sydney Morning Herald* in 1848, stating his side of the argument. The battle became known as 'The Iron Pot Case', and in John Smith's family the humble pot was called the £1,000 pot, because of the cost of litigation.[94] John Smith, Henry Dangar[95] and William Tom Junior were all prepared to fight on to the bitter end if their integrity was questioned and when they believed they were being unfairly treated.

William Selwood, a miner turned farmer, spent years fighting a bitter battle relating to a boundary on his land near Orange. He expressed a view similar to that of Smith and Tom when he stated:

> I have my own ideas and I take my stand upon them. You
> know a man who does that is always charged with
> eccentricity.[96]

This stubbornness, this spirit of determination and refusal to give up was not confined to Cornish men. It was also evident in Cornish women such as Ann Webb. When her husband died suddenly, leaving her with a young family of eight children aged between seventeen years and one year, she continued to manage the farm at Mutton Falls with only the help of her older children. During the goldrush, she established a store beside her home at Mutton Falls, again running this enterprise efficiently on her own, and on several occasions she faced bushrangers without fear.[97]

The distinctly Cornish sense of humour which came with Cornish immigrants to South Australia is captured in Oswald Pryor's cartoons.[98] Evidence of its existence amongst Cornish settlers in New South Wales was hard to find, because it was not generally recorded in written sources, but anecdotal evidence suggested strongly that it existed amongst the Cornish in New South Wales, as elsewhere.

The qualities seen by themselves and others as typically Cornish, and their pride in being a separate ethnic group, as well as their recognisable accent and dialect, set the Cornish apart from other settlers. This difference was sufficiently obvious for others, outside the close-knit group, to use the name Cornishtown or Cornish Settlement to describe the places where they chose to settle together. Although though they were possessed by some other immigrants as well, stubborness, determination, initiative, adaptability, love of music and clannishness, emerged as characteristics common amongst the Cornish in New South Wales, as they did amongst the Cornish in Victoria and South Australia. Their involvement in Methodism was also seen as a Cornish characteristic, and while Cornish Methodism was a

93    J.W. Tom, *Cornish Settlement: reminiscences, 1941*, typescript in the possession of Mr B.W. Thomas, p.8. See J. Rule, *The cradle of a nation: the truth about Ophir's gold discovery in 1851*, the author, Yagoona, N.S.W., 1979.

94    B. Mac. Smith (ed.), *Quench not the spirit: merino heritage*, Hawthorn Press, Melbourne, 1972, p.60.

95    Henry Dangar's battles of honour are well documented in biographies which are listed in the bibliography.

96    W. Selwood, 'Diary', in the possession of Mrs P. Trevena, p.30. John Trewren of Kelso was yet another Bathurst Cornishman who was not afraid to speak out when faced with the threat of 'being trampled upon by any sect or party'. He refrained from taking legal action against his opponent only because the man was a Catholic and Trewren felt that because of this, his motives for such legal action could be misconstrued as bigotry. (*BFP*, 12 November 1859, p.2.)

97    Her sister-in-law Mary Mutton, proprietor of a store near Bathurst, (which she also had continued to run following her husband's death), stood her ground when confronted by Ben Hall and his gang during an attempted hold up of her store in 1863. (K. Muggleston, *William and Ann Webb: a family history*, the author, [Tarana, N.S.W.?], 1990, pp.6-11.) This incident was also described in an undated newspaper cutting sent by Mrs Joan Edgar.

98    For example, O. Pryor, *Cornish pasty: a selection of cartoons*, Rigby, Adelaide, 1976.

distinctly recognisable type, in New South Wales Methodism was more correctly a community group made up of individuals from different ethnic groups. In their involvement in Methodism in New South Wales, the Cornish took the first steps towards eventual integration into the wider community.

The Cornish clusters in New South Wales, which were seen as different by the Cornish themselves and also by other settlers, were caused partly by occupational factors, but also by cultural, personal and family influences, and through the choice of the Cornish people involved. Their patterns of chain migration, while in no way exclusive to Cornish immigrants, were further outward indications of their clannish nature and of their conscious choice to remain together in New South Wales. The movement and contact between Cornish clusters in New South Wales and in other colonies, and with Cornwall itself, was another sign of this personal choice. Intermarriage between Cornish families, which often occurred over a period of several generations, showed that Cornish immigrants chose to settle and then to remain together. Although occupational and other outside forces were sometimes very important influences and also often offered an element of choice, the major determinants on Cornish settlement patterns in New South Wales were personal preference and choice.

PLATE 44.     A Cornish family in Bathurst.

The Tremain family of Bathurst. Like most other Cornish immigrant families, they were involved in intermarriage across the Cornish clusters; and in chain migration with members of the extended family coming from Cornwall to join family members already in New South Wales. (Photograph courtesy of Miss Grace Tremain.)

PLATE 45.                     Cornish 'characters'.

From Ian Glanville's *St Just's Point*, published by the author, Bendigo, 1990, p.24. (Courtesy of Ian Glanville.)

# CHAPTER EIGHT

## CORNISH AUSTRALIANS: THE WIDER COMMUNITY

*So, I'm proud to be Australian*
*And Cornish all in one,*
*And I'm glad I've not forgotten*
*From where and who I am.*[1]

The Cornish clusters across New South Wales were an outward sign of the clannish attitude which characterised Cornish immigrants the world over. The clustering occurred, in spite of their individualistic and independent natures, when Cornish immigrants were a minority group within a larger community. They 'immediately made good citizens' in America where their democratic natures helped them to adapt quickly to American society and many joined community organisations like Oddfellows and Freemasonry.[2] A similar pattern occurred in South Australia and Victoria, and in both these colonies Methodism was an important aspect of the Cornish communities.[3]

For the Cornish in New South Wales, too, Methodism was an important influence. It was a familiar community organisation to which many had belonged in Cornwall, a membership which they continued in their adopted land. In New South Wales they settled in their clannish clusters, while at the same time becoming 'good citizens' who were involved in various community organisations and in local and colonial politics. With their democratic nature, and their background in Methodism where lay members were able to reach positions of authority and responsibility, and to play an active and important part, they adapted easily to New South Wales society.

Cornish Methodists in Victoria were a distinct type characterised by their enthusiastic and emotional involvement in chapel services, and by their love of music.[4] In New South Wales also, many Cornish immigrants were Methodists, and a number of Methodist ministers were Cornishmen. As at least one nineteenth century newspaper remarked:

> How great must be the advantage and how very great the
> comfort to the Cornish emigrant on landing on his southern
> home, to find a Cornish clergyman on the spot for his friend
> and pastor.[5]

The Rev Walter Lawry and the Rev Benjamin Carvosso were the second and third Wesleyan missionaries to come to New South Wales. They had been friends in Cornwall, and provided mutual support in the important roles both played in the foundation of Methodism in New South Wales.[6] In 1854, four more Cornish Wesleyan missionaries

---

1  'Cornish Australian', words and music by Richard Gendall.
2  A.L. Rowse, *The Cornish in America*, Macmillan, London, 1969, pp.15-17.
3  P.J. Payton, *The Cornish miner in Australia: Cousin Jack Down Under*, Dyllansow Truran, Redruth, 1984, pp.79-83. A. Colman, 'Colonial Cornish: Cornish immigrants in Victoria, 1865-1880', M.A., University of Melbourne, 1985, chapter 4.
4  A. Colman, 'Colonial Cornish', pp.132-4.
5  *RCG*, 21 February 1851, p.5, c.3. Although this referred to the Cape Colony, the sentiments of Australian immigrants were doubtless similar.
6  Although he made only two journeys to the Bathurst district in its infancy, Lawry had married into the Hassall family, who were instrumental in the settlement of the Tom, Lane, Hawke and Glasson families there. See chapter 1.

arrived in the colony. Thomas Angwin, William Kelynack, William Curnow and John Gale travelled together aboard *American Lass* to begin pastoral duties in New South Wales.[7]

Cornish Christians of all denominations were doubtless comforted to have a Cornish clergyman ministering to them, and many Cornish clergymen served in at least some of the areas of settlement where the Cornish clustered. As would be expected, many were Methodist clergymen, and amongst these were were Thomas Adams, Thomas Angwin, Benjamin Carvosso, William Curnow, Eldred Dyer, John Gale, Gustavus Glasson,[8] William Glasson, Richard Jennings,[9] William Kelynack D.D., Stephen Kessell, Walter Lawry, Matthew Maddern, J. Sweetnam Thomas,[10] John Thomas, Francis Tuckfield, and William Henry Williams. Most of these men were Wesleyans. Some of these ministers remained in Australia permanently, but others eventually returned to Cornwall.

Among the Cornish Anglican clergy were Charles Bice, John Fletcher, Lyndon Athol Kelynack,[11] John Wright Pope, and Alfred Teed Puddicombe.[12] The Congregational clergymen in New South Wales included Cornishmen Edward Adams, Edward Tremayne Dunstan, John Brown Gribble, and Palmer Law.[13] The only Presbyterian clergyman known to be of Cornish descent was Richard Jennings, who had previously been a Primitive Methodist minister.[14]

Cornish clergyman from all these denominations served in most of the Cornish clusters. In the Bathurst district were Curnow, Dyer, Kessell, Kelynack and Maddern while in the Hunter region were Adams, Bice, Curnow, Dyer, Fletcher, Jennings, Kelynack, Kessell and Tuckfield. In the Cornish areas of Sydney were Adams, Curnow, Jennings, Kelynack and Pope, with Gribble at Adelong. In the coastal areas were Kelynack, Kessell and Puddicombe.

The Wesleyan Church was the first, and major, branch of Methodism in nineteenth century New South Wales. There were later congregations of Primitive Methodists in Newcastle, Sydney, Goulburn, Crookwell, Mudgee, Kempsey and Camden. Smaller and more localised groups, the United Free Methodist Church and the Lay Methodist Church, occurred in New South Wales also. Bible Christians moved to Broken Hill from South Australia, but there were no other organised groups of this branch of Methodism in New South Wales, and individual Bible Christians joined other Methodist branches in the colony.[15]

Phyllis Tibbs argued that New South Wales inherited a divided Methodism from Britain, but not the causes of the divisions. She also argued that in the colony the differences between Wesleyan and Primitive Methodists diminished and thus brought about an early

---

7   Gale resigned from the ministry to become a tutor after his marriage in 1857. He was a pioneer of the Canberra region. (*ADB* 4, pp.227-8.) Angwin spent much of his ministry in Bathurst and Mudgee. Curnow was at Bowenfels near Bathurst in 1858. Later he was editor of *Christian Advocate and Wesleyan Record*, eventually becoming editor of the *Sydney Mail* in 1885, and of the *Sydney Morning Herald* from 1886 until his death in 1903. (Information from the Rev E.G. Clancy.) Kelynack spent two appointments at Bathurst. He was famed as a preacher and lecturer, was awarded an honorary Doctor of Divinity degree in the United States, and became President of Newington College from 1887 until his death in 1891. (*ADB* 5, p.11)

8   He was born in Bathurst, but was of Cornish descent.

9   Jennings was the son of Cornish immigrants. (See appendix VI.)

10  He was born in Guyong, but was of Cornish descent.

11  He was born in Sydney, but was of Cornish descent, the son of the Rev William Kelynack D.D.

12  Entries for the clergyman named appear in appendix VI.

13  G. Lindsay Lockley, *A biographical card index of Congregational ministers in Australia 1798-1977*, a photocopied and bound volume at UCA. There may have been more, but many of the entries do not record birthplaces. However, a number of such entries are for names such as Odgers, Northey, Rowe and Tonkin which suggest Cornish descent.

14  B. Bridges and M. Prentis, 'A biographical register of Presbyterian ministers in New South Wales 1823-1865', in *Church Heritage*, vol.3, no.3, March 1984, pp.185-208.

15  Whitby, K. and Clancy, E.G., (eds.), *Great the heritage: the story of Methodism in N.S.W.:1812-1975*, N.S.W. Methodist Conference, Sydney, 1975, p.14.

Methodist union.[16] The movement of Cornish lay Methodists between these two divisions of Methodism certainly occurred in New South Wales. The less rigid divisions between the two meant that the choice between Wesleyan or Primitive Methodism sometimes depended less on doctrine than on convenience, or on individual preference for a particular minister.[17] There is also evidence of movement between other Protestant denominations as well. For example Gale, Law and Jennings were clergymen who changed denomination,[18] and family information provided by descendants indicated that movement of lay people between Protestant denominations was quite common in New South Wales.

Methodism certainly helped sustain Cornish clannishness, but it did not necessarily exclude the non-Cornish from their Cornish groups. For example, there was early co-operation between Methodists and other Protestant denominations in the Bathurst district,[19] a co-operation which continued as the settlement grew. Joseph C. Stanger and his family arrived in Bathurst in 1841.[20] They were Baptists, but were treated so kindly by the Methodist community that they became Methodists.[21]

The well-documented story of Methodism in the Bathurst district clearly shows strong Cornish involvement, and emphasises the central role Methodism played in their lives. Cornish involvement in the birth and growth of Methodism there was tremendous, but at the same time they worked closely and harmoniously with non-Cornish Methodists. In particular, the families at Cornish Settlement were pioneers of Methodism, initiating what would be a long and strong record of Methodism in the Bathurst district. After the Rev Orton's visit to the Bathurst district in the early 1830s,[22] the Rev Frederick Lewis was appointed there in 1836[23] and held the first quarterly meeting which was attended by William Lane, William Tom, George Hawke, John Hughes and John Trewren.[24] Lewis was replaced by the Rev D.J. Draper in 1840. On a visit to Cornish Settlement in that year, Draper:

> rode to Springfield ... and preached to a very respectable and attentive congregation ... The whole of the families in this neighbourhood are emigrants from Cornwall, who, having been some years in the Colony, are pretty well established. About thirty persons attended the preaching, most of whom are young persons, for whose salvation I was much led out in prayer.[25]

During Draper's ministry, the little chapel, measuring only 24 feet by sixteen feet, was built at Cornish Settlement on land given by John Glasson. The cost of the building was met by 'Mr Glasson and other friends' and incurred no expense to the Methodist Church.[26]

---

16  P. Tibbs, 'Illawarra Methodism in the nineteenth century: a comparative study of Wesleyan and Primitive Methodism in Wollongong, 1838-1902', B.A. (Hons.), University of Wollongong, 1981.

17  Discussion with the Rev E.G. Clancy.

18  See appendix VI.

19  A Nonagenarian (Mrs A. Busby), *Bathurst in the thirties: some memories of the early days*, A.J. Dowse, Bathurst, N.S.W., 1902, p.4.

20  J.C. Stanger, *A journey from Sydney over the Blue Mountains to Bathurst forty years ago*, G. Whalan, Bathurst, N.S.W., 1882, pp.1-31.

21  Information supplied to the author at the Webb family reunion at Tarana, February 1990.

22  See chapter 1.

23  R.H. Doust, *After one hundred years: the centenary of Methodism in Bathurst and the west of N.S.W. 1832-1932*, G.W. Brownhill, Bathurst, N.S.W., 1932, p.23.

24  Ibid, p.25. John Hughes had arrived in the colony in 1833, and after several years in Parramatta, brought his family to Bathurst. His property, 'Sussex Farm' was about six miles from 'Orton Park'. Cornishman John Trewren settled at Kelso in the 1830s. (Ibid, pp.95-97.)

25  J. Colwell, *The illustrated history of Methodism: Australia 1812 to 1855*, New South Wales and Polynesia 1856 to 1902, William Brooks, Sydney, 1904, p.249.

26  R.H. Doust, *After one hundred years*, p.31.

The Rev Samuel Wilkinson was the next minister appointed to the Bathurst Circuit from 1843 to 1845, during which time he noted financial assistance from 'our friend Wm. Lane, Esq.'.[27] When Wilkinson was replaced by the Rev Benjamin Hurst, membership had grown from the original class of five at Cornish Settlement to 188 people.[28] In 1848 services began at Guyong when a member moved there from Cornish Settlement.[29]

The importance of the Methodist clergyman's position and the need for him to understand and emphathise with his flock was shown in the antagonism towards the Rev Hurst which grew during his time in Bathurst. He was appointed for a fourth year, when it was the usual practice that Wesleyan ministers were moved on after a three year term. This caused great dissatisfaction at Cornish Settlement where the members felt so strongly about the issue that they separated temporarily from the circuit.[30]   John Glasson wrote to his parents in September 1849 to inform them of the seriousness of the situation:

> we shall be one and all out of the Society, and that not for
> violating Mr Wesley's rules but for daring to appeal to them
> against those whose business it is to see that they are obeyed
> and to respect them themselves.[31]

It was clear that the Rev Hurst did not understand the Cornish, for their main complaints about him were his tendency to gossip about, and his unfair treatment of, members of his flock, and his 'uncourteous manner'. They had been prepared to tolerate him for the three year period of his appointment. When this was completed John Glasson (as chapel steward at Cornish Settlement) 'earnestly requested him to take another circuit on his own account as well as those to whom his ministry was not likely to do good'. Hurst's refusal to take this advice, and even worse, the subsequent appointment of a young assistant preacher of his choice was the last straw for the Cornish. Although they treated his choice with courtesy, they:

> cannot on principle receive him being planned and sent by
> Mr Hurst. We do not recognise his right to send anymore
> than to come'.[32]

Fortunately, Hurst's replacement, the Rev Benjamin Chapman, arrived and was able to mend the rift by dealing more courteously with the Cornish.

Not all the Cornish, however, shared this antipathy towards Hurst. William Lane wrote, in September 1849, to a cousin planning to emigrate from Cornwall, that on arrival in Sydney he should visit the Rev B. Hurst, 'a particular friend of mine'.[33] Lane's youngest child was called Edwin Hurst Lane, presumably because of this friendship.[34] This custom of naming their children after their clergyman was not uncommon amongst the Cornish, and shows the feelings of respect and friendship held for these men by their communities.

As the population grew, chapels sprang up throughout the Bathurst district. There were Cornish people amongst the founders and members of almost every Wesleyan

---

27  Ibid, p.33.
28  They were living in areas as scattered as King's Plains (Blayney), Emu Swamp and Pretty Plains, Fish River, Hartley Vale, Summer Hill, Carcoar and Macquarie Plains as well as the established groups at Bathurst and Kelso, Orton Park and Cornish Settlement. (Ibid, p.33.)
29  Ibid, p.35.
30  Ibid, p.37.
31  John Glasson, *Letters 1828-1857*, with introduction by his grand-daughter, Mrs O. Phillips, typescript copy held at Bathurst Historical Society, letter 10 September 1849, p.111.
32  Ibid, letter 10 September 1849, pp.109-111.
33  P. Hohnen, *A history of the Lane, Tom and Dale families*, the author, Canberra, [n.d.], p.22.
34  Other of William Lane's children were given the Christian names Lewis and Draper, presumably after the Methodist ministers at Bathurst at the times of their baptisms. (Information from Mr Peter Hohnen.)

congregation in the area.[35] In the early years in the Bathurst district, the Methodist church relied heavily on its Cornish local (lay) preachers. 'Parson' Tom, William Lane, George Hawke and others, ensured that services in widely scattered locations could carry on,[36] and those whose strength was not preaching worked in other ways for the expansion of the church. In Bathurst John Trewren, an early class leader and chapel steward, held prayer meetings at his home. The Hon. Edmund Webb was a generous benefactor and represented the Bathurst circuit at wider functions.[37] Cornish Methodists worked in the choir, Sunday school and other organisations within the Bathurst church,[38] and were involved in the development of the south Bathurst church as well.[39]

Lay involvement continued to be an important part of Methodism in the Bathurst district. In 1852, for example, the Bathurst ministers were assisted by lay preachers Fulton, Rowe, Whalan, Sweetnam, Parker, S. Sweetnam, Walker and Trevarton [sic], and exhorters Tom and Hawke. Lay preachers rostered for Cornish Settlement services included Cornishmen Rowe, Trevarton [sic],[40] Tom and Hawke.[41] Methodism also relied on the dedication of other Cornish laymen like Captain Henry Cock of Blayney. Whenever he:

> took charge of a mine and found no Methodist cause
> represented near, it was not long before he had one, as he
> would get to work at once and gather the children for a
> Sunday School, and write to the nearest Methodist minister
> to come.[42]

The population around Orange had grown sufficiently in 1848 to support a Wesleyan church, and regular services were held there and at the newly opened Molong copper mines.

---

35  Perthville church at Queen Charlotte's Vale was close to 'Orton Park' where the Rev Orton had preached in 1832, and of the ten original trustees of the church built there in 1863, John Short and Reuben Robert Tremain were of Cornish descent. In addition, Josiah Parker Junior and Glyndwr Whalan were from families 'accepted' into the Cornish group, as was Peter Furness, superintendent of the Sunday School for 30 years. White Rock church was built in 1858, and amongst the Cornish families who worked towards its establishment and maintance were those of Samuel and Walter Short, and the Sloggetts, while Thomas Starr was from an 'accepted' family. Dennis Island church was given in 1857 by William Sweetnam, member of an 'accepted' family. The first church trust included three members of the Sweetnam family and Josiah Parker. Cornishman William Bryant was an early worker for this church. Caloola and Cow Flat were mining settlements close to Dennis Island and during Cow Flat's copper boom, when the mine employed 500 men, a church was built there, and members of the Cornish Kessel family were involved. Dunkeld church, built in 1871, had a number of Cornish members: Sandry/Saundry, Northey, Hunking, Harris and Eade. The Isons belonged to an 'accepted' family. Cornishman Christopher Armstrong worked for the Rockley church, as did the 'accepted' Stanger family, and the Nancarrow family helped to establish Wattle Flat church. (R.H. Doust, *After one hundred years*, pp.109-17.)

36  John C. White, a Londoner, was registered as a local preacher in New South Wales from 1843 to 1904. Originally a teacher, he became the proprietor of *The Bathurst Free Press and Mining Journal*. Other local preachers were Josiah Parker of Kelso, Thomas Starr of White Rock, Glyndwr Whalan and William Sweetnam, whose families were 'accepted' by the Cornish, and Cornishmen Thomas Bonear and Baker Banks Carvosso, who was the first teacher at Bathurst National School. Samuel Paul, James Burgess and Christopher Armstrong were all Cornishmen and William Pascoe was from neighbouring Devonshire. The other pioneer local preachers were Robert Knott, Henry Naylor, Aubrey Hunt, John N. Makepeace, John Lew, D. Tuckwell and William Gentle. (R.H. Doust, *After one hundred years*, pp.72-8.)

37  Samuel Bray, William Tremain, James James, Samuel Lean, William Trezise, John Burns, H.B. Thomas, Frank Glasson, Samuel and Hannah Paul, and their son William Henry Paul, were all stalwart members. Others who were accepted by the Cornish families included Joseph Carey Stanger, who was English, but his wife's maiden name was Pollard, suggesting Cornish descent. (Information from Mr Garry Howard.) George Palmer, Isaac and George Toole, John Hughes and Peter Furness were 'accepted' by the Cornish. (R.H. Doust, *After one hundred years*, pp.99-104.)

38  These included Kessel, Pearce, Plummer, Pascoe, Harris, Bonear, Lane, Yeo, Glasson, Webb, James, Bray and Paul, and some of the 'accepted' families, Stanger, White and Toole. (Ibid, pp.79-104.)

39  Ibid, pp.105-108.

40  This was Captain James Trevarthen of Carangara mine. (Information from Mrs Mary Nesbitt.)

41  *Wesleyan Preachers' Plan, Bathurst, 1852*, ML Am123-2, item 7.

42  *The Methodist*, 15 August 1908, p.6, c.3-4.

Again, the families from Cornish Settlement were instrumental in its formation and maintenance, and most of these services were conducted by the local preachers from Cornish Settlement.[43] The Rev John Pemell, one of the Wesleyan ministers at Bathurst from 1849 to 1851, described some of the hazards of the journey from Cornish Settlement to Orange:

> One Sunday morning my appointment was at Cornish
> Settlement and in the afternoon at Orange.  The lucid
> directions for getting to my destination, were given to me by
> Mr Hawke,  "Get around the Canoblas ... and keep the sun
> on your left shoulder".

> There were not any roads, not even a sheep track, but at last
> I got to the town of Orange, and found no congregation, they
> had all left.[44]

At that time Orange consisted of 'but one store, an hotel, smithy, and a miserable hut or two'.[45]  The Rev Pemell recalled:

> On another occasion, going from Cornish Settlement ... my
> first time, and at night, I was told  "In about a mile you
> should come to a broad expanse of sand; go straight across
> that, and pick up the track again".  I failed, but I had taken
> the three stars of 'Orion's belt' as my guide, and by so doing
> was able to get back to the track.[46]

However, Methodism was such an important part of their lives, that such difficulties of transport and terrain did not deter the Cornish from attending services or from keeping in close contact with others in the district, and numbers at Orange continued to grow until it became a separate circuit in 1860.  The first minister there was Cornishman Thomas Angwin, and his fellow-Cornishmen were instrumental in the early work of the Orange church.[47]

Like the rest of the colony, the Bathurst district was changed drastically by the discovery of gold at Ophir in 1851 and by the ensuing rushes to the diggings.  Those already resident in the district were inundated by the dramatic growth in population caused by the influx of hopeful diggers.  This affected local farmers, trades and businesspeople alike, and soon increased postal and coaching services were needed.  In the township of Bathurst drunkenness was referred to in the local press as 'the usual Bathurst charge' long before the goldrush[48] but it was even more prevalent afterwards.[49]  In contrast, the strong Wesleyan influence at Cornish Settlement ensured that no policeman ever needed to be stationed there,

43   E.G. Clancy, *'More precious than gold': commemorating the 100th anniversary of the Orange circuit of the Methodist Church 1860-1960*, Central Western Daily, Orange, 1960, chapter 1, [no page numbers].
44   J. Pemell, 'The life of an early Methodist preacher', ML A425, pp.9-10.
45   Ibid, p.10.
46   Ibid, p.10.
47   They were William Tom, George Hawke, Henry Thomas, Fred Hawke and William Rowe, who were assisted by other Cornishmen John Tom Lane, T.G. Lane, G.R. Glasson, T.G. Webb and F. Cornwall.  Other early Cornish Methodists around Orange were the pioneer orchardists John Hicks and Joseph Watts at Canobolas, and William and Jane Johns (nee Gartrell).  Later Cornish local preachers included A. Baker, W. Selwood, W. Mutton and P. Floyd.  (Information from Mr Will Hawke.  E.G. Clancy, *'More precious than gold'*, chapter 2, [no page numbers].)  Peter Floyd came via Victoria, South Australia and Queensland, as a miner to Cornish Settlement during the 1860s, settling eventually as a farmer at Lucknow.  He was a dedicated local preacher who often preached three services in widely scattered areas on Sundays.  He returned to Cornwall several times to attend Methodist functions, leaving his wife to care for their 10 children.  (*CWD*, 6 November 1984, p.4.)
48   *BA*, 11 March 1848, p.3, c.1.
49   B. Greaves (ed.), *The story of Bathurst*, Angus and Robertson, Sydney, 3rd edition, 1976, pp.38-39.

no licensed premises ever existed, and there is no knowledge of the presence at any time of sly-grog shops.[50]

The Rev Chapman and the Rev Pemell, Wesleyan ministers at Bathurst, quickly joined the rush to Ophir, but in search of souls rather than gold. They were the first clergy to visit the diggings, and ensured that public worship was held at Ophir on 'the first Sunday after they were generally known, and while there were only a few hundreds of miners on the creeks'.[51] Amongst these miners were the Tom brothers from Cornish Settlement. Pemell remembered:

> I wore a white hat, and a blouse made of brown holland, washed white, there were no silk coats in those days; as I passed down the creek leading my pony, men were at alluvial work, rocking a cradle with one hand and dipping up, and pouring water on the washdirt with the other. I was saluted with "Good evening, Jack" and a little further on "Good evening, Jack". I thought I had known him in Sydney and that he had evidently left his good manners the other side of the Blue Mountains - so I said, "Good evening. I am going to preach at that Gum tree at 10 o'clock tomorrow, come and help me with the singing." All was changed - it was the want of clerical garb.

> ... I went on until I reached Mr Toms son's tent, tied my pony to a sheoak and placed a rug on him. I saw a large tent, in which was a table made of three sticks stuck in the ground, with a sheet of bark on top. Upon this was a tin baking dish with a boiled leg of mutton, and damper - I was invited in, "Come Mr Pemell where's your pocket knife? Help yourself." This I did, and found that the mutton and damper were not the best I had ever tasted - there was also quart pot tea, without milk, sweetened with black sugar, which materially intensified its colour. At night a large opossum rug was spread on the grass; eight men lay on that I made the ninth, there were no pillows, and one rug was over all. Two of the men snored, and the scent of that tent was not that of 'Arabi the blest'.[52]

Soon though, the Methodists at the diggings found that this earlier, innocent camaraderie had altered. The Rev Chapman reported:

> After the first few weeks the wicked men were emboldened to sin with little fear. Sad immoralities were practised, the Sabbath awfully desecrated. We continue to preach there as often as possible. By many we were cordially welcomed and generally obtained large and attentive congregations.[53]

Many New South Wales Methodists had left their own congregations during the early months of the goldrush, without joining any local Society. Attempts were made to form

---

50    Information from Mr Will Hawke.

51    R.H. Doust, *After one hundred years*, p.40.

52    J. Pemell, 'The life of an early Methodist preacher', pp.7-9.

53    R.H. Doust, *After one hundred years*, p. 40.

Methodist Societies at the diggings, with the help of such members already there.[54]  The Rev Chapman's report from the Turon diggings made it clear that their evangalism was needed:

> Here also, as at Ophir, immorality abounds, and a wide
> scope is presented for the exercise of Christian sympathy.[55]

The Cornish residents in the Bathurst district had been involved in the gold rush since its infancy, with the gold discovery at Ophir by the Tom brothers and Lister.  Cornish Methodists adapted to the rapidly changing circumstances and co-operated with Methodists of other ethnic groups to bring their Christian faith to others on the goldfields.

Of course some Cornish settlers chose to be members of denominations other than Methodism, and many of these were devout members of the Church of England, and made important contributions to it.[56]  Although the Cornish Methodists in the Bathurst district were part of a minority religion, it was a religion which was vital and dynamic, and a central part of their everyday lives.  It was a basis for friendship groups, marriages and business relationships and emphasised their Cornishness as they worshipped together and shared the moral and religious values of their homeland.  At the same time, as a community group, it brought them into close contact with Methodists from other ethnic groups, and to eventual assimilation into the wider community.

As they did in the Bathurst district, Cornish Methodists gathered in other clusters in the colony.  Similar detail is not available on Cornish contributions in these clusters, but it is clear that Cornish involvement did occur.  In 1840 the first Wesleyan missionary, the Rev Jonathan Innes, was stationed at Maitland, and he was soon able to report an enthusiastic congregation at Patrick's Plains (Singleton), and a congregation of 100 at Newcastle.[57]  The majority of Methodists in the hinterland were Wesleyans, although the more radical Primitive Methodists from the industrial north of England, and from Wales and Cornwall, went to Newcastle.  It developed as a non-conformist stronghold, with a higher percentage of non-conformist religions and a lower percentage of Catholics than in New South Wales as a whole.[58]  The first Primitive Society was formed there in 1852,[59] and the United Free Methodists established churches there in the 1870s.[60]

During the 1850s the strength of Methodism in the Hunter hinterland increased, and by 1854 there were two Wesleyan ministers based at Maitland, one of whom was a Cornishman, the Rev Francis Tuckfield.  In 1855 a minister was stationed at Newcastle for the first time.  He was a Cornishman, the Rev William Curnow.[61]  As the mining townships appeared, so did Methodist preachers.

54    Minutes of the meeting of Australian [Wesleyan] districts 1846-1854, *General Returns 1852*, p.466. [UCA].
55    J. Colwell, *The illustrated history of Methodism*, p.255.
56    The Harveys at Oberon were Methodists when they first arrived, but were soon involved in working to build St Thomas' Church of England there.  The Hon. John Smith of 'Gamboola' was instrumental in the development of Molong Church of England, although his wife was 'Parson' Tom's daughter Mary, and Tom often used his daughter's home for Methodist services. (Information from Mrs Netta Stoneman and Mr B.W. Thomas.)
57    J. Colwell, *The illustrated history of Methodism*, p.261.
58    J.M. Sloggett, 'Temperance and class: with particular reference to Newcastle and the South Maitland coalfields, 1860-1928', M.A., University of Newcastle, 1989, pp.56-8.
59    N.F. Charge and E.K. Lingard, *Glory be: commemorating the 100th anniversary of the opening of the first Wesleyan chapel in Newcastle 1845-1945*, the organising committee, Newcastle, N.S.W., 1945, p.15.
60    Ibid, p.19.
61    H. Charleston, T. Moase and D.N. Morison, *Seventy years of Newcastle Methodism 1834-1904*, [no publisher], Newcastle, N.S.W., 1904, pp.2-3.

As soon as a township began to appear, a Methodist emissary would be there. A stump, a mound or a convenient corner did service for a pulpit, from which the "local" held forth. Next a room would be hired and then a primitive chapel built of slabs would be the forerunner of the more stately church.[62]

Singleton had its own clergyman appointed in 1854, and he was a Cornishman, the Rev Thomas Angwin, who also ministered in the Bathurst district. In 1856 Singleton became a separate circuit, under the Rev Pemmell who had earlier served in the Bathurst district during the early years of the gold rush.[63] This shows that though ministers moved from one circuit to another, the movement was often between inter-related areas, and in the close, minority society of Methodism the clergymen and many of their flock were known by repute, if not personally, in districts other than their own.

Although the Dangars in Singleton were not Methodist, other Cornish settlers were. For example, William and Melinda Burnett who arrived in Singleton in 1863 were dedicated Methodists. For 50 years William worked as a lay preacher and trustee in the district, and in the wider field as a representative to the Annual Conference of the Methodist Church.[64]

The numbers of Cornish recorded amongst the Hunter Wesleyan Methodist registers were much fewer than expected, but it is very likely that many Cornish settlers in Newcastle followed the Primitive Methodist denomination, for which few New South Wales records survive.

In Sydney too, Methodism was strong amongst the Cornish. As early as 1826, there were three Wesleyan circuits in New South Wales - Sydney, Parramatta and Windsor,[65] and the Primitive Methodist Church began in Sydney much later, in 1845.[66] Information from the Cornish marriages on the Sydney data base was used to examine the prevalence of Methodism there. Examination of the denominations in which Cornish men and women in Sydney chose to marry gave an indication of the comparative strength of Methodism amongst the Sydney Cornish. Those Cornish marriage partners who stated their residence as other than Sydney were discarded, and the remainder totalled 238 persons resident in Sydney at the time of their marriage. Of these 238 persons, 60 percent were non-conformists: 47 percent being married according to the rites of one of the branches of Methodism, while eight percent were Presbyterian and five percent were Congregational. The remaining 40 percent were Church of England. See Table 2.14.

There was no evidence of Cornish clusters in certain areas of Sydney based on religion alone. The Methodists did not congregate in any particular suburbs, and neither did the members of other denominations. This indicated that the Cornish in Sydney were not settling in groups primarily according to their religious faith. It suggested that the major reason for their clustering was personal choice, and that they preferred to be with other Cornish people, regardless of their denomination.

---

62   H. Charleston, T. Moase, D.N. Morison, *Seventy years of Newcastle Methodism*, p.10.

63   T. Oades (compiler), *Two streams meet: the story of the Uniting Church Parish of Singleton 1835-1985*, Uniting Church, Singleton, N.S.W., 1985,      pp.13-15.

64   Ibid, p.15. At nearby Goorangoola, Simon Richards was a staunch Methodist, as were his children. (Information from Mrs Peggy Richards and Mrs Shirley Richards.) In Maitland and Morpeth, the Cornish Jory, Short, Caddy, Lightfoot and Boulden families were Methodists. (Information from descendants.) In Newcastle William Lightfoot was a local preacher for many years. James Avery of Adamstown, William Hicks, the Bear family and Richard Leathlean were all Methodists of long standing. (Obituaries of Richard Leathlean, *Methodist*, 21 September 1907, p.10, c.1, and *NMH*, 2 July 1907, p.6, c.8. Information from descendants.)

65   K. Whitby and E.G. Clancy, *Great the heritage*, p.9.

66   Discussion with the Rev E.G. Clancy.

The Methodist Church 'geared itself to a particular function: evangelism'.[67] The suburbs of Redfern and Chippendale were amongst those in Sydney which supported Cornish clusters,[68] and during the early 1870s the residents of these suburbs were visited by a zealous Methodist evangelist. The door knocker recorded the responses in Morehead and Walker Streets in November 1874.

> Fourth [visit].   Mrs B [Church of England] ... conversed with her at the door, spoke faithfully and kind to her, asking her to seek religion and enjoy it in her heart, not to rest satisfied with a nominal profession, she too thanked me when leaving.

> Fifth   Mrs H. ...   Congregationalist an aged woman spoke to her of the love of Christ urged to seek to have it shed abroad in her heart after which I prayed with her.

> Sixth   Mrs D. ...   Baptist, during conversation found she had been attending our Services in the Country, and occasionally here at Cleveland St, asked her to seek redemption through the Blood of Christ not to rest satisfied with anything short of this. I gave an affectionate invitation to our Services, this took place at the door.

> Seventh and 8th   Roman Catholics sought a conversation with them at the door, subject of conversation with one The Prodigal Son, tried to set before her the character of the Sinner, and the Fathers willingness to recieve [sic] all such that come to him, listened very attentively as I tried to apply it.   In the other case dealt equally faithful was kindly received.[69]

Apart from the evangelical side though, Methodism met other needs. Just as the Cornish at home embracing Methodism were able to find a way of overcoming harsh physical conditions in the present, some of those living in overcrowded and unhealthy conditions in nineteenth century Sydney continued to find security, comfort and hope in their Christian faith. Wesleyans George and Elizabeth Crothers of Surry Hills suffered the loss, from scarlatina and convulsions, of their baby son in 1864. Their strong faith obviously brought them through the unbearable tragedy of losing three more of their children (aged three, five and seven) within a period of five days in April 1876 - all from complications following scarlatina. They were able to include, at the end of the death notice of the third child, the message: 'For of such is the Kingdom of heaven'.[70]

As well as its immense value to immigrants as a means of bringing comfort and hope in such dreadful circumstances, the happier role of the Methodist network in Cornish emigration was obvious. An example is the case of Joseph and Susannah Wearne of Ponsanooth, who arrived with their eleven children aboard *Harbinger* in 1849. They were close friends of the Rev. Benjamin Carvosso and his father, who lived in the same part of Cornwall, and Joseph Wearne came to the colony with employment already organised in

---

67    K. Whitby and E.G. Clancy, *Great the heritage*, p.22.

68    See chapter 4.

69    'Pastoral visitation, 1873/4', Anonymous, Methodist Church papers, ML 5015, no.81.

70    *SMH*, 7 April 1876, p.1, c.1 and p.12, c.1, and 11 April 1876, p.1, c.1.  Death certificates of Joseph Crothers (*NSWRGI* 1864, no.2177 ) and Henry, Rosina and Elizabeth Louisa Crothers. (*NSWRGI* 1876, nos.00812, 00835, 00836).

Pemell's flour mill at Glebe. Although not Cornish, the Methodist proprietor was a relative of the Rev. John Pemell, and gave land near his mill at Glebe for a chapel.[71] The emigration and settlement of this large family was obviously organised through the Lawry-Carvosso-Hosking Cornish Methodist network. It is interesting to find this link still flourishing almost twenty years after it had assisted the emigration of Tom, Lane, Hawke and Glasson before 1830.[72] An even earlier proponent of emigration to New South Wales was George Worgan, the eccentric surgeon who brought his piano with him in 1788 with the First Fleet. On his return to Liskeard, Worgan was heavily involved in the Methodist church and constantly advocated the benefits of emigration to New South Wales.[73]

Methodism was strong amongst all the Cornish clusters in mining districts and in non-mining areas as well. In Adelong almost half the Cornish males and almost all of the Cornish females who died there between 1856 and 1905 were Methodists.[74] In the Adelong Wesleyan church:

> A special point of interest is the gallery built at the back of
> the Church which was added as a result of the great influx of
> Cornishmen who came to work on the mines. These men
> were keen singers and formed the Methodist choir.[75]

In Cobar, too, many of the Cornish were Methodists. Their first church burned down in 1881, but 'quickly those Cornishmen got together and built another church, a wooden and iron building'.[76] According to the death registrations of the Cobar Cornish, approximately half were buried with a Methodist ceremony. See Table 2.28.

Evidence of devotion to Methodism was found in all the New South Wales clusters, but of course some Cornish Australians were devout adherents to other denominations. However, many were staunch Methodists whose Christian faith was an important part of their lives which had come with them from the homeland. In New South Wales they became involved in all facets of the Church, from the humblest level to the high office and distinction achieved by the Rev William Kelynack D.D.[77]

Membership of the Methodist Church tended to encourage membership of related community groups. Anne Colman found that Methodists in Victoria were often members of temperance societies, and friendly societies. These groups were organised with a hierarchical structure similar to Methodism which allowed any members who wished, to hold office. She argued that such membership was an important outward sign of having achieved a respectable place in their community.[78]

In New South Wales, the Cornish remained in clannish groups yet saw membership of the wider community as important, and were involved in many aspects of it. Like their Victorian cousins, they joined the Band of Hope: for example, the first anniversary of the Bathurst Band of Hope was celebrated with a concert and tea in the Wesleyan Church in 1860. It offered 'temperance pieces ... sung by the Band of Hope Choir' and a recitation of 'The Trial of John Barleycorn' with the aim of 'saving the young from habits of intemperance'.[79]

---

71  Telephone conversation with Mrs Val Wearne-Frost.
72  John Hosking was one of the three original lay Methodists in Sydney who agitated in 1812 for the appointment of a Wesleyan missionary to the colony. His son John was a staunch Methodist later. (Discussion with the Rev E.G. Clancy.) John Hosking Senior died in Truro. John Junior was the first mayor of Sydney. (Information from Mr Warwick Adams.)
73  Information from Mrs Thelma Freeman.
74  See Table 2.23.
75  R.J. Bird, *Adelong: glimpses at the past*, Stewart Press, Hornsby, N.S.W., 1976, p.45.
76  Interview with Mr W. Snelson.
77  See appendix VI.
78  A. Colman, 'Colonial Cornish', pp.162-6.
79  *BFP*, 4 August 1860, p.3, c.5.

The first friendly society in New South Wales began in 1830 and within thirty years they were widespread, offering freedom from worry about loss of wages and cost of medical care in the case of illness or accident. They also offered social activities.[80]    Although membership was common to other ethnic groups, friendly societies appealed to the Cornish who valued the concepts of self-help and independence upon which the operation of friendly societies were based.    The Cornish were familiar with similar ideas upon which the conributory 'mine doctor' schemes were based in Cornwall and in New South Wales mining settlements at Cadia and Cobar, and in New England.    However, evidence of the friendly society membership of individual Cornish Australians in New South Wales was difficult to find, and it is impossible to be sure just what proportion of Cornish immigrants belonged to such societies.[81]

Gollan stated that 'The Oddfellows, Druids, and Foresters existed in Newcastle from the mid-1830s'.[82] McEwen's research showed that New Lambton was the only coalmining town which did not have more than one friendly society between 1860 and 1900.[83] In this 40 year period, attempts were made by thirteen different groups to establish 40 lodges.    They were:

> four orders of Oddfellows: Manchester Unity, Grand United,
> The Independent Order of N.S.W. and the American Order,
> as well as the Druids, Rechabites, Sons of Temperance, Free
> Gardeners, Foresters, Buffaloes, Ancient Britons, and the
> Protestant Alliance Friendly Society.[84]

Many Cornishmen in the Hunter were members of at least one lodge or friendly society.[85] In the Bathurst district some were Masons, Druids, Orangeman or members of Manchester Unity, the Foresters' Lodge, or other friendly societies.[86] In Orange itself, Cornishmen were amongst members of the Foresters' Lodge.[87] In Sydney, Cornishmen whose membership of a lodge or friendly society was mentioned in death or funeral notices, or recorded on their gravestones, were generally members of the Masonic Lodge, and the occupations of these men varied from builder, stonemason and dairy proprietor, to warder in an asylum.    Others were members of the Ancient Order of Foresters, the Oddfellows and the Loyal Orange Lodge.    Where information from descendants included lodge membership, it was generally of the Masonic Lodge.[88]

---

80  D. Green and L. Cromwell, *Mutual aid or welfare state: Australia's friendly societies*, Allen & Unwin, Sydney, 1984, p.xiii.

81  This has depended largely on obituaries, biographies, death notices and gravestone inscriptions, but it is not certain that every member of such a society had this recorded in such places.  I have also relied heavily on information sent to me by descendants, and again, individual membership of such groups is not always handed down as part of the oral tradition in families, and is very difficult information for descendants to find several generations later.  Unfortunately, no collection like that of Victorian friendly society records held at ANUBLA, exists for New South Wales, and so it was not possible to use Dr Price's estimation system.

82  R. Gollan, *The coalminers of New South Wales: a history of the union 1860-1960*, Melbourne University Press in association with the Australian National University, Melbourne, 1963, p.28.

83  E. McEwen, 'The Newcastle coalmining district of New South Wales, 1860-1900', PhD., University of Sydney, 1979, p.159.

84  E. McEwen, 'The Newcastle coalmining district', p.159.

85  J.D. Barklay of Muswellbrook, for instance, was one of the founders of the local Masonic Lodge.(*MM*, 26 March 1889, p.5, c.5.)    William H. Langsford of Singleton was a member of the Loyal Orange Lodge, the Protestant Alliance and the Manchester Unity Order of Oddfellows. (*MM*, 15 March 1918, p.4, c.6.)    William H. Manuell had worked through all the chairs of office in the Druids.  (*Daily Telegraph*, 10 July 1894, p.5, c.6.)    He was also a respected member of the Loyal Orange Lodge, which recorded an inscription to that effect on his tombstone.  (SAG Sandgate cemetery transcpripts. NLA MCN 823.)

86  Many Cornish miners in Butte, Montana, were involved with Masonry, which they saw as a symbol of upward mobility, and were also Oddfellows. (Discussion with Dr John Rowe.)

87  F.S. Bone (ed), *Orange district guide 1908*, facsimile reprint G. and C. Reynolds, Millthorpe, N.S.W., 1983, p.100.

88  This type of information was unlikely to have been passed down through several generations in a family, and

There was friendly society membership in the smaller mining settlements also. For example, in Adelong, at the opening of the MUIOOF Lodge with 58 members in 1862, and said to be the largest lodge yet opened in the colony, two of the elected office bearers were Cornishmen Messrs Prowse and Treweek.[89] Most of the usual Friendly Societies existed in Glen Innes, including the Foresters, Independent Oddfellows, Grand United Oddfellows and Rechabites and the Masonic Lodge.[90] George Trewhella Jnr, of Torrington, was a member of the Oddfellows Society.[91] Many Cornishmen were members of the Masonic Lodge in Cobar where 'the mine captains dressed in morning coats, cutaway and tails, and across their stomachs was the heavy gold watch chain with the Masonic emblem on, and they wore a little goatee beard'. Cornish funerals in Cobar, particularly those of Cornish Masons, were led by brass bands with muffled drums and instruments wreathed in black, while the members of the walking procession wore black arm bands.[92]

In South Australia, Cornish immigrants did become involved in unionism.[93] Therefore it is very likely that Cornishmen in New South Wales did also, although evidence of this was somewhat sketchy. Membership would be expected in such a strong unionist district as Newcastle which also had regular contact with the South Australian copper triangle.

Gollan stated that a coal miners' union was formed in Newcastle in May 1860, although there had been a type of miners' organisation earlier. He credited friendly societies with being 'the nucleus from which union activity sprouted'.[94] The coalmining strike of 1861 was 'the most extensive and bitter industrial dispute that had occurred in the colony up to that time',[95] and after unsuccessful attempts to import strike breaking miners from Britain as assisted emigrants, the mine owners brought hardrock miners from Victoria and South Australia in an attempt to destroy the union. Coming as they did from the hardrock mining areas, it is likely that many of these men were Cornish. However, many of them refused to work when they realised they were being used as strike breakers, and as a result they were pursued and then hounded by the proprietors for breaking their contracts. In a second attempt to provide extra labour to break the strike, an official travelled incognito to Burra Burra and Wallaroo, but had great difficulty in persuading men to sign contracts for employment in Newcastle. Eventually, a group of about 80 men was contracted, 'the majority of them Cornishmen, who proved if anything less tractable than the men from Victoria'.[96]

Another important union activity at this time was the establishment of a co-operative mine by James Fletcher and other union leaders. Cornish unionist, William Henry Manuell had arrived as a small child in 1849, with his family, and from the age of six was employed as a surface worker at the coal mines in Newcastle. He became a railway carriage fitter and was an active supporter of James Fletcher, who also worked for improved conditions for the railway unions. Manuell was a member of the Topmen's Society, and President of the

would be difficult for descendants to locate three or four generations later.

89  Tumut Family History Society, (comps.), *Transcripts of the Perkins Papers 1823-1954*, typescript, NLA MS 7231, no.3, pp.309-310.

90  E.C. Sommerlad and E. St Clair, *The Beardies' heritage: a history of Glen Innes and district*, Glen Innes Municipal Council, Glen Innes, N.S.W., 1972, pp.200-202.

91  C. Alt, (comp.), *Old Torrington: a history of Torrington and district 1881-1981*, 'Back to Torrington Weekend' Committee, Torrington, N.S.W., 1981, p.57.

92  Interview with Mr W. Snelson.

93  P.J. Payton, *The Cornish miner in Australia*, chapter 4.

94  R. Gollan, *The coalminers of New South Wales*, p.28.

95  Ibid, p.38.

96  Ibid, p.44.

Railway and Tramway Employee's Association, and treasurer of the Confederation Senate of Railway Employees.[97]

New England was said to be a 'bastion of non-unionism',[98] but there were at least pockets of unionism there. For example, Captain William Martin of Hillgrove was a member of Hillgrove Miners' Association and had been elected President several times. A hundred members marched in his funeral procession, as did the members of the Masonic Lodge in full mourning regalia. The funeral procession was led by the local brass band and:

> the Miners came next, the Masons, then the hearse and three
> mourning coaches, then the Oddfellows and townspeople;
> 32 carriages and several horsemen followed the procession.[99]

There was unofficial 'union' activity at Molong copper mine amongst the Cornishmen who had arrived under contract with Captain Clymo in 1848. After their arrival, they found their contracted incomes were low by local standards. They wanted to break their contracts without attracting heavy penalties, so:

> being eminently practical mining men, they ... worked on
> what is termed "the hide" of the lode. The expenses went on
> week by week without any result cheering to the
> management ... the rumour going forth that in reality the
> deposit was slight, and one that could not be profitably
> worked.

The company officials were not experienced miners, and when Captain Clymo suggested that his contract and those of his miners be terminated, the officials gladly agreed.[100]

Records of union membership in nineteenth century Sydney are sparse and it seems likely that Cornishmen in Sydney were not employed in jobs which had strong unions during this period. They were more likely to be working in self-employed situations where possible, in small business and trades which gave them the independence they preferred, and if in such employment they would not have wished to become union members.[101]

Most Cornish settlers were involved in community organisations. The Dangars and Cooks of course were outstanding in this way, acting for the benefit of individuals and the local and wider community as well.[102] The Dangar family obviously felt more than just the responsibility of employers towards workers. For example, when the coal mines near

---

97  W.H. Manuell's obituary, *NMH*, 27 August 1917, p.6, c.7. *Daily Telegraph*, 10 July 1894, p.5, c.6. While it is likely that other Cornishmen were active unionists in Newcastle, I have found little evidence of this. However, this is not necessarily because they were not unionists, rather that it was not information recorded in death notices and not handed down orally in the family. So many of them were involved in other political and community activities that it is reasonable to assume they were amongst the unionists as well.

98  R.B. Walker, *Old New England: a history of the Northern Tablelands of New South Wales 1818-1900*, Sydney University Press, 1966, p.165.

99  *The Hillgrove Guardian*, 24 June 1899, p.3.

100  J.C.L. Fitzpatrick, *The good old days of Molong*, Cumberland Argus, Parramatta, N.S.W., 1913, pp.97-8.

101  The use of Dr Price's system was attempted to estimate the strength of Cornish union membership, using the union records held at ML and ANUBLA. However, very few membership lists could be located for nineteenth century unions in New South Wales. So the results were inconclusive, but suggested that Cornishmen were not generally working in jobs which had strong unions at this period. In Sydney, the only union with many Cornish members' names was the Coopers' Union. In the city, coopers would have been employees of a brewery rather than self employed tradesmen. (Federated Coopers of Australia, New South Wales Branch, ANUBLA, E100/1, E100/6, E100/8.)

102  See appendix VI.

Morpeth (in which they had a financial interest) closed down, they moved their unemployed miners to the newly opened Cobar copper mines, in which they also had a financial interest.[103]

However, many other Cornish men and women in the Hunter contributed to their communities in valuable ways according to their interests and abilities. For example, William Burnett frequently wrote to the Singleton newspaper, earning the reputation for possessing a 'facile and forceful pen',[104] while his wife, Melinda, was 'a woman of deeds rather than words'.[105] In Sydney, too, many Cornish immigrants belonged to community organisations according to their interests and abilities. For example, William Vial was a member of the Sydney Volunteer Fire Company No.2.[106]

Joseph and Susannah Wearne, assisted immigrants who arrived in 1849 with their eleven children, settled first at Glebe and later at Liverpool. They enjoyed a successful life in the colony, and their children and grandchildren became prominent in professional, business and political fields. A son, Joseph Wearne, was a member of the New South Wales Legislative Assembly. Three of his daughters became schoolmistresses: one, Minnie Flora Wearne M.A., was the first headmistress of the Methodist Ladies' College, Burwood. Another son of Joseph and Susannah, Thomas Wearne J.P., was an alderman in Liverpool. A grandson, Walter Ernest Wearne, of Bingara, became a member of the New South Wales Parliament, and Minister for Lands.[107]

Lieutenant-Colonel Thomas Rowe arrived as an assisted immigrant with his family aboard *Steadfast* in 1849, aged twenty. He became a respected architect in Sydney, having a small street off Pitt Street renamed Rowe Street in his honour.[108] He was one of the founders of the New South Wales Institute of Architects and President of this organisation for many years, and a Fellow of the Royal Institute of British Architects. He was active in local government, a J.P.,[109] and Superintendent of Dowling Street Wesleyan Sunday School for thirty years. Also he was involved with the Church of England church in Manly and at Darling Point.[110]

In Cobar a similar pattern of community involvement emerged. For example, Captain Dunstan was the first Chairman of Cobar Hospital Board. Captain Lean resigned in 1874 to become a grazier, but continued the paternal interest in the community which had characterised his time as mine captain, and which was continued by his successor. Captain Lean:

> remained in the Cobar district for the remainder of his days
> being much in demand from other mining companies ... as a
> consultant and adviser.

103 Information from Mr Peter Dangar.
104 *Singleton Argus*, 3 February 1916, p.3, c.2.
105 *Weekly Advocate* 31 May 1890, p.91. John Cundy was a member of Aberdeen School Board. (Information from Mrs Enid Farnham.) Simon Richards was a foundation member of Singleton Bowling Club and one of its first life members. He 'supported all measures for the advancement of the town and district'. (Information from Mrs Peggy Richards and Mrs Shirley Richards.) Mr G. Hicks of Carrington was a longtime member of the railway male voice choir and had been involved in choral societies in the Newcastle district. (*NMH*, 4 May 1925, p.7, c.4.)
106 *SMH*, 6 August 1878, p.8, c.1. Emily Kate Juleff was a tireless worker for her local Church of England church, and also met immigrant women on their arrival and helped them to settle into their new lives. (Information from Mrs Jean Juleff Roy.) It is believed that Green Park and Greens Road in Paddington are named after James Green J.P., a businessman in Paddington from 1865 until the turn of the century. (Information from Mrs Pat McCormack.)
107 V. Wearne-Frost, *Wearne of Cornwall and Australia*, the author, Blaxland, N.S.W., 1981. This information is contained in the genealogical charts 1-16 at the end of the book.
108 Rowe believed that the renaming of Pitt Street itself would have been more appropriate. (N. Rowe Best, *The Mumford Rowes*, the author, Fairlight, N.S.W., 1987, p.25.)
109 *AMM*, series 1, vol.1, pp.353-6.
110 N. Rowe Best, *The Mumford Rowes*, pp.23-8.

He was also a member of the Masonic Lodge, the elder
Justice of the Peace and was appointed to the Licensing
Board and the Local Land Board when they were first
constituted. He seldom missed a sitting and, although in
latter years was much handicapped by defective hearing, he
was held in such high respect that no exception was taken by
the Cobar people to this failing.[111]

Cornish community involvement was also evident on the south coast. For instance,
Nicholas Craig of Kiama was a founder of Kiama Agricultural Society, and a committee
member for fifteen years. His son, C.W. Craig, became chairman of directors of the
Jamberoo Dairy Company, and was mayor of Kiama in 1889, as well as mayor of Jamberoo
for nineteen years, declining future terms.[112]

Cornish people from the Bathurst district were prominent in local and colonial life.
William Lane's son, John Tom Lane, was the first police magistrate in Orange and 'took a
prominent part in all public matters'.[113] The Hon. John Smith of 'Gamboola' and 'Llanarth'
was appointed a J.P. in 1850. He stood once as a parliamentary candidate for Molong but
was defeated by six votes. He chose never to make another attempt, but was appointed to the
Upper House of the New South Wales parliament in 1880.[114] The Hon. Edmund Webb of
Bathurst began his own business as a storekeeper in Bathurst in 1851 at the age of 21. It
grew into a very prosperous enterprise, and he used his wealth to help public projects in the
Bathurst district. He was prominent in the Wesleyan church, founded the Bathurst School of
Arts, and was an alderman in Bathurst, serving as mayor on five occasions. He was elected
to the Legislative Assembly in 1870 (as an independent member), and was appointed to the
Legislative Council in 1882.[115] His son Edmund Tom Webb also served as an alderman and
as mayor on several occasions.[116]

A natural extension of Cornish involvement in general community groups was the
move into local politics, and many Cornishmen were members of their local councils.[117]

111 W. Clelland, *Cobar founding fathers: an illustrated history of the pioneering days in the copper mining district
of Cobar, New South Wales*, Western Heritage Series no. 7, Macquarie Publications Pty Ltd, Dubbo, N.S.W.,
1984, pp.50 and 71.

112 W.A. Bayley, *Blue Haven: a history of Kiama municipality New South Wales*, Kiama Municipal Council,
Kiama, N.S.W., 1976, pp.136, 139 and 162-3. Charles Crapp of Moruya was a founder of the Pastoral and
Agricultural Society there. His son, Charles, represented Kiola on Moruya's Progress Committee in 1889.
(H.J. Gibbney, *Eurobodalla: history of the Moruya district*, LAH in association with the Council of the Shire
of Eurobodalla, Sydney, 1980, pp.128, 181.) The Good Samaritan stained glass window in St Andrew's
church, Wollongong, is dedicated to William James and his wife as a result of a 'Good Samaritan' action on
their behalf. (Information from Mrs Lorna Spackman.)

113 E.G. Clancy, *'More precious than gold'*, chapter 2, [no page numbers].

114 B. Mac. Smith (ed.), *Quench not the spirit: merino heritage*, Hawthorn Press, Melbourne, 1972, pp.61 and 63.

115 *AMM*, series 1, vol.1, pp.84-86.

116 G.S. White (comp.), *Back to Bathurst Week: official souvenir containing the history and progress of Bathurst
and district 1813-1923*, Direct Publicity Co., for the Committee of the Back to Bathurst Week, Sydney, 1924,
p.55. Other businessmen of Cornish descent in Bathurst acted as aldermen. A.B. James, William Tremain,
W.H. Paul and Frederick Crago all served long terms, and Crago was mayor in 1891. (Ibid, pp.51 and 55.
Information from Miss Grace Tremain.) John Trewren acted as one of two trustees for the Ebenezer Mining
Company. (*BA*, 30 June 1849, p.1, c.1.) W.H. Couch was involved in public life at Molong. He was
appointed a J.P. and in this capacity sat on the local Bench of Magistrates between 1892 and 1904. He was
elected an alderman in 1894 and remained in office until 1898. Information from Mr David Rutherford. Mr
J.M. Paul served as mayor of Orange. (*BP*, 15 March 1887, p.2, c.1.) John Watts and T. Oates were
councillors on Canoblas Shire Council and B. Penhall served as an alderman on East Orange Municipality.
(F.S. Bone (ed.), *Orange district guide*, pp.76-78.) William Dale was a president of the Orange Show Society.
(*Orange and district illustrated*, first published 1928, facsimile reprint by Orange City Council, Orange,
N.S.W., 1989, p.75.) Henry Oliver, who discovered gold on his small farming block, became a large
landholder and his son R.M. Oliver was later a mayor of Blayney. (G. Reynolds, *The Kings colonials: the
story of Blayney and district*, the author, Millthorpe, N.S.W., 1982, p.26.)

117 However, most evidence for involvement in local politics comes from biographies and from information from
descendants, who are not necessarily aware of an ancestor's involvement in local councils, or of other

The following examples are typical of the involvement found in Sydney. Nicholas Hawken had been an alderman and mayor of Darlington before his election as a member of the Legislative Assembly.[118] A builder, George Crothers, of Portreath, served as an alderman on Petersham Council from 1887 to 1895,[119] and fellow Cornishmen on Petersham Council were brothers Frederick and William Langdon, who operated a local timber business.[120] John White, a builder, was an alderman in Paddington.[121]

W.H. Phillips, a city produce merchant and former blacksmith and publican, was asked several time to stand as an alderman, but withstood the temptation.[122] Lieutenant-Colonel Thomas Rowe was an alderman for Bourke ward from 1872, and later an alderman and mayor of Manly.[123] It was during his term as the first mayor of Manly that the landmark Norfolk pines were planted along the Ocean Beach.[124] This pattern of involvement in local government was repeated in other cluster areas.[125]

Some Cornishmen became involved in the wider world of colonial politics, and many of those who did so espoused the liberal political view which predominated in Cornwall. George Hawke's strong opposition to James Martin of Orange, later Sir James Martin and Premier of New South Wales, was typical of this attitude. His opposition to Martin was partly because his parents:

> were Irish Roman Catholics and I have been informed that
> they kept a public house in Sydney of rather a low order. I
> should say, not above a third class.

This was not a serious complaint about Martin though. The main reason for his hostility towards Martin was disapproval of his principles and judgement:

> his views and actions have been anything but liberal. I
> know not a liberal measure which has been brought into
> Parliament that he has not opposed.[126]

---

community involvement.

118 *Cyclopaedia of New South Wales: an historical and commercial review*, McCarron Stewart, Sydney, 1907, p.82.

119 *AMM*, series 1, vol.2 appendix, p.41. R. Cashman and C. Meader, *Marrickville: rural outpost to inner city*, Hale and Iremonger, Petersham, N.S.W., 1990, p.210.

120 R. Cashman and C. Meader, *Marrickville*, p.178.

121 *AMM*, series 1, vol.2 appendix, p.27.

122 *AMM*, series 1, vol.2 appendix, p.26.

123 *AMM*, series 1, vol.1, p.355.

124 I am indebted to Mr David Rutherford for this information.

125 W.T. Dangar was an alderman at Kempsey for fifteen years, and was mayor on three occasions. (J.H. Watson, 'Kempsey: early settlement of the Macleay River', in *JRAHS*, vol.VII 1921 part 4, p.210.) In Cobar, Mr Jeffery was an alderman, and Captain Dunstan, who was an alderman on Cobar's first Municipal Council, was nominated as mayor, but declined. (Interview with Mr W. Snelson.) Dairy farmer Evan Evans of Dapto worked towards the formation of the Municipality of Central Illawarra, and was elected to represent his district in 1859. (A. Brown, *The Evans family history*, the author, Epping, N.S.W., 1987, p.23.) William James of Shellharbour was an alderman on Shellharbour Council between 1859 and 1888, and mayor in 1870 and 1871. (*Illawarra pioneers: pre 1900*, Illawarra Family History Group Inc., Wollongong, N.S.W., 1988, p.91.) A number of Cornishmen became actively involved in local politics in the Hunter region. For example, William Burnett in Singleton served as an alderman and as mayor. (*Singleton Argus*, 3 February 1916, p.3, c.2.) In Newcastle William Henry Manuell was an alderman and served twice as mayor of Hamilton. (*NMH*, 27 August 1917, p.6, c.7, and *Daily Telegraph*, 10 July 1894, p.5, c.6.) William Lightfoot was one of the first aldermen on Lambton Council. (Information from Mr Daryl Lightfoot.) In 1844 Henry Dangar was elected as Singleton's representative on the newly formed District Council. (E.C. Rowland, 'The life and times of Henry Dangar', in *JRAHS*, vol.XXXIX, 1953, p.70.)

126 George Hawke, *Colonial experience: diary of George Hawke of Orange*, typescript, NLA MS 227, pp.97 and 99.

Other Cornishmen in the Bathurst district had joined George Hawke in supporting the liberal policies of Thomas Mort in his candidacy for the 1856 election.[127]

Augustus Morris was born in Tasmania in 1820, the son of a Cornishman. As an adult he took up property in the Riverina district of New South Wales, and represented Balranald in the New South Wales Legislative Assembly between 1859 and 1865. He was instrumental in T.S. Mort's development of refrigeration techniques for fresh meat.[128] Other Cornishmen, or Australians of Cornish parentage, in the New South Wales Parliament after 1856, included Russell Barton, James Bligh, Henry Cooke, Henry C. Dangar, Otho Dangar, Thomas Dangar, Ernest Durack, John Gale, Nicholas Hawken, William Paul, Jeremiah Brice Rundle, Fergus Jago Smith, John Smith, Harold Stephen, Josiah Thomas, Joseph Wearne, Walter Wearne, Edmund Webb and James Webb.[129]

In northern New South Wales, O.O. Dangar, Australian born brother of Cornishman W.T. Dangar of Kempsey, represented the Hastings and Macleay electorate in the New South Wales Legislative Assembly.[130] William Burnett stood as a Labor candidate but later changed his views.[131] W.H. Manuell of Newcastle made at least two attempts to enter parliament. As a carriage fitter at Redfern Railway Workshops, he was 'dismissed in 1891 for contesting the election at Redfern as one of the freetrade bunch'. In 1894 he stood unsuccessfully as the 'selected freetrade candidate' for the Sydney seat of Darlington.[132]

The Dangar family was involved in colonial politics over a long period. Henry Dangar stood unsuccessfully for the Legislative Council in 1843, then served as member for Northumberland between 1845 and 1851. His son, Henry Cary Dangar, was the member in the Legislative Assembly for West Sydney between 1874-1877, for East Sydney between 1880 and 1882, and was appointed to the Legislative Council in 1883.[133] Henry's brother Thomas Dangar was member for the Upper Hunter in the Legislative Assembly between 1861 and 1864.[134] While visiting his electorate in 1862 he was met:

> with every demonstration of joy and attachment wherever he presents himself. His manly uncompromising straightforwardness and independence of character have tended to give him a lasting home in the hearts of the electors. Friends and foes join in wishing him well.[135]

Jeremiah Brice Rundle, (son of J.B. Rundle who was a partner of R.C. Dangar), was a member of the New South Wales Legislative Council.[136]

In the Cobar district, Russell Barton was the member for Bourke in the New South Wales Legislative Assembly between 1880 and 1886. He was born in Penzance in 1830 and as a child, emigrated to South Australia with his parents. He overlanded cattle for the Burra Burra mine to New South Wales, and eventually settled in western New South Wales as a pastoralist and mining speculator. He was chairman of the Great Cobar Copper Mining Co. in 1883 and became involved in fourteen other mining companies.[137]

---

127 *BFP*, 14 June 1856, p.1, c.1-2. Mort supported immigration, public education through the National system, revision of the judicial system, railways to the interior, and universal suffrage. Members of his committee included Baker, Barratt, Corse, Lane, Glasson, Rowe, Short, Sloggett, Trevarthen, Hawke and Bryant.

128 *AMM*, series 1, vol.2, pp.305-10.

129 See appendix VI.

130 J.H. Watson, 'Kempsey: early settlement of the Macleay River', in *JRAHS*, vol.VII, 1921, part 4, p.208.

131 *Singleton Argus*, 3 February 1916, p.3., c.2.

132 *Daily Telegraph*, 10 July 1894, p.5, c.6.

133 *ADB* 4, p.14.

134 *ADB* 1, p.281.

135 *MM*, 18 February 1862, p.2, c.1.

136 E.M. Dangar, *The Dangars from St Neot, Cornwall*, John Dangar Christian Reid? Sydney, 1966, p.30.

137 C.N. Connolly, *Biographical register of the New South Wales Parliament 1856-1901*, Australian National University Press, Canberra, 1983, pp.16-17.

In Sydney, James Frederick Harvey of Paul, who arrived in New South Wales in 1879, was a member of the Legislative Assembly 1894-1900.[138] Joseph Wearne also became a member of the New South Wales Legislative Assembly, and Walter Ernest Wearne of Bingara was a member of the New South Wales Parliament, and Minister for Lands.[139] Also in Sydney, Nicholas Hawken (born in St. Austell in 1836), held liberal political views, and represented Newtown in the Legislative Assembly from 1887 to 1891. He was defeated 'while defending a great principle, consequently he went down with honour'. His defeat was due to the new Labor Party, and to his disagreement with the pledge of its candidates to be bound by secret caucus decisions, which he believed to be a 'menace to the freedom of representation'. Subsequently, he was nominated as a member of the Legislative Council.[140]

The Cornish who were involved in New South Wales politics generally held the liberal views which predominated in Cornwall and which were also brought with the Cornish to South Australia. Some who were attracted by the aims of the Labor Party supported it in its early days, but were apparently quickly disillusioned by a perceived threat to their religious independence. The Rev E.G. Clancy detailed the strong involvement of New South Wales lay Methodists and clergy in the development of the Labor Party during the early 1890s, and argued that some Methodists turned away from it because of the binding caucus decisions which they believed threatened their religious freedom.[141]

A Cornish coachbuilder, William Vial of Castlereagh Street, was unwittingly involved in colonial politics while part of the crowd observing the Duke of Edinburgh's visit to Clontarf (near Manly) in 1868, when his bravery and quick action saved the prince's life. He 'sprang upon the dastardly assailant, pinioned his arms to his side, and thus the aim of the pistol was diverted'.[142] Later Vial was thanked publicly for his courageous actions, which had 'saved Australasia from the disgrace which would have inevitably attached to it if the act of the assassin had proved fatal'.[143] A reminder of Vial's part in the event was carved on his tombstone at Rookwood cemetery.[144]

Other Cornish Australians in New South Wales made important individual contributions to the community of their adopted country. They were men who excelled in their chosen fields: Lietenant-Colonel Thomas Rowe in architecture, the Rev William Kelynack in religion, the Rev William Curnow in journalism, the Hon. Edmund Webb in commerce, the Hon. John Smith in merino breeding, William Henry Wesley in mining, Henry Dangar in exploration and surveying, Alfred Goninan in engineering, and the Tom brothers in the discovery of payable gold. In politics were Augustus Morris, Russell Barton and Nicholas Hawken, amongst others. Thousands of other Cornish men and women who settled in New South Wales during the nineteenth century became 'good citizens' and although never destined to become rich or famous they contributed in their own way to their adopted country, according to their own talents and interests.

Although its membership was not confined to the Cornish, Methodism was an important facet of their lives which had come with them from the homeland, and which influenced their friendships, marriage and social life in the colony. However, it was a community group, and its members in New South Wales were drawn from various ethnic groups. Through active involvement in Methodism, and then in other community groups as

---

138 Information from Mrs Jean Saunders.
139 V. Wearne-Frost, *Wearne of Cornwall and Australia*. This information is contained in the genealogical charts 1-16 at the end of the book.
140 *AMM*, series 1, vol.2 appendix, p.10. *The Cyclopaedia of New South Wales*, p.82.
141 E.G. Clancy, 'Methodism and the New South Wales Labor Party in the early 1890s', in *Church Heritage*, vol.7, no.1, March 1991, p.26.
142 *SMH*, 13 March 1868, p.5, c.1.
143 *SMH*, 31 March 1868, p.5, c.3.
144 William Vial's tombstone inscription, *Rookwood monumental inscriptions*, Wesleyan cemetery, NLA MCN 781. He died 5 August 1878.

diverse as temperance societies and politics, the Cornish were able to maintain their clannish behaviour which set them apart as Cornish, while at the same time they were able to adapt to become part of the wider New South Wales community.

Anne Colman argued that Cornish membership of such community groups in Victoria was an attempt to achieve respectability. It was much more than this, however. Far from being out of character for these clannish people, it was a clear sign of that clannishness and its adaptation to the new community. The Cornish who were intending to settle permanently in New South Wales wanted to belong to their new community. So they joined community groups where people in the adopted homeland, regardless of their ethnic background, shared their interests. This was merely another form of clustering. Membership of respectable groups was certainly a way to achieve respectability, but such membership was also fulfilling the basic need the Cornish had to group together with people like themselves and which was epitomised by their clannish behaviour. In the wider Australian community they were able to achieve this by joining community groups in which they were interested, and in which they often played a high profile role. In turn this gave them status within the new community and helped them to feel an important and necessary part of it. They were still fulfilling the need to cluster with other Cornish, while being 'good citizens' in the wider community. They were able to belong to both communities successfully, without losing their Cornishness. They showed their feelings of loyalty to their adopted home by joining and working hard in these groups, while still publicly retaining their love for their homeland, and their Cornish identity.

PLATE 46.    Cornish-Australians ...

...... in Australia ....

... and in Cornwall.

# CONCLUSION

There is no doubt that nineteenth century Cornish immigrants clustered in identifiable groups in mining areas in New South Wales, gathering in transplanted Cornish communities as they did in other emigrant destinations throughout the world. It is clear that they clustered in the mining areas of the Bathurst district, in the Hunter region coal mining district, and in the mining communities of Adelong, Cobar and New England. However, they also clustered where mining was not a factor: in Sydney, in coastal New South Wales, and in farming communities in the Bathurst district and in the Hunter hinterland.

The evidence for these conclusions was found in three diverse sources: in published and official records (such as local histories, biographies, birth, death, marriage and shipping records), in family information, and in the name counting of distinctive Cornish names to provide an estimate of the Cornish density in certain localities. All three sources supported the conclusion that the Cornish clustered in certain mining and non-mining areas of New South Wales. As well, they settled in even greater density in pockets within the larger settlement areas, and even within certain sections of the mining townships.

There were several reasons why Cornish immigrants established and maintained these cohesive groups. One was their sense of Cornish identity and their difference from English settlers, which had developed through their separate ethnic background and culture. Centuries of isolation from the rest of Britain had contributed to the survival of the Cornish language and of Cornish customs. The isolation, and the physical formation of Cornwall, along with its traditional occupations of farming, fishing, mining and associated trades, contributed towards the Cornish character. Their Celtic background and culture also helped to mark the Cornish in New South Wales as different from immigrants of other ethnic groups. An outward sign of this difference was the clannishness which typified Cornish immigrants to the colony. Methodism, which was a strong influence on the Cornish throughout the nineteenth century, came with Cornish immigrants to New South Wales.

Apart from their Cornish background and identity, another reason for clustering was the influence of occupations, and in particular of shared job skills in farming, mining and trades. Some Cornish settlers in New South Wales certainly clustered in recognisable and cohesive groups around the mines which supplied their livelihood. There was usually an element of choice available in the selection of the place of settlement even when, as with these miners, occupation was a major determinant. However, many other Cornish immigrants lived and worked in agricultural districts, while others settled in urban and suburban areas. In addition, miners often moved away from mining and into other occupations. Movement of immigrants between Cornish clusters within New South Wales and between other colonies was common, and not confined to any particular occupational group. In the case of Adelong, though, there was a definite Cornish migration to that mining settlement from certain parts of the Victorian goldfields, by individuals who had come from the same part of Cornwall.

The occupation of mining offered independence, and in non-mining areas (and amongst those in the mining areas who were not miners), the occupations chosen were also those which offered independence. Thus Cornish immigrants tended to choose occupations such as farming, or trades where they could be self-employed, as well as positions as storekeepers, hotelkeepers and carriers. Cornish immigrants showed adaptability in their moves across occupations, and often into quite different occupations from those in which they had worked before emigrating.

Specific recruitment of miners, clergymen, servants and farm labourers certainly occurred, but there was little evidence of this happening on a large scale. This is not necessarily because it did not occur, however, and anecdotal evidence suggested that it happened unofficially without being permanently recorded.

Other factors important in Cornish clustering were chain migration and intermarriage. Information, from all three categories of sources used, showed clearly that chain migration and intermarriage within the Cornish community in New South Wales occurred frequently. They occurred amongst all classes of immigrants, and it made little difference whether they were assisted or unassisted passengers, or in which part of the colony they had settled. Chain migration and intermarriage which occurred over several generations provided firm evidence that all Cornish clusters in New South Wales were influenced to some degree by personal choice.

It would be expected that another strong reason for the formation of clusters in New South Wales would be the shared experiences of the long voyage. It is reasonable to assume that such experiences would bond members of an ethnic group, such as the Cornish, who were travelling together to New South Wales. However, evidence of such bonding was anecdotal, and little proof was found of friendships and relationships actually being formed on the voyage. There was certainly evidence that persons travelling on the same ships went to the same settlement areas after arrival, but anecdotal evidence suggests that relationships were cemented rather than formed during the voyage, because many Cornish emigrants already knew, or at least knew of, their fellow travellers before embarkation. Nevertheless, the voyage was the beginning of their new lives in New South Wales, and many Cornish immigrants who travelled together remained friends and neighbours in their adopted country.

This long voyage was common to all nineteenth century immigrants arriving in the colony, and the Cornish used a variety of methods to meet the expenses of the voyage. They came as assisted, unassisted and recruited passengers to New South Wales, or they came through other colonies, sometimes as assisted immigrants.

Assisted immigrants arriving between 1837 and 1877 apparently came from many parts of Cornwall. Their places of birth were spread through their homeland, and do not indicate a migration only from mining areas, or from any particular region. These assisted immigrants made good use of the schemes giving assistance with the passage to New South Wales. Many took advantage of the schemes which were offered, by presenting themselves as possessing the qualities which were preferred in immigrants at a given time. The majority of assisted immigrants were not miners, but those who claimed to be labourers and tradesmen.

Cornish settlers established clannish, self-contained and recognisably Cornish groups in the colony. However, they were quite prepared to accept others into these Cornish groups, as they did in the Bathurst district where intermarriage and friendship occurred with 'accepted' families. This helped in the transition from Cornish immigrant to Cornish-Australian.

As well as all these factors, discussed above, which affected Cornish clustering in the colony, another major reason emerged from this study - that of personal choice. In the non-mining areas, Cornish settlers gathered in the same locality, not because of shared occupations or religions, but simply because they wanted to be with other Cornish settlers. This aspect of choice was also clear in the mining areas, even where occupation *was* a major factor. The Cornish were not dispersed through the general population in the mining towns, but chose to cluster in certain parts, like Cornishtown in Adelong and Hill End, which were named by others who perceived them as a separate group. Even in Cornish Settlement itself, the Cornish miners' camp was separate from the other miners.

Surprisingly, only a minority of assisted immigrants stated they were Methodists, although after arrival many of them were active members of Methodist communities across

New South Wales. Their Methodist faith was a contributing factor to Cornish clannishness, but Methodism in New South Wales consisted of members from various ethnic groups. Membership of the Methodist community in New South Wales was often the first step towards assimilation into the wider community in the colony.

Evidence pointed to a strong Cornish participation in community organisations in New South Wales, as well as in the Methodist church. Anecdotal evidence, for instance, suggested that the liberal political tradition which was obvious amongst the Cornish in South Australia was also present in New South Wales, and there was a small amount of documentary evidence available which supported the view that Cornish immigrants who were involved in unions and politics generally shared a liberal (as distinct from socialist or conservative) viewpoint.

The wide Cornish involvement in community organisations could be seen, on the surface, as being at odds with their strong need to cluster throughout New South Wales, in groups whose Cornishness was their common bond. In fact, this was merely another form of clustering, adapted to the new environment. It was a continuation, into the wider New South Wales community, of the clannish behaviour which marked them as Cornish. In fact they were able to be part of both communities very successfully, becoming part of their adopted country without losing their Cornish identity.

Cornish immigrants showed their intention of permanent settlement, and their feelings of responsibility towards their adopted home, in their vigorous participation in these community groups. They were able to do this without losing, or disguising, their love and respect for their homeland. These deep feelings were permanently and publicly declared in the simple phrase 'native of Cornwall' which was inscribed on so many of their tombstones in New South Wales, half a world away from their homeland.

## PLATE 47.    Landscapes: Cornwall and New South Wales

Contrasting views: Cornish Settlement in New South Wales and the Camborne-Redruth mining area of Cornwall.

# APPENDIX I
## METHODOLOGY

This exploration of Cornish settlement patterns was never intended to be an intensive demographic study, because statistical evidence of Cornish immigration and settlement in New South Wales is very patchy and often non-existent. The reason for this scarcity is that Cornish immigrants were included in English statistics. Cornish-born settlers can be identified with certainty only when birthplace was required in official records, or was provided gratuitously in obituaries or in newspaper notices or elsewhere, or has been traced by Cornish Australians. One official source which consistently supplied the country or county of birth was the Archives Office of New South Wales shipping lists for assisted immigrants arriving in New South Wales. These often gave specific birthplaces in Cornwall, as well as the county name.

I began by searching the arrivals of assisted immigrants between 1837 and 1877 and found 3898 persons who stated they had been born in Cornwall, or who were travelling in a family group with someone who had been born in Cornwall. These immigrants were asked about their relatives already in the colony and their answers suggested definite areas of Cornish settlement. I entered details of each immigrant on a data base which was sorted on each of the answers which individuals had given to immigration officials.

Next, I wrote to the Cornish Associations in Australia and New Zealand, to Australian genealogical and family history societies, and to historical societies in each of the settlement areas. I asked these associations to publish my interest in their journals and newsletters. Similar contact was made with the Cornwall Family History Society, and I phoned or wrote to libraries and archives in the settlement areas, and many of them publicised my request for information. Subsequently, many people willingly shared the results of their own research and I have often been able to reciprocate with information or contacts. Only one reply indicated an unmistakeable lack of interest: one gentleman (the bearer of a distinctively Cornish name) wrote, 'My grandfather was Irish, my grandmother was Scottish and I am a dinkum Aussie. Thank you'.

I researched each area of settlement separately, and although the general approach was similar, modifications were needed in each area because of the different records and facilities available. It soon became evident though, that those of the 3898 assisted immigrants able to be traced were only a minority of the total Cornish in these settlement areas.

Apart from using diaries, letters and biographies of known Cornish immigrants, the basic method used in each settlement area was to make initial contact with the historical and/or family history society and the library, and then to visit that area. In each area I spent time reading any local newspapers which were not held at the National Library of Australia, and looking through locally-held cemetery transcriptions, to find those which recorded individuals as having been born in Cornwall. Cemetery transcriptions (held in local and also in centralised repositories) for those born in Cornwall were followed to death and funeral notices in the newspapers, and to obituaries where these existed.

In all settlement areas I was very fortunate to have personal contact with local people who were interested in my research and who were most helpful. In Cobar and in Adelong, with the help of local historical societies, I gained access to the Clerk of Petty Sessions civil registers. In other areas I had to rely on marriage records held by the Uniting Church Archives, and on copies of church marriage registers microfilmed by the Society of Australian Genealogists and held in the National Library of Australia. Marriage registers after 1856 should show place of birth, residence, parentage and occupation of both parties but few clergymen bothered to record exact birthplaces until the mid-1870s and merely wrote 'Australia' or 'New South Wales', 'England', 'Ireland', 'America' and so on. Thus, proof of several generations of Cornish-born immigrants marrying in New South Wales before the 1870s was often lost because they were included with the English. Although the registers examined were church registers, the references to those included in the text of the book are given their civil registration numbers because these appear in the New South Wales Registrar General's Index to Births, Deaths and Marriages and this index is widely available on microfiche.

Research in the settlement areas did not give an indication of the numbers of Cornish amongst the total population in each area. The system of counting distinctive Cornish names, compiled by Dr C.A. Price, provided a method of estimating their density in each region. This method is explained in appendix III and the results of the name counts of distinctive Cornish names are included there.

Explanatory tables were compiled when other statistics were available, such as those from my Sydney data base, and from the Clerk of Petty Sessions registers at Adelong and Cobar, but there is no claim that these represent all Cornish immigrants.

A computerised index to nineteenth century Bathurst newspapers has been compiled, and a printout copy is held in the National Library. Unfortunately not all the Bathurst newspapers are held there, and at the time of research some were available only at Bathurst Historical Society. Bathurst Historical Society and Bathurst Family History Society have comprehensive card indexes which I searched for Cornish entries, and I wrote to individuals who had expressed an interest in finding information on a Cornish person. The Orange Historical Society and the Orange City Library have local history collections. Nineteenth century Orange newspapers were destroyed by floods early this century, but the *Central Western Daily* newspaper had run regular articles on personalities and places of historical interest, and these were on file at the Orange Historical Society.

In Sydney, I began with the Archives Office of New South Wales shipping lists, using the names of relatives or prospective employers, given by assisted Cornish immigrants (1837-1877) at the Immigration Board examinations on arrival. Sometimes a suburb was given, sometimes a particular street, sometimes merely 'Sydney'. These relatives may not have been Cornish, but the fact that their names were given as relatives suggests that they were part of the Cornish community in the colony. Sometimes disposal information noted the address of the employer, (who was not necessarily Cornish), which would be the future residence of the Cornish servant.

The Sydney marriage registers examined were the Church of England, Methodist, Congregational and Presbyterian records held at the National Library of Australia on microfilm, and the remaining original Methodist registers at the Archives Office of New South Wales and the Uniting Church Archives. Time constraints prevented me from examining Catholic registers, as experience has shown that the few Cornish entries located in Catholic records do not repay the time spent searching. By comparing details of place and date of birth, and parents' names, on the marriage certificates with similar information given by assisted immigrants on arrival, sometimes it was possible to match these up, to establish the whereabouts of assisted immigrants in Sydney, and sometimes to follow them from arrival to death many years later.

Next I searched microfiche cemetery transcriptions of Sydney's Camperdown and Rookwood cemeteries, reading every Protestant demominational transcript to locate those showing natives of Cornwall. Then I searched the transcriptions of other Sydney cemeteries held at the Society of Australian Genealogists. Here I was permitted to examine the transcribers' unchecked sheets for Waverley cemetery. (Unfortunately the transcribing of the huge Field of Mars cemetery at Ryde was still in progress at the time of research and unavailable to me.) The dates of death of these Cornish people, and sometimes of their families, were used to find *Sydney Morning Herald* death or funeral notices, which often gave the deceased person's address and relatives, and occasionally gave an occupation, or the name of a lodge or friendly society to which the deceased had belonged. Although I used the arbitrary cut-off point of 1900 in marriage searches,[1] I attempted to follow the names of all Cornish located in cemetery transcriptions, as those born in Cornwall before 1877 may well have lived until the 1930s or even later.

Finally, I attempted to locate and follow all the known Cornish in *Sands Sydney directory* between 1858 and 1898. Again, time constraints prevented any attempt to check through every year. I examined 1858/9, 1861, 1863, 1866, 1869, 1873, 1877, 1882, 1886, 1892 and 1898. This was sufficient to locate those who remained in Sydney, and also to note long-term moves within or between suburbs. This method might not have picked up the short-term relocations, or those who were temporary residents of Sydney. Multiple-entry names like Williams and Thomas were discarded when it was unclear which were the Cornish ones. More straightforward methods of locating the Sydney (and other) Cornish, were publications such as *Australian Men of Mark*,[2] and through information supplied about Cornish settlers by their descendants.

The information obtained from all these sources was entered on a Sydney data base, with separate fields for each column on the marriage certificate, and also details of arrival in the colony. Although the data base contained 1875 entries, some individuals have only one entry, while others may have several: arrival, marriage, directory entries, death and funeral notices.

In the Methodist marriage registers for the Cobar district (1880-1902) in the Uniting Church Archives, I found records of the marriages of 31 Cornish persons, which indicated the possibility of a cluster there late in the century. After contacting Cobar Historical Society, I visited Cobar, interviewed local people and examined the Clerk of Petty Sessions registers for the years between 1880 and 1907. The information extracted from these registers has been used only to compile statistics and not to identify any individual.

Adelong Methodist marriage registers at the Uniting Church Archives and the Church of England registers on microfilm in the National Library of Australia were examined. Through initial contact with the Tumut Family History Group, meetings with local residents were arranged and permission was gained for me to examine the civil birth, death and marriage records at Tumut. The registers held at Tumut were for Tumut (including Adelong) from 1856, and for Adelong separately from 1872. I had hoped to take advantage of the rare opportunity to examine the civil registers at Adelong and to use the civil marriage registers there (which included marriages of all denominations) to compare Adelong marriages with those in Sydney, and to make a comparison of the numbers marrying in each denomination in Adelong. Unfortunately, the Adelong official had, inexplicably, ignored the columns for place of birth of the parties at marriages until the late 1890s, so it was not possible. Some comparison could be made, though, by using Church marriage registers and also the civil birth registers, because the birthplaces of both parents and their date and place of marriage were recorded on the birth registrations of their Adelong-born children.

Names of Cornish-born persons in Adelong are used in the text, but only where the information has been obtained from published or archival sources, from descendants, from Tumut Family History Group files, or from church marriage registers. The birth, death and marriage registrations have been used only to compile non-identifying statistical information, and not to identify individuals.

I made a brief visit to Glen Innes, Deepwater, Torrington and Emmaville, which included a tour of these mining districts, discussions with residents and a visit to Glen Innes Historical Society library and archives.

---

1   If the marriage register volume continued to 1903, for example, Cornish marriages found there were recorded.
2   There was a complication using this publication, because it appears to consist of two volumes, but there are several quite different 'volume 2' volumes. Some of the 'volume 2' publications have appendices which consist of short biographical entries. There is no way of distinguishing any one of these from the others, except by the contents. The volumes in the ML are arranged as series 1, series 2 and series 3. The volumes in NLA appear to be the same as the ML series 1. The 'volume 2' in the Newcastle Region Public Library appears to be different from any of the 'volume 2' publications in the ML.

During my research, I compiled three data bases: the emigrant file, the Adelong file and the Sydney file. All other entries were kept in a biographical and a geographical card index and each entry was duplicated so persons could be found under their names or their place of residence. This was a more useful system than having one overall data base. It had the advantage that sections of it could be taken to libraries or to settlement areas when required, and could be added to continually without new, lengthy printouts being required.

No attempt was made to document or even to locate every Cornish person who came to nineteenth century New South Wales. Theoretically, this would have been possible if I had been allowed access to the New South Wales Registrar General's birth, death and marriage registers, because from 1856 onwards death certificates showed place of birth and marriage, place of residence and the residence in colonies other than New South Wales. Birth and marriage registers give further information.

No attempt was made to detail immigration regulations and procedures. They are referred to only where relevant to the arrival and settlement of the assisted Cornish immigrant component.

Fascinating as they are in their own right, there was no attempt to produce local or family histories of the areas of Cornish settlement. On occasion both are relevant to the Cornish clusters and are mentioned in this context.

Broken Hill was a definite cluster in New South Wales, but I did not attempt to include it because it was more correctly an extension of the South Australian copper triangle and has been thoroughly covered by Dr Philip Payton as part of his research on the Cornish in South Australia.

Several factors influenced the methods used in my research. First was the constant problem of finding satisfactory proof of Cornish birth or descent. Lack of access to the Registrar General's centralised records made such identification unnecessarily and frustratingly difficult. Even when individuals had typically Cornish names, this was proof only of probable Cornish descent. Dr Price's system, of estimating the percentage of persons of Cornish descent in the population, assisted in overcoming this difficulty.

Another associated frustration, with Church marriage records, was the clergy's habit of leaving blank the column for place of birth of parties to a marriage, or of writing merely 'England' or 'New South Wales', with no other details. This meant that many marriages of Cornish individuals were never found. A similar problem was that some biographical publications gave only 'England' as a place of birth, and Cornish ethnicity was thus disguised. As well, there was no way of proving the Cornish descent of Cornish-Australians unless it was stated, or found through the research of their descendants.

# APPENDIX II

## TABLES

Tables in this appendix are not numbered according to the chapter in which reference is made to them. This is because reference to some tables is made in more than one chapter. Consequently, they are organised according to arrival and then setlement areas and are numbered accordingly. Percentages in all tables have been rounded.

### TABLE 2.1

| CORNISH ASSISTED IMMIGRANTS TO NEW SOUTH WALES 1837-1877. | | |
|---|---|---|
| 1837-1851 | 1122 | 29% |
| 1852-1859 | 1648 | 42% |
| 1860-1877 | 1128 | 29% |
| Total immigrants | 3898 | |

### TABLE 2.2

| AGES OF CORNISH ASSISTED IMMIGRANTS TO NSW 1837-1877 | | |
|---|---|---|
| under 12 | 1149 | 29% |
| 13-17 | 265 | 7% |
| 18-29 | 1685 | 43% |
| 30-39 | 530 | 14% |
| 40-49 | 168 | 4% |
| 50-59 | 34 | 3% |
| 60-70 | 17 | |
| No age given | 50 | |
| TOTAL | 3898 | 100% |

Note that 97% were under 50 years of age and 79% were under 30 years of age.

### TABLE 2.3

| ASSISTED CORNISH FAMILY GROUPINGS 1837-1877. | | | | | |
|---|---|---|---|---|---|
| Years | Total numbers | Adults with children | Single females | Single males | Married couples (no children) |
| 1837-51 | 1122 | 78% | 5% | 8% | 9% |
| 1852-59 | 1648 | 54% | 5% | 27% | 14% |
| 1860-77 | 1128 | 64% | 8% | 17% | 11% |
| TOTAL | 3898 | | | | |

### TABLE 2.4

| STATED OCCUPATIONS OF CORNISH ASSISTED IMMIGRANTS 1837-1877. | |
|---|---|
| Farm labourer | 535 |
| Labourer | 220 |
| Trades | 436 |
| Miner | 413 |
| Women | (had occupations recorded) 630 |
| TOTAL | 2234 |

**TABLE 2.5**

| STATED OCCUPATIONS: CORNISH ASSISTED WOMEN IMMIGRANTS 1837-1877. | |
|---|---|
| Domestic servants | 282 |
| Trained occupations* | 135 |
| Skilled domestics** | 91 |
| Farm servants | 71 |
| Unpaid occupations | 43 |
| Mine work | 8 |
| TOTAL | 630 |

\* Trained occupations were tailoress, teacher, safety fuse maker, milliner, and weaver.
\*\* Skilled domestics were those doing specfic domestic work (cook, housekeeper, laundress, parlourmaid or nursemaid.)

**TABLE 2.6**

| STATED RELIGIONS OF CORNISH ASSISTED IMMIGRANTS 1837-1877. | |
|---|---|
| Church of England | 2297 |
| Methodist denominations | 1103 |
| Protestant | 253 |
| Roman Catholic | (mostly children born in Cornwall but of Irish parentage.) 61 |
| Baptist | 48 |
| Episcopalian | 45 |
| None stated | (mostly children) 43 |
| Independent | 17 |
| Dissenter | 10 |
| Presbyterian | 7 |
| Other Protestant | 6 |
| Congregational | 5 |
| Church of Scotland | 1 |
| Jewish | 1 |
| Non-conformist | 1 |
| TOTAL | 3898 |

**TABLE 2.7**

| STATED METHODIST DENOMINATIONS: CORNISH ASSISTED IMMIGRANTS 1837-1877 | |
|---|---|
| Wesleyan | 958 |
| Methodist | 109 |
| Bible Christian | 16 |
| Primitive Methodist | 14 |
| Free Church | 6 |
| TOTAL METHODIST | 1103 |
| | |
| TOTAL IMMIGRANTS | 3898 |

**TABLE 2.8**

## SUBURBAN CORNISH COMMUNITY IN SYDNEY
## TOTAL SUBURBAN NUMBERS WERE 881

| | | |
|---|---|---|
| Surry Hills | 114 | |
| Woolloomooloo | 71 | |
| Darlinghurst | 33 | |
| Total | 218 | 25% |
| | | |
| Redfern | 56 | |
| Newtown | 46 | |
| Chippendale | 23 | |
| Waterloo | 20 | |
| Darlington | 18 | |
| Alexandria | 8 | |
| Total | 171 | 19% |
| | | |
| Balmain | 40 | |
| Glebe | 42 | |
| Pyrmont/Darling Harbour | 32 | |
| Forest Lodge | 14 | |
| Ultimo | 6 | |
| Annandale | 5 | |
| Total | 139 | 16% |
| | | |
| Petersham | 36 | |
| Burwood | 22 | |
| Leichhardt | 14 | |
| Marrickville | 13 | |
| Ashfield | 12 | |
| Strathfield | 5 | |
| Dulwich Hill | 4 | |
| Stanmore | 3 | |
| Summer Hill | 3 | |
| Total | 112 | 13% |
| | | |
| Paddington | 55 | |
| Woollahra | 20 | |
| Waverley | 20 | |
| Total | 95 | 11% |
| | | |
| North Shore | 55 | |
| Parramatta/Ryde | 38 | |
| Botany | 27 | |
| Total | 120 | |
| Total: | 855 | |

North Shore entries include North Sydney, Willoughby, Millers Point, Chatswood, Eastwood, Gladesville, Gordon, Lindfield, St Ives, Manly, Middle Harbour. The remaining suburban residents lived in Alexandria, Annandale, Arncliffe, Auburn, Belmore, Bexley, Bankstown, Concord, Camperdown, Croydon, Canterbury, Cooks River, Double Bay, Dulwich Hill, Darling Point, Drummoyne, Enfield, Enmore, Fivedock, Granville, Homebush, Hurstville, Kogarah, Liverpool, McDonaldtown, Rushcutters Bay, Randwick, Stanmore, St George, St Peters, Strathfield, Summer Hill, Tempe, Ultimo.

Evidence of the residences chosen by Cornish immigrants was compiled from information gathered from many sources. An explanation of the methodology is given in the methodolody appendix. The 1875 entries on the data base was sorted by locality but those entries which stated only 'Sydney' were excluded, as were those which were burial entries for Sydney cemeteries. Entries which were obviously the same person at the same address in different years were counted as one only, while entries for the same person moving within the same suburb or to another suburb were counted as separate entries. The 1053 entries remaining comprised 172 or 16% within the city of Sydney, and 881 or 84% in the suburbs. The early suburbs such as Surry Hills, Woolloomooloo, Darlinghurst, Redfern, Chippendale were included in the suburban count.

**TABLE 2.9**

| CORNISH SUBURBAN GROUPINGS | | | |
|---|---|---|---|
| **DISTRICT** | **SUBURBS** | **CORNISH** | |
| North-west | Balmain, Leichhardt, Glebe. | 90 | 16% |
| West-central | Newtown, St Peters, Camperdown, MacDonaldtown. | 65 | 12% |
| East central | Redfern, Darlington, Waterloo, Botany, North Botany, Alexandria. | 129 | 23% |
| West | Ashfield, Burwood, Concord, Enfield, Fivedock, Drummoyne, Marrickville, Petersham, Strathfield. | 100 | 18% |
| South | Canterbury, Hurstville, Kogarah, Rockdale. | 8 | 1% |
| East | Paddington, Woollahra, Randwick, Waverley. | 99 | 18% |
| North Shore | North Sydney, Willoughby, Manly, Ryde, Hunter's Hill. | 62 | 11% |
| **Total entries** | | **553** | |

The number in this example decreased to 553 entries because Kelly's division of suburbs excluded some inner suburbs as part of the city of Sydney.

**TABLE 2.10**

| CORNISH OCCUPATIONS ACCORDING TO SYDNEY SUBURBS | |
|---|---|
| ALEXANDRIA | cooper, builder. |
| ANNANDALE | miner, carpenter, joiner. |
| ARNCLIFFE | stonemason, tailor. |
| ASHFIELD | storeman, bookseller, grocer, nurseryman, fancy goods store. |
| AUBURN | carpenter |
| BALMAIN | draper, builder, clerk, engineer, grocer, mariner, stone mason, master mariner, shipwright. |
| BANKSIA | tailor. |
| BOTANY | florist, market gardener, dairyman. |
| BURWOOD | farrier, groom, miner, grocer, domestic servant, auctioneer, headmistress. |
| CHIPPENDALE | carpenter, engineer, coachbuilder, domestic servant, quarryman, laundress, brickmaker. |
| CONCORD | farm labourer. |
| COOKS RIVER | grocer, builder. |
| CROYDON | miller, grocer. |
| DARLING HARBOUR | miner. |
| DARLINGHURST | druggist, military officer, blacksmith, storekeeper, grocer, builder, architect, commercial traveller, carpenter, produce dealer, stonemason, Wesleyan minister, tailor, caneworker, banker, miner. |

| DARLING POINT | surveyor, grazier, architect, President of Water & Sewage Board. |
|---|---|
| DARLINGTON | fireman, builder, grocer, commission agent, cooper, carpenter, carriage fitter, signwriter. |
| DOUBLE BAY | servant. |
| DULWICH HILL | hospital superintendent, domestic duties, chemist. |
| ENFIELD | quarry labourer. |
| ENMORE | plasterer, solicitor. |
| FIVEDOCK | butcher, solicitor, surgeon. |
| FOREST LODGE | clerk, butcher, labourer |
| GLADESVILLE | warder in asylum. |
| GLEBE | private life, provision agent, civil servant, coachbuilder, mason, blacksmith, engineer, Newcastle Steamship Co., living with mother, bricklayer, builder, dyer, photographer, clerk, miner, plasterer, ironmonger, traveller, produce merchant, milk carter, housemaid, cook & laundress. |
| HURSTVILLE | mason. |
| KOGARAH | cooper, warehouseman, farmer, clerk. |
| LEICHHARDT | nurseryman, galvanizer, private life, banker, chemist. |
| LEWISHAM | builder. |
| LIVERPOOL | miller, hotelkeeper, railway porter, butcher. |
| McDONALDTOWN | bricklayer, carpenter, brickmaker, cordial manufacturer, baker. |
| MARRICKVILLE | laundress, laundry proprietor, manager, plasterer, captain. |
| MERRYLANDS | brickmaker. |
| MOORE PARK | private life, iron fitter. |
| NEWTOWN | builder, accounts clerk, domestic servant, labourer, cordial manufacturer, domestic, labourer, constable, editor, engineer, miner, civil engineer, superintendent, brick manufacturer, carpenter, tannery proprietor, private life, carpenter, builder, cooper, painter. |
| NORTH SHORE | coalminer, architect, dressmaker, builder, farmer, puntman, merchant, clerk, saddlers' ironmongery, warehouseman, captain, carrier, storekeeper, miller, accountant, stationer/tobacconist. |
| PADDINGTON | carpenter, engineer, coachpainter, private life, labourer, mine manager contractor, coachbuilder, bootmaker, commission agent, stonemason, plumber, accountant, painter/glazier, oil/colourman, fruiterer, builder, captain, mason, at home, compositor. |
| PARRAMATTA | grocer, plasterer, miner, draper, miller, stonemason, labourer, engineer, dressmaker, watchmaker, mine captain, nurseryman, fruitgrower, cooper, orchardist, accountant, master mariner, boatman, lighterman. |
| PETERSHAM | stonemason/builder, cab proprietor, schoolmistress, mason, carpenter, |

| | |
|---|---|
| | builder, housemaid, timber merchant, builder, ironfounder. |
| POTTS POINT | boat proprietor, architect. |
| PYRMONT | householder, labourer, sailmaker, cab proprietor, stonemason, boatbuilder, publican, ballastman, home duties, mason, shipwright, draper, smith, coppersmith, storekeeper, warehouseman. |
| RANDWICK | domestic servant. |
| REDFERN | clerk, baker, carpenter, clicker, farrier, machinist, dray proprietor, engineer, stonemason, wood & coal merchant, blacksmith, fruiterer, confectioner, ovenmaker, cabinetmaker, butcher, restauranteur, dyer, mariner, baker, grocer, auctioneer, dressmaker, bootmaker, hairdresser, builder, engine driver. |
| ROCKDALE | quarryman. |
| RUSHCUTTERS BY | greengrocer, builder. |
| ST PETERS | brick manager, builder, drainer, moulder. |
| STANMORE | captain. |
| STRATHFIELD | carpenter, gardener. |
| SUMMER HILL | saleswoman, salesman. |
| SURRY HILLS | stonecutter, foreman, storekeeper, at home, builder, blacksmith, domestic duties, assayer, plasterer, labourer, miner, blacksmith, mason, stonemason, M.B., cabinetmaker, cab driver, clerk, dressmaker, publican, grocer, collector, warehouseman, labourer, general house servant, cook, plasterer, engine driver, gardener, laundress, bootmaker, shingler, slater, fuel dealer, contractor, pawnbroker, dealer, cabinetmaker, woodcarver, coachbuilder, miller, brickmaker. |
| ULTIMO | bootmaker, coachbuilder. |
| WATERLOO | miner, private life, carpenter, cooper, engineer. |
| WAVERLEY | gentleman's servant, mason, miner, constable, CE minister, clerk, mason, carpenter, builder, monumental mason, builder, storekeeper. |
| WOOLLAHRA | dressmaker, metropolitan transport commission, gardener, stonemason, cab proprietor, fire chief, confectioner, toll keeper, grocer, greengrocer, coachbuilder. |
| WOOLLOOMOOLOO | stonemason, builder, fish trade, dyer, printer, bootmaker, builder, carpenter, plasterer, dealer, joiner, housekeeper, cabinetmaker, mine manager, commission agent, ironmonger, dairy proprietor, miner, joiner, general servant, HM Customs officer, shoemaker, publican, builder, cane worker, housemaid, decorator, painter, housemaid, bricklayer, blacksmith. |

Those in the city of Sydney, and those in unpaid occupations were not included.

## TABLE 2.11

### RANKED OCCUPATIONS OF CORNISH IMMIGRANTS IN SYDNEY.

| RANK 1 | 7% of total |
|---|---|

accountant, architect, assayer, banker, brick manager, captain, chemist, civil engineer, dentist, druggist, editor Sydney Morning Herald, gentleman, grazier, lady, M.B., M.D. merchant, military officer, minister C of E, minister Wesleyan, mine captain/manager(5), mining engineer, master mariner, naval officer, President of Water & Sewage Board, schoolmaster, solicitor, superintendent of dockyard, superintendent of hospital, surgeon, surveyor, tannery proprietor, teacher.

| RANK 2 | 22% of total |
|---|---|

builder & stonemason, boat proprietor, bookseller, builder(39), butcher(7) cab proprietor, civil servant, clerk(11), commission agent, confectioner, contractor, draper(6), dray proprietor, estate agent, fancy goods store, farrier, fire chief, fish trade, foreman, Darling Harbour, fruiterer, fuel dealer, furniture warehouse, general dealer, greengrocer, grocer(21), hay & corn store proprietor, Her Majesty's Customs, hotel keeper(5), ironmonger, laundry proprietor, market gardener, Newcastle Steamship Co., nurseryman, ovenmakers, pawnbroker, photographer, produce dealer/merchant(5), proprietor of bonded stores, provision agent, publican(6), railway foreman, restauranteur, saddlers' ironmonger, salesman, saleswoman, stationer & tobacconist, storekeeper(9), timber merchant, tobacconist, wholesale fruiterer, wood & coal merchant.

| RANK 3 | 40% of total |
|---|---|

baker(5), blacksmith(20), boatbuilder, bootmaker(11), brewer & cooper, bricklayer, brickmaker, boot & shoemaker, cabinetmaker(20), carpenter(47), carriage fitter, coachbuilder(12), coachbuilder & wheelwright, coachmaker, coachpainter, coalminer, compositor, constable, cooper(7), coppersmith, cordial manufacturer, dyer, engine driver, engineer(11), iron fitter, ironfounder, jeweller, joiner, mason(19), miller(7), milliner, miner(45), moulder, Oil & colourman, painter(11), painter & glazier, patternmaker, plasterer/plaister(10), police constable, policeman, printer, sailmaker, shingler, shipwright, shoemaker, signwriter, silver smelter, slater and shingler, smith, stonemason(30), tailor(5), tailoress, tanner, upholsterer, vocalist, watchmaker, whitesmith, wheelwright, wheelwright & blacksmith, woodcarver.

| RANK 4 | 22% of total |
|---|---|

ballastman, boatman, cab driver, cane worker, caretaker, carrier, collector, commercial traveller, cook, cook & laundress, cook & steward, decorator, drainer, dressmaker(15), domestic, domestic servant(10), drainer, ferryman, fireman, florist, footman, gardener(7), furniture warehouseman, galvaniser, garden labourer, general house servant(5), general servant, gentleman's servant, groom, groom & coachman, hairdresser, housekeeper(8), housemaid(12), house servant(8), labourer(46), laundress, lighterman, machinist, mariner, Metropolitan Transport Commission employee, milk carter, needlewoman, nursemaid, postal department, puntman, quarry labourer, quarryman, railway employee, railway porter, sawyer, seaman, servant(5), stoker, stonecutter, storeman, tollkeeper, traveller, vanman, warder in asylum, warehouseman(5).

| RANK 5 | 9% of total |
|---|---|

agricultural labourer(10), farm house servant, farm labourer(46), farm servant, farm & wharf labourer, farmer(8), fruit grower, herdsman, orchardist, selector.

| OTHER | not included in total |
|---|---|

at home(6), home duties, householder, living with mother, none(44), private life(12), schoolgirl, widow.

| | |
|---|---|
| Total occupations | 223 |
| Total entries | 909 |
| Minus OTHER (74) | 835 |

| | |
|---|---|
| Rank 1 | 7% |
| Rank 2 | 22% |
| Rank 3 | 40% |
| Rank 4 | 22% |
| Rank 5 | 9% |

NOTES ON TABLE 2.11

To establish occupational classification of the Sydney Cornish, information on the occupations of individuals in the city and the suburbs on the data base was sorted. Entries which were obviously the same person, in the same occupation, at the same address in different years were counted as one. Entries were counted separately where the person changed occupation, or remained in the same occupation and changed the place of residence.

Shirley Fitzgerald has classified the occupations of Sydney residents into five categories, and for convenience I have adopted her classifications.[1] Rank 1 consisted of professional, semi-professional and some commercial occupations. Rank 2 included other white-collar workers and also persons such as market-gardeners who owned property. Rank 3 consisted of all skilled workers. Rank 4 included the semi-skilled and unskilled occupations. Rank 5 included all non-urban workers. Although Cornish miners had no formal apprenticeship, they were highly skilled and were recognised for their expertise throughout the world, so I have classified them as Rank 3, amongst tradesmen and other skilled workers. Tradesmen have been allocated to Rank 3. If they had operated their own businesses they should be classified as Rank 2, but generally this could not be established with certainty. This was the case for other occupations as well, for example, the puntman would be in one category if he had been merely an employee, and in another if he had been the proprietor. Where an occupation had five or more entries, the number of entries is beside it in brackets.

## TABLE 2.12

| BIRTHPLACES OF SPOUSE OF CORNISH PARTNER | | | | | | | | |
|---|---|---|---|---|---|---|---|---|
| **SPOUSE** | **Cornish Partner** | | | | | | | |
| **BIRTHPLACE** | **Bachelors** | | **Widowers** | | **Spinsters** | | **Widows** | |
| Other Australian colonies | 14 | 9% | 5 | 16% | 1 | 1% | 2 | 10% |
| New Zealand | 5 | 3% | - | - | - | - | - | - |
| Ireland | 8 | 5% | 3 | 9% | 1 | 1% | - | - |
| London | 5 | 3% | 1 | 3% | 5 | 7% | 1 | 5% |
| England | 10 | 6% | 7 | 22% | 19 | 25% | 4 | 20% |
| Channel Is & Isle of Man | 2 | 1% | - | - | - | - | 2 | 10% |
| Wales | 1 | 0.5% | - | - | 2 | 3% | - | - |
| Scotland | 2 | 1% | 1 | 3% | 1 | 1% | - | - |
| Europe | 1 | 0.5% | - | - | 1 | 1% | 1 | 5% |
| At sea | - | - | - | - | - | - | 1 | 5% |
| Not stated | 3 | 2% | - | - | 2 | 3% | - | - |
| Devon | 3 | 2% | - | - | 1 | 1% | 1 | 5% |
| NSW | 77 | 49% | 12 | 38% | 19 | 25% | 3 | 15% |
| Cornwall | 26 | 17% | 3 | 9% | 24 | 32% | 5 | 25% |
| | | | | | | | | |
| TOTALS | 157 | 100% | 32 | 100% | 76 | 100% | 20 | 100% |
| TOTAL CORNISH MALES | | | | | | | | 189 |
| TOTAL CORNISH FEMALES | | | | | | | | 96 |

NOTE

Twenty six (17%) of the Cornish bachelors married spouses also born in Cornwall. Three (9%) of the Cornish widowers, 24 (32%) of the Cornish spinsters and five (25%) of the Cornish widows chose spouses also born in Cornwall. On a total of 285 occasions, one partner was born in Cornwall. However, since sometimes both partners were born in Cornwall, this does not represent 285 marriages.

---

1    S. Fitzgerald, *Rising damp:Sydney 1879-90*, Oxford University Press, Melbourne, 1987, p.117.

**TABLE 2.13**

| STATED OCCUPATIONS: CORNISH MARRIAGES, SYDNEY | | | |
|---|---|---|---|
| **Occupation** | **Occupation of Father** | **Occupation of Spouse** | **Occupation of Spouse's Father.** |
| Bricklayer | Miner | None | Gardener |
| Cab driver | Labourer | At home | Sawyer |
| Carpenter | Builder | Domestic Servant | Builder |
| Contractor | Mine Manager | None | Farmer |
| Dentist | Doctor | Private Life | Accountant |
| Engineer | Engineer | Private Life | Engineer |
| Farrier | Farmer | Private Life | Bootmaker |
| Gardener | Bootmaker | Domestic | Labourer |
| Labourer | Foreman of Works | Cook | Carpenter |
| Mariner | Tailor | Dressmaker | Publican |
| Miller | Miller | None | Farmer |
| Miner | Miner | None | Farmer |
| Plasterer | Plasterer | None | Plasterer |
| Police Constable | Cabinetmaker | None | Bus Proprietor |
| Salesman | Builder | Private Life | Bootmaker |
| Schoolmaster | Minister | Governess | Builder |
| Stonemason | Stonemason | At home | Sawyer |
| Timber merch | Builder | None | Contractor |
| Tobacconist | Stock dealer | None | Grocer |
| Warehouseman | Carrier | Music teacher | Tanner |

This random sample was selected from male spouses only, because the majority of females had no occupation given.

**TABLE 2.14**

| RELIGIONS: CORNISH MARRIAGES, SYDNEY | | |
|---|---|---|
| Methodist | 112 | 47% |
| CE | 95 | 40% |
| Presbyterian | 20 | 8% |
| Congregaional | 11 | 5% |
| | | |
| TOTALS | 238 | 100% |

NOTE
Sorting on the Sydney data base on the marriage field produced 285 occasions between 1856 and 1900 where one partner was born in Cornwall. On 235 occasions the resicence of the Cornish partner was given as Sydney. Residences in New South Wales but outside Sydney were: Adelong, Barraba, Bathurst, Bingara, Blayney, Byng, Cobar, Coonabarabran, Cootamundra, Dapto, Dungog, Forbes, Goulburn, Harden, Hill End, Junee, Liverpool Plains, Muswellbrook, Newcastle, Nymagee, Richmond River, Robertson. Sofala, Shoalhaven, Tambaroora, Tamworth and Temora. Queensland entries were Brisbane, Charters Towers, Mackay and Warwick.

It should be remembered that these statistics are for the religion in which the ceremony was performed and not necessarily the religion of both partners.

**TABLE 2.15**

| BIRTHS TO CORNISH PARENTS IN ADELONG | |
|---|---|
| **Year** | **Births to Cornish parents of total births** |
| 1873 | 12% |
| 1874 | 20% |
| 1875 | 13% |
| 1876 | 18% |
| 1877 | 13% |
| 1878 | 18% |
| 1879 | 17% |
| 1880 | 19% |
| 1881 | 17% |
| 1882 | 10% |
| 1883 | 9% |
| 1884 | 13% |
| 1885 | 10% |
| 1886 | 6% |
| 1887 | 6% |
| 1888 | 9% |

NOTE
Total births to Cornish parents between 1856 and 1888 were 277. Of these, 33 were in the Tumut register before the Adelong register began.

**TABLE 2.16**

| CAUSES OF CORNISH DEATHS IN ADELONG 1856-1905. | | | | |
|---|---|---|---|---|
| **Cause** | **Male** | | **Female** | |
| Lung complaints | 4 | 19% | 4 | 44% |
| Heart/circulatory | 4 | 19% | 2 | 22% |
| Accidents* | 6 | 29% | | |
| Other** | 7 | 33% | 1 | 11% |
| Childbirth | | | 2 | 22% |
| TOTALS | 21 | 100% | 9 | 100% |

\* accidents included drowning, falling from a horse, being struck by lightning. None were obvious mine accidents.
\*\* included sunstroke, liver and kidney disease, and unstated causes.

**TABLE 2.17**

| AGES AT DEATH OF ADELONG CORNISH 1856-1905. | | | | |
|---|---|---|---|---|
| **Ages** | **Male** | | **Female** | |
| Under 20 | | | | |
| 20-29 | 4 | 19% | 2 | 22% |
| 30-39 | 2 | 10% | 1 | 11% |
| 40-49 | 8 | 38% | 1 | 11% |
| 50-59 | 4 | 19% | 3 | 33% |
| 60-69 | 3 | 14% | 2 | 22% |
| TOTAL | 21 | | 9 | |

## TABLE 2.18

| YEARS RESIDENT IN THE AUSTRALIAN COLONIES | | | | |
|---|---|---|---|---|
| **ADELONG CORNISH DEATHS 1856-1905.** | | | | |
| **Years** | **Males** | | **Females** | |
| Less than 15 | 6 | 29% | 4 | 44% |
| Fifteen or more | 10 | 48% | 5 | 56% |
| Not stated | 5 | 24% | | |
| Resident in more than one colony | 4 | 19% | 2 | 22% |
| TOTAL | | 21 MALES | | 9 FEMALES |

## TABLE 2.19

| OCCUPATIONS: CORNISH DEATH REGISTRATIONS | | | | |
|---|---|---|---|---|
| **ADELONG 1856-1905.** | | | | |
| **Occupation** | **Male** | | **Female** | |
| Miner | 15 | 71% | | |
| Labourer | 1 | 5% | | |
| Engine driver | 1 | 5% | | |
| Carter | 1 | 5% | | |
| Builder | 1 | 5% | | |
| Solicitor | 1 | 5% | | |
| Shoemaker | 1 | 5% | | |
| None stated | | | 8 | 89% |
| Dressmaker | | | 1 | 11% |
| TOTAL | 21 | | 9 | |

**TABLE 2.20**

| OCCUPATIONS OF PARTIES IN CORNISH MARRIAGES AT ADELONG | | | |
|---|---|---|---|
| **Cornish partner** | **Father** | **Spouse** | **Spouse's father** |
| Assistant at home | Miner | Miner | Farmer |
| Draper | | None | Clerk |
| Goldminer | Tin dresser | None | Goldminer |
| Goldminer | Engineer | None | Farmer |
| Goldminer | Goldminer | None | Baker |
| Miner | Miner | None | Tailor |
| Miner | Blacksmith | None | Farmer |
| Miner | Miner | None | Tailor |
| Miner | Miner | Private life | Miner |
| Miner | Miner | None | |
| Miner | Merchant | Dressmaker | Miner |
| Miner | Miner | None | Gentleman |
| Miner | Miner | None | Stonemason |
| Miner | Blacksmith | None | Engineer |
| Miner | Miner | None | Publican |
| Miner | Miner | None | Timber merchant |
| Miner | Farmer | None | Farmer |
| Miner | Miner | Private life | Carter |
| Miner | Miner | None | Mariner |
| Miner | Miner | Seamstress | Miner |
| Miner | Farmer | None | Customs officer |
| Miner | Miner | None | Miner |
| Miner | Miner | None | Farmer |
| Miner | Farmer | None | Farmer |
| Miner | Miner | None | Miner |
| Miner | Wheelright | None | Miner |
| Miner | Miner | None | Shoemaker |
| Miner | Carpenter | None | Miner |
| None | Engineer | Miner | Blacksmith |
| None | Miner | Miner | Carpenter |
| None | Farmer | Miner | Blacksmith |
| None | Miner | Miner | Miner |
| None | Farmer | Teacher | Miner |
| None | Miner | Miner | Miner |
| None | Customs officer | Miner | Farmer |
| None | Farmer | Miner | Farmer |
| Teacher | Miner | None | Farmer |

NOTE

The marriages are those recorded in Church of England and Methodist marriage registers. Those held at Adelong C.P.S. were not used as place of birth of the parties was not recorded, and so Cornish-born persons could not be identified.

**TABLE 2.21**

| PLACE OF MARRIAGE OF CORNISH PARENTS:ADELONG. | | |
|---|---|---|
| Adelong | 126 | 46% |
| Cornwall | 57 | 21% |
| Victoria | 47 | 17% |
| New South Wales (excluding Adelong) | 39 | 14% |
| Illegitimate | 5 | 2% |
| South Australia and United States | 3 | 1% |
| TOTAL BIRTHS | 277 | 100% |

**TABLE 2.22**

| ADELONG MARRIAGES | | | | |
|---|---|---|---|---|
| BIRTHPLACES OF SPOUSES OF CORNISH PARTNERS. | | | | |
| **Birthplace** | **Males** | | **Females** | |
| Other colonies | 1 | 11% | 4 | 14% |
| Ireland | - | | 1 | 4% |
| London | - | | 1 | 4% |
| England | - | | 3 | 11% |
| Channel Is | 1 | 11% | - | |
| India | - | | 1 | 4% |
| NSW | - | | 9 | 32% |
| Cornwall | 7 | 78% | 9 | 32% |
| TOTAL | 9 | 100% | 28 | 100% |

Total                              9 Cornish females                              28 Cornish males
9 male spouses of Cornishwomen.    28 female spouses of Cornishmen.
NOTE
The majority of Cornish women (or seven of the nine) in Adelong married Cornish men, while nine of the 28 males married Cornishwomen.

**TABLE 2.23**

| RELIGIONS:ADELONG DEATHS 1856-1905. | | | | |
|---|---|---|---|---|
| **Religion** | **Male** | | **Female** | |
| Wesleyan/Methodist | 9 | 43% | 7 | 78% |
| Church of England | 7 | 33% | 1 | 11% |
| Not stated | 5 | 24% | | |
| Presbyterian | | | 1 | 11% |
| TOTAL | 21 | 100% | 9 | 100% |

**TABLE 2.24**

| OCCUPATIONS: CORNISH DEATHS COBAR 1880-1907. | | | | |
|---|---|---|---|---|
| **Occupation** | **Male** | | **Female** | |
| Miner | 18 | 69% | | |
| Labourer | 2 | 8% | | |
| Farmer | 1 | 4% | | |
| Hotelkeeper | 1 | 4% | | |
| Cordial manufacturer | 1 | 4% | | |
| Engine driver | 1 | 4% | | |
| Storekeeper | 1 | 4% | | |
| None | 1 | 4% | 11 | 85% |
| Nurse/matron | | | 2 | 15% |
| TOTAL | 26 | | 13 | |

TABLE 2.25

| CAUSES OF DEATH: CORNISH REGISTRATIONS COBAR 1880-1907. | | | | |
|---|---|---|---|---|
| **Cause of death** | **Male** | | **Female** | |
| Lung complaints | 12 | 46% | 1 | 8% |
| Heart/circulatory disease | 7 | 27% | | |
| Accident | 5 | 19% | 1 | 8% |
| Other | 2 | 8% | 7 | **54% |
| Childbirth | | | 4 | 31% |
| TOTAL | 26 | 100% | 13 | 100% |
| ** These included suicide, cancer and peritonitis. | | | | |

TABLE 2.26

| AGES AT DEATH: CORNISH REGISTRATIONS COBAR 1880-1907. | | | | |
|---|---|---|---|---|
| **Ages** | **Males** | | **Females** | |
| Under 20 | | | | |
| 20-29 | 1 | 4% | 2 | 15% |
| 30-39 | 5 | 19% | 3 | 23% |
| 40-49 | 3 | 12% | 2 | 15% |
| 50-59 | 9 | 35% | 2 | 15% |
| 60-69 | 7 | 26% | 1 | 8% |
| 70-80 | 1 | 4% | 3 | 23% |
| TOTAL | 26 | 100% | 13 | 100% |

TABLE 2.27

| CORNISH DEATH REGISTRATIONS COBAR 1880-1907. YEARS OF RESIDENCE IN THE AUSTRALIAN COLONIES. | | | | |
|---|---|---|---|---|
| **Time** | **Males** | | **Females** | |
| Less than 15 years | 2 | 8% | 2 | 15% |
| Fifteen years or more | 22 | 84% | 11 | 85% |
| Unknown | 2 | 8% | | |
| TOTAL | 26 | 100% | 13 | 100% |
| Resident in more than one colony | 11 | 42% | 4 | 31% |

TABLE 2.28

| RELIGIONS: CORNISH DEATH REGISTRATIONS, COBAR 1880-1907. | | | | |
|---|---|---|---|---|
| **Religion** | **Males** | | **Females** | |
| Wesleyan/Methodist | 13 | 50% | 7 | 54% |
| Church of England | 10 | 38% | 1 | 8% |
| None stated | 3 | 12% | 2 | 15% |
| Roman Catholic | | | 1 | 8% |
| Presbyterian | | | 2 | 15% |
| TOTAL | 26 | 100% | 13 | 100% |

# APPENDIX III
## NAME COUNT TABLES

NOTES ON NAME COUNTS
Name counts were done according to the system devised by Dr C.A. Price, and are explained at the end of this appendix. The tables in this appendix are not numbered according to the chapters in which reference is made to them. This is because some tables are referred to in more than one chapter. Consequently they are arranged in chronological order. Percentages were rounded to hundredths in the *Sands* Sydney name count, and in the other name counts the first two numbers after the decimal point were recorded without rounding.

### TABLE 3.1

| SANS SYDNEY DIRECTORIES 1859-1898 | | |
|---|---|---|
| YEAR | TOTAL | % CORNISH |
| 1858/9 | 9234 | 0.60 |
| 1861 | 10004 | 1.00 |
| 1863 | 10999 | 0.73 |
| 1866 | 14858 | 0.84 |
| 1869 | 17490 | 1.09 |
| 1873 | 20984 | 0.81 |
| 1877 | 28482 | 1.04 |
| 1882 | 41234 | 1.14 |
| 1886 | 58780 | 1.17 |
| 1892 | 79417 | 1.21 |
| 1898 | 81761 | 1.33 |

NOTE ON TABLE 3.1
The years selected were those for which I used *Sands* to find entries for the Sydney database, in which I followed Sydney residents or their relatives, to locate their residences and occupations.

I am indebted to the late Mrs Joan Northey who did these namecounts from *Sands*, and the calculations, to establish the percentage of Cornish residents in Sydney in selected years between 1859 and 1898. Attempting to estimate the total number in *Sands* and other directories is difficult because of the advertisements which appear on some pages, and which are not uniform in size or placement, whereas electoral rolls state the number of voters in each electorate.

### TABLE 3.2

### CORNISH PERCENTAGE IN CENSUS OF NEW SOUTH WALES 1828

| Total | % Cornish |
|---|---|
| c.36 500[1] | 0.35 |

---

1    M.R. Sainty and K.A. Johnson (eds.) *Census of New South Wales November 1828*, LAH, Sydney, 1985, p.14.

**TABLE 3.3**

| 1859/60 ELECTORAL ROLL, NEW SOUTH WALES | | |
|---|---|---|
| **Electorate** | **Total** | **% Cornish** |
| Camden | 1737 | 1.15 |
| Canterbury | 3028 | 0.99 |
| Central Cumberland | 1693 | 0.59 |
| Eden | 769 | 1.30 |
| The Glebe | 1584 | 0.94 |
| Goulburn | 501 | 1.99 |
| Gwydir | 657 | 1.52 |
| Hawkesbury | 1477 | 2.36 |
| Hume | 918 | - |
| Hunter | (767+222)  989 | 2.03 |
| Lower Hunter | 679 | - |
| Ipswich | 841 | 1.18 |
| West Moreton | 710 | - |
| Morpeth | 749 | 0.66 |
| Mudgee | 2015 | 0.99 |
| Parramatta | 1208 | 1.65 |
| Paterson | 441 | 2.26 |
| St Leonards | 1476 | 0.33 |
| Shoalhaven | 916 | 3.82 |
| East Sydney | 7568 | 1.38 |
| West Sydney | 6418 | 0.54 |
| Tenterfield | 264 | - |
| Tumut | 778 | 0.64 |
| Yass Plains | 737 | - |

NOTES ON TABLE 3.3

The namecount was done from the microfilm copy of the New South Wales Electoral Office *Revised list* of persons qualified to vote for the election of members of the Legislative Assembly 1859-60, ML Q324.241/1. However, examination of the electoral map for the same election shows that some electorates are missing from the electoral roll. Unfortunately they include the Bathurst and Orange areas, and it has not been possible to find them elsewhere.

PLATE 48.    Map of the electoral districts of NSW 1859

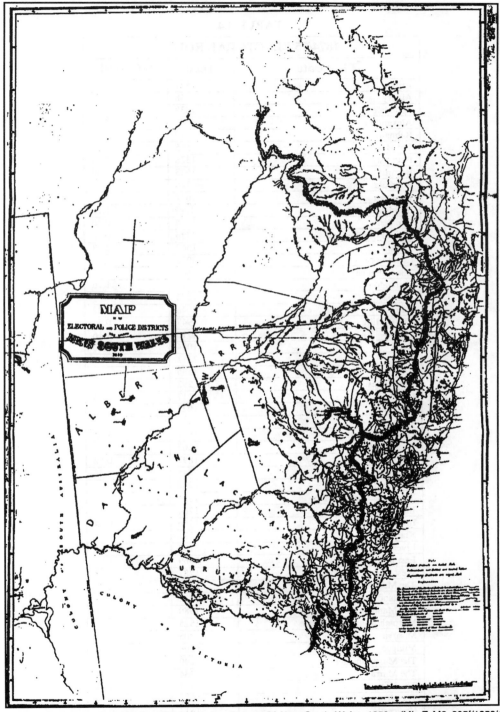

*Map of the Electoral and Police Districts in the Colony Of New South Wales 1859.* (ML Z M3 805f/1859/1.
Courtesy of the State Library of New South Wales.)

## TABLE 3.4

| 1874/75 ELECTORAL ROLL[2] | | |
|---|---|---|
| **Electorate** | **Total** | **% Cornish** |
| Argyle | 2521 | - |
| Albury | 748 | 1.33 |
| Armidale | 1038 | - |
| Alexandria | 1667 | 2.09 |
| Balmain | 2040 | 0.73 |
| The Barwon | 565 | 3.53 |
| Bathurst | 1328 | 1.88 |
| Berrima | 1623 | 0.30 |
| Bombala | 748 | - |
| Boorowa | 1647 | - |
| Braidwood | 2149 | 1.16 |
| Camden | 1239 | 0.40 |
| Central Cumberland | 2756 | 0.18 |
| Cassilis | 1362 | 0.73 |
| Canterbury | 3052 | 0.16 |
| The Clarence | 1644 | - |
| Clarendon | 1717 | 1.16 |
| Cooma | 1373 | - |
| Carcoar | 2046 | 1.22 |
| The Darling | 947 | 0.52 |
| Dubbo | 1716 | 1.16 |
| Eden | 1064 | 1.40 |
| Forbes | 2211 | - |
| The Glebe | 1535 | - |
| Glen Innes | 1292 | 0.38 |
| Goulburn | 1117 | 2.23 |
| Grafton | 925 | - |
| Grenfell | 1143 | - |
| Gulgong | 1897 | 1.05 |
| The Gwydir | 1263 | - |
| Hartley | 1897 | 0.52 |
| The Hawkesbury | 745 | 1.34 |
| The Hume | 1942 | - |
| The Hunter and Paterson | 1551 | 2.57 |
| Illawarra | 1284 | - |
| Inverell | 1446 | 0.34 |
| Kiama | 1171 | - |
| Liverpool Plains | 3193 | 0.62 |
| East Macquarie | 2869 | 1.56 |
| West Macquarie | 1287 | 3.88 |
| The Macleay | 1169 | 1.28 |
| Maitland West | 1232 | 1.21 |
| The Manning/Port Macquarie | 1980 | 1.01 |
| Morpeth/Raymond Terrace | 1525 | 0.32 |
| Moruya | 805 | 0.62 |
| Mudgee | 4006 | 1.49 |
| The Murrumbidgee | 1290 | |
| The Murray | 1234 | 0.81 |
| The Namoi | 1587 | 0.94 |
| The Nepean | 1088 | 2.29 |
| Newcastle | 1614 | 0.61 |
| New England | 1539 | 0.32 |

---

2  *New South Wales Electoral Roll 1875*, NLA mfm N273.

| | | |
|---|---|---|
| Newtown | 2382 | 0.41 |
| Northumberland and East Maitland | 1464 | 1.70 |
| Orange | 2090 | 3.58 |
| Oxley | 1153 | - |
| Paddington | 1991 | 1.25 |
| Parramatta | 1492 | 1.67 |
| Patrick's Plains | 1545 | - |
| Queanbeyan | 1248 | 1.60 |
| Redfern | 2489 | 0.80 |
| The Richmond | 1693 | 0.29 |
| Scone | 1241 | 0.40 |
| East Sydney | 11409 | 0.83 |
| West Sydney | 8853 | 1.18 |
| Shoalhaven | 1492 | 1.34 |
| St Leonards | 1662 | 0.30 |
| Tambaroora and Hill End | 1503 | 3.99 |
| Tenterfield | 1324 | 1.88 |
| The Tumut | 1965 | 1.01 |
| Waratah | 2272 | 0.22 |
| Wellington | 1200 | 1.25 |
| Windsor | 1165 | 3.80 |
| The Williams | 1195 | 2.09 |
| Wollombi | 1028 | 1.45 |
| Yass Plains | 1552 | 0.96 |
| Young | 1815 | - |

NOTE

The accompanying 1873 electoral map has been used because an 1875 electoral map could not be found.

PLATE 49.    Electoral map of New South Wales 1873

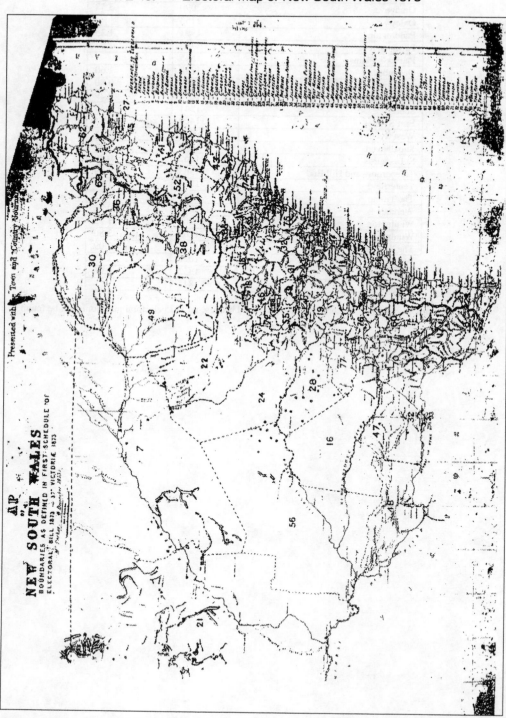

Map of New South Wales shewing boundaries as defined in first schedule of electoral bill 1873.  (ML Z M2 810 fbe/1873/1.  Courtesy of the State Library of New South Wales.)

## TABLE 3.5

| Greville's official post office directory and gazetteer of New South Wales 1875 to 1877 | | | |
|---|---|---|---|
| **District** | **Town** | **Totals** | **% Cornish** |
| BATHURST | Bathurst | 700 | 3.57 |
| | Byng | 46 | 32.60 |
| | Cadia | 80 | 6.25 |
| | Caloola | 50 | 10.00 |
| | Canonbar | 170 | 2.94 |
| | Cow Flat | 120 | 16.60 |
| | Dunkeld | 100 | 10.00 |
| | Forest Reefs | 110 | 9.09 |
| | Graham | 50 | 10.00 |
| | Guyong | 120 | 12.50 |
| | Hill End | 550 | 10.00 |
| | Icely | 100 | 15.00 |
| | Junction Point | 70 | 7.14 |
| | Kelso | 150 | 3.33 |
| | Lucknow | 130 | 11.53 |
| | Mt Macquarie | 60 | 8.33 |
| | Oberon | 130 | 7.69 |
| | Ophir | 80 | 6.25 |
| | Orange | 650 | 1.53 |
| | Rockley | 150 | 3.33 |
| | Tambaroora | 80 | 6.25 |
| | Trunkey Creek | 130 | 3.84 |
| | Turon Lower | 30 | 16.60 |
| | Wellington | 280 | 5.35 |

Note that

| | Tambararoora and Hill End combined | 630 | 9.52 |
|---|---|---|---|

| **District** | **Town** | **Totals** | **% Cornish** |
|---|---|---|---|
| MUDGEE | Home Rule | 300 | 1.66 |

| **District** | **Town** | **Totals** | **% Cornish** |
|---|---|---|---|
| DUBBO | Coonamble | 150 | 3.33 |
| | Dubbo | 190 | 2.63 |
| | Obley | 80 | 6.25 |
| | Parkes | 530 | 0.94 |
| | Tenandra | 55 | 9.09 |

| **District** | **Town** | **Totals** | **% Cornish** |
|---|---|---|---|
| HUNTER | Blandford | 130 | 3.84 |
| | Cassilis | 120 | 4.16 |
| | Dungog | 200 | 7.50 |
| | Largs | 140 | 7.14 |
| | Lewinsbrook | 50 | 30.00 |
| | Maitland East | 380 | 1.31 |
| | Maitland West | 850 | 0.58 |
| | Murrurundi | 330 | 1.51 |
| | Newcastle | 1200 | 1.25 |
| | Stockton | 130 | 3.84 |
| | Tamber Springs | 55 | 27.27 |
| | Wallsend | 480 | 1.04 |
| | Wickham | 130 | 3.84 |

| District | Town | Totals | % Cornish |
|---|---|---|---|
| SYDNEY | Appin | 130 | 7.69 |
| | Botany | 150 | 3.33 |
| | Hornsby | 60 | 8.33 |
| | Parramatta | 640 | 0.78 |
| | Picton | 130 | 3.84 |

| District | Town | Totals | % Cornish |
|---|---|---|---|
| NEPEAN-HAWKESBURY[3] | Eastern Creek | 60 | 8.33 |
| | Emu [Plains] | 60 | 8.33 |
| | St Mary's | 80 | 6.25 |

| District | Town | Totals | % Cornish |
|---|---|---|---|
| NEW ENGLAND AND NORTHERN TABLELANDS | Bingara | 100 | 5.00 |
| | Dalmorton | 50 | 10.00 |
| | Elsmore | 50 | 10.00 |
| | Inverell | 400 | 2.50 |
| | Oban | 70 | 7.14 |
| | Quirindi | 80 | 6.25 |
| | Stanborough | 70 | 7.14 |
| | Tamworth | 350 | 1.42 |
| | Tenterfield | 350 | 2.85 |
| | Tingha | 230 | 4.34 |
| | Vegetable Creek | 150 | 3.33 |
| | Wallabadah | 150 | 3.33 |

| District | Town | Totals | % Cornish |
|---|---|---|---|
| ADELONG-TUMUT | Adelong | 230 | 13.04 |
| | Clarendon | 120 | 4.16 |
| | Gundagai South | 130 | 7.69 |
| | Hillas Creek | 90 | 5.55 |
| | Reedy Flat | 140 | 3.57 |
| | Tumut | 240 | 4.16 |

| District | Town | Totals | % Cornish |
|---|---|---|---|
| COBAR | Cobar | 24 | 20.83 |

| District | Town | Totals | % Cornish |
|---|---|---|---|
| NORTH COAST | Bookookoorara | 150 | 10.00 |
| | Kempsey | 130 | 7.69 |
| | Kempsey East | 80 | 6.25 |
| | Kempsey West | 80 | 6.25 |
| | Lionsville | 110 | 4.54 |

| District | Town | Totals | % Cornish |
|---|---|---|---|
| SOUTH COAST | Bega | 190 | 7.89 |
| | Burrier | 50 | 10.00 |
| | Eden | 80 | 6.25 |
| | Fig Tree | 110 | 9.09 |

---

3   A few assisted immigrants had relatives in the Hawkesbury-Nepean district west of Sydney, but I found no evidence of large clusters there. It is possible there was an earlier Cornish group in that area, with the King and Lethbridge families as the nucleus.

| District | Town | Totals | %Cornish |
|---|---|---|---|
| SOUTHERN TABLELANDS | Bowning | 80 | 6.25 |
| | Currawang | 130 | 11.53 |
| | Goulburn | 800 | 3.12 |
| | Hoskinstown | 90 | 22.22 |
| | Major's Creek | 150 | 3.33 |
| | Molonglo | 80 | 6.25 |
| | Mooroowoolen | 130 | 3.84 |
| | Mummel | 100 | 5.00 |
| | Taralga | 200 | 2.50 |

| District | Town | Totals | %Cornish |
|---|---|---|---|
| OTHER | Albury | 450 | 1.11 |
| | Bartletts Camp | 80 | 12.50 |
| | Hay | 180 | 2.77 |
| | Junee | 90 | 5.55 |
| | Mathoura | 50 | 10.00 |
| | Moama | 70 | 14.28 |
| | Picton | 130 | 3.84 |
| | Wagga Wagga | 1100 | 0.45 |
| | Wanganella | 60 | 8.33 |
| | Young | 630 | 0.79 |

Exact numbers are not shown in this publication, which is a directory and not a list of electors. Estimation is made difficult by the intermittent placement of advertisements. The estimated totals were calculated by counting ten pages and averaging the number of names, giving about 50 per column or 100 per page. In some of the smaller settlements fewer entries were spread over one or two columns and so the estimate was adjusted accordingly. The results from settlements with a small population of 40 or 50 and only one Cornish name should be treated with caution.

## TABLE 3.6

| SELECTED ELECTORATES 1899/1900 ELECTORAL ROLL[4] | | |
|---|---|---|
| **Electorate** | **Total** | **% Cornish** |
| Armidale (Armidale) | 1784 | 0.56 |
| Armidale (Guy Fawkes) | - | - |
| Armidale (Hillgrove) | 1133 | 3.97 |
| Armidale (Hillgrove West) | 63 | 7.93 |
| Bathurst (city) | 2649 | 2.64 |
| Bega (Bega) | 1714 | 2.04 |
| Bega (Cobargo) | - | - |
| Broken Hill | 3397 | 9.42 |
| Cobar (Byerock) | - | - |
| Cobar (Cobar) | 1514 | 4.62 |
| Cobar (Coolabah) | 198 | 2.52 |
| Cobar (Curranyalpa, Drysdale, Louth, Girilambone) | - | - |
| Cobar (Nyngan) | 863 | 1.73 |
| Glen Innes (Emmaville) | 608 | 5.75 |
| Glen Innes (Glen Innes) | 1003 | 0.99 |
| Glen Innes (Guyra) | - | - |
| Glen Innes (Kookaburra) | 172 | 5.81 |
| Inverell (Ashford, Graman, Yetman, Little Plain and Bonshaw) | - | - |
| Inverell(Elsmore) | 235 | 10.59 |
| Inverell (Inverell) | 1208 | 1.24 |
| Inverell (Little Plain) | | |
| Macquarie (Oberon) | 443 | 3.38 |
| Macquarie (Sunny Corner) | 606 | 6.60 |
| Macquarie (Tarana) | 582 | 0.85 |
| Macquarie (Peel and Sofala) | | |
| West Macquarie | - | - |
| Mudgee (Gulgong) | 770 | 5.8 |
| Orange (Orange) | 2111 | 3.07 |
| Orange (The Forest) | 281 | 1.79 |
| Orange (Lucknow) | 733 | 7.50 |
| Orange (Lewis Ponds) | 102 | 9.80 |
| Orange (Ophir) | 52 | - |
| Tumut (Adelong) | 814 | 1.22 |

---

4    *New South Wales Electoral Roll 1899/1900*, NLA mfm N273

## EXTRACT FROM AN ADDRESS TO THE CORNISH ASSOCIATION OF THE AUSTRALIAN CAPITAL TERRITORY IN DECEMBER 1990

### BY CHARLES A PRICE, M.A. D.Phil

### USING CORNISH NAMES TO ESTIMATE THE CORNISH POPULATION OF AUSTRALIA AND ITS REGIONS OR DISTRICTS

Statistical information on the Cornish in Australia is difficult to obtain. Australian censuses, though giving England, Scotland, Ireland and Wales as distinct birthplaces since 1846, have always included Cornwall in England. Language statistics are also useless because Celtic Cornish had ceased to be the language of common use before emigration to Australia began. Religious statistics are occasionally helpful (most Cornish being Methodist) though only in places where English and Welsh Methodists were absent. Statistics of assisted passages, when they show county of origin, are also helpful, but these are very incomplete and show only totals arriving, not where the persons settled.

Apart from intensive work on family and regional records, this leaves only one method, viz, that of the distinctive surnames, a method used in the USA early this century when census officials were estimating the ethnic make-up of the population for purposes of immigration quotas. The method works as follows. First, make a list of distinctive surnames, ie surnames which belong to one ethnic group only; eg. names such as MacDonald, Campbell, Douglas and Menzies for the Scottish, or O'Neill, Donoghue, Moran and Sullivan for the Irish. Then use Scottish or Irish electoral, parish, ratepayer or similar lists existing at the time of mazimum emigration to estimate what proportion of all Scottish or Irish names are distinctive in the country of origin, say one in four. Then, assuming emigrants to Australia were drawn proportionately from families with distinctive and non-distinctive names, work through electoral, rate-payer, telephone and other lists in Australia, counting distinctive surnames. Then multiply the total of distictive names by the proportion, one in four. So, if in the western districts of Victoria, we find 200 dinstinctive Scottish surnames in a total of 2400 surnames we estimate the Scottish proportion to be 200 multiplied by 4 divided by 2400 which equals 33.3 per cent.

For the Cornish I constructed a list of 199 distinctive surnames, with the aid of G. Pawley White's *Cornish Surnames* (1972) and Basil Cottle's Penguin *Dictionary of Surnames* (1967); not just those comprising a Cornish word prefixed with a traditional Cornish prefix (such as Tre, Pol, Pen, Ros, Lan, Car) but other distinctive surnames such as Angove, Bonython, Nancekivell, Pascoe, Retallick. I then compared this with a list of nineteenth century Cornish emigrants to Australia compiled from the name indexes in Philip Payton's *Cornish Miner in Australia* (1984) and *Cornish Farmer in Australia* (1987), and from the list of Cornish pioneers held by the S.A. Genealogical Society in Adelaide; 618 surnames in all. Of these, 128 were distinctive, ie 1:4.83 or, in round figures, one in five. (The proportion was only one in five because many Cornish had surnames based on non-distinctive personal names – Adam, Arthur, Martin, Matthew, Paul, Richards, Thomas, etc – or surnames derived from Cornish words but identical with Welsh or other Celtic names – Harvey, Powell, Price – or else, fortuitously, with names derived from quite different Anglo-Saxon words; Bray, Hancock, Harris, Rouse, etc.)

I then (rightly as it happened) assumed the 71 distinctive surnames not appearing on this emigrant list might well appear elsewhere in Australia – the Payton books were primarily concerned with families going first to South Australia – and that it would be best to take them on a 1:5 basis also. I then used this list of 199 distinctive surnames to examine electoral and telephone lists in the various regions of South Australia, NSW and Tasmania as a basis for estimating the total of Cornish family names in the total of all names.

We must take great care when drawing conclusions from this method. First, the method is quite straightforward where dealing with first-generation immigrants, such as

Cornish miners at Kapunda in the 1840s, Bendigo in the 1850s or Moonta in the 1870s. We can simply assume that the proportion of Cornish surnames to other surnames represents the strength of the Cornish element in the population.

With later generations things become more difficult. Cornish immigrants arriving single may marry non-Cornish women, producing children who, though bearing Cornish surnames, are ethnically half-Cornish; if there are more immigrant males than females – as was the case in many mining areas – this will not be counterbalanced by Cornish women marrying non-Cornish men. Things get still more complicated when third generation men who are only one-quarter Cornish, but have Cornish surnames, marry women who may be three-quarters Cornish but do not have Cornish surnames; and vice versa. There are numerous situations of a similar kind.

Experiments with model family trees, covering various genealogical outcomes and ethnic fractions, may be constructed. In doing this we have to remember the three main ethnic measures. The Pure or Unmixed total covers those of unmixed Cornish descent. Second, Total Descent covers all persons who have any Cornish in them, even if that be only one thirty-second. Third, Ethnic Strength counts pure Cornish persons as one but others fractionally; eg four persons who are one-quarter Cornish count as only one in the total. This last is the best measure for comparing the relative strength of the various ethnic contributions to the total population.

In general the genealogical models suggest that the proportion of Cornish surnames is a reasonable measutre of Ethnic Strength but is far too high as a measure of those of unmixed Cornish descent – mainly because the great mass of Cornish immigration was in the mid nineteenth century and very few of those families have, down the generations, married into Cornish families only. Conversely, the surname count greatly understated the number of persons with some Cornish ancestry (ie Total Descent).

Preliminary estimates suggest that the Unmixed Cornish population of Australia is about 12,000, Ethnic Strength is about 215,000 and Total Descent about 630,000 which matches quite well with estimates based on assisted passsage records. Further work may increase the Cornish element a bit, as work on SA electoral records gives somewhat higher totals.

(The address then examined the surname counts in various parts of SA, NSW and Tasmania, drawing conclusions about the Cornish element in the population of those areas.)

# APPENDIX IV
## SELECT MINING TERMS

I am indebted to Mr Richard Hancock of Adelaide for his assistance with this appendix. Unless otherwise stated, the information has been provided by Mr Hancock, who is a mining engineer, and a direct descendant of the legendary Captain H.R. Hancock of Moonta Mines. I am also indebted to Mr Mel Davies, Department of Economics, The University of Western Australia, for his explanation of the differences between blast, draught and reverbatory furnaces.

**ADIT**            A horizontal or near horizontal opening driven from the surface for working or dewatering a mine. If it is driven right through a hill, it becomes a tunnel.

**ALLUVIUM**            The material deposited by stream or wave action. Alluvial deposits may be concentrated into fractions according to density (specific gravity) or size.

**BATTERY**            Literally a set or series of similar machines and generally refers to a set of stamps, commonly in multiples of five. Typically a ten stamp battery for crushing (gold) ore.

**BLAST FURNACE**            The blast, by mechanical means, forces air by high pressure into the body of the furnace to provide great heat. It generates greater heat than the draught furnace. The heating agent (wood, charcoal, some types of coal) is in contact with the copper ore.[1]

**BUDDLE**            A circular device with an obtusely conical surface commonly three to ten metres in diameter excavated in the ground and into the centre of which is delivered finely crushed ore in water. The heaviest particles bed down and are washed to the peripheral launders where gravity separation can be achieved. The lightest (tailings) fraction is carried over the rim. The whole can be agitated by rotating rakes or an umbrella type frame. The earliest types were powered by a horse whim (capstan).

**DEEP LEAD**            A lead is generally an alluvial gold deposit in an old river bed. A deep lead is as above, but where the river bed is buried below sediments and/or magmatic (basaltic) flow.

**DRAUGHT FURNACE**            Apertures in the wall of the furnace draw air (by free entry) into the chamber which help to increase the heat in the furnace. It is not as efficient as a blast furnace. The heating agent (wood, charcoal, some types of coal) is in contact with the copper ore.[2]

**LEVEL**            A depth (horizon) at which an ore body is opened up. It provides access by cross cuts to the ore body and, as required, drives along it. A plat or platform is established at the shaft at each level to facilitate the landing of men and materials.

**LODE (VEIN)**            The line or place, of the mineralised zone or ore body, generally in quartz or other hard rock. A vein has a more or less regular length, width and height and is often tabular.

**REEF (BLANKET)**            Primarily a South African term describing a planar sedimentary ore deposit of varying widths, often in conglomerate and extending over considerable distances. A reef may dip considerably from the horizontal.

**REVERBERATORY (OR REVERBATORY) FURNACE**            This involves the separation of the heating agents from the ores, and this is usually done to avoid noxious materials contained in the fuel from contaminating the ores. The ores are spread over a low ceilinged floor and separated from the fuel which is in a separate combustion chamber. The hot gases from the combustion chamber escape over a wall separating the body of ore and they 'bounce' or reverberate over the ores which are thus smelted.[3]

**STAMPER (STAMP)**    A mechanical form of large mortar and pestle, used for crushing and grinding. The heavy pestle (shoe, stem and tappet) is lifted on the tappet by the rotary action of a cam and allowed to fall, onto the ore to be treated, in the mortar block.

**STOPE**            An underground excavation (mining area other than development working) made in the extraction of ore. The nature of the deposit determines the method of extraction (stoping method), and ground support needed and therefore the size, shape and type of the stope.

**TIN IN NEW ENGLAND**

Tin ore or cassiterite in which the mineral was compounded with oxygen and when pure made up of 78.6 per cent of the total weight was found distributed in various forms in New England.

---

1    Mr Mel Davies, The University of Western Australia.
2    Mr Mel Davies.
3    Mr Mel Davies.

In the margins of the acid portions of the granite rocks which had intruded into the sedimentary rocks of the Palaeozoic era the ore was found in veins a few feet wide and deep, also in 'stockworks' which were a mass of minute veins, and in curiously formed 'pipes' which might be four to five feet in diameter but rarely descended far beneath the surface. As the sedimentary and granite rocks had eroded, the cassiterite had been washed out to be deposited in stream beds which in the course of time had been overlaid by sandy drift and sometimes capped by a flow of basaltic lava, securely sealing in the stanniferous material. These gravels belonging to the Tertiary period geologically were known to miners as 'deep leads'. Later in the Pleistocene epoch tin had been deposited in the alluvial terraces bordering the watercourses that we know today and ... the beds of these rivers had collected further deposits of the tinstone. To the first diggers this 'stream tin' - in or near the water that they needed for their sluice boxes and either on the surface of the ground or but thinly covered over - was the most attractive form of deposit although it was also recognized that it would be the first to be worked out. Tin was also widely if patchily disseminated in areas just below the surface of the ground from the grass roots to two feet down. Usually such low-grade deposits could only be worked profitably, if at all, by ground sluicing, for it would not pay to carry the ore to the box.

Although there is no continuous series of production figures it is apparent that in the nineteenth century most of the ore produced came from the stream tin and alluvium, with the deep leads holding second place and the veins, or lodes, making a poor third. This major dependence on shallow easily worked deposits explains why New South Wales exported large quantities in the first dozen years, reaching a maximum of 9,123 tons in 1883, and thereafter declined steadily to a mere 916 tons in 1900. Practically all the tin produced in this colony came from the New England district and it helped to make Australia the largest tin producer in the world between 1873 and 1882, from 1872 to 1883 inclusive New South Wales tin exports were worth £5.9 million.[4]

**TRIBUTE**      A method of employment whereby a group of miners (usually two, three or four) bid for the ground to be worked (usually for a two month period) for a set percentage of the value of the ore won. 'Tributers' therefore were not only skilled miners but had to be shrewd in their appraisal of the trends of the ore body.

---

4    R.B. Walker, *Old New England: a history of the northern tablelands of New South Wales 1818-1900*, Sydney University Press, 1966, pp.93-94.

# APPENDIX V
## GEOGRAPHICAL NOTES

Where possible, entries are based on *Bailliere's New South Wales gazetteer and road guide, 1866, (BGNSW)*, or on *Greville's official post office directory and gazetteer of New South Wales, 1875-1877, (GPDNSW)*.

**ADELONG** ... a postal mining township ... being the chief town of the Adelong goldfields ... The district is a mining one, quartz and alluvial, the former being worked on numerous reefs in the neighbourhood, and the latter for 20 miles upwards along the the banks of the creek ... the communication with Sydney is by cross road to the Adelong crossing place, 12 miles distant on the great Southern-road, and then by the mail coach to Picton, whence trains run several times a day. The total distance is 252 miles ... The surrounding country consists of elevated ranges of hills, running from N. to S. There is not much land available for agricultural purposes ... The population of the township numbers about 400 settled inhabitants.[1]

**ADELONG CREEK** ... an important auriferous stream ... flowing N. about 45 miles through the Adelong gold fields and the township of Adelong. To the N. of the latter it expands into a large swampy lagoon ... This creek is worked from about 30 miles from its source to its fall into the Murrumbidgee ... There is little or no agricultural ground ... until below the swamp above named, but after that the land on both sides the creek is taken up by numerous settlers, chiefly for small farms, many of them of less than 100 acres.[2]

**ADELONG GOLD-FIELD** ... a vast tract of auriferous country lying to the S. of the Murrumbidgee river and along the course of the Adelong creek and the W. bank of the Tumut river ... and is both quartz and alluvial. The quantity of gold received by escort from the Adelong gold-fields during the year 1864 was 18,720 ozs ... total value of £72,696.19s.7d.[3]

**ALEXANDRIA** an area of South Sydney which became a borough independent from Waterloo in 1868.[4]

**AMERICAN CREEK** ... a beautiful stream, flowing from the Coast range, opposite Wollongong. It is celebrated for the kerosene works which have recently been established on its banks.[5]

**ANNANDALE** an area in the Petersham district of Sydney.[6]

**ARALUEN** ... a postal mining township, in the ... police district of Braidwood ... in the valley of the Araluen creek ... The district is an alluvial mining one ... the number of miners being about 1200, inclusive of 100 Chinamen ... The population of Araluen numbers about 3,500 persons.[7]

**ARMIDALE** ... the central town of the New England district ... situated in an agricultural, pastoral, and alluvial mining district ... The means of communication with Sydney, 313 miles S., are by mail coach to Singleton, thence by rail to Newcastle, and then to Sydney by steamer, or by horse or dray to Grafton, 130 miles along a bad road, and thence by steamer ... The surrounding country is elevated and mountainous, the country being rugged and well grassed and timbered. It occasionally, however, suffers severely from long droughts and heavy frosts, which cause a scarcity in meat and dairy produce. The soil is rich and productive ... There are numerous sheep stations in the district ... The population of the township numbers about 1,000 persons.[8]

**ARNCLIFFE** a Sydney suburb in Rockdale municipality.[9]

**ASHFIELD** ... a postal village and railway station, in the parish of Petersham ... on the road and railway from Sydney to Parramatta ... The district is an agricultural one ... well suited for market gardening ... and is a great resort of persons in search of health and a change of air ... a favourite place of residence for merchants and others having their business in town ... The population numbers about 1000.[10]

**AUBURN** an agricultural area in the Parramatta district until 1877, when land speculators subdivided and sold land in the district.[11]

**BALMAIN** ... one of the suburbs of Sydney ... a peninsula; on three sides it is bounded by water ... Balmain owes much of its progress, and this has been considerable within the last few years, to the dry dock ... the property of Mr. T.S. Mort. The undertaking, considered as the result of private enterprise, ranks among the greatest in the colony ... From the number and extent of the various works in and about Balmain, it may be inferred that a very large proportion of its inhabitants are mechanics ... Shipwrights, boat builders, engineers, boiler makers, carpenters, &c., will thus form the bulk of the population. Not by any means a small portion, however, consists of clerks and

1    *BGNSW*, p.2.
2    Ibid, pp.2-3.
3    Ibid, p.3.
4    Brian Kennedy and Barbara Kennedy, *Sydney and suburbs: a history and description*, Reed, Frenchs Forest, N.S.W., 1982, pp.118-9.
5    *BGNSW*, p.7.
6    Brian Kennedy and Barbara Kennedy, *Sydney and suburbs*, p.91.
7    *BGNSW*, pp.9-10.
8    Ibid, p.12.
9    Brian Kennedy and Barbara Kennedy, *Sydney and suburbs*, p.112.
10   *BGNSW*, p.14.
11   Brian Kennedy and Barbara Kennedy, *Sydney and suburbs*, pp.12-14.

mercantile men who, although occupied in the city, have been attracted to Balmain by its proverbial healthiness and agreeable scenery. Communication is effected between Sydney and Balmain by means of steam ferries, three in number - by small watermen's boats, and an omnibus ... The population of Balmain is stated at about 4000.[12]

**BATEMAN'S BAY** ... township in the ... electoral district of Eden ... The district is agricultural and pastoral, the Mogo diggings (alluvial and quartz), being 8 miles distant.[13]

**BATHURST** ... the principal town in the W. district of New South Wales, and one of the most important in the colony ... The district in which Bathurst is situated is agricultural, pastoral and mining. Most of the surrounding country consists of large and valuable estates, and in this respect the district may be said to contain a larger numer of wealthy men than any other in the colony, that is, estimating property as wealth, some of the estates being almost princely ... As a wheat growing country it is second to the district of Orange, but with this exception is inferior to no part of the colony. The extent of cultivated land is very great ... Many of the farms are purchased, others rented, and 31,320 acres have been allotted to 561 free selectors ... The gold fields ... workings are extensive, and afford employment to about 1700 miners, of which number about two-thirds are Chinese. The mining population is settled as follows: - Mitchell's creek, about 100; Napoleon reef, 150; Winburndale creek and its tributaries, 100; Glanmire, 350; King's plains, 300; Flyers's creek, 50; Millewa, 100; and Rockley, about 550 ... The population of Bathurst numbers about 5000 persons.[14]

**BEARDY PLAINS** ... a large tract of fine pastoral country lying to the N.E. of glen Innis [sic] and consisting of open undulating downs well grassed, and watered by the Beardy waters and its tributaries.[15]

**BEGA** ... a postal township ... The district is an agricultural and pastoral one. It is occupied by a number of farmers and graziers on a small scale ... Considerable quantities of grain, cheese, butter and wool, of excellent quality, are exported. The river lands are equal, in their producing capabilities, to any in the colony. Coal and kerosene shale mines have been discovered about 10 miles distant ... the nearest gold diggings are ... distant 51 miles.[16]

**BELLINGEN** on the Bellinger river, was proclaimed a village in 1870.[17]

**BELLINGER RIVER** ... a small stream ... flowing ... through low swampy cedar country into the ocean about 24 miles N. of Trial bay. It has a shallow shifting channel at its mouth and is only frequented by small vessels trading in cedar[18]

**BELUBULA GOLD FIELD** ... a tract of auriferous country lying on the upper part of the Belubula River, between Blayney and Carcoar.[19]

**BINGARA** ... a postal township in the ... police district of Warialda ... The district is agricultural, pastoral and mining. The gold workings are alluvial ... Sydney 356 miles S.E. ... The population of Bingera [sic] township numbers about 150 persons.[20]

**BLAYNEY** ... a postal township ... on the Belubula River, 144 miles W. from Sydney, and 22 miles S.W. from Bathurst ... The district ... is an agricultural, pastoral, and mining one. The soil ... is suited to the growth of wheat, which is grown in abundance, and of excellent quality. The entire country abounds in fine pasture lands. There are gold workings, alluvial and quartz, within 4 or 5 miles ... The population of the township numbers 91 persons.[21]

**BOTANY** ... is situated on Cook's River and the N. shore of Botany bay ... Botany is an agricultural district, the principal industry being market gardening. It also contains a tannery, a fell-monger's yard, a slaughtering establishment, and the Sydney water works. The latter are situate about 5 miles from Sydney, and occupy an area of 30 acres, the water reserves being fed by many springs in Randwick and the vicinity. The quantity of water supplied to the city is about 18 millions of gallons per week. The water is exceedingly pure and sweet, and is pumped to the Sydney reservoir, in the Surry Hills, by means of three powerful beam engines, of a collective power of 250 horses, each engine being capable of delivering 8 tons of water per minute, and forcing it to an elevation of 215 feet, at a distance of 4½ miles. Sydney is 5 miles distant ... the communication being by means of a two-horse omnibus, which runs twice per day ... The country surrounding Botany consists of swamps and sand hills, with occasional patches of rich alluvial soil. The population numbers about 700 persons.[22]

**BOURKE** ... a postal township ... on the Darling river ... the furthest inland town in New South Wales ... The district ... is strictly a pastoral one, and is unsurpassed in the colony in the variety and luxuriance of its pasturage, the grassy plains being intersected by immense belts of valuable salt bush. To the north of the township, good specimens of gold have been obtained, but the country has never been properly prospected ... steamers ply for a great portion of the year, up the Darling, supplying this enormous district with stores, chiefly from South Australia, and taking produce in return. With Sydney, 576 miles, the communication is by horse, to Molong or Dubbo, each

12    *BGNSW*, pp.20-1.
13    Ibid, p.30.
14    Ibid, pp.30-1.
15    Ibid, p.33.
16    Ibid, p.34.
17    J. Kay Donald, *Exploring the north coast and New England*, a Heritage Field Guide, Kangaroo Press, Kenthurst, N.S.W., 1987, p.57.
18    *BGNSW*, p.36.
19    Ibid, p.37.
20    Ibid, pp.46-7.
21    Ibid, p.52.
22    Ibid, p.73.

distant about 400 miles S.E., thence by Cobb's coach to Penrith, and thence by rail; the former is the mail route, and takes 8 days ... The population of Bourke and the immediate neighbourhood numbers about 300.[23]

**BRAIDWOOD**     ... an important postal township ... The district is both agricultural and pastoral, gold mining, chiefly alluvial, being also carried on to a great extent ... The population numbers about 1000 persons.[24]

**BROULEE**     ... a small agricultural township lying a few miles N. of the Moruya River. It is celebrated for the excellence of the potatoes grown there.[25]

**BULLI**     ... a small hamlet on the coast road from Wollongong to Sydney; lying about 8 miles N. of the former place. It is noted as a coal mining hamlet.[26]

**BURWOOD**     ... a postal roadside village, and railway station, forming a pleasant suburb of Sydney ... between Sydney and Parramatta ... There are a few small dairy farms and market gardens in Burwood, but no mills or manufactures of any kind ... The population of Burwood is 548 persons, and the neighbouring villages may be roughly estimated at about 2000 persons, scattered over a large extent of country, and, excepting the resident gentry, who carry on their businesses in Sydney, subsisting by tillage, farming, woodcutting, or brickmaking ...[27] Burwood had an early Cornish connection. It was named by Cornishman Captain Thomas Rowley, who sold the land in 1812 to a Sydney businessman.[28]

**BYNG CREEK**     ... a small W. tributary of the upper part of Lewis' ponds, flowing through land held by R. Glasson, into the main stream at the township of Byng.[29]

**CADIA**     ... a private postal township in the ... police district of Orange. It is situated on the Cadiangullong rivulet (locally called the Oaky creek), and on an E. spur of the Canobolas mountains, the watershed draining into the Belubula river. The Cadiangullong Consolidated Copper company have extensive workings in the neighbourhood, which employ a large number of hands. A considerable portion of the land in the district is highly fit for cultivation, the only obstacle being the heavy timber growing upon it. A good poor man's diggings has been in existence for about three years, on Flyers's or Errobinbang creek, about 5 miles S.E. of the township. The nearest places are Orange, 12 miles N. by a bridle track, or 15 miles by dray road; Carcoar, 16 miles S.; and Bathurst 34 miles E. With these places there is communication by horse only, the road to Orange and Carcoar being over boggy creeks and heavy sidelings, and that road being frequently altered by free selectors placing fences across the track. The road to Bathurst is, however, a surveyed one ... There is no hospital in Cadia, but there is a resident medical man, and the greater portion of the population being employed by the copper mining company, pay a weekly subscription, which entitles them to gratuitous medical assistance when needed ... Cadia being the private property of the Cadiangullong Mining Company, all residents are subject to the control of the board of directors of that company ... The population numbers about 600 persons. The following is the latest report of the mines at Cadia:- "Since our last notice of the Cadiangullong copper mines, very important progress has been made, the prospects of the company being now very encouraging. Upon the N. lode the adit has been extended, and the lode in the end is large and orey. Revena's [sic], or the engine shaft, has been sunk 12 fathoms below the adit level, and levels are being drawn E. and W. on the course of the lode struck, which is over 6 feet wide, easy to quarry, and yields fine pale yellow ore. It has been decided to sink at once upon this lode another 12 fathoms, and it is confidently believed that at this depth some good discovery will be made, as the lode has improved from the surface downwards. The lode in the various slopes [sic] in this section of the mine are, generally speaking, producing ores throughout the greater portion of them, and the lode ranges from 6 to 10 feet wide, which augers well for the yield in the next leads. On the S. lode, the erection of the large engine, with the pumping, crushing, and dressing machinery, has been completed. This is one of the largest and finest pieces of machinery out of Sydney, the building enclosing it being substantially erected of stone. The engine shaft on the S. side is now being sunk deeper; it is 4 fathoms below the 16 fathom level, and though not so productive as it has been, there are indications of an early improvement. The whole of the stopes in this part of the mine are more or less yielding ore; indeed this may be said of every portion of the mine. The smelting works are in full operation, giving full work to another furnace that has been recently completed. The company have about 90 tons of fine copper on the road to Sydney and at the mines; and it is calculated that the rise in the price of copper will make a difference close upon £4000 on the copper held by the company in the colony or on its way to England.[30]

**CADIANGULLONG RIVULET**     is a N. tributary of the Belubula creek, rising in the S. of the Canobolas cluster of hills, and flowing S. about 20 miles through rough scrubby country, much of which is taken up for agricultural and pastoral purposes.[31]

**CALOOLA**     ... a postal hamlet ... 140 miles W. from Sydney, on the main line of road between Bathurst, Tuena, and Goulburn ... Agricultural and pastoral pursuits are followed in the neighbourhood, and alluvial gold mining is also carried on ... The population numbers about 150 persons, including those on the surrounding farms.[32]

---

23    Ibid, pp.74-5.
24    Ibid, pp.78-9.
25    Ibid, p.87.
26    Ibid, p.93.
27    Ibid, p.107.
28    Brian Kennedy and Barbara Kennedy, *Sydney and suburbs*, p.34.
29    *BGNSW*, p.109.
30    Ibid, p.111.
31    Ibid, p.111.
32    Ibid, p.113.

**CANDELO** ... a newly surveyed agricultural township ... about 12 miles S.W. of the township of Bega. The communication is by horse and dray only. The surrounding population is scattered, and consists of small free selection settlers.[33]

**CANOBOLAS, THE** ... a group of lofty mountains in the Macquarie range, consisting of several peaks ... The highest altitude of these mountains is 4610 feet above the level of the sea. They are exceedingly rugged and covered with dense scrub and heavy timber, and present a conspicuous appearance from the towns of Orange, Ophir, Blayney and Carcoar. The Canobolas lie on the S. of the road from Orange to Molong ... There are rich beds of copper in these mountains, and a mine has been worked and yielded as much as 2000 tons of ore per annum.[34]

**CARCOAR** ... a postal township in the ... electoral and police districts of Carcoar. It is situated on the Belubula river ... 3 miles from mount Macquarie, a high peak having snow on its summit nearly the whole of the winter months. There are two flour mills in Carcoar, the district being a splendid agricultural one, with tolerably good pastoral country all round. There are alluvial gold workings ... in the neighbourhood ... The surrounding country is mountainous, and well timbered ... The population numbers about 6000 persons in the entire district.[35]

**CARGO CREEK** is a N. tributary of the Belubula river.[36]

**CASINO** ... a postal township ... on the ... main stream of the Richmond river ... The district is an agricultural and pastoral one solely ... The population numbers about 150 persons. The climate is suited to the growth of cotton.[37]

**CESSNOCK** ... a postal hamlet in the ... police district of Maitland ... The district is an agricultural one, dairy farming, and the growth of cereals being carried on to a great extent ... Cessnock proper consists only of 2 houses, and a population of 11 persons, but the surrounding agricultural district contains the small farms of a great number of settlers. The surrounding country is generally flat, the land being occasionally encumbered with dense scrub and heavy timber.[38]

**CHIPPENDALE** ... a portion of Sydney, within the city boundary, and lying between Parramatta-street and Redfern, on the W. side of the railway line.[39]

**CLARENCE RIVER** ... the largest river known on the E. coast, and has 13 feet of water on its bar. There are large quantities of rich alluvial plains, cedar brushes, and swamps on it ... Copper has been found in several places, also coal of good quality ... The course of the Clarence river is about 240 miles, and it drains an area of 8000 square miles of country, generally rough and scrubby. Towards its lower end there are rich beds of coal and large tracts of exceedingly productive soil, mostly alluvial ... taken up by small settlers.[40]

**COBAR** ... small hamlet 698 miles west from Sydney.[41]

**CONCORD** ... one of the original districts ... bounded on the S. side by the Sydney road ... on the N. side by the Parramatta river.[42]

**COOK'S RIVER** ... a fine stream falling into the head of the N. arm of Botany bay.[43]

**COOMA** ... a postal township ... With Sydney, 296 miles N.N.E., the communication is by Cobb's coach, via Goulburn to Picton, and thence by rail ... The height above sea level is 2637 feet ... The surrounding country is mountainous to the S., with undulating plains to the E. Much of the available agricultural land is taken by free selectors ... The population numbers 370 persons. Cooma gold field lies in the neighbourhood.[44]

**CORNISH SETTLEMENT** ... a small village, lying near the township of Guyong. There is a copper mine in the village, which is, however, not worked at present.[45]

**COW FLAT** ... is 155 miles west from Sydney, and 11 miles from Bathurst ... An agricultural district.[46]

**CROYDON** an area near Burwood, in Sydney.[47]

**CURRAWANG** a small township in the police district, electorate, and county of Argyle, is 149 miles from Sydney ... Chiefly agricultural pursuits. Copper is found near Lake George.[48]

**DAPTO** ... a postal village, the centre of an agricultural district ... at the E. foot of the Illawarra range of mountains. The district is almost exclusively an agricultural one, the principal industry being dairy farming ... There is, however, some good grazing country, used chiefly for the fattening of cattle.[49]

**DARLING HARBOUR** ... a S. arm of port Jackson ... This bay divides the suburbs of Balmain, Pyrmont, and the Ultimo estate from Sydney.[50]

---

33   Ibid, p.119.
34   Ibid, p.119.
35   Ibid, p.121.
36   Ibid, p.122.
37   Ibid, pp.124-5.
38   Ibid, p.128.
39   Ibid, p.130.
40   Ibid, p.132.
41   *GPDNSW*, p.162.
42   *BGNSW*, p.142.
43   Ibid, p.145.
44   Ibid, pp.147-8.
45   Ibid, p.154.
46   *GPDNSW*, p.190.
47   Brian Kennedy and Barbara Kennedy, *Sydney and suburbs*, p.34.
48   *GPDNSW*, p.208.
49   *BGNSW*, p.170.

**DARLINGHURST** ... a portion of the city of Sydney, lying on the hill, on the E. side.[51]
**DARLINGTON**     a municipality of Sydney, incorporated in 1864.[52]
**DEEPWATER**     ... a small agricultural village ... 28 miles N. of Glen Innis, on the great N. road, the communication being by horse and dray only ... has a population of about 40 persons.[53]
**DENNIS ISLAND**   ... an agricultural settlement, lying about 12 miles W. of Bathurst, on the Queen Charlotte vale creek.[54]
**DOUBLE BAY**    ... a fine indentation in the S. side of port Jackson ... a favourite place of suburban residence ... on a sloping piece of land, between the New South Head road on the S. and E., the waters of the bay on the N. ... the surrounding district is rocky, rugged, and scrubby, although in a valley to the S.E. of the village ... is a tract of fine alluvial and rather swampy land, highly cultivated as market gardens, and watered by a small creek, draining from the high lands of Waverley ... the population numbers about 230 persons.[55]
**DULWICH HILL**   an area in the Petersham district of Sydney.[56]
**DUNDEE** see Severn.
**DUNGOG**     ... a postal ... township in the parish of Dungog ... in an agricultural district, and contains 2 flour mills (1 driven by steam, and 1 by water), 2 tanneries, and 2 tobacco manufactories, the cultivation of that article of produce having been extensively gone into of late in the neighbourhood. The chief produce of the district is, however, cereals, very fine wheat, barley, and maize being grown in great abundance, and large quantities of hay being sent down to the Sydney market ... There is a population numbering about 500 persons.[57]
**DUNKELD**    ... a small village in the ... police district of Bathurst, lying about 3 miles N. of Evans' plains, the nearest post office.[58]
**EDEN**     ... on the N. shore of Twofold bay, and is the port for the whole of the S.E. districts of New South Wales ... The district is an agricultural and pastoral one, whaling being carried on to a considerable extent during the proper season, and a number of fishermen gaining a livelihood on the bay ... communication ... with Sydney, 283 miles N., by the steamers ... once a fortnight ... The surrounding country is rugged and scrubby ... The population numbers about 200 persons[59]
**ELSMORE**     a small township 398 miles north from Sydney.[60]
**EMMAVILLE**     See Vegetable Creek
**EMU PLAINS**     a tract of fine fertile undulating country, lying about 35 miles W. of Sydney, and mostly taken up in agricultural and grazing farms. The great Western road and railway cross these plains, which are watered by the river Nepean. The towns of Emu and Penrith are both in the neighbourhood, and there is a fine tweed factory, which gives employment to a large number of the residents.[61]
**ENFIELD**     ... a small postal village ... on the main line of Southern road from Sydney ... The district is chiefly an agricultural (dairy farming and market gardening) one, with some good pasture land ... Sydney, 7 miles distant N. ... The population of Enfield numbers about 409 persons.[62]
**ENMORE**     ... portion of the municipality of Newtown ... It consists of suburban residences, and the farms of a few dairymen.[63]
**EVANS' PLAINS**   ... a postal village in the ... police district of Bathurst ... a tract of excellent agricultural country, noted particularly for the excellence of the wheat grown there, and belongs wholly to the mount Pleasant estate, except a reserved Government village known as mount Pleasant. Cherry Tree hill and mount Apsley gold fields are each about 1 mile distant E. from Evans' plains, which are 4 miles W. of the town of Bathurst ... There is no regular booking office, but many teamsters reside on the plains, who carry goods to all parts of the country. There is a large 3 storey brick-built steam flour mill in the village.[64]
**FAL BROOK** ... a small N. tributary of the Hunter river. It flows past the township of Camberwell, and is fed by the Carron and Goorangoola creeks, and the Foy brook.[65]
**FISH RIVER** ... the E. head of the Macquarie river. It rises in the W. slope of the Australian alps, and flows N. and W. through good pastoral and agricultural country, into the main stream about 4 miles S. of Bathurst. Much of the land on and near this river is taken up as agricultural land ... The land along the river consists of a rich deep soil,

---

50   Ibid, pp.171-2.
51   Ibid, p.172.
52   Brian Kennedy and Barbara Kennedy, *Sydney and suburbs*, p.119.
53   *BGNSW*, p.176.
54   Ibid, p.180.
55   Ibid, pp.184-5.
56   Brian Kennedy and Barbara Kennedy, *Sydney and suburbs*, p.92.
57   *BGNSW*, pp.190-1.
58   Ibid, p.191.
59   Ibid, pp.194-5.
60   *GPDNSW*, p.240.
61   *BGNSW*, p.199.
62   Ibid, p.200.
63   Ibid, p.200.
64   Ibid, p.204.
65   Ibid, p.205.

black, fertile, and containing scarcely any stones ... The water is clear, and the stream well supplied with excellent fish, whence its name.[66]

**FIVEDOCK**   ... a rural district ... on the Parramatta river, 6 miles W. from Sydney, and on the main road from that place to Parramatta ...  There is a salting and boiling-down establishment ... in full work in Five Dock, the district being an agricultural one, producing large quantities of dairy produce and fruit and vegetables for the Sydney market ...  With Sydney the communication is from Ashfield by rail, trains running each way 11 times per day, and by the river steamers, which call 3 times per day.[67]

**FOREST REEFS**   a settlement 182 miles west from Sydney.[68]

**FOY BROOK** ... a small N. tributary of the Hunter river, flowing through good agricultural ground.[69]

**GEORGE LAKE**   ... the largest and most important of the inland lakes of New South Wales. It lies about 25 miles S.W. from the city of Goulburn ... 21 miles in length, with an average width of 7 or 8 miles. It is situated on the top of the table land of the dividing range, 2129 feet above sea level.[70]

**GLEBE**   ... a suburban municipality, adjoining the city of Sydney ... a populous suburb, and a favourite place of residence for merchants, and others having business in town ...  Communication with Sydney may be had by 'bus every 5 minutes ...  The population is estimated at 3712.[71]

**GLEN INNES** ... a postal township in the electoral district of Tenterfield ... in an agricultural and pastoral district, chiefly the latter ...  A gold field, known as Glen Elgin, gives fair average returns. It is within 20 miles E. of the town ...  The surrounding country is partly elevated and mountainous, and partly low and flat, with plains here and there all over the district. The plains are generally well grassed and lightly timbered, and the mountains thickly scrubbed and heavily wooded ...  The population numbers about 350 persons.[72]

**GOULBURN** ... an episcopal city ... an assize town, the chief place in the S. district, and one of the most important towns in the colony ...  Goulburn lies at the N. end of an extensive plain ...  Copper is obtained ... in the neighbourhood, and gold at various places in the district.[73]

**GRAFTON**   ... a postal town ... a seaport ... on the Clarence river ... 55 miles W. from the sea ...  The district is agricultural and pastoral ...  Gold mining has, for some time past, also been carried on with considerable success, the whole of the head waters of the Clarence being auriferous, and being worked over a length of 100 miles ...  The population of Grafton is about 1500.[74]

**GRESFORD**   ... a postal village ... situated on the Paterson river, about 15 miles N. from the Paterson township ... The district is an agricultural one, tobacco and corn being grown in large quantities in the neighbourhood. The vine is also extensively cultivated, the soil being admirably suited to its growth. Some of the best colonial wine made in New South Wales is manufactured at Gresford ...  The population is tolerably large, but scattered all over the district.[75]

**GUYONG**   ... a postal township in the parish of Colville, and electoral and police district of Orange. It is situated on the source of the Lewis Ponds creek, about 16 miles S. of the Ophir diggings, and the confluence of the Summerhill creek. The Great Western road from Bathurst to Wellington, via Lucknow and Orange, passes by Guyong, upon which road runs daily Cobb and Co.'s coaches to and from Sydney, carrying the mails. There is a steam flour mill at Frederick's valley, 5 miles W. of Guyong, also copper smelting works about 2 miles N. (at present idle). The district is well adapted for agricultural and pastoral purposes, both of which are extensively followed. It also abounds in gold, copper, lead, black sand, (auriferous), and sulphur; and in asbestos, limestone, freestone, and slate. There are 4 copper mines in the vicinity viz.: the Carangara, Brown's creek, Ophir and Icely. The Carangara mine, in addition to its rich copper lodes, is celebrated for the production of a black oxide, called the Carangara hair restorer, which is said to prevent and cure baldness, and which is largely used for that purpose. The Brown's creek and Ophir copper mines are not being worked at present. The Icely mine is situated 5 miles N.E. on 1183 acres of land leased from C. Icely Esq.; in this mine 8 distinct lodes have been discovered and traced for more than a mile. One lode is 3 feet 6 inches wide, 8 fathoms deep, and of solid grey ore, containing 58 per cent. of copper; another is 3 feet wide, and contains green and blue carbonates, red oxide, and grey ore, of from 43 to 45 per cent., the other lodes being of a similar general character. There are, also, thousands of tons of gozzan on the surface, yielding 15 dwts. of gold to the ton. This mine is pronounced by competent authorities to be one of the richest and most extensive ever discovered in the colony, and is leased by a company, consisting of Messrs. Tom Brothers, Stevens, and Sturt. A rich quartz reef is being worked at King's plains, 9 miles S. of Guyong, at which the proprietors have 1000 tons of quartz ready for crushing. The nearest towns are Lucknow, 7 miles W.; Orange, 12 miles W.; Blayney, 10 miles S.; and Bathurst, 22 miles E.  There is also an old settlement of considerable note, about 3 miles N., on the Lewis ponds creek, where there are the residences of several gentlemen, prominent amongst whom are the well-known old colonists, Messrs Tom, Hawke, Lane and Glasson. Cobb's coaches run daily to and

---

66   Ibid, p.206.
67   Ibid, p.207.
68   *GPDNSW*, p.256.
69   *BGNSW*, p.211.
70   Ibid, pp.216-7.
71   Ibid, p.223.
72   Ibid, p.225.
73   Ibid, pp.233-4.
74   Ibid, pp.236-7.
75   Ibid, p.241.

from Bathurst, Lucknow, and Orange. With Sydney, 141 miles E., the communication is by Cobb's coach to Penrith, and thence by rail. Guyong has a Wesleyan chapel, a national school, and a temperance society. The nearest hotels are, Oates's, 2 miles W.; and Butler's, 2 miles E., both on the Western road. The surrounding country is generally high land; to the N. and E. it is of a mountainous character, well-grassed, and watered by many small creeks and swamps between the hills, which are of trap and granite formation and deposit. There is abundance of timber of almost all kinds, principally, however, gum, box, apple, and stringybark, the latter being the most useful for building and fencing purposes.[76]

**GUYRA** a town in New England whose development began in the 1880s.[77]

**HANGING ROCK** ... a postal township in the ... police district of Tamworth ... The district is principally a mining one, both alluvial and quartz ... there are numerous cattle stations in the surrounding district ... Nundle, 4 miles W ... communication is by horse or dray, over bush roads only ... The want of good roads is a drawback to the district ... The population of Hanging Rock ... amounts to about 200 persons.[78]

**HARGRAVE** see Louisa Creek.

**HILL END** a township ... 180 miles north-west from Sydney ... The township, which is three miles distant from Tambaroora and 40 miles from Bathurst, is the locality of very extensive gold workings, principally quartz of great richness ... The district forms a portion of an immense tract of auriferous country, through which run the Turon and Macquarie rivers and their tributaries. The country is exceedingly mountainous and unfit for agricultural purposes, except to the eastward, where there is an occasional combination of agricultural and pastoral pursuits.[79]

**HINTON** ... a postal township, in the ... police district of Maitland ... at the junction of the Paterson and Hunter rivers ... The population numbers about 200 persons, chiefly engaged in farming.[80]

**HOMEBUSH** ... a small village on the Parramatta-road, about 10 miles W. from Sydney.[81]

**ICELY COPPER MINE** see Guyong.

**ILLAWARRA**... a fertile, beautiful, and romantic district in new South Wales, about 50 miles S. from Sydney ... extends in a N. and S. direction ... along the sea coast ... comprising about 150,000 acres. The Illawarra mountain is a lofty and precipitous range, running parallel to the coast, and supporting the elevated table land to the W. The view is indescribably beautiful and magnificent. The district of Illawarra consists of a belt of land enclosed between the mountain and the ocean, increasing in breadth to the S., thickly wooded, and for the most part of exuberant fertility ... There are exceedingly rich coal mines in the N. part of the district; in the neighbourhood of Wollongong these mines are best known as the mount Keira, Bellambi, and Bulli mines. On the American creek, a fine stream of water flowing from the W. ranges, a bed of kerosene shale has lately been discovered. The Illawarra district is celebrated for its dairy farming, and the excellence of its butter is well-known all over Australia. The chief towns are Wollongong, Kiama, and Dapto.[82]

**INVERELL** ... a township ... on the Mcintyre river, 383 miles N.W. of Sydney ... in a district unsurpassed in the colony for agriculture, which is being rapidly developed; the cultivation of the grape is attracting particular attention ... The country is also remarkable for its great grazing capability ... The first land in the township was sold in 1859 ... The population numbers about 250 persons.[83]

**KELSO** ... a postal township in the ... police district of Bathurst ... The district is chiefly an agricultural one, embracing three-fourths of the Bathurst plains, whose soil is for agricultural and pastoral purposes, unequalled in the colony. The plains cover an area of about 10 miles square, and are surrounded by high ranges, so that they form the bottom of an immense basin. The land is all more or less auriferous, particularly so near the ranges, but it is only of late that its golden resources, both alluvial and quartz, have attracted proper attention ... Kelso was the site of the first settlement W. of the Blue mountains, the Government stockade, with the commandant's offices being established on the opposite side of the river, about the centre of the present town of Bathurst. Kelso was set apart for free settlers, and is now the residence of many of the wealthiest inhabitants and largest landowners of the district ... There are several good vineyards near the town, producing excellent wine ... The population numbers about 500 persons.[84]

**KEMPSEY** ... a postal government township ... situated on the Macleay river, which divides it into East and West Kempsey, and lies about 240 miles N. of Sydney ... The district of the Macleay is principally an agricultural one, maize being grown in very large quantities, and the land being admirably adapted for the growth of the sugar cane, the cultivation of which is creating considerable attention amongst the settlers. Pastoral pursuits are followed in the outlying part of the district, and cattle, horses, and sheep all thriving well ... The population of East Kempsey numbers 145 persons, that of West kempsey 230, and that of the surrounding district about 1650.[85]

---

76  Ibid, p.251-2.
77  J. Kay Donald, *Exploring the north coast*, p.135.
78  *BGNSW*, p.254.
79  *GPDNSW*, p.340.
80  *BGNSW*, p.265.
81  Ibid, p.265.
82  Ibid, p.273.
83  Ibid, p.276.
84  Ibid, p.294.
85  Ibid, p.295.

**KIAMA** ... a small and pleasantly situated seaport town in the ... police district of Kiama ... The district is an agricultural and pastoral one, mostly occupied by small dairy farmers. The district is justly celebrated for the excellence of the butter it produces ... The population numbers about 700.[86]

**KIANDRA** ... a postal township in ... Monaro ... The district is an alluvial mining one, formerly of considerable importance but having fallen off for the last few years ... Tumut, 60 miles N.W., ... communication ... is now by horse or dray, the coaches which in the palmy days of the Kiandra diggings having been withdrawn, the mail is conveyed on horseback ... The surrounding country is mountainous ... The population, including that of the diggings ... numbers about 230 persons.[87]

**KINGDON PONDS** ... a tributary stream at the head of the Dart brook.[88]

**KINGDON PONDS** ... a small agricultural village on the creek of the same name. It is situated 6 miles N. of Scone.[89]

**LAKE GEORGE** see George, Lake.

**LARGS** (or DUNMORE) ... a small postal village adjoining the Bolwarra estate, 4 miles N. from Maitland. It contains a small agricultural population.[90]

**LEICHHARDT** ... a surveyed village, in the parish of Petersham, and electoral district of Canterbury.[91]

**LEWISHAM** an area in the Petersham district of Sydney.[92]

**LEWIS' PONDS CREEK** ... a rich auriferous stream, which has its rise in the mountainous country near Guyong ... The townships of Guyong, Byng and Ophir are situtated on this stream ... The principal gold field on this creek is that of Ophir. There are numerous tributary creeks, nearly all of which are auriferous.[93]

**LIVERPOOL** ... a postal borough town ... on the main road to the S. districts, 20 miles S.W. of Sydney. The district is an agricultural and pastoral one, principally the former, the chief industry being dairy farming ... The population numbers about 600 persons.[94]

**LOB'S HOLE** ... a deep valley near the crossing of the road from Kiandra to Tumberumba, over the Tumut river ... Ores of copper abound ... promising a profitable field of labour and enterprise.[95]

**LOUISA CREEK GOLD FIELDS** ... an extensive tract of auriferous country, lying on the Louisa creek and its tributaries. The chief town is Hargraves. The quantity of gold received by escort from the Louisa creek gold fields during the year 1864 was 8167 ozs ... total value £31,826 7s 9d.[96]

**LUCKNOW** ... a roadside mining village on the main road from Bathurst to Orange, lying about 7 miles W. of Guyong. The Lucknow or Wentworth diggings are on private land, on the side of the hills rising from Frederick's valley.[97]

**MACDONALD TOWN** [sic] ... a small village lying on the Cook's River road, between Newtown and Tempe.[98]

**MACLEAY RIVER** ... a magnificent stream ... flowing in an E. and S.E. direction, through rugged country, splendidly timbered with cedar and other valuable trees, for a distance of about 200 miles into the ocean at Trial Bay.[99]

**MACQUARIE PLAINS** a settlement and railway station in the police district of Bathurst ... 138 miles west from Sydney ... the district, which is a pastoral one, consists of a plain, which is undulating in character.[100]

**MAITLAND, EAST** ... a municipal borough and postal town ... on Wallis' creek, which divides it on its W. side from West Maitland, and on the Hunter river which flows on its N. side. East Maitland was laid out by the Government on a flat between the Hunter river and a range of low sloping hills, in a pleasant but unsuitable site ... The district is an agricultural and pastoral one, chiefly the former, the cultivation of maize, lucerne, and garden produce being one of the principal industries. There are coal mines ... horse and cattle market and sale yards ... The population numbers about 2000 persons.[101]

**MAITLAND, WEST** ... a borough and postal town ... The district is wholly agricultural, the soil being well adapted for the growth of wheat, maize, barley, lucerne, and also of fruit and vegetables. Within 3 miles of Maitland there are several coal mines at work ... The population ... is ... 5694.[102]

---

86 Ibid, pp.297-8.
87 Ibid, p.298.
88 Ibid, p.300.
89 Ibid, p.300.
90 Ibid, p.312.
91 Ibid, p.313.
92 Brian Kennedy and Barbara Kennedy, *Sydney and suburbs*, p.92.
93 *BGNSW*, pp.313-4.
94 Ibid, p.318.
95 Ibid, p.320.
96 Ibid, pp.322-3.
97 Ibid, p.323.
98 Ibid, p.324.
99 Ibid, pp.325-6.
100 *GPDNSW*, p.435.
101 *BGNSW*, pp.329-30.
102 Ibid, p.330.

**MAJOR'S CREEK** ... a small postal digging township ... on Major's creek, on the table land immediately above the coast range, about 10 miles S. from Braidwood ... The district is an alluvial mining one ... The surrounding country is elevated and mountainous. The population of Major's creek numbers about 200 persons.[103]

**MANLY** ... a pleasant suburban village, lying between Manly beach and the Pacific ocean ... much frequented by visitors on Sundays and at holiday times.[104]

**MARRICKVILLE** ... a municipal village, suburban to Sydney, in the parish of Petersham ... about 4 miles S.W. of the Sydney post office ... There are 2 soap and candle factories, 3 brick yards, and a tannery in Marrickville, and the land, which is generally fine alluvial soil, is laid out for market gardens, a pursuit for which it is well adapted ... the population numbers about 800 persons.[105]

**MOLONG**: ... a postal township ... the Canobolas mountains lie about 18 miles S. Molong lies in an agricultural and pastoral district, abounding in minerals, principally copper. Mines were worked some time since, but have been abandoned, although it is contemplated by a private company now forming to re-open one of them ... population ... numbers 277.[106]

**MORPETH** ... is situated at the head of the navigation of the Hunter river, 96 miles N. of Sydney, the Paterson joining that river half a mile E. of the township. The district is an agricultural and coal mining one, there being 4 coal pits opened and in full operation.[107]

**MORUYA** ... a postal seaport town, in the electoral district of Eden ... an agricultural and quartz mining district. The mines are situated about 4 miles to the S.W. of the township ... There are 2 quartz-crushing mills, a steam engine for raising quartz, a steam flour mill, and a tobacco factory ... The surrounding country consists of fine, rich, alluvial flats, mostly under cultivation, and good undulating forest land.[108]

**MURRURUNDI** ... a postal township in the electoral district of the upper Hunter ... an agricultural district, surrounded by mountains ... The population numbers 322 persons.[109]

**MUSCLEBROOK** (or MUSWELLBROOK) ... on the Hunter river ... The district is agricultural and pastoral, principally in the former, in the immediate neighbourhood of the town ... The surrounding country is mostly flat, with a few undulating rises. It is well grassed and timbered ... the town ... has a population of about 600 inhabitants, that of the entire police district being about 2000.[110]

**MUTTON'S FALLS** ... a postal township ... on the Fish river, near its junction with the Macquarie river ... The district is thickly grassed, well timbered, and admirably adapted for agricultural pursuits, which are extensively followed in the neighbourhood ... Oberon, 10 miles S.E.; and Bathurst, 25 miles N.W. With these places, the communication is by horse or dray, the mail being conveyed weekly on horseback ... The surrounding country is slightly elevated, hilly, but not mountainous ... The population of the neighbourhood numbers about 500 persons.[111]

**NEWCASTLE** (or KINGSTOWN) ... the second port in the colony ... The district in which Newcastle is situated is especially a coal mining one, the principal mines in the neighbourhood being those of Lambton, Borehole, Wallsend, and Minmi ... In the neighbourhood of Newcastle agriculture is carried on to a considerable extent, large quantities of maize, barley, and lucerne being grown, the land along the river banks being especially productive ... The port, although inferior in natural advantages to port Stephens, has monopolised the whole of the trade of the Hunter district, as well as that of the pastoral country beyond, and the railway from Newcastle to the N. interior has tended to consolidate and confirm that supremacy ... The mineral resources of the district may be looked upon as inexhaustible, and the facilities available at Newcastle alone, permit the easy shipment of 3000 to 4000 tons of coal per day. The extraction of coal has doubled in the last 5 years, and amounted in 1864 to half a million of tons.[112]

**NEW ENGLAND** ... a pastoral district in a vast tract of grazing country ... It forms an immense table land, at an elevation of about 3000 feet above sea level, and has an area of 13,100 square miles. The climate is mild, and much of the soil is well adapted for agriculture.[113]

**NEWTOWN** ... a large and important suburb of Sydney, in the parish of Petersham ... The population numbers between 6000 and 7000 persons.[114]

**NUNDLE**... a postal town in the ... police district of Tamworth ... The district is an agricultural one, with alluvial and quartz workings in the neighbourhood ... The surrounding country is generally mountainous, with undulating plains of good pastoral country ... The population numbers about 500 persons.[115]

**OBERON**: ... a small postal township in the ... police district of Bathurst ... situated in an agricultural district; the Native Dog creek and Brisbane valley diggings, both alluvial, being, respectively, 8 and 7 miles W ... The

---

103  Ibid, p.332-3.
104  Ibid, p.335.
105  Ibid, pp.338-9.
106  Ibid, pp.359-60.
107  Ibid, pp.369-70.
108  Ibid, p.371.
109  Ibid, p.389.
110  Ibid, p.390.
111  Ibid, pp.391-2.
112  Ibid, pp.406-9.
113  Ibid, pp.409-10.
114  Ibid, p.423.
115  Ibid, p.430.

surrounding country consists of a table land, surrounded by mountains and heavily timbered ... The population numbers about 30 persons.[116]

**O'CONNELL** ... a postal township on the Fish river, the Blue mountain range being about 20 miles distant. The district is agricultural, pastoral, and alluvial mining, there being one steam flour mill in the township. Bathurst is the nearest place, being 12 miles distant, there being no regular means of conveyance, and the mails being carried on horseback twice a week ... The surrounding country is mountainous ... The population numbers about 300 persons.[117]

**OPHIR** ... a postal mining township ... near the Summer hill creek ... Ophir is the oldest gold field in New South Wales ... The district is surrounded by sheep and cattle stations, and there are also several nice farms of small extent in the neighbourhood of the town ... Orange, distant 16 miles W.; Bathurst, 36 miles S. ... the communication being by horse or dray ... There are no coach or carrying offices, but drays are continually passing through the town for all the neighbouring places. The surrounding country is mountainous, and surrounded by slate and quartz ridges ... The population, which is a variable one, averages about 150 Europeans and 200 Chinese. There are fine veins of copper in the district, and a mine; the old Ophir mine has yielded large returns. A new mine (Icely's), adjoining the old Ophir, has been worked some time, and continues to give very great promise. Several fine lodes have been opened upon, some of which are of great size, and are yielding very rich ore, particularly one which runs from the Ophir mine, and is believed to be part of the lode formerly worked.[118]

**ORANGE**: ... a postal and municipal township, in the electoral and police district of Orange ... the surrounding district ... is one of the finest agricultural ones in the colony. Gold and copper are found in the district, the Ophir and Wentworth diggings being the principal gold diggings, and the old Ophir, Icely's Carangara, Cadiangullong, and Canobolas, the principal copper mines. From these mines 1800 tons of ore ... were taken during the year 1864 ... The neighbourhood of Orange is as rich in mineral wealth as any part of the colony. Gold, silver, copper, and lead have been found in it, the copper-producing country having been traced from the Canobolas mountains, E., for a distance of 30 miles, in a belt 10 or 12 miles in width. Coal exists only in thin seams, and its production is immaterial, except for the smelting of iron, copper smelting being better carried on with wood ... The district is mountainous and rugged ... The population numbers about 600 persons.[119]

**PADDINGTON** ... a township ... suburban to Sydney, and lying on the high land to the E. of the city ... It is a favourite place of residence for persons having business in Sydney, being salubrious and pleasant ... The communication with Sydney is by 'busses, which run throughout the day ... The population of Paddington numbers 2692 persons.[120]

**PANBULA** [sic] ... a postal township in the ... police district of Eden ... The district is both agricultural and pastoral ... The population ... numbers about 300 persons.[121]

**PARRAMATTA** ... a postal and municipal and electoral township, (the oldest in the colony with the exception of Sydney) ... on the Parramatta river ... The district is agricultural, the soil being, however, unsuitable to farming pursuits generally, but admirably adapted to the growth of fruit, particularly oranges, of which there are large orchards within a short distance, yielding large returns ... With Sydney, 14 miles by railway, 15 miles by road, and 16 miles by water, the communication is by rail 7 times per day, and by river steamer thrice per day. There is no regular conveyance along the road, although drays, &c., are continually passing ... The population numbers about 6000 persons.[122]

**PARRAMATTA RIVER** ... is the name applied to the inland continuation of port Jackson, an arm which stretches to the W. for about 18 miles ... There is steamboat communication along this arm to Parramatta, which is the head of the navigation ... The Parramatta river ... is celebrated for the beauty of its scenery ... The villages of Hunter's hill and Gladesville, and the township of Ryde, lie upon the N. bank (places celebrated for the splendid quality of their orangeries and orchards, many of which descend to the river bank in sloping terraces, and impart a tranquil beauty to a scene otherwise somewhat wild and rugged).[123]

**PATERSON** ... a postal township in the ... police district of Paterson ... The district is essentially an agricultural one, the soil being rich and well cultivated. It produces maize, wheat, barley, oats, lucerne, potatoes, pumpkins, melons, cucumbers, tobacco, and all kinds of esculent roots and farm and garden produce in abundance. Fruits of all kinds, there being large vineyards, orangeries, and orchards in the neighbourhood ... The surrounding country is extremely mountainous, but to the S. and W. are extensive flats ... The population numbers about 400 persons.[124]

**PATRICK'S PLAINS** ... a large tract of fine pastoral and agricultural country, lying on both sides the Hunter river, near Singleton. The district is celebrated for its dairy produce, and for its fattening capability for cattle.[125]

---

116  Ibid, p.433.
117  Ibid, pp.433-4.
118  Ibid, pp.435-6.
119  Ibid, pp.436-7.
120  Ibid, pp.440-1.
121  Ibid, pp.442-3.
122  Ibid, pp.444-6.
123  Ibid, p.446.
124  Ibid, pp.447-8.
125  Ibid, pp.448-9.

**PEEL**    ... a postal township in the police district of Bathurst ... There are mountains within half a mile of Peel, and running in almost every direction. The district is a pastoral, agricultural, and mining one, the latter both alluvial and quartz, and the diggings surrounding the township on every side.[126]

**PETERSHAM**... a small postal township, suburban to Sydney ... on the Parramatta or Great Western road and railway ... There is but little agriculture in Petersham, which, before the railway was established, was a roadside township of considerable importance, but since then has subsided into a mere place of residence for persons occupied in Sydney, but living out of town ... The population is small and scattered.[127]

**PORT MACQUARIE**    ... the embouchure of the Hastings river ... a bar harbour, and is dangerous of access.[128]

**POTTS POINT**    ... a rocky promontory on the S. shore of port Jackson ... a favourite place for suburban residences.[129]

**PRETTY PLAINS** ... a tract of fine agricultural land ... on the road from Bathurst to Orange, about 9 miles S.E. of Orange ... mostly taken up by small settlers, under the new Land Act.[130]

**PYRMONT**    ... a suburb of Sydney ... on a tongue of land which divides the Blackwattle cove from Darling harbour, the latter separating it from Sydney ... The Australian Steam Navigation Company's patent slip and engineering yard for the repair of steamers, lies to the N.E. opposite Balmain. The number of men and boys employed in this establishment is 350 ... every convenience [is supplied] for carrying on all branches of the marine engineering business, blacksmiths, coppersmiths, plumbers, moulders, carpenters, joiners, pattern makers, and mechanists of all kinds requisite being employed.[131]

**QUEANBEYAN**    ... a postal township ... on the Queanbeyan river ... The district is pastoral and agricultural ... The population numbers about 550 persons.[132]

**RAYMOND TERRACE** ...a postal township ... on the E. bank of the Hunter river ... an agricultural district, the cultivation of the grape being extensively carried on, and the soil being eminently suited to vine growing ... The population numbers about 300 persons.[133]

**REDFERN**    ... a postal and municipal suburb of Sydney ...    The railway terminus adjoins it on the N. The population numbers about 4000 persons.[134]

**RICHMOND RIVER**    ... a fine stream ... flowing through rugged pastoral country for about 120 miles, during which course it drains an area of 2400 square miles ... like all small rivers along this coast, this has also a bar across the entrance, which is constantly shifting.[135]

**ROCKLEY**    ... a postal township ... 22 miles S. of Bathurst ... 2000 feet above the level of the sea ... situated in a district principally agricultural, although having some large sheep runs in the locality ... Gold mining, chiefly alluvial, employs an average population of about 400 persons, which has, however, varied from 200 to 1300 during the last four years' digging ...    The entire country is very mountainous, even the township itself being hilly ... Copper has been found in large quantities at the Bathurst copper mines (now idle), 5 miles N. Silver and lead mines were also worked at one time ... There are 2 quarries of a stone called soap stone, which ... retains heat for a longer time than fire-bricks, and is very valuable for furnaces and similar purposes. There is a large population in the neighbourhood, but owing to the mountainous character of the country it is very much scattered. In the township itself are about 130 souls.[136]

**ROCKY RIVER**    ... a postal mining village in the ... police district of Armidale. It is the postal head quarters of the Rocky river gold field, which extends from the township of Uralla ... The crest of the main dividing range is distant about 2 miles E., and reaches an elevation of 4000 feet above sea level. The surrounding country is lightly timbered and grassed ...    Only a small portion of the land is suitable for agriculture. Gold mining is the chief interest, and is confined to alluvial workings, chiefly by means of shafts and tunnels ... the population numbers about 500 Europeans and 350 Chinese, scattered over the diggings ... A feature of this gold field is the masses of huge granitic rock piled one on another in wild confusion.[137]

**RUSHCUTTERS BAY**    ... an indentation on the S. shore of port Jackson ... between Darling and Pott's points.[138]

**ST. LEONARD'S**    ... a suburban township to Sydney, situated on the N. shore of port Jackson ... The inhabitants are chiefly persons whose business lies in Sydney, but there are also a number of quarrymen, ballastmen, and ferrymen resident in and near the township ... The population of St. Leonard's and the vicinity number about 2000 persons.[139]

---

126  Ibid, pp.449-50.
127  Ibid, p.453.
128  Ibid, p.461.
129  Ibid, p.462.
130  Ibid, p.462.
131  Ibid, pp.465-6.
132  Ibid, pp.466-7.
133  Ibid, pp.472-3.
134  Ibid, pp.473-4.
135  Ibid, pp.476-7.
136  Ibid, pp.479-80.
137  Ibid, pp.481-2.
138  Ibid, p.485.
139  Ibid, pp.488-9.

**ST. PETERS** ... a postal village in the parish of Petersham ... The district is an agricultural one, but a considerable number of the inhabitants are engaged in brickmaking and limeburning ... The population numbers about 600 persons.[140]

**SCONE** ... a postal township on the Kingdon ponds ... the Hunter river 7 miles N.E. ... Scone is almost totally surrounded by mountains ... The township lies at an elevation of about 870 feet above sea level ... The population of Scone numbers about 400 persons. The surrounding country, known as the Kingdon Ponds plain, is gently undulating, and is adapted for agriculture.[141]

**SEVERN** (postal name DUNDEE) ... A postal village in the ... police district of Wellingrove ... The district is a pastoral and agricultural one, principally the former ... The population numbers about 60 persons.[142]

**SHELLHARBOUR**... a small postal township ... on the coast, about 4 miles ... N. of Kiama ... The district is a dairy farming one, and the population is small and scattered.[143]

**SHOALHAVEN RIVER** ... the largest and most important river on the coast side of the dividing range to the S. of Sydney ... Its upper part is highly auriferous ... The Shoalhaven river is about 260 miles in length.[144]

**SIDMOUTH VALLEY CREEK** ... a small S. tributary of the Fish river, rising in the rich pastoral country to the S. of Mutton's falls ... The soil in the valley through which this stream flows is exceedingly fertile.[145]

**SINGLETON** ... a postal town ...on the Hunter river ... in a rich agriultural and pastoral district. There are no manufactories ... The population of the town and suburbs ... numbers about 2000 persons; that of the entire district ... about 10,000.[146]

**SOFALA** ... a postal mining township ... on the Turon river ... The district in which Sofala is situated is essentially a mining one, both alluvial and quartz workings being extensively carried on ... The nearest places are Bathurst, 30 miles, and Peel, 21 miles distant, with both of which places there is daily communication by Cobb's 4-horse American coach ... The surrounding country is generally mountainous ... The population of the township numbers about 1000 persons, and of the diggings, of which it is the chief centre, about 3000 more.[147]

**STANMORE** ... a suburb of Newtown, lying to the S. of the railway line ... occupied by dairymen, and has numerous suburban residences.[148]

**SURRY HILLS** ... a residential suburb of Sydney, included in the electoral district of Paddington, and in the metropolitan police district. It lies on the S. side of Sydney and is within the city boundary.[149]

**TAMBAROORA** ... a postal mining township ... on the Tambaroora creek. W. from Tambaroora, at a distance of 10 miles, runs the Macquarie river ... This river is being worked by numerous parties of gold miners. The only mills in operation are two quartz-crushing machines, which are nearly always working night and day. The district is entirely a mining one, and both alluvial and quartz mining are carried on to a considerable extent ... The distance from Bathurst, 38 miles, is by a bridle path, exceedingly rough, and quite impassable for wheeled conveyances, which have to travel by a different route a distance of 65 miles ... The district is very mountainous, and entirely unfit for agricultural purposes, except to the E., where small portions of land are occupied by settlers, who combine agricultural with pastoral pursuits. The population of the town is not more 400 [sic], but that of the district may be fairly estimated at 3500.[150]

**TAMWORTH** ... a postal township ... on the Peel and Cockburn rivers, in an undulating, pastoral, and agricultural district ... Tamworth is surrounded by large tracts of excellent agricultural land, and since the new land act has come into operation, has progressed rapidly ... The surrounding country is undulating, and hemmed in by mountain ranges at some distance ... The population numbers about 650 persons, including that of the environs.[151]

**TARANA** a small township and station ... 126 miles west from Sydney.[152]

**TENT HILL** a settlement in the police district of Wellingrove ... 395 miles north from Sydney ... A pastoral district with fine agricultural land on the plains and lower areas, which are also well-grassed; the mountainous portions being thickly scrubbed and timbered.[153]

**TINGHA** a settlement in the ... pastoral district of New England, is 344 miles north from Sydney.[154]

**TRUNKEY CREEK** a small township in the police district of Bathurst ... 182 miles west from Sydney ... An agricultural and mining district.[155]

---

140  Ibid, p.489.
141  Ibid, pp.492-3.
142  Ibid, p.496.
143  Ibid, p.498.
144  Ibid, pp.499-500.
145  Ibid, p.500.
146  Ibid, p.501.
147  Ibid, p.504.
148  Ibid, p.510.
149  Ibid, pp.514-5.
150  Ibid, pp.529-30.
151  Ibid, p.530.
152  *GPDNSW*, p.695.
153  Ibid, p.705.
154  Ibid, p.711.
155  Ibid, p.720.

**TUENA** ... a postal township ... on the Tuena creek ... the locality is mountainous for many miles round, and is rich in gold, silver, copper, and iron; also, in marble and limestone. The district is agricultural and mining. It produces in perfection wheat, and all other cereals; also, potatoes of the best quality, and vegetables in abundance. The fruits are of the finest flavour, consisting of apples, pears, peaches, plums, apricots, almonds, and splendid grapes. Tobacco also grows to perfection. Its mines are both alluvial and quartz; they have been very rich, and are still undeveloped for the want of capital ... The carrying trade of Tuena ... is by horse teams and bullock drays, chiefly belonging to the neighbouring settlers ... The surrounding country is very mountainous ... The population numbers about 1500 persons, including the diggers.[156]

**TUMUT** ... a postal township ... The district ... is essentially an agricultural one ... There are also some diggings (alluvial) ... The population numbers about 520 persons.[157]

**TURON DIGGINGS**    ... the numerous and extensive gold workings on the Turon river and its tributary auriferous crecks. The various diggings, large and small, are exceedingly numerous, and have been for a long time, and still are richly payable. They are chiefly alluvial, although in several places good quartz is obtained. Sofala is the chief town on these gold fields.[158]

**TWOFOLD BAY**    ... the principal harbour on the S. part of the coast of the colony ... the port of the Monaro country, and has the fine flourishing township of Eden built on its N. bank.[159]

**ULLADULLA** ... situated on the sea, 120 miles by sea S. of Sydney ... The harbour is one of the safest in New South Wales ... The surrounding country is undulating and has good soil, dairy farming being carried on to a considerable extent ... The population numbers about 90 persons.[160]

**ULTIMO** ... a tract of land, lying between Parramatta-street and Pyrmont, Black Wattle cove and Darling harbour[161]

**URALLA** ... a postal township ... on the Rocky river ... There is a large lake, known as Dangar's lagoon, about 2½ miles from Uralla, S.E., from which a water race is cut, for the use of miners at Burying Ground gully, near Uralla ... The district is agricultural, pastoral and mining. Alluvial gold mining is carried on to a great extent, by means of shafts and tunnels. The gold field is distant about 2 miles W. of Uralla ... The country is generally flat and undulating ... The population numbers about 120 persons.[162]

**VEGETABLE CREEK**    a settlement in the police district of Wellingrove ... 401 miles north from Sydney ... a pastoral district.[163]

**WALLSEND** ... a postal coal mining village, in the ... police district of Newcastle ... The district is a coalmining one ... The population numbers about 2000 persons.[164]

**WARATAH**    ... a postal village in the ... police district of Newcastle ... Coal mining is carried on extensively in the village and neighbourhood ... The surrounding district is hilly ... The population of Waratah, including miners and others, numbers about 500 persons.[165]

**WATERLOO** ... suburban municipality ... on the road from Sydney to Botany ... There is a large wool washing establishment ... several boiling down establishments, and a sugar works, also a newly erected rope works ... The population numbers about 1700 persons.[166]

**WATTLE FLAT**    ... a postal mining township ... on the line of road from Bathurst to Sofala, and on a table land lying 2000 feet above the level of the sea ... The district is a mining one (alluvial and quartz), forming portion of the Turon diggings, there being 2 quartz-crushing mills on the flat ... The population numbers about 2000 persons in the whole district.[167]

**WAVERLEY** ... a postal village, suburban to Sydney ... about 4 miles E. of Sydney ... chiefly occupied by the villa residences of gentlemen having business in the city ... There are, also, 4 quarries of excellent freestone. With Sydney there is communication by 'bus every hour ... The district is elevated, and has a population of about 900 persons.[168]

**WELLINGROVE**    ... a postal township ... on the Wellingrove creek, the Beardy river being 12, and the Severn river 20 miles distant. The district is solely pastoral, the nearest diggings (the Bingara) being 77 miles distant S.W. ... the population numbers about 50 persons[169]

**WELLINGTON**    ... a postal town in the electoral and police districts of Wellington ... Within the last few years, the neighbourhood has become an extensive agricultural one. Gold mining is also carried on ... The country is generally mountainous, with large alluvial flats and forest land ... The population of Wellington is about 400, including Montefiores. The capability of the country for agriculture is very great ... Fruit of every description is

---

156  *BGNSW*, pp.554-5.
157  Ibid, pp.556-7.
158  Ibid, p.560.
159  Ibid, pp.561-2.
160  Ibid, p.564.
161  Ibid, p.565.
162  Ibid, pp.567-8.
163  *GPDNSW*, p.743.
164  *BGNSW*, pp.579-80.
165  Ibid, pp.583-4.
166  Ibid, p.591.
167  Ibid, p.593.
168  Ibid, p.593.
169  Ibid, pp.597-8.

grown, and the vine flourishes to an extent not surpassed in any part of the world. Copper and iron stone also exist, but have not been worked.[170]

**WOLLONGONG** ... seaport town ... justly celebrated for the beauty of its scenery and the salubrity of its climate ... The district is an agricultural and coal mining one ... The population numbers about 1500 persons.[171]

**WOOLAHRA** [sic] ... suburban municipality ... a favourite place of residence for merchants and others having business in Sydney, from which it lies distant about 4 miles, the communication being by 'buss.'[172]

**WOOLLOOMOOLOO** ... an E. suburb of Sydney, lying within the city boundary ... principally a place of residence.[173]

---

170 Ibid, pp.598-9.
171 Ibid, p.618.
172 Ibid, p.621.
173 Ibid, p.622.

# APPENDIX VI
## BIOGRAPHICAL NOTES

\*     member of the New South Wales Parliament.          +     clergyman.

**+ADAMS**     Edward, Congregational minister, was born in Cornwall in 1843. He entered the ministry in 1875, and served at Wallsend, Waterloo, Willoughby, Glebe, Manly, and Southport (Queensland).[1]

**+ADAMS**     Thomas, Wesleyan minister, was born in 1821 at Laneast, and arrived in New South Wales in 1847 en route to Tonga as a missionary. He served in Parramatta and in Tonga before returning to Britain in 1861.[2]

**+ANGWIN**     Thomas, Wesleyan minister, was born in 1832 at St Agnes, and arrived in New South Wales in 1854. He served at West Maitland-Singleton, Parramatta, Goulburn, Bathurst-Orange, Mudgee, and Kiama. He died in 1867.[3]

**\*BARTON**     Russell, was born in 1830, and emigrated to South Australia in 1839. He became a pastoralist in western New South Wales, a mining entrepreneur, and chairman of the Great Cobar Copper Mining Co. He was MLA for Bourke from 1880 to 1886.[4]

**+BICE**     Charles, Anglican minister, was born in 1844 at St Enoder. He served at Murrurundi, Raymond Terrace, West Maitland, Stockton and Neutral Bay (Sydney). He died in Sydney in 1922.[5]

**\*BLIGH**     James William, was born in Bodmin in 1810. A solicitor in Cornwall, he emigrated to South Australia in 1839, and began practising in New South Wales in 1841. He was a J.P. in 1852, the first chairman of Willoughby Council 1865-7, an elected member of the old Legislative Council 1851-6, and MLC 1856-59.[6]

**+CARVOSSO**     Benjamin, Wesleyan minister, was born at Gluvian [sic] in 1789. He was the son of William Carvosso, a fisherman and farmer who was a class leader and local preacher for 60 years. Benjamin was accepted as a candidate for the ministry in 1814 and served in New South Wales between 1820 and 1825, before moving to Hobart. He returned to Britain in 1830, and died at Tuckingmill, Cornwall in 1854. He was buried at Ponsanooth. While in Sydney he was one of the founders of the *Australian Magazine*.[7]

**\*COOKE**     Henry Harry, was born in St Martin's in 1840. He emigrated to Victoria in 1857, living at Bendigo and Beechworth and came to New South Wales in 1861. He settled in Parkes (then known as Currajong) and is credited with bringing Sir Henry Parkes to the town and hanving it renamed in his honour. He was a miner, storekeeper, newspaper proprietor and editor, farmer and vigneron. He was an alderman at Parkes, and the first mayor. He was MLA for Forbes 1880-82, and 1887-91. He set up business as a merchant banker, establishied the first newspaper in the region, set up a school on his property, served as a magistrate and as a mining warden and is believed to have grown the first wheat in the area. His brother Albert emigrated in 1878. Methodist.[8]

**+CURNOW**     William, Wesleyan minister, was born in 1832 at St Ives, son of a miner. He arrived in New South Wales in 1854 and served at West Maitland, Parramatta, Oberon, Ipswich (Queensland), Balmain, Bourke Street (Sydney) and Goulburn. He was known as a 'prince of preachers' but a throat complaint forced a change of occupation. He was co-editor of *Christian Advocate and Wesleyan Record* betweeen 1864 and 1868, and from 1871 to 1873. In 1875 he was a member of the editorial staff of *Sydney Morning Herald*, and editor of *Sydney Mail*, in 1885. He was editor of the *Sydney Morning Herald* from 1886 until his death in 1903.[9]

## DANGAR

Members of the Dangar family of St Neot became involved in all areas of Hunter region life. Six Dangar brothers, Henry, William, Thomas, Charles Cary, John Hooper, Richard Cary and their sister and brother-in-law Elizabeth Cary and Samuel W. Cook emigrated between 1821 and 1837.[10]

Henry Dangar arrived in the colony in 1821 and was employed as assistant Government Surveyor. The majority of his survey work was carried out in the Hunter region and further north.[11] By 1826 he had surveyed and

1     G. Lindsay Lockley, *A biographical card index of Congregational ministers in Australia 1798-1977*, photocopied, and bound into a volume at UCA. The index does not give his birthplace, but his tombstone in Wallsend general cemetery (Newcastle) does.
2     E.G. Clancy, 'Biographical notes on early Wesleyan ministers in New South Wales', manuscript, UCA.
3     E.G. Clancy, 'Early Wesleyan ministers'.
4     C.N. Connolly, *Biographical register of the New South Wales Parliament 1856-1901*, ANU Press, Canberra, 1983, pp.16-17.
5     K.J. Cable and L. Cable, 'Biographical register of Anglican ministers in Australia', in the possession of Professor and Mrs K.J. Cable.
6     C.N. Connolly, *Biographical register of the New South Wales Parliament 1856-1901*, pp.24-5.
7     E.G. Clancy, 'Early Wesleyan ministers'.
8     C.N. Connolly, *Biographical register of the New South Wales Parliament 1856-1901*, p.61. Information from Mr William Georgans.
9     E.G. Clancy, 'Early Wesleyan ministers'. *SMH*, 15 October 1903, p.6, c7.
10    E.M. Dangar, *The Dangars from St Neot,Cornwall*, John Dangar Christian Reid? Sydney, 1966, pp.27-9.
11    E.C. Rowland, 'The life and times of Henry Dangar', in *JRAHS*, vol.XXXIX, 1953, part II, pp.3-4.

laid out King's Town, surveyed the Hunter River and its tributaries, and the Port Stephens area. He was rewarded with grants of land near Patrick's Plains (Singleton) which he called 'Neotsfield'.[12]

Henry's younger brothers William and Thomas arrived in the colony in 1825. William received a grant of land near Scone, which he named 'Turanville'. He also supervised his brother's properties while Henry continued work as a surveyor. Another brother, Thomas, had moved to Scone by 1836, becoming the district's first postmaster.[13]

Henry Dangar became involved in a dispute over land he had chosen for himself and in 1827 was officially reprimanded. He returned to Britain to appeal against what he believed was unfair treatment, using the months on the voyage to write his *Index and Directory to the Hunter River and Emigrants' Guide*. On arrival, he used family contacts with Anthony Rogers and Lord Eliot in Cornwall to support his appeal,[14] and eventually he was permitted to reselect the same number of acres as those confiscated. While in Cornwall Henry married Grace Sibley, also of St Neot. He was offered employment as the Australian Agricultural Company's surveyor, and returned to the colony in that capacity with his wife and small son in 1830.[15]

While in the employ of the company, Henry surveyed the Hastings River area, explored the route to the Liverpool Plains and surveyed the area which was to become the company's grants of Warrah and Goonoo Goonoo.[16] He left the company on amicable terms in 1833 and returned to 'Neotsfield'. In the following years he acquired over 300,000 acres in New England and other parts of New South Wales. He was elected to the Legislative Assembly from 1845 to 1851. On his return from a visit to Cornwall in 1855, he retired to his home 'Grantham' at Woolloomooloo and died there in 1861.[17]

Henry's brother, John Hooper Dangar, arrived in the colony in 1829, and went to William Dangar at 'Turanville'. Another brother Richard Cary Dangar arrived in 1837. He opened a general store at Muswellbrook with financial help from Henry, and then formed a partnership with their relative Jeremiah Brice Rundle and later (with other relatives) established the firm of Dangar, Gedye and Malloch Ltd.[18]

Henry Dangar's survey work and his *Emigrants' guide* were valuable contributions to the colony of New South Wales. However, all seven Dangars and in many cases, their children, made important contributions to the areas of the Hunter and New England in which they settled. Members of the family were involved in local and colonial politics and had input into almost every aspect of life in the Hunter region. They were involved in exploration, agricultural and pastoral settlement and expansion, in business and industry, and also in the life of the community. In Scone, Singleton and Goorangoola they were respected as country squires. They (like Tom, Lane, Glasson and Hawke in the Bathurst district), encouraged kinsfolk and other Cornish people to join them in New South Wales.

Although they had extended their property holdings in the Hunter region and in New England to over 300,000 acres by 1850, Henry and Grace Dangar lived at 'Neotsfield' until their visit to Cornwall, from which they returned in 1855.[19] He also became involved in business ventures, often in partnership with one or another of his immediate or extended family. The businesses included boiling down works at 'Neotsfield' and in Newcastle,[20] a meat preserving works in Newcastle, and inns and stores in the Hunter district.[21]

Henry Dangar was a considerate employer whose 'warm humanity and generous treatment of his employees were long remembered'. This was reflected in 'the proud boast of his employees, and of their children and grandchildren, that they were "Dangar men"'.[22]

Henry Dangar's children continued the example he had set. For example, his fourth son, Albert Augustus, who had spent several years as a pupil at Truro Grammar School, in Cornwall, managed family properties in New South Wales, and then acquired 'Baroona' at Goorangoola near Singleton. He became a successful pastoralist, and a generous benefactor to the people of Singleton.[23] He donated the Dangar Cottage Hospital to the district,[24] and contributed a great deal of money towards the rebuilding of All Saints' Church Singleton, on the understanding that the tower would be an exact replica of the church tower of St Neot.[25]

He was respected as an employer who 'throughout the whole course of his long life never had any litigation with an employee'. He was known for his acts of generosity to local people in need, for example after a severe flood he sent a bag of gold to the Rector of Singleton for distribution where relief was most needed. He was an

---

12    E.M. Dangar, *The Dangars from St Neot*, p.11.
13    Ibid, pp.25-7.
14    E.C. Rowland, 'The life and times of Henry Dangar', pp.49-52.
15    E.M. Dangar, *The Dangars from St Neot*, p.11.
16    E.C. Rowland, 'The life and times of Henry Dangar', pp.53-6.
17    E.M. Dangar, *The Dangars from St Neot*, pp.11-13.
18    Ibid, pp.28-9
19    Ibid pp.11-13.
20    E.M. Dangar, *William Dangar of Turanville*, Scone historical monograph no.1, Scone & Upper Hunter Historical Society, Scone, N.S.W., 1968, p.12.
21    *ADB* 1, p.281.
22    *ADB* 1, pp.281-2.
23    *ADB* 4, p.15.
24    E.C. Rowland, 'The life and times of Henry Dangar', pp.75-6.
25    Information from Mr Peter Dangar.

example that 'a man could be successful without violating any of those customs by which a Christian gentleman should order his conduct'.[26]

A.J. Greenhalgh presented the Dangar family as a benevolent and caring 'squirearchy in action' in the district until the beginning of World War I. It was a 'tradition-directed situation based on an English model' with 'two generations of Australian experience behind it'. As late as 1903, after a trip to Europe, A.A. Dangar and his family were enthusiastically welcomed back under an archway of flowers by employees who were motivated 'by affection and not by fear'.[27]

Like the original landholders at Cornish Settlement who brought siblings to join them, Henry Dangar's sister and brothers came to New South Wales. His sister Elizabeth and her husband Samuel Cook arrived in the colony in 1837, living first with William Dangar at 'Turanville', before moving to their own property near Tamworth.[28] They retired to the area of Newcastle, Cook's Hill, which now bears their name.[29] Their son Thomas Cook managed 'Turanville' for William Dangar, and eventually inherited it. He carried on the family tradition of successful property management, developing a respected horse-breeding stud.[30] He also continued the family tradition as a public benefactor. He was known as 'the Father of Scone' and the 'Squire of Turanville', and was revered as the district's greatest benefactor.[31]

**\*DANGAR** Henry C., was born at Port Stephens New South Wales, son of Henry and Grace Dangar. He was on the committee of the Australian Jockey Club, being chairman on three occasions. He was Commodore of the Royal Sydney Yacht Squadron, a foundation member of the National Rifle Association of New South Wales, and acted as secretary, vice-president and trustee. He was a director of Royal Prince Alfred Hospital, a trustee for the Art Gallery, on the council of the New South Wales Academy of Art, and a founder and trustee of the Union Club. He was MLA for West Sydney 1874-77, for East Sydney 1880-82, and MLC 1883-1917. CE.[32]

**\*DANGAR** Otho Orde, was born in 1842 at the Hastings River, northern New South Wales. He was a storekeeper, austioneer, land and estate agent, valuator and insurance agent at Kempsey. He was MLA for The MacLeay 1889-93.[33] He was a brother of Cornishman W.T. Dangar of Kempsey (see Chapter Six),[34] and a devout Methodist.[35]

**\*DANGAR** Thomas, was born in 1807 at St Neot. He emigrated in 1825, and was the first postmaster at Scone. He was a storekeeper, mail contractor and carrier, and squatter. He was MLA for the Upper Hunter 1861-64. CE.[36]

**\*DANGAR** Thomas Gordon Gibbons, was born in Sydney in 1829, and became the stepson of Thomas Dangar. He was MLA for The Gwydir 1865-80, and for The Namoi 1880-90. CE.[37]

**+DUNSTAN** Edward Tremayne, Congregational minister, was born in 1861 in Cornwall. He was a Wesleyan minister in South Africa before coming to West Australia, then to New South Wales and eventually moving to the United States. He was Chairman of the Congregational Union of New South Wales in 1896 and 1897.[38]

**\*DURACK** Ernest, was born in 1882 at Mutton Falls near Bathurst, son of Thomas Durack and Mary Webb. Labor. He was MLA for Bathurst 1913-17.[39] He was a grandson of William and Ann (Mutton) Webb who emigrated from Altarnun to Mutton Falls in 1839.[40]

**+DYER** Eldred, Wesleyan minister, was born in 1862 in Cornwall and came to New South Wales during the 1880s. He served in New South Wales in Newcastle, Bathurst and Wagga, and also in Queensland.[41]

**+FLETCHER** John, Anglican minister, was born c.1817 at Quethiock, the son of a clergyman. He served in Newcastle and Sydney between 1861 and 1868. He died in Plymouth in 1886.[42]

**+\*GALE** John, Wesleyan minister, was born in 1831 at Bodmin, the son of an excise officer. He completed an apprenticeship with a newspaper in Monmouthshire, and later became a Wesleyan minister. He arrived in Sydney in 1854 and served at Yass and Queanbeyan before resigning to become a tutor in 1857. He was one of the

---

26 N. Gray, *The promised land: a summary of early settlement in the Shire of Scone*, Scone historical monograph no.3, Scone and Upper Hunter Historical Society, Scone, N.S.W., 1975, p.53.

27 A.J. Greenhalgh, *Times's subjects: the story of Goorangoola*, published by the author, Roseville, N.S.W., 1982, pp.226-7.

28 E.M. Dangar, *The Dangars from St Neot*, p.29.

29 Ibid, p.29.

30 N. Gray, *Thomas Cook of Turanville*, Scone historical monograph no.5, Scone and Upper Hunter Historical Society, Scone, N.S.W., 1977, p.26.

31 N. Gray, *Thomas Cook of Turanville*, p.37, p.49.

32 C.N. Connolly, *Biographical register of the New South Wales Parliament 1856-1901*, p.75.

33 Ibid, p.76.

34 J.H. Watson, 'Kempsey: early settlement of the Macleay River', in *JRAHS*, vol.VII 1921, part 4, p.208. He was not related to the St Neot Dangars.

35 Information from the Rev. E.G. Clancy.

36 C.N. Connolly, *Biographical register of the New South Wales Parliament 1856-1901*, p.76.

37 Ibid, p.76.

38 G. Lindsay Lockley, *A biographical card index of Congregational ministers*.

39 H. Radi, P. Spearritt and E. Hinton, *Biographical register of the New South Wales Parliament 1901-1970*, ANU Press, Canberra, 1979, pp.81-2.

40 K. Muggleston, *William and Ann Webb: a family history*, the author, [Tarana, N.S.W.?], 1990, p.11.

41 Information from Mrs Dorothey Fellowes.

42 K.J. Cable and L. Cable, 'Biographical register of Anglican ministers in Australia'.

first aldermen on Queanbeyan Council. He joined the Presbyterian church in 1871, and about 1904 rejoined the Methodists, and acted as a lay preacher in both churches. He died in 1919 in Queanbeyan and was buried in the Presbyterian cemetery after a Wesleyan service.[43]

John Gale was involved in free selectors' associations, and he was President of the New South Wales Land Law Reform Alliance for three terms, a member of the Land Board, a founder of Queanbeyan Pastoral Agricultural and Horticultural Association, first secretary of Queanbeyan District Hospital, coroner for more than 40 years, an elder of Queanbeyan Presbyterian Church, and a leader of the movement advocating Canberra as the site for a national capital. He was MLA for The Murrumbidgee 1887-9. Methodist and Presbyterian.[44]

**GLASSON**     John Glasson was born into the farming family of 'Tremearne' and 'Ledgereth' in Breage, in 1803. He was the eldest of ten children, and seven of his brothers and sisters eventually joined him in New South Wales. A sister Eliza remained in Cornwall and married a Mr Treweeke but some of their children joined their aunts and uncles in New South Wales.[45] John sailed from London aboard the *Australia* in November 1829, arriving in Sydney the following April. He was granted 640 acres at Cornish Settlement in November 1830, and built his first wattle and daub home at 'Newton' (later 'Bookanon'). A new Georgian style home was begun in 1842 at 'Bookanon', and completed in three stages over the next seven years. Earlier, Glasson had sold part of his property to George Hawke, who called his section 'Pendarves'. The two men grew wheat and raised cattle and pigs.[46] In 1834 Glasson and Hawke imported brewing equipment from Cornwall and built a malt house as a money-making venture, intending to share the profits.[47] By 1849 John Glasson had diversified his interests. 'I make more now of fruit and wine than of wheat which used to be everything to me.'[48] The other Cornish families also brewed ale and made wine for their own use and for sale.[49]

In 1833 John Glasson was delighted to welcome his Cornish servant Edward Bishop to New South Wales. His arrival coincided with John's journey to the Sydney markets with his first load of produce. Bishop, a servant of the Glassons in Breage, had been sent to help John at 'Bookanon', and he brought welcome news of home to John Glasson, who still regarded New South Wales as only a temporary home, and stated his intention to return to Cornwall eventually, to marry.[50]

Like the other families at Cornish Settlement, John Glasson was acquainted with the Rev Walter Lawry. When planning to emigrate, Glasson had reassured his parents of the Cornish network in the colony which had existed at least since the arrival of the Toms and Lanes in 1823.

> From Mr Lawry I can get advice, from his friend Mr Hockin in London I
> can have assistance in procuring a passage, and the pleasure of advice from
> Mr Carvosso in the Colony.[51]

In addition, he carried letters of introduction to the merchant, John Hosking Junior, in Sydney.[52] He had some kind of cordial financial arrangement with Lawry, at least for his first years in the colony. He hoped Lawry would 'consent to wait awhile for the money, as he is not in want of it, and as it is of such consequence to me, just getting comfortably settled.'[53]

In December 1834 Glasson married Annie Evans, a Welsh girl he had met in Sydney.[54] They had three children, John, Robert and Mary Anne. The family left 'Bookanon' in 1857 and moved to New Zealand in an attempt to improve Annie's failing health. John retained ownership of 'Bookanan' and one of his sons eventually returned to it from New Zealand, married a niece of George Hawke and lived there until its sale in 1874.[55]

---

43  E.G. Clancy, 'Early Wesleyan ministers'.

44  C.N. Connolly, *Biographical register of the New South Wales Parliament 1856-1901*, p.116-7.

45  Information from Mr B.W. Thomas.

46  Information from Mr Will Hawke.

47  John Glasson, *Letters 1828-1857*, with introduction by his grand-daughter Mrs O. Phillips, typescript held at Bathurst Historical Society, letter, 21 March 1834, p.45.

48  Ibid, letter 19 January 1849, p.103.

49  Before leaving Cornwall, John Glasson had written to his uncle Robert 'warning him against drinking'. (Ibid, letter 10 November 1829, p.11,) yet he seems to have seen no conflict between brewing ale and making wine and his Methodist beliefs. This is possibly because John Wesley did not forbid the drinking of wine and the working man's drink, ale, in moderation. The Temperance movement did not really gain strength in the Methodist church in New South Wales until the 1840s. (Discussion with the Rev E. G. Clancy, archivist, UCA.)

50  John Glasson, *Letters*, letter 21 March 1834, p.46.

51  Ibid, letter, April 1828, p.3. In 1820 Walter Lawry had been joined by another Cornishman, Benjamin Carvosso, the third Methodist missionary to be sent to New South Wales. (Discussion with the Rev E.G. Clancy.)

52  John Glasson, *Letters*, letter 18 November 1829, p.16.

53  Ibid, letter 10 September 1834, pp.50-1.

54  Ibid, letter 1 January 1835, pp.53-5.

55  Ibid, p.iii. This son, John, married Hannah Truscott Hawke, who had arrived at Cornish Settlement during the 1850s from America with her family. Her father was George Hawke's brother. (Information from Mr Will Hawke.)

George Hawke described his lifelong friend John Glasson in 1872, commenting that although they had lived and worked side-by-side for thirty years, they had never quarrelled.

> His personal appearance carried a very manly bearing, and commanded respect in every company. He was from five feet eight inches to five feet ten high, rather strongly built, more bony than fleshy, and his face rather inclined to an oval shape. His nose stood out prominently and projected at the extremity more than is usual. When in a sedate mood his countenance carried an appearance of sternness, but his manner was very agreeable and pleasant, and in his conversation he displayed more than an ordinary share of intelligence. His temper, though naturally quick, was good, and he had more than an ordinary degree of self-control. He possessed a very ready and pleasant wit, I think more so than I ever saw in any other ... I attribute our long friendship to his good temper, disposition and forbearance with my infirmities. I believe there was never any other man who could exercise so great an influence over me as he could.[56]

**+GLASSON**   Gustavus Richard, Wesleyan minister, was born in Bathurst in 1839[57] and entered the ministry in 1873. He died in 1894 at Liverpool, NSW.[58]

**+GLASSON**   William, Wesleyan minister, was born in Cornwall in 1839 and entered the ministry in 1872. He died in Sydney in 1923.[59]

**GONINAN**   Alfred, was born in St Just in 1865, the son of a mine captain, and was apprenticed in the machine shop of Holmans Engineering Works.   He established the engineering firm 'Goninans' in Newcastle in 1899, which became a landmark and 'a great engineering concern' with a capital of £500,000 in 1926. He died in 1953.[60]

**+GRIBBLE**   John Brown, Congregational minister, was born in Redruth in 1847 and came to Victoria as a child. He entered the United Free Methodist church before moving to the Congregational church.   He served in West Australia, Victoria and in New South Wales, including Batlow near Adelong between 1890 and 1892.[61]

**HAWKE** George was born at Bedruthan in 1802, into a family of yeoman farmers, but he was apprenticed to a woolstapler because he was a delicate child and his parents were concerned that he would not survive the active life of a farmer.[62]   At the age of 22 he began his own business as a woolstapler with his brother Robert, but in the first of many disappointments George was to suffer in his life, the business failed. Robert returned to farming, and George decided to emigrate to New South Wales.[63]

In 1872, aged 70, he wrote a detailed autobiographical letter to a nephew in Cornwall. He suggested that a suitable title for the story of his life could be 'A Triumph over Disappointments, Losses, Trials and Bodily Suffering', and stated emphatically that he would never have succeeded at anything if he had given up after the first attempt.[64]

In his decision to emigrate, Hawke was helped with information about the colony by the Rev Walter Lawry,[65] who organised his steerage passage aboard the *Jessie Lawson* in 1828, and arranged for several other Cornish people to travel with him.[66]

On 12 January 1828, George Hawke went to Plymouth to put his luggage aboard the *Jessie Lawson*, and returned to his lodgings. The following day he discovered that the ship had run aground overnight in a fierce storm

---

56   George Hawke, *Colonial experience: diary of George Hawke of Orange*, typescript, NLA MS 227, pp.72-3.

57   He was a member of the Glasson family which emigrated from Breage. (Information from Mr B.W. Thomas.)

58   '"In memorium", ministers who have laboured in New South Wales and in the mission fields', in *New South Wales Methodist Conference Minutes 1943-45*, pp.365.

59   '"In memorium", ministers who have laboured in New South Wales and in the mission fields', 1944, Appendix E, p.368.

60   *Memoirs of Alfred Goninan (1865-1953)*, by L.E. Fredman, (ed.), introduction and typescript unpublished, from the original manuscript in the possession of Mrs Markovitch, Chatswood.

61   G. Lindsay Lockley, *A biographical card index of Congregational ministers*.

62   George Hawke, *Colonial experience*, p.4.

63   Ibid, p.23.

64   Ibid, pp.7-8. The nephew to whom the letter was written was William Hawke, who later came to Cornish Settlement and married his cousin (Jane and George Hawke's daughter and only child.) Their descendants still farm at Byng. (Information from Mr Will Hawke.)

65   George Hawke, *Colonial experience*, p.24.   Lawry's family lived near Mevagissey, and his pastoral district at that time was St Austell, neither place more than twenty miles from Hawke's home at Bedruthan. Lawry had been the second Wesleyan missionary sent to the colony, and in 1819 he had married Mary Hassall, sister of Samuel, James and the Rev Thomas Hassall.   Walter and Mary Lawry were sent as missionaries to Tonga, returning to Sydney and Parramatta between November 1823 and August 1824, at the time when the Lane and Tom families had just arrived in the colony.   In 1825 Mary Lawry died in childbirth at St Austell.   Walter remained in Cornwall for some years before returning to the Pacific Islands, and eventually to Parramatta where he died in 1859. (M. Reeson, *Currency Lass*, 2nd edition, Albatross Books, Sutherland N.S.W., 1988, pp.85, 212-27, 250-62.)

66   George Hawke, *Colonial experience*, p.24.

and was too badly damaged to put to sea. His second attempt was successful, and he sailed aboard the *Henry Wellesley* on 16 June 1828 accompanied by the same group as before.

Hawke soon became concerned for the welfare of J. Hicks, who suffered from deep depression throughout the voyage, often threatening suicide. As soon as he arrived in Sydney, Hawke went immediately to Parramatta to make the acquaintance of the Hassall family, relatives of the Rev Walter Lawry. He still felt responsible for Hicks, who had become 'quite mad' so Hawke returned to Sydney and took him to the Hassalls at Parramatta, who with the help of the Rev Marsden had the unfortunate Hicks admitted to Parramatta Hospital.[67]

Hawke then, through no fault of his own, found himself financially embarrassed. His letters of credit from Lawry were useless since 'Lawry's pastoral interests had not been liquidated'[68] but again the Hassall family came to his assistance and he was employed by the Rev Thomas Hassall as superintendent of his property at the Cowpastures in December 1828.[69] In April 1829 Hassall sent Hawke to 'Lampeter' at O'Connell Plains. Hawke soon moved to nearby Tarana, to the Toms and Lanes, to whom he carried letters of introduction from mutual Cornish friends. The families offered him a position as tutor to their children,[70] and when the Tom family moved to Cornish Settlement, George Hawke went with them as tutor.[71]

Hawke bought part of John Glasson's property which he called 'Pendarves' and which he was to 'pay for in cows'. Soon after, he left the Toms' employ and went to live at 'Newton' with John Glasson.[72] The two men formed a cordial working partnership and a strong friendship which lasted throughout their lives, even though the Glasson family later moved to New Zealand.[73]

Hawke and Glasson ran dairy cattle, made cheese and butter and grew wheat, working hard and 'getting into comfortable circumstances' until Hawke felt he could support a wife.[74] He knew that his uncle planned to emigrate from Cornwall with his family, and Hawke hoped to marry his cousin Jane. These plans were thwarted by the unexpected death of the uncle and his son, so after discussion with John Glasson, Hawke wrote to his cousin Jane and proposed. She accepted on the condition that he came to Cornwall within two years to collect her. After organising a superintendent who was to be supervised (without charge to Hawke) by John Glasson, he set sail for Cornwall.[75]

The ship, the *James Laing* left Sydney in August 1836, sailing via Hokianga, New Zealand.[76] It ran onto rocks as it entered the harbour and was forced to return to Sydney, and again Hawke's first attempt was doomed to failure. He expected the repairs and return journey to take only a few weeks, so decided to stay at the Wesleyan mission until the ship returned. The damage was much worse than realised and the ship limped back to Sydney where the captain was drowned in a boating accident and the ship was condemned. So Hawke was stranded in New Zealand with no likelihood of a replacement ship arriving for months. Typically though, he did not waste the unexpected time in New Zealand and became actively involved in the work of the mission and worked with another Cornishman, the Rev William Woon, printing the Wesleyan Testament and Hymn Book.[77] Eventually, the *Pyramus*, (which brought the Rev Samuel Marsden to the mission) called the following February en route to Plymouth and Hawke was able to arrange a passage.[78]

On arrival, he went directly to Bedruthan where he 'found my love at my father's house'. He and Jane were married in March 1838 at Bedruthan, and sailed for New South Wales on board *Florentia*. Once again, his plans were thwarted by outside influences and the ship fought unfavourable winds until it was forced back to Plymouth. Again, the second attempt was successful and the newly-married couple travelled uneventfully to New South Wales.[79]

Hawke had thought Cornish Settlement would be a favorable spot to raise fruit trees and while in Cornwall had bought more than two thousand trees and plants, but they all died because of delays in their shipment from Penzance to Sydney, and further delay between there and Cornish Settlement. The cask of hawthorn haws, which he brought back with him on board *Florentia*, also died, thwarting his plans to introduce hawthorn hedges as fences.

Yet Hawke refused to be defeated and bought from Van Diemen's Land replacement haws, fruit trees and other trees reminiscent of home, including oak, ash, elm, sycamore, lime, olive, beech, poplar and cyprus.[80] Again, his second attempt was successful and he developed his interest into a successful business, becoming known as the

---

67  Much later, this same J. Hicks became a successful market gardener at Botany. (Ibid, pp.36-9.)
68  E. Ramsden, 'George Hawke of Pendarves: a pioneer of the Cornish Settlement', in *JRAHS*, vol.XXIII, 1937, p.170
69  George Hawke, *Colonial experience*, p.40.
70  Ibid, pp.42-4, 46-9.
71  Ibid, p.51.
72  Ibid, p.52.
73  Ibid, p.73.
74  Ibid, p.55.
75  Ibid, p.58.
76  E. Ramsden, *Marsden and the missions, prelude to Waitangi*, Angus and Robertson, Sydney, 1936, p.142.
77  E. Ramsden, 'George Hawke of Pendarves', pp.172-3.
78  George Hawke, *Colonial experience*, p.60. E. Ramsden, *Marsden and the missions*, p.145.
79  George Hawke, *Colonial experience*, pp.63-5.
80  Ibid, pp.66-7.

father of the fruitgrowing industry in western New South Wales.[81]   As early as 1850 he advertised the sale of hawthorns for fencing.[82]

George and Jane Hawke remained at 'Pendarves' for the rest of their lives.[83] Although they had only one child, born 12 years after their marriage,[84] their family included several other young people:- a nephew Frederick Hawke, another nephew John Hawke and his sister whom they brought up after the mother's death, and a daughter of Mr and Mrs William Rowe of Bodmin.[85]

George Hawke was thinly built, with a sallow complexion.  He was about five feet six inches tall and maintained a weight of 140 pounds for most of his life.  He was:

> active for one seventy years of age and over, with a very light grey head, fast approaching to white; with a pair of light blue eyes of ordinary size, deeply set in the head under heavy eyebrows, and a very prominent forehead; a deep furrow or wrinkle from above each nostril to the corners of the mouth ... My beard is gray (though not so light as my head) and hangs several inches from my chin, but shaved from both upper and lower lip. My nose, (which is a very prominent part of the human countenance in everyone) is quite up to the ordinary size if not above, though by no means of the aquiline or hooked state, as it stands most prominent at the point, but there is a perceptible lump about the middle, occasioned by the kick of a cow which cracked it a bit.  My voice in ordinary speaking is rather sharp or high and sonorous, particularly when in argument on a subject on which I feel much interest.[86]

George Hawke believed that one should 'always prepare for the worst, but hope for the best'.[87]  He was a man of great determination, stubbornly overcoming his many disappointments and trying again each time, until he was successful.  He also had the foresight and adaptability to diversify into orcharding and storekeeping.

*\*HAWKEN    Nicholas, was born in 1836 at St Austell.  He arrived in 1854, and was initially employed clearing timber on the south coast.  In Sydney he became a storeman, then manager of a produce business, before establishing his own firm of produce merchants.  He was an alderman in Darlington for fifteen years, and served as mayor.  He was MLA for Newtown 1887-91.  Methodist.[88]

**HOSKING**    John Senior, arrived in Sydney in 1809.  He had been a woollen manufacturer, but was a teacher in a Wesleyan school when asked by the Rev Samuel Marsden to come to New South Wales to take charge of the Orphan School at Parramatta.  He returned to Britain in 1819 and died in Truro in 1850.[89]

**HOSKING**    John Junior, was born in 1806 and arrived in the colony with his parents in 1809.  He returned to Britain with them in 1819, but came back to New South Wales in 1825.  He was a successful merchant and the first elected mayor of Sydney in 1842.  He died near Penrith in 1892.[90]

**+JENNINGS**    Richard, Primitive Methodist and then Presbyterian minister, was born in the colony in 1856.  His Cornish parents, John Jennings and Peggy Richards, had emigrated two years earlier.[91]  He entered the ministry in 1876 and served at Sydney, Crookwell, Newcastle, Marrickville and Bowral, before resigning in 1884 to enter the Presbyterian ministry.[92]

**+KELYNACK**    Lyndon Athol, Anglican clergyman, was born in 1885 in Sydney, son of Wesleyan minister William Kelynack D.D.  He served as curate in West Monaro in 1909.[93]

**+KELYNACK** William D.D., Wesleyan minister, was born in 1831 at Newlyn, the son of a sea captain.  He arrived in New South Wales in 1854 and served at Bathurst, Braidwood, Yass, Chippendale, Parramatta, Wollongong, Sydney, and Goulburn.  He was Overseas Missions Secretary from 1882 to 1886, and President of Newington College from 1887 until his death in 1891.  He was awarded the degree of Doctor of Divinity by the University of New Orleans in 1877.[94]  He was President of the New South Wales and Queensland Wesleyan Conference in 1880.[95]

---

81   E. Ramsden, 'George Hawke of Pendarves', p.169.

82   *BFP*, 18 May 1850, p.1, c.1.

83   Information from Mr Will Hawke.

84   John Glasson, *Letters*, letter, 10 September 1849, p.111.  Information from Mr Will Hawke.

85   George Hawke, *Colonial experience*, pp.81-2.  William Rowe, his wife Eleanor and their children Mary aged 4 and Rebecca aged 7 were passengers aboard the *Florentia*, as were Samuel and Elizabeth Hawke, and their children Thomas aged 2 and John aged 1.  (AONSW shipping lists for *Florentia* 1838, AO reel 1290.)

86   George Hawke, *Colonial experience*, p.5.

87   Ibid, p.4.

88   C.N. Connolly, *Biographical register of the New South Wales Parliament 1856-1901*, p.139-40.

89   Information from Mr Warwick Adams.

90   Information from Mr Warwick Adams.

91   P. Lay, 'Clotted cream and chapel: the Mullis family in Cornwall and New South Wales', Dip. FHS., Society of Australian Genealogists, Sydney, 1988, p.44.  AONSW shipping lists *Lady Kennaway* 1854, AO reel 2466.

92   E.G. Clancy, 'Biographical register of Primitive Methodist ministers in New South Wales 1847-1902', in *Church Heritage*, vol.4, no.2, September 1985, p.129-30.

93   Biographical card index of Anglican ministers in Australia, in the possession of Professor K.J. Cable.

94   E.G. Clancy, 'Biographical notes on early Wesleyan ministers'.

+**KESSELL**    Stephen, Primitive Methodist minister, was born in 1864 in Redruth and came to New South Wales as a child. He was a teacher before entering the ministry in 1890. He served in Penrith, Mudgee, Wallsend, Wollongong and Corowa before transferring to South Australia in 1905.[96]

**LANE**    William and Catherine (nee Tom) arrived in Sydney with the Tom family in 1823. William Lane went as overseer to 'Lampeter' farm, at O'Connell Plains (between Bathurst and Oberon), owned by the Rev Thomas Hassall.[97]

The Lane family remained in the Hassalls' employ, gaining 'colonial experience' before taking up their own family property.[98] William Lane had received an unsatisfactory land grant at the Fish River and in 1824 asked for it to be exchanged for another in the Hunter River region,[99] but in 1828 the Lanes were at 'Tarranah' near Oberon where William owned 1,000 acres, 82 cattle and 1,076 sheep. Hannah Davey who had emigrated with them in 1823 was still with them.[100] Later, the family moved closer to Bathurst where Lane was granted land on which he first built a small brick farmhouse,[101] and later a more imposing home named 'Orton Park' to honour the Wesleyan missionary the Rev Joseph Orton who visited in November 1833.[102] The Lane family remained at 'Orton Park', farmed the property very successfully and acquired further property elsewhere in New South Wales.[103] William and Catherine maintained close links with their relatives at Cornish Settlement and with the Bathurst Methodist community. They had a family of twelve children between 1820 and 1849, Mary Tom, John Tom, Thomas Tom, William Hannibal, James Barrett, Nicholas Olver, Charles Wesley, Catherine Tom, Mary Tom Lewis, Frederick Lewis, Jane Draper, and Edwin Hurst. Catherine Lane died in 1854, William died in 1855 and both are buried in Bathurst cemetery.[104]

+**LAW**    Palmer, Congregational minister, was born in Penryn and arrived in South Australia in 1878. He served in Woollahra (Sydney), between 1881 and 1883 before entering the Anglican church.[105]

+**LAWRY**    Walter, Wesleyan minister, was born in 1793 at Rutheren [sic], the son of a farmer. He came to New South Wales in 1818, as chaplain aboard the convict ship *Lady Castlereagh*. He served in Sydney and Parramatta, and married Mary Cover Hassall (daughter of Rowland Hassall) in 1819. They pioneered the Wesleyan mission in Tonga in 1822 and in 1825 went to Cornwall. Mary died in St Austell. In 1844 he returned to Tonga and New South Wales and died in Parramatta in 1858.[106]

+**MADDERN**    Matthew, Wesleyan minister, was born in Zennor in 1844 and entered the ministry in 1867. He died in Sydney in 1924.[107]

***MORRIS**    Augustus, was 'born in Tasmania in 1820', son of an early Cornish settler. He was MLA for Balranald between 1859 and 1865.[108] He held stations on the Murrumbidgee, and while there in 1857 he:

> first conceived the idea of the possibility of utilising artificial cold for the preservation of fresh meat, and of conveying it to Europe in a frozen condition. Unsparing ridicule was cast on this idea by the Melbourne and Deniliquin newspapers when he first broached it. He never abandoned it, however, until he had, in 1866, induced the late Mr. Thomas S. Mort to make it his own, and announce that by means of artificial cold there should be "no more waste".

***PAUL**    William Henry, was born in 1846 at Richmond New South Wales, (son of Cornish immigrants Samuel Paul and Betsey Walkom) and became a saddler, harnessmaker, auctioneer in Bathurst. He was a J.P., vice-president of Bathurst Hospital, and was active in religious and other local organisations, including friendly societies. He was an Orangeman. He was MLA for Bathurst 1889-91. Methodist.[109]

---

95   *TCJ*, 31 January 1880, p.209, c.1.
96   E.G. Clancy, 'Biographical register of Primitive Methodist ministers in New South Wales' [1847-1902], in *Church Heritage*, vol.4, no.2, September 1985, p.130.
97   P. Hohnen, *A history of the Lane, Tom and Dale families*, the author, Canberra, [n.d.], pp.6-7. Hassall, an Anglican, was married to Anne, a daughter of the Rev Samuel Marsden and, like Marsden, was sympathetic towards Methodists. (E. Ramsden, 'George Hawke of Pendarves', pp.167-8.  E. Ramsden, *Marsden and the missions*, p.145.)
98   P. Hohnen, *A history of the Lane, Tom and Dale families*, p.16.
99   AONSW Col.Sec. 'Memorial of William Lane', 1824, p.383, AO mfiche 3097. Hassall papers, ML A1677-2, pp.1343-4.
100  M.R. Sainty and K.A Johnson (eds.), *Census of New South Wales November 1828*, LAH, Sydney, 1985, pp.116, 229 and 432.
101  P. Hohnen, *A history of the Lane, Tom and Dale families*,  p.16.
102  Information from Mr Peter Hohnen.
103  P. Hohnen, *A history of the Lane, Tom and Dale families*, p.19.
104  Information from Mr Alan Lane.
105  G. Lindsay Lockley, *A biographical card index of Congregational ministers*.
106  E.G. Clancy, 'Early Wesleyan ministers'.
107  '"In memorium", ministers who have laboured in New South Wales and in the mission fields', pp.369.
108  *AMM*, series 1, vol.2, pp.305-10.
109  C.N. Connolly, *Biographical register of the New South Wales Parliament 1856-1901*, p.264.

**+POPE**   John Wright, Anglican minister, was baptised in Germoe in 1859.  He came to Australia for health reasons and served in Sydney, and at Waverley and Bondi from 1886 until his death in 1892.[110]

**+PUDDICOMBE**   Alfred Teed, Anglican minister, was born in Cornwall c.1837 and served in New South Wales in Goulburn and Moruya.  He returned to Cornwall and was buried at Morwenstow in 1904.[111]

**\*RUNDLE**     Jeremiah BRICE, was born in 1816 in Cornwall, and arrived in 1835.  He was a storekeeper at Murrurundi, then merchant and commission agent in partnership with members of the Dangar family.  He was director and chairman of the Australian Joint Stock Bank, director of Sydney Meat Preserving Company, Moruya Silver Mining Company, United Fire and Marine Insurance Company, and a J.P.  He was MLC 1881-93.  CE.[112]

**\*SMITH**    Fergus Jago, was born in 1843 in New South Wales, son of Cornish immigrants John Smith and Mary Tom, and became a pastoralist and sheep and horse breeder.  He was a J.P., a director of the Australian Bank of Commerce and Newcastle Wallsend Coal Company, on the committee of the Sheepbreeders' Association, and vice-president of the Federal Convention, Bathurst 1896.  He was a member of the Union Club, the Protestant Federation, and Bathurst Church of England Synod.  He was MLA for West Macquarie 1887-9, and MLC 1895-1924.  CE.[113]

**\*SMITH**     John, was born in 1811 at St Keverne, and arrived in 1836.  He was employed as a station superintendent near Wellington, and later took up his own property and began the 'Gamboola' sheep stud.  He was a J.P., involved in establishment of the church and school at Molong, president of the first show, and a foundation member of the Union Club in 1857.  He was MLC 1880-1895.  CE.[114]

**\*STEPHEN**       Harold Wilberforce Hindmarsh, a nephew of Sir Alfred Stephen, was born in 1841 in Penzance, son of George Milner Stephen.  He was a journalist and editor, including editor of *Sydney Punch*.  He was MLA for Monaro 1885-7, 1889.[115]

**\*THOMAS**      Josiah, was born c.1864 in Cornwall and went as a child to Mexico then returned to Cornwall.  He arrived in the 1880s and worked as a miner at Broken Hill, becoming a mine captain by 1890.  He was active in the Amalgamated Miners' Association and led the union in the 1892 strike.  He was a Wesleyan local preacher and circuit steward.  He left the Labor Party over the conscription issue.  He was MLA for Alma 1894-1901.  He entered Federal politics at Federation and was MHR for Barrier 1901-17, Senator 1917-22, 1925-29.  He served as Postmaster-General 1908-9 and 1910-11, and as Minister for External Affairs 1911-13.  Methodist.[116]

**+THOMAS**      J. Sweetnam, Wesleyan minister, was born in 1870 at Guyong, and entered the ministry in 1894.  He died in 1927 in Sydney.[117]  He was a descendant of the Thomas family from St Keverne.[118]

**TOM**       William, was born in Blisland, North Cornwall, in 1791,[119] and married Ann Lane in 1817.[120]  Her family, of yeoman farming stock, lived near Launceston on the borders of Devon and Cornwall.[121]  Ann's brother William Lane married William Tom's sister Catherine,[122] and in 1823 both couples emigrated to New South Wales.  With William and Ann Tom were their three children, John, James and Mary.  William and Catherine Lane had two children, Catherine Tom and John Tom Lane.  Accompanying the two families were Ann Tom's nephew James Bray,[123] and Miss Hannah Davey, a friend and companion of Catherine Lane.[124]

William and Ann Tom's fourth child, William, was born at sea shortly before their arrival.  The ship was damaged in a storm off Hobart, and the two families stayed in Hobart for a short time with a recently arrived Wesleyan missionary, the Rev Ralph Mansfield, before travelling on to New South Wales in another vessel.[125]  After their arrival in Sydney, the Tom family spent several months in Parramatta.[126]  In December 1824 William Tom was 'Superintendent of the Estate and Property, at Bathurst, of the Rev^d Walter Lawry, and Mr Jonathon Hassall'.[127]  When land on the Bathurst side of the Macquarie River became available for settlement, William Tom was impressed by the valley 28 miles west of Bathurst, and the family was most likely resident there in 1829[128] but certainly by 1st April 1831 when another son, Charles, was born.[129]

110  K.J. Cable and L. Cable, 'Biographical register of Anglican ministers in Australia'.
111  Ibid.
112  C.N. Connolly, *Biographical register of the New South Wales Parliament 1856-1901*, p.290.
113  Ibid, pp.306-7.
114  Ibid, p.308.
115  Ibid, p.316.
116  Ibid, p.331.
117  '"In memorium", ministers who have laboured in New South Wales and in the mission fields', pp.369.
118  Information from Mr B.W. Thomas.
119  W.H. Webb, *The life of the late William Tom Senr.*, A.K.Murray & Co., Paddington, N.S.W., 1922, p.3.
120  Information from Mr Alan Lane.
121  Information from Mr Peter Hohnen.
122  Information from Mr Alan Lane.
123  W.H. Webb, *The life of the late William Tom Senr.*, p.3.
124  P. Hohnen, *A history of the Lane, Tom and Dale families*, p.1.
125  Ibid, p.6.
126  W.H. Webb, *The life of the late William Tom Senr.*, p.4.
127  AONSW Col.Sec. 'Memorial of William Tom', 1824, p.1253, AO mfiche 3114.
128  J.W. Tom, *Cornish Settlement: reminiscences, 1941*, typescript in possession of Mr B.W. Thomas, p.1.
129  W.H. Webb, *The life of the late William Tom Senr.*, p.5.

Their first home was a simple five-roomed dwelling equipped with a loft which was used as sleeping accommodation by the Tom boys and their tutor, George Hawke.[130]   By 1840, William and Ann Tom had thirteen children, Mary, John, James and William (all born prior to the family's arrival in New South Wales), and Thomas, Henry, Nicholas, Charles, twins Helen Wesley and Emma Fletcher, and Selina Jane Jones,[131] Wesley and Annie. In 1847 the two-storey stone home at 'Springfield' was built to accommodate the large Tom family.[132] The rich, black soil at 'Springfield' produced excellent wheat crops, and in addition, William Tom raised livestock, mainly cattle.[133] Although he and his sons accumulated other property in New South Wales,[134] William and Ann lived at Cornish Settlement for the rest of their lives.

Their grandsons J.W. Tom and W.H. Webb remembered Ann and William Tom with affection. Ann Tom was 'quite pretty, with rosy cheeks'. She never lost her love of Cornwall and preferred it to her adopted country. Once, when referring to native trees, she said, 'You call your trees Evergreen? - I call them Nevergreen'. In a letter to her parents in 1827 she wrote:

> Perhaps I may see England once more, the Lord's will be done, if I do it
> will be when my children are grown up, I should wish them to marry in
> England and live my later days there.[135]

Her hopes were never realised, and although a son, Wesley, did make his home in London as a barrister, he did not marry and Ann Tom never returned to Cornwall.[136]

Letters from the Glassons and those of the Tom and Lane families quoted in Peter Hohnen's book, as well as George Hawke's own reminiscences, were peppered with references to the importance to them of the very personal relationship they enjoyed with God through his son Jesus Christ. Also vitally important to them was the state at any given moment of personal salvation - both theirs and that of their readers. John Glasson reported to his parents on the progress of his brother Joe and sister Mary, and added that he hoped they were 'travelling heavenwards'.[137]

William Tom retained his Cornish dialect throughout his life and often told stories of Cornwall, including those of his own experiences as a Customs officer. When preaching, he spoke slowly and clearly so that his sermon (generally from the Old Testament) would be heard. He:

> always spoke of God as his greatest friend; considered Him in all his
> actions of Life, and really believed his prayers were answered.[138]

He was held in high esteem by a variety of people. Once when travelling to Sydney he stayed overnight at a hotel at the Fish River, and during the night he was attacked and robbed. When the robbers recognised him as 'Parson' Tom his property was returned to him immediately.

> They did this because they knew that while he had three convicts, he never
> flogged them but treated them well.  One station house was built of
> freestone and had two rooms, a heavy door and a window merely a square
> about nine inches, and a wall 18 inches thick.  We called it "The Lockup",
> but he never used it for locking up any man.[139]

William Tom attributed his success to 'the mercy and help of God' but he was also willing to work hard. After arriving in Cornish Settlement he had been 'broke' three times, but each time had managed to survive and eventually to prosper.  As well as having his fair share of Cornish determination, he also had foresight and adaptability, which enabled him to diversify, sending his sons overland through virgin country in Gippsland to sell cattle at a good profit when prices in New South Wales were poor, and when others had resorted to boiling down their stock for a meagre return.[140]

---

130  Ibid, p.6.
131  The Jones was given to her in honour of a Mr Jones in Sydney who had promised to make the child his heir, but eventually the fortune went to Newington Methodist College. (R. Cashman and C. Meader, *Marrickville: rural outpost to inner city*, Hale & Iremonger, Petersham, 1990, pp.55 and 96.
132  W.H. Webb, *The life of the late William Tom Senr.*, p.7.
133  Ibid, pp.6-7.
134  Ibid, pp.8-9.
135  Letter from Ann Tom to her parents from Sidmouth Valley, 14 November, 1827. Quoted in P. Hohnen, *A history of the Lane, Tom and Dale families*, p.39.  Members of all four Cornish Settlement families made reference in their letters to 'England' rather than 'Cornwall', but never referred to people as English, always Cornish.
136  P. Hohnen, *A history of the Lane, Tom and Dale families*, p.41.
137  John Glasson, *Letters*, letter 12 June 1847, p.88.
138  J.W. Tom, *Reminiscences*, p.2.
139  W.H. Webb, *The life of the late William Tom Senr.*, p.11.
140  J.W. Tom, *Reminiscences*, pp.1-3.  W.H. Webb, *The life of the late William Tom Senr.*, pp. 8-14.

+**TUCKFIELD**     Francis, Wesleyan minister, was born in 1808 in Germoe, and entered the ministry in 1835. He served in Sydney and in the Hunter Valley. He was involved in pioneering mission work with Aborigines in Victoria. He died in Victoria in 1865.[141]

**VIAL**     William, was born in Kenwyn and arrived with his wife aboard *Walter Morrice* in 1849 as an assisted immigrant. He stated he was a wheelwright aged 27, and a Wesleyan.[142] He was a coachbuilder of Castlereagh Street when in 1868 he saved the life of the Duke of Edinburgh at Clontarf.[143] He died in Paddington in 1878, aged 57.[144]

**VIAL**     Samuel, was:

> born in Cornwall, England, in 1815. His father, Captain Vial, well known in Cornwall mining circles, met his death in Mexico. Mr Vial was captain of a mine in Wales for some time, and landed in Sydney in 1848. Finding no scope for the exercise of his profession, he started a coachbuilding factory with his brother in Castlereagh-street, and after twelve years at this trade he was induced to accept the management of the Buckinbar Copper Mine. This position he held until the mine was abandoned, on his return to Sydney in 1876. Mr Vial was the best authority on copper mining in the colony.[145]

\***WEARNE**     Joseph, was born in 1832 at St Levan, and arrived in 1849 as an assisted immigrant aboard *Harbinger*.[146] He was a flour miller in Liverpool and Sydney, and a mining speculator and businessman. He was involved in the Benevolent Society, the Protestant Political Association, the Loyal Orange Institution, Freemasonry, Sons of Temperance, and the Methodist church. He was MLA for West Sydney 1869-74, and for Central Cumberland 1875. Methodist.[147]

\***WEARNE**     Walter Ernest, was born in 1867 in Sydney, son of Cornish emigrant James Teare Wearne. He was an auctioneer, commission agent, council clerk at Bingara, and became a farmer and grazier. He was MLA for Namoi 1917-27, for Barwon 1927-30, and acted as Minister for Lands and for Forests 1921, 1922-25. Methodist.[148]

\***WEBB**     Edmund, was born at Liskeard in 1830, arrived in the colony in 1847 and went to Bathurst in 1850. He began his own business there in 1851 and built it into a highly successful enterprise. He was involved in community affairs in Bathurst, including the local council on which he served as mayor. He was a founder of Newington College (Sydney), and a J.P. He was MLA for West Macquarie 1870-1874, and for East Macquarie 1878-1882. MLC 1882-1899.[149]

\***WEBB**     James Eli, was born in 1887 in Pyrmont in Sydney, son of Eli Webb and Emma Smitham, who was a Cornish emigrant.[150] He was a doctor, and an alderman at Hurstville, and served a period as mayor. He was MLA for Hurstville 1932-9. CE.[151]

**WESLEY**     William Henry

> J.P. ... born at St Just, Cornwall ... 1845 ... He received one year's schooling at Sancreed Public School, and began to work hard in the mines of Cornwall at the age of nine years. ... At the age of eighteen he was appointed Underground Engineer at Wheal Hearl Tin and Copper Mine, St Just, and a year later became Mining Manager of the same mine. In the intervals of labour he attended evening classes with so much application and success that at the examination of the Science and Art department at South Kensington, in 1867, he passed, taking the Queen's Prize in Mineralogy, second class, and in Mining, third class ... Mr Wesley came into contact with a party of returned Victorian gold miners about to start again for Victoria. ...he decided to go out with them ... went at once to the Jim Crow diggings at Daylesford, and got gold in the first hole sunk. ...

141  E.G. Clancy, 'Biographical notes on early Wesleyan ministers'.
142  AONSW shipping list *Walter Morrice* 1849, AO reel 2460.
143  *SMH*, 13 March 1868, p.5, c.1.
144  *SMH*, 6 August 1878, p.8, c.1.
145  *AMM*, series 1, vol.2 appendix, p.38.
146  AONSW shipping list *Harbinger* 1849, AO reel 2459.
147  C.N. Connolly, *Biographical register of the New South Wales Parliament 1856-1901*, pp.352-3.
148  H. Radi, P. Spearritt and E. Hinton, *Biographical register of the New South Wales Parliament 1902-1970*, p.288.
149  C.N. Connolly, *Biographical register of the New South Wales Parliament 1856-1901*, pp.353-4. AMM, series 1, vol.1, pp.84-86.
150  *SMH* 7 February 1917, p.9, c.1, funeral notices for Mrs Emma Smitham. AONSW shipping lists *La Hogue* 1877, AO reel 2488, arrival of James and Emma Smitham and their daughter Emma.
151  H. Radi, P. Spearritt and E. Hinton, *Biographical register of the New South Wales Parliament 1902-1970*, p.289.

In the following year he left ... to take the position of Mining Surveyor under H.R. Hancock, in the Moonta Copper Mines, South Australia ... until 1872, when he received an appointment to travel as a Mine Inspector in New South Wales and Queensland. This he held for about eighteen months, when he rejoined his old firm ... at Wallaroo Copper Mine ... he again resigned to take the post of Superintendent of the Great Britain Tin Mine, at Vegetable Creek, New England, and agent for Sir Thomas Elder. While he held this post he reported to his Adelaide firm on many of the mines of the district, and recommended the selection of land for deep alluvial tin-mining. A representative sent up to confer with Mr Wesley agreed with him that there were good prospects. A company was formed, and 320 acres selected. From his knowledge of geology, and observation of the alluvial operations for gold in Victoria, he was led to form a pronounced opinion on the result of the smae workings for tin. His firm, however, deterred by the low price of tin, declined to take the land, and Mr Wesley solicited permission to retain 180 acres on his own account ... until 1878, when he left his brothers to carry on that work, and went to Tasmania to open the West Bischoff Tin Mine ... In November 1879 he received a telegram calling on him to return to New England, as good tin had at last been discovered ... after working with his brothers for about three months, during which time he took many thousands of pounds out of the mine, they sold three-fourths of the property for £30,000 cash, retaining one-fourth. He then gave over the management to the company and came to Sydney. In 1880 he visited England with his family with a view to settling down. But after spending two years in Penzance, Cornwall, and other seaport towns in England, he decided on returning to Australia, where his sons might have as good a chance as himself. He returned to Sydney in 1883, and has since settled dowm in a pleasant residence among the orange groves of Parramatta ... Mr Wesley is a Justice of the Peace. He has at present a business connection as a Mining Expert, and his reports are always considered as of special value.[152]

+**WILLIAMS** William Henry, Wesleyan minister, was born in Cornwall in 1851 and entered the ministry in 1875. He died in Sydney in 1920.[153]

---

152 *AMM*, series 1, vol.2, pp.223-5.
153 '"In memorium", ministers who have laboured in New South Wales and in the mission fields', p.368.

# APPENDIX VII
## STATED BIRTHPLACES OF ASSISTED IMMIGRANTS 1837-1877

The 3898 Cornish assisted immigrants who arrived between 1837 and 1877 were required to state their places of birth to government immigration officials. Although over a quarter were recorded simply as being born in Cornwall, the remainder gave birthplaces which ranged across the length and breadth of their homeland, as shown below. The numbers in brackets beside native places represent the number of immigrants who stated that location as being their birthplace. Only those places given by five or more are numbered. It must be remembered that these were immigrants' places of birth, but not necessarily their places of residence prior to emigration.

Some names were obvious attempts at interpretation of a parish name by colonial officials unfamiliar with the Cornish dialect and accent. For example, Cindizie [St Issey], Aisle [Hayle], Allegon [Illogan], Camblin, Cambrien [Camborne], St Alary Mary's Zion [Marazion, St Hilary?], St Henner [St Enoder], Tordraff, Towdrath [Tywardreath], and the many variations of Helston and of Gwennap.

## TABLE 7.1

### BIRTHPLACES OF ASSISTED IMMIGRANTS 1837-1877

Advent, Agniscarra, Aisle, Albaston, Allegon,

Baldal, Barrion, Bedworth [Redruth?] (16),Beerferris, Bethskinnell, Blisland, Boconnoc, Bodmin (15), Boyton, Brack, Breage (34), Breek, Bridgerule, Brigg Churchtown, Broadford, Broadoak, Broadwoodwidger, Bucks Head, Bude, Budock (13), Budock Water, Buryan (23) And St Buryan (13),

Caher, Callington (8), Calstock (14), Camblin, Camborne (70), Cambrien, Camelford, Caraden, Cardinham, (6), Carharrack, Caridon, Cawsand, Chacewater (12), Charlestown, Cindizie, Coe, Coldwind, Comerford, Comerva, Constantine (18), Cormibis, Cranden, Crantock, Creed , Crowan (18), Cruth, Cubert, Cury (6), Cornwall (1114), Davidstow, Duloe (6),

Egloshayle (7), Ellstone, Elston (6), Elstone (6), Elstown,

Falmouth (27), Fellock, Feock, Fillack, Forrerbury, Fowey/Foy/Fie (9), Frogwell,

Ganmar, Germa, Germo, Gerrans, Gluvias, Goldsithney, Gorans, Gorran, Grade, Gramor, Grampound (7), Green Plat (5), Guinock, Gulval (25), Gunnislake, Gunwaller, Gwennack, Gwennap (93), Gwinder, Gwinear (12), Gwithian, Gwyndon, Gynop,

Hale Foundry, Hatherop, Hayle, Helland, Helston (30), Helstone (7), High Luggan,

Illogan/Illuggan (24),

Jacobstow (8),

Kea (20), Kenwill/Kenwin/Kenwyn (62), Kenyan, Kerr, Kilkhampton, Kingsand,

Ladock (10), Lanark, Lanarth, Landawadniak, Landraff, Landrake (5), Landsells, Lanhydrock, Lanlivery, Lanner, Lanock, Lanrath, Lansallo, Lant, Lanteglos (6), Lanteglos Near Fowey, Launceston (18), Launeret, Lelant (5), Lewannick, Lewis, Lewiton, Linkinhorne, Liskeard (40), Little Colum, Litton, Lizard (8), Llanarth, Landrath, Lostwithiel (6), Ludgvan (11), Luggan (16), Luxulyan,

Mabe, (10), Madden/Marden/Madron (27), Maker, Manaccan/Manackin (7), Marazion, Marden, Marramchurch, Marzon, Mawgan (19), Mawgan West Cornwall, Mawnan, Menheniot, Merther (9), Mevagissey (7), Michaelstow, Midross, Minster, Minstow, Mitchell, Mornan, Morryl, Morvauh, Motwen, Mount Charles, Mullion (23), Mylor (15),

Near Penzance, Near St Erth, Near Truro, New Passage (5), Newchurch, Newland/Newlyn (13), Newmills, Newnan, Newquay, North Hill, North Petherwin,

Padstow, Paran, Parnarble, Parran Near Truro, Parranuthnoe, Paul (5), Pelynt, Penmarth, Penrin/Penryn (45), Penstutton, Penthero, Penzance (75), Perin/Perran/Perrin (14), Perran Worran/ Perranaworthal (5), Perranuthnoe (7), Perranzabelo/ Perranzabuloe/Perranziblough (8), Perrannwarf, Phillack/Pillack (23), Pillaton, Pole, Poleshill, Polperro, Ponsongay, Pool (8), Porthleven, Poundstock, Probus (19),

Quethiock (6),

Redruth (68), Roche (11), Roseland St Just, Ruan (5), Ruan Major, Ruan Minor, Saltash, Sancreed (5), Sarrens, Scilly, Sennen, Sethnell, Shalon, Shortlanesend, Sithney (11), Skillegate [Roskilly Gate, St Keverne][1,] South Cornwall, South Hill (5), South Petherwin,

St Agnes (34), St Aitt, St Alary Mary's Zion, St Allan/St Allen, St Andrews, St Ann, St Anne's, St Anthony, St Austell/St Austin/St Oswald/Oswall/St Tossall (44), St Aval, St Blazey (6), St Braig/Bragg/Braock (5), St Breward (6), St Brigg, St Catherine's, St Cleer (5), St Clements (8), St Columb (32), St Columb Major, St Columb Minor (9), St Crum, St Day, St Dennis (12), St Dominic, St Eagle, St Eleanor, St Ellen (5), St Enoder (18), St Erme, St Erth (9), St Eves, St Ewe, St Germans (24), St Ginniter, St Ginnes, St Gluvias, St Guineas, St Helens, St Henner, St Herm, St Hilary (8), St Ive, St Ives (11), St John/S, St Just (27), St Just Treward (7), St Keverne (45), St Kew, St Levan, St Lewis (8), St Mabyn (6), St Martin/S (5), St Mawgan, St Mellion, St Michael Penkivell, St Neot (15), St Nicholas, St Pinic (7), St Pyth, St Stephens (28), St Stephens Coombe, St Stephens In Brammel, St Teath (19), St Tew, St Thomas, St Tudy, St Twain, St Veep (7), St Vudock, St Wenn, St Winnow (5),

Stithian/s (19), Stokeclimsland (7), Stratton (7), Sunning,

Tillis, Tintagel (5), Tordraff, Torpoint, Towdrath, Treglossack, Tregony, Treleigh, Trematon Castle, Trenaugh, Trendon, Trewen, Truro (106), Tuckingmill, Tywardreath (14),

Ulston/E, Uny Lelant,

Veryan (6),

Wadebridge, Warbstowe, Warleggan, Wendron (14), West Cornwall, Whitecross, Windern, Winnock, Withern/Withiel/Wyther (5), Woodbridge, Wyndham,

Zennor, Zouna

## TABLE 7.2

| BIRTHPLACES OF FIVE OR MORE ASSISTED IMMIGRANTS 1837-1877 |
| --- |

*Bedworth [Redruth?] (16), Bodmin (15), Breage (34), Budock (13), Buryan/St Buryan (46),

Callington (8), Calstock (14), Camborne (70), Cardinham (6), Chacewater (12), Constantine (18), Crowan (18), Cornwall (1114), Cury (6),

Duloe (6),

Egloshayle (7), Elston (6), Elstone (6),

Falmouth (27), Fowey/Foy/Fie (9),

Grampound (7), Green Plat (5), Gulval (25), Gwennap (93), Gwinear (12),

Helston (30), Helstone (7),

Illogan/Illuggan (24),

Jacobstow (8),

Kea (20), Kenwin/Kenwyn (62),

Ladock (10), Landrake (5), *Lanteglos (6), Launceston (18), Lelant (5), Liskeard (40), *Lizard (8), Lostwithiel (6), Ludgvan (11), Luggan (16),

Mabe (10), Madron (25), Manaccan/Manackin (7), *Mawgan (19), Merther (9), Mevagissey (7), Mullion (23), Mylor (15),

*New Passage (5), *Newland/Newlyn (10),

Paul (5), Penrin/Penryn (45), Penzance (75), *Perin/Perran/Perrin (14), Perran Worran/ Perranaworthal (5), Perranuthnoe (7), Perranzabelo/Perranziblough/Perranzabuloe (8), Perrannwarf, Phillack/Pillack (23), *Pool (8), Probus (19),

Quethiock (6),

Redruth (68), Roche (11), *Ruan (5),

Sancreed (5), Sithney (11), South Hill (5),

St Agnes (34), St Austell/St Austin/St Oswald/Oswall/St Tossall (44), St Blazey (6), St Braig/Bragg/Braock (5), St Breward (6), St Cleer (5), St Clements (8), St Columb (32), St Columb Minor (9), St Day, St Dennis (12), St Dominic, St Ellen (5), St Enoder (18), St Erth (9), St Germans (24), St Hilary (8), St Ives (11), St Just (27), *St Just Treward (7), St Keverne (45), *St Lewis (8), St Mabyn (6), *St Martin/S (5), St Neot (15), St Pinic (7), *St Stephens (28), St Teath (19), St Veep (7), St Winnow (5), Withiel (5),

Stithian/S (19), Stokeclimsland (7), Stratton (7),

Tintagel (5), Truro (106), Tywardreath (14),

Veryan (6),

Wendron (14),

NOTE    Those places marked * have not been included on the accompanying map, generally because there were several places with similar names in Cornwall, and it was unclear exactly which one was meant.

Parishes of birth of some of the assisted immigrants were not recorded at the examination on arrival. The official simply wrote 'Cornwall'. Some parishes of birth have been established by their descendants, and so are included on the accompanying map.

---

1    This place of birth was given by an ancestor of Mr B.W. Thomas, who decoded it during family history research.

PLATE 50.     Map of Cornish parishes of birth.

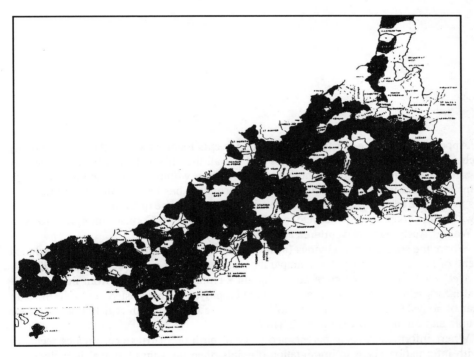

Map showing the parishes of birth of Cornish assisted immigrants to New South Wales 1837-1877.

Appendix VIII is a collection of names and events found or supplied to me during my research. It has come from various sources and not all the information in it has necessarily been verified. It is included in the hope that information within may be used as a jumping off point for others in their research. Enough information has been included here to allow readers to find the events listed in greater detail. Names are those of Cornish born persons or those with some connection (marriage, employment etc) with a Cornish immigrant to New South Wales. Australian-born children are not generally included.

Where the source is not obvious (as in births, marriages, burials) it has been included at the end of the relevant entry, for example the names of newspapers such as *SMH, BT, BA, CWD, Methodist*. Where names of an immigrant's employer was taken from the AONSW disposal information, then the immigrant and the employer are both listed, and also the ship and year of arrival. The references to 'NSW births' are the first birth registration found for that couple and can be followed up in *NSWRGI*.

Where information about parents and place of birth on marriage certificates seems to tally with information given to immigration officials, then the ship of arrival is included in brackets. Finally, the name of any person who has provided information is added at the end of the entry about which they have given information

# APPENDIX VIII

## A MISCELLANY: SOME CORNISH IMMIGRANTS TO NEW SOUTH WALES.

### A

**Abrahams** Annie M married Alexander Dingle Sandoe, 1891, CE, Sydney.

**Adams** Edward Congregational minister. Born Corwall 1843. Buried Wallsend Cemetery 1907.

**Adams** Eunice Martha married Charles Thomas Aubrey Lane, Cowra, 1893.

**Adams** Richard per 'Ninevah' in 1877. Appears to be brother of Mary Ann Dingle also on board.

**Addicott** Annie married Alfred Harvey, Adelong, CE, 1881.

**Addicott** James and Annie, of Adelong 1879. NSW births.

**Addlington** Alice married John Thomas Tresidder, Bulli, 1886.

**Ah Tim** married Jenny Maria Hilson Tippett, Tambaroora, 1874.

**Aitcheson** Samuel married Mary Callaghan, Bathurst, Wesleyan, 1841. NLA MS 3290

**Alchin** Annie married Thomas Oliver, Sydney, Wesleyan, 1883.

**Aldrich** William married Frederica E. Garling, Darlinghurst, CE, 1860. He was of Dungog.

**Alford** Lucy married James Thompson, Emmaville, Wesleyan, 1884.

**Allen** Alexander married Agnes Murley, Newcastle, CE, 1892.

**Allen** Frank of Adelaide. Uncle of Charlotte Richards per 'Washington Irving' 1857.

**Allen** Jane married William Chenhall, Stockton, CE, 1892.

**Allen** W H of Blayney. Brother of Mary A. Dudley per 'St Lawrence' 1877.

**Allen** of Peel Point. A relative of Alice and Honor Thomas per 'Wallasea' 1865. See William Westaway.

**Allison** Agnes married William Henry Nancarrow, West Maitland, Wesleyan, 1860.

**Allison** Stockton married Mary Tucker, Newcastle, CE, 1860. She came per 'Mataoka' 1857.

**Allwood** Emily Martha married William Anderson Brown, Liverpool, CE, 1876.

**Ambler** Elizabeth married James Warren, West Maitland, Methodist, 1900.

**Amor** Isaac married Ann Haines, Cornish Settlement (Bathurst) Wesleyan, 1840. At home of William Tom.

**Amy** James per 'Lochee' 1878. Of Nattai, and Wagga. Valma Murray.

**Anderson** Agnes married Albert Read, Sydney, CE, 1893.

**Anderson** Lucy married James Peter Best (per 'Sea' 1849), Woolloomoolo, Presbyterian, 1860.

**Andrew** Absalom and Elizabeth, of Adelong 1874. NSW births.

**Andrew** Bennett married Annie Hurley, Newcastle, CE, 1889.

**Andrew** Edward married Annie Leggo, Adelong, Wesleyan, 1876.

**Andrew** Elizabeth see Elizabeth Goldsworthy.

**Andrew** John died Cobar aged 53, 1882. Buried Cobar Wesleyan.

**Andrews** Henrietta of Alexandria, married Samuel Thomas Holliday, Chippendale, Wesleyan, 1896.

**Andrews** Rebecca married John Crase, Leichhardt, Wesleyan, 1885.

**Angove** Elizabeth Jane married Alfred Rundle, Vegetable Creek, Wesleyan, 1881.

**Angwin** Rev Thomas married Elizabeth Jane Parker, Bathurst, Wesleyan, 1859.

**Anstiss** Thomas married Charlotte Lee, Bathurst, Wesleyan, 1873.

**Archer** Lucetta V married Alfred Burns (per 'Jerusalem' 1875), Darlinghurst, CE, 1889.

**Arnold** Richard married Susannah Jane Forrester, Richmond, CE, 1883.

**Arthur** James at Patterson. Uncle of James Arthur per 'Kapunda' 1877. ( A James Arthur came per 'Alfred' 1839.)

**Arthur** of Adelaide. Brother of William Arthur per 'St Vincent' 1849.

**Ashenden** Mary married William Miller, Bathurst, 1843.

**Ashworth** Susan Wadsworth married William Henry Rowe, Bathurst, 1864.

**Asprey** William married Isabella McMullen, Bathurst, 1842.

**Austin** Alice married Ernest Butler, Surry Hills, CE, 1865.

**Avery** Isabella? of Clarence River. Sister of Mary Ann Haynes, per 'Julindar' 1849.

**Avery** James of Newcastle, per 'Ellora' 1878. Beryl Mason.

**Avery** Samuel of Clarence River. Brother of Robert Avery per 'Emma Eugenie' 1849.

**Avery** Samuel of Clarence River. Brother of Anthony Avery per 'Sea' 1849. (Samuel came per Wm Turner 1841)

**Avery** Samuel and Isabella per 'William Turner' 1841. employed by Mr Sandiman at Clarence River.

**Axford** Joel of Glebe. Brother of Mary Chapman per 'Commonwealth' 1877.

### B

**Bailey** Louisa married John Francis Mitchell, Orange, 1866.

**Baither** Emily Alice married John Channon, Adelong, Wesleyan, 1875.

**Baker** Alice A married Richard Bunt, Newcastle, CE, 1877.

**Baker** Elizabeth see Elizabeth French.

**Ball** Thomas John per 'Peterborough' 1878. Went to Forest Lodge, Sydney. Reg Ball

**Ball** William Arthur buried Rookwood CE 1888 aged 40. Wife Mary buried 1922 aged 73.

**Ball** William aged 79, of Petersham. SMH 27 May 1885.

**Bamfield** Henry Rashleigh of Crookwell, 70 years. Methodist, 31 December 1910.

**Bampton** Maria married George Gilbert (per 'Fitzjames' 1857), Singleton, CE, 1865.

**Banfield** Mary married John Prisk (per 'Zemindar' 1857), East Maitland, CE, 1860.

**Banns?** John cousin of Charles Doble, both aboard 'Lady Ann' 1854.

**Barber** Susan married George Octavius Osborne,

Albury, Wesleyan, 1872.

**Barden** Albert married Charity Jane Pryor, Cooks River, CE, 1885.

**Barfett** family, Victoria. Venerable T. Barfett.

**Bargwanna** Elizabeth Jane married John Job, Orange, 1864.

**Bargwanna** Henry married Elizabeth Ann Eslick, Orange, 1879

**Bargwanna** Mary Ann married James Joseph Buckley, Cobar, Wesleyan, 1883.

**Bargwanna** Thomas married Mary Jane Gill, Orange, 1889.

**Barklay** John Daniel married Elizabeth Meyn, Singleton, CE, 1872.

**Barklay** John Daniel died 24 March 1889, buried Muswellbrook.

**Barkle** Rachel see Rachel McFadden.

**Barnes** Walter married Matilda Cock, Bathurst, 1890.

**Barnett** James married Emma Cornish, Sydney, Wesleyan, 1873.

**Barrett** Adelaide Margaret married Henry Trevethan, Forest Lodge, Wesleyan, 1891.

**Barrett** John married Elizabeth Webb nee Hean, Newtown, Presbyterian, 1898.

**Barron** James married Emily Rule, Cobar, Wesleyan, 1886.

**Bartle** Harriet died 1902 aged 53, buried Adelong Presbyterian.

**Bartle** James per 'Samuel Plimsoll' 1877, brother of Susan Robert aboard the same ship.

**Bartle** James of Orange, died 7 October 1938 aged 86. Wife Jane died 1932, aged 82. Buried Orange Methodist.

**Bartle** James and Jane, of Adelong, 1881. NSW births.

**Bartle** Lena Jane married Robert King, Adelong, 1898.

**Bartle** Samuel and Harriet, of Adelong, 1884. NSW births.

**Bartle** Samuel died Adelong 1890 aged 42, buried Adelong Wesleyan.

**Barton** Undine Una died Cobar aged 25, 1888, buried Cobar Presbyterian.

**Basanko** family, arrived in NSW, went to Victoria and South Australia. Eveline Madden.

**Basset ?** Mary see Brissett, Mary.

**Bassett** William of Hinton. Samuel & Loveday, per 'Robert Small' 1856. Associated with Christian, Bulmore, Cardell families. Marianne Eastgate.

**Bate** Richard H of Moruya. Died Moruya 1892 (56 yrs). Arrived 1854. Methodist, 3 September 1892.

**Bateman** Thomas and Mary Ann, of Adelong 1873. NSW births.

**Bath?** Anne see Anne Martin.

**Batten** Samuel a carpenter of Chippendale. Brother of Jane Edwards per 'Fitzjames' 1857.

**Bawden** Athelia nee Woolcock. A widow with seven children. Arrived per 'Ninevah' 1876. Margaret Playford.

**Bawden** Fanny Gray married Cyrus Osborne, Albury, Wesleyan, 1888.

**Bawden** William Lemon married Sarah Amelia Evans, Ashfield, Wesleyan, 1891.

**Baws** Mary see Bews

**Baynard** family of Maitland. Came per 'St Vincent' 1849. Bob Nelder.

**Beale** Captain John of 4 Jamison St, Sydney. Cousin of Mary Juleff per 'Lord Hungerford' 1855.

**Bear** Nicholas died Newcastle, 1900. Buried Sandgate.

**Bear** William per 'Fairlie' 1848. Died 1926 aged 86. Buried Sandgate cemetery, Newcastle.

**Bear** William of Newcastle. Brother of Emanual Bear/Beer per 'Eastern Empire' 1862.

**Beasley** Samuel married Eliza Smith, Bathurst, Wesleyan, 1841.

**Beel** John of Jamison St, Sydney. Brother of Francis Beel per 'Lady Ann' 1854.

**Beer** Mrs William of Gundagai. 1910. Methodist, 31 December 1910.

**Beer** William see William Bear

**Bellamy** James married Amelia Nettle, Bathurst, 1859.

**Bellamy** Robert married Hannah Nettle, Bathurst, 1875.

**Bellamy** Robert married Amelia Nettle, Bathurst, 1857.

**Bellman** Vincent with wife Jane (Dawe) per 'Amelia Thompson' 1839. Went to Parramatta. David Hall.

**Bennett** Captain Charles of Juliet St, Marrickville. SMH, 6 May 1919.

**Bennett** Charles Reath died 1919 (70 yrs). Buried Waverley cemetery.

**Bennett** Edward of Stanley St, Wooloomooloo. Nephew of William Goodman per 'Kate' 1856.

**Bennett** Elizabeth married Henry Pearce, Surry Hills, CE, 1893.

**Bennett** Elizabeth of Juliet St, Marrickville. SMH 6 July 1925.

**Bennett** Ellen see Ellen Gibbons.

**Bennett** Emma nee Hockey, married John Ellis, Byng, 1889.

**Bennett** James married Rebecca Davis, Bathurst, Wesleyan, 1865.

**Bennett** John married Rachel Rebecca Penfold, West Maitland, CE, 1880.

**Bennett** Mary of Rushcutters Bay. Sister of Richard Ball per 'Talavera' 1853.

**Bennett** William of Pyrmont. Brother of Elizabeth Crewes per 'Rajasthan' 1855.

**Bennetts** Joseph married Louisa Jane Jolly, Bathurst, Wesleyan, 1885.

**Bensley** Emma married Richard Francis Gartrell, Orange, 1894.

**Berriman** Andrew per 'Gloriana' 1855. Settled in Mogo, then Moruya. Died in Moruya 1904. Estelle Neilson.

**Berriman** John per 'St Vincent' 1849. Went to Victoria, then Mogo and Sydney. Settled in Marrickville. Estelle Neilson.

**Berriman** John in Melbourne. Brother of Andrew and Joseph Berriman per 'Gloriana' 1855.

**Berriman** Joseph per 'Gloriana' 1855. Settled in Ballarat, Victoria. Died 1889. Estelle Neilson.

**Berriman** Richard buried Rookwood cemetery, 1905

**Berryman** Edward Pooley and Mary Ann, of Adelong, 1864. NSW births.

**Berryman** Edward per 'Persia' 1863. Went to his brother James at Adelong Reef.

**Berryman** Eliza Ann per 'Persia' 1863. Went to James Berryman at Adelong Reef.

**Berryman** James of Adelong married Jane Peters, Sydney, CE, 1862.

**Berryman** James of Adelong Reefs. Brother of Edward Berryman per 'Persia' 1863.

**Berryman** James and Jane, of Adelong, 1863. NSW births.

**Berryman** Richard husband of Margaret, Lewisham. SMH 22 March, 1905.

**Berryman** Richard and Alice, of Adelong, 1863. NSW births.

**Best** Anna Maria wife of Gervase Best. She died 1860 (aged 28). Buried Pioneer Memorial Park, Botany.

**Best** Cyrus buried Waverley with Gervase, no date.

**Best** Edwin Carncross married Elizabeth Cock, Parkes, Wesleyan, 1897.

**Best** Elizabeth widow of James. Of Woolloomooloo. SMH 23 May, 1878.

**Best** Elizabeth wife of James. Buried Rookwood Independent 1878 (24 yrs)

**Best** George came per 'Sea' 1849. Married Ellen

Stuart, Woolloomooloo, Wesleyan, 1860.

**Best** George married Mary Riley, Cooks River, Congregational, 1879.

**Best** George of Darlinghurst, 1889. SMH 6 August, 1889.

**Best** Gervase of Darlinghurst, aged 72, 1903. SMH 11 August, 1903.

**Best** Gervase born Helston (Cornwall) 1831. Buried Waverley 1903 (72 yrs). Cyrus Best in same grave.

**Best** James P of North Willoughby, died at Woolloomooloo 1884. SMH 16 August 1884

**Best** James Peter buried with James Best, Rookwood Independent 1884 (51 yrs)

**Best** James Peter (per 'Sea' 1849). Married Lucy Anderson, Woolloomooloo, Presbyterian, 1860.

**Best** James buried Rookwood Independent 1872 (72 yrs)

**Best** James of Woolloomooloo, formerly of Helston, Cornwall. Funeral, 1872. SMH 30 August 1872.

**Best** Lewin James buried with James Best, Rookwood Independent 1930 (57 yrs).

**Best** Mary of Rockdale SMH 20 May 1885.

**Best** Walter Cyrus of Darlinghurst. SMH 18 March 1904.

**Best** see lewin Wood.

**Betheras** James Ellicott and Jessie, of Adelong, 1876. NSW births.

**Bews** Mary wife of Simon and supposed to be in Sydney. Sister of Charles Keverne per 'Julindar' 1849.

**Biddick** Sarah married John Arthur Kenny, Surry Hills, CE, 1899.

**Birch** Mary Annie G married John Henry Cook, Cobar, Wesleyan, 1884.

**Birch** Sarah married Frederick Sutton, Bathurst, 1863.

**Birch** William Williams and Grace, of Adelong, 1873. NSW births.

**Bishop** Jane married James Henry Tucker, Orange, 1867.

**Blacker** Mary married John Strongman, Croydon Park, Wesleyan, 1885.

**Blacklock** Alice married Charles Teague (per 'Mary Pleasants' 1858), Macleay River, Wesleyan, 1873.

**Blackwell** Sarah Jane married James Jory, Adelong, Wesleyan, 1876.

**Blake** Catherine married James Sheridan, Cornish Settlement (Bathurst) 1841.

**Blake** Charles married Ellen Knapman, Sydney, 1861.

**Blamey** Louis Rowe married Ellen Williams of Moruya, Glebe, Wesleyan, 1884.

**Blamey** Margaret per 'Harbinger' 1849. Daughters Eliza Northey & Mary Ann Treneman on board. Settled in Bathurst. Marjorie Jesse

**Blamey** related to Northey, Trebilcock, Rowe, Treneman. Marjorie Jesse

**Blewett** Charles Nicholas married Catherine Uren, Hill End, 1873.

**Blewett** John married Clara Woolley, Hamilton, Wesleyan, 1892.

**Blight** Mary Elizabeth married Brenton James (per 'Australia' 1853), Macleay River, Wesleyan, 1873.

**Bliss** William of Riversdale near Kiama. Brother-in-law of Alexander Bosanko per 'Harbinger' 1849

**Boaden** Joseph married Lucy Ann Harris, Bathurst, Wesleyan, 1883.

**Bole** Harriet Ann married Thomas Morris of Redfern, Marrickville, Wesleyan, 1886.

**Bolt** Walter William (per 'Dunbar Castle' 1877) married Ellen Rowe, Kempsey, Wesleyan, 1880.

**Bolton** Margaret married John Francis Trewnick, Cobargo, Wesleyan, 1884.

**Bone** Jabez married Constance Emeline Ann Nute, Rockdale, Methodist, 1902.

**Bone** Thomas of Cobar, married Margaret Lamont, Sydney, Wesleyan, 1896.

**Bonney** Ann per 'Herefordshire' 1857, niece of Anna Hoskyn per 'Tartar' 1857.

**Booth** John innkeeper of Windsor Rd. Employer of Rhoda Pidwell per 'Lady Kennaway' 1841.

**Bosanko** Alexander per 'Harbinger' 1849. Went to Victoria and South Australia. Eveline Madden.

**Bossistow** two brothers of William Bossistow per 'Sultana' 1855, but no places of residence given.

**Bosustow** Diana nee Courtis, per 'Julindar' 1849, mother of James Bosustow per 'Walter Morrice' 1849.

**Bosustow** son of Diana & Jacob Bosustow per 'Julindar' 1849. No place of residence given.

**Bosustow** daughter of Diana & Jacob Bosustow per 'Julindar' 1849. No place of residence given.

**Bott** Ellen died 1911 (84 yrs). Buried Waverley cemetery in same grave as George and Minnie Mair.

**Bott** Ellen widow of Lt George Bott RN. Woollahra. SMH 4 January 1911.

**Bottrel** family per 'Lord Hungerford' 1855, parents & family of Thomas Bottrel per 'Bermondsey' 1855.

**Boulden** John married Mary Sophia Williams, Burwood, CE, 1886.

**Boulden** Mary married Nicholas Henry Harris, Burwood, CE, 1883.

**Boulden** Samuel and wife Susan (Willey) per 'Herald of the Morning' 1858. Settled in Newcastle. Margaret Bauer.

**Boundy** Dorothy wife of John. She died Newcastle 1908. Buried Sandgate cemetery.

**Boundy** John married Alice Reid, Newcastle, CE, 1861.

**Bourne** Edna nee Truscott. Married Edward John Quine, Surry Hills, Primitive Methodist, 1891.

**Bourne** Rosa married William Henry Manuell (per 'Lady Amherst' 1849), Newcastle, CE, 1871.

**Bowden** Charles labourer living 8 miles from Sydney. Uncle of John Bowden per 'Himalaya' 1865.

**Bowden** Elizabeth Ann married Simon S Tucker, Muswellbrook, CE, 1875.

**Bowden** Hannah of Telegherry died after a short illness. Wife of Thomas Bowden Senior. Methodist 12 August 1905.

**Bowden** Jane married Thomas Couch, Singleton, Methodist, 1868.

**Bowden** John of West Maitland. Died 1901 (89 yrs). Methodist 24 August 1901, 23 November 1901.

**Bowden** John per 'Lady Amherst' 1849 went to West Maitland.

**Bowden** John labourer living 8 miles from Sydney. Uncle of John Bowden per 'Himalaya' 1865.

**Bowden** Thomas Richards married Mary Langmaid, Muswellbrook, CE, 1884.

**Bowden** William C of Sydney, brother of Mary Jane Pearce (widow) per 'Trevelyan' 1877.

**Bowen** Catherine of Hunter St Sydney, sister of Georgiana Beer per 'Montrose' 1864.

**Boyle** Hector Allen married Mary Gribble nee Dudley, Surry Hills, CE, 1901.

**Boyle** Maggie May married Ernest Victor Knight, Redfern, Wesleyan, 1895.

**Boyle** Martha married James Simmons, Grafton, Wesleyan, 1890.

**Brabyn** Captain John of Windsor. Captain Royal Veteran Co. Arrived 1796. Betty McGrath.

**Brabyn** John died Windsor 1835. Buried Windsor.

**Bradford** Camellia Elene married Charles Soady (per 'Earl Dalhousie 1877), Murrurundi, Wesleyan, 1883.

**Bradley** family, of Molong. David Rutherford.

**Bramble** James married Mary Lloyd, Darlinghurst, CE, 1888.

**Bray** Abdiel Went to South Australia. Chris Wright.

**Bray** Elizabeth married William Henry Paul, Bathurst, 1867.

**Bray** Eva married Alfred Stanhope Swift, a Wesleyan minister, Bathurst, 1874.

**Bray** James per 'William Metcalfe' 1844 apprenticed

to Mr Dent, ship's carpenter, Circular Quay.

**Bray** James marriage of R. Brooking & S. Trembath at his residence, 635 George St Sydney, 1884.

**Bray** John married Margaret Ellen Calloway, America Creek Wollongong, Primitive Methodist, 1887.

**Bray** John of Icely, copper miner. Husband of Mary Ann Bray per 'Samuel Plimsoll' 1875.

**Bray** Mary per 'William Metcalfe' 1844 employed by Mr Moore, Liverpool.

**Bray** Mrs of Bathurst. Palmer, Bayliss and Paul connections. BDT 4 May 1883.

**Bray** Phillip per 'Willim Metcalfe' 1844. Residing with stepfather Samuel Warren who is employed at government works.

**Bray** Samuel married Joanna Jane Pearse of Cornish Settlement, Bathurst, Wesleyan, 1844. NLA MS 3290.

**Bray** Samuel tailor & draper, married Ann Trestrain, Bathurst, Wesleyan, 1839. NLA MS 3290.

**Bray** William of Cooks River married Elizabeth Rowles nee Hobbs, Cooks River, CE, 1859.

**Brechin** Gertrude Margaret married William Thomas, Balmain, Wesleyan, 1880.

**Brenton** James married Maria Elizabeth Blight, Macleay River, Wesleyan. 1873.

**Brenton** James from near Adelaide, South Australia. Brother of Thomas Brenton per 'Australia' 1853.

**Brenton** John from near Adelaide, South Australia. Brother of Thomas Brenton per 'Australia' 1853.

**Brett** George of Botany Town, uncle of Edward Mount per 'Lord Stanley' 1850.

**Brett** George of Surry Hills, 1885. SMH 11 June 1885.

**Brewer** Henry (per 'Alfred' 1857) married Fanny Hawke (per 'Conrad' 1841), Maitland, CE, 1863.

**Brewer** Nicholas (per 'Alfred' 1857) married Mary Ann Stephens, Morpeth, CE, 1858.

**Brewer** Nicholas (per 'Alfred' 1857) married Eliza Hawke, Wingham. CE, 1865. (She was sister of Fanny, wife of his brother Henry Brewer).

**Brickwood** see Chubb.

**Bridgewater** Elizabeth Ann married Thomas John Mumford, Surry Hills, CE, 1892.

**Bridwell** May J of Sydney. Sister of Edwin Forrest per 'Trevelyan' 1877. He went to Bathurst.

**Brissett** Mary married John Hollow, Sydney, Congregational, 1883.

**Bristier** Charlotte Anne married William James Rowe, Sydney, Presbyterian, 1877.

**Bristow** Kate married Richard Wellington, Adelong, 1888.

**Briton** Agnes married Frederick Lawrence Langdon of Petersham, Sydney, Presbyterian, 1896.

**Broad** Albert Edward died 1904 aged 39. Buried Waverley cemetery.

**Broad** Elizabeth died 1909 aged 69. Buried Waverley cemetery. Wife of Albert.

**Broadbent** Jane nee Wearne. Died 1902, Redfern. Methodist 1 October 1892.

**Broadleck** Nicholas residence unknown. Brother of John Broadbent per 'Fitzjames' 1857.

**Brock** Elizabeth nee Farmer married John Moloney, Surry Hills, CE, 1899.

**Bromley** James Thomas married Mignonette Mary Rowe, Hillgrove, Wesleyan, 1891.

**Brookes** Ann married Richard Kestall, Bathurst, 1843.

**Brookes** John married Lucy Elizabeth Chambers, Bathurst, 1843. NLA MS 3290

**Brooking** Richard of Nymagee married Sarah Martin Trembath, Sydney, Wesleyan, 1884.

**Brooking** Sarah Jane married Joseph Edwin Roberts, Cobar, Methodist, 1905.

**Brooking** Thomas Henry married Elizabeth Jane Harvey, Cobar, Wesleyan, 1883.

**Brooks** Thomas married Eliza Hawkins, Wallsend,

Methodist, 1901.

**Brown** Catherine married William Henry Harris, Wollombi, Wesleyan, 1868.

**Brown** Eliza married Frederic Morcom, Maitland, CE, 1861.

**Brown** Elizabeth Ann nee Plummer. Funeral, Bathurst, 1926. BT 31 July 1926.

**Brown** F of Newcastle, brother-in-law of Ellen Trenerry per 'Forest Monarch' 1858.

**Brown** F of Newcastle, sent for Susan Mill/s per 'Forest Monarch' 1858. She was not a relative.

**Brown** Frederick married Mary J. Trenerry (per 'Ellenborough' 1853) in 1856. NSW BDM 1856 12486

**Brown** John of Adelong. Uncle of James Williams per 'Commonwealth' 1877.

**Brown** Rebecca married John Moffatt (per 'Plantaganet' 1857), Woolloomooloo, CE, 1862.

**Brown** Rose Ann married William Evan Thomas, Surry Hills, CE, 1897.

**Brown** Susannah nee Daw, married William James Worth, Pyrmont, Presbyterian, 1891.

**Brown** Thomas married Mary Louise Sara, Cornish Settlement, Wesleyan, 1856.

**Brown** William Anderson married Emily Martha Allwood, Liverpool, CE, 1876.

**Bruggmann** Carl H F married Susan Grigg, Parramatta, Wesleyan, 1890.

**Bryant** Dorothy married John Whalan, Fish River (Bathurst), 1856.

**Bryant** Elizabeth per 'St Lawrence' 1877, married John Frederick Thomas, Petersham, CE, 1886.

**Bryant** Mary Barrett married Isaac John Thomas, Fish River (Bathurst) 1856.

**Bryant** Walter and wife Mary nee Barrett per 'Earl Grey' 1841. Settled in Oberon. Robyn Ambascheer

**Bryant** Walter of Bathurst. Uncle of Thomas Bryant per 'Kate' 1856.

**Buckett** John married Caroline Woodbridge, Adelong, Wesleyan, 1880.

**Buckley** George married Emma Darlington Pearce, Cobar, Methodist, 1903.

**Buckley** Grace Ann died Cobar 1884 aged 43, buried Cobar.

**Buckley** James Joseph married Mary Ann Bargwanna, Cobar, Wesleyan, 1883.

**Budden** Arthur married Sarah Stanger, Bathurst, 1859.

**Budge** William of Melbourne, Victoria. Father of John Budge per 'Sultana' 1855.

**Bullock** Edwin brother of William Bullock per 'Lord Hungerford' 1855.

**Bullock** Edwin per 'Cressy' 1856. Had moved to Victoria by 1860. Pauline Hartman.

**Bullock** John in colony, whereabouts unknown. Brother-in-law of William Butson per 'Rajasthan' 1855.

**Bullock** John whereabouts uncertain. Husband of Jane Bullock nee Butson per 'Africana' 1866.

**Bullock** John supposed to be in Ballarat, Victoria. Father of Mary J Bullock per 'Africana' 1866.

**Bullock** William per 'Lord Hungerford' 1855. Went to Victoria. Pauline Hartman

**Bullock** William Per 'Lord Hungerford' is brother of Edwin Bullock per 'Cressy' 1856.

**Bunn** Mary Ann died Cobar aged 79, 1891, buried Cobar Wesleyan.

**Bunney** Arthur died 1908 (38 yrs), buried Rookwood CE. In same grave; wife Catherine Bunney & Mary Glanfield.

**Bunney** Arthur murdered Gladesville, 1908. Husband of Catherine A. Bunney. SMH 22 December 1908.

**Bunney** Catherine Allen died 1938 (72 yrs), buried Rookwood CE.

**Bunney** Mary per 'Admiral Lyons' 1858, mother of Thomas Perry also on board.

**Bunt** Edward residence not given. Brother of

Richard Bunt per 'Sarah' 1849.

**Bunt** Elijah per 'St Lawrence' 1877. Brother of James Bunt. Went to Sydney & Lithgow. See Truscott. Joy Hadfield.

**Bunt** James per 'St Lawrence' 1877. Brother of Elijah Bunt. Went to Sydney & Lithgow. See Truscott. Joy Hadfield.

**Bunt** John per 'General Hewitt' 1848. Farmer at Hinton near Morpeth. Vi Rose.

**Bunt** Richard Bartlett married Alice Amelia Baker, Newcastle, CE, 1877.

**Bunt** W H died Carrington 1907 (44 yrs).

**Burge** John gave consent for marriage of William Barry Burge Cooke, Brown's Creek, 1861.

**Burgess** Jane married Henry Nancarrow per 'Equestrian' 1848, West Maitland, Wesleyan, 1880.

**Burley** Charles married Mary Jane Longbottom, Bandongrove, CE, 1858.

**Burley** Charles per 'Alfred' 1839, widower, married Eliza Norris, Allyn River, CE, 1864.

**Burnett** Joseph married Mary Ann Ford, Newtown, Wesleyan, 1888.

**Burnett** Melinda arrived 1860. Died 1890, buried Singleton.

**Burnett** Melinda sister of Richard Kent per 'Coldstream' 1863.

**Burnett** Melinda of Campbelltown. Niece of Thomas Langsford per 'Coldstream' 1863.

**Burnett** William John married Jane Killin, Singleton, Wesleyan, 1890.

**Burnett** William arrived 1860. Died Singleton 1916.

**Burnett** family, Singleton. Peggy Richards.

**Burns** Alfred (per 'Jerusalem' 1875) married Lucetta V Archer, Surry Hills, CE, 1889.

**Burns** Ann married John Dumble of Tambaroora, Sydney, CE, 1872.

**Burns** James married Ann Drew Darke, Sydney, Presbyterian, 1862.

**Burns** John (per 'Zemindar' 1857) of Bathurst, brother of Alfred Burns per 'Jerusalem' 1875. Brother Richard also aboard 'Zemindar'.

**Burns** John marble mason, Bathurst, 1888. AMM

**Burns** John married Ellen Surridge nee Whalan, Bathurst, Wesleyan, 1867.

**Burns** John of Newcastle. Brother of Henry Burns per 'Samuel Plimsoll' 1874.

**Burns** John of Newcastle. Brother of James Burns per 'Samuel Plimsoll' 1874.

**Burns** Richard of Newcastle. Brother of Thomas Burns per 'Jerusalem' 1874.

**Burridge** William married Harriet Hodge, Kempsey, Wesleyan, 1880.

**Burrows** Grace Marshall per 'Andromache' 1837, sister of William Burrows also on board.

**Burrows** William per 'Andromache' 1837, brother of Grace Marshall Burrows also on board.

**Burt** Peter and Hester, of Adelong, 1879. NSW births.

**Burton** Elizabeth married John Sandry, Bathurst, 1879.

**Burton** Henry married Elizabeth Ginn, Newcastle, CE, 1895.

**Butler** Ernest married Alice Austin, Surry Hills, CE, 1885.

**Butson** Mary per 'Rajasthan' 1855. Of Milton. Died 1896. Methodist 2 May 1896.

**Butson** William boot & shoemaker of Ulladulla. Brother of Jane Bullock per 'Africana' 1866.

**Buttle** William John per 'Dunbar Castle' 1877. Went to Maitland, Bathurst, Orange. Roma Blackhall.

**Button** Charles residence unknown. Uncle of John D. Pethick per 'Golconda' 1858.

**Buzza** J produce merchant of Sydney, 1873 +. AMM

**Buzza** James of Redfern, 1890. SMH 25 April 1890.

**Buzzacott** Marion Sarah (Minnie) of Camperdown 1899. SMH 3 November 1899.

# *C*

**Caddy** Henry per 'Tartar' 1857 married Tamar Thomas, Hinton, Wesleyan, 1861.

**Caddy** James and wife Eliza per 'Orient' 1839. Went to Morpeth. Dianne Minnican.

**Cagny** Angeline see Angeline Walton.

**Caldwell** Isabella married Joseph Wearne (per 'Harbinger' 1849), Liverpool, Wesleyan, 1857.

**Caldwell** Martha married William Carvosso Wearne (per 'Harbinger' 1849), Liverpool, Wesleyan, 1856.

**Caldwell** Rebecca married William Weeks, Wollongong, Wesleyan, 1892.

**Caldwell** Rev Richard married Lucy Ellen Stanger, Bathurst, Wesleyan, 1864.

**Callaghan** John married Priscilla Paul, Bathurst, Wesleyan, 1861.

**Callaghan** Mary married Samuel Aitcheson, Bathurst, 1841.

**Calloway** Anne see Thomas Evans.

**Calloway** James (per 'Cressy' 1856), of Wollongong. Cousin of James Uren per 'Trevelyan' 1877.

**Calloway** Margaret Ellen married John Bray, Wollongong, Primitive Methodist, 1887.

**Calloway** in Sydney - Sussex St. Three daughters of Anne Calloway per 'Cressy' 1856.

**Calloway** Sydney. Three brothers of James & Moses Calloway per 'Cressy' 1856.

**Campbell** Elizabeth married John Pearn, Raymond Terrace, CE, 1856.

**Cannon** Joseph of Newcastle, born 1858. Margaret Cannington.

**Capel** Alice married Martin Guy, Adelong, 1897.

**Carbis** family, in Victoria from 1872. See Crispin. Graham Gape.

**Carder** William Monk of Blayney, married Jemima Westlake of Paddington, Surry Hills, CE, 1897.

**Carkeek** Ann Maria nee Eden, married John Plummer, Hill End, 1877.

**Carkeek** Anna Maria married William Chellew, Hill End, 1873.

**Carkeek** Mary Jane married George Jeffree, Hill End, 1876.

**Carlyon** Charles died 1942 (59 yrs). Buried Sandgate cemetery, Newcastle.

**Carlyon** Julia Annie married Thomas Lodwick, Newcastle, Methodist, 1886.

**Carlyon** Sarah Jane died 1967 (82 yrs). Buried Sandgate cemetery, Newcastle.

**Carlyon** Tamsin married Thomas Carlyon, Hamilton, Wesleyan, 1881.

**Carlyon** Thomas married Tamsin Carlyon, Hamilton. Wesleyan, 1881.

**Carlyon** Thomas died 1908 (68 yrs). Buried Sandgate cemetery, Newcastle.

**Carlyon** Thomasine died 1933 (87 yrs). Buried Sandgate cemetery, Newcastle.

**Carlyon** William married Mary Williams, Hamilton, Wesleyan, 1881. Her mother was Catherine Carlyon. He is brother of Thomas Carlyon.

**Carmichael** Archibald Jennings of Brisbane, married Ferd. Louise Pacelle of Brisbane, Surry Hills, 1890.

**Carslisle** James in service of James Duigan/Dwyer? brother of Grace Harris per 'Maitland' 1856.

**Cartes** R of Gardners Creek Victoria, brother-in-law of Henry Myers, soldier, per 'Highflyer' 1864.

**Carthew** Edwin and Margaret, of Adelong 1874. NSW births.

**Carthew** Thomas married Amelia Richards, Orange, 1863.

**Carveth** Jane near Sydney, sister of John Carveth and cousin of his wife Mary nee Carveth per 'Sultana' 1855.

**Carveth** John and wife Maria Lightfoot (nee Carveth) per 'Eliza' 1855. Settled in Balmain. J. Harvey.

**Carveth** John and wife Mary (nee Carveth) per 'Sultana' 1855. Settled in Balmain. See Cavill. J. Harvey.

**Carveth** Mary A of Balmain. Sister of John Carveth and cousin of his wife Mary nee Carveth per 'Sultana' 1855.

**Carveth** family from St Breock, settled in Sydney. J. Harvey.

**Carvosso** Baker Banks married Elizabeth Vines Evenis, Bathurst, Wesleyan, 1862.

**Casley** Henry married Jane Niggleworth nee Rowley, Gunnedah, Wesleyan, 1880.

**Casley** William died Adelong 1878 aged 45, buried Adelong CE.

**Cater** Ernest born Launceston, Cornwall. Died Sydney 1888 (32 yrs). Buried Waverley cemetery.

**Cater** Ernest funeral, Sydney, 1881. SMH 1 March 1888.

**Catren** Albert Henry married Amy Middleton, Redfern, CE, 1897.

**Cavery** Elizabeth married Charles Pascoe (per 'Commonwealth' 1877) of Manly, Redfern, CE, 1900.

**Cavill** John and wife Mary Ann (nee Carveth) per 'Andromache' 1839. Settled Balmain. J. Harvey.

**Cavill** John builder and contractor of Balmain. AMM

**Cavill** Syria of Balmain. Died 1854 (32 yrs). Buried Camperdown with John Cavill & his wife. J. Harvey.

**Cavill** family, settled in Sydney. See Carveth. J. Harvey.

**Cawrse** John near Hunter River, uncle of James Cawrse & John Cawrse, both per 'General Hewitt' 1848.

**Chadban** William married Ada Ellery, Murrurundi, Methodist, 1899.

**Chambers** Lucy Elizabeth married John Brookes, Bathurst, 1843.

**Champion** John married Elizabeth Jeffery nee Hartwell, Surry Hills, CE, 1898.

**Channon** Elizabeth Tregidza died Adelong 1890 (62).

**Channon** John married Emily Alice Baither, Adelong, Wesleyan, 1875.

**Channon** John and Emily, of Adelong 1878. NSW births.

**Chapman** Georgiana married Walter John Trathen, Kempsey, Primitive Methodist, 1879.

**Chapman** Martha per 'Telegraph' 1858 went to her sister-in-law (Hawke) at Hartley.

**Chapman** William per 'Lord Stanley' 1850 appears to be brother of Mary Truscott aboard the same ship.

**Chapman** William see William Chadban.

**Chapple** James and Eliza, of Adelong 1864. NSW births.

**Charles** A of Ballarat. A relative of John Richards per 'Robert Small' 1856.

**Charleston** Ellen married Charles Martel, Newcastle, CE, 1885.

**Charters** Annie Ethelwyn married Francis Everard Hunt of Sydney, Redfern, Wesleyan, 1899.

**Chate** Alfred married Alarina Paul, 1855. NSW RG 1855 942 43

**Chegwidden** Frederick and wife Agnes. Rex Chegwidden.

**Chegwidden** Frederick of Orange, died 1927 (81 yrs). Methodist 9 July 1927.

**Chegwidden** Frederick and wife Agnes (nee Stephens). Lived in Orange and Sydney. Phyllis Trevena.

**Chegwidden** Frederick and wife Agnes. Relative of William J and Joseph W Chegwidden. Rex Chegwidden.

**Chegwidden** Joseph Weeks per 'Sabraon' 1868. Brother of William James Chegwidden. Rex Chegwidden.

**Chegwidden** William James per 'Lady Ann' 1854. Settled in Wollongong/Candelo. Brother of Joseph W Chegwidden. Rex Chegwidden.

**Chellew** William married Anna Maria Carkeek, Hill End, 1873.

**Chenhall** William married Jane Allen, Stockton, CE, 1892.

**Chenoweth** Mary Elizabeth married Sydney Arnold Wilson, Newtown, Wesleyan, 1896.

**Chenoweth** Salome married Joseph Sharp, Newtown, Wesleyan, 1895.

**Chenoweth** William married Amelia Ann Davis, Newtown, Wesleyan, 1886.

**Chew** Mary Ann married William B B Cooke, Bathurst, Methodist, 1861.

**Chubb** Robert of Sydney. Cousin of Damaris Miller per 'Victoria' 1849.

**Chubb** Robert cousin of Ann Colley (nee Brickwood) per 'Victoria' 1849.

**Chudleigh** William Best married Mary McManous, Parramatta, Wesleyan, 1856.

**Churchill** Sarah married John Thomas Williams (per 'Pericles' 1877), Newtown, Congregational, 1883.

**Chynoweth** Richard of Crown Flat, Araluen. Husband of Mary Chynoweth per 'Morning Star' 1864.

**Clark** Alice sister of Johanna Teague per 'Mary Pleasants' 1858. Connected with Francis and Parkin.

**Clark** Eliza Gossip married Christopher Lean, Dungog, CE, 1859.

**Clark** Harriet married Alfred Duence of Chippendale, Redfern, Wesleyan, 1892.

**Clarke** John married Susan Jane Wiltshire, Adamstown, Wesleyan, 1896.

**Cleave** Albert Ernest died 1917 (49 yrs). Buried Rookwood CE with Edmund & Martha.

**Cleave** Edmund of Pyrmont, (per 'Malvina Vidal' 1853) died 1887 (64 yrs). Buried Rookwood CE.

**Cleave** Edmund of Pyrmont. Death, 1887. SMH 21 November 1887.

**Cleave** Emily died 1929 (66). Buried Rookwood CE with Edmund & Martha.

**Cleave** Martha wife of Edmund. Died 1913 (88 yrs). Buried Rookwood CE.

**Cleave** Martha wife of Edmund. Died Neutral Bay 1913. SMH 14 November 1913.

**Cleworth** Carolyn married John Tamblyn Hawkey, Singleton, CE, 1868.

**Clift** Mary Agnes married John Dunstan Harry, Adelong, Wesleyan, 1878.

**Clifton** Mary Ann married James Roach, Ultimo, Primitive Methodist, 1885.

**Cline** Daisy married Alfred John Gray, Surry Hills, CE, 1898.

**Clough** James married Elizabeth Ann Dennis, Woolloomooloo, CE, 1863.

**Clyde** Sarah married James Rowe (both of Liverpool) Sydney, Presbyterian, 1870.

**Clymo** James Budge Mine Captain of Molong. Went to Irrawaddy River. Steve Bartlett.

**Clymo** James of Molong. Brother of Mary Terrill per 'Garland' 1851.

**Coad** William John (per 'Rajasthan' 1855) married Mary Turner, Surry Hills, Congregational, 1878.

**Coad** family. See Paul.

**Coates** William of Cargo/Carcoar? uncle of Christopher Sydney per 'Jeruslaem' 1875.

**Cock** Edwin of Wellington. Death, 1902. Methodist, 25 October 1902.

**Cock** Edwin and Susanna (Stephens). Mrs Phyllis Hohnen.

**Cock** Elizabeth J married Edmund Carncross Best, Parkes, Methodist, 1897.

**Cock** Ethel of Burwood. Married 1914. Methodist, 18 April 1914.

**Cock** Henry of Blayney 1908. Methodist, 15 August 1908.

**Cock** James and wife Christiana per 'Sir George Seymour' 1852, brother of Ann Parker per 'Andromache' 1839.

**Cock** James and Christiana. Grahame Thom.

**Cock** John of Gunnedah. Death aged 60. Methodist, 15 January 1898.

**Cock** John of Sydney, brother of James Cock per 'Pericles' 1877.

**Cock** Jonathon G and wife Phillips, of Bathurst. Brother-in-law of Benjamin Parkins per 'Walmer Castle' 1848.

**Cock** Jonathon G of Bathurst. Brother-in-law of Samuel Parkins per 'Walter Morrice' 1849.

**Cock** Mary Jane married Frank Pendray, Bathurst, 1867.

**Cock** Matilda J married George H. Weakley, Gunnedah, Wesleyan, 1893. Methodist, 7 October 1893.

**Cock** Matilda married Walter Barnes, Bathurst, 1890.

**Cock** Mrs E of Wellington. Death, 1912, aged 70. Methodist, 17 August 1912.

**Cock** Phillipa of Bathurst, wife of Johathon G. Cock, sister of Benjamin Parkins per 'Walmer Castle' and Samuel Parkins per 'Walter Morrice' 1849.

**Cock/s** James (per 'Amelia Thompson' 1838) married Laura Crofts, Surry Hills, 1888.

**Cocking** Sarah nee Mitchell married John Henry Jenkin (both of Charters Towers QLD), Surry Hills, CE, 1891.

**Cocking** Sidney John married Florence M Killingsworth, Marrickville, CE, 1902.

**Cocks** George Whitehouse of Milton. Birth of a daughter, 1900. Methodist, 13 January 1900.

**Cocks** Julia married Nathaniel Dyer, Newtown, Wesleyan, 1888.

**Cocks** Thomas died Sydney 1918 (born 1852 Cornwall). Buried Waverley cemetery. Also Muriel Helen & Muriel Grace.

**Cocks** Thomas of Dulwich Hill. Died 1918. SMH 4 November 1918.

**Cocks** W H B of Parkes. Death aged 61. Methodist, 8 May 1897.

**Cocks** William recognition of 30 years as a Methodist local preacher, 1897. Methodist, 17 July 1897.

**Cocks** William of Kiama. Died 1892 aged 52. Had lived in Orange & Bathurst. Methodist 25 June 1892.

**Coe** Anthony James married Mary Elizabeth Trethowen (per 'Earl Dalhousie' 1877), Enmore, CE, 1886.

**Cole** David and Mary Jane, of Adelong 1882. NSW births.

**Cole** John and Martha, of Adelong 1876. NSW births.

**Coleman** Emma married Henry Tom, Cornish Settlement, 1859.

**Coleman** Henry married Mary McDowell, Parramatta, Wesleyan, 1880.

**Coleridge** Derwent married Emma Taylor, Woolloomooloo, Congregational, 1879.

**Colless** Elizabeth married Joseph Stephens, Emu Plains, CE, 1857.

**Colley** Amelia married John Trebilcock, Bathurst, 1857.

**Colley** Thomas Chubb per 'Victoria' 1849. Went to Cornish Settlement, Bathurst and Hargraves. Sally Colley.

**Collins** Harriet married William John Polglase, Cobar, Wesleyan, 1880.

**Collins** John of Botany in the 1880s. S.L. Adams.

**Collins** John of Botany, married Alice Augusta Favell, Arncliffe, Wesleyan, 1884.

**Collins** John of Sydney, uncle of Susan Caddy per 'Tartar' 1857.

**Collins** Percy married Olivia Maud Mary Knight, Redfern, Wesleyan, 1897.

**Collins** Robert of Sydney, uncle of Susan Caddy per 'Tartar' 1857.

**Congdon** Samuel of Woolloomooloo. Involved in the fish trade 1854+. AMM

**Conley** Charlotte see Charlotte Jeffery.

**Connor** Edward F married Bessie Rogers, Darlinghurst, CE, 1890.

**Cook** Charlie married Annie Hocking, Armidale, Wesleyan, 1894.

**Cook** Harriet married Richard E Cook, Glebe, Wesleyan, 1896. NSW BDM 1896 7329

**Cook** John Henry married Mary Annie Georgina Birch, Cobar, Wesleyan, 1884.

**Cook** Richard E married Harriet Cook, Glebe, Wesleyan, 1896 NSW BDM 1896 7329

**Cook** Samuel W died Newcastle 1881 (82 yrs). Brother-in-law of Henry Dangar. AMM

**Cook** Thomas married Caroline Paul, Woolloomooloo, Wesleyan, 1879.

**Cook** Thomas residence unknown, brother of Henry Cook per 'Plantaganet' 1857.

**Cooke** William Barry Burge married Mary Ann Chew, Brown's Creek (Bathurst) Wesleyan, 1861. With consent of guardian, John Burge.

**Coombe** William died Cobar aged 32, 1904, buried Cobar CE.

**Copp** Mary Ann per 'Parsee' 1853, of Market St, Sydney, sister of Henry Francis per 'Blenheim' 1855.

**Cord** Ann married Alexander McDonald, Bathurst, 1871.

**Cornish** Emma nee Hall, married James Barnett, Sydney, Wesleyan, 1873.

**Cornish** John married Mary Ann Robyns, Adelong, Wesleyan, 1874.

**Cornish** John and Mary Ann, of Adelong 1875. NSW births.

**Cornish** family, Sydney. A. T. Thomas.

**Cornwall** Mrs Annie died Cornish Settlement, 1894. Methodist 29 December 1894.

**Corse** William and Mary Ann, of Adelong 1873. NSW births.

**Cory Ferrett** family per 'William Turner' 1841 employed by Mr Currie of Currie Vale.

**Costelloe** Annie Beatrice married George Rens (both of Temora), Sydney, CE, 1890.

**Couch** Edith Jane married John Parslow, Molong, 1887.

**Couch** Elizabeth Mary married Henry Ayers Parslow, Molong, 1893.

**Couch** Elizabeth married John Maddison, Orange, 1864.

**Couch** Grace of Molong. Died 1897 aged 60. Buried Molong. Wife of WH Couch.

**Couch** Hester of Yass. Sister of Joseph Watts per 'Lady Ann' 1854.

**Couch** Thomas married Jane Bowden, Singleton, Methodist, 1868.

**Couch** W H of Molong. David A. Rutherford.

**Couch** W H died 1910 aged 74, Molong. Buried Molong.

**Couch** William H of Orange, Cargo and Molong. CWD, 15 May 1984.

**Courter** Henry married Elizabeth Annie Gibb, Glen Innes, Wesleyan, 1895.

**Courtis** Diana see Bosustow, Diana.

**Courtis** William of Port Phillip, Victoria, a cousin of James Bosustow per 'Walter Morrice' 1849.

**Cox** Mr see Marianne Johns.

**Cox** Phillipa see Cock, Phillipa.

**Crago** Ann of Yass. Sister of Jane Stephens per 'Morning Star' 1864.

**Crago** Ann of Yass. Sister of Sidonia Stephens per 'Morning Star' 1864.

**Crago** Charlotte see Charlotte Crego.

**Crago** Edward married Charlotte Dalzell, South Singleton, Wesleyan, 1890.

**Crago** Francis per 'Hornet' 1865, of Yass, Singleton and Bathurst. AMM

**Crago** Francis per 'Hornet' 1865. Died 1907 aged 59. Buried Rookwood CE with Mary Ann & Percival

Crago and Edith Lewis.

**Crago** Jane Meredith wife of Edward. Died 1886 aged 32. Buried Rookwood Independent.

**Crago** Mary Ann died 1934. Buried Rookwood CE with Francis Crago.

**Crago** Percival George died 1937 aged 42. Buried Rookwood CE with Francis & Mary Ann Crago.

**Crago** Petherick T of Yass, lately clerk to Mr Godfrey, Yass. Son of William & Elizabeth Crago, per 'Hornet' 1865.

**Crago** Petherick T of Yass, lately clerk to Mr Godfrey, Yass. Brother of William, John & Francis Crago, per 'Hornet' 1865.

**Crago** Petherick T per 'Castillian' 1858.

**Crago** family Lesley Evans.

**Crago** see James Dunstan.

**Crago** see Edith Lewis.

**Crago** Crago Flour Mills, Bathursrt - article. NA 15 August 1890.

**Crago** Crago fountain, Bathurst. BT 15 & 24 December 1891.

**Cramp** Sara nee Jeffrey, married Lewis Pritchard, Grafton, 1868.

**Crane** Mary Jane married William Henry Tresidder, Bulli, Primitive Methodist, 1888.

**Cranstone** John married Eliza Poppins, Bathurst, Wesleyan, 1841.

**Crapp** Charles of Broulee (per 'Australia' 1853?), brother of John Crapp per 'Sultana' 1855.

**Crapp** Edwin Arnold of Uralla, married Ellen Alice Leece, Uralla, 1905. Methodist, 1 July 1905.

**Crapp** John Thomas of Uralla. Death aged 60, 1894. Methodist, 15 September 1894.

**Crapp** John supposed to be in Sydney, brother of Mary Ann Mortimer per 'Harbinger' 1849.

**Crapp** Martha of Uralla. Died 1898. Methodist, 15 January 1898.

**Crapp** Martha of Uralla, wife of William. Memorial service. Methodist, 12 February 1898.

**Crapp** Miss of Uralla. Farewell, 1897. Methodist, 12 June 1897.

**Crapp** Mrs J S of Armidale. Methodist, 8 November 1902.

**Crapp** Serrana Mary of Glen Innes. Wife of WH Crapp. Died 1910. Methodist, 25 February 1911.

**Crase** John married Rebecca Andrews, Leichhardt, Wesleyan, 1885.

**Crego** Charlotte married Ernest F. New, Surry Hills, CE, 1892.

**Crispin** family, in Victoria from 1872. See Carbis. Graham Gape.

**Crofts** Laura married James Cock/s (per "Amelia Thompson' 1838), Surry Hills, CE, 1888.

**Cronin** Patrick J and wife Amelia nee Woolcock. Margaret Playford.

**Cross** Margaret married Stephen Curnow, Bathurst, Methodist, 1857.

**Crossman** Elizabeth died Cobar aged 34, 1904, buried Cobar Methodist.

**Crothers** Annie see Lockwood, Annie.

**Crothers** Elizabeth Louisa married James Thomas Williams, Lewisham, Methodist, 1900.

**Crothers** Elizabeth Opie nee Jennings. Wife of George. Died 1915. Buried Rookwood Wesleyan.

**Crothers** George of Petersham. Died 1909. Buried Rookwood Wesleyan.

**Crothers** George of Petersham. AMM

**Crothers** George of Lewisham. Died 1909. SMH 29 November 1909.

**Crouch** Elizabeth Ann married John Wilmot May Pearson, Parramatta, CE, 1889.

**Crowther** John per 'Salisbury', a relative of Edward Howarth per 'Dunbar Castle' 1877.

**Cullen** Dominick married Mary Maddern, Vegetable Creek, Wesleyan, 1875.

**Cundy** Diana see Diana Hughes.

**Cundy** John of Hunter River, brother-in-law of John Goog, per 'Forest Monarch' 1858.

**Cundy** John Muswellbrook, Aberdeen. Brother of Samuel Cundy per 'Fitzjames' 1858. See William Cundy.

**Cundy** John and Catherine, per 'Duchess of Northumberland' 1838. Settled in Muswellbrook, Scone & Merriwa. Sr Juliana Googe.

**Cundy** Samuel and wife Marianne, per 'Fitzjames' 1858. Settled in Muswellbrook, Scone, Merriwa. Sr Juliana Googe & Enid Farnham.

**Cundy** William Muswellbrook, Aberdeen. Brother of Samuel Cundy per 'Fitzjames' 1858. See John Cundy.

**Curnow** Alice Mary married Richard Prout, Bathurst, 1885.

**Curnow** John Richard of Warwick QLD married Katherine Celia Marshall, Enmore, Wesleyan, 1886.

**Curnow** John of West Kempsey, uncle of James Gilbert, per 'Pericles' 1877.

**Curnow** John married Betsey Jane Johns, Burwood, Wesleyan, 1891.

**Curnow** Peter a cousin of Peter Floyd, Orange. CWD, 6 November 1984.

**Curnow** Rev William married Matilda Weiss, Sydney, Wesleyan, 1858.

**Curnow** Stephen married Margaret Cross, Bathurst, Wesleyan, 1857.

**Curnow** see Kerno.

**Currie** Mr (Cory?) of Currie Vale, employed Cory Ferrett family per 'William Turner' 1841.

**Currie** Mr of Currie Vale, employed Elizabeth Eastcote, per 'William Turner' 1841.

**Currie** Mr of Currie Vale, employed Mary & William Moyse per 'William Turner' 1841.

**Currie** Mr of Currie Vale, employed John & Susan Turner per 'William Turner' 1841.

**Curtis** William see Courtis, William.

# D

**Dainty** Mary A married Christopher Knight, Redfern, CE, 1884.

**Dale** William and wife Dorothea per 'Earl Grey' 1841. Peter Hohnen.

**Dalley** George Henry married Bessie Matilda Venning Tabb, Sydney, Wesleyan, 1881.

**Daly** Ellen married Richard Roberts, (both of Dapto), Redfern, United Free Methodist, 1898.

**Dalzell** Charlotte married Edward Crago, South Singleton, Wesleyan, 1890.

**Dangar** Grace nee Sibly. Wife of Henry Dangar. Died Singleton 1869.

**Dangar** Henry born St Neot, Cornwall, 1798. Died Sydney 1861. AMM

**Dangar** John Charles married Angelina Walton nee Cagny, Sydney, CE, 1869.

**Dangar** Thomas Colin Cunningham.

**Dangar** family. Peter Dangar.

**Dargin** James of Windsor, employed George family per William Metcalfe' 1844.

**Dargin** William married Mary Short Mutton, Bathurst, Wesleyan, 1860.

**Darke** Ann Drew married James Burns, Sydney, Presbyterian, 1862.

**Datson** William Thomas and wife Susan and family per 'Wanata' 1864, went to 19 Norton St (Sydney).

**Davey** Grace married James Rule, Cobar, Wesleyan, 1887.

**Davey** Hannah died Cobar aged 31, 1881, buried Cobar.

**Davey** Mary see Mary Maddern.

**Davey** Walter died Cobar aged 58, 1884, buried Cobar CE.

**Davey** William appears to be brother of James Davis,

both per 'Trevelyan' 1877.

**Davey** William died Cobar aged 32, 1883, buried Cobar Wesleyan.

**Davey** Willliam of Vegetable Creek, brother of Samuel Dunstan per 'Jerusalem' 1875.

**Davies** Annie Elizabeth married William John Pearce, Glebe, 1883.

**Davies** James Thomas married Emmeline Downing, Cobar, Wesleyan, 1882.

**Davis** Amelia Ann married William Chenoweth, Newtown, Wesleyan, 1886.

**Davis** George married Eliza Smith, Bathurst, 1841.

**Davis** James appears to be brother of William Davey, both per 'Trevelyan 1877.

**Davis** John married Jane Haywhite, Bathurst, Wesleyan, 1841.

**Davis** Julie Annie married William Edward Ward, Chippendale, Wesleyan, 1892.

**Davis** Mary Ann married Stephen Grose (per 'Kate' 1854), Newcaslte, CE, 1888.

**Davis** Mary Hannah married Thomas Gaynor, Newcaslte, CE, 1897.

**Davis** Mrs Elizabeth of Bungarribee, employed Elizabeth Trebilcock per 'Hawkesbury' 1871.

**Davis** Rebecca married James Bennett, Bathurst, 1865.

**Davis** William of Vegetable Creek, brother of Susan Prisk per 'Earl Dalhousie' 1877.

**Daw** Susannah see Susannah Brown.

**Dawe** Joseph married Ellen Thomas, Sydney, CE, 1887.

**Dawes** Adelaide married William Charles Jenkin, Darlinghurst, CE, 1893.

**Dawes** William Henry of Goulburn & Yass, per 'Herefordshire' 1857. Died 1908. A. Jaeger, & J. Dawes.

**Dawson** Isabella married William Northey, Kelso, 1885.

**Dawson** Mary Ann married William Evans, Newcaslte, CE, 1862.

**Dawson** Sarah Elizabeth married Richard Sandry, Dunkeld, 1876.

**De Mamul** Norah married William Stephen Harper, Sydney, CE, 1891. Both of Inner Junction.

**Deacon** William of Waverley, 1870s. P.J. Stemp.

**Deeble** Mary widow, per 'Ninevah' 1876. Relative of Emily & James Whittle also on board.

**Delbridge** James of Adelaide, relative of Josiah Phillips per 'Harbinger' 1849. See Veal, Thomas.

**Delbridge** William of Adelaide, relative of Josiah Phillips per 'Harbinger' 1849. See Veal, Thomas.

**Dellacour** Caroline married Thomas Niclan, Surry Hills, 1888.

**Dengate** Emily married James Tare Wearne (per 'Harbinger' 1849), Parramatta, Wesleyan, 1863.

**Dennis** Ann of Cow Flat (Bathurst). Sister of Elizabeth Jenkin (nee Grenfell) per 'Ninevah' 1877.

**Dennis** Charles married Catherine Joan Sampson, Chippendale, Wesleyan, 1874.

**Dennis** Elizabeth Ann (per 'Sultana' 1855) married James Clough, Sydney, CE, 1863.

**Dennis** Elizabeth of Sydney, per 'Sultana' 1855. Robert Hay.

**Dennis** George of Cow Flat. Son-in-law of Alice Grenfell per 'Ninevah' 1877. Connection with Jenkins also on board.

**Dennis** George of Bathurst brother-in-law of John Dennis per 'Jerusalem' 1874.

**Dennis** Henry of Cootamundra (per Samuel Plimsoll 1874) married Lucy Holdsorthy, Granville, CE, 1884.

**Dennis** John married Louisa Kemp, Bathurst, Wesleyan, 1882.

**Dent** John of Surry Hills, uncle of William Timmins per 'Lady Ann' 1854.

**Dent** Mr of Circular Wharf, employed James Bray per 'William Metcalfe' 1844 as apprentice ship's carpenter.

**Dent** Sarah of Sydney, aunt of Edward Timmins per 'Golconda' 1857. See Timmins.

**Dent** Thomas married Susan Hooper, Hamilton, CE, 1890.

**Diehm** Catherine married William Thomas Anderson Pascoe, Wellington, 1901.

**Dingle** John married Frances Jane Melville, Adamstown, Free Methodist, 1887.

**Dingle** Mary Ann per 'Ninevah' 1877. See Adams, Richard.

**Dingle** Samuel Seccombe died 1924 aged 58. Buried Woronora CE cemetery.

**Dingle** Samuel Seccombe death 1924. SMH 25 November 1924.

**Doble** Charles per 'Lady Ann' 1854, cousin of John Banns? also on board.

**Doble** John of Sydney, 1883. Anne Carolan.

**Doble** John Maxwell of Paddington. 1885. SMH 19 October 1885. Buried Waverley.

**Doidge** John (per 'Ninevah' 1877) married Mary Woodcock, Redfern, Methodist, 1877.

**Dorrington** Francis of North Richmond, uncle of John Dorrington per 'Waconsta' 1855.

**Douglass** G Esq. of Douglass Park, employed Edward & Elizabeth Tregoning per 'Hornet' 1859.

**Douglass** Mary Jane see M.J. Gill.

**Douglass** Susan married Joseph Kent, Sydney, Wesleyan, 1885.

**Dower** John and Ellen Margaret, of Adelong 1881. NSW births.

**Dower** Michael of Barraba, married Frances Jane Stevens, Paddington, Methodist, 1900.

**Downing** Eliza Jane (per 'Sameul Plimsoll' 1877) married John Stacey, Cobar, Wesleyan 1881.

**Downing** Elizabeth (per 'Samuel Plimsoll' 1877) married Joseph Henry Thomas, Cobar, Wesleyan, 1882.

**Downing** Emmeline (per 'Samuel Plimsoll' 1877) married James Thomas Davies, Cobar, Wesleyan, 1882.

**Downing** Frederic Harry of Mountain Top, married Georgina Margaret Maguire, Sydney, CE, 1890.

**Downing** Mary see Rowe, Thomas.

**Driscoll** Dennis of Surry Hills, son of Michael Driscoll per 'Fitzjames' 1857.

**Driscoll** Miriam married Henry Rickard, Cobar, Wesleyan, 1884.

**Dudley** Mary see Mary Gribble.

**Duence** Alfred married Harriet Clark, Redfern, Wesleyan, 1892.

**Dumble** John of Tambaroora, married Ann Burns, Sydney, CE, 1872.

**Dumble** Lavinia married Charles Rhodes, Sydney, CE, 1885.

**Dunn** Sarah see Dent.

**Dunnett** Dianah married Thomas Henry Merrett, Sydney, Wesleyan, 1893.

**Dunsford** Maude married William Millett (of Charters Towers QLD), Waverley, Wesleyan, 1886.

**Dunstan** Captain James of Roseville, died 1912 aged 77. SMH 29 August 1912.

**Dunstan** Captain James died 1912, buried Enfield CE.

**Dunstan** Henry died Cobar aged 60, 1902. Buried Cobar Wesleyan.

**Dunstan** James of Port Phillip, cousin of Phillipa Williams nee Crago per 'Emigrant' 1849.

**Dunstan** John JP Chatswood, died 1924, aged 73. SMH

**Dunstan** John died Broken Hill 1894. Buried Gore Hill Methodist cemetery, with Grace Dunstan.

**Dunstan** Mary Ann see Mary Ann George

**Dunstan** Nicholas John married Clara Tredinnick, Ashfield, Wesleyan, 1896.

**Dunstan** Richard Henry died Cobar aged 55, 1880, buried Cobar CE.

**Dunstan** Stephen P died 1881 aged 26. Buried Inverell cemetery.

**Dunstan** William of Hillgrove, died 1899, aged 60. Methodist, 4 February 1899.

**Dunston** Ann of Melbourne. Sister of Edward Martin per 'Sultana' 1855.

**Dunstone** Jane cousin of Jane Tregoning per 'Victoria' 1849.

**Dutton** Hannah married John Tonking, Adelong, Wesleyan, 1874.

**Dyer** Alice married John Trewhella, Burwood, Weslwyan, 1895.

**Dyer** Nathaniel married Julia Cocks, Newtown, Wesleyan, 1888.

**Dyer** Nathaniel married Susan Catherine Turner nee Hitchcock, St Peters, Wesleyan, 1895.

**Dyer** Rev Eldred Wesleyan minister. Dorothy Fellowes.

**Dyer** William Calvin died 1871 aged 91. Buried Morpeth Methodist cemetery.

**Eade** Josiah and wife Sarah (nee Johns) per 'Lady MacDonald' 1856. Went to Byng. Marion Thompson.

**Eade** Rosina Jane married William Charles Jury Ford, Dunkeld, 1885.

**Eade** William per 'Fairlie' 1848. Went to Bathurst district. Pat Eade.

**Eade** of Bathurst, brother of Joseph & Theophilus Eade per 'Phoebe Dunbar' 1856.

**Eade** family, Bathurst. Pat Eade

**Eastcote** Elizabeth per 'William Turner' 1841, employed by Mr Currie, of Currie Vale.

**Eastcote** Jane per 'William Turner' 1841, employed by Mr Jerroe, Pitt St.

**Easton** Hannah married Edward Harris (per 'Commonwealth' 1877), St Peters Congregational, 1885.

**Eckhardt** Elizabeth died 1915 aged 74. Buried Rookwood CE with Thomas Newport. (Her first husband?)

**Eckhardt** Elizabeth formerly Newport, wife of Thomas Newport. Woolloomooloo, 1915. SMH 8 November 1915.

**Eddy** Alfred died 1892 aged 52 at Forest Reefs. CWD, 21 August 1984.

**Eddy** Christopher of Forbes, uncle of John Berryman per 'Glendower' 1868.

**Eddy** Christopher of Forbes, husband of Catherine Eddy & father of George and Jane Eddy, all per 'Glendower' 1868.

**Eddy** George Grenfell (per 'Glendower' 1868) of Forbes, married Letitia Johnston, Darlinghurst, Wesleyan, 1894.

**Eddy** Richard married Jane Hewson, Adelong, Wesleyan, 1879.

**Eddy** Richard and Jane, of Adelong 1880. NSW births.

**Eddy** William and Elizabeth, of Adelong 1875. NSW births.

**Ede** Josiah per 'Lady McDonald' 1856 appears to be brother of the Eade brothers per 'Phoebe Dunbar' 1856.

**Ede** of Bathurst, brother of Josiah Ede per 'Lady McDonald' 1856.

**Eden** Ann Maria see Ann Maria Carkeek.

**Edmonds** Charles Henry died 1899 aged 26 at his uncle's residence at Inverell. Buried Inverell.

**Edwards** Edward uncle of William Edwards per 'Alfred' 1857.

**Edwards** Joseph of Parramatta Rd, living with brother? Thomas, is son of James Edwards per 'Fitzjames' 1857.

**Edwards** Octavius supposed to be in Sydney, brother of Edward Edwards per 'Fitzjames' 1857.

**Ellason** brother of Mary Ellason per 'James Pattison' 1838 and said to be on board the same ship.

**Ellery** Ada married William Chadban, Murrurundi, Wesleyan, 1899.

**Ellery** Benjamin of Scone, brother of James T. Ellery per 'Dunbar Castle' 1877.

**Ellery** Mark Pascoe of Mount Macquarie. AMM

**Ellery** family and Poyner family per 'Orient' 1839. Settled in Sydney. Robert Sutton.

**Ellicott** Richard of Maitland, cousin of John Lee per 'Hydaspes' 1852.

**Ellicott** Richard married Rebecca Threadgate, West Maitland, 1871.

**Ellis** Arthur married Sarah Green, Orange, Wesleyan, 1890.

**Ellis** John married Emma Bennett, Orange, Wesleyan, 1889.

**Ellis** Margaret Hannah married John Thomas, Tambaroora, 1877.

**Ellis** Mary of Adelaide, relative of Mary Trenemon per 'Harbinger' 1849.

**Ellis** Peter brother of Anna Grenfell per 'Kate' 1856.

**Ellis** Sampson died Adelong 1861 aged 26, buried Adelong CE,

**Emblem** Mary nee Parkins (per 'Walter Morrice' 1849) married Henry Osborne, Tamworth, Wesleyan, 1896.

**Endean** John of Sydney, father of Henry Endean per 'Shackamaxon' 1863.

**Englebrecht** Annie married Henry Lord, Muswellbrook, CE, 1880.

**Eslick** Edith Harriet died 1944 aged 62, buried Orange. Wife of John Eslick.

**Eslick** Eliza Jane of Millthorpe, 1908 aged 55. Methodist, 15 August, 1908.

**Eslick** Elizabeth Ann married Henry Bargwanna, Orange, 1879.

**Eslick** Elizabeth wife of George Eslick, Orange. Died 1877 aged 62, buried Orange.

**Eslick** George married Elizabeth Ann Nicholls, Bathurst, Wesleyan, 1885.

**Eslick** George per 'Jerusalem' 1874, husband of Elizabeth. Died 1877 aged 65, buried Orange.

**Eslick** George of Bathurst, grandfather of Ann Verran per 'Corona' 1877. Her parents Thomas & Eliza Verran also on board.

**Eslick** John died 1958 aged 81, buried Orange. Husband of Edith.

**Eslick** Mary Anne died 1921 aged 81, buried Orange. Wife of Simon Eslick.

**Eslick** Mary Anne nee Hocking (per 'Kate' 1854). Wife of Simon Eslick. CWD 28 August 1984.

**Eslick** Simon died 1909 aged 76, buried Orange.

**Eslick** Simon married Mary Ann Hocking, Cornish Settlement, 1858.

**Eslick** Simon settled at 'Sparnick', Bloomfield, Orange. CWD 28 August 1984.

**Eslick** Simon of Orange, brother of Sarah, Stephen & Christopher Eslick per 'Wallasea' 1865.

**Eslick** Simon of Orange, son of George Eslick per 'Jerusalem' 1874.

**Eslick** Thomas married Sarah Law, Orange, 1879.

**Eslick** family. Settled in Orange. Roma Blackhall.

**Euler** Mary Josephine married John Thomas, Inverell, Wesleyan, 1880.

**Eva** George at Moreton Bay, brother of Ann Eva, per 'Kate' 1856.

**Eva** Louisa died Adelong 1882 aged 28, buried Adelong Wesleyan.

**Eva** Thomas and Mary Ann, of Adelong 1864. NSW births.

**Eva** William Henry and Louisa, of Adelong 1880. NSW births.

**Evans** Annie Louisa married James Henry Gartrell, Orange, 1888.

**Evans** David per 'Andromache' 1839, went to St

Leonards. A.J. Brown.
**Evans** David   and wife Eliza (nee Woolcock, per 'Hotspur' 1862) went to Forbes and Sydney. Margaret Playford.
**Evans** David   near Wollongong, brother of Mary Ann Williams per 'Australia' 1853.
**Evans** Elizabeth Jane married William Charles Mitchell, Stanmore, Wesleyan, 1886.
**Evans** Evan R near Wollongong, brother of Mary Ann Williams per 'Australia' 1853.
**Evans** Evan Robert and wife Sarah (nee Roberts) per 'Andromache' 1839, went to Dapto and Kiama. A.J. Brown.
**Evans** Henry   died Cobar aged 44, 1884.  Buried Cobar.
**Evans** John   and wife Mary (nee Calloway) per 'Bolton 1853, went to Milton. A.J. Brown.
**Evans** John   per 'Joseph Soames' 1852, brother of Henry Evans per 'Herald of the Morning' 1858.
**Evans** John   per 'Joseph Soames' 1852, of Bathurst, brother of William Evans per 'Lady Ann' 1854.
**Evans** Joseph Barnes and wife Alice (nee Mildren) per 'William Metcalfe' 1844, went to Mannus and Corryong. A.J. Brown.
**Evans** Joseph   near Wollongong, brother of Mary Ann Williams per 'Australia' 1853.
**Evans** Joseph   Wollongong?   brother-in-law of Elizabeth Palamountain per 'Trafalgar' 1853.
**Evans** Mary   married Andrew Mikelson, Orange, 1867.
**Evans** Mary   of Orange. Ward of John Tom Lane JP. CWD 28 August 1984.
**Evans** Mrs Thomas of Wollongong, sister of Mary Calloway per 'Trafalgar' 1853.
**Evans** Mrs Thomas sister & daughter of the Calloway family per 'Cressy' 1856.
**Evans** Mrs  of Guyong, relative of Samuel Evans per 'Fairlie' 1863.
**Evans** Samuel   per 'Fairlie' 1863 went to Mrs Evans at Guyong.
**Evans** Sarah Amelia married William Lemon Bawden, Ashfield, Wesleyan, 1891.
**Evans** Thomas   and wife Ann (nee Calloway) per 'Andromache' 1839, went to Camden and Wollongong. A.J. Brown.
**Evans** Thomas   near Wollongong, brother of Mary Ann Williams per 'Australia' 1853.
**Evans** Thomas   of Sydney, son-in-law of Anne Calloway per 'Cressy' 1856. She also has 3 daughter living in Sussex St.
**Evans** William   married Mary Ann Dawson, Newcastle, CE, 1862.
**Evans** William married Mary James, Orange, 1859.
**Evans**   of Stanley St, Woolloomooloo, brother of Theresa Williams per 'Hornet' 1859.
**Evans** family. B. and J. Smith.
**Eveleigh** George Martin per 'Lady McNaughton' 1840. Died 1911, buried Singleton.
**Eveleigh** William   per 'Lady McNaughton' 1830, settled at Lostock. E.D. Eveleigh.
**Eveleigh** William   died 1932 aged 76.  Buried Singleton.
**Evenis** Elizabeth Vines married Baker Banks Carvosso, Bathurst, 1862.
**Everingham** Priscilla   Edith   married   William Plummer, Hill End, 1873.
**Everson** John James married Catherine Teague nee Keass?, Surry Hills, 1893.
**Eyre** Maria   of Port Phillip, sister of John Eyre per 'Sarah' 1849.

**F**

**Fardon** Annie   Maria   married Hezekiah Taylor, Adelong, 1877.

**Fardon** Caroline Janet married Thomas White, Adelong, Wesleyan, 1870.
**Farmer** Elizabeth   see Brock.
**Farmer** Matilda   married Daniel Harresky, Bathurst, 1863.
**Farrell** Jessy   married John George, Surry Hills, CE, 1893.
**Faull** Thomas   married Mary Jane Poole, Sydney, CE, 1885.
**Favell** Alice Augusta married John Collins of Botany, Arncliffe, Wesleyan, 1884.
**Favell** Ellen   married Sampson Hawke, Orange, Wesleyan, 1887.
**Fayle** Anna Maria married William James Paul, Sydney, Presbyterian, 1856.
**Ferrett** family, see Cory Ferrett.
**Finch** Josephine A married John H. Nettle, Newcastle, CE, 1873.
**Findlay** Isabella   married Walter Vivian (per 'Tartar' 1857), Taree, CE, 1886.
**Fisher** Elizabeth Louisa (widow) married John Henry (of Richmond River) Darlinghurst, CE, 1884.
**Fisher** Emma Elizabeth married James Charles White, Castlereagh, CE, 1876.
**Fisk** Henry   married Susannah Siberley, Surry Hills, CE, 1892.  Both of Coonabarabran.
**Fitzgibbons** Johanna   married Edward Soars, Bathurst, 1844.
**Fitzsimmons** Arthur   of Sydney, brother-in-law of Edward Johnson per 'Shackamaxon' 1863.
**Fitzsimmons** Mary   Ann married Thomas Rodgers, Orange, 1883.
**Flack** Frederick William married Mary Grace Williams, Maitland, Wesleyan, 1885.
**Fleming** Grace   see Grace Plummer.
**Fleming** Joseph A see Joseph Pleming.
**Fletcher** Ernest Lyon died 1906 aged 30.  Buried Rookwood CE.
**Floyd** Peter   of Orange, died 1919 aged 80.  Buried Orange Methodist. CWD 6 November 1984.
**Floyd** Susannah   wife of Peter Floyd. Died 1921 aged 71.  Buried Orange Methodist.
**Ford** Elizabeth   married John Thomas Treloar, Glen Innes, Wesleyan, 1882.
**Ford** Mary Ann married Joseph Burnett, Newtown, Wesleyan 1888.
**Ford** William Charles Jury married Rosina Jane Eade, Dunkeld, 1885.
**Ford**   one of two cousins of Richard Bodilly per 'Emigrant' 1849.
**Forrest** Edwin   per 'Trevelyan' 1877, went to Bathurst. Brother of May J. Bridwell of Sydney.
**Forrester** Susannah Jane married Richard Arnold, Richmond, CE, 1883.
**Forster** Mary   Alice married Charles Thomas Truscott, Emmaville, Methodist, 1902.
**Forster** William   of Clarence River employed Samuel Warren per 'William Metcalfe' 1844.
**Forsyth** Amy Amelia married Anthony Charles Knight, Willoughby, Methodist, 1902.
**Fortescue** George   married Ellen C. O'Brien, Surry Hills, CE, 1865.
**Foss** William   married Clara A.C. Leach, Marrickville, Congregational, 1889.
**Foster** William Thomas married Annie Emma Robey, Forest Lodge, Wesleyan, 1897.
**Francis** Grace   sister of Johanna Teague per 'Mary Pleasants' 1858. See Parkin and Clark.
**Fraser** Ada   married William Trethowan (per 'Earl Dalhousie' 1877?) Newtown, Wesleyan, 1895.
**Freeman** Edward   died Cobar aged 52, 1899, buried Cobar CE.
**Freeman** Thomas   and wife Amelia nee Jeffree. In Hill End by 1871. Marlene Reid.
**French** Elizabeth nee Baker, married Richard Hosken Senior (per 'Tartar 1857), Tenterfield, Wesleyan, 1878.

**Frethey** Thomas went from Sydney to New Zealand before 1840. John Wilson.

**Furlong** Mary Ann see Jacobs.

**Furness** Peter married Jane Hannah Paul, Bathurst, 1860.

**Furney** Celia married George Harvey, Bathurst, 1842.

## G

**Gale** Albert C. Tizzard.

**Gale** Christopher Parrah drowned Tweed Heads 1875 aged 49. C. Tizzard.

**Gale** Christopher per 'Golden Era' 1855. Went to Queanbeyan, Grafton and Redfern. C. Tizzard, & V. Smith.

**Gale** Eliza sister of John Gale of Queanbeyan. Died 1869 Sydney. C. Tizzard.

**Gale** Francis Peter died 1892 aged 68, buried Maclean Methodist cemetery. Brother of John Gale. C. Tizzard.

**Gale** George alderman, Woollahra. Son of Joseph Gale, buried with him Waverley cemetery.

**Gale** John of Narellan, brother of Gale family per 'Chance' 1860.

**Gale** John born 1831 Cornwall. Died Queanbeyan 1929 C. Tizzard.

**Gale** John of Berrima, brother of Christopher Gale per 'Golden Era' 1855.

**Gale** Joseph died Woollahra 1890 (75 yrs). Buried Waverley cemetery.

**Gale** Mary Jane married Timothy Starr, died Dalton 1874 (54 yrs). Sister of John Gale. C. Tizzard.

**Gale** William died Redfern 1871 (58 yrs). Brother of John Gale. C. Tizzard.

**Gale** family per 'Chance' 1860. Went to brother, John Gale, at Narellan.

**Gardiner** Elizabeth married William Henry Langsford, Singleton, Wesleyan, 1871.

**Garling** Frederica E married William Aldrich of Dungog, Darlinghurst, CE, 1860.

**Gartrell** Absolom married Grace Randell, Bathurst, Wesleyan, 1888.

**Gartrell** Edwin born Cornwall 1843, died 1910, buried Waverley CE cemetery. Jane & James in same grave.

**Gartrell** Edwin son of Richard. Arrived per 'Annie H. Smith' 1877. Living in Sydney 1944. CWD, 22 January 1985.

**Gartrell** Francis married Minnie Haselden, Orange, 1886.

**Gartrell** Frederick Norman of Paddington. SMH 3 September 1901.

**Gartrell** James Henry married Annie Louisa Evans, Orange, Wesleyan, 1888.

**Gartrell** James see Edwin Gartrell.

**Gartrell** James of Orange, per 'Annie H Smith' 1877. CWD, 22 January 1985.

**Gartrell** Jane see Edwin Gartrell.

**Gartrell** Richard of Orange, per 'Annie H Smith' 1877. CWD, 22 January 1985.

**Gartrell** Richard Francis married Emma Bensley, Orange, 1894.

**Gartrell** W H died 1916 aged 66. Buried Waverley cemetery with wife Emma, children Frederick, Francis, Minnie.

**Gartrell** William Henry of Chatswood. SMH 5 April 1916.

**Gartrell** William J son of Richard. Per 'Annie H Smith' 1877. Died 1944 aged 74. CWD 22 January 1985.

**Gartrell** see Johns

**Gatherick** Emily of Cooma, Maneroo, no relation but a contact of William Brown per 'Herefordshire' 1857.

**Gay** John Bennett married Mary Jane Tresidder,

Wollongong, Primitive Methodist, 1886.

**Gay** Richard living in the country, uncle of Thomas Gay per 'Lady Ann' 1854.

**Gaynor** Thomas married Mary Hannah Davis, Newcastle, CE, 1897.

**Geake** Catherine of Pendarves married John Jones of Sydney, Cornish Settlement, 1840.

**Geake** John brother-in-law of Richard Lane of Byng. Went to Victoria c.1849.

**Geard** Frederick died 1894 aged 68, buried Rookwood CE.

**Geddye** Richard in employ of Mr Dangar, cousin of William Greenaway per 'Fitzjames' 1857.

**George** Amelia nee Stephens, married Rossiter Smaldon, Sydney, Presbyterian, 1876.

**George** Amelia married John Robins, Adelong, CE, 1873.

**George** Edward in the colony, father of William George per 'Alfred' 1857.

**George** Eliza married Janmes Ross, Orange, 1885.

**George** Emma Jane married John Guy, Adelong, 1897.

**George** James per 'Lady Elgin' uncle of Thomas Thomas per 'Lady Ann' 1854.

**George** John married Jessey Farrell, Surry Hills, CE, 1893.

**George** Mary Ann nee Dunstan, (per 'Earl Dalhousie' 1877) married Arthur Richards, Redfern, CE, 1891.

**George** Richard of Sydney, father of Elizabeth George per 'Lord Stanley' 1850.

**George** Samuel per 'Lady Elgin' uncle of Thomas Thomas per 'Lady Ann' 1854.

**George** William of Sydney, uncle of Elizabeth and Phillippa Bray per 'Walter Morrice' 1849.

**George** family per 'William Metcalfe' 1844 employed by James Dargin at Windsor.

**George?** of Chippendale, uncle of Henry Lord per 'Fitzjames' 1858.

**Gerathy** Michael of Carcoar?, cousin of Maria Gilbert per 'Sirocco' (2) 1864.

**Gibb** Elizabeth Annie married Henry Courter, Glen Innes, Wesleyan, 1895.

**Gibbons** Cuthbert married Clara Richardson nee Richards, Hamilton, Methodist, 1900.

**Gibbons** Ellen Jane nee Bennett. Died 1901. SMH 12 November 1901.

**Gibney** Thomas and Ann, of Adelong 1874. NSW births.

**Gidley** Thomas of Gulgong, uncle of John Coffin/Coppin per 'Samuel Plimsoll' (2) 1874.

**Gilbert** Eli of Hunter River, brother of Elizabeth Tregoning per 'Hornet' 1859.

**Gilbert** George of Hunter River, brother of Elizabeth Tregoning per 'Hornet' 1859.

**Gilbert** George (per 'Fitzjames' 1857) married Maria Bampton, Singleton, CE, 1865.

**Gilbert** Mrs near Bathurst. Aunt of James Harvey per 'Lady Ann' 1854.

**Gilbert** Thomas near Cooma, uncle of Thomas Gilbert per 'Lady Elgin' 1854.

**Gilbert** of Brisbane, two brothers/sons of Gilbert family per 'Ascendant' 1858.

**Gilbert** of Sydney, brother of John Gilbert per 'Persia' 1856.

**Giles** Edwin James married Catherine Stevens nee Merrin, Sydney, CE, 1892.

**Gill** Caroline died Cobar aged 32, 1899, buried Cobar Wesleyan.

**Gill** Mary Jane nee Douglass married Thomas Bargwanna, Orange, 1889.

**Gill** Richard married Marriser Mary Jackson, Sydney, CE, 1889.

**Gill** William married Caroline Warren, Cobar, Wesleyan, 1886.

**Gillam** Lilian married Alfred Keen Watson, Burwood, Wesleyan, 1887.

**Ginn** Elizabeth A. M. married Henry Burton, Newcastle, CE, 1895.

**Gladding** Joseph of Melbourne, uncle of William Gladding per 'Sultana' 1855.

**Glanfield** Mary Frances died 1958 (59 yrs), buried Rookwood CE. See Bunney.

**Glanville** Peter Henry of Surry Hills, 1884. SMH 2 August 1884.

**Glanville** William of Maneroo, cousin of James Glanville per 'Alfred' 1857.

**Glanville** brother of Harry Glanville per 'City of Edinburgh' 1837, said to be aboard same ship.

**Glasson** Charles Bennett married Grace Martin, Bathurst, Wesleyan, 1861.

**Glasson** Elizabeth Jane married Henry Curtois Hosie, Limestone Flat, Methodist, 1862.

**Glasson** Elizabeth sister of John. Married Thomas Stephens. CWD 12 February 1985.

**Glasson** Frank funeral, 1912. BT 8 January 1912.

**Glasson** Henry of Orange. AMM

**Glasson** Henry brother of John. CWD 12 February 1985.

**Glasson** James married Mary Jane Gordon, Tamworth, Methodist, 1900.

**Glasson** John of Cornish Settlement. CWD 12 February 1985.

**Glasson** Joseph Henry married Sarah Miller, Bathurst, 1867.

**Glasson** Joseph Kemp married Emma Helen Webb, Bathurst, 1900.

**Glasson** Joseph married Mary Anne Sweetnam, Cornish Settlement, 1863.

**Glasson** Joseph brother of John Glasson. CWD 12 February 1985.

**Glasson** Mary sister of John Glasson. Married John Lane. CWD 12 February 1985.

**Glasson** Richard brother of John Glasson. CWD 12 February 1985.

**Glasson** Robert died Adelong 1862 aged 24, buried Adelong Wesleyan.

**Glasson** Selina of Waterloo, 1883. Wife of William. SMH 3 December 1883.

**Glasson** Stephen of Sydney, uncle of William Glasson per 'Ninevah' 1877.

**Glasson** Susan sister of John. CWD 12 February 1985.

**Glasson** Susan Read Russel married William Hill, Blayney, 1865.

**Glasson** William brother of John Glasson. CWD 12 February 1985.

**Glasson** William (Rev) married Elizabeth Barbara Stanger, Bathurst, 1876.

**Glinn** Elizabeth per 'Sultana' 1855, married William Harman, Sydney, CE, 1857.

**Gluyas** Francis died Cobar aged 30, 1881. Buried Cobar Wesleyan.

**Godfrey** Martha married John Phillips, Bathurst, 1896.

**Goldsworthy** Elizabeth nee Andrew, married William Roberts, Sydney, Presbyterian, 1878.

**Goldsworthy** Richard relative of Mary Williams (nee Gill) per 'Meteor' 1853.

**Good** Jane married Ruben Robert Tremain, Bathurst, 1882.

**Goodfellow** Richard married Mary Kinsella, Sydney, Wesleyan, 1882.

**Goodman** Jane Gidley married Henry Lancelot Smith, Cooks River, CE, 1862.

**Goodsell** Edward Cook married Laura Anna Melluish, Redfern, CE, 1898.

**Googe** John and wife Eliza (nee Cundy) per 'Forest Monarch' 1858 went to Scone, Merriwa, Muswellbrook. Sr Juliana Googe, Enid Farnham.

**Gooth** T see Joseph Niness.

**Gootsall** Elizabeth Jane married James Harvey, Cornish Settlement, 1842.

**Gordon** Mary Jane married James Glasson, Tamworth, Methodist, 1900.

**Goyen** Martha wife of Nicholas, of Paddington, 1917. SMH 7 June 1917, buried Rookwood Independent.

**Goyen** Nicholas died 1927, buried Rookwood. SMH 17 January 1927.

**Grace** Ernest H married Nanny Mitchell, Surry Hills, CE, 1896.

**Graham** Samuel married Caroline Treneman, Dunkeld, Wesleyan, 1874.

**Gray** Alfred John married Daisy Cline, Surry Hills, CE, 1898.

**Greaves** Edward married Caroline Strongman (per 'Samuel Plimsoll' 1874) Sydney, Presbyterian, 1878.

**Green** Evie married Albert Ernest Townsend, Annandale, 1898.

**Green** Frederick married Mary Hart, Orange, 1887.

**Green** George Thomas and Mary Ann, of Adelong 1871. NSW births.

**Green** James of Sydney & Cooma?, brother-in-law of John Paul per 'Lady Elgin' 1854.

**Green** James and Mary per 'Petrel' 1849, of Darlinghurst. Pat McCormack

**Green** Mary of Sydney, sister of Alarina Paul & Elizabeth Paul per 'Garland' 1851.

**Green** Mary of Sydney, sister of John Paul per 'Lady Elgin' 1854.

**Green** Sarah married Arthur Ellis, Orange, 1890.

**Green** Walter David married Elizabeth Maud Nancarrow, Surry Hills, CE, 1885.

**Gregg** Elizabeth married William Guy Higgs, Manning River, CE, 1860.

**Grenfell** Catherine per 'Northampton' 1881, married William Mackey, Nymagee, Wesleyan, 1883.

**Grenfell** David per 'Ninevah' 1877, married Harriet Hampton, Nymagee, Wesleyan, 1882.

**Grenfell** John of Cadia?, uncle of Elizabeth & Sarah Ann Grenfell per 'Ninevah' 1877.

**Grenfell** John of Cadia?, uncle of William and David Grenfell per 'Ninevah' 1877.

**Grenfell** Lavinia married Alexander Jones, Cobar, Wesleyan, 1897.

**Grenfell** Richard buried Byng 1873 aged 86. CWD 19 March 1985.

**Grey** Francis Charleston married Annie Hawke, Surry Hills, CE, 1891.

**Gribble** John of Hartley Vale, son of Susan Gribble (widow) per 'Earl Dalhousie' 1877.

**Gribble** Mary nee Dudley, married Hector Allen Boyle, Surry Hills, CE, 1901.

**Gribble** Richard married Grace Plummer, Parramatta, Wesleyan, 1875.

**Grieve** Isabella married William Harvey, Pyrmont, Wesleyan, 1897.

**Griffin** Ellen Maria married Sydney Hugh Maclean, Gladesville, Wesleyan, 1883.

**Griffith** Winifred Sarah Ann married William John McNamara, Surry Hills, CE, 1895.

**Griffiths** Richard G married Lydia Whalan (widow), Fish River, Wesleyan, 1859.

**Grigg** Susan per 'Malvina Vidal' 1853 married Carl Bruggmann, Parramatta, Wesleyan, 1890.

**Grills** John per 'Orpheus' 1825, settled in West Maitland. Joan Grills.

**Grose** Joseph Henry married Martha Kershaw, Newtown, Congregational, 1886.

**Grose** Richard of Newcastle. Convict per 'Royal Sovereign' 1835. Dorothy Heber.

**Grose** Stephen (per 'Kate' 1856) married Mary Ann Davis, Newcastle, CE, 1858.

**Grose** Stephen per 'Kate' 1856. Settled in Newcastle, son of Richard. Dorothy Heber.

**Guard** William per 'Star of India' 1876. Went to Thirroul, then Sydney. Enid Wheeler.

**Gumb** Daniel of Wallsend, 1909, aged 81. Methodist 7 August 1909.

**Gun** William married Caroline Esther Turner, Sydney, Wesleyan, 1881.

**Gunn** George married Mary Jane Tresidder, Bulli, Primitive Methodist, 1887.

**Gunning** John married Catherine Sloggett, Fish River, 1882.

**Guy** Elizabeth Ann of Adelong 1886. NSW births.

**Guy** John Thomas married Emma Jane George, Adelong, Wesleyan, 1897.

**Guy** Martin Hosking married Alice Sophia Capel, Adelong, CE, 1897.

**Guy** Thomas and Louisa, of Adelong 1878. NSW births.

## H

**Haines** Ann married Isaac Amor, Cornish Settlement, 1840.

**Haley** James and John Haley both per 'Commonwealth' 1877 appear to be brothers of William Hayley on board.

**Haley** John see James Haley.

**Hall** Emma see Emma Cornish.

**Hall** Mary married James Nicholls (both of Robertson), Sydney, CE, 1892.

**Hall** Sophie (nee Read) married George Osborne, Newcastle, Free Methodist, 1884.

**Hall** Winifred Frances see Winifred Frances Munro.

**Hallicott** Richard see Richard Ellicott.

**Hambly** Albert son of William, brother of Francis and Amos, Sydney, 1894. SMH 19 February 1894.

**Hambly** Amos see Albert Hambly.

**Hambly** Caroline widow of Thomas, Darlington, 1911. SMH 18 September 1911.

**Hambly** Emma Jane (per 'Forest Monarch' 1858) married Amos Richard Saxby, Botany, Wesleyan, 1868.

**Hambly** Emma Jane death in Bathurst, aged 15, 1882. BT 25 September 1882.

**Hambly** Francis see Albert Hambly.

**Hambly** James market gardener, Botany, 1888. AMM.

**Hambly** Mark (per 'Forest Monarch' 1858) married Annie Amelia Johnston, St Leonards, Wesleyan, 1880.

**Hambly** Mary Ann wife of William, Botany, 1901. SMH 11 July 1901.

**Hambly** Thomas of Darlington, 1904. SMH 7 June 1904.

**Hambly** Thomas of Botany H. Hambly.

**Hambly** Thomas see Thomas Hanley.

**Hambly** Walter of Tempe, 1914. SMH 17 October 1914.

**Hambly** William John of Burwood, formerly of Botany. Died 1893 aged 45. Methodist 2 September 1893.

**Hambly** William see Albert Hambly.

**Hambly** William husband of Catherine Grace, of Botany, 1916. SMH 6 July 1916.

**Hambly** William and son James, market gardeners, Botany, 1853+ AMM

**Hambly** William of Botany H. Hambly.

**Hamilton** Maude married John Painter, Lucknow?, 1885.

**Hamlet** Henry of Icely, brother of Bessie Lee per 'Tyburnia' 1874.

**Hammond** Ann daughter of Rachel Pearce & stepdaughter of William Pearce per 'Rajasthan' 1855. Also Betsey, John & Leo.

**Hampton** Elizabeth per 'Scythia' 1871, employed by Richard Kelly, Woolloomooloo.

**Hampton** Elizabeth married William May, Nymagee, Wesleyan, 1883.

**Hampton** Harriet married David Grenfell (per 'Ninevah' 1877), Nymagee, Wesleyan, 1882.

**Hampton** Mary see Mary Smith.

**Hancock** William of Moreton Bay, brother of Thomas Hancock per 'Winifred' 1856.

**Hanford** Rebecca married Nicholas Charles Moyle, Cobar, Wesleyan, 1876.

**Hanley** Ann died Cobar aged 43, 1897, buried Cobar Wesleyan.

**Hanley** Thomas near Sydney, brother of Elizabeth Hocken per 'Kate' 1856.

**Hardman** Florence G married John Lee, Surry Hills, CE, 1893.

**Harman** William married Elizabeth Glinn (per 'Sultana' 1855), Surry Hills, CE, 1857.

**Harper** William Stephen married Norah De Mamul, Sydney, CE, 1891.

**Harresky** Daniel married Matilda Farmer, Bathurst, 1863.

**Harris** Edward (per 'Commonwealth' 1877) married Hannah Easton, St Peters, Congregational, 1885.

**Harris** Elizabeth per 'Sabraon' 1870 employed by Rev Thomas Smith, Glebe.

**Harris** Jane married Joseph Thomas, Sunnycorner, Wesleyan 1891.

**Harris** John per 'Trevelyan' 1877 went to Bathurst.

**Harris** John married Amelia Hunking (per 'Malvina Vidal' 1853) Bathurst, 1865.

**Harris** John in South Australia 1863, in Bathurst 1873 (Cow Flat & Forest Reefs). David Rutherford.

**Harris** Joseph Chappell married Adela Jane Wellington, Burwood, Wesleyan, 1883.

**Harris** Lucy Ann married Joseph Boaden, Bathurst, 1883.

**Harris** Maria Chapple died 1908 aged 82, buried Rookwood Methodist with William Dalley Harris.

**Harris** Maria widow of William D. Harris, Burwood, 1908. SMH 6 March 1908.

**Harris** Nicholas Henry married Mary Boulden, Burwood, CE, 1883.

**Harris** Richard of Cobar and Nyngan. AMM.

**Harris** Thomas of Parramatta, employed Tippett family per 'Hornet' 1859.

**Harris** William Dalley died 1900 aged 67, buried Rookwood Methodist with Maria Chapple Harris.

**Harris** William Henry married Catherine Brown, Singleton, Wesleyan, 1868.

**Harris** William bootmaker, Oxford St., Darlinghurst, 1874+ AMM

**Harrison** Louise married John Nicholls, Paddington, Wesleyan, 1888.

**Harry** Emily wife of James, Waverley, 1924. SMH 25 October 1924.

**Harry** Ethel daughter of James & Emily, of Waverley, 1911. SMH 28 December 1911.

**Harry** James husband of Emily, monumental mason, Waverley, 1907. SMH 24 December 1907.

**Harry** James died 1907 (aged 58), buried Waverley cemetery with Emily and Ethel.

**Harry** John Dunstan married Mary Agnes Clift, Adelong, Wesleyan 1878.

**Hart** Mary married Frederick Green, Orange, 1887.

**Hartwell** Elizabeth see Elizabeth Jeffery.

**Harvey** Alfred married Mary Hawke, (per 'Conrad' 1841) Maitland, CE, 1865.

**Harvey** Alfred married Annie Addicott, Adelong, CE, 1881.

**Harvey** Alfred and Annie, of Adelong 1881. NSW births.

**Harvey** Edmund per 'Upton Castle' 1838, unassisted. Settled at Oberon. Netta Stoneman.

**Harvey** Elizabeth Jane married Thomas Henry Brooking, Cobar, Wesleyan, 1883.

**Harvey** Ellen married Francis Jenkins, Cadia, 1865.

**Harvey** George married Celia Furney, Cornish Settlement, 1842.

**Harvey** James F and Elizabeth. He was MLA, Sydney, 1879. Jean Saunders.

**Harvey** James married Elizabeth Jane Gootsall,

Cornish Settlement, 1842.

**Harvey** Peter stonemason, Geelong, brother-in-law of Harriet Wallis per 'Caribou' 1859.

**Harvey** Richard and Caroline, in South Australia. Parents of Elizabeth Jane Goldsworthy per 'Annie H Smith' 1877.

**Harvey** Robert of Pyrmont, brother of Thomas Harvey per 'Tartar' 1857.

**Harvey** Samuel of Pyrmont, brother of Thomas Harvey per 'Tartar' 1857.

**Harvey** Thomas sister of Elizabeth Harvey per 'Samuel Plimsoll (2)' 1874, aboard same ship?

**Harvey** William married Isabella Grieve, Pyrmont, Wesleyan, 1897.

**Haselden** Minnie married Francis Gartrell, Orange, 1886.

**Hasset** Christina sister of William Perry per 'Dunbar Castle' 1877.

**Hawke** Ada of Lucknow, died aged 28. Daughter of Frederick Hawke. Methodist 1 September 1894.

**Hawke** Annie married Francis Charleston Grey, Surry Hills, CE, 1891.

**Hawke** Charlie of Orange, died 1889 aged 23, buried Orange Methodist.

**Hawke** Eliza married Nicholas Brewer, Wingham, CE, 1865.

**Hawke** Emily Gertrude married William Northey Warren, Bathurst, 1890.

**Hawke** Fanny per 'Conrad' 1841, married Henry Brewer (per 'Alfred' 1857) Maitland 1863.

**Hawke** Frederick of Orange, died 1867 aged 46. CWD 4 June 1985.

**Hawke** George married Rebecca Rowe, Pendarves, Cornish Settlement, 1863.

**Hawke** George of Sydney, cousin of Robert Hawke per 'Herefordshire' 1857.

**Hawke** George of Cornish Settlement, died 1882 aged 80. CWD 21 May 1985.

**Hawke** John per 'Conrad' 1841, went to Singleton and Glen Innes. Dot Clayworth.

**Hawke** John of Dubbo. Came to Bathurst from Cornwall c. 1847. AMM

**Hawke** John nephew of George Hawke. Of Orange. CWD 4 June 1985.

**Hawke** Mary per 'Conrad' 1841, married Alfred Harvey, Maitland, CE, 1865.

**Hawke** Mary sister of Robert Hawke & family per 'City of Edinburgh' 1837.

**Hawke** Mrs George died 1917 Orange aged 79. Obituary. BT 11 June 1917.

**Hawke** Phebe Esther married Rev George Woolnough, Bathurst, 1875.

**Hawke** Richard of Orange. Married Anne Treneman 1867. CWD 4 June 1985.

**Hawke** Robert brother of Mary Hawke, all per 'City of Edinburgh' 1837.

**Hawke** Sampson married Ellen Favell, Orange, Wesleyan, 1887.

**Hawke** Sampson orchardist at Canobolas. Brother of Thomas. CWD 4 June 1985.

**Hawke** Samuel Baker (per 'Conrad' 1841) married Sarah Thompson, Wingham, CE, 1867.

**Hawke** Susannah per 'Conrad' 1841, married William Spencer, Maitland, CE, 1865.

**Hawke** Thomas orchardist at Canobolas. CWD 4 June 1985.

**Hawke** Tom married Millicent J S O Martin, Orange, 1879.

**Hawke** at Hartley, sister-in-law of Martha Chapman per 'Telegraph' 1858.

**Hawke** sister of John Hawke, per 'Lord Stanley' 1850.

**Hawken** John settled on south coast c.1851. Dorothy Heber.

**Hawken** John of Coolangatta, death aged 70. Methodist 17 August, 26 October 1895.

**Hawken** John per 'Amelia Thompson' 1838. Settled in Bathurst. Selwyn Hawken.

**Hawken** Nicholas of Darlington. Mayor, MLA for Newtown. AMM

**Hawken** Nicholas married Mary Jane Vance, Kiama, Wesleyan 1861.

**Hawker** Mary Ann Gardner, married Thomas Sandry, Jerry's Plains, CE, 1884.

**Hawkey** John Tamblyn of Singleton. Dot Clayworth.

**Hawkey** John Tamblyn married Caroline Cleworth, Singleton, CE, 1868.

**Hawkin** Nicholas of Sydney, brother of Charles Hawkin per 'Castillian' 1858.

**Hawkins** Anna Maria nee Lane, married Richard Newton, Branxton, Methodist, 1903.

**Hawkins** Eliza nee Thomas married Thomas Brooks, Wallsend, Methodist, 1901.

**Hawkins** Jane per 'Light of the Age' 1857. Ann Shaunessy.

**Hawkins** William of Wallsend, died 1893 aged 40. Methodist 18 November 1893.

**Hawthorne** Lily Cameron married George Richards, Sydney, CE, 1895.

**Haydon** James married Lavinia Frances Sweetman, West Maitland, CE, 1879.

**Haydon** Mary Ann married Charles Rogers, Armidale, Wesleyan, 1878.

**Hayley** see Haley.

**Haywhite** Jane married John Davis, Bathurst, 1841.

**Hean** Elizabeth see Elizabeth Webb.

**Heather** Mary Ann married Richard Rodda, Adelong, CE, 1876.

**Hebblewhite** Mrs of Mosman, 1905. Methodist 8 August 1905.

**Hender** Jemima see John Henry Hender.

**Hender** John Henry died 1918 aged 65. Buried Waverley CE cemetery. Wife Jemima.

**Hender** John Henry of Paddington. Died 1918. SMH 15 June 1918.

**Hennessy** Ann married William Charles Rogers, Sydney, Presbyterian, 1856.

**Henry** John of Richmond River married Elizabeth Louisa Fisher (widow), Darlinghurst, CE, 1884.

**Henton** Dora of Adelong 1872. NSW births.

**Henwood** James of Adelong 1870. NSW births.

**Henwood** Nahami per 'Alfred' 1837. Left the ship without being employed.

**Herbert** James (of Guyong) married Elizabeth Jane Tregenza, Paddington, Wesleyan, 1885.

**Hewson** Jane married Richard Eddy, Adelong, 1879.

**Hick** William per 'Racehorse' 1866, went to William Lobb, market gardener, Botany.

**Hicks** Caroline married John Thomas, Orange, 1891.

**Hicks** James at Cadia mines, son of Catherine Hicks per 'Racehorse' 1866.

**Hicks** John at Cadia mines, son of Catherine Hicks per 'Racehorse' 1866.

**Hicks** John per 'Lady Ann' 1854. Settled at Canobolas. CWD 16 July 1985.

**Hicks** John brother of Joseph Solomon Hicks. Settled at Canobolas. CWD 16 July 1985.

**Hicks** Joseph Solomon per 'Lady Ann' 1854. Settled at Canobolas. CWD 16 July 1985.

**Hicks** Joseph of Botany, uncle of Joseph Thomas per 'Lady Elgin' 1854.

**Hicks** Joseph of Petersham, uncle of Eliza Thomas per 'David McIvor' 1858.

**Hicks** Richard of Cargo, died 1897 aged 78, buried Cargo.

**Hicks** Sabrina Mary of Teglecherry, aged 17. Buried Stroud. Methodist 22 April 1893.

**Hicks** Sarah Ann married Henry Powley, Canobolas, 1887.

**Hicks** William of Newcastle. In Victoria c.1877. J. Carter-Smith.

**Higgs** William Guy married Elizabeth Gregg,

Manning River, CE, 1860.

**Higman** Matilda  see Matilda White.

**Higman?**  of Goulburn, see Hyland.

**Hill** Captain  of West Kempsey, brother of Arabella Stevens per 'La Hogue' 1877.

**Hill** Emma  nee Merrett, married William Henry Wicks, Sydney, Congregational, 1896.

**Hill** George William married Maria Richards, Surry Hills, CE, 1896.

**Hill** Phillip C near Kempsey, son of Phillip C. Hill per 'La Hogue' 1877.

**Hill** William  married Susan Read Russell Glasson, Blayney, Wesleyan, 1865.

**Hilton** Eliza Jane married Francis Johns, St Leonards, Wesleyan,1882.

**Hines** Ann  married George Hopgood, Bathurst, 1842.

**Hitchcock** Susan  see Susan Turner.

**Hitchens** William Francis married Barbara Morris, Newtown, Wesleyan, 1882.

**Hobbs** Elizabeth  see Elizabeth Rowles.

**Hobbs** Willliam  per 'Dirigo' 1860, went to friend Susan Reid, Sydney.

**Hobley** Vernal  married Jane Price, Gullen (Crookwell?), Methodist, 1881.

**Hockey** Emma  see Emma Bennett.

**Hocking** Anne  daughter of William & Anne Hooper per 'Agenoria' 1849.  Died 1861 aged 28.  Buried Sydney Burial Ground.

**Hocking** Annie  married Charlie Cook, Armidale, Wesleyan, 1894.

**Hocking** Grace  (per 'Ninevah' 1876?) married John Spooner, CE, Forster, 1890.

**Hocking** Grace  married John William West, Cobar, Wesleyan, 1897.

**Hocking** John  of Summer Hill, Bathurst, husband of Mary A. Hocking and father of Elizabeth, John, Mary A & Susan all per 'Kate' 1854.

**Hocking** John  of Orange, died 1896 aged 79.  Buried Orange Methodist with wife Mary Anne.

**Hocking** John  to South Australia per 'Aden' 1849. Settled in Orange.  Wife Mary (nee Pascoe) arrived 1854.  Trevor Pascoe.

**Hocking** John  of Orange 1853+. CWD 10 September 1985.

**Hocking** Mary Anne of Orange, died 1900 aged 83, buried Orange Methodist with husband John.

**Hocking** Mary Anne married Simon Eslick, Cornish Settlement, 1858.

**Hocking** Mary Anne of Orange. CWD 10 September 1985.

**Hocking** Richard  at Thomas Hambly, Botany, cousin of John Tretheway per 'Herefordshire' 1857.

**Hocking** Sarah Sophia married William Williams, Parkes, Wesleyan, 1883.

**Hocking** Sarah  married Frederick Noakes, Leichhardt, Wesleyan, 1899.

**Hocking** William  married Annie Pascoe (widow), Bathurst, 1877

**Hocking**  family, per 'Trevelyan' 1877, went to Grafton.

**Hockley** Joseph Emalane cousin of James Jolly per 'Lord Stanley' 1850.

**Hodge** Harriet  married William Burridge, Kempsey, Wesleyan 1880.

**Hodge** Mary  married Edward Spencer, Muswellbrook, CE, 1888.

**Hodges** Ethel May married William Eatham Melleuish, Paddington, Wesleyan, 1897.

**Holds** James  see James Olds.

**Holdsworthy** Lucy  married Henry Dennis of Cootamundra (per 'Samuel Plimsoll' 1874), Granville, CE, 1884.

**Holliday** Samuel Thomas married Henrietta Andrews, Chippendale, Wesleyan, 1896.

**Hollow** John  married Mary Brisset, Sydney, Congregational, 1883.

**Holman** Catherine  cousin of James Heath per 'Herefordshire' 1857.

**Holman** Elizabeth  wife of Josiah Holman. Died 1898 aged 74, buried Cadia. CWD 1 October 1985.

**Holman** Josiah  mine captain then farmer, of Cadia, died 1893 aged 71.  Buried Cadia. CWD 1 October 1985.

**Holman** Stephen  of Gloucester, uncle of John Edgecombe per 'Rajasthan' 1855.

**Holmes** Thomas  married Lorrima Williams, Surry Hills, 1895.

**Holt** Jane Elizabeth married Arthur Odgers, Newcastle, Primitive Methodist, 1900.

**Homan** Ann Gluyas nee Bunny per 'Agincourt' 1848, went to West Maitland/Wollombi. E. Williams.

**Honey** John  per 'Tartar', uncle of Jane Levers per 'Vocalist' 1857.

**Honey** William John married Ada Eliza Lane, Glebe, Wesleyan, 1891.

**Hooper** Ann  per 'Agenoria' 1849, died 1864 aged 67, buried Sydney Burial Ground.

**Hooper** Anne  see Anne Hocking

**Hooper** Annie Maria married John Nankivell Mitchell of Bathurst, at Croydon, Wesleyan, 1885.

**Hooper** Julia Mary married Charles Rickard, Orange, 1879.

**Hooper** Mrs Ann of Paddington, funeral 1864. SMH 16 February 1864.

**Hooper** Susan  married Thomas Dent, Hamilton, CE, 1890.

**Hooper** William John per 'Agenoria' 1849, died 1864 aged 33, only son of William & Ann.  Buried Sydney Burial Ground.

**Hooper** William John of Paddington, death 1864. Compositor on SMH. SMH 19 August 1864.

**Hooper** William  died 1854 Sydney aged 57.  Buried Sydney Burial Ground (Wesleyan) with Ann, William, & Anne Hocking.

**Hopgood** George  married Ann Hines, Bathurst, 1842.

**Hordern** John H per 'Persia' 1863, went to a cousin at Castlereagh St, Sydney.

**Hore** Mary  nee Parnell, married Frank Mountrion, Sydney, CE, 1888.  Both of Shoalhaven.

**Horn** Mary  married James Martin Kerkin, Harrington, CE, 1882.

**Horrell** John  married Ada Roylance nee Smith, Orange, 1892.

**Hosie** Henry Curtois married Elizabeth Jane Glasson, Limestone Flat, 1862.

**Hosken** Joseph  and Emma, of Adelong 1876.  NSW births.

**Hosken** Richard Senior (per 'Tartar' 1857?) married Elizabeth French, Tenterfield, Wesleyan, 1878.

**Hoskin** Mary Ann per 'David McIvor' 1858  went to her brother at Melbourne.

**Hoskin** Thomas  of New Caledonia married Hessy Jane Philips, Sydney, Congregational, 1883.

**Hoskin** William  of Melbourne, brother of Stephen Hoskin per 'Tartar' 1857.

**Hoskin** William  died Adelong 1890 aged 61, buried Adelong CE.

**Hoskin/g** Edwin  of Tambaroora, uncle of Emma Richards and Mary Hosking per 'Dunbar Castle' 1872.

**Hosking** Elizabeth  see Elizabeth Robertson.

**Hosking** Joseph  of Adelong, uncle of George Tippett per 'Samuel Plimsoll' 1877.

**Hosking** Mary Ann married William Henry Powell of Adelong, Sydney, CE, 1862.

**Hosking** Mary  relative of Emma Richards, both aboard 'Dunbar Castle' 1872.

**Hosking** Richard  of Benalla, Victoria, brother of Thomas Hoskin (sic) per 'David McIvor' 1858.

**Hosking** Thomas  of Benalla, Victoria, brother of Thomas Hoskin (sic) per 'David McIvor' 1858.

**Hosking** William  of Armidale? brother of James Hosking per 'Cressy' 1856.

**Hosking** of Sydney, a brother and a sister of William Hosking per 'Parsee' 1853.

**Hoskins** William of Woolloomooloo, brother of Margaret Darcy per 'Fitzjames' 1857.

**Hoskyn** Anna per 'Tartar' 1857, aunt of Ann Bonney per 'Herefordshire' 1857.

**Hotten** William Mankin died Adelong 1896 aged 69, buried Adelong Wesleyan.

**Houlding** Lucy Hannah of Darlinghurst, married Rev William Kelynack, Redfern, Wesleyan, 1862.

**Howard** Albert William married Annie Wood nee Hugo, Lewisham, Methodist, 1904.

**Howarth** Edward per 'Dunbar Castle' 1877, a relative of John Crowther per 'Salisbury' 1877.

**Howell** Mary see Mary Powell.

**Huggins** Richard Thomas and Mary Harvey (Wellington) of Adelong 1885. NSW births.

**Hughes** Clementia married Charles Whalan, Dennis Island, 1862.

**Hughes** Diana nee Cundy, married Richard Michell, Guyong, 1867.

**Hugo** Annie see Howard and Wood.

**Hunking** Amelia married John Harris, Bathurst, 1865.

**Hunking** Mary Ann married Arthur Frederick Wilkinson, Bathurst, Methodist, 1861.

**Hunt** Francis married Annie Ethelwyn Charters, Redfern, Wesleyan, 1899.

**Hunter** James married Elizabeth Skinner (per 'Harriet' 1853), Sydney, Presbyterian, 1856.

**Hurley** Anna of Sydney, sister of Joseph Juleff, per 'Kate' 1856.

**Hurley** Annie married Andrew Bennett, Newcastle, CE, 1889.

**Hurley** Mary A of Sydney, sister of Margaret Pollard, per 'Commonwealth' 1877.

**Hutchinson** Henry married Ellen Spike, Yass, Wesleyan, 1876.

**Hyland?** of Goulburn, uncle of John Higman per 'General Hewitt' 1848.

*i*

**Inch** David Jeffree married Hannah Pattinson, Hill End, 1877.

**Inch** Mary Elizabeth married Frederick Henry Trevenen, CE, Surry Hills, 1887.

**Inch** see Jeffree.

**Ireland** Alice Mabel married William Jeffery, CE, Newcastle, 1900.

**Isaac?** William of Sydney, brother of Richard Nettle, per 'Harbinger' 1849.

**Ison** Alfred married Harriet Treblecock, Bathurst, 1883.

**Ison** Isaac married Eliza Ann Treblecock, Bathurst, 1879.

**Ison** James Thomas married Rosina Northey (per 'Harbinger' 1849) Bathurst, 1867.

**Ison** William Thurgood married Mary Jane Jenstes, Bathurst, 1872.

**Ivey** Elizabeth White (per 'Samuel Plimsoll' 1877) died 1941 aged 65. Buried Gore Hill CE cemetery with Francis Ivey.

**Ivey** Ethel May wife of James, of Balmain, 1898. Aged 20. SMH 10 November 1898.

**Ivey** Francis per 'Samuel Plimsoll' 1877. Died 1914 aged 65. Buried Gore Hill CE cemetery.

**Ivey** Francis of Lindfield, died 1914. SMH 5 October 1914.

**Ivey** Malinda Angelina died 1951 aged 57. Buried Gore Hill CE cemetery with Francis Ivey.

**Ivey** Maria per 'Samuel Plimsoll' 1877, wife of Francis. Died 1898, buried Gore Hill CE cemetery with Francis.

**Ivey** Maria of Balmain, wife of Francis, death 1898 aged 47. SMH 10 November 1898.

*J*

**Jacka** John and Mary (nee Edmonds), settled in Hay. Kathy Wills.

**Jacka** John died 1933 aged 84, buried Hay. Kathy Wills.

**Jacka** Mary wife of John, died 1928 aged 74, buried Hay. Kathy Wills.

**Jackett** Clara married Harvey Thyer, CE, Redfern, 1896.

**Jackson** Eliza per 'Lady Ann' 1854, sister of Samuel Mayne per 'Lady Elgin'.

**Jackson** Elizabeth Ann married Henry Coad Trethowen, Cooks River, CE, 1870.

**Jackson** Marriser Mary marrried Richard Gill, Sydney, CE, 1889.

**Jacobs** John married mary Anne McKay, Bathurst, 1841.

**Jacobs** Mary Ann nee Furlong, married William Henry Rundle, Surry Hills, Primitive Methodist, 1887.

**James** Ann known as Nancy O'Hearn, died Cobar aged 79, 1907, buried RC Mt Drysdale.

**James** B of Sydney, died 1908. Methodist, 19 December 1908.

**James** David per 'Palmyra' 1859 sent on to Norfolk Island.

**James** Edwin of Cobar, farewell 1905. Methodist 14 October 1905.

**James** Emma per 'Palmyra' 1859 sent on to Norfolk Island.

**James** Henry of Sydney, husband of Maria, father of Ann, Caleb, Henry, per 'Mangerton' 1855.

**James** James per 'Thomas Arbuthnot' 1849, settled in Bathurst. Brother of William James. Mary Nesbitt.

**James** John and Mary Maria of Adelong 1876. NSW births.

**James** Joseph came to South Australia then Hill End. Died Hill End 1903. Lorna James.

**James** Joseph drowned Hill End 1903. BT 28 May 1903.

**James** Joseph of Turon Diggings, Bathurst, father of Thomas James per 'Washington Irving' 1857.

**James** Mary Ann married Samuel Wilmot (per 'Lord Elgin' 1854), Murrurundi, Congregational, 1868.

**James** Mary per 'Palmyra' 1859 sent on to Norfolk Island.

**James** Mary married William Evans, Orange, 1859.

**James** Mrs H of Mudgee 1900. Methodist 29 December 1900.

**James** William married Elizabeth Sarah Menham?, Kiama, Wesleyan, 1863.

**James** William of Springhurst, Victoria, married Elizabeth Raymont, Kogarah, Wesleyan, 1900.

**James** William came to South Australia then Bathurst. Died Guyong 1870 aged 72. Mary Nesbitt.

**James** William and Maria nee Kernick, per 'Australia' 1853, settled in Kiama. Lorna Spackman.

**James** William per 'Rajasthan' 1855, cousin of William and John Rashleigh per 'Lady Ann'.

**James** Willliam of Dapto, cousin of Edward Kernick per 'Lady Elgin' 1854.

**Jane** of Newcastle, brother of James Jane per 'Lady Ann' 1854.

**Jane** of Sydney, brother of William Jane per 'Alfred' 1858.

**Jeffery** Charlotte nee Conley, per 'Devon' 1881. Settled in Darlington. Marie Lute.

**Jeffery** Elizabeth nee Hartwell, married John Champion, Surry Hills, CE, 1898.

**Jeffery** James of Bathurst. William John per 'Ocean Empress' 1864 went to him from the ship.

**Jeffery** John and Mary Giles, of Adelong 1879. NSW births.

**Jeffery** William married Alice Mabel Ireland, Newcastle, CE, 1900.

**Jefferys** James of Bathurst, husband of Sarah Jeffreys nee Pascoe per 'Ocean Empress' 1864.

**Jeffree** Caroline nee Inch & 5 children per 'Admiral Lyons' 1858. went to husband Phillip Jeffree at Hill End. Marlene Reid.

**Jeffree** George married Mary Jane Carkeek, Hill End, Wesleyan, 1876.

**Jeffree** Phillip and wife Caroline nee Inch, of Hill End. Harold Jeffree.

**Jeffrey** John married Mary Giles Prowse, Adelong, Wesleyan, 1878.

**Jeffrey** Sara see Sara Cramp.

**Jeffrey** William married Emily Teague, (per 'Mary Pleasants' 1858), Macleay River, Wesleyan, 1871.

**Jelbart** Eliza married Hugh Kelly, Macquarie Plains, 1864.

**Jelbart** Ellen married John Wilson Lew, Bathurst, 1883.

**Jelbart** James of Parkes, 1897. Methodist 27 February 1897.

**Jelbart** Mrs of Parkes and Bathurst, (nee Spicer) death 1899. Methodist 30 September & 4 November 1899.

**Jenkin** John Henry married Sarah Cocking nee Mitchell (both of Charters Towers), Surry Hills, CE, 1891.

**Jenkin** John married Elizabeth Robertson nee Hosking, Sydney, CE, 1898.

**Jenkin** John cousin of Thomas Leatham per 'Fitzjames' 1857.

**Jenkin** John brother of Philadelphia Jenkin, both per 'Cressy' 1856.

**Jenkin** Philadelphia sister of John Jenkin, both per 'Cressy' 1856.

**Jenkin** William Charles married Adelaide Dawes, Surry Hills, CE, 1893.

**Jenkin** William married Emily Littlewood, Paddington, Wesleyan, 1898.

**Jenkins** Ellen Trenerry wife of James, died 1886 aged 43, buried Waverley CE.

**Jenkins** Francis married Ellen Harvey, Cadia, 1865.

**Jenkins** James died Adelong 1876 aged 40, buried Adelong.

**Jenkins** John son-in-law of Alice Grenfell, both per 'Ninevah' 1877. George Dennis of Cow Flat also a son-in-law.

**Jenkins** John of Guyong, brother of Francis/Thomas? Jenkins per 'Malvina Vidal' 1853.

**Jenkins** Mary A widowed mother of Ann Williams & Lavinia Matthews all per 'Commonwealth' 1877.

**Jenkins** Susan married James Rogers, Armidale, Wesleyan, 1896.

**Jenkins** wife of James Jenkins, Paddington, 1886. SMH 30 April 1886.

**Jenkyn** William of Orange, wife of Jane, father of Mary & Tabetha, all per 'Hornet' 1865.

**Jenkyns** Tabitha married Robert Northey, Hill End, 1878.

**Jenkyns** William Joseph of Hill End, married Mary Ann Perrett, Glebe, Wesleyan, 1884.

**Jennings** Eliza aunt of Mary Ann Williams per 'Alfred' 1857. She also has an uncle William Jennings in Sydney.

**Jennings** John of Surry Hills, funeral, aged 19, 1869. SMH 15 December 1869.

**Jennings** John of Rushcutters Bay, death aged 53, 1875. SMH 14 December 1875.

**Jennings** John per 'Lady Kennaway' 1854, died 1875 aged 53, buried Rookwood Wesleyan.

**Jennings** John and Mary, of Melbourne, uncle & aunt of Amy Crisp per 'Constitution' 1855.

**Jennings** Joseph of Bendigo, brother of William Jennings per 'Alfred' 1857.

**Jennings** Mary see John Jennings.

**Jennings** Phillippa per 'Hornet' 1859, employed by H. Roberts of Crown Street.

**Jennings** Simon and Selina, per 'Hornet' 1859, went to Benjamin Mountcastle of North Shore.

**Jennings** William of Sydney, uncle of Mary Ann Williams per 'Alfred' 1857. She also has an aunt Eliza Jennings.

**Jennings** of Morpeth, two brothers of Simon Jennings per 'Hornet' 1859.

**Jenstes** Mary Jane married William Thurgood Ison, Bathurst, 1872.

**Jerroe** Mr of Sydney, employed Jane Eastcote per 'William Turner' 1841.

**Job** John married Elizabeth Jane Bargwanna (per 'Harbinger' 1849), Orange, 1864.

**Job** William per 'Elphinstone' 1849. Settled in Orange. Jenny King.

**John** William per 'Ocean Empress' 1864, went to James Jeffery at Bathurst.

**Johns** Betsey Jane married John Curnow, Burwood, Wesleyan, 1891.

**Johns** Bradford died Adelong 1888 aged 60, buried Adelong CE.

**Johns** Elizabeth married Seth Junot Winsten, Tuena, 1889.

**Johns** Francis married Eliza Jane Hilton, Sydney, Wesleyan, 1882.

**Johns** Jane of Orange, aunt of the Gartrell family per 'Annie H Smith' 1877.

**Johns** Marianne in service of Mr Cox, Penrith, daughter by her first husband of Susan Rees per 'Robert Small' 1856.

**Johns** Stephen and Jane of Adelong 1881. NSW births.

**Johns** Thomas John married Mary Powell, Newcastle, Wesleyan, 1891.

**Johns** William and Jane (nee Gartrell) sent to India by his mining company then to NSW in 1848. Settled Orange. E. Clancy, 'More precious than gold' Ch.2.

**Johns** William uncle of Amelia Adams per 'Ninevah' 1877.

**Johns** family per 'Trevelyan' 1877 went to Murrumburrah for Young.

**Johnson** Mary Anne nee Palfrey, married Joseph Short, Sydney, Presbyterian, 1870.

**Johnson** Mary see Mary Short.

**Johnston** Annie Amelia married Mark Hambly, late of Botany, (per 'Forest Monarch' 1858), Sydney, Wesleyan, 1880.

**Johnston** Letitia married George Grenfell Eddy of Forbes (per 'Glendower' 1868) at Darlinghurst, Wesleyan, 1894.

**Joiner** John married Susan Watts nee Rapson, (per 'Kate' 1856), Manning River, CE, 1867.

**Jolly** Ann married John Waters, Hill End, 1873.

**Jolly** Louisa Jane married Joseph Bennett/s, Bathurst, 1885.

**Jonas** Catherine of Adelaide, sister of Susannah Wearne per 'Harbinger' 1849.

**Jones** Alexander married Lavinia Grenfell (per 'Northampton' 1881), Cobar, Wesleyan, 1897.

**Jones** Charlotte married William Henry Pascoe, Wattle Flat, Bathurst, 1893.

**Jones** John married Catherine Geake, Cornish Settlement, 1840.

**Jones** Mary married Stephen Stainer, Nowra, Wesleyan, 1895.

**Jones** Samuel died Cobar aged 37, 1881. Buried Cobar CE.

**Jones** Sarah Anne marrried Alfred Edwin Sleeman, Paterson, CE, 1858.

**Jory** Elizabeth Jane died Adelong 1901 aged 59, buried Adelong Wesleyan.

**Jory** Elizabeth Ann died Adelong 1875 aged 22, buried Adelong Wesleyan.

**Jory** James married Sarah Jane Blackwell, Adelong, Wesleyan, 1876.

**Jory** James and Sarah Jane, of Adelong 1879. NSW

births.
**Jory** James and Elizabeth Ann, of Adelong 1875. NSW births.
**Jory** John of Morpeth, per 'Fairlie' 1838. Victor Jory.
**Jory** Josiah and Elizabeth Jane, of Adelong 1873. NSW births.
**Jory** Margaret Frances married Theopilus Lightfoot, Morpeth, 1906.
**Jose** Mary see Mary Richards.
**Joseph** Mr Henry of George St, Sydney, employed Mary A. Rogers alias Whatson per 'Dunbar Castle' 1871.
**Judge** Hugh Hector married Jane Thomas Rowe, Armidale, Wesleyan, 1893.
**Juleff** Michael Broad per 'Lady Elgin' 1854, went to Redfern. Jean Juleff Roy.
**Julian** Ellen wife of Joseph, of Windsor, 1886. SMH 24 August 1886.
**Julian** John and Elizabeth, per 'William Metcalfe' 1844, employed by John McDonald of Pitt Town.
**Julian** John of Pitt Town, Windsor, brother of Joseph Julian per 'Thomas Arbuthnot' 1849.
**Julian** Joseph per 'Thomas Arbuthnot' 1849, proprietor of Newtown tannery 1888. AMM

# K

**Kain** Elizabeth Thirza wife of Thomas, of Darlinghurst, 1914 aged 80. SMH 17 August 1914.
**Kain** Elizabeth Thirza wife of Thomas, died 1914 aged 79, buried Waverley cemetery.
**Kain** Margaret wife of Thomas Kain, Surry Hills, 1886. SMH 28 August 1886.
**Kain** Thomas of Darlinghurst, 1906 aged 76. SMH 8 January 1906.
**Kain** Thomas died 1906 aged 76, buried Waverley cemetery.
**Keass** Catherine see Catherine Teague
**Kellaway** Alf married Louisa Maria Lord, Parramatta, Wesleyan, 1884.
**Kelley** Joseph James and Grace, of Adelong 1880. NSW births.
**Kelly** Hugh married Eliza Jelbert (per 'Fairlie' 1848) , Bathurst, 1864.
**Kelly** Mr Richard of Palmer St, Woolloomooloo, employed Elizabeth Hampton per 'Scythia' 1871.
**Kelynack** Lucy died 1932 aged 88, buried Rookwood Wesleyan.
**Kelynack** Rev William married Lucy Houlding, Redfern, Wesleyan, 1862.
**Kelynack** Rev William, biography of, Methodist, 27 April 1912.
**Kelynack** Rev William died 1891 aged 59, buried Rookwood Wesleyan, with wife Lucy and Laura & Philip Phillips.
**Kemp** Louisa married John Dennis, Bathurst, 1882.
**Kemp** William Chynoweth married Frances Paddison, Bathurst, 1879.
**Kendall** Louise Jane married Thomas Henry Rule, Cobar, Wesleyan, 1881.
**Kendall** Thomas per 'Herefordshire' 1857, first cousin of Edward Mitchell (per 'Tartar' 1857) of Twofold Bay.
**Kenny** John Arthur married Sarah Biddick, Surry Hills, CE, 1899.
**Kent** Frank married Louisa Taylor, Cobar, Wesleyan, 1890.
**Kent** Henry married Caroline Warren (per 'William Metcalfe' 1844, Cooks River, CE, 1857.
**Kent** Hugh married Anne Martin, Sydney, Wesleyan, 1873.
**Kent** John of Hill End, uncle of Thomas Kent per 'Commonwealth' 1877.
**Kent** Joseph married Susan Douglass, Glebe, Wesleyan, 1885.

**Kent** Richard per 'Coldstream' 1863, went to Singleton.
**Kerkin** James Martin married Mary Horn, Harrington, CE, 1882.
**Kerkin** James Martin of Drummoyne 1918. SMH 31 May 1918.
**Kernick** Edward of Temora, died 1894 aged 61. Methodist 22 September 1894.
**Kernick** see William James.
**Kerno** Mrs of Sydney, aunt of Jane Anne Martin per 'Lady Ann' 1854. See Maria Simcocks, same ship.
**Kerno** Mrs of Sydney, aunt of Maria Simcocks per 'Lady Ann' 1854. See Jane A. Martin, same ship.
**Kershaw** Martha married Joseph Henry Grose, Newtown, Congregational, 1886.
**Kessell** Elizabeth Mary married Alfred James Sweetnam, Bathurst, 1889.
**Kessell** Elizabeth married Richard Trefry, Orange, Methodist, 1861.
**Kestall** Richard married Ann Brookes, Bathurst, 1843.
**Kestall** Stephen of Bathurst, husband of Maria & father of Elizabeth, Mary & Stephen per 'Mangerton' 1855.
**Keyes** Jane married Thomas Geake Webb, Parramatta, Wesleyan, 1874.
**Killey** Joseph James and Grace, of Adelong 1880. See Kelley. NSW births.
**Killin** Jane married William John Burnett, Singleton, Wesleyan, 1890.
**Killingsworth** Florence M nee Pitt married Sidney John Cocking, Marrickville, CE, 1902.
**King** Edward Richard arrived before 1873. Lived in Gulgong then Sydney. Bonnie Churchill.
**King** Mr R of Wallsend 1895. Methodist 27 July 1895.
**King** Robert married Lena Jane Bartle, Adelong, 1898.
**Kinsella** Mary married Richard Goodfellow, Sydney, Wesleyan, 1882.
**Kitto** Walter and Hannah, of Adelong 1858. NSW births.
**Knapman** Ellen married Charles Blake, Sydney, 1861.
**Knapman** Frederick died 1912, buried Waverley CE. SMH 6 August 1912.
**Knapman** Mary wife of Frederick. Died 1924, buried Waverley CE.
**Knight** Anthony Charles married Amy Amelia Forsyth, Willoughby, Methodist, 1902.
**Knight** Christopher married Mary A Dainty, Redfern, CE, 1884.
**Knight** Ernest Victor married Maggie May Boyle, Redfern, Wesleyan, 1895.
**Knight** Louisa Jane married John Wheeler, Waterloo, Wesleyan, 1898.
**Knight** Olivia Maud Mary married Percy Collins, Redfern, Wesleyan, 1897.
**Knight** William and (H)annah nee Ward per 'Fitzjames' 1858. Ronald Knight.
**Knight** William of Bathurst, uncle of Robert Truscott per 'Earl Dalhousie' 1877.
**Knuckey** Benjamin of Sydney (per 'Sultana' 1855) brother of John Knuckey per 'Fitzjames' 1858.
**Knuckey** Benjamin Waverley. SMH 8 September 1877.
**Knuckey** Hugh died Sydney 1936. NSW Probate index.
**Knuckey** John Henry of Peak Hill, died 1915. NSW Probate index.
**Knuckey** Thomas Nicholas of Leichhardt 1914. SMH 3 December 1914.
**Knuckey** William died Mulwala 1899. NSW Probate index.
**Krouge** Henry of the Lachlan, uncle of Elizabeth A. Pearce and Elizabeth Jane Pearce per 'St Lawrence'

1877. (Cobar connection?)

**Kulmar** Elizabeth married Alfred Charles Westcott, Summer Hill, Wesleyan, 1886.

**Kyle** David married Harriet Ellen Markwell, Newcastle, Free Methodist, 1893.

# L

**Ladkin** Annie married Martin Lampshire, Parramatta, CE, 1882.

**Lake** Catherine of Rushcutters Bay, daughter of Thomas Russell per 'Morning Star' 1864.

**Lake** Elizabeth Jane B married Henry Mitchell, Dulwich Hill, Primitive Methodist, 1900.

**Lambert** John married Elizabeth Sloggett, Bathurst, 1877.

**Lambrick** Nicholas (per 'Julindar' 1849), father of Sophia & Richard Lambrick per 'Walter Morrice' 1849.

**Lambrick** Richard per 'Walter Morrice' 1849, son of Nicholas & Susannah Lambrick per 'Julindar' 1849.

**Lambrick** Richard brother of Sophia Lambrick per 'Walter Morrice' 1849.

**Lambrick** Sophia per 'Walter Morrice' 1849, sister of Richard Lambrick on same ship.

**Lambrick** Sophia per 'Walter Morrice' 1849, daughter of Susannah & Nicholas Lambrick per 'Julindar' 1849.

**Lamont** Margaret married Thomas Bone of Cobar, Sydney, Wesleyan, 1896.

**Lampshire** Martin married Annie Ladkin, Parramatta, CE, 1882.

**Lamrock** Elizabeth married Thomas Richard Wills, Bathurst, 1881.

**Landers** Harriet F married Thomas Rowe, (per 'Fitzjames' 1858), Macleay River, Wesleyan, 1869.

**Lane** Ada Eliza married William John Honey, Glebe, Wesleyan, 1891.

**Lane** Anna Maria see Anna Maria Hawkins.

**Lane** Charles Thomas A married Eunice Martha Adams, Cowra, 1893.

**Lane** Charles Wesley married Selina Lane, Bathurst, 1857.

**Lane** E H of Bathurst. AMM.

**Lane** Harriet died 1927 aged 86, buried with Robert Lane, Sandgate.

**Lane** J B of Bathurst. AMM.

**Lane** Jane Jones W married Thomas Sargeant Pearse, Cornish Settlement, 1866.

**Lane** John Tom married Mary Rundle Lane, Bathurst, 1844.

**Lane** Mary Rundle married John Tom lane, Bathurst, 1844.

**Lane** Robert died 1891 aged 51, buried Sandgate Primitive Methodist, Newcastle.

**Lane** Selina married Charles Wesley Lane, Bathurst, 1857.

**Lane** Thomas Geake married Jane Peirce, Cornish Settlement, 1866.

**Lane** family, of Bathurst and Byng. Alan Lane.

**Langdon** Frederick Lawrence married Agnes Briton, Petersham, Presbyterian, 1896.

**Langmaid** Mary married Thomas Richards Bowden, Muswellbrook, CE, 1884.

**Langsford** Thomas died 1869, buried Singleton.

**Langsford** William Henry married Elizabeth Gardiner, Singleton, 1871.

**Langsford** William Henry died 1918, buried Singleton.

**Langsford** family of Singleton. Peggy Richards.

**Langsford** family per 'Coldstream' 1863 went to Singleton.

**Lathlean** Richard of Newcastle, aged 60, 1907. Methodist 21 September 1907.

**Lavers** Fanny married Arthur James Sargeant, Redfern, CE, 1900.

**Law** Sarah married Thomas Eslick, Orange, 1879.

**Lawrey** John married Frances Platt, Sunny Corner Bathurst, Wesleyan, 1890.

**Lawry** Henry died Adelong 1864 aged 44, buried Adelong Wesleyan.

**Lawry** Rev W Methodist 13 April 1895.

**Lawry** Thomas Samuel married Margaret Meyn, Singleton, CE, 1866.

**Leach** Clara A. C. married William Foss, Marrickville, Congregational, 1889.

**Lean** Ann of Bathurst, cousin of Amelia Nettle per 'Harbinger' 1849. See Trewren.

**Lean** Christopher married Eliza Gossip Clark, Dungog, CE, 1859.

**Lean** Christopher died Dungog 1886. NSW Probate index.

**Lean** John of Bathurst, cousin of Amelia Nettle per 'Harbinger' 1849. See Trewren.

**Lean** Mary married Lorenzo Dixon Marshall, Bathurst, 1886.

**Lean** Nicholas of Gunning and Sydney, per 'Dunbar Castle' 1877. David Lean.

**Lean** Olivia per 'Dunbar Castle' 1877. Sister of Nicholas also on board and Samuel already in Bathurst. David Lean.

**Lean** R of Ashfield 1896. Methodist 26 December 1896.

**Lean** Richard of Sydney 1913. Methodist 11 October 1913.

**Lean** Robert at Bathurst? Mary Row per 'Mangerton' 1855 came under engagement to him.

**Lean** Samuel of Bathurst, cousin of Amelia Nettle per 'Harbinger' 1849. See Trewren.

**Lean** Samuel of Bathurst, died 1872. NSW Probate index.

**Lean** Samuel married Margaret Martin, Bathurst, Wesleyan, 1865.

**Lean** Samuel of Bathurst, husband of Eliza and father of Richard & Samuel per 'Jerusalem' 1875.

**Lean** Samuel of Bathurst, brother of Nicholas Lean per 'Dunbar Castle' 1877.

**Lean** Stephen of Bellinger River 1910. Methodist 10 September 1910.

**Lean** Thomas died Cobar 1901. NSW Probate index.

**Leavers** Lily married Richard James Thomas, Cobar, Wesleyan, 1881.

**Lee** Charlotte married Thomas Anstiss, Bathurst, 1873.

**Lee** John married Florence Hardman, Surry Hills, CE, 1893.

**Leece** Ellen Alice married Edwin Arnold Crapp, Uralla, 1905. Methodist, 1 July 1905.

**Leggo** Annie married Edward Andrew, Adelong, Wesleyan, 1876.

**Leggo** Grace (wife of William), died 1885 aged 71. Buried Waverley cemetery. SMH 17 December 1885.

**Letcher** James of Louisa Creek, husband of Anne, father of Elizabeth, Mary Jane & William per 'Northern Light' 1858.

**Letcher?** James of Adelaide. Cousin of James Barry per 'Walmer Castle' 1848.

**Lethlean** family of Orange. Jean Gibson.

**Levers** Jane per 'Vocalist' 1857, niece of John Honey per 'Tartar' 1857.

**Lew** John Wilson married Ellen Jelbart, Bathurst, Wesleyan, 1883.

**Lewis** Edith M died 1909 aged 27. Buried Rookwood CE with Francis & Mary Ann Crago.

**Liddicoat?** Harriet of Bathurst, cousin of Amelia Nettle per 'Harbinger' 1849. See Trewren and Lean.

**Liffey?** Robert of West Maitland, uncle of George Philips per 'Samuel Plimsoll (2)' 1874.

**Lightfoot** James married Emma Vercoe, West Maitland, Wesleyan, 1861.

**Lightfoot** Jessie married Jonathan Wilson, Maitland, 1886.

**Lightfoot** John see Varcoe.
**Lightfoot** John per 'Cressy' 1856, went to Newcastle and Maitland. Daryl Lightfoot.
**Lightfoot** John per 'Cressy' 1856, brother of William Lightfoot per 'Truro' 1855.
**Lightfoot** Theophilus married Margaret Jory, Morpeth, Methodist, 1906.
**Lightfoot** William per 'Truro' 1855, went to Newcastle and Maitland. Daryl Lightfoot.
**Lightfoot** William per 'Truro' 1855, brother of John & Grace Lightfoot per 'Cressy' 1856.
**Lindsay** Annie Annis married William Henry Odgers, Minmi, Primitive Methodist, 1891.
**Lintern** Elizabeth married John Strugnell, Woollahra, Wesleyan, 1876.
**Lintern** George per 'Eliza' 1855 settled in Woolloomooloo. Sue Lamrock.
**Lintern** Henry of Woolloomooloo, brother of George Lintern per 'Eliza' 1855.
**Lintern** Henry died 1887 aged 69. Buried Waverley cemetery.
**Lister** Annie Caroline married William Henshaw Rowe, Guyong, 1865.
**Littlewood** Emily married William Jenkin, Paddington, Wesleyan, 1898.
**Livermore** Lydia married John Thomas, Redfern, United Free Methodist, 1898.
**Lloyd** Mary married James Bramble, Darlinghurst, CE, 1888.
**Lobb** Catherine married John Woolcock (arrived c.1838), and settled in Murrurundi. D V H Lobb.
**Lobb** John of near Sydney, brother-in-law of Willliam Hambly per 'Forest Monarch' 1858.
**Lobb** Mary Ann of Auburn, 1910. SMH 22 March 1910.
**Lobb** Thomas Francis died 190? aged 69, buried Rookwood Methodist.
**Lobb** William George of Annandale, 1911. SMH 31 May 1911.
**Lobb** William of near Sydney, brother-in-law of Willliam Hambly per 'Forest Monarch' 1858.
**Lobb** William market gardener of Botany, employed William Hick per 'Racehorse' 1866.
**Lockwood** Annie nee Crothers, daughter of George & Elizabeth. Died 1892. Buried with parents, Rookwood Wesleyan.
**Lockwood** Fred W husband of Annie Crothers. Died 1943. Buried with Crothers family, Rookwood Wesleyan.
**Lockyer** Clara Australia, granddaughter of Richard Rowe, buried with him at Sydney Burial Ground. She died 1858 aged 5 months.
**Lodwick** Thomas married Julia Annie Carlyon, Newcastle, Wesleyan, 1886.
**Longbottom** Mary Jane married Charles Burley, Hunter River, CE, 1858.
**Lord** George of Chippendale uncle of Henry Lord per 'Fitzjames' 1858.
**Lord** Henry married Annie Englebrecht, Muscle Creek, CE, 1880.
**Lord** Louisa Maria married Alfred Kellaway, Parramatta, Wesleyan, 1884.
**Lord** Martha married John Stansfield, Bathurst, 1843.
**Lord** William arrived in NSW and went to WA. E. J. Lord.
**Loutit** Margaret married James Wearne (per 'Harbinger' 1849) of Bingara, at Surry Hills, Wesleyan, 1881.
**Lucas** John of Sydney, uncle of Charles Lukies/Lucas per 'Kapunda' 1877.
**Lucas** William of Emu Plains died 1892 aged 82. Methodist 23 January 1892.
**Lukey** Charles William of Sydney, died 1900 aged 66. SMH 22 February 1900.
**Lukey** Elizabeth Snow of Sydney, died 1909 aged 73. Buried with Charles William Lukey. SMH 10

November 1909.
**Lukies** William of Chippendale, brother of Henry Lukies per 'Lady Ann' 1854.
**Lutey** Thomas Lorey married Amy Smith, Burwood, Primitive Methodist, 1887.
**Lytton** J of Surry Hills, brother of Mary Back per 'Star of India' 1876.

# M

**Mackay** James buried Rookwood Wesleyan 1886 aged 58.
**Mackay** James buried Rookwood Wesleyan 1907 aged 58. In same grave as James Mackay buried 1886.
**Mackay** Mary Anne married John Jacobs, Bathurst, 1841.
**Mackey** William married Catherine Grenfell (per 'Northampton' 1881), Nymagee, Wesleyan, 1883.
**Maclean** Sydney Hugh married Ellen Maria Griffin, Gladesville, Wesleyan, 1883.
**Maddern** Mary nee Davey, married Dominick Cullen, Vegetable Creek, Wesleyan, 1875.
**Maddison** John married Elizabeth Couch, Orange, Wesleyan, 1864.
**Maddock** Emanuel of Ovens Diggings, Victoria, brother of John Maddock per 'Kate' 1856.
**Maguire** Georgina Margaret married Frederic Harry Downing of Mountain Top, Sydney, CE, 1890.
**Mair** George of Woollahra 1908. SMH 17 April, 1908. Buried Waverley with wife Minnie and Ellen Bott.
**Manners** Ann of Windsor, a relative of William Sutton per 'Australia' 1853. William Soper also a relative.
**Manners** Ann see William Soper.
**Manners** James? of the Hunter, brother of Mary Kelly, per 'Lord Stanley' 1850.
**Manners** see Miners.
**Manning** Mary Ann married John Thomas, Hamilton, Wesleyan, 1892.
**Manuel** family, of Newcastle. Elaine Linfoot.
**Manuell** Thomas married Ellen Urquart, Newcastle, CE, 1861.
**Manuell** William Henry married Rosa Bourne, Newcastle, 1871.
**Mardons** Joseph see Joseph Martins.
**Marks** Ellen Jane married Gideon Patten of Granville, Pennant Hills, Wesleyan, 1899.
**Marks** Emily died 1893 aged 65, buried Rookwood Wesleyan with son Thomas. SMH 12 October 1893.
**Marks** John husband of Alice. Of Glebe, 1898. SMH 29 November 1898.
**Marks** Thomas died 1919 aged 60, buried Rookwood Wesleyan with mother Emily.
**Marks** Thomas married Mary Mullin, Burwood, Wesleyan, 1881.
**Markwell** Harriet Ellen nee Matthews, married David Kyle, Adamstown, Free Methodist, 1893.
**Maroney** Patrick and Ellen per 'Palestine' 1842, employed on shore as agricultural labourer.
**Marshall** Katherine Celia married John Richard Curnow of Warwick Queensland, Enmore, Wesleyan, 1886.
**Marshall** Lorenzo Dixon married Mary Lean, Bathurst, 1886.
**Marshall** Margaret married Richard Rowe (per 'Lady Ann' 1854) Sydney, Presbyterian, 1861.
**Marshall** Richard arrived 1883 unassisted. Lived Bathurst, Surry Hills, North Sydney. Farmer & coach builder. Gwen King.
**Martel** Charles married Ellen Charleston, Newcastle, CE, 1885.
**Martin** Anne nee Bath?, married Hugh Kent, Sydney, Wesleyan, 1873.
**Martin** Catherine of Adelaide, relative of James

Peters per 'Harbinger' 1849.

**Martin** Emily see Emily Ponsonby.

**Martin** Grace married Charles Bennet Glasson, Bathurst, Wesleyan, 1861.

**Martin** J H of O'Connells Plains, the destination of the Martin family per 'Severn' 1863.

**Martin** Jane and Maria Simcocks, both per 'Lady Ann' 1854 appear to be related.

**Martin** Janie married Edward Abraham Wright, Bathurst, 1890.

**Martin** Job of Mitchells Creek, brother of William H Martin per 'Severn' 1863.

**Martin** Margaret married Samuel Lean, Bathurst, 1865.

**Martin** Martha Jane married William Henry Martin, Inverell, Wesleyan, 1882.

**Martin** Martha Nicholls died 1895 aged 65, wife of B C Martin. Buried Tingha cemetery.

**Martin** Mary Ann of Botany, 1906. SMH 8 January 1906.

**Martin** Millicent Jane S O married Tom Hawke, Orange, 1879.

**Martin** Millicent died 1900, buried Orange Methodist. Wife of late John? Martin, mother of Mrs Tom Hawke.

**Martin** Mrs of Rylestone, 1899 aged 71 years. Methodist 9 September 1899.

**Martin** Richard died Cobar aged 60, 1901, buried CE Cobar.

**Martin** Susan married Thomas Syer, Bathurst, 1869.

**Martin** W H per 'Severn' 1863, went to Bathurst area. Deborah Shuker.

**Martin** W H per 'Severn' 1863, went to Bathurst and then Hillgrove. Jodi Goman.

**Martin** William Henry per 'Severn' 1863, married Martha Jane Martin, Inverell, Wesleyan, 1882.

**Martin** William went from NSW to Melbourne c.1849. Maria Sullivan.

**Martins** Joseph of New England, uncle of James Trembath per 'Commonwealth' 1877.

**Matthew** Harriet Ellen see Harriet Ellen Markwell.

**Matthews** Charles cousin of William Manual per 'Lady Amherst' 1849.

**Matthews** Harriet Ellen see Harriet Ellen Markwell.

**Matthews** J of Berrima, destination of William H Richards per 'Queen of the East' 1864.

**Matthews** John Thomas died Cobar 1897 aged 54, buried Cobar Wesleyan.

**Matthews** Joseph Palmer married Anna Maria Thompson nee Nerkell? Sydney, CE, 1891.

**Matthews** Lavinia daughter of Mary A Jenkins, sister of Ann Williams. All per 'Commonwealth' 1877.

**Matthews** Thomas of Paddington, uncle of Ann May per 'Herefordshire' 1857.

**Matthews** William Guy and Levinia, of Adelong 1878. NSW births.

**Matthews** William cousin of William Manual per 'Lady Amherst' 1849.

**May** George of Bathurst? 1888. AMM

**May** John arrived 1870, settled in Inverell. AMM

**May** Joseph married Bessie O'Connor, Sydney, CE, 1892.

**May** William Henry per 'David McIvor' 1858, married Eliza Hicks Thomas, Balmain, CE, 1863.

**May** William married Elizabeth Hampton, Nymagee, Wesleyan, 1883.

**Mayne** Samuel per 'Lady Elgin', brother of Eliza Jackson per 'Lady Ann' 1854.

**Mayne** William emigrated to Victoria then NZ in 1861. Settled in Cargo near Bathurst. AMM.

**McAlister** Sarah married John Rogers Tangye, Bathurst, 1868.

**McAuley** Sarah married Robert Webb, Bathurst, 1871.

**McAuliffe** Ellen married William Paul, Bathurst, 1863.

**McCoombe** Robert per 'Highflyer' 1864. Sent to assist in work of 40 pounder Armstrong guns in the colony.

**McDonald** Alex at Garlicks. Uncle of Maria Cowles per 'Samuel Plimsoll' 1876.

**McDonald** Alexander married Catherine Miller, Bathurst, 1844.

**McDonald** Alexander widower, married Ann Cord, Bathurst, 1871.

**McDonald** Alexander farmer of Dubbo, 1888 AMM

**McDonald** Jane died Cobar 1902 aged 51, buried Cobar Wesleyan.

**McDonald** John of Pitt Town, employed John & Elizabeth Julian per 'Willim Metcalfe' 1844.

**McDowell** Mary married Henry Coleman, Parramatta, Wesleyan, 1880.

**McFadden** Rachel (nee Barkle) married Alfred Edward Penno, Cobar, Methodist, 1906.

**McFadyen** Mary married Abraham Prout Woodward, Gunnedah, Wesleyan, 1888.

**McKay** Mary Anne married John Jacobs, Bathurst, 1841.

**McLauchlan** Mrs of Princes St (Newcastle?) sister of Ada & Amelia Woodey per 'Kapunda' 1877.

**McLean** Emily Harriet married Thomas Wing Willman, Bathurst, 1887.

**McLean** John married Harriet Emma Trewren, Kelso, Wesleyan, 1856.

**McLean** Mary see Mary Twine.

**McManous** Mary married William Best Chudleigh, Parramatta, Wesleyan, 1856.

**McMillen** Adeline married John Tremain, Wellington, 1904.

**McMullen** Elizabeth of Molong, wife of William, died 1896 aged 61, buried Molong.

**McMullen** Isabella married William Asprey, Bathurst, 1842.

**McNamara** Williiam John married Winifred Sarah Ann Griffith, Surry Hills, CE, 1895.

**McNeil** Sarah died 1904, buried Waverley, wife of John Stuart McNeil. SMH 30 March, 1904.

**Meadham** James married Susan Trevena, Cobar, Wesleyan, 1888.

**Meek** Martha married Warwick Wilce, Newtown, Wesleyan, 1889.

**Melleuish** Laura Ann married Edward Cook Goodsell, Redfern, CE, 1898.

**Melleuish** William Eatham married Ethel May Hodges, Paddington, Wesleyan, 1897.

**Mellow** Thomas of Wollongong, brother of Elizabeth Bassett per 'Salisbury' 1877.

**Melville** Frances Jane married John Dingle, Newcastle, Free Methodist, 1887.

**Menham?** Elizabeth Sarah married William James, Kiama, Wesleyan, 1863.

**Merratt** family per 'Burlington' 1857, to George Wallis, Copperminer, near Orange.

**Merrett** Emma see Emma Hill.

**Merrett** Thomas Henry married Dianah Dunett, Sydney, Wesleyan, 1893.

**Merrin** Catherine see Catherine Stevens.

**Meyn** Elizabeth married John D. Barklay, Singleton, CE, 1872.

**Meyn** Margaret married Thomas Samuel Lawry, Singleton, 1866.

**Michell** Charles c. 1858+, Uralla. Beryl Michell.

**Michell** Charles c. 1880+, Bingara. Beryl Michell.

**Michell** Richard married Diana Hughes, nee Cundy, Guyong, 1867.

**Michell** Stephen c. 1854, Victoria. Mary Devonshire.

**Middleton** Amy married Albert Henry Catren, Redfern, CE, 1897.

**Middleton** George married Mary Warren (per 'Hawkesbury' 1872), Sydney, Presbyterian, 1877.

**Middleton** James per 'Earl Dalhousie' 1876. See William Turner, Tamworth.

**Middleton** Stephen brother of James Middleton per 'Earl Dalhousie' 1876. See William Turner.

**Mikelson** Andrew married Mary Evans, Orange, Wesleyan, 1867.

**Miller** Catherine married Alexander McDonald, Bathurst, 1844.

**Miller** Sarah married Joseph Henry Glasson, Dennis Island 1867.

**Miller** William married Mary Ashenden, Bathurst, Wesleyan, 1843.

**Millett** William of Charters Towers, married Maude Dunsford, Waverley, Wesleyan, 1886.

**Mills** Susan per 'Forest Monarch' 1858. Sent for by F. Brown of Newcastle. Not a relative.

**Milne** George married Emily Walkom. Bathurst, Wesleyan, 1882.

**Milne** James Beehan married Elizabeth Ann Bennett Trevarthen, Bathurst, 1866.

**Miners** Ann of Redfern, sister of Elizabeth Butson per 'Ellenborough' 1853. See William Soper.

**Miners** James of Bega, nephew of John P. Northey per 'Pericles' 1877. See Tenby.

**Miners** James married Ethel Ada Wallis, Woolloomooloo, Wesleyan, 1892.

**Mitchell** Anne per 'Tartar' 1857, aunt of Thomas Kendall per 'Herefordshire' 1857.

**Mitchell** Charles of Rocky River, Armidale. Brother of Richard Mitchell per 'Herefordshire' 1857.

**Mitchell** Edmund of Twofold Bay, son of Edward Mitchell per 'Tartar' 1857.

**Mitchell** Edmund of Eden, per 'Gloriana' 1855. Lyn Lyon.

**Mitchell** Edward of Eden, per 'Tartar' 1857. Father of Edmund Mitchell per 'Gloriana' 1855. Lyn Lyon.

**Mitchell** Edward of Twofold Bay, first cousin of Thomas Kendall per 'Herefordshire' 1857.

**Mitchell** Elizabeth Jane married James Opie, Sydney, 1878.

**Mitchell** Emma married Henry James Woodley of Liverpool Plains, at Sydney, CE, 1858.

**Mitchell** Henry married Elizabeth J.B. Lake, Dulwich Hill, Primitive Methodist, 1900.

**Mitchell** John Francis married Louisa Bailey, Orange, Wesleyan, 1866.

**Mitchell** John Nankivell married Annie Maria Hooper, Croydon, Wesleyan, 1885.

**Mitchell** Mrs Jane of Twofold Bay, sister of Eliza Nicholas per 'Fitzjames' 1857.

**Mitchell** Nanny of Randwick married Ernest Herbert Grace, Surry Hills, CE, 1896.

**Mitchell** Richard of Bathurst, brother of William Mitchell per 'Earl Dalhousie' 1876.

**Mitchell** Robert marriet Harriet Westlake (both of Blayney) at Surry Hills, 1896.

**Mitchell** Sarah see Sarah Cocking.

**Mitchell** William Arthur married Sarah Anne Rowe, Parramatta, Wesleyan, 1885.

**Mitchell** William Charles married Elizabeth Jane Evans, Stanmore, Wesleyan, 1886.

**Mitchell** William married Winifred Frances Munro nee Hall, Sydney, Methodist, 1900.

**Moffatt** John per 'Plantaganet' 1857, married Rebecca Brown, Woolloomooloo, CE, 1862.

**Moloney** John married Elizabeth Brock nee Farmer, Surry Hills, CE, 1899.

**Moore** Mr of Liverpool, employed Mary Bray per 'William Metcalfe' 1844.

**Morcom** Frederick W A of Maitland 1860s+. Doris Black.

**Morcom** Frederick William A married Eliza Brown, Maitland, CE, 1861.

**Morcombe** Jane see Jane Snell.

**Morison** Henrietta married William Richards, Sydney, Presbyterian, 1894.

**Morley** Charles married Annie Scully (both of Mackay, QLD), Darlinghurst, CE, 1894.

**Morris** A Balranald 1859. Of Sydney 1888. AMM.

**Morris** Barbara married William Francis Hitchens, Newtown, 1882.

**Morris** Jane per 'Kate' 1859, states she has a brother on board (William Morris?).

**Morris** Thomas married Harriet Ann Bole, Marrickville, Wesleyan, 1886.

**Morris** William D of Castlereagh ST Sydney, brother of Grace Bryant, uncle of Elizabeth & Grace Bryant, all per 'St Lawrence' 1877.

**Morris** William per 'Kate' 1856, brother of Jane Morris aboard same ship?

**Morriss** George and Louisa, of Adelong 1880. NSW births.

**Mountcastle** Benjamin of North Shore, destination of Simon & Selina Jennings per 'Hornet' 1859.

**Mountrion** Frank married Mary Hore nee Parnell, Sydney, CE, 1888. Both of Shoalhaven.

**Moyle** Bridget married Richard Trudgeon of Adelong, Sydney, Wesleyan, 1865.

**Moyle** Charles T. M. died 1884 aged 48. Buried Rookwood Independent with Elizabeth Honor, Thomas and Elizabeth H. Moyle. SMH 2 August 1884.

**Moyle** Elizabeth H died 1926 aged 57. Buried Rookwood Independent with Charles T.M. Moyle.

**Moyle** Elizabeth Honor died 1896 aged 57. Buried Rookwood Independent with Charles T.M. Moyle. SMH 11 August 1896.

**Moyle** John of Wattle Flat, brother -in-law of Eliza Martin per 'Wallasea' 1865.

**Moyle** Nicholas Charles married Rebecca Hanford, Cobar, Wesleyan, 1876.

**Moyle** Thomas A. M. died 1919 aged 59. Buried Rookwood Independent with Charles T.M. Moyle.

**Moyse** Mary and William per 'William Turner' 1841, employed by Mr Currie of Currie Vale.

**Muir** Hilda Maria married William Henry Phillips of Muswellbrook, Surry Hills, CE, 1894.

**Mullin** Mary married Thomas Marks, Burwood, Wesleyan, 1881.

**Mullis** Jonathon died 1892, buried Rookwood Wesleyan.

**Mullis** Mary died 1904, buried Rookwood Wesleyan. Wife of Jonathon.

**Mumford** Thomas John married Elizabeth Ann Bridgewater, Surry Hills, CE, 1892.

**Munro** Winifred Frances nee Hall, married William Mitchell, Sydney, Methodist, 1900.

**Murley** Agnes married Alexander Allen (per 'Pericles' 1877?), Newcastle, CE, 1892.

**Murphy** Timothy near Adelaide, brother of William Murphy per 'Walmer Castle' 1848.

**Mutton** Edward Henry married Anne Palmer, Bathurst, 1862.

**Mutton** Mary Short married William Dargin, Bathurst, 1860.

**Mutton** Richard and wife Mary (nee Short and sister of Walter Short who arrived 1829), arrived 1827. Settled in Bathurst. Dave Short.

**Mutton** Richard and wife Mary nee Short, per 'Elizabeth' 1827. Settled in Bathurst. Peg Edgar.

**Nancarrow** Elizabeth Maud married Walter David Green, Surry Hills, CE, 1885.

**Nancarrow** George of Adelong, brother of William H. Nancarrow per 'Star of India' 1877.

**Nancarrow** Henry (per 'Equestrian' 1848) married Jane Burgess, West Maitland, Wesleyan, 1880.

**Nancarrow** Mrs E Waverley 1899. Methodist 11 March 1899.

**Nancarrow** R of Woolloomooloo, uncle of William & Richard Nancarrow, both per 'Earl Dalhousie' 1877.

**Nancarrow** Richard Merrifield of Woolloomooloo,

1888 aged 61. SMH 17 August 1888.

**Nancarrow** William Henry (per 'Equestrian' 1848) married Agnes Allison, West Maitland, Wesleyan, 1860.

**Nancarrow** William Henry and Lydia, of Adelong 1878. NSW births.

**Nancarrow** William married Clara Simpson, Bathurst, Methodist, 1909.

**Nance** Amy Grace death 1902, Petersham. Granddaughter of James Bennett. SMH 8 February 1902.

**Nance** Eliza (per 'William Metcalfe' 1844), married Edward Osborne Woolford, Macleay River, Wesleyan, 1866.

**Nance** family per 'William Metcalfe' taken into temporary employment by the government after 11 days on board.

**Nankarvis** John and Elizabeth, of Adelong 1881. NSW births.

**Nankevell** John and Elizabeth per 'Walmer Castle' 1848. Went to Molong until the mine closed and then to Moonta. James Nankivell.

**Nankivell** Edward of Broken Hill c.1900. James Nankivell.

**Nelson** Caroline Elizabeth married William Henry Rowe (per 'Hindustan' 1857), Macleay River, Wesleyan, 1870.

**Nemonitch** John married Christian Sampson, Murrurundi, Wesleyan, 1880.

**Nerkell?** Anna Maria see Anna Maria Thompson.

**Nettle** Amelia married James Bellamy, O'Connell Plains, 1859.

**Nettle** Amelia married Robert Bellamy, Bathurst, Wesleyan, 1857.

**Nettle** Elizabeth Jane married William Pretyman Petit, Bathurst, Wesleyan, 1856.

**Nettle** Hannah married Robert Bellamy, Bathurst, 1875.

**Nettle** John Henry married Josephine Alice Finch, Newcastle, CE, 1873.

**Neville** Thomas (adopted son of William Pearce) married Grace Williams, Bathurst, 1883.

**New** Ernest F married Charlotte Crego, Surry Hills, CE, 1892.

**Newport** Ellen died 1879 aged 7 months. Buried Rookwood CE with Thomas Newport.

**Newport** Mrs of Sydney, relative of Benjamin Bone per 'Samuel Plimsoll (1)' 1874.

**Newport** Mrs of Sydney, daughter of Elizabeth Bone per 'Samuel Plimsoll (1)' 1874. Relative of Mrs Rowe, Newcastle.

**Newport** Mrs of Sydney, relative of John & Mahala Ellis per 'Samuel Plimsoll (1)' 1874.

**Newport** Thomas died 1886 aged 38. Buried Rookwood CE with Ellen Newport & Elizabeth Eckardt. SMH 17 April 1886.

**Newton** Edward died Cobar aged 52, 1896, buried Cobar CE.

**Newton** Richard married Anna Maria Hawkins, Branxton, Methodist, 1903.

**Nial** James married Mary Ann Simmons, Maitland, CE, 1898.

**Nicholas** Augustus Francis of Redfern c. 1887. Robyn Singh.

**Nicholas** Eliza of Bathurst, sister of Richard Badcock per 'Earl Dalhousie' 1876.

**Nicholas** George Charles of Redfern c. 1887. Robyn Singh.

**Nicholas** James and Rebecca, of Adelong 1861. NSW births.

**Nicholas** William John and Mary Jane, of Gosford, c.1880+. Barry Ridge.

**Nicholas** William John married Clara Witten, West Maitland, Methodist, 1893.

**Nicholls** Edward John died Cobar aged 29, 1902. Buried Cobar Wesleyan.

**Nicholls** Edward near Bathurst, cousin of Elizabeth Retallack per 'Joseph Somes' 1852.

**Nicholls** Elizabeth Ann married George Eslick, Orange, Wesleyan, 1885.

**Nicholls** H Goldsmith of Paddington, aged 47, 1883. SMH 8 November 1883.

**Nicholls** Henry Goldsmith married Susanna Richards (per 'Bermondsey' 1856), Paddington, Wesleyan, 1862.

**Nicholls** Henry Goldsmith died 1883 aged 48. Buried Waverley CE with Susannah Nicholls.

**Nicholls** J died Cobar aged 61, 1900, buried Cobar Wesleyan.

**Nicholls** James married Mary Hall, Sydney, CE, 1892. Both of Robertson.

**Nicholls** James per 'Victoria' 1849, went to Orange. Pam Body, Merle Robinson, Mark Gordon.

**Nicholls** James married Mary Ann Tippett, Bathurst, 1883.

**Nicholls** John married Louise Harrison, Paddington, Wesleyan, 1888.

**Nicholls** Mary married Arthur Small of Cobar, Paddington, Wesleyan, 1898.

**Nicholls** Richard of Newcastle, brother of John Nicholls per 'Commonwealth' 1877.

**Nicholls** Richard of Royal Hotel Stores. Uncle of Frances Manuel per 'Tartar' 1857.

**Nicholls** Robert of Royal Hotel Stores. Uncle of Frances Manuel per 'Tartar' 1857.

**Nicholls** Sampson of Rouse Hill, aged 68, 1881. SMH 16 August 1881.

**Nicholls** Susannah died 1918 aged 75, buried Waverley CE with Henry G. Nicholls.

**Nicholls** Susannah wife of Henry Goldsmith Nicholls, of Paddington, 1918. SMH 26 August 1918.

**Nicholls** Thomas Yates died Cobar aged 30, 1882, buried Cobar Wesleyan.

**Nicholls** Thomas of Mt Hirst, husband of Catherine per 'Sandringham' 1864.

**Nicholls** William of Sydney. Hotel keeper, ex-miner. AMM.

**Nichols** Minnie married William Wheeler, Cobar, 1898.

**Niclan** Thomas married Caroline Dellacour, Surry Hills, CE, 1888.

**Nigglesworth** Jane nee Rowley, married Henry Casley, Gunnedah, 1880.

**Niness** Edwin died 1889 aged 20. Buried Rookwood CE with parents Joseph & Charlotte.

**Niness** Joseph (per 'Lady Ann' 1854) of Double Bay - Mr T. Gooth - brother of John Niness per 'Stebonheath' 1858.

**Niness** Joseph of Railway Place, Sydney, 1890. SMH 21 August 1890.

**Niness** Joseph (per 'Lady Ann' 1854) died 1890 aged 58. Buried Rookwood CE.

**Niness** Mary A, widow of John Crummy Niness, of Waterloo 1901. SMH 11 November 1901.

**Ninness** Charlotte died 1889 aged 50. Buried Rookwood CE with Joseph Niness.

**Ninniss** William Henry and Jane, of Adelong 1880. NSW births.

**Noakes** Frederick married Sarah Hocking, Leichhardt, Wesleyan, 1899.

**Norris** Eliza married Charles Burley (per 'Alfred' 1839), Allyn River, CE, 1864.

**Northey** Elizabeth Ann wife of Martin, died 1898 aged 51. Buried with Martin Northey, Waverley.

**Northey** Elizabeth (per 'Harriet' 1853) at Mrs Preddy, Castlereagh St, sister of James Northey & Susan Northey, daughter of Susan Northey all per 'Sultana' 1855.

**Northey** Elizabeth of Sydney, cousin of Elizabeth Dennis, per 'Sultana' 1855.

**Northey** Martin died 1928 aged 80. Buried with Elizabeth Ann Northey, Waverley.

**Northey** Mary married John Warren, Bathurst, 1867.

**Northey** Richard per 'Pericles' 1877, went to Bathurst and later to Lithgow,. BT 4 January 1928.
**Northey** Robert married Tabitha Jenkyns, Hill End, 1878.
**Northey** Robert per 'Lobelia' 1863, married Sarah Ann Wood, Bathurst, Wesleyan, 1899.
**Northey** Rosina married James Thomas Ison, Bathurst, 1867.
**Northey** William near Bathurst, brother of Robert Northey per 'Lobelia' 1863.
**Northey** William married Isabella Dawson, Kelso, 1885.
**Northey** William and Eliza nee Blamey & Trebilcock stepchildren per 'Harbinger' 1849. Went to Mt Pleasant, Bathurst. Connected with Blamey, Treneman, Rowe. Marjorie Jesse.
**Northey** per 'Harriet' 1853 and 'Sultana' 1855. Settled in Sydney. Robert Hay.
**Nute** Constance Emeline A married Jabez Bone, Rockdale, Methodist, 1902.

**Oak** Susan of Brougham Place, Sydney, cousin of Abraham Hicks per 'Herefordshire' 1857.
**Oates** Eliza daughter of William & Mary Thomas, all per 'Blundell' 1853.
**Oates** Emily sister of Joseph Oates, both per 'Herald' 1856.
**Oates** Florrie of Byng. Obituary 1899. Methodist 9 December 1899.
**Oates** John (per 'Blundell' 1853) brother of Thomas Oates per 'Fitzjames' 1858.
**Oates** Joseph brother of Emily Oates, both per 'Herald' 1856.
**Oates** Mrs Annie near Maitland, sister of Mary Pearce per 'Sultana' 1855.
**Oates** Thomas and Elizabeth nee Thomas, per 'Fitzjames' 1858. B.W. Thomas.
**Oates** Thomas married Elizabeth Thomas, Guyong, 1864.
**Oates** Thomas per 'Fitzjames' 1858. Anne Oates.
**Oates** Thomas of Sydney, brother of Emily & Joseph Oates, both per 'Herald' 1856.
**Oates** Thomas of Millthorpe, 1906. Methodist 21 September 1906.
**Oates** William of Orange, 1888. AMM.
**Oates** William (per 'Blundell' 1853) brother of Thomas Oates per 'Fitzjames' 1858.
**Oates** William and Eliza per 'Blundell' 1853. BW Thomas.
**Oates** of Orange. Four sons, blacksmiths & farmers, of Elizabeth Oates per 'Hornet' 1865.
**Oats** John and Jane, of Adelong 1874. NSW births.
**Oats** Richard of Bathurst? 1888. AMM.
**Oats** William and Jane, Adelong, 1874. NSW births.
**O'Brien** Ellen Carne married George Fortescue, Sydney, CE, 1865.
**O'Brien** William D P and Caroline Jane (Hynes nee Wellington) of Adelong 1880. NSW births.
**O'Connor** Margaret Bessie married Joseph May, Sydney, CE, 1892.
**Odgers** Arthur married Jane Elizabeth Holt, Newcastle, Primitive Methodist, 1900.
**Odgers** Mary Toni Martino.
**Odgers** William Henry married Annie Annis Lindsay, Minmi, Primitive Methodist, 1891.
**O'Hearn** Nancy see Ann James.
**Oldham** George William married Mary Ann Richards, Woollahra, Wesleyan, 1882.
**Olds** George G married Marie Annie Richardson, Sydney, Wesleyan, 1883.
**Olds** James of Sydney, brother-in-law of Thomas Jenkin per 'Shackamaxon' 1863.
**Oliver** Benjamin married Ellen Richards, Newcastle

Region Library.
**Oliver** John cousin of Philip Williams per 'Meteor' 1853.
**Oliver** John of Victoria, brother of Charles Oliver per 'Lord Stanley' 1850.
**Oliver** Thomas married Annie Alchin, Sydney, Wesleyan, 1883.
**Opie** James married Elizabeth Jane Mitchell, Sydney, CE, 1878.
**Opie** John died Cobar aged 54, 1907, buried Cobar Wesleyan.
**O'Reilly** Mary married James Pascoe, Sydney, Presbyterian, 1877.
**Organ** Francis of Melbourne, father of Nicholas Organ per 'Fitzjames' 1857.
**Osborne** Cyrus married Fanny Gray Bawden, Albury, Wesleyan, 1888.
**Osborne** George Octavius married Susan Barber, Albury, Wesleyan, 1872.
**Osborne** George married Sophie Hall, Newcastle, Methodist Free Church, 1884.
**Osborne** Henry married Mary Emblem (nee Parkins per 'Walter Morrice' 1849), Tamworth, Wesleyan, 1896.
**Osborne** John married Teresa Tucker, Bathurst, 1888.
**Osborne** Thomas Rawlings married Eugenie Stackhouse, Glebe, Wesleyan, 1875.
**Osler** Edward of Sydney, 1875. SMH 5 April 1875.
**Otter** Sarah married William Braddon Ward (per 'Kate' 1854), Sydney, CE, 1859.
**Ould** James of Melbourne, brother of Jane William per 'Thomas Arbuthnot' 1850. Also has cousin James Richards.

**Pacelle** Ferderiandine L married Archibald Jennings Carmichael, Surry Hills, CE, 1890.
**Paddison** Frances married William Chynoweth Kemp, Bathurst, 1879.
**Page** Charlotte married Samuel Wilmot (per 'Lady Elgin' 1854), Murrurundi, Congregational, 1865.
**Page** Edward of Sydney, brother of Eliza Reed per 'Walmer Castle' 1848. She is also sister of Henry Page per 'Rajasthan' 1855.
**Paine** Emily Jane married Frederick Parks, Hunter, CE, 1872.
**Painter** Francis of Turon, brother of Richard Painter per 'Washington Irving' 1857. Also brother of John Painter.
**Painter** Francis per 'Lady Ann' 1854, married Mary Tregonning, Newcastle, Wesleyan, 1857.
**Painter** John husband of Ellen & father of W. John Painter & brother of Richard Painter per 'Washington Irving' 1857. Also brother of Francis Painter per 'Lady Ann' 1854.
**Painter** John married Maude Hamilton, Lucknow? 1885.
**Palfrey** Mary see Mary Johnson.
**Palmer** Anne married Edward Henry Mutton, Bathurst, Wesleyan, 1862.
**Pankhurst** Henry died 1930 aged 63, buried Rutherford Methodist with Samuel Pankhurst.
**Pankhurst** Phillippa died 1941, buried Rutherford Methodist with Samuel Pankhurst.
**Pankhurst** Samuel died 1904 aged 62? buried Rutherford Methodist with wife Sarah & Henry & Phillippa Pankhurst.
**Pankhurst** Sarah died 1920 aged 76, buried Rutherford Methodist with Samuel Pankhurst.
**Parker** Elizabeth Jane married Rev Thomas Angwin, Bathurst, Wesleyan, 1859.
**Parker** John and Ann per 'Andromache' 1839. Settled in Parramatta. Grahame Thom.

**Parker** John (arrived 1838?) "of Parramatta, brother-in-law of James Cock per 'Sir George Seymour' 1852.

**Parkin** Elizabeth sister of Johanna Teague (nee Winsor) per 'Mary Pleasants' 1858. She also has sisters Alice Clark & Grace Francis.

**Parkin** of Bathurst & Nundle, per 'Walmer Castle' 1848 and 'Walter Morrice' 1849. Gwen Griffin.

**Parkins** Benjamin of Sydney, per 'Walmer Castle', brother of Samuel Parkins per 'Walter Morrice'. Also has a sister Phillipa Cox, Bathurst.

**Parkins** Mary see Mary Emblem.

**Parks** Frederick James married Emily Jane Paine, Hunter, CE, 1872.

**Parnell** Frederick George married Catharine Matilda Tippett, Sunny Corner, Wesleyan, 1890.

**Parnell** Mary see Mary Hore.

**Parslow** Henry Ayers married Elizabeth Mary Couch, Molong, 1893.

**Parslow** John married Edith Jane Couch, Molong, 1887.

**Parslow** Mary E nee Couch, fourth daughter of G & W Couch, died 1897 aged 25. Buried Molong.

**Parsons** Mrs Selina said to be aboard 'Lady Kennaway', sister of Jane Gibbons per 'Waconsta' 1855.

**Pascoe** Annie (widow), married William Hocking, Bathurst, 1877.

**Pascoe** Charles (per 'Commonwealth' 1877) married Elizabeth Cavary, Redfern, CE, 1900.

**Pascoe** James married Mary O'Reilly, Sydney, Presbyterian, 1877.

**Pascoe** John of Melbourne, uncle of James Sims, per 'Trevelyan' 1877.

**Pascoe** John of Hill End, died c.1911. Leslie Thurling.

**Pascoe** John and Eliza, of Adelong 1862. NSW births.

**Pascoe** John died Adelong 1864 aged 25, buried Adelong Wesleyan.

**Pascoe** Mark Wiles of Carcoar, brother of Miriam Sandry per 'La Hogue' 1877.

**Pascoe** Mark brother of Charles Pascoe per 'Commonwealth' 1877.

**Pascoe** Mary Anne married James Williams, Burrowa, Wesleyan, 1877.

**Pascoe** Mary Jane married Thomas Richard Edward Williams, Bathurst, 1886.

**Pascoe** Mrs Jane of Neville, death aged 103, 1910. BT 9 November 1910.

**Pascoe** Sampson of Neville, and Jenifer (nee Tom) and Pascoe/Saundry/Ellery relatives per 'Samuel Plimsoll', 'Earl Dalhousie' and 'Erato' all 1878. Trevor Pascoe.

**Pascoe** Thomas and Grace. Trevor Pascoe.

**Pascoe** William Henry married Charlotte Jones, Bathurst, Wesleyan, 1870.

**Pascoe** William Henry of Broken Hill, White Cliffs and South Australia. Arrived NSW 1891 via USA. Trevor Pascoe.

**Pascoe** William Thomas A married Catherine Diehm, Wellington, 1901.

**Pascoe** William married Mary Ann Plummer, Bathurst, 1870.

**Pascoe** William and Catherine, of Adelong 1865. NSW births.

**Pascoe** William and Elizabeth, of Adelong 1871. NSW births.

**Patten** Gideon married Ellen Jane Marks, Pennant Hills, Wesleyan, 1899.

**Pattinson** Hannah married David Jeffree Inch, Hill End, 1877.

**Paul** Alarina (per 'Garland' 1851) married Alfred Chate, 1855. NSW RG 1855 942 43

**Paul** Caroline married Thomas Cook, Woolloomooloo, Wesleyan, 1879.

**Paul** Elizabeth (per 'Garland' 1851) married John Maxell 1851. NSW RG 1851 218 80

**Paul** Elizabeth of Richmond, sister of Charles Walkom per 'Plantaganet' 1857. He also has a brother Jonathon Walkom, residence unknown.

**Paul** Emily Ann married James William Smith, Bathurst, 1878.

**Paul** Jane Hannah married Peter Furness, Bathurst, Wesleyan, 1860.

**Paul** Mr T of Petersham, formerly of Windsor. Brother of Samuel Paul of Bathurst. Death, 1895. Methodist 24 August 1895.

**Paul** Mrs of Bathurst, 1893. Methodist, 21 January 1893.

**Paul** Mrs of Bathurst, obituary 1893 BDT 5 & 6 January 1893.

**Paul** Priscilla married John Callaghan, Bathurst, Wesleyan, 1861.

**Paul** Samuel of Bathurst, death 1868. BT 16 May 1868.

**Paul** William Henry married Elizabeth Bray, Bathurst, Wesleyan, 1867.

**Paul** William James married Anna Maria Fayle, Sydney, Presbyterian, 1856.

**Paul** William married Ellen S. McAuliffe, Bathurst, Wesleyan, 1863.

**Paul** and Coad families, per 'Lord Eldon' 1838, 'Lady McNaughton' 1840 & 'Pattinson' 1838, went to Windsor & Bathurst. Allan Richards. Peter Procter.

**Paull** Martha nee Trezes, married Alexander F.H. Thompson, Surry Hills, CE, 1893.

**Paull** William and Mary Jane (Hitchens), 1869 Victoria. Went to Nundle and Tamworth. Eunice Traise.

**Pearce** Elizabeth per 'St Lawrence' 1877 is a niece of Henry Krouge of Lachlan. (Cobar connection?)

**Pearce** Emma Darlington married George Buckley, Cobar, Methodist, 1903.

**Pearce** Henry married Elizabeth Bennett, CE, Surry Hills, 1893.

**Pearce** James died Cobar aged 65, 1899, buried Cobar Wesleyan.

**Pearce** John of George St, Sydney, uncle of Richard Nicholas per 'Lady Ann' 1854.

**Pearce** John and Mary Ann per 'Sultana' 1856. Settled at Bathurst. Jean Wright.

**Pearce** Joseph of Hay. Police magistrate. 1896. Methodist 25 January 1896.

**Pearce** Mary Jane and children per 'Trevelyn' 1877, settled at Glebe. Maidee Smith.

**Pearce** Mrs of Hay, widow of late Mr J.E. Pearce, Police Magistrate. 1899. Methodist 14 October 1899.

**Pearce** Samuel died Cobar aged 77, 1899, buried Cobar Wesleyan.

**Pearce** Selina married Wilson Tyas, Ultimo, Primitive Methodist, 1884.

**Pearce** Thomas Henry married Isabella Rafelle, Cobar, Wesleyan, 1886.

**Pearce** William John married Annie Elizabeth Davies, Glebe, Wesleyan, 1883.

**Pearce** see Thomas Neville.

**Pearn** John married Elizabeth Campbell, Raymond Terrace, CE, 1856.

**Pearn** John married Elizabeth Campbell, Newcastle, CE, 1856.

**Pearse** Ann Agnes died 1863 aged 66. Buried Morpeth CE with John Pearse.

**Pearse** Elizabeth Bray married Thomas Stephens, Cornish Settlement, 1859.

**Pearse** Elizabeth died 1891, buried Morpeth CE with John & Ann Agnes Pearse.

**Pearse** Joanna Jane married Samuel Bray, Bathurst, 1844.

**Pearse** John died 1863 aged 67, buried Morpeth CE.

**Pearse** Thomas Sargeant married Jane Jones Wilkinson Lane, Cornish Settlement, 1866.

**Pearse** Thomas died 1885, son of John. Buried Morpeth CE with John Pearse.

**Pearse** William H married Sarah Todd, Paddington, Wesleyan, 1880.

**Pearse** William son of John & Ann Agnes, died 1849 aged 18, buried with parents Morpeth CE.

**Pearson** John Wilmot M married Elizabeth Ann Crouch, Parramatta, CE, 1889.

**Peat** John of Pyrmont, son of Charles Peat per 'Corona' 1877.

**Peil** Jane Mary died 1875 aged 58, buried Waverley CE with John Ninis Peil. SMH 10 April 1875.

**Peil** John Ninis died 1885 aged 73, buried Waverley CE, with Jane Mary Peil. SMH 26 May 1885.

**Peirce** Jane married Thomas Geake Lane, Cornish Settlement, 1866.

**Pellow** William of Sydney, brother of Thomas Pellow per 'Lady Elgin' 1854. States he has a sister in Sydney and brother John and family aboard 'Lady Elgin'.

**Pemmell** Rev J obituary 1910. Methodist 17 September 1910.

**Pendray** Frank married Mary Jane Cock, Bathust, 1867.

**Penfold** Rachel Rebecca married John Bennett, West Maitland, CE, 1880.

**Penglase** Henry of Newcastle, brother of Phillipa Penglase per 'Ida' 1864.

**Penglase** Henry and wife Elizabeth of Newcastle. Newcastle Region Library.

**Penglease** Philippa Newcastle Region Library.

**Penhall** Digory Ackerley and Susan, of Adelong 1874. NSW births.

**Penhall** Robert of Millthorpe, brother of William Penhall living Lumpy Swamp when William arrived 1878. Trevor Pascoe.

**Penhall** William and Ellen nee Berriman per 'Erato' 1878, of Millthorpe. Trevor Pascoe.

**Penney** Edward arrived Newcastle c.1860, went to Mudgee. Connections with Sandry. Vic Wilkinson.

**Penno** Alfred Edward married Rachel McFadden nee Barkle, Cobar, Methodist, 1906.

**Pepper** William Belville married Matilda Jewell White (nee Higman), Narranderah, Methodist, 1900.

**Perrett** Mary Ann nee Trew, married William Joseph Jenkyns of Hill End, Glebe, Wesleyan, 1884.

**Perry** Ada J married Edward Rapson, Newcastle, CE, 1876.

**Perry** Thomas son of Mary Bunney per 'Admiral Lyons' 1858 (both on board.)

**Perry** William says he is per 'Dunbar Castle' brother of Christina Hassett per 'Pericles' 1877.

**Peters** Jane per 'Abyssinian' 1862, married James Berryman of Adelong, Sydney, CE, 1862.

**Peters** Robert see Samuel Peters.

**Peters** Samuel, Thomas and Robert, all brothers of James Peters per 'Harbinger' 1849. He also has a sister, Catherine Martin, living in Adelaide.

**Peters** Thomas see Samuel Peters.

**Pethick** Martha per 'Herefordshire' 1857, married Thomas Wright, Maitland, CE, 1869.

**Petit** William Pretyman married Elizabeth Jane Nettle, Bathurst, Wesleyan, 1856.

**Philips** Hessy Jane married Thomas Hoskin of New Caledonia, Sydney, Congregational, 1883.

**Phillips** John married Martha Godfrey, Bathurst, Wesleyan, 1896.

**Phillips** John on board ship 'Albemarle' at Pot Phillip, is father of Mary Phillips per 'Malvina Vidal' 1853.

**Phillips** Laura died 1912. Buried Rookwood Wesleyan with Rev William & Lucy Kelynack & Philip W. Phillips.

**Phillips** Philip Wesley died 1919 aged 49, buried Rookwood Wesleyan with Rev William & Lucy Kelynack.

**Phillips** W H of Adelong, then Sydney, per 'Zemindar' 1857? AMM

**Phillips** W H produce merchant of Darlinghurst. Death of his father in Cornwall 1873. SMH 10 May

1873.

**Phillips** William Henry of Muswellbrook, married Hilda Maria Muir, Surry Hills, CE, 1894.

**Phillips** William J pioneer blacksmith of Sutherland, died 1927 aged 64. Buried Woronora CE.

**Phillips** William cabinetmaker of Sydney, cousin of John George per 'Victoria' 1849.

**Phillips** William died Adelong 1865 aged 32. Buried Adelong.

**Phillips** family per 'William Metcalfe' 1844, taken into temporary employment by the government after 11 days on board.

**Phoebe** Alice Ann married Nicholas Henry Winn, Lucknow, 1888.

**Pickering** George Felton married Elizabeth Whalan, Fish River, 1857.

**Pidwell** Rhoda per 'Lady Kennaway' 1841 employed by John Booth, innkeeper, Windsor Road.

**Pinch** George Arthur settled on NSW south coast 1879+ Valda Pinch.

**Piner** Francis of Middle Harbour, Sydney. Uncle of Reuben & George Harris per 'Northern Light' 1858. See Poyner.

**Pitt** Florence M see Florence M Killingsworth.

**Platt** Frances married John Lawrey, Sunnycorner, Wesleyan, 1890.

**Pleming?** Joseph A married Elizabeth Carlton Robertson, Albury, Methodist, 1903.

**Plint** George of Melbourne, father of Susan Datson per 'Wanata' 1864.

**Plummer** Grace nee Fleming, married Richard Gribble, Parramatta, Wesleyan, 1875.

**Plummer** Hannah Eva married William Richard Plummer, Hill End, 1875.

**Plummer** James and family per 'Plantaganet' 1857 to Bathurst and Hill End. Pat Sheriff.

**Plummer** John married Ann Maria Carkeek nee Eden, Hill End, 1877.

**Plummer** Mary Ann married William Pascoe, Bathurst, 1870.

**Plummer** Mrs M. A. (per 'Plantaganet' 1857) aged 90, 1912. Mother of Mrs Pascoe of Bathurst. BT 27 January 1912.

**Plummer** Mrs of Manning River 1898. Methodist 12 & 26 November 1898.

**Plummer** William Richard married Hannah Eva Plummer, Hill End, 1875.

**Plummer** William married Priscilla Edith Everingham, Hill End, 1873.

**Plummer** William and Grace, of Bathurst, parents of James Plummer per 'Plantaganet' 1857.

**Plummer** brother of William Plummer per 'Walter Morrice' 1849.

**Polglase** William John married Harriet Collins, Cobar, Wesleyan, 1880.

**Polglase** of Sydney, brother of Joseph Polglase per 'Ascendant' 1858.

**Pollard** Caroline widow, mother of Christopher Pollard, both per 'Salisbury' 1877.

**Pollard** Christopher son of Caroline Pollard, both per 'Salisbury' 1877.

**Pollard** Lily married Samuel Searston, Newcastle, CE, 1885.

**Pollard** Woodman married Harriet Dorcas Reeves, West Maitland, Wesleyan, 1889.

**Pollard** of Melbourne, brother of Thomas Pollard per 'Gloriana' 1855.

**Pomroy** William Osborne married Josepha Wesley, Vegetable Creek, Wesleyan, 1875.

**Ponsonby** Emily nee Martin, married William Stevens, Bathurst, 1882.

**Pool** John of Tambaroora? brother of William Pool per 'Ninevah' 1877.

**Pool/e** John of Sydney, brother of James Pool per 'Lady Ann' 1854.

**Poole** Mary Jane married Thomas Faull, Sydney, CE,

1885.
**Pooley** John  per 'Trevelyan' 1877 went to Bathurst.
**Pope** James  per 'Trevelyan' 1877 went to Warrah.
**Pope** Jane  see Jane Trewartha.
**Pope** Rev John Wright died 1892 aged 33, buried Waverley CE.
**Poppins** Eliza  married John Cranstone, Bathurst, 1841.
**Porton** Joseph Christopher married Mabel Grace Trounce, Wellington, Methodist, 1902.
**Potter** George  married Mary Richards (per 'Ellenborough' 1853) nee Jose, Newcastle, CE, 1873.
**Powell** Mary Ann died Adelong 1881 aged 42, buried Adelong CE.
**Powell** Mary  married Thomas John Johns, Adamstown, Wesleyan, 1891.
**Powell** William Henry of Adelong, married Mary Ann Hosking, Sydney, CE, 1862.
**Powell** William Henry and Mary Ann, of Adelong 1872. NSW births.
**Powley** Henry  married Sarah Ann Hicks, Canobolas, 1887.
**Poyner** Francis  general dealer of Surry Hills, uncle of Louisa & Celia Harris per 'Northern Light' 1858.
**Poyner**  per 'Orient' 1839. Robert Sutton.
**Price** Jane  married Vernal Hobley, Crookwell?, 1881.
**Priest** George  of Melbourne, uncle of Eliza/beth Glinn/Glynn per 'Sultana' 1855.
**Priest** Phillip  of Melbourne, uncle of Eliza/beth Glinn/Glynn per 'Sultana' 1855.
**Prior** James  married Mary Taylor, Albury, Wesleyan,. 1882.
**Prisk** Christian  see Christian Sampson.
**Prisk** John  (per 'Zemindar' 1857) of Hanging Rock, married Mary Banfield, East Maitland, CE, 1860.
**Prisk** Paul  of Hanging Rock, brother of John Prisk per 'Zemindar' 1857.
**Prisk** Paul  and Mary, of Nundle. Anne Massey.
**Prisk**  to Bathurst & Nundle. Gwen Griffin.
**Pritchard** Lewis  married Sara Cramp, Grafton, Wesleyan, 1868.
**Prout** Richard  married Alice Mary Curnow, Bathurst, Wesleyan, 1885.
**Prowse** James  of Adelong. AMM.
**Prowse** James  and Mary Ann, of Adelong 1865. NSW births.
**Prowse** John  of Adelong Reefs, husband of Matilda, father of Mary & Levinia all per 'Himalaya' 1865.
**Prowse** John  and Matilda, of Adelong. John is uncle of Thomas G. Williams and Matilda is sister of Thomas H. Williams, all per 'Commonwealth' 1877.
**Prowse** John  died Adelong 1879 aged 45, buried Adelong Wesleyan.
**Prowse** John  and Matilda, of Adelong 1875. NSW births.
**Prowse** Lavinia  married Thomas Trudgeon, Adelong, Wesleyan, 1875.
**Prowse** Mary Giles married John Jeffrey, Adelong, Wesleyan, 1878.
**Prowse** Richard  married Matilda Jane Quarmby, Adelong, Wesleyan, 1876.
**Prowse** Richard  and Matilda Jane, of Adelong 1877. NSW births.
**Prowse** family. Irwin Prowse.
**Pryor** Charity Jane married Albert Barden, Cooks River, CE, 1885.
**Pryor** Martha Ann married John Henry Cock Roberts, Plattsburg, Primitive Methodist, 1898.
**Pryor** Richard  per 'Lady Elgin' 1854 of Bathurst and Chewton (Victoria). Joan Brown.

## Q

**Qualming** Mary  married Matthew Quinter, Molong, 1878.

**Quarmby** Matilda Jane married Richard Prowse, Adelong, Wesleyan, 1876.
**Quine** Edward John married Edna Bourne nee Truscott, Surry Hills, Primitive Methodist, 1891.
**Quinter** Matthew  married Mary Qualming, Molong, 1878.

## R

**Raffelle** Isabella  married Thomas Henry Pearce, Cobar, Wesleyan, 1886.
**Randell** Grace  married Absolom Gartrell, Bathurst, 1888.
**Randle** James  of Rushcutters Bay, funeral 1864. SMH 26 May 1864.
**Randle** James  Williams died 1864 aged 33, buried Camperdown CE.
**Rapson** Edward  married Ada Jane Perry, Newcastle, CE, 1876.
**Rapson** Sampson  of Dungog, per 'Tory' 1849. Newcastle Region Library.
**Rapson** Sampson  of Paterson River, brother of Susan Watts per 'Kate' 1856.
**Rapson** Susan  see Joiner.
**Rashleigh** John  per 'Lady Ann' 1854, cousin of William James per 'Rajasthan' 1855.
**Rashleigh** William  cousin of William James per 'Rajasthan' 1855.
**Rashleigh** William  of Camperdown, brother of John Rashleigh per 'Lady Ann' 1854.
**Raymont** Elizabeth  married William James of Springhurst Victoria, Kogarah, Wesleyan, 1900.
**Read** Albert  married Agnes Anderson, Sydney, CE, 1893.
**Read** Sophie  see Sophie Hall.
**Read** Thomas  of Sussex St, Sydney, uncle of John Woodgate per 'Abyssinian' 1859.
**Readett** Mary Elizabeth died 1883, buried Morpeth CE. Sister of W.C. Dangar.
**Reed** Mrs  of Bathurst, sister of Henry Page per 'Rajasthan' 1855.
**Reed** Thomas  and Susan (Woodgate) per 'Robert Small' 1856. Went to Bathurst, Blayney, Araluen. Kenneth Plumb.
**Reed** William  of Bathurst c.1895. L.B. Galbraith.
**Reedy** John  married Mary Jane Teague (per 'Mary Pleasants' 1858), Macleay River, Wesleyan, 1860.
**Reeves** Harriet Dorcas married Woodman Pollard, West Maitland, Methodist, 1889.
**Reid** Alice  married John Boundy (per 'Ascendant' 1858), Newcastle, CE, 1861.
**Reid** Susan  of Sydney, name given as a friend of John Rickard & William Hobbs, both per 'Dirigo' 1860.
**Reilly** Kate  married Edward Rickard (both of Tamworth), Sydney, CE, 1881.
**Rens** George  married Annie B. Costelloe, Sydney, CE, 1890. Both of Temora.
**Rescorl** Emily  married Nicholas Stick (of Newcastle) at Glebe, Wesleyan, 1894.
**Reylin** Louisa  married John White, Adelong, 1877.
**Reynolds** Richard  of Sussex St, Sydney, husband of Mary A Reynolds and father of Mary Martha, both per 'Samuel Plimsoll' 1877.
**Rhodes** Charles  married Lavinia Dumble, Sydney, CE, 1885.
**Richards** Amelia  married Thomas Carthew, Orange, 1863.
**Richards** Ann  wife of James, Died 1903 aged 83. Buried Rookwood Wesleyan.
**Richards** Ann  of NSW. Sister of Stephen Glasson per 'Herefordshire' 1857.
**Richards** Ann  of Norton St, Surry Hills, sister of William Thomas Datson per 'Wanata' 1864.
**Richards** Ann  of Surry Hills, aged 84, 1903. SMH 24 August 1903.

**Richards** Arthur P married Mary Ann George (nee Dunstan), per 'Earl Dalhousie' 1877, Redfern, CE, 1891.

**Richards** Bartholomew and Thomas, carpenters of Paddington, relatives of James Johns per 'Bermondsey' 1856.

**Richards** Clara see Clara Richardson.

**Richards** Elizabeth married Samuel Rule, Cobar, Wesleyan, 1888.

**Richards** Ellen married Benjamin Oliver, Newcastle Region Library.

**Richards** Emma nee Hosking, relative of Mary Hosking, both per 'Dunbar Castle' 1872.

**Richards** George married Lily Cameron Hawthorne, Sydney, CE, 1895.

**Richards** Honour of Bathurst, cousin of Jane Evans per 'Joseph Somes' 1852.

**Richards** James died 1873 aged 52, buried Rookwood Wesleyan with wife Ann.

**Richards** James husband of Ann, Surry Hills, 1873. SMH 10 May 1873.

**Richards** James (name crossed out) brother of Edwin Richards per 'Ninevah' 1877.

**Richards** James cousin of Jane William nee Ould per 'Thomas Arbuthnot' 1850. She also has a brother James Ould in Melbourne.

**Richards** James of Bathurst, uncle of James & Henry Harry, both per 'Zemindar' 1857.

**Richards** James per 'Bolton', brother of Richard Richards per 'Ellenborough' 1853.

**Richards** James died Cobar aged 64, 1903. Buried Cobar Wesleyan.

**Richards** Jane died 1899 aged 94. Buried Rookwood Wesleyan with husband Thomas. SMH 24 November 1899.

**Richards** John of Mt Pleasant, brother of Samuel Richards per 'Washington Irving' 1857.

**Richards** John blacksmith of Carcoar, died 1866. Topsy Motten.

**Richards** John of Spring Grove, Bathurst. Brother of William Richards, uncle of Emily, Helen & Thomas H. Richards, all per 'Ninevah' 1876.

**Richards** John of Spring Grove, Bathurst, uncle of Bessie & Jane Richards per 'Ninevah' 1876.

**Richards** John of Bathurst, first cousin of Samuel Hammond per 'Plantaganet' 1857.

**Richards** Joseph Henry married Margaret Spiker, Albury, Wesleyan, 1882.

**Richards** Maria married George William Hill, Surry Hills, CE, 1896.

**Richards** Mary Ann married George William Oldham, Woollahra, Wesleyan, 1882.

**Richards** Mary nee Jose, married George Potter, Newcastle, CE, 1873.

**Richards** Simon of Singleton, (per 'Lady Ann' 1854). Kingsley Richards.

**Richards** Susanna per 'Bermondsey' 1856, married Henry Goldsmith Nicholls, Paddington, Wesleyan, 1862.

**Richards** Thomas died 1878, buried Rookwood.

**Richards** Thomas near Bathurst, farmer, brother of Henry Richards per 'Joseph Somes' 1852.

**Richards** Thomas of Paddington, husband of Jane Richards per 'Bermondsey' 1856. She complained about Surgeon's treatment of her son Henry.

**Richards** Thomas of Paddington, 1878. SMH 30 January 1878.

**Richards** Thomas farmer, of Guyong. BW Thomas.

**Richards** Thomas of Guyong, 1888. AMM.

**Richards** Thomas married Mary Ann Thomas, Guyong, Wesleyan, 1858.

**Richards** Thomas of Paddington, brother of Eliza Richards per 'Bermondsey' 1856.

**Richards** Thomas of Paddington. See Bartholomew Richards.

**Richards** William H per 'Queen of the East' 1864 went to J. Matthews at Berrima.

**Richards** William per 'Bolton', brother of Richard Richards per 'Ellenborough' 1853.

**Richards** William married Henrietta Morison, Sydney, Presbyterian, 1894.

**Richards** William relative of Edwin Richards per 'Tyburnia' 1874.

**Richards** of Sydney, brother of Charles Richards per 'Earl Dalhousie' 1877.

**Richardson** Clara nee Richards, married Cuthbert Gibbons, Hamilton, Methodist, 1900.

**Richardson** Marie Annie married George Gelbert Olds, Sydney, Wesleyan, 1883.

**Richardson** Thomas married Mary Jane Wanten, Balmain, Wesleyan, 1879.

**Rickard** Charles married Julia Mary Hooper, Orange, 1879.

**Rickard** Edward married Kate Reilly (both of Tamworth), Sydney, CE, 1881.

**Rickard** Henry died Cobar aged 45, 1897, buried Cobar Wesleyan.

**Rickard** Henry married Miriam Driscoll, Cobar, Wesleyan, 1884.

**Rickard** John per 'Dirigo' 1860 went to friend Susan Reid in Sydney.

**Riddell** George Charles married Alice Jane Wathers, Surry Hills, CE, 1881.

**Riley** Mary married George Best (per 'Sea' 1849), Cooks River, Congregational, 1879.

**Rixon** Caroline Matilda married John Gartrell Thomas, Darlington. Primitive Methodist, 1899.

**Roach** John married Mary Ann Clifton, Ultimo, Primitive Methodist, 1885.

**Roach** John of Adelong Reefs, husband of Mary E. Roach per 'Ninevah' 1877.

**Roach** John and Mary Eddy of Adelong 1878. NSW births.

**Robards** Martha married Joseph Sloggett, Orange, Wesleyan, 1856.

**Robert** Susan sister of James Bartle, both per 'Samuel Plimsoll' 1877.

**Roberts** Betsey of Adelaide, relative of Mary Trenemon per 'Harbinger' 1849.

**Roberts** H of Crown St, Sydney, employed Phillipa Jennings per 'Hornet' 1859.

**Roberts** John Henry Cock married Martha Ann Pryor, Newcastle, Primitive Methodist, 1898.

**Roberts** John of Lucknow, per 'Plantaganet' 1857. Chris Wright.

**Roberts** John died Merewether 1928 aged 72, buried Newcastle.

**Roberts** John of Camden, cousin of Phillip Roberts per 'Castillian' 1858.

**Roberts** Joseph Edwin married Sarah Jane Brooking, Cobar, Methodist, 1905.

**Roberts** Philip butcher & restaurant keeper of Redfern. Per 'Castillian' 1858? AMM.

**Roberts** Richard married Ellen Daly, both of Dapto, at Redfern United Free Methodist, 1898.

**Roberts** Thomas and Susan of Adelong 1876. NSW births.

**Roberts** William married Elizabeth Goldsworthy nee Andrew, Sydney, Presbyterian, 1878.

**Roberts** William of Peel River, brother of Francis Roberts per 'Samuel Plimsoll' 1876.

**Roberts** of Sydney 1788+ Robert Sutton.

**Robertson** Elizabeth Carlton married Joseph A. F/Pleming, Albury, 1903.

**Robertson** Elizabeth nee Hosking, married John Jenkin (both of Carlingford), Sydney, CE, 1898.

**Robey** Annie Emma married William Thomas Foster, Glebe, Wesleyan, 1897.

**Robins** John and Amelia of Adelong 1874. NSW births.

**Robins** John married Amelia George, Adelong, CE, 1873.

**Robins** Mary died Adelong 1881 aged 58, buried Adelong Wesleyan.

**Robins** Nicholas married Lucy Tanswell, Adelong, Wesleyan, 1877.

**Robins** Nicholas and Lucy (Tanswell) of Adelong 1878. NSW births.

**Robins** Thomas married Sarah Tanswell, Adelong, Wesleyan, 1874.

**Robins** Thomas and Sarah (Tanswell) of Adelong 1879. NSW births.

**Robins** Thomas married Sarah Tanswell, Adelong, Wesleyan, 1874.

**Robyns** Mary Ann married John Cornish, Adelong, Wesleyan, 1874.

**Rodd** B C solicitor, aged 80, 1898. SMH 28 November 1898.

**Rodd** Brent Clements died 1898 aged 88, buried Rookwood CE.

**Rodd** Trebartha B died 1883 aged 1. Buried Rookwood CE with Brent Clements Rodd. SMH 4 December 1883.

**Rodda** Richard of Adelong, husband of Margaret, father of Mary Ellen, Richard & Thomasine, all per 'Light Brigade' 1867.

**Rodda** Richard married Mary Ann Heather, Adelong, CE, 1876.

**Rodda** Richard and Mary Ann of Adelong 1876. NSW births.

**Rodda** Thomasine Thomas married Richard Henry Rowe, Adelong, Wesleyan, 1871.

**Rodgers** Thomas married Mary Ann Fitzsimmons, Orange, 1883.

**Rogers** Bessie married Edward F. Connor, Darlinghurst, CE, 1890.

**Rogers** Charles married Mary Ann Haydon, Armidale, Wesleyan, 1878.

**Rogers** James married Susan Jenkins, Armidale, Wesleyan, 1896.

**Rogers** John Major married Catherine Williams, Albury, Wesleyan, 1888.

**Rogers** Joseph of Bathurst. V.L. Nicholson.

**Rogers** Mary A alias Whatson, per 'Dunbar Castle' 1871, employed by Mr Henry Joseph of George St, Sydney.

**Rogers** Richard and Elizabeth of Adelong 1877. NSW births.

**Rogers** Walter James Paull married Mary Smith nee Hampton, Petersham Congregational, 1881.

**Rogers** William Charles married Ann Hennessy, Sydney, Presbyterian, 1856.

**Rogers** of Adelaide, brother & sister of John Rogers per 'Thomas Arbuthnot' 1849.

**Rooke** Henry and Mary (White) of Adelong 1878. NSW births.

**Rosewarne** William son of Jane Rosewarne per 'Julindar' 1849.

**Ross** James married Eliza George, Orange, Wesleyan, 1885.

**Ross** Margaret married Samuel Toye, Redfern, CE, 1900.

**Rossiter** Edward per 'Rajasthan' 1855, brother of Walter Rossiter per 'Lady Ann' 1854.

**Rossiter** Henry of Pitt St, Sydney, husband of Eliza, father of Eliza, Emily, Walter & William, all per 'Coldstream' 1863.

**Rossiter** Walter per 'Lady Ann', brother of Edward Rossiter per 'Rajasthan' 1855.

**Row** Mary per 'Mangerton' 1855 is under engagement to Robert Lean (of Bathurst?)

**Rowe** Annie nee Lister, of Guyong 1906. Methodist 24 August 1906.

**Rowe** Colonel Thomas of Darling Point, aged 60, 1899. SMH 21 January 1899.

**Rowe** Elizabeth married James Greive Searle, Orange, 1893.

**Rowe** Ellen married Walter William Bolt (per 'Dunbar Castle' 1877), Kempsey, Wesleyan, 1880.

**Rowe** Emily per 'Hindostan' 1857, married John H. Seccomb, Kempsey, Wesleyan, 1872.

**Rowe** Henry of Surry Hills 1877. SMH 7 June 1877.

**Rowe** Henry died 1877 aged 28, buried Rookwood CE.

**Rowe** Henry of Princes St (Newcastle?), uncle of Elizabeth Bone per 'Northern Light' 1858.

**Rowe** James married Sarah Clyde, Sydney, Presbyterian, 1870.

**Rowe** Jane Thomas married Hugh Hector Judge, Armidale, Wesleyan, 1893.

**Rowe** John and Mary of Adelong 1874. NSW births.

**Rowe** John died Adelong 1887 aged 41, buried Adelong CE. Husband of Mary.

**Rowe** John married Mary Killalea, Adelong, 1873.

**Rowe** Lt Colonel of Darling Point, architect, Mayor of Manly. Per 'Steadfast' 1849. AMM.

**Rowe** Margaret Sargent of Bathurst, aged 76, 1890. Relict of William Rowe of Guyong, sister of Mrs Samuel Bray, Bathurst. BT & NA 15 August 1890.

**Rowe** Mignonette Mary married James Thomas Bromley, Hillgrove, Wesleyan, 1891.

**Rowe** Mrs of Newcastle, sister of Elizabeth Bone per 'Samuel Plimsoll (1)' 1874. She also has a daughter, Mrs Newport, in Sydney.

**Rowe** Rebecca married Joseph Warne, Newcastle, CE, 1859.

**Rowe** Rebecca married George Hawke, Cornish Settlement, 1863.

**Rowe** Richard H and Thomasine Thomas (Rodda) of Adelong 1872. NSW births.

**Rowe** Richard Henry married Thomasine Thomas Rodda, Adelong, Wesleyan, 1871.

**Rowe** Richard per 'Lady Ann' 1854, married Margaret Marshall, Sydney, Presbyterian, 1861.

**Rowe** Richard and children per 'Steadfast' 1849. Settled in Sydney. N. Rowe Best.

**Rowe** Richard per 'Steadfast' 1849, died 1853 aged 56. Buried Sydney Burial Ground, Wesleyan, with Clara Lockyer.

**Rowe** Sarah Anne married William Arthur Mitchell, Parramatta, Wesleyan, 1885.

**Rowe** Thomas and Mary (Downing) per 'Enmore' 1843, went to Liverpool and Marulan. L. Meeth.

**Rowe** Thomas married Harriet Frances Landers, Macleay River, Wesleyan, 1869.

**Rowe** Thomas at Macleay River, uncle of Thomas Rowe per 'Fitzjames' 1858.

**Rowe** Thomas at Macleay River, uncle of John Rowe per 'Samuel Plimsoll' 1877.

**Rowe** Walter cousin of John Albert Arthur per 'Salisbury' 1877. He has another cousin, Edward Williams.

**Rowe** William Green of Waratah, Newcastle, 1870+ Dennis Rowe.

**Rowe** William H of Cargo 1900. Methodist 20 January 1900.

**Rowe** William Henry (per 'Hindostan' 1857) married Caroline Elizabeth Nelson, Macleay River, Wesleyan 1870.

**Rowe** William Henry of Paddington, aged 50, 1911. SMH 11 September 1911.

**Rowe** William Henry married Susan Wadsworth Ashworth, Bathurst, 1864.

**Rowe** William Henry husband of Susan Wadsworth Rowe, died 1891 aged 50. Buried Waverley.

**Rowe** William Henshaw married Annie Caroline Lister, Guyong, 1865.

**Rowe** William James married Charlotte Anne Bristier, Sydney, Presbyterian, 1864.

**Rowe** William per 'Florentia' 1838, went to Mt Pleasant, Bathurst. Marjorie Jesse.

**Rowett** Emma wife of William of Manly, 1888. SMH 22 October 1888.

**Rowett** William died 1899 aged 75, buried Waverley.

**Rowett** William of Manly 1890. SMH 20 January 1890.

**Rowlandson** Jessie Sarah married Richard Francis Thomas, Adelong, Wesleyan, 1875.

**Rowles** Elizabeth nee Hobbs, married William Bray, Cooks River, CE, 1859.

**Rowley** Jane see Jane Nigglesworth.

**Rowse** John brother of Joseph Rowse per 'Star of India' 1876.

**Roylance** Ada nee Smith, married John Horrell, Orange, 1892.

**Rule** Emily married James Barron, Cobar, Wesleyan, 1886.

**Rule** James married Grace Davey (per 'Trevelyan' 1877), Cobar, Wesleyan, 1887.

**Rule** Samuel married Elizabeth Richards, Cobar, Wesleyan, 1888.

**Rule** Thomas Henry married Louise Jane Kendall, Cobar, Wesleyan, 1881.

**Rundle** Alfred married Elizabeth Jane Angove, Vegetable Creek, Wesleyan, 1881.

**Rundle** Mrs Elizabeth of Wallsend 1909. Methodist 7 August 1909.

**Rundle** William Henry married Mary Ann Jacobs, Surry Hills, Primitive Methodist, 1887.

# S

**Sackham** see Seccombe.

**Salls** Mrs near Sydney, sister of Mary Hurley per 'Samuel Plimsoll' 1874.

**Sampson** Catherine Joan married Charles Dennis, Chippendale, Wesleyan, 1874.

**Sampson** Christian nee Prisk, married John Nemonitch, Murrurundi, Wesleyan, 1880.

**Sampson** Rachel married Richard H. H. Treweeke, Surry Hills, CE, 1893.

**Sampson** Stephen died 1863 aged 29, buried Camperdown CE.

**Sampson** W H died 1881 aged 45, buried Murrurundi.

**Sampson** William Henry son of WH Sampson, died 1906 aged 45. Buried with father, Murrurundi.

**Sandiman** Mr employed Samuel & Isabella Avery per 'William Turner' 1841, at Clarence River.

**Sandoe** Alexander Dingle married Annie Margaret Abrahams, Sydney, CE, 1891.

**Sandry** John married Elizabeth Burton, Bathurst, 1879.

**Sandry** Richard married Sarah Elizabeth Dawson, Bathurst, 1876.

**Sandry** Thomas married Mary Ann Gardner Hawker, Singleton, 1884.

**Sandry** William per 'Fitzjames' 1857, of Mudgee. Vic Wilkinson.

**Sanguinetto** Francis married Jane Trewartha, Stroud, CE, 1897.

**Sara** Mary Louise married Thomas Brown, Bathurst, Wesleyan, 1856.

**Sara** William cousin of John Sara per 'Sultana' 1855.

**Sara?** Martin cousin of Alfred Sara per 'Fitzjames' 1857.

**Sara?** Nicholas cousin of Alfred Sara per 'Fitzjames' 1857.

**Sara?** William cousin of Alfred Sara per 'Fitzjames' 1857.

**Sargeant** Arthur James married Fanny Lavers, Redfern, CE, 1900.

**Saundry** Thomas and Phillipa (Thomas) per 'Herefordshire' 1857, to Bathurst. Lorna Stephens.

**Saundry** William brother of Thomas Saundry per 'Herefordshire' 1857. Also has an uncle Robert Taylor in Chippendale.

**Sawle** James Junior of Botany 1904. SMH 31 October 1904

**Sawle** James per 'Fitzjames' 1857, of Botany, dairy farmer, with his sons. AMM.

**Sawle** William Henry of Ryde 1906. SMH 22 February 1906.

**Saxby** Amos Richard married Emma Jane Hambly (per 'Forest Monarch' 1858), Botany, Wesleyan, 1868.

**Scott** Thomas Henry married Harriet Treneman, Bathurst, Wesleyan, 1874.

**Scott** Thomas Henry and Frances Caroline of Adelong 1878. NSW births.

**Scully** Annie married Charles Morley (both of Mackay, QLD) at Darlinghurst, CE, 1894.

**Searle** James Greive married Elizabeth Rowe, Orange, 1893.

**Searston** Samuel married Lily Pollard, Newcastle, CE, 1885.

**Seccomb** John H married Emily Rowe (per 'Hindustan' 1857), Kempsey, Wesleyan, 1872.

**Seccombe** Roger and Mary per 'William Metcalfe' 1844, employed by James Shepherd of Hen & Chicken Bay.

**Secomb** Sophia of Kempsey, died 1894. Methodist 29 December 1894.

**Secombe** Edward of Kempsey, leaving for Tamworth 1910. Methodist 30 July 1910.

**Secombe** James of Kempsey 1909. Methodist 26 June 1909.

**Secombe** Maude of Kempsey 1905. Methodist 4 February 1905.

**Secombe** Roger brother-in-law of Miles Berry per 'Sarah' 1849.

**Selby** Hannah died 1896 aged 79, buried Rookwood Wesleyan with John Selby.

**Selby** John died 1890 aged 78, buried Rookwood Wesleyan with wife Hannah. SMH 25 April 1890.

**Sellwood** William per 'Hannah More' 1860. Of Byng and Cadia. Phyllis Trevena.

**Sellwood** William of Lague near Orange, brother of Joseph Sellwood per 'St Hilda' 1865.

**Sharp** Joseph married Salome Chenoweth, Newtown, Wesleyan, 1895.

**Shepherd** James of Hen & Chicken Bay, employed Roger & Mary Seccombe per 'William Metcalfe' 1844.

**Shepparbottom** James married Catherine Williams, Cobar, Wesleyan, 1881.

**Sheppard** Louisa died Cobar aged 37, 1899, buried Cobar Wesleyan.

**Sheridan** James married Catherine Blake, Cornish Settlement, 1841.

**Shindler** Doris of Adelong 1870. NSW births.

**Short** Cecil James of Surry Hills, death aged 3 years, 1896. Methodist 1 August 1896.

**Short** Jane married Thomas Starr, Bathurst, Wesleyan, 1856.

**Short** Jane stepsister of Walter Short. Of White Rock, Bathurst. David Short.

**Short** John Andrew married Ann Selina Sloggett, Bathurst, Wesleyan 1856.

**Short** John Andrew married Elizabeth Townsend, Bathurst, 1899.

**Short** Joseph married Mary Anne Johnson nee Palfrey, Sydney, Presbyterian. 1870.

**Short** Mary Eliza nee Johnson, married Richard Sloggett, Bathurst, 1886.

**Short** Samuel and Jane, per 'Amelia Thompson' 1839, to Maitland and Grafton. Bonnie Bush.

**Short** Samuel (brother of Walter Short) and Agnes, per 'William Jardine' 1841. David Short and margaret Woods.

**Short** Thomas Wilkinson married Bessie Johns Trevena, Bathurst, 1874.

**Short** Walter per 'Elizabeth' 1829, to White Rock, Bathurst. David Short.

**Siberley** Susannah married Henry Fisk, Surry Hills, CE, 1872. Both of Coonabarabran.

**Silk** Isabella Ann married Charles Wesley Wearne (per 'Harbinger' 1849), Redfern, Wesleyan, 1870.

**Simcocks** Maria and Jane Martin, both per 'Lady Ann' 1854, appear to be related.

**Simmons** James married Martha Boyle, Grafton, Wesleyan, 1890.

**Simmons** Mary Ann married James Nial, Maitland, CE, 1898.

**Simpson** Clara married William Nancarrow, Bathurst, 1909.

**Sims** James and family per 'Trevelyan' 1877 went to Hill End.

**Sims** Richard of Gosford, brother of Elizabeth & Maria Sims, both per 'Garland' 1851.

**Sims** William per 'Trevelyan' 1877, went to Hill End.

**Sincock** Edward died 1889 aged 62. Buried Rookwood CE with wife Sarah. SMH 28 June 1889.

**Sincock** Sarah E wife of Edward. Died 1910 aged 75, buried Rookwood CE.

**Skewes** Samuel Jordan died Cobar aged 56, 1898, buried Cobar CE.

**Skinner** Elizabeth per 'Harriet' 1853, married James Hunter, Sydney, Presbyterian, 1856.

**Sleeman** Alfred Edwin married Sarah Anne Jones, Paterson, CE, 1858.

**Sleep** Catherine see Sloggett.

**Sleep** James Pauley of Crookwell 1909 aged 72. Methodist 26 June 1909.

**Sleep** James (per 'Tartar' 1857) of Cambewarrah, brother of Eliza Sleep per 'Samuel Plimsoll (2)' 1874.

**Sleep** William uncle of James Sleep per 'Tartar' 1857, and of Eliza Sleep per 'Samuel Plimsoll (2)' 1874.

**Sloggett** Ann Selina married John Andrew Short, White Rock Bathurst, Wesleyan, 1856.

**Sloggett** Catherine Jane married John Gunning, Bathurst, 1882.

**Sloggett** Elizabeth married John Lambert, Bathurst, 1877.

**Sloggett** Joseph and wife Catherine (nee Sleep) per 'Argyle' 1839, settled in Oberon. Jennifer Sloggett.

**Sloggett** Joseph married Martha Robards, Orange, Wesleyan, 1856.

**Sloggett** Richard married Mary Eliza Short nee Johnson, White Rock Bathurst, Wesleyan, 1886.

**Sloggett** Thomas per 'Argyle' 1839 with wife Catherine nee Sleep. P. Garnsey.

**Sloggett** William settled at Oberon. Jennifer Sloggett.

**Smaldon** Rossiter married Amelia George (nee Stephens), Sydney, Presbyterian, 1876.

**Small** Arthur of Cobar, married Mary Nicholls, Paddington, Wesleyan, 1898.

**Smith** Ada see Ada Roylance.

**Smith** Amy married Thomas Lorey Lutey, Burwood, Primitive Methodist, 1887.

**Smith** Edward Werren married Caroline Taylor, Minmi, Wesleyan, 1886.

**Smith** Eliza of Newcastle, sister-in-law of Edwin Richards per 'Abyssinian' 1859.

**Smith** Eliza married Samuel Beasley, Bathurst, 1841.

**Smith** Eliza married George Davis, Bathurst, 1841.

**Smith** Emma see Emma Taylor.

**Smith** Francis of Bathurst, uncle of William Thomas per 'Harbinger' 1849.

**Smith** Francis died near Dubbo 1887 (born 1818 St Keverne). B W Thomas

**Smith** Henry Lancelot married Jane Gidley Goodman, Cooks River, CE, 1862.

**Smith** James William married Emily Ann Paul, Bathurst, 1878.

**Smith** John Ballantyne married Mary Thomas, Albury, Wesleyan, 1880.

**Smith** John uncle of William Thomas per 'Harbinger' 1849.

**Smith** John of Gamboola, Molong. Brother of Francis & Robert. Died 1895, born 1811 St Keverne. BW Thomas.

**Smith** Mary nee Hampton, married Walter James Paull Rogers, Petersham, Congregational, 1881.

**Smith** Rev Thomas of St Barnabas, Glebe, employed Eliza Harris per 'Sabraon' 1870.

**Smith** Robert uncle of William Thomas per 'Harbinger' 1849.

**Smith** Robert per 'Florentia' 1838, died Bathurst 1851. Brother of John & Francis. BW Thomas.

**Smith** Sheldon and Ellen (Kemp) of Adelong 1863. NSW births.

**Smith** Thomas Henry and Mary Elizabeth (Grenfell) of Adelong 1884. NSW births.

**Smith** William Duncan and Elizabeth Ann (Powell) of Adelong 1865. NSW births.

**Smitham** Emma M died 1917 aged 75, buried Waverley. SMH 6 February 1917.

**Smitham** James of Pyrmont 1898. SMH 29 December 1898.

**Smitham** James died 1898 aged 55, buried Waverley with wife Emma.

**Sneesby** Emma Elizabeth married John Marshall Williams, Paddington, Wesleyan, 1896.

**Snell** Jane of Adelaide, mother of Elizabeth Pinsent per 'Emily' 1850.

**Snell** Jane per 'Maidstone' 1853 appears to be the sister of William Morcombe on the same ship.

**Snow** Catherine married John Pearce Spargo, Cobar, Wesleyan, 1882. Both of Girilambone.

**Snow** Samuel and Ellen, lived at Bathurst and Hillgrove. John Redman.

**Soady** Charles (per 'Earl Dalhousie' 1877) married Camellia Elene Bradford, Murrurundi, Wesleyan, 1883.

**Soars** Edward married Johanna Fitzgibbons, Summer Hill Bathurst, 1844.

**Solomon** William married Maria Wood, Merrylands, Wesleyan, 1884.

**Soper** Alice married Thomas Pascoe, buried Sandgate Newcastle. Trevor Pascoe.

**Soper** William of Redfern, brother of Elizabeth Butson per 'Ellenborough' 1853. She also has a sister Ann Miners in Redfern.

**Soper** William of Windsor, a relative of William Sutton per 'Australia' 1853. Another relative is Ann Manners (Miners?) of Windsor.

**Soper** of Redfern, brother of Thomas Soper per 'Lady Ann' 1854. He also has two sisters in the colony.

**Spargo** James Martin per 'Andromache' 1838, went to Penrith and Wellington. AMM

**Spargo** John Pearce married Catherine Snow, Cobar, Wesleyan, 1882. Both of Girilambone.

**Spencer** Edward married Mary Hodge, Muswellbrook, CE, 1888.

**Spencer** William married Susannah Hawke (per 'Conrad' 1841) , Maitland, CE, 1865.

**Spike** Ellen married Henry Hutchinson, Yass, Wesleyan, 1876.

**Spike?** William married Mary Catherine Touss?, Sydney, Wesleyan, 1873.

**Spiker** Margaret married Joseph Henry Richards, Albury, Wesleyan, 1882.

**Spooner** John married Grace Hocking (per 'Ninevah' 1877?), Forster, CE, 1890.

**Sprague** Thomas died Adelong 1896 aged 56, buried Adelong Wesleyan.

**Stacey** John married Eliza Jane Downing, Cobar, Wesleyan, 1881.

**Stackhouse** Eugenie married Thomas Rawlings Osborne, Glebe, Wesleyan, 1875.

**Stainer** Stephen married Mary Jones, Nowra, Wesleyan, 1895.

**Stanger** Elizabeth Barbara married Rev William Glasson, Bathurst, Wesleyan, 1876.

**Stanger** J C death in Bathurst aged 81, 1892. Methodist, 6 August 1892.

**Stanger** Lucy Ellen married Rev Richard Caldwell, Bathurst, Wesleyan, 1864.

**Stanger** Sarah married Arthur Budden, Bathurst, 1859.

**Stansfield** John married Martha Lord, Bathurst, 1843.
**Stanway** William Henry went to New Zealand c.1875. Helen Dyson.
**Star?** Mrs of Paterson, sister of Alfred Sleeman per 'Sarah' 1851.
**Starr** Mr T and Mrs of Bathurst, 1902. Methodist 17 May 1902.
**Starr** Thomas married Jane Short, Bathurst, 1856.
**Steer** Joseph of Carcoar, died 1911. H. Preston.
**Steer** Louisa daughter of Stephen & Maryann, buried Gresford 1883.
**Steer** Maryann Susannah died 1884, buried Gresford. Wife of Stephen.
**Steer** Stephen died 1890, buried Gresford.
**Stein?** Mrs see Mrs Star.
**Stephens** Amelia see Amelia George.
**Stephens** Ann married William Trezise, Bathurst, 1876.
**Stephens** Annie Maria married William Trenerry, Hill End, 1877.
**Stephens** Jane married John Tinney, Yass, Wesleyan, 1864.
**Stephens** John and Maria, near Broulee, parents of Anne Richards per 'Sultana' 1855. See John Stevens.
**Stephens** John brother of Thomas Stephens, both per 'Lady Ann' 1854.
**Stephens** Joseph married Elizabeth Colless, Emu Plains, CE, 1857.
**Stephens** Mary Ann married Nicholas Brewer (per 'Alfred' 1857), Morpeth, CE, 1858.
**Stephens** Thomas brother of John Stephens, both per 'Lady Ann' 1854.
**Stephens** Thomas married Elizabeth Bray Pearse, Cornish Settlement, 1859.
**Stephens** of Broulee, brother of James Stephens per 'Malvina Vidal' 1853. He also has a sister & brother-in-law elsewhere.
**Stevens** Catherine nee Merrin, married Edwin James Giles, Sydney, CE, 1892.
**Stevens** Frances Jane married Michael Dower (of Barraba), Paddington, Methodist, 1900.
**Stevens** James and Anne, parents of Zephania Stevens per 'Persia' 1856.
**Stevens** John near Broulee, brother-in-law of Anne Crapp per 'Australia' 1853.
**Stevens** Nancy died Adelong 1880 aged 33, buried Adelong Wesleyan.
**Stevens** Susanna married John Watts, Orange, 1867.
**Stevens** Thomas and Nancy of Adelong 1880. NSW births.
**Stevens** William married Emily Ponsonby (nee Martin), Bathurst, Wesleyan, 1882.
**Stick** James settled in Victoria. Jean Davies.
**Stick** Nicholas married Emily Rescorl, Glebe, 1894.
**Stodden** Nathaniel H died 1882, buried Rookwood Wesleyan. SMH 13 December 1882.
**Stokes** Jane Miller married Albert Hodge White, Balmain, Wesleyan, 1893.
**Stone** John of Bathurst, brother of Glanville Stone per 'Annie H Smith' 1877.
**Stoneman** James Warren and Mary A (nee Pascoe) per 'Lord Hungerford' 1855, settled in Redfern. Netta Stoneman.
**Stoneman** Thomas of Chippendale, brother of James Stoneman per 'Lord Hungerford' 1855.
**Strickland** Susannah married William John Truscott, Lithgow, 1883.
**Strongman** Benjamin of Petersham 1876. SMH 3 March 1876.
**Strongman** Caroline (per 'Samuel Plimsoll' 1874) married Edward Greaves, Sydney, Presbyterian, 1878.
**Strongman** Caroline of Sydney, sister of Ellen Hodge per 'Jerusalem' 1875. Her parents are said to be on board also.
**Strongman** John married Mary Blacker, Croydon Park, Wesleyan, 1885.

**Strongman** John at W. Barker Esq, Solicitor, Newcastle, brother of Mary Jane Rooke and son of Benjamin & Mary Strongman, all per 'Jerusalem' 1875.
**Strugnell** John married Elizabeth Lintern, Woollahra, Wesleyan, 1876.
**Stuart** Ellen married George Best (per 'Sea') 1849, Woolloomooloo, Wesleyan, 1860.
**Surridge** Ellen (nee Whalan) married John Burns, Bathurst, 1867.
**Sutton** Frederick married Sarah Birch, Bathurst, Wesleyan, 1863.
**Sutton** George and Matilda (Noble) per 'Petrel' 1849, went to Bathurst. Merle Bedwell, Dulcie Davies.
**Swan** William of Newcastle, husband of Mary Swan per 'Spitfire' 1863.
**Sweetman** Lavinia married James Haydon, West Maitland, CE, 1879.
**Sweetnam** Alfred James married Elizabeth Mary Kessell, Bathurst, Wesleyan, 1889.
**Sweetnam** Mary Anne married Joseph Glasson, Cornish Settlement, 1863.
**Swift** Alfred Stanhope` married Mary Eva Bray, Bathurst, Wesleyan, 1874.
**Syer** Thomas married Susan Martin, Bathurst, Wesleyan, 1869.

# T

**Tabb** Bessie Matilda Venning, married George Henry Dalley, Sydney, Wesleyan, 1881.
**Tangye** John Rogers married Sarah McAlister, Bathurst, Wesleyan, 1868.
**Tanswell** Lucy married Nicholas Robins, Adelong, Wesleyan, 1877.
**Tanswell** Sarah married Thomas Robins, Adelong, Wesleyan, 1874.
**Tarromina** Margaret of Surry Hills, sister of William Trethowan (aged 12, travelling with his mother) per 'Earl Dalhousie' 1877. Says his father Nicholas is living at Newtown.
**Tarvuig** James of Bathurst, married Sarah Ward, Surry Hills, CE, 1891.
**Taylor** Caroline married Edward Werren Smith, Minmi, Wesleyan, 1881.
**Taylor** Edward per 'Roxburgh Castle' 1836 settled at Sodwalls near Bathurst. Aileen Roberson.
**Taylor** Emma nee Smith married Derwent M Coleridge, Sydney, Congregational, 1879.
**Taylor** Hezekiah married Annie Maria Fardon, Adelong, Wesleyan, 1877.
**Taylor** Hezekiah died Cobar aged 47, 1898, buried Cobar Wesleyan.
**Taylor** Hezekiah and Annie Maria of Adelong 1877. NSW births.
**Taylor** Louisa married Frank Kent, Cobar, Wesleyan, 1890.
**Taylor** Mary Ann died 1872 aged 69, buried Rookwood Independent with Robert Taylor.
**Taylor** Mary married James Prior, Albury, Wesleyan, 1882.
**Taylor** Mary wife of Robert of Chippendale, funeral 1872. SMH 11 November 1872.
**Taylor** Robert per 'Andromache' 1839, of Chippendale, died 1878 aged 77. Buried Rookwood Independent. SMH 7 June 1878.
**Taylor** Robert per 'Andromache' 1839, coachbuilder of Chippendale. Margaret Watts.
**Taylor** Robert coachbuilder of Chippendale, uncle of Thomas Saundry per 'Herefordshire' 1857. He also has a brother, William Saundry.
**Taylor** Robert uncle of William Sandry per 'Fitzjames' 1857.
**Teague** Catherine (nee Keass?) married John James Everson, Surry Hills, CE, 1893.
**Teague** Charles married Alice Blacklock, Macleay

River, Wesleyan, 1873.

**Teague** Emily per 'Mary Pleasants' 1858, married William Jeffrey, Macleay River, Wesleyan, 1871.

**Teague** Mary Jane per 'Mary Pleasants' 1858, married John Reedy, Macleay River, Wesleyan, 1860.

**Tenby** James of Vegetable Creek, brother of Elizabeth Northey per 'Pericles' 1877.

**Terrell** Samuel and Rose Mary of Adelong 1873. NSW births.

**Thomas** Alfred John buried Gore Hill Methodist 1921.

**Thomas** Alfred John of Gordon, aged 58. SMH 17 January 1921.

**Thomas** Ambrose of Sydney, brother of Mary Bennett per 'Lord Hungerford' 1855.

**Thomas** Charles Henry of Surry Hills aged 67, 1893. SMH 24 October 1893.

**Thomas** Charles died 1893 aged 64, buried Waverley CE with Jane Gardner Thomas.

**Thomas** Eliza Hicks (per 'David McIvor' 1858) married William Henry May, Balmain, CE, 1863.

**Thomas** Eliza see Eliza Hawkins.

**Thomas** Eliza per 'David McIvor' 1858 went from the ship to an uncle in Sydney.

**Thomas** Elizabeth married Thomas Oates, Guyong, 1864.

**Thomas** Ellen married Joseph Dawe, Sydney, CE, 1887.

**Thomas** Francis of Guyong, per 'Blundell' 1853. BW Thomas.

**Thomas** Frederick John married Elizabeth Bryant (per St Lawrence' 1877) at Petersham, CE, 1886.

**Thomas** Henry of Marrickville 1910. Methodist 31 December 1910.

**Thomas** Henry brother of Eliza Oates and son of William & Mary Thomas all per 'Blundell' 1853.

**Thomas** Henry per 'Harbinger' 1849. BW Thomas.

**Thomas** Henry and Margaret of Adelong 1874. NSW births.

**Thomas** Isaac John married Mary Barrett Bryant, Fish River, 1856.

**Thomas** Isaac and family per 'Emma Eugenie' 1849, settled at Mutton Falls. Juanita Carroll.

**Thomas** Jane Gardner buried Waverley CE with husband Charles Thomas.

**Thomas** Jane of Guyong, per 'Blundell' 1853. BW Thomas.

**Thomas** John Arthur bush missionary, came to Hill End via NZ. Died 1895 aged 45. Methodist 9 November 1895.

**Thomas** John Frederick married Elizabeth Bryant, Petersham, CE, 1886.

**Thomas** John Gartrell married Caroline M Rixon, Darlington, Primitive Methodist, 1899.

**Thomas** John Rule per 'Blundell' 1853. BW Thomas.

**Thomas** John married Lydia Livermore, Redfern, United Free Methodist, 1898.

**Thomas** John married Mary Josephine Euler, Inverell, Wesleyan, 1880.

**Thomas** John married Mary Ann Manning, Hamilton, Wesleyan, 1892.

**Thomas** John married Margaret Hannah Ellis, Tambaroora, 1877.

**Thomas** John married Caroline Hicks, Orange, 1891.

**Thomas** Joseph married Jane Harris, Sunny Corner, Wesleyan, 1891.

**Thomas** Joseph married Elizabeth Downing, Cobar, Wesleyan, 1882.

**Thomas** Margaret Mary of Randwick, 1929. SMH 22 April 1929.

**Thomas** Margaret wife of Martin Thomas, buried with him at Waverley RC.

**Thomas** Martin of Randwick, 1920. SMH 21 October 1920.

**Thomas** Martin buried Waverley RC 1920 aged 80.

**Thomas** Mary Ann per 'Blundell' 1853. BW Thomas.

**Thomas** Mary Ann married Thomas Richards, Guyong, 1858.

**Thomas** Mary married John Ballantyne Smith, Albury, Wesleyan, 1880.

**Thomas** Mrs of Sydney, sister of Jane Parkin per 'Plantaganet' 1857.

**Thomas** Mrs Loana of Orange 1907. Methodist 28 September 1907.

**Thomas** Richard Francis married Jessie Sarah Rowlandson, Adelong, Wesleyan, 1875.

**Thomas** Richard Francis and Jessie Sarah of Adelong, 1878. NSW births.

**Thomas** Richard James married Lily Leavers, Cobar, Wesleyan, 1881.

**Thomas** Richard of Woolloomooloo, husband of Jane, father of Albert and Frederick per 'Stebonheath' 1858.

**Thomas** Richard of Sydney, publican, brother of John Thomas per 'Africana' 1866.

**Thomas** Stephen per 'Harbinger' 1849. Went to Victoria and South Australia. Eveline Madden.

**Thomas** Tamar married Henry Caddy, Hinton, Wesleyan, 1861.

**Thomas** Thomas per 'Lady Ann' 1854, nephew of James and Samuel George, both per 'Lady Elgin' 1854.

**Thomas** Thomas and Bridget of Adelong 1861. NSW births.

**Thomas** Thomasine per 'Blundell' 1853. BW Thomas.

**Thomas** William Evan married Rose Ann Brown, Surry Hills, CE, 1897.

**Thomas** William married Gertrude Margaret Brechin, Balmain, Wesleyan, 1880.

**Thomas** William brother of Eliza Oates and son of William & Mary Thomas all per 'Blundell' 1853.

**Thomas** William from South Australia to NSW 1856. A.T. Thomas.

**Thomas** William married Elizabeth Uren, Hill End, 1873.

**Thomas** William living with Dr Williams, uncle of John Williams per 'Bermondsey' 1855. He also has an aunt Phillipa in Riley St.

**Thomas** William per 'Harbinger' 1849. BW Thomas.

**Thomas** William and Mary (nee Coplin) per 'Blundell' 1853. BW Thomas.

**Thomas** William and Mary, parents of Eliza Oates, all per 'Blundell' 1853.

**Thomas** William cousin of James Eddy per 'Fairlie' 1863.

**Thomas** the married brother of William H Thomas per 'Malvina Vidal' 1853.

**Thomas** family of Sydney. A.T. Thomas.

**Thompson** Alexander F H married Martha Paull nee Trezes, Surry Hills, CE, 1893.

**Thompson** Anna Maria nee Nerkell? married Joseph Palmer Matthews, Sydney, CE, 1891.

**Thompson** James married Lucy Alford, Emmaville, Wesleyan, 1884.

**Thompson** Joseph married Selina Helen Webb, Bathurst, 1880.

**Thompson** Mary married Rowland Samuel Williams, Vegetable Creek, Wesleyan, 1878.

**Thompson** Sarah married Samuel Baker Hawke (per 'Conrad' 1841) at Wingham, CE, 1867.

**Threadgate** Rebecca married Richard Ellicott (per 'Sarah' 1849), West Maitland, Methodist, 1871.

**Thyer** Harvey married Clara Jackett, CE, Redfern, 1896.

**Tim** Ah married Jenny Maria Hilson Tippett, Tambaroora, 1874.

**Timmins** James of Melbourne, father of Edward Timmins per 'Golconda' 1857. He also has an aunt, Sarah Dent/Dunn? in Sydney. Edward is brother of William Timmins per 'Lady Ann' 1854.

**Timmins** Thomas Senior Surry Hills 1898. SMH 14 February 1898.

**Timmins** William per 'Lady Ann' 1854, brother of Edward Timmins per 'Golconda' 1857.

**Tinney** John married Jane Stephens (per 'Morning Star' 1864), Yass, Wesleyan, 1864.

**Tippett** Catherine M married Frederick G Parnell, Sunnycorner, Wesleyan, 1890.

**Tippett** Francis of Bathurst and Currawang. Edna Townsend.

**Tippett** George died Adelong 1879 aged 22. Buried Adelong CE.

**Tippett** Jenny Maria Hilson, married Ah Tim, Tambaroora, 1874.

**Tippett** Mary Ann married James Nicholls, Bathurst, 1883.

**Tippett** family of Victoria. Thelma Weston.

**Tippett** family per 'Hornet' 1859, employed by Thomas Harris of Parramatta.

**Todd** Sarah married William Henry Pearse, Paddington, Wesleyan, 1880.

**Tom** Henry married Emma Coleman, Cornish Settlement, 1859.

**Tom** William (Parson) of Byng, article 1911. Methodist 24 June 1911.

**Tom** William son of 'Parson' Tom. AMM

**Tom** William and Ann (Lane) of Byng. Pat Ruffels, Alan Lane, Selwyn Hawken, Peter Hohnen.

**Tom** William of Springfield. Death of an old resident. BDT 28 September 1883.

**Tonkin** Henry died 1934, Newcastle. Killed in a rock fall. NMH 18 September 1893.

**Tonkin** James of Adelaide, cousin of Jane Orchard per 'Emperor' 1848.

**Tonkin** James per 'Lady Ann' is brother of John Tonkin per 'Rajasthan' 1855.

**Tonkin** John per 'Rajasthan' 1855 is brother of James Tonkin per 'Lady Ann'.

**Tonking** John married Hannah Dutton, Adelong, Wesleyan, 1874.

**Tonking** John and Hannah of Adelong 1875. NSW births.

**Tonking** Mary Margaret married Abednego Uren, Adelong, Wesleyan, 1874.

**Touss?** Mary Catherine married William Spike?, Sydney, Wesleyan, 1873.

**Townsend** Albert Ernest married Evie Green, Annandale, 1898.

**Townsend** Elizabeth married John Andrew Short, Bathurst, 1899.

**Toye** Samuel married Margaret Ross, Redfern, CE, 1900.

**Trace** Ellen and James per 'Trevelyan' 1877 went to Morpeth.

**Trambath** see Trembath.

**Trathen** Mrs Susan of Orange, died 1893 aged 60. Methodist 5 August 1893.

**Trathen** Walter John married Georgiana Chapman, Kempsey, Primitive Methodist, 1879.

**Travis** family arrived in NSW c.1854 via South Australia and NZ. AT Thomas.

**Trebilcock** Elizabeth per 'Hawkesbury' 1871, employed by Mrs Elizabeth Davis of Bungarribee.

**Trebilcock** Elizabeth sister of Thomas Trebilcock, both per 'Hawkesbury' 1871.

**Trebilcock** John Blamey married Amelia Colley, Bathurst, Wesleyan, 1857.

**Trebilcock** Thomas brother of Elizabeth Trebilcock, both per 'Hawkesbury' 1871.

**Trebilcock** of Sydney? sister of William Trebilcock per 'Lord Hungerford' 1855. Says he has a brother in Sydney also.

**Trebilcock** of Sydney, brother of William Trebilcock per 'Lord Hungerford' 1855. Says he has a sister.

**Trebilcock** of Sydney, brother of Eliza Trebilcock per 'Florentia' 1853.

**Treblecock** Eliza Ann married Isaac Ison, Bathurst,

1879.

**Treblecock** Henrietta married Alfred Ison, Bathurst, 1883.

**Tredinnick** Clara married Nicholas John Dunstan, Ashfield, Wesleyan, 1896.

**Tredinnick** James and Susan Ann (Woolcock) arrived Sydney c.1871 via South Australia. Margaret Playford.

**Tredinnick** James died 1875 aged 46, buried Rookwood Wesleyan with Susan Ann Tredinnick.

**Tredinnick** John died 1888 aged 67, buried Rookwood Wesleyan with Maria Tredinnick.

**Tredinnick** Maria died 1885 aged 62, buried Rookwood Wesleyan with John Tredinnick. SMH 22 May 1885.

**Tredinnick** Susan Ann died 1888, aged 50, buried Rookwood Wesleyan with James Tredinnick. SMH 20 October 1888.

**Tredrea** B of Orange, died 1913. Methodist 18 October 1913.

**Tredrea** B of Forbes, farewell. Methodist 26 November 1898.

**Tredrea** Edith May of Orange, only daughter of Mr & Mrs B. Tredrea, death aged 4, 1903. Methodist 15 August 1903.

**Trefry** Richard married Elizabeth Kessel, Orange, 1861.

**Trefry** Richard of Orange, uncle of George Trefry per 'Dunbar Castle' 1877.

**Tregenza** Elizabeth Jane married James Herbert of Guyong at Paddington, Wesleyan, 1885.

**Tregenza** John Henry died 1903 aged 59, buried Waverley.

**Tregenza** John cab proprietor of Pyrmont, 1903. SMH 12 January 1903.

**Tregoning** Edward and Elizabeth per 'Hornet' 1859 employed by G. Douglass Esq of Douglass Park.

**Tregonning** Mary married Francis Painter (per 'Lady Ann' 1854), Sydney, Wesleyan, 1857.

**Treleavan** John of Liverpool St, Sydney, brother of William Treleavan per 'Hotspur' 1863.

**Treloar** John Thomas married Elizabeth Ford, Glen Innes, Wesleyan, 1882.

**Tremain** Cuthbert of Maitland, per 'Lysander' 1849 to Melbourne. Joyce Watt.

**Tremain** Elizabeth of Bathurst 1898. Methodist 18 June 1898.

**Tremain** Elizabeth of Bathurst. Methodist 13 June 1896.

**Tremain** John of Maitland, per 'Lysander' 1849 to Port Phillip. Carol Foster.

**Tremain** John of Bathurst 1897. Methodist 5 June 1897.

**Tremain** John married Adeline McMillen, Wellington, Methodist, 1904.

**Tremain** John of Bathurst 1897. Methodist 3 July 1897.

**Tremain** Mary married William Tremain, Wellington, 1902.

**Tremain** Mr memorial service, Bathurst, 1898. Methodist 28 May 1898.

**Tremain** Mrs William of Bathurst 1895. Methodist 27 July 1895.

**Tremain** Richard per 'William Jardine' 1841, of Surry Hills. Betty Bridges.

**Tremain** Robert per 'Queen of the East' 1864 went to R. Tremain in Pitt Street.

**Tremain** Ruben Robert married Jane Good, Bathurst, 1882.

**Tremain** William married Mary Tremain, Wellington, 1902.

**Tremain** William of Bathurst. Methodist 18 June 1898.

**Tremain** William of Sydney, uncle of Henry Doney per 'Dunbar Castle' 1877.

**Tremaine** R carpenter of Pitt St, uncle of Robert

**237**

Tremaine per 'Queen of the East' 1864. Went to him from the ship.

**Trembath** James Martin (per 'Commonwealth' 1877?) married Elizabeth Jane White, Adelong, Wesleyan, 1881.

**Trembath** Sarah Martin married Richard Brooking, of Nymagee, Sydney, Wesleyan, 1884.

**Trembath** William lived Newcastle and Charters Towers. Chris Wright.

**Trembath** William and Lucinda of Adelong 1860. NSW births.

**Trenally** Mary of Bathurst, sister of Elizabeth Pryor per 'Lady Elgin' 1854.

**Treneman** Anne see Richard Hawke.

**Treneman** Caroline married Samuel Graham, Dunkeld, 1874.

**Treneman** Harriet married Thomas Henry Scott, Dunkeld, 1874.

**Treneman** Thomas and Mary Ann (Blamey) per 'Harbinger' 1849, settled in Bathurst, related to Northey, Trebilcock, Blamey & Rowe. Marjorie Jesse.

**Trenemon** Emily married William H Wilson, Bathurst, 1873.

**Trenerry** Mary J (per 'Ellenborough' 1853?) married Frederick Brown in 1856. NSW BDM 1856.

**Trenerry** William married Annie Maria Stephens, Hill End, 1877.

**Trenery** Mary Jane of Bathurst, sister of Edwin Trenery per 'Lady Elgin' 1854. Relative of F. Brown, Newcastle.

**Trenery** William per 'Trevelyan' 1877, went to Bathurst.

**Trescott** Captain of Sydney, uncle of William Hicks per 'Samuel Plimsoll (1)' 1874.

**Treseder** John G nurseryman, of Sydney, 1892. Methodist 25 June 1892.

**Treseder** John G of Ashfield 1890. Mavis James.

**Treseder** Peter per 'Trevelyan' 1877, went to Bathurst.

**Treseder** of Sydney. Doris Black.

**Tresidder** John Thomas married Alice Addlington, Bulli, Primitive Methodist, 1886.

**Tresidder** Mary Jane married John Bennett Gay, Wollongong, Primitive Methodist, 1886.

**Tresidder** Mary Jane married George Gunn, Bulli, Primitive Methodist, 1887.

**Tresidder** Philip Orchard of Bulli. Doris Black.

**Tresidder** William Henry married Mary Jane Crane, Bulli, Primitive Methodist, 1888.

**Trestrail** Edward of Girilambone via South Australia. Link Van Ummerson.

**Trestrain** Ann married Samuel Bray, Bathurst, 1839.

**Trethowan** Nicholas of Newtown, husband of Ann & father of Charles, Laura, Mary, Phillipa, Priscilla & William, all per 'Earl Dalhousie' 1877. See Tarromina.

**Trethowan** William John died 1910 aged 34, buried Woronora CE cemetery. SMH 8 January 1910.

**Trethowan** William married Ada Fraser, Newtown, Wesleyan, 1895.

**Trethowen** Henry Coad married Elizabeth Ann Jackson, Cooks River, CE, 1870.

**Trethowen** Mary Elizabeth per 'Earl Dalhousie' 1877, married Anthony James Coe, Enmore, CE, 1886.

**Trevarthen** Elizabeth Ann Bennett married James B. Milne, Bathurst, 1866.

**Trevarthen** James per 'Joseph Somes' 1852, to Bathurst, Byng, Molong & Currawang. Mary Nesbitt.

**Trevaskis** Joel and Bridget of Adelong 1875. NSW births.

**Trevaskis** Rosanna A M married Ernest Stein c.1893 Raymond Terrace. E. Coulin.

**Trevaskis** family. Dr KG Pont.

**Trevathan** James died 1927, aged 74, buried Rookwood Methodist.

**Trevena** Bessie John married Thomas Wilkinson Short, Bathurst, 1874.

**Trevena** Bessie Johns of Bathurst, per 'Bee' 1856, married Thomas Short. Grace Short.

**Trevena** Samuel of Hill End. Phyllis Trevena.

**Trevena** Susan married James Meadham, Cobar, Wesleyan, 1888.

**Trevena** Thomas of Sydney, brother of Joseph Trevena per 'Blundell' 1853.

**Trevena** William Francis died Cobar aged 54, 1902, buried Cobar CE.

**Trevenen** Frederick Henry married Mary Elizabeth Inch, Surry Hills, CE, 1887.

**Treveskes** see Trevaskis.

**Trevethan** Henry married Adelaide Margaret Barrett, Glebe, Wesleyan, 1891.

**Trevethan** Isaac of St Issey. Albie Willett.

**Trevethan** Richard brother of William Trevethan per 'Lady Ann' 1854.

**Trevethan** Robert of Sydney c.1877. Laurence Turtle.

**Trevethan** William of Paddington 1875. SMH 24 June 1875.

**Trew** Mary Ann see Perrett.

**Trewartha** Jane nee Pope, married Francis Sanguinetto, Stroud, CE, 1897.

**Treweek** James John and Maria (Powell) of Adelong, 1858. NSW births.

**Treweek** William died Adelong 1862 aged 46. Buried Adelong Wesleyan.

**Treweeke** Richard H H married Rachel Sampson, Surry Hills, CE, 1893.

**Trewen** see Truin.

**Trewern** William of Woolloomooloo, husband of Emily Trewern per 'Boanerges' 1857.

**Trewesks** see Trevaskis

**Trewhella** John married Alice Dyer, Burwood, Wesleyan, 1895.

**Trewnick** John Francis married Mary Bolton, Cobargo, Wesleyan, 1884.

**Trewren** see Truin.

**Trewren** Alfred John obituary 1917, Bathurst. BT 22 March & 6 April 1917.

**Trewren** Catherine married Richard Mutton Webb, Kelso, Wesleyan, 1861.

**Trewren** Harriet Emma married John McLean, Kelso, Wesleyan, 1856.

**Trewren** John property for sale, Bathurst. BT and BFP 10 July 1872

**Trewren** John of Kelso, funeral 1888. BDT 6 February 1888.

**Trewren** Mary Elizabeth married William Webb, Kelso, 1869.

**Trewren** Mary of Bathurst, cousin of Amelia Nettle per 'Harbinger' 1849. See Ann Lean.

**Trewren** Mr of Kelso, has brickmaking machine 1858. BFP 30 October 1858.

**Trewren** Susannah Ada married Glyndwr Whalan, Kelso, Wesleyan, 1868.

**Trewren** William of Kelso, funeral 1897. BT 16 November 1897.

**Trewren** family of Bathurst. Garry Howard.

**Trewren** home missionary at Bombala 1895. Methodist 16 November 1895.

**Trezes** Martha see Paull.

**Trezise** William married Ann Stephens, Bathurst, Wesleyan, 1876.

**Trigg** Joseph cousin of William Oliver per 'Panama' 1850.

**Trounce** Mabel Grace married Joseph Christopher Porton, Wellington, 1902.

**Trudgen** Margaret died Adelong 1894 aged 56, buried Adelong Wesleyan.

**Trudgen** Richard and Margaret of Adelong 1873. NSW births.

**Trudgen** Richard died Adelong 1905 aged 69, buried Adelong Methodist.

**Trudgen** Thomas and Lavinia (Prowse) of Adelong

1880. NSW births.

**Trudgeon** Richard of Adelong, married Bridget Moyle, Sydney, Wesleyan, 1865.

**Trudgeon** Richard of Adelong Reefs, brother of William Trudgeon per 'General Caulfield' 1865.

**Trudgeon** Thomas F of St Austell. Olive Trudgeon.

**Trudgeon** Thomas married Lavinia Prowse, Adelong, Wesleyan, 1875.

**Trudgeon** Thomas of Adelong 1908. Methodist 30 October 1908.

**Trudgian** Joseph came to Brisbane via NZ. Helen Trudgian.

**Truin** John of Bathurst Plain, cousin of Henry Martin per 'Thomas Arbuthnot' 1849.

**Truscott** Captain see Captain Trescott.

**Truscott** Charles Thomas married Mary Alice Forster, Emmaville, Methodist, 1902.

**Truscott** Edna see Edna Bourne.

**Truscott** James H of Orange, a relative of Elijah & Amanda Bunt per 'St Lawrence' 1877.

**Truscott** Mary appears to be a sister of William Chapman, both per 'Lord Stanley' 1850.

**Truscott** Mrs William of Wheeo, per 'Lord Stanley' 1850. Died 1893 aged 80. Methodist 11 November 1893.

**Truscott** Robert per 'Earl Dalhousie' 1877, of Sydney. Joy Hadfield.

**Truscott** William John married Susannah Strickland, Bathurst, Wesleyan, 1883.

**Tucker** Annie Jane married Stephen Taylor Williams, Junction Point, 1873.

**Tucker** James Henry married Jane Bishop, Orange, 1867.

**Tucker** John of Sydney, cousin of Emily Snell per 'Ninevah' 1877.

**Tucker** Mary (per 'Mataoka' 1857) married Stockton Allison, Newcastle, CE, 1860.

**Tucker** Simon Summers married Elizabeth Ann Bowden, Muswellbrook, CE, 1875.

**Tucker** Teresa married John Osborne, Bathurst, 1888.

**Tucker** William of Sydney, cousin of Emily Snell per 'Ninevah' 1877.

**Turner** Caroline Esther married William Gun, Sydney, Wesleyan, 1881.

**Turner** George of George St, Sydney, husband of Maria and father of George, both per 'Pericles' 1877.

**Turner** John and Susan per 'William Turner' 1841 employed by Mr Currie of Currie Vale.

**Turner** Mary married William John Coad (per 'Rajasthan' 1855), Surry Hills, Congregational, 1878.

**Turner** Susan Catherine (nee Hitchcock) married Nathaniel Dyer, St Peters, Wesleyan, 1895.

**Turner** William a builder of Tamworth, son of Eliza Turner per 'Earl Dalhousie' 1877. Her son-in-law James Middleton is also on board.

**Turner** William of Tamworth, brother of Caroline Middleton per 'Earl Dalhousie' 1877. See Stephen Middleton.

**Twine** Mary of Croydon 1898. Methodist 15 January 1898.

**Tyas** Wilson married Selina Pearce, Ultimo, Primitive Methodist, 1884.

**Tylerleigh** Francis of Sydney, husband of Mary, father of Ellen, Francis, Henry and Thomas all per 'Himalaya' 1865.

**Uhr** Richard first cousin of Richard Thomas per 'Fitzjames' 1857.

**Uhren** Henry husband of Elizabeth, father of Catherine & Elizabeth, all per 'Dunbar Castle' 1872.

**un-named** relative of Thomas Bowden per 'Star of the West' 1877.

**un-named** relative at Darling Downs, cousin of George Cliff per 'John Davis' 1855.

**un-named** relative in NSW, sister of Mary Clymer per 'British Empire' 1859.

**un-named** relative in Adelaide, sister of Stephen Common per 'Walter Morrice' 1849.

**un-named** relative in Parramatta, a cousin, Joseph, of Jane Coad per 'Kate' 1851.

**un-named** relative in Port Macquarie, a sister of Jane Gilbert per 'Persia' 1856.

**un-named** relative in Broulee, a sister of Phillip Jeffery per 'General Hewitt' 1848.

**un-named** relative in Melbourne, two sisters of Mary Jenkin per 'Cressy' 1856.

**un-named** relative in Woolloomooloo, relatives of Richard Jenkins per 'Samuel Plimsoll' 1875.

**un-named** relative in Moreton Bay, sister of Samuel Jenkins per 'Ascendant' 1858.

**un-named** relative sister & brother-in-law of Ann Kessell per 'Rajasthan' 1855.

**un-named** relative in Moreton Bay, an uncle of James Laity per 'Shackamaxon' 1859.

**un-named** relative in Sydney, a sister of Thomas Pellow per 'Lady Elgin' 1854.

**un-named** relative in Sydney, cousins of John Penno per 'Ascendant' 1858.

**un-named** relative in Sydney, an uncle of Thomas Peters per 'Artemesia' 1854.

**un-named** relative in South Australia, uncle and aunt of James Rogers per 'Thomas Arbuthnot' 1849.

**un-named** relative in Sydney, sister of Phillip Salmon per 'Phoebe Dunbar' 1856.

**un-named** relative brother-in-law & sister of Alfred Sherman, all aboard 'Commonwealth' 1877.

**un-named** relative in Redfern, sisters and a brother of Thomas Soper per 'Lady Ann' 1854.

**un-named** relative of Thomas Thompson per 'Hawkesbury' 1872.

**un-named** relative of Marianne Trengrove per 'Fitzjames' 1858.

**un-named** relative brother and sister (both married) of Jane Watts per 'Kate' 1856.

**Uren** Abednego married Mary Margaret Tonking, Adelong, Wesleyan, 1874.

**Uren** Catherine married Charles Nicholas Blewett, Hill End, 1873.

**Uren** Elizabeth married William Thomas, Hill End, 1873.

**Uren** James amd family per 'Trevelyan' 1877 went to Wollongong.

**Uren** John died Cobar aged 65, 1885, buried Cobar.

**Urquhart** Ellen married Thomas Manuell, Newcastle, CE, 1861.

**Vallack** Mary Ordish buried Rookwood Wesleyan with Richard Vallack. No death date on headstone.

**Vallack** Richard Glinn died 1896 aged 71, buried Rookwood Wesleyan with Mary Ordish Vallack.

**Vallack** Richard Glinn Snr of Castle Hill 1896. SMH 4 January 1896.

**Vallack** William of Balmain 1875. SMH 8 December 1875.

**Vance** Mary Jane married Nicholas Hawken of Sydney at Kiama, Wesleyan, 1861.

**Varcoe** John of West Maitland, brother of Grace Lightfoot per 'Cressy' 1856.

**Veal** Thomas of Adelaide, relative of Josiah Phillips per 'Harbinger' 1849. He says William & James Delbridge of Adelaide are also relatives.

**Vercoe** Emma married James Lightfoot, West Maitland, Wesleyan, 1881.

**Verran** family, Queensland 1883+ Margaret Verran.

**Vial** Caroline Augusta wife of William, died 1874

aged 51, buried with William. SMH 7 September 1874.

**Vial** Samuel   coachbuilder & mine captain, brother of William. AMM

**Vial** William   died 1878 aged 57. Buried Rookwood Wesleyan. Inscription "Saved the life of the Duke of Edinburgh at Clontarf". SMH 6 August 1878.

**Vincent** John   of Waverley, uncle of Henry Vincent per 'Samuel Plimsoll' 1877.

**Vivian** Walter   (per 'Tartar' 1857) married Isabella Findlay, Taree, 1886.

**Vrendall?**   of Sussex St, Sydney, brother of Jemima Hocking per 'Ninevah' 1876.

# w

**Wackford** Thomas   of Sydney, brother of Alfred Wackford per 'Lady Ann' 1854.

**Walkom** Charles   and Elizabeth per 'Plantaganet' 1857, of Bathurst. Harold Frape.

**Walkom** Charles   and Elizabeth per 'Plantaganet' 1857, of Bathurst, brother of Betsy Paul of Richmond. Liz Ayscough.

**Walkom** Emily   married George Milne, Bathurst, 1882.

**Walkom** Jonathon   per 'Lady McNaughton' 1840, of Windsor and Parkbourn. AMM

**Walkom** Jonathon   brother of Charles Walkom per 'Plantaganet' 1857. He also has a sister Elizabeth Paul at Richmond.

**Wall** Ann   of Adelaide, relative of Mary Trenemon per 'Harbinger' 1849.

**Wall** Rose   of Adelaide, relative of Mary Trenemon per 'Harbinger' 1849.

**Wall** Thomas   of Adelaide, relative of Mary Trenemon per 'Harbinger' 1849.

**Wallis** Alfred   of Adelong, brother of Elizabeth Wallis per 'Canning' 1873.

**Wallis** Alfred   and Grace (Tonkin) of Adelong 1865. NSW births.

**Wallis** Elizabeth   of Adelong 1875. NSW births.

**Wallis** Ethel Ada   married James Miners, Woolloomooloo, Wesleyan, 1892.

**Wallis** George   copperminer, near Orange, was the destination of William Henry Wallis and the Merratt family, all per 'Burlington' 1867.

**Wallis** Jane   sister of Mary Warren per 'Hawkesbury' 1872.

**Wallis** Mrs Jane   of Lucknow, mother of Grace & Sarah Wallis per 'Hawkesbury' 1872.

**Wallis** Thomas   died Adelong 1887 aged 54, buried Adelong CE.

**Walton** Angelina   nee Cagny married John Charles Dangar, Sydney, CE, 1869.

**Wanten** Mary Jane   married Thomas Richardson, Balmain, 1879.

**Ward** Bratton   of Upper Riley St, Sydney, uncle of Walter Vivian per 'Tartar' 1857.

**Ward** Sarah   married James Tarvuig, of Bathurst, Surry Hills, CE, 1891.

**Ward** William Bratton   (per 'Kate' 1854) married Sarah Otter, Surry Hills, CE, 1859.

**Ward** William Edward   married Julie Annie Davis, Chippendale, Wesleyan, 1892.

**Ward** William   and Jane (both per 'Trafalgar' 1853) of Happy Vale Public House, South Head Road, are parents of William Ward per 'Kate' 1854.

**Warne** Joseph   (per 'Plantaganet' 1857) married Rebecca Rowe, Newcastle, CE, 1859.

**Warren** Caroline Edine   per 'William Metcalfe' 1844, married Henry Kent, Cooks River, CE, 1857.

**Warren** Caroline   died Cobar aged 60, 1884, buried Cobar Wesleyan.

**Warren** Caroline   married William Gill, Cobar, 1886.

**Warren** James   married Elizabeth Ambler, West Maitland, Methodist, 1900?

**Warren** John   married Mary Northey, Bathurst, Wesleyan, 1867. Her sister Rosina married James Ison on the same day.

**Warren** Mary   per 'Hawkesbury' 1872, married George Middleton, Pyrmont, Presbyterian, 1877.

**Warren** Mrs   sister of Keziah Newton per 'Samuel Plimsoll' 1875.

**Warren** Mrs   of Alstonville 1914 aged 88. Methodist 6 June 1914.

**Warren** Samuel   and family (including Bray stepchildren) per 'William Metcalfe' 1844, employed by William Forster of Clarence River.

**Warren** Susan   of Sydney, sister of James Warren per 'Star of India' 1876.

**Warren** William Northey   married Emily Gertrude Hawke, Bathurst, 1890.

**Warwick** Richard   died Cobar aged 64, 1904, buried Cobar CE.

**Waters** John   married Ann Jolly, Hill End, 1873.

**Wathers** Alice Jane   married George Charles Riddell, Surry Hills, CE, 1881.

**Watson** Alfred Keen   married Lilian Gillam, Petersham, Wesleyan, 1887.

**Watts** John   per 'Lady Ann' 1854, of Orange, aged 95 in 1937. CWD 16 July 1985.

**Watts** John   married Susanna Stevens, Orange, 1867.

**Watts** Joseph   and Harriett per 'Lady Ann' 1854, of Orange. Joseph died 1898. CWD 16 July 1985.

**Watts** Susan   nee Rapson, per 'Kate' 1856, sister of Sampson Rapson per 'Tory' 1849.

**Watts** Susan   nee Rapson, married John Joiner, Wingham, CE, 1867.

**Weakley** George   married Matilda Cock, Gunnedah, Wesleyan, 1893.

**Wearne** C W   of Rockdale 1905. Methodist 21 January 1905.

**Wearne** Charles Wesley   per 'Harbinger' 1849, married Isabella Ann Silk, Sydney, Wesleyan, 1870.

**Wearne** I   of Sydney, wife of late Joseph Wearne, 1901. Methodist 6 July 1901.

**Wearne** J T   of Rydal 1914 aged 74. Methodist 22 August 1914.

**Wearne** James Tare   per 'Harbinger' 1849, married Emily Dengate, Parramatta, Wesleyan, 1863.

**Wearne** James   of Bingara, married Margaret Loutit, Surry Hills, Wesleyan, 1881.

**Wearne** Joseph   per 'Harbinger' 1849, married Isabella Caldwell, Liverpool, Wesleyan, 1857.

**Wearne** Miss Amy BA   assistant to headmistress, Burwood College. Methodist 9 December 1899.

**Wearne** Miss M A   headmistress of Burwood College 1899. Methodist 9 December 1899.

**Wearne** Susannah   widow of Joseph, of Surry Hills, 1886. SMH 26 August 1886.

**Wearne** Thomas JP   of Sydney and Liverpool 1914 aged 80. Methodist 13 June 1914.

**Wearne** Thomas John   cousin of Selina Glasson per 'Ninevah' 1877?

**Wearne** William Carvosso   married Martha Caldwell, Liverpool, Wesleyan, 1856.

**Weary** Abel   (per 'Garland' 1851) cousin of Thomas Weary per 'Malvina Vidal' 1853.

**Weary** Abel   (per 'Garland' 1851) cousin of Edward Coppin per 'Castillian' 1858.

**Weary** Lucy   per 'Malvina Vidal' 1853 with husband Thomas. Died Casino 1893 aged 78. Methodist 23 December 1893.

**Weary** Thomas   of Kiama, (per 'Malvina Vidal' 1853), cousin of Edward Coppin per 'Castillian' 1858.

**Webb** Edmund MLC   funeral 1899. NA 27 June 1899.

**Webb** Edmund Tom JP   of Bathurst. AMM.

**Webb** Elizabeth   nee Hean, married John Barrett, Sydney, Presbyterian, 1898.

**Webb** Emma Helen   married Joseph Kemp Glasson, 1900.

**Webb** Evelyn of Narromine, aged 10, 1898. Methodist 1 January 1898.

**Webb** James A per 'Trevelyan' 1877, went to Lithgow.

**Webb** Jane nee Keyes, of Byng, 1897. Methodist 3 July 1897.

**Webb** John H and Mary, per 'Trevelyan' 1877, went to Bathurst.

**Webb** Mr E of Bathurst. AMM, ADB.

**Webb** Mrs Edmund of Bathurst, 1913. ("An early westerner.") BT 19 December 1913.

**Webb** Mrs T J obituary 1897. BT 12 June 1897.

**Webb** Mrs Ann of Mutton Falls, Bathurst, aged 98, 1906. Methodist 28 July 1906.

**Webb** Richard Mutton married Catherine Trewren, Kelso, 1861.

**Webb** Robert married Sarah McCauley, Bathurst, 1871.

**Webb** Selina Helen married Joseph Thompson, Bathurst, 1880.

**Webb** Thomas Geake married Jane Keyes, Parramatta, Wesleyan, 1874.

**Webb** Thomas Geake aged 52, 1879. BT 29 November 1879.

**Webb** William and Elizabeth per 'Elizabeth' 1829, of Tarana Bathurst. Kevin Webb.

**Webb** William married Mary Elizabeth Trewren, Kelso, 1869.

**Webb** Wilson William of Narromine, aged 25, 1897. Methodist 13 November 1897.

**Webb** family of Bathurst. Jenny King.

**Webber** John of Sydney, brother of William Webber per 'Star of the West' 1877.

**Weeks** William married Rebecca Caldwell, Wollongong, Wesleyan, 1892.

**Weiss** Matilda Susanna married Rev William Curnow, Sydney, Wesleyan, 1858.

**Wellington** Adela Jane married Joseph Chappel Harris, Burwood, Wesleyan, 1883.

**Wellington** Joseph died Adelong 1887 aged 43. Buried Adelong.

**Wellington** Joseph and Catherine, of Adelong 1877. NSW births.

**Wellington** Joseph died Adelong 1887 aged 43, buried Adelong Wesleyan.

**Wellington** Richard married Kate Bristow, Adelong, Wesleyan, 1888.

**Wellington** Richard and Kate, of Adelong 1874. NSW births.

**Wellington** Walter and Mary Ann, Adelong, 1873, NSW births.

**Wellington** Walter and Sarah, of Adelong 1863. NSW births.

**Wescott** Alfred Charles married Elizabeth Kulmar, Petersham, Wesleyan, 1886.

**Wesley** Josepha married William Pomroy, Vegetable Creek, Wesleyan, 1875.

**Wesley** W H of Vegetable Creek and Parramatta. AMM.

**Wesley** W H of Vegetable Creek, sister of Ann Wesley per 'Commonwealth' 1877.

**Wesley** W H of Vegetable Creek, cousin of Francis Ivey per 'Samuel Plimsoll' 1877.

**West** John William married Grace Hocking, Cobar, Wesleyan, 1897.

**Westaway** William of Newcastle, brother-in-law of John & Jane Odgers per 'Wallasea' 1865. See Allen.

**Westaway** William of Newcastle, brother-in-law of Alice and Honor Thomas per 'Wallasea' 1865. See Allen.

**Westaway** William of Peel River, son-in-law of William Thomas per 'Wallasea' 1865.

**Westcott** Alfred Charles married Elizabeth Kulmar, Petersham, 1886.

**Westlake** Harriet married Robert Mitchell, (both of King's Plains Blayney) Surry Hills, Ce, 1896.

**Westlake** Jemima married William Monk Carder, of Blayney, at Surry Hills, CE, 1897.

**Whalan** Charles married Clementia Hughes, Bathurst, Wesleyan, 1862.

**Whalan** Elizabeth married George Felton Pickering, Fish River, 1857.

**Whalan** Ellen see Ellen Surridge.

**Whalan** Glyndwr married Susannah Trewren, Kelso, 1868.

**Whalan** John married Dorothy Bryant, Fish River, 1856.

**Whalan** Lydia (widow) married Richard Glewin Griffiths, Fish River, 1859.

**Whalan** Mrs of Oberon, obituary 1899 aged 89. Her husband discovered Jenolan Caves. Methodist 29 April 1899.

**Whatson** Mary A see Mary A Rogers.

**Wheeler** John married Louisa Jane Knight, Waterloo, Wesleyan, 1898.

**Wheeler** William married Minnie Nichols, Cobar, Wesleyan, 1898.

**White** Albert Hodge married Jane Miller Stokes, Balmain, Wesleyan, 1893.

**White** Elizabeth Jane married James Martin Trembath, Adelong, Wesleyan, 1881.

**White** Elizabeth Jane sister of John White and Honor White, all per 'Samuel Plimsoll' 1875.

**White** Elizabeth married John Wilson, Marrickville, Methodist, 1902.

**White** Elizabeth of Sydney, sister of Eliza Colensa per 'Samuel Plimsoll' 1876.

**White** Elizabeth married John Wilson, Marrickville, Methodist, 1902.

**White** Honor sister of Elizabeth Jane and John White, all per 'Samuel Plimsoll' 1875.

**White** Honor of Sydney, cousin of Maria Ivey per 'Samuel Plimsoll' 1877.

**White** James Charles married Emma Elizabeht Fisher, Castlereagh, CE, 1876.

**White** James of Cow Flat, husband of Ann and father of Annie, Elizabeth, James & William per 'Pericles' 1877.

**White** John and Louisa, of Adelong 1879. NSW births.

**White** John of Paddington, builder 1888. AMM.

**White** John married Mary Louise Reylin, Adelong, CE, 1877.

**White** John brother of Elizabeth Jane and Honor White, all per 'Samuel Plimsoll' 1875.

**White** Matilda Jewell nee Higman, married William Belville Pepper, Narranderah, Wesleyan, 1900.

**White** R of Adelong, brother of Thomas White per 'Persia' 1863.

**White** Richard and Sarah Jane of Adelong 1862. NSW births.

**White** Richard died Adelong 1903 aged 67, buried Adelong Methodist.

**White** Thomas Wearne of Dubbo 1888. AMM.

**White** Thomas married Caroline Janet Fardon, Adelong, Wesleyan, 1870.

**White** Thomas and Caroline of Adelong 1873. NSW births.

**White** William of Bathurst, brother of Thomas White per 'Samuel Plimsoll (2)' 1874. Their sister Elizabeth Harvey is also on board.

**White** William of Byng, brother of Elizabeth Harver per 'Samuel Plimsoll (2)' 1874.

**White** at Adelong Reefs, destination of Thomas White per 'Persia' 1863.

**Whiting** Thomas draper, of Parramatta, uncle of Thomas Penno per 'Herefordshire' 1857.

**Whittaker** William brother of James Whittaker per 'Lady Ann' 1854.

**Whittle** Emily sister of Mary Deeble, both per 'Ninevah' 1876.

**Wicks** William Henry married Emma Hill nee

Merrett, Sydney, Congregational, 1896.

**Wilce** Frederick of Dungog, died 1896. NSW Probate index.

**Wilce** Jonathon and Susan, per 'Orient' 1839. Settled in Dungog. AMM.

**Wilce** Jonathon died Dungog 1897. NSW Probate index.

**Wilce** Jonathon of Dungog. Newcastle Region Library.

**Wilce** Warwick married Martha Meek, Newtown, Wesleyan, 1889.

**Wilkinson** Arthur Frederick married Mary Ann Hunking, Bathurst, Wesleyan, 1861.

**Willcock** Nicholas of Burra mines, South Australia, cousin of Charles Arthur per 'Steadfast' 1849.

**William** Rogester and James Williams, both per 'Thomas Arbuthnot' 1850 appear to be brothers.

**Williams** Ann daughter of Mary A Jenkins and sister of Lavinia Matthews, all per 'Commonwealth' 1877.

**Williams** Catherine married James Shepparbottom, Cobar, Wesleyan, 1881.

**Williams** Catherine married John Major Rogers, Albury, Wesleyan, 1888.

**Williams** Daniel died Tumut 1871 aged 42, buried Tumut.

**Williams** Edward cousin of John Albert Arthur per 'Salisbury' 1877. He also has a cousin Walter Rowe.

**Williams** Edward of Millthorpe 1899 aged 64. Methodist 4 February 1899.

**Williams** Ellen of Moruya, married Louis Rowe Blamey, Glebe, Wesleyan, 1884.

**Williams** Grace married Thomas Neville, Bathurst, 1883.

**Williams** H of Dixon St, Sydney, uncle of Caroline Strongman & John Strongman per 'Samuel Plimsoll (1)' 1874.

**Williams** James Thomas married Elizabeth Louisa Crothers, Methodist, Lewisham, 1900.

**Williams** James married Mary Anne Pascoe, Frogmoor (Boorowa?), Wesleyan, 1877.

**Williams** James and Rogester William both per 'Thomas Arbuthnot' 1850 appear to be brothers.

**Williams** James of Sydney, father of Louisa, Violetta, Edith and Mary Williams per 'Pericles' 1877.

**Williams** James and Zachariah, of Sydney, both uncles of William Mills per 'Lady Ann' 1854.

**Williams** James and Mary Ann (Pascoe) of Adelong 1880. NSW births.

**Williams** James and Jane (Grenfell) of Adelong 1885. NSW births.

**Williams** John Marshall married Emma Elizabeth Sneesby, Paddington, Wesleyan, 1896.

**Williams** John Thomas per 'Pericles' 1877, married Sarah Churchill, Sydney, Congregational, 1883.

**Williams** John (or John Wills?) of Blayney, uncle of George Williams per 'Alfred' 1857.

**Williams** Joseph per 'Sir Robert Sale' 1867, went to Richard Williams at Wentworth near Orange.

**Williams** Lorrima married Thomas Holmes, Surry Hills, CE, 1895.

**Williams** Louisa Ann of Darlinghurst, wife of Richard Williams, ironmonger, funeral 1870 SMH 6 June 1870.

**Williams** Louisa Ann died 1870, wife of Richard Williams, buried Rookwood Independent..

**Williams** Luke supposed to be at Port Phillip, brother of William Williams per 'Emigrant' 1849.

**Williams** Mary Grace married Frederick Flack, West Maitland, Wesleyan, 1885.

**Williams** Mary of Forest Lodge, 1914, widow of Philip Coleman Williams. SMH 30 March 1914.

**Williams** Mary married Willliam Carlyon, Hamilton, Wesleyan, 1881.

**Williams** Mary Sophia married John Boulden, Burwood, CE, 1886.

**Williams** Mr of Goulburn, brother-in-law of George Dennis per 'Samuel Plimsoll (1)' 1874.

**Williams** Mrs of Currawang, Goulburn, sister of Grace Dennis per 'Samuel Plimsoll (1)' 1874.

**Williams** Peter and Theresa (nee Eva), per 'Hornet' 1859, settled in Moruya. M. Porter.

**Williams** Peter and Theresa per 'Hornet' 1859, no employment agreements, went to Stanley St (Woolloomooloo).

**Williams** Philip Coleman of Forest Lodge 1911. SMH 27 March 1911.

**Williams** Philip Coleman per 'Meteor' 1853, died 1911 aged 81, buried Rookwood Wesleyan with wife Mary.

**Williams** Philip of Dixon St, Sydney, uncle of Caroline Strongman & John Strongman per 'Samuel Plimsoll (1)' 1874.

**Williams** Richard of Petersham, died 1913 aged 81, buried Rookwood Independent with wife Louisa Ann Williams.

**Williams** Richard of Orange, brother of Joseph Williams per 'Sir Robert Sale' 1867.

**Williams** Richard at Wentworth near Orange, destination of Joseph Williams per 'Sir Robert Sale' 1867.

**Williams** Richard of Petersham, 1913. SMH 4 April 1913.

**Williams** Richard of Norton St, Glebe, husband of Louisa A Williams per 'Bermondsey' 1856.

**Williams** Richard of Sydney, cousin of Elizabeth Oke per 'St Vincent' 1849.

**Williams** Rowland Samuel married Mary Thompson, Vegetable Creek, Wesleyan, 1878.

**Williams** Samuel of Sydney, cousin of Edwin Bushell per 'Winifred' 1856.

**Williams** Stephen Taylor married Annie Jane Tucker, Junction Point, Primitive Methodist, 1873.

**Williams** Theresa per 'Hornet' 1859, going with friends. Conduct very good.

**Williams** Thomas Richard E married Mary Jane Pascoe, Bathurst, Wesleyan, 1886.

**Williams** Thomas and Mary Ann (nee Evans) per 'Australia' 1853, went to Campbelltown. AJ Brown.

**Williams** Thomas of Goulburn & Bowral via Ballarat & Bendigo. Merle Walker.

**Williams** Thomas of Dapto, brother of Joseph Williams per 'Bermondsey' 1855.

**Williams** Thomas of Melbourne, cousin of Jenifer Pethick per 'Herefordshire' 1857.

**Williams** Thomas of Penrose Vale, Dapto, uncle of William J. Hosking per 'Earl Dalhousie' 1877.

**Williams** Thomas of Sydney, no relative of Richard Carbines per 'Spitfire' 1863.

**Williams** Thomas of Woolloomooloo, cousin of Elizabeth Anthony per 'Scythia' 1871.

**Williams** William Henry and Mary Jane of Adelong 1880. NSW births.

**Williams** William married Sarah Sophia Hocking, Parkes, Wesleyan, 1883.

**Williams** William of Newcastle via South Australia. Margaret Cannington.

**Williams** William coppperminer of Cow Flat, son of Mary Williams per 'Kapunda' 1877.

**Williams** William of Cow Flat copper mines, brother of Mary Jane Williams per 'Kapunda' 1877.

**Williams** Zachariah and James, of Sydney, both uncles of William Mills per 'Lady Ann' 1854.

**Williams** family of Orange. Jean Gibson.

**Williams** and Lethlean families of Orange. Jean Gibson.

**Williams** of Sydney, uncle of Allen Maker per 'Star of India' 1877.

**Williams** per 'Anglia' 1850. Helen Belcher.

**Williams** of Sydney. AT Thomas.

**Willis** Charles and Sophia (Dunston) of Adelong 1874. NSW births.

**Willis** William of Sydney, brother of Elizabeth Coad per 'Rajasthan' 1855.

**Willman** Thomas Wing married Emily Harriet McLean, Bathurst, Wesleyan, 1887.

**Wills** John see John Williams.

**Wills** John of Frogmore Copper Mines, uncle of Thomas Wills per 'Commonwealth' 1877.

**Wills** John and Nanny (Calloway) per 'Hydaspes' 1852 settled in Ashfield. Grace Thrush.

**Wills** John uncle of Clara and Thomas Wills per 'Commonwealth' 1877.

**Wills** John of Blayney, see Williams.

**Wills** Jonathon of Sydney, uncle of Elijah Wills per 'Tartar' 1857.

**Wills** Phillippa Ann died Cobar aged 52, 1905, buried Cobar Presbyterian.

**Wills** Samuel and Phillapa Ann (Green) of Adelong 1880. NSW births.

**Wills** Thomas Richard married Elizabeth Lamrock, Bathurst, Wesleyan, 1881.

**Wills** William of Parramatta, cousin of Mary Deeble per 'Ninevah' 1877 (and therefore a cousin of Emily Whittle also on board and sister of Mary Deeble.)

**Wills/Willis** family per 'Trevelyan' 1877 went to Bathurst.

**Wilmot** Samuel (per 'Lady Elgin' 1854) married Charlotte Page, Murrurundi, Congregational, 1868.

**Wilmot** Samuel (per 'Lady Elgin' 1854) married Mary Ann James, Murrurundi, Congregational, 1868.

**Wiloe** Jonathon see Jonathon Wilce. AMM

**Wilson** John Jardine married Elizabeth White, Marrickville, Methodist, 1902.

**Wilson** Jonathon Otley married Jessie Lightfoot, Maitland, CE, 1886.

**Wilson** Sydney Arnold married Mary Elizabeth Chenoweth, Newtown, Wesleyan, 1896.

**Wilson** William H married Emily Trenemon, Bathurst, Wesleyan, 1873.

**Wiltshire** Susan Jane married John Clarke, Adamstown, Wesleyan, 1896.

**Winn** Catherine died Cobar 1904 aged 74, buried Cobar CE.

**Winn** Nicholas married Alice Ann Phoebe, Orange, 1888.

**Winn** of Moghill Creek, are husband and son of Mary Winn per 'Shackamaxon' 1859.

**Winsten** Seth Junot married Elizabeth Johns, Tuena, Wesleyan, 1889.

**Wise** Sarah Ann see Sarah Ann Wood.

**Witten** Clara married William John Nicholas, West Maitland, Methodist, 1893.

**Wood** Alfred married Annie Hugo, Burwood, Wesleyan 1893.

**Wood** Annie nee Hugo, married Albert William Howard, Lewisham, Methodist, 1904.

**Wood** Lewin buried with Best family, Rookwood Independent, 1897 (66 yrs). SMH 2 March 1897.

**Wood** Maria married William Solomon, Merrylands, Wesleyan, 1884.

**Wood** Sarah Ann nee Wise, married Robert Northey of Blayney, at Bathurst, 1899.

**Woodbridge** Caroline married John Buckett, Adelong, Wesleyan, 1880.

**Woodcock** Alice Sarah married William John Woodcock, Ryde, CE, 1875.

**Woodcock** Mary married John Doidge (per 'Ninevah' 1877) at Redfern, Methodist, 1902.

**Woodcock** Stephen of Parramatta River, orchardist 1853+ AMM.

**Woodcock** William John married Alice Sarah Woodcock, Ryde, CE, 1875.

**Woodey** Robert of Sydney, son of John Woodey per 'Kapunda' 1877.

**Woodley** Henry James married Emma Mitchell, Sydney, 1858.

**Woodward** Abraham Prout married Mary McFadyen, Gunnedah, Wesleyan, 1888.

**Woolcock** Edward of Redfern, "per 'Tyburnia' 1874. Margaret Playford.

**Woolcock** Edward of Redfern, Relative of Ethelia Bawden (widow) and 7 children, per 'Ninevah' 1876.

**Woolcock** Eliza per 'Hotspur' 1862. Connection with Evans family.

**Woolcock** John see Lobb.

**Woolcock** family. Margaret Playford. Lesley Evans.

**Woolford** Edward Osborne married Eliza Nance (per 'William Metcalfe' 1844), Macleay River, 1866.

**Woolley** Clara married John Blewett, Hamilton, Wesleyan, 1892.

**Woolnough** James married Phebe Esther Hawke, Bathurst, Wesleyan, 1875.

**Worden** Grace died 1911 aged 62, buried Gore Hill CE.

**Worth** William James married Susannah Brown nee Daw, Pyrmont, Presbyterian, 1891.

**Wright** Edward Abraham married Janie Martin, Bathurst, Wesleyan, 1891.

**Wright** Thomas Henry married Martha Williams Pethick (per 'Herefordshire' 1857), Maitland, CE, 1869.

**Wynn** of Moreton Bay, father of Mary Laity per 'Shackamaxon' 1859.

**Yeo** James and Mary (Mitchell) of Adelong 1873. NSW births.

**Young** James and Lydia nee Woolcock per 'Hotspur' 1862. Margaret Playford.

**Youren** William of Maldon, brother of David Youren per 'Samuel Plimsoll' 1876.

PLATE 51. Cornish coastline.

# SELECT BIBLIOGRAPHY
## I. PRIMARY SOURCES

**A.  In institutions**
1.  Archives Office of New South Wales
2.  Australian National University Archives of Business and Labour.
3.  Bathurst Family History Society
4.  Bathurst District Historical Society
5.  Cobar Clerk of Petty Sessions
6.  Glen Innes Historical Society
7.  Mitchell Library
8.  National Library of Australia
9.  Newcastle Region Public Library
10.  Orange Historical Society
11.  Singleton Historical Society
12.  Society of Australian Genealogists
13.  Tumut Clerk of Petty Sessions
14.  Uniting Church Archives and Research Centre
15.  National Maritime Museum, Greenwich
16.  Cornwall Record Office, Truro
17.  Cornish Studies Library, Redruth
18.  Royal Institution of Cornwall, Truro

**B.  In private collections**
**C.  Official publications**
**D.  Contemporary books, articles, journals**
**E.  Contemporary newspapers**
**F.  Directories, guides and gazetteers**
**G.  Interviews and telephone discussions**

## II. SECONDARY SOURCES

**A.  Reference works and guides**
**B.  Books and articles**
**C.  Newspapers and periodicals**
**D.  Theses**

## III. FAMILY INFORMATION

# I  PRIMARY SOURCES

## A.) IN INSTITUTIONS

### 1.)                    ARCHIVES OFFICE OF NEW SOUTH WALES

i.    Immigration Records      (Microfilm reel numbers are given because original material is not issued after it has
      been microfilmed.)
Col. Sec., Reports of vessels arrived 1826-1853
      AO COD 20-106.
      AO reels 1263-1280.
Immigrant ships arriving in New South Wales 1837-1877
      Assisted (bounty) immigrants 1837-1842, AO reels 1287-1349.
      Assisted immigrants (Board's lists) 1848-1877, AO reels 2458-2488.
      Assisted immigrants (Agent's lists) 1838-1877, AO reels 2134-2140.
      AO 4/1149.1, 'Other papers and notes', *Sir Charles Napier* 1842, *Panama* 1850.
      AO 4/1881.3, 'Other papers and notes', *Plantaganet* 1854.
      AO 9/6212, 'Other papers and notes', *Mary Ann, Fitzjames* 1857.
      AO 9/6213, 'Other papers and notes: matron's diary', *Herefordshire* 1857.
      AO 9/6276-6289, 'Other papers and notes'' 1848-1873.
      Shipping arrivals, AO reels 699, 2654-2668.
Immigration deposit journals 1853-1900, AO reels 2668A-2676.
Shipping master's office: passengers arriving, AO reels 399-436.
Wage agreements and entitlement certificates 1844-45, AO reels 2449-2456.

ii.    Methodist Marriage Registers
Armidale 1860-1895, 5/3916 5/3920.
Ashfield 1866-1895, 5/3915.
Balmain 1885 1893-1900, 5/3929, 5/3924.
Bathurst: Carcoar 1864-67, 5/3953.
Bega 1866-1897, 5/3916.
Branxton-Greta 1863-1893, 5/3922.
Burwood 1878-1906, 5/3944.
Cobar 1880-1901, 5/3920. Rev G. Cocks private register.
Cobargo-Tilba 1890-1905, 5/3981.
Cooma-Bombala 1872-1906, 5/3976-7.
Emmaville 1881-82, 5/3979.
Glebe 1864-97, 5/3944, 5/3951.
Glen Innes 1880-1896, 5/3925, 5/3980.
Hamilton 1876-1901, 5/4014.
Hill End 1873-94, 5/3922.
Kempsey 1864-82, 1894-9, 5/3915.
Kiama 1857-73, 5/4009.
Leichhardt 1895-1902, 5/3951.
Lewisham-Petersham 1884-1895, 5/3915.
Maitland 1856-1880, 5/3914, 5/4027, 5/3953, 5/3922.
Moama 1890-1900, 5/4009, SAG reel 0128.
Molong 1875-1892, 5/3979.
Morpeth 1860-77, 5/3922.
Moruya-Tilba 1859-1882, 1895-98, 5/3934.
Newcastle 1876-1901, 5/4014.
Nowra 1858-1898, 5/3951 5/3953.
Orange 1859-1894, 5/3931 5/3934.
Paddington 1880-1895, 5/3951 5/3997.
Parramatta 1856-87, 5/3914.
Primitive Methodists
      Rev Gilby 1876-1902, 5/3944.
      Rev Holden 1886-1902, 5/3857-8.
      Rev Harrison 1888-1896, 5/3843.
      Rev Rudd 1882-1891, 5/3968.
      Rev Penman 1887-1897, 5/3995.
      Rev Kessell 1901-04, 5/3838.
Raymond Terrace 1889-1906, 5/3932.
Rockdale 1883-1900, 5/3999.
Rockley and Burraga 1872-92, 5/3978.
Ryde 1870-72, 1875-87, 5/3914.
Singleton 1857-1896, 5/3915 5/3918.

Spring Hill and Millthorpe, 1882-1897, 5/3999.
Stanmore 1896-1904, 5/4013.
South Sydney: Chippendale,     1856-73, 5/3834.
                             1877-90. 5/3897.
South Sydney: Cleveland St., 1881-94, 5/3897.
South Sydney: Redfern, 1881-94, 5/3897-8.
South Sydney: Waterloo, 1878-93, 5/3898.
Sydney: Bourke St., 1856-65, 5/4011.
                    1881-90, 5/3897.
                    1883-95, 5/4000.
                    1897-1902, 5/3858.
Sydney: Prince and York St 1896-1900, 5/3949.
Sydney: Pyrmont and Ultimo 1881-95, 5/3943.
Taree 1858-89, 5/3934.
Tenterfield 1865-92, 5/3922.
United Free Methodists:    1879-1901, 5/3997.
Uralla 1895-97, 5/3917.
Wollongong 1856-76, 5/3921.
             1879-99,5/3915,5/3919


ii.    Other.

Col. Sec., 'Memorial of William Lane', 1824, p.383, AO microfiche 3097.
Col. Sec., 'Memorial of William Tom'', 1824, p.1253, AO microfiche 3114.

## 2.)    AUSTRALIAN NATIONAL UNIVERSITY ARCHIVES OF BUSINESS AND LABOUR

i.    Trade Unions.
Amalgamated Engineering Union, E209/6, Central Branch donation and sick benefit book 1893-1896.
Australian Coal and Shale Employees Federation, E165/16 and 18, Illawarra 1893-1916, ledger.
Australian Federation of Locomotive Enginemen, NSW division, E99/26, contribution book Picton 1889-1905, Sydney 1899-1903.
Baking Trade Employees Federation of Australia, NSW branch T13/4, Sydney Branch contribution books 1905-1940.
Boilermakers and Blacksmiths Association of Australia, Federal office N24/20, Boilermakers' Federated Funeral Fund 1902-1915, N24/46 Boilermakers' Federated Funeral Fund 1903-1911.
Federated Coopers of Australia, NSW branch E100/1, minutes 1886-96 (Sydney), E100/6, contributions book 1881-1924, E100/8, memo of levies c.1890.
Operative Plasterers and Plaster Workers Federation of Australia, NSW branch, E235/1-5, minutes 1875-1905, E235/30, contribution book 1901-1910.
Operative Stonemasons Society of Australia, NSW branch, N55/18-19, handbill blacklist 1893, 1899, T46/1, 7-15, minutes, T46/18-20, cashbooks, rule book, T46/26-27, contribution books.
Printing and Kindred Industries Union, NSW branch T39/12-14, subscription books 1896-1905 and applications for membership 1888-1896.
Sheet Metal Working, Agricultural Implement and Stovemaking Industrial Union of Australia, NSW branch, E196/7/1-2, contribution books 1888-1902.

## 3.)    BATHURST FAMILY HISTORY SOCIETY

Biographical index of Bathurst and district families.
Cemetery transcripts for Bathurst district cemeteries.
Files of Bathurst families.

## 4.)    BATHURST DISTRICT HISTORICAL SOCIETY

Biographical index to Bathurst personalities.
Files on Bathurst personalities and events.
Glasson, John, *Letters 1828-1857*, with introduction by his grand-daughter, Mrs O. Phillips, typescript.
Thomas, B.W. *Notes on some historic places in old Cornish Settlement district*, typescript, 1974.
Webb, R.W. *Pioneers of Bathurst district*, typescript, Webb papers.
Webb, R.W. *Concerning my mother*, typescript, Webb papers.

## 5.)    COBAR CLERK OF PETTY SESSIONS.

Birth, death and marriage records 1880-1905.

**6.) GLEN INNES HISTORICAL SOCIETY**

Biographical index of Glen Innes personalities.

**7.) MITCHELL LIBRARY**

*Alfred*, weekly ship's newspaper 1839, A1680.

*'Andromache* 1837', T.W. New papers 1837-63, A1967.

Boilermakers and Blacksmiths Society of Australia 1876-1909, ML MSS 2422, K 52391.

*City of Edinburgh 1837*, Ac123.

Dangar, Albert A., 'Log, *La Hogue'*, 1856-7, A2565, CY 1573

Glasson, Hannah Truscott (nee Hawke), *Reminiscences 1845-1922*, typescript, MSS 3523.

H., Mrs, 'Diary aboard *Lady Kennaway* 1841', FM4/1447.

Hartas, Joseph, 'Diary aboard *Pericles* 1877 and later in the Orange district to 1900', MSS 2096.

Hartley District Miners' Mutual Protective Association 1886-1900, MSS 1692.

Hawke, George, letters to Rev T. Hassall, 8 May, 16 May 1829, Hassall papers, A1677-3, vol.3, pp.1941 and 1957, CY938.

Hawke, George, 'Extracts from diary 1836-37', B847.

Henderson, John, 'Logbook of *Florentia'*, 1838, B740.

Hunt and Stevens, *Map of the City of Sydney 1868*, ZM4 811.17/1868/1.

Jevons, W.S., 'A social survey of Sydney 1858', B864, CY1045.

Lane, W., 'Petition to grant of extra land', Hassall papers, A1677-2, pp.1343-4.

Lang, Rev John Dunmore, Papers, vol.1, A2221, CY869.

*Map of the electoral and police districts in the colony of New South Wales 1859*, ML ZM3 805f/1859/1.

*Map of New South Wales shewing boundaries as defined in first schedule of electoral bill 1873*, ML ZM2 810 fbe/1873/1.

Marshall, letter to Bowman *City of Edinburgh* 1837, 10 March 1837, DOC 376.

Muir, R., 'Diary aboard *Alfred*" 1838-9, B1496, CY1153.

Orton, Rev. J., 'Journal', CY 1119.

'Pastoral visitation, 1873/4', Anonymous, Methodist Church papers, 5015, no.81.

Pemmell, Rev J., 'The life of an early Methodist preacher', MSS A425.

'Prospectus for *Moffatt*' 1841, ML FM1/AUST PACKET SHIP.

Read, John H., 'Surgeon's journal, *Steadfast*', 1849, MSS 991 FM3/648.

Sydney Progressive Society of Carpenters and Joiners 1846-1896. A2784, CY266 .

Tom, W., Gold mining papers 1851-1873, A856, CY812.

United Labourers' Protective Society 1861-1906, MSS 262, item 6, (7).

Wellings, H., 'Diary aboard *David McIvor* 1858', MSS 1963, CY1684.

Wells, W.H., *Map of the City of Sydney, 1843*, ML ZM2 811.17/1843/1.

*Wesleyan preachers' plan, Bathurst 1852*, Am 123-2, item 7.

Wilson, H.M., 'Diary aboard *Sarah* 1849', B1535, CY1024.

Womens's Christian Temperance Union, Sydney membership books 1898-1958, 1882-1902, 1889-1897, cash book 1882-1890, MSS 3641 MLK 1985.

**8.) NATIONAL LIBRARY OF AUSTRALIA**

Bloxsome, O., 'Journal of a voyage to New South Wales 1838', MS 336.

Hawke, George, *Colonial experience: diary of George Hawke of Orange*, typescript, MS 227.

Martens, Conrad, 'View of the Molong mine, N.S.W.', watercolour 1848. PIC T371 NK229 LOC811.

New South Wales Church Registers, Society of Australian Genealogists microfilms. SAG reels, 0001, 0003, 0014, 0015, 0034, 0037, 0064, 0076, 0094, 0101, 0102, 0103, 0106, 0128, 0129, 0134, 0145, 0148, 0171, 0182, 0192, 0227, 0229, 0230.

Newcastle Diocese parish registers. [NLA mfm N 236 reels 1-8.]

'Plan of *Florentia*', Rawson papers, MS 204, folder 3.

Rawson, Samuel, 'Diary of the voyage aboard *Florentia*' 1838, Rawson papers, MS 204/1.

Registers of baptisms, burials and marriages 1787-1856 [N.S.W.]. [NLA mfm N229.]

'Scale of victualling in government emigrant ships, 1839', CO 384/87, circulars 1817-51, p.337. [AJCP reel 5132.]

Tumut Family History Society (comps.), *Transcripts of the Perkins papers 1823-1954*, typescript, MS 7231.

'Wesleyan Chapel Bathurst, marriage register 1839-1844', MS 3290.

**9.) NEWCASTLE REGION PUBLIC LIBRARY**

Alphabetical files on personalities and events.

Newcastle region cemetery transcripts.

Smith, L., The Rapson family, Williams River Valley, typescript.

**10.) ORANGE HISTORICAL SOCIETY**

Alphabetical files on personalities and events.

Orange and district cemetery transcripts.

**11.)**    **SINGLETON HISTORICAL SOCIETY**

Files on personalities and events.

**12.)**    **SOCIETY OF AUSTRALIAN GENEALOGISTS**

i.    Cemetery transcripts
Botany, B/7/11/94 and P.R.4/4395.
Chinamens Bend, Orange, reel 3215, 3219.
Cobar, SAG reel 3207.
Gore Hill, SAG reel 3207, and manuscript transcripts.
Gresford, SAG reel 3217.
Hobbys Yards, SAG reel 3207.
Millthorpe, SAG reel 3219.
Morpeth, SAG reel 3208.
Oberon, SAG reel 3209 and P.R.4/508.
Scone, SAG reel 3212.
Waverley, transcribers' manuscript sheets (unchecked).

**13.)**    **TUMUT CLERK OF PETTY SESSIONS**

Tumut-Adelong birth, death and marriage records 1856-1900.

**14.)**    **UNITING CHURCH ARCHIVES AND RECORD SOCIETY, PARRAMATTA.**

i.    Methodist Marriage registers
Adamstown 1890-1896.
Adelong 1865-1882.
Albury 1869-1903.
Annandale 1893-1900.
Armidale and Uralla 1891-1894.
Balmain 1869-1880.
Bathurst 1856-1895.
Bega 1885-1888, 1898-1902.
Bulli 1894-1910.
Burwood 1886-1898, 1908.
Cobar 1881-1902.
Dubbo-Wellington 1881-1895.
East Maitland 1877-1893.
Emmaville 1896-1900.
Glen Innes 1896-1900.
Hillgrove 1891-92, 1898-1900.
Inverell 1872-1901.
Kempsey 1871-72, 1882-1905.
Kiama 1874-1901.
Lambton 1895-1900, (Lay Methodist.)
Leichardt 1899-1903.
Maclean 1870-1902.
Milton-Ulladulla 1858-1891.
Muswellbrook 1884-1897.
Newcastle 1875, 1894-96.
Newtown 1874-1905.
Oberon 1856-1900.
Paddington 1886-93.
Parramatta 1898-1902.
Stanmore 1882-1908.
South Sydney: Redfern 1897-98.
Sydney: Bourke Street 1861-86.
Sydney: Prince and York Streets 1838-75.
Sydney: William Street 1880-89, 1891-1900.
Wallsend 1872-92.
Waverley 1864-89.
Wellington 1890-1900.

Private registers:    Rev W.H Beale

ii.   Other

Clancy, E.G., 'Biographical notes on early Wesleyan ministers in New South Wales', manuscript.

Clancy, E.G., *The Ranters' Church*, typescript.

Dangar, O.O., *Account of Methodism on the Macleay River*, typescript.

Lockley, G. Lindsay, *A biographical card index of Congregational ministers in Australia 1798-1977*, photocopied, and bound into a volume.

Methodist church histories: filed and boxed alphabetically.

Minutes of the meetings of Australian [Wesleyan] districts 1846-1854.

### 15.)      NATIONAL MARITIME MUSEUM, GREENWICH

`The *Florentia* passing through Tellicherry Roads 1825', painting.

### 16.)      CORNWALL RECORD OFFICE, TRURO

*A map of the ecclesiastical parishes in Cornwall*, Cornwall County and Diocesan Record Office, Truro, 1990.

### 17.)      CORNISH STUDIES LIBRARY, REDRUTH

1841-1881 censuses of Cornwall.

### 18.)      ROYAL INSTITUTION OF CORNWALL, TRURO

Extracts from the *West Briton* and *Royal Cornwall Gazette* relating to Cornish emigration in the nineteenth century.

## B.) IN PRIVATE COLLECTIONS

Bathurst district cemetery transcripts: Mrs Helen Jeuken, Bathurst, N.S.W.

Cable, K.J., and Cable, L., (comps.), 'Biographical register of Anglican ministers in Australia': Professor K.J. and Mrs L. Cable, Sydney.

Cadia engine house, photographs: Mr Roger Thomas, Gosford, N.S.W.

Clements, Hanbury, Station book, 'Summer Hill' 1848, photocopy of manuscript: Mrs G. Kelly, Queanbeyan, N.S.W..

Cobar personalities and events, files, photographs and biographical information: Mrs Joy Prisk, Cobar, N.S.W.

Cornish Settlement and Guyong map: Mr B.W. Thomas, Orange, N.S.W.

Hawken, Lane and Barrett family correspondence: Mr Selwyn Hawken, Cannonvale, Queensland.

Lawry, Rev Walter, *Diary 1818-1825*, typescript: Mrs Mavis James, Lawson, N.S.W.

Lane family correspondence: Mr Peter Hohnen, Canberra.

McLelland, M.H., *The Lane family*, typescript: M.H. McLelland, Sydney.

Maitland district cemetery transcripts: Mrs Mavis Newcombe, Maitland, N.S.W.

*Memoirs of Alfred Goninan (1865-1963)*, L.E. Fredman (ed.), introduction and typescript unpublished, from the original manuscript in the possession of Mrs Marcovitch, Chatswood: Professor L.E. Fredman, Newcastle, N.S.W.

*Newcastle Morning Herald*, card index: Mr Don Baker, Newcastle, N.S.W.

Peters, Thomas, letter to William Rowe of Bathurst, 23 February 1852: Mrs Marjorie Jesse, Sydney.

Rowe, Rebecca, letter from `Pendarves' to her father at Ophir diggings 7 October [1851?]: Mrs Marjorie Jesse, Sydney.

Selwood, William, 'Diary': Mrs Phyllis Trevena, Orange, N.S.W.

Thomas, B.W., *Guyong Wesleyan Church (1857) - site lost and found, 1971*, typescript: Mr B.W. Thomas, Orange, N.S.W.

Tom, J.W., *Cornish Settlement:reminiscences, 1941*, typescript: Mr B.W. Thomas, Orange, N.S.W..

Towzey, John (Hawken), letter to his parents in Padstow, Cornwall, 12 May 1860: Mr Robert Jeremy, Maryborough, Queensland.

## C.) OFFICIAL PUBLICATIONS

i.   British Parliamentary Papers

First and second reports from the Select Committee on Emigrant Ships with the minutes of evidence taken before them, Emigration 7, 1854, Irish University Press, Shannon, 1968.

General reports of the Colonial Land and Emigration Commissioners with appendices, Emigration 10, 1842-48, Irish University Press, Shannon, 1969.

General reports of the Colonial Land and Emigration Commissioners with appendices, Emigration 11, 1849-52, Irish University Press, Shannon, 1969.

General reports of the Colonial Land and Emigration Commissioners with appendices, Emigration 12, 1852-55, Irish University Press, Shannon, 1969.

General reports of the Colonial Land and Emigration Commissioners with appendices, Emigration 13, 1856-58,

Irish University Press, Shannon, 1969.

General reports of the Colonial Land and Emigration Commissioners with appendices, Emigration 14, 1859-61, Irish University Press, Shannon, 1969.

General reports of the Colonial Land and Emigration Commissioners with appendices, Emigration 15, 1862-64, Irish University Press, Shannon, 1969.

General reports of the Colonial Land and Emigration Commissioners with appendices, Emigration 16, 1865-66, Irish University Press, Shannon, 1969.

General reports of the Colonial Land and Emigration Commissioners with appendices, Emigration 17, 1867-70, Irish University Press, Shannon, 1969.

General reports of the Colonial Land and Emigration Commissioners with appendices, Emigration 18, 1871-73, Irish University Press, Shannon, 1969.

Reports correspondence and papers relating to emigration from the United Kingdom to the colonies 1828-38, Emigration 19, Irish University Press, Shannon, 1969.

Reports correspondence and papers relating to emigration to and from the United Kingdom 1839-41, Emigration 20, Irish University Press, Shannon, 1970.

Correspondence and papers relating to emigration and Crown Lands in the colonies 1842-43, Emigration 21, Irish University Press, Shannon, 1970.

Reports returns and correspondence relating to emigration from the United Kingdom with appendices 1843-53, Emigration 22, Irish University Press, Shannon, 1971.

Correspondence and papers relating to emigrant vessels and emigration to the British colonies 1854-59, Emigration 23, Irish University Press, Shannon, 1970.

Reports correspondence and papers relating to emigration from the United Kingdom with appendices, Emigration 24, 1860-71, Irish University Press, Shannon, 1971.

Reports correspondence and statistics relating to emigration and immigration with appendices, 1872-81, Emigration 25, Irish University Press, Shannon, 1971.

ii.    New South Wales Parliamentary Papers

Daw, James, 'Petition respecting claim as discoverer of tin in New South Wales', 18 September 1873, *New South Wales Legislative Assembly Votes and Proceedings*, 1873-74, vol.4, p.781.

Deloitte, W.S. Esq., 'Minutes of evidence taken before the Committee on Immigration, 17 August 1838', *New South Wales Legislative Council Votes and Proceedings*, 1838, pp.843-5.

*Noxious and offensive trades inquiry commission: to inquire into the nature and operations of, and to classify noxious and offensive, within the city of Sydney, and its suburbs, and to report generally on such trades*, New South Wales Royal Commission, New South Wales Legislative Council, 2nd session 1883. [ML Q628.52 1A1.]

'Papers relative to geological surveys', *New South Wales Legislative Council Votes and Proceedings 1851*, vol.2.

'Report on the condition of the working classes of the metropolis', *New South Wales Legislative Assembly Votes and Proceedings 1859/60*, vol.4, pp.1265-1461.

'Report on tin-bearing country, New England', *New South Wales Legislative Assembly Votes and Proceedings*, 1873-4, vol.4, pp.771-80.

iii.    Electoral rolls

N.S.W. Electoral Office, *Revised list of persons qualified to vote for the election of members of the Legislative Assembly 1859-60*. [ML Q324.241/1, FM4/9467.]

*N.S.W. electoral rolls 1875*. [NLA mfm N273 reels 2-4.]

*N.S.W. electoral rolls 1899-1900*. [NLA mfm N273 reels 17-22.]

## D.) CONTEMPORARY BOOKS, ARTICLES, JOURNALS

*Australian men of mark*, 2 vols., Charles F. Maxwell, Sydney, 1889. [NLA N920.01 AUS.]

Baring-Gould, S., *A book of the west being an introduction to Devon and Cornwall*, vol.2, Cornwall, Methuen, London, 1899.

'Bathurst', in *Sydney Gazette*, 17 January 1832, p.3, c.2.

Bensusan, S.L., 'Recent copper extracting processes', in *Royal Society of New South Wales Journal*, 1876, pp.135-45. [ML 506/R.]

Buller, J., *A statistical account of the parish of Saint Just in Penwith in the County of Cornwall*, first published 1842, facsimile edition, Dyllansow Truran, Redruth, 1983.

Campbell, W.S., *Extracts from reports on certain agricultural districts of New South Wales*, New South Wales Government Printer, Sydney, 1888. [ML 630.991C.]

Carew, R., *The survey of Cornwall*, first published 1602, F.E. Halliday, (ed.), republished Andrew Melrose, 1953, Adams and Dart, London, 1969.

Carter, H., *The autobiography of a Cornish smuggler: Captain Harry Carter of Prussia Cove 1749-1809*, first published 1894, Barton, Truro, 1971.

Collins, Wilkie, *Rambles beyond railways, or notes in Cornwall taken afoot*, first published 1851, Westaway Books, London 1948.

Couch, J., *The history of Polperro*, first published 1871, condensed edition, Dyllansow Truran, Redruth, 1965.

Dangar, H., *Index and directory to map of the ... River Hunter: the lands of the Australian-Agricultural Company, with the ground plan and allotments of King's Town, New South Wales: ... a complete emigrant's guide*, Joseph Cross, London, 1828. [NLA FRM F1184.]

Daniell, J.J., *A compendium of the history and geography of Cornwall*, 3rd edition, Netherton and Worth, Truro, 1894.

*Deed of settlement of the Cadiangullong Consolidated Copper Mining Company Limited*, Clarson, Shallard and Co., Sydney, 1864. [ML 622.343/1A1.]

'An excursion from Bathurst to Wellington Valley', in *Sydney Gazette*, 19 January 1832, p.3, c.1-2.

Garran, A. (ed.), *Australia: the first hundred years*, facsimile copy of *The picturesque atlas of Australasia*, 2 vols, first published 1886, Ure Smith, Sydney, 1974.

Henwood, G., *Cornwall's mines and miners: nineteenth century studies*, R. Burt, (ed.), Barton, Truro, 1972.

Hood, J. *Australia and the East: a journal narrative of a voyage to New South Wales in an emigrant ship with a residence of some months in Sydney and the bush in the years 1841 and 1842*, John Murray, London, 1843. [ML 981/H].

Jevons, W.S., 'Sydney in 1858', in *Sydney Morning Herald*, 6, 9, 13, 16, 23, 30 November and 7 December 1929.

Lang, Rev J.D. 'Moreton Bay and separation once more' in *The Empire*, 7 August 1857, p.6, c.3-5..

Lang, Rev J.D., 'Notes of a visit to the Clarence and Richmond Rivers,' in *The Empire*, 4 November 1865, p.5, c.2-6.

Lean, T., *On the steam engines in Cornwall*, first published 1839, reprinted Barton, Truro, 1969.

La Meslee, E.M., *The new Australia*, first published 1883, translated and edited by Russell Ward, Heinemann Educational, Melbourne, 1979.

Meredith, Mrs C., *Notes and sketches of New South Wales during a residence in that colony from 1839 to 1844*, first published 1844, facsimile edition, Penguin Books, Ringwood, Victoria, 1973.

A Nonagenarian, [Mrs A. Busby], *Bathurst in the thirties: some memories of the early days*, A.J. Dowse, Bathurst, N.S.W., 1902. [ML 991.6/8A1.]

Norden, J., *Speculi Britanniae Pars: a topographical and historical description of Cornwall, with a map of the county and each Hundred*, first published 1728, facsimile reprint by F. Graham, Newcastle upon Tyne, 1966. [SLNSW NQ 942.37/3.]

An old Methodist, [George Hawke], *Wesleyan Methodism in New South Wales*, Fred H. Earle, Falmouth, 1879. [ML 287.1/H.]

Plummer, J., *The mineral products of New South Wales*, New South Wales Court, International Exhibition of Mining and Metallurgy, London 1890, Department of Mines and Agriculture, Sydney, 1890. [ML 553P.]

Polsue, J., *Lakes's parochial history of the County of Cornwall*, 4 vols., first published 1867-1873, facsimile reprint EP Publishing in collaboration with Cornwall County Library, Truro, 1974.

Ryan, J.T., *Reminiscences of Australia: containing 70 years of his own knowledge and 35 years of his ancestors*, first published 1894, facsimile reprint by Nepean Family History Society, South Penrith, N.S.W., 1982.

'The Sanitary state of Sydney', in *Sydney Morning Herald*, 1, 8, 15, 22 February, 1, 8, 15, 22, 29 March, 5 April 1851.

Stanger, J.C., *A journey from Sydney over the Blue Mountains to Bathurst forty years ago*, G. Whalan, Bathurst, N.S.W., 1882. [ML 981.5/W and 042/Pa 407.]

*The Star of Peace Gold Mining Company Ltd.*, Hawkins Hill, Tambaroora, with phototype and plans, Jarrett and Co., Sydney, 1880. [ML 662.3S.]

Stockdale, F.W.L., *Excursions through Cornwall 1824*, reprinted Barton, Truro, 1972.

Walker, W., *Reminiscences (personal, social and political) of a fifty years' residence at Windsor on the Hawkesbury*, first published 1890, facsimile reprint, Library of Australian History, North Sydney, 1977.

Windross, J. and Ralston, J.P., *Historical records of Newcastle 1797-1897*, first published 1897, facsimile reprint Library of Australian History, North Sydney, 1978.

## E.) CONTEMPORARY NEWSPAPERS

*Adelong Argus*, Tumut and Gundagai Advertiser, Adelong.

*The Adelong Mining Journal and Tumut Express*, [NLA Nx 330.]

*Australian Town and Country Journal*, Sydney.

*The Bathurst Advocate*, Bathurst.

*The Bathurst Free Press and Mining Journal*, Bathurst.

*The Bathurst Post*, Bathurst.

*The Bathurst Times*, Bathurst.

*Bulletin*, Sydney.

*The Christian Advocate and Wesleyan Record*, Sydney.

*Daily Telegraph*, Sydney.

*The Empire*, Sydney.

*The Gundagai Times*, Gundagai.

*The Hillgrove Guardian*, Hillgrove.

*The Illustrated Sydney News*, Sydney.

*The Times*, London.

*Maitland Mercury*, Maitland.
*The Methodist*, Sydney.
*Newcastle Morning Herald and Miner's Advocate*, Newcastle.
*The Royal Cornwall Gazette*, Truro.
*Singleton Argus*, Singleton.
*Sydney Gazette and New South Wales Advertiser*, Sydney.
*Shipping Gazette and Sydney General Trade List, 1844-1860*, Sydney. [NLA MCN 700.]
*Sydney Morning Herald*, Sydney.
*The Weekly Advocate*, Sydney.
*West Briton*, Truro.

## F.) DIRECTORIES, GUIDES AND GAZETTEERS

*Bailliere's New South Wales gazetteer and road guide*, Bailliere, Sydney, 1866. [NLA 919.44 BAI.]

*Bathurst directory and almanac 1862*, published for the proprietor by E.G. Wilton, Bathurst, 1862. [NLA F6797.]

Ford, W. and F., *Sydney commercial directory for the year 1851*, first published 1851, facsimile reprint Library of Australian History, North Sydney 1978.

*The gazetteer of New South Wales 1866*, Sherriff and Downing, Sydney.

*Greville's official post office directory and gazetteer of New South Wales 1875-1877*, Greville and Company, Sydney, 1877. [NLA 919.44 GRE.]

Maclehose, J., *Picture of Sydney and strangers' guide in N.S.W. for 1839*, first published 1839, republished John Ferguson in association with the Royal Australian Historical Society, Sydney, 1977.

Middleton, A. and Maning, F.B., *Bathurst and Western District directory and tourist's guide and gazetteer 1886-7*, first published 1886, facsimile reprint Library of Australian History, North Sydney, 1978.

Pulleine, F.A., *The Australasian mining directory*, W.H. Lacey, Sydney, 1888. [ML 622.06/P.]

*Sands Sydney and N.S.W. directory 1858-1933*. [NLA MCN B3.]

Symons, R., *Gazetteer of Cornwall*, F. Rodder, Penzance, 1884. [Royal Institution of Cornwall.]

Waugh J.W., *The stranger's guide to Sydney*, first published 1861, facsimile reprint Library of Australian History, North Sydney, 1978.

## G.) INTERVIEWS AND TELEPHONE DISCUSSIONS

Mr Bill Broadsmith, Molong, N.S.W.
Mrs L. Cable, Sydney.
Mr A.W. Cameron, Glen Innes, N.S.W.
The Rev. E.G. Clancy, Sydney.
Mr Rex Chegwidden, Sydney.
Mrs Dot Clayworth, Singleton, N.S.W.
Mr Mel Davies, The University of Western Australia.
Mr Bernard Deacon, Cornwall.
Mr Dominic Eagan, Cobar, N.S.W.
Dr Shirley Fitzgerald, Sydney.
Professor L.E. Fredman, The University of Newcastle, N.S.W.
Mrs Thelma Freeman, Melbourne, Victoria.
Mrs Jan Gendall, Cornwall.
Mr Richard Gendall, Cornwall.
Ms Robin Haines, Flinders University, Adelaide, South Australia.
Mr Richard Hancock, Adelaide, South Australia.
Mr Will Hawke, Byng, N.S.W.
Mr Peter Hohnen, Canberra.
Mrs Phyllis Hohnen, Canberra.
Mrs Helen Jeuken, Bathurst, N.S.W.
Mr Ross Maroney, Orange, N.S.W.
Mrs Mavis Newcombe, Maitland, N.S.W.
Mrs Mary Nesbitt, Bathurst, N.S.W.
Mr W. Newby, Cornwall.
Mr Trevor Pascoe, Beneree, N.S.W.
Dr Philip Payton, Cornwall.
Dr C.A. Price, Australian National University, Canberra.
Mrs Joy Prisk, Cobar, N.S.W.
Mr Ken Prowse, Tumut, N.S.W.
Mrs Lyn Quince, Tumut, N.S.W.
Dr Richard Reid, Australian National University, Canberra.
Mrs Peggy Richards, Singleton, N.S.W.
Mrs Aileen Roberson, Cowra, N.S.W.
Mrs Beth Robertson, Sydney.
Mr Dennis Rowe, Newcastle, N.S.W.
Dr John Rowe, Cornwall.
Miss Jennifer Sloggett, Newcastle, N.S.W.
Mr W. Snelson, Cobar, N.S.W.
Mrs Netta Stoneman, Bathurst, N.S.W.
Mr B.W. Thomas, Orange, N.S.W.
Mr Roger Thomas, Gosford, N.S.W.
Mrs Catherine Tizzard, Queanbeyan, N.S.W.
Mrs V. Wearne-Frost, Katoomba, N.S.W.
Mrs Elizabeth Wiedemann, Inverell, N.S.W.

# II. SECONDARY SOURCES

## A.) REFERENCE WORKS AND GUIDES

Andrighetti, J., *Labour records in the Mitchell Library*, State Library of NSW, State Library of New South Wales, Sydney, 1989.

Ansell, L.J., (ed.), *Register of church archives*, 2nd edition, Church Archivists' Society, Toowoomba, Queensland, 1985.

*ANU Archives of Business and Labour list of holdings*, Canberra, 1990.

*Australian Dictionary of Biography*, 10 vols., Melbourne University Press, Melbourne, 1966-86.

*Australian Historic Records Register*, mfiche, NLA, Canberra, 1989. [NLA RM MCN 805.]

Bathurst City Library, (comp.), *Bathurst newspaper index*, Bathurst, N.S.W., 1986-87, [NLA NEF 016.0799445 B332.]

Broxam, G. and Nicholson, I., *Shipping arrivals and departures: Sydney 1841-1844*, vol.3, Roebuck Books, Canberra, 1988.

Champion, B.W., (comp.), *Hunter Valley register, registers 1-4, 1843-1905*, the author, Newcastle, N.S.W., 1973-1978. [NLA Nf+ 079.944 2016.].

Connolly, C.N., *Biographical register of the New South Wales Parliament 1856-1901*, Australian National

University Press, Canberra, 1983.

*Cyclopaedia of New South Wales: an historical and commercial review*, McCarron Stewart, Sydney, 1907. [ML Q991C Refl.]

Eslick, C., Hughes, J. and Jack, R.I., *Bibliography of New South Wales local history: an annotated bibliography of secondary works published before 1982 and New South Wales directories 1828-1950: a bibliography*, New South Wales University Press, Sydney, 1987.

Ferguson, J.A., *Bibliography of Australia 1780-1900*, 7 vols., National Library of Australia, Canberra, 1975-86.

Gibbney, H.J, and Burns, N., (comps.) *A biographers' index of parliamentary returns (New South Wales, Queensland and Victoria) 1850-1889*, Department of History (Australian Dictionary of Biography), Institute of Advanced Studies, Australian National University, Canberra, 1969.

Gray, N., (ed.), *Gravestone inscriptions in the Upper Hunter Valley, New South Wales*, Scone and Upper Hunter Historical Society, Scone, N.S.W., 1987. [NLA NLq 989.5099444.G776.]

Gray, N., (ed.), *Murrurundi memorials: gravestone inscriptions in the Upper Hunter Valley, New South Wales*, Scone and Upper Hunter Historical Society, Scone, N.S.W., 1987. [NLA NLq 929.5099444 M984.]

*Guide to shipping and free passenger records*, guide no.17, 2nd edition, Archives Office of New South Wales, Sydney, 1984.

Guilford, E., (comp.), *Hunter Valley directory: 1841*, Hunter Valley Publications, Newcastle, N.S.W., 1987.

Hughes, J., (ed.), *Local government ... local history: a guide to N.S.W. local government minute books and rate records*, Royal Australian Historical Society, Sydney, 1990.

*Illawarra pioneers: pre 1900*, Illawarra Family History Group Inc., Wollongong, N.S.W., 1988.

*Index to N.S.W immigration deposit journals 1853-1900*, microfiche, Pastkeys, Sydney, 1988.

Jones, E., (comp.), *Register of pioneer families of Lithgow and district (pre 1856)*, vol.1, Lithgow and District Family History Society Inc., Lithgow, N.S.W., 1988.

*Manuscript material relating to immigrant voyages to Australia*, National Library of Australia, Canberra, 1984.

*New South Wales Registry of Births, Deaths and Marriages index 1787-1900*, microfiche, New South Wales Registrar General, Sydney.

*Newspapers in Australian libraries: a union list*, part 2, Australian newspapers, 4th edition, National Library of Australia, Canberra, 1985.

Nicholson, I. H., *Shipping arrivals and departures: Sydney 1826-1840*, Roebuck Society, Canberra, reprinted 1981.

Peskett, H., (comp,), *Guide to the parish and non-parochial registers of Devon and Cornwall 1538-1837*, Extra Series vol II, Devon and Cornwall Record Society, Torquay, 1979.

*Probate index 1800-1938*, Supreme Court of N.S.W, microfiche, [NLA MCN 481.]

Radi, H., Spearritt, P. and Hinton, E., *Biographical register of the New South Wales Parliament 1901-1970*, Australian National University Press, Canberra, 1979.

Richards, A., *Guide to books relating to Cornwall in Canberra libraries*, the author, Canberra, 1989.

Richards, J.A., Garnsey, H. and Phippen, A., *Index to the microform collection of the Society of Australian Genealogists*, Society of Australian Genealogists, Sydney, 1990.

*Rookwood monumental inscriptions*, index and inscriptions, microfiche, Society of Australian Genealogists, 1988. [NLA MCN 781.]

Sainty, M.R. and Johnson, K.A., (eds.), *Census of New South Wales, November 1828*, Library of Australian History, Sydney, 1985.

*Sandgate cemetery burials 1881-1985*, microfiche, Newcastle Region Public Library, Newcastle, N.S.W., 1989. [NLA MCN 783.]

Stemp, P.J., (comp.), *Index of depositors for emigrants resident in Cornwall 1853-1900*, compiled from Archives Office of New South Wales immigration deposit journals 1853-1900, computer printout: in the possession of the author.

Stuckey, G, and Archer, P., (eds.), *Adelong cemetery 1861-1987*, Tumut Family History Group, Tumut, N.S.W., 1988.

*St Stephens Church of England, Camperdown*, index and transcripts, microfiche, Society of Australian Genealogists, Sydney, [n.d.].

## B.) BOOKS AND ARTICLES

Abbott, J.H.M., 'Mount Wingen: the Burning Mountain of the Kingdon Ponds Valley, its story during the last century', in *Royal Australian Historical Society Journal and Proceedings*, vol.VII, 1921, part 3, pp.131-47.

Alt, C., (comp.), *Old Torrington: a history of Torrington and district 1881-1981*, `Back to Torrington Weekend' Committee, Torrington, N.S.W., 1981.

Andrews, E.C., *Report on the Hillgrove gold-field*, Department of Mines and Agriculture, mineral resources no.8, New South Wales Government Printer, Sydney, 1900.

Andrews, E.C., *Report on the Cobar copper and gold-field*, 2 vols., Department of Mines, mineral resources nos.17-18, New South Wales Government Printer, Sydney, 1913-1915.

*Armidale 1863-1938: 75th anniversary of the Municipality*, Pogonoski, Newcastle, N.S.W., 1938. [NLA Nq 994.44 A729.]

Armstrong, J., (ed.), *Shaping the Hunter: a story of engineers, and the engineering contribution to the development of the present shape of the Hunter Region, its rivers, cities, industries and transport arteries*, Institution of Engineers Australia, Newcastle division, Newcaste, N.S.W., 1983.

Atkinson, A., *Camden: farm and village life in early New South Wales*, Oxford University Press, Melbourne, 1988.

*Back to Maitland Week Souvenir Book*, C. Brock, Maitland N.S.W., 1927. [NLA JAFp HIST 812].

*Back to Molong celebrations 1928: official souvenir*, Back to Molong Executive Committee, Sydney, 1928. [NLA JAFp HIST 878.]

Baker, R.G.V., *Historic Sofala: a goldfield that changed a nation, 1851-1943*, Centrepak Research, Cronulla, N.S.W., 1985.

Balchin, W.G.V., *Cornwall: an illustrated essay on the history of the landscape*, Hodder and Stoughton, London, 1954.

Barry, J.A., *The city of Sydney: the story of its growth from its foundation to the present day*, 3rd edition, New South Wales Bookstall, Sydney, 1902. [NLA MCL HIST 663.]

Barton, D.B., *Essays in Cornish mining history*. 2 vols., Barton, Truro, 1968-71.

Barton, R.M., (ed.), *Life in Cornwall in the mid-nineteenth century being extracts from the West Briton newspaper in the two decades from 1835 to 1855*, Barton, Truro, 1971.

Barton, R.M., (ed.), *Life in Cornwall in the late nineteenth century being extracts from the West Briton newspaper in the two decades from 1855 to 1875*, Barton, Truro, 1972.

Barton, R.M., (ed.), *Life in Cornwall at the end of the nineteenth century being extracts from the West Briton newspaper in the years from 1876 to 1899*, Barton, Truro, 1974.

Barwood, W., (ed.), *Cobar Public School Centenary 1878-1978*, [Cobar P. and C. Association ?], Cobar, N.S.W., 1978.

*Bathurst neswpaper cuttings*, vol.46. [MLQ991/N.]

Bayley, W.A., *Blue Haven: history of Kiama Municipality New South Wales*, 2nd edition, Kiama Municipal Council, Kiama, N.S.W., 1976.

Bayley, W.A., *Shoalhaven: history of the Shire of Shoalhaven, New South Wales*, revised edition, Shoalhaven Shire Council, Nowra, N.S.W., 1975.

Bennett, A., *Cornwall through the mid nineteenth century*, Kingfisher Railway Productions, Southampton, 1987.

Berresford Ellis, P., *The story of the Cornish language*, Tor Mark Press, Truro, [n.d.].

Berry, C., *Portrait of Cornwall*, 2nd edition, Robert Hale, London, 1974.

Best, N. Rowe, *The Mumford Rowes*, the author, Fairlight, N.S.W., 1987.

Birch, A. and Macmillan, D., (eds.)., *The Sydney scene 1788-1960*, first published 1962, Hale and Iremonger, Sydney, 1982.

Bird, R.J., *Adelong: glimpses at the past*, Stewart press, Hornsby, N.S.W., 1976.

Bird, S., *The book of Cornish villages*, Dovecote Press, Dorset, 1988.

Blainey, G., *A land half won*, revised edition, Sun Books, Melbourne, 1983.

Blainey, G., *The tyranny of distance: how distance shaped Australia's history*, revised edition, Sun Books, Melbourne, reprinted 1988.

Boden, E.G., 'Tempe Wesleyan chapel', in *Australian Methodist Historical Society Journal*, vol.VIII, no.24, part 2, January 1940, pp.375-86.

Bone, F.S., (ed.), *Orange district guide 1908*, facsimile reprint, G. and C. Reynolds, Millthorpe, N.S.W., 1983.

Bowd, D.G., *Macquarie country: a history of the Hawkesbury*, revised edition, Library of Australian History, Sydney, 1982.

Braithwaite, N. and Beard, H., (eds.), *Pioneering in the Bellinger Valley*, Bellinger Valley Historical Society, Bellingen, N.S.W., c.1978.

Brayshay, M., 'Government assisted emigration from Plymouth in the nineteenth century', in *Transactions of the Devonshire Association*, vol.112, pp.185-213, December 1980.

Bridges, B. and Prentis, M., 'A biographical register of Presbyterian ministers in New South Wales 1823-1865', in *Church Heritage*, vol.3, no.3, March 1984.

Brodsky, I., *Sydney's little world of Woolloomooloo*, Old Sydney Free Press, Neutral Bay, N.S.W., 1966.

Brown, A., *The Evans family history*, the author, Epping, N.S.W., 1987, reprinted 1989.

Brown, H. Miles, *The Church in Cornwall*, Oscar Blackford, Truro, 1964.

Brown K., 'Australian Cornish and other beam engines, part I' in *The Trevithick Society newsletter*, the Trevithick Society, [Callington ?] no.47, November 1984, pp.4-5.

Brown, Martyn, *Australia bound! the story of West Country connections 1788-1988*, Ex Libris Press, Bradford on Avon, 1988.

Buckley, G.C., *Of toffs and toilers: from Cornwall to New Zealand: fragments of past*, Ross, Auckland, 1983.

Buckley, K. and Wheelwright, T., *No paradise for workers: capitalism and the common people in Australia 1788-1914*, Oxford University Press, Melbourne, 1988.

Burke, G., 'The Cornish diaspora of the nineteenth century', in S. Marks and P. Richardson, (eds.), *International labour migration: historical perspectives*, University of London Institute of Commonwealth Studies, London, 1984, pp.57-75.

Burt, R., (ed.), *Cornish mining: essays on the organisation of Cornish mines and the Cornish mining economy*, David and Charles, Newton Abbot, 1969.

*Burwood Municipal Jubilee: official souvenir: containing history* of the Municipality of Burwood 1874-1924 together with a record of the early history of the district, Madden and Grano for the Municipality of Burwood, Sydney, 1924. [NLA MCL HIST 351.]

Button, P. M., *The Button family: from Blisland to Burren and beyond*, the author, Canberrra, 1997.

Cameron, A.W., *A short history of Glen Innes*, Glen Innes and District Historical Society, Glen Innes, N.S.W., 1987.

Carne, J.E., *The copper-mining industry and the distribution of copper ores in New South Wales*, 2nd edition, Department of Mines, mineral resources no.6, New South Wales Government Printer, Sydney, 1908.

Carne, J.E., *The tin-mining industry and the distribution of tin ores in New South Wales*, New South Wales Department of Mines, mineral resources no.14, New South Wales Government Printer, Sydney, 1911.

Cashman R. and Meader C., *Marrickville: rural outpost to inner city*, Hale and Iremonger, Petersham, N.S.W., 1990.

Charge, N.F. and Lingard, E.K., *Glory be: commemorating the 100th anniversary of the opening of the first Wesleyan chapel in Newcastle 1845-1945*, the organising committee, Newcastle, N.S.W., 1945. [UCA].

Charleston, H., Moase, T. and Morison, D.N., (comps.), *Seventy years of Newcastle Methodism*, [no publisher], Newcastle, N.S.W., 1904. [UCA].

Charlwood, D., *The long farewell: the perilous voyages of settlers under sail in the great migrations to Australia*, Penguin, Ringwood, Victoria, 1983.

Chesher, V., *Industrial housing in the tin and copper mining areas of Cornwall: later 18th & 19th centuries*, Trevithick Society, [Penzance ?], 1981.

Chesher, V.M, and Chesher, F.J., *The Cornishman's house: an introduction to the history of traditional domestic architecture in Cornwall*, Barton, Truro, 1968.

Chubb, W., (comp.), *Jubilee souvenir of the Municipality of Newtown 1862-1912*, Austral Press and Advertising Ltd., Sydney, 1912. [NLA Nq+ 994.41 CHU.]

Chuk, F., *The Somerset years: government-assisted emigrants from Somerset and Bristol who arrived in Port Phillip Victoria 1839-1854*, Pennard Hill Publications, Ballarat, Victoria, 1987.

Clancy, E.G., *'More precious than gold': commemorating the 100th anniversary of the Orange Circuit of the Methodist Church 1860-1960*, Central Western Daily, Orange, N.S.W., 1960. [NLA JAFp HIST 1050.]

Clancy, E.G., 'Orange Circuit centenary', in *Australian Methodist Historical Society Journal*, no.76, May 1961, pp.1023-4.

Clancy, E.G., 'The Primitive Methodist Church in New South Wales: piccaninny daylight - 1847-1854', in *Church Heritage*, vol.2, no.4, September 1982, pp.305-39.

Clancy, E.G., (comp.), 'Biographical register of Primitive Methodist ministers in New South Wales' [1847-1902], in *Church Heritage*, vol.4, no.2, September 1985, pp.122-41.

Clancy, E.G., 'Methodism and the New South Wales Labor Party in the early 1890s', in *Church Heritage*, vol.7, no.1, March 1991, pp.13-35.

Clarke, R.M., 'The early days of the Rev William Clarke', in *Journal and Proceedings of the Australian Methodist Historical Society*, vol.XL, no.37, part 3, July 1943, pp.518-37.

Clegg, J., *Carcoar, historic village*, Robert Brown and associates, Bathurst, N.S.W., 1979.

Clelland, W., *Cobar founding fathers: an illustrated history of the pioneering days in the copper mining district of Cobar, New South Wales*, Western Heritage Series no.7, Macquarie Publications, Dubbo, N.S.W., 1984.

Clune, F., *Serenade to Sydney: some historical landmarks*, Angus and Robertson, Sydney, 1967.

*Cobar Copper Centenary 1869-1969*, The Cobar Copper Centenary Celebrations Committee, Cobar, N.S.W., 1969.

Coe, T.B., (ed. and comp.), *The northern districts of New South Wales, descriptive and illustrative: Tamworth, Manilla, Quirindi, Armidale, Hillgrove, Uralla, Glen Innes, Tenterfield, Inverell, etc., etc.*, Samuel E. Lees, Sydney, [1907 ?]. [ML Q981.8C.]

Colwell, J., *The illustrated history of Methodism: Australia 1812 to 1855, New South Wales and Polynesia 1856 to 1902*, William Brooks, Sydney, 1904.

'Copper Hill', in *The Molong Historian*, vol.I, no.18, Molong Historical Society, Molong, N.S.W., February 1975, pp.2-5.

'The Copper Hill story', in *The Molong Historian*, vol.I, no.24, Molong Historical Society, Molong, April 1976, pp.1-3.

*Cornwall*, Cornwall County Council, Truro, 1989.

Coupe, S., *Concord: a centenary history*, The Council of the Municipality of Concord, Concord, N.S.W., 1983.

Cowls, B., 'Cornish Settlement in Australia' in *Old Cornwall: journal of the Federation of Old Cornwall Societies*, vol.IX, no.1, Federation of Old Cornwall Societies, [Penzance ?], 1979, pp.22-4.

Dangar, E.M. *The Dangars from St Neot, Cornwall*, John Dangar Christian Reid ?, Sydney, 1966. [NLA JAFp 929.2 D182.]

Dangar, E.M., *William Dangar of Turanville*, Scone historical monograph no.1, Scone and Upper Hunter Historical Society, Scone, N.S.W., 1968.

Daniell, S., *Old Cornwall: life in the county about a century ago*, Tor Mark Press, Truro, [n.d.].

Daniell, S., *The story of Cornwall*, Tor Mark Press, Truro, [n.d.].

*Darlington Public School 1878-1978*, Darlington Public School Parents and Citizens Association, Darlington, N.S.W., 1978. [NLA Npf+ 371.0099441 D22.]

Deacon, B., 'Migration and the mining industry in East Cornwall in the mid nineteenth century', in *Journal of the Royal Institution of Cornwall*, vol.X, part 1, 1986-87, pp.84-104.

Deacon, B., George, A. and Perry, R., *Cornwall: at the crossroads: living communities or leisure zone?*, The Cornish Social and Economic Research Group, Redruth, 1988.

Deacon, B., 'The pattern of migration in nineteenth century Cornwall', lecture at the Fifth British Family History Conference, Newquay, Cornwall, 1 April 1990.

Dexter, T.F.G., *Cornish names*, first published 1926, reprinted Barton, Truro, 1968.

Dickason, G.B., *Cornish immigrants to South Africa: the Cousin Jacks' contribution to the development of mining* and commerce 1820-1920, Balkema, Cape Town, 1978.

Donald, J. Kay, *Exploring the north coast and New England*, a Heritage Field Guide, Kangaroo Press, Kenthurst, N.S.W., 1987.

Donald, J. Kay, and Hungerford, M.E., *Exploring the Hunter Region*, a Heritage Field Guide, Kangaroo Press, Kenthurst, N.S.W., 1984.

Doust, R., *After one hundred years: the centenary of Methodism in Bathurst and the west of N.S.W. 1832-1932*, G.W. Brownhill, Bathurst, N.S.W., 1932.

Dowd, B.T., 'The genesis of Nundle', in *Royal Australian Historical Society Journal and Proceedings*, vol.XXXI 1945, pp.41-5.

Driscoll, W.P., *The beginnings of the wine industry in the Hunter Valley*, Newcastle history monographs no.5, Newcastle Public Library, Newcastle, N.S.W., 1969.

Du Maurier, D., *Vanishing Cornwall*, Penguin, Harmondsworth, 1972, reprinted 1986.

Duncan, R., 'Case studies in emigration: Cornwall, Gloucestershire and New South Wales 1877-1886', in *The Economic History Review*, vol.XVI, 1963-4, pp.272-89.

Dygemysker, 'Cornish Notes' in *An Baner Kernewek: the Cornish Banner*, vol.2, no.4, 1978. [NLA Sq 320.94237 COR.]

Edwards, M.S., *The divisions of Cornish Methodism 1802 to 1857*, The Cornish Methodist Historical Society Association, occasional publication no.7, [Redruth ?], 1964.

Elder, B., *Blood on the wattle: massacres and maltreatment of Australian Aborigines since 1788*, Child and Associates, Frenchs Forest, N.S.W., 1988.

Elkin, A.P., 'Some early chaplains and churches in the Hunter River Valley', in *Royal Australian Historical Society Journal and Proceedings*, vol.XXIII, 1937, pp.122-48.

Elkin, A.P., *Morpeth and I*, first published 1937, facsimile reprint, Library of Australian History, North Sydney, 1979.

Ellis, H., *Views and reviews: a selection of uncollected articles 1884-1932*, first series 1884-1919, Harmsworth, London, 1932.

Emanuel, U.R., 'The history and decline of the village of Byng', in *The Australian Geographer*, vol.I part 2, November 1929, pp.79-81. [ML Q980/A.]

Faull, J., *Cornish heritage: a miner's story*, the author, Adelaide, 1980.

Faull, J., *The Cornish in Australia*, AE Press, Melbourne, 1983.

Fitzgerald, S., *Rising damp: Sydney 1870-90*, Oxford University Press, Melbourne, 1987.

Fitzgerald, S., *Writing a history of the City of Sydney, working papers in Australian Studies, no.45*, Sir Robert Menzies Centre for Australian Studies, Institute of Commonwealth Studies, University of London, 1989.

Fitzgerald, S., *Chippendale: beneath the factory wall*, Hale and Iremonger, Sydney, 1990.

Fitzgerald, S. and Keating, C., *Millers Point: the urban village*, Hale and Iremonger, Sydney, 1991.

Fitzpatrick, J.C.L., *The good old days of Molong*, Cumberland Argus, Parramatta, N.S.W., 1913. [NLA N+ 994.45 FIT.]

Folster, W., *Newspaper cuttings, Orange New South Wales*, [ML Q991.6/O].

Folster, W., *Lucknow 1851-1933*, Orange Advocate, Orange, N.S.W., 1933. [NLA JAFp HIST 811.]

Foott, S., (ed.), *Methodist celebration: a Cornish contribution*, Dyllansow Truran, Redruth, 1988.

Fox, A., *South west England*, Thames and Hudson, London, 1964.

Freame, W., *Chronicles of the past: being newspaper cuttings from 1827 to 1914 relating to Australian history, biography, topography and literature*. [ML F991/4A1.]

Fredman, L.E., (ed.), *Sir John Quick's notebook*, Pogonoski, Newcastle, N.S.W., 1965.

Fredman, L.E., (ed.), *A history of Maitland*, Council of the City of Maitland, Maitland, N.S.W., 1983.

Fudge, C., *The life of Cornish*, Dyllansow Truran, Redruth, 1982.

Gibbney, H.J., *Eurobodalla: history of the Moruya district*, Library of Australian History in association with the Council of the Shire of Eurobodalla, Sydney, 1980.

Glanville, I., *St Just's Point*, the author, Bendigo, 1990.

Glanville, I., *St Just's Point No.2*, the author, Bendigo, n.d.

Glasson, M., (comp.), *The Glasson saga*, the author, Orange, N.S.W., [1982 ?].

Glasson, W.R., *Australia's first goldfield: an address delivered to the Rotary CLubs of Wellington, Orange and Bathurst, N.S.W.*, Australasian Medical Publishing Company Limited, Sydney, 1944. [NLA MCL HIST 244a.]

Glasson, W.R., *Early western glimpses*, Orange Leader, Molong, N.S.W., 1933. [NLA MCL HIST 246.]

Glasson, W.R., *Ophir revisited*, Australasian Medical Publishing Company Limited, Sydney, 1947. [NLA MCL HIST 566.]

Glasson, W.R., *Our shepherds*, Australasian Medical Publishing Company Limited, Sydney, 1942. [NLA Np 636.0835 GLA.]

*Glebe School Centenary 1958*, the Centenary Committee of the Glebe School, Glebe, N.S.W., 1958. [NLA Np 372.99441 G554.]

Gollan, R., *The coalminers of New South Wales: a history of the union, 1860-1960*, Melbourne University Press in association with the Australian National University, Melbourne, 1963.

Goold, W.J., 'The port of Newcastle', in *Royal Australian Historical Society Journal and Proceedings*, vol.XXIV, 1938, pp.43-73.

Goold, W.J., 'Churches of the Newcastle district', in *The Newcastle and Hunter District Historical Society Journal*, vol.IX, pp.81-128, May 1955, part VIII. [ML 991.4/2.]

Graham, F., *Smuggling in Cornwall*, Nigel Clarke Publications, Lyme Regis, [n.d.].

Gray, N., *The promised land: a summary of early settlement in the Shire of Scone*, Scone historical monograph no.3, Scone and Upper Hunter Historical Society, Scone, N.S.W., 1975.

Gray, N., *Thomas Cook of Turanville*, Scone historical monograph no.5, Scone and Upper Hunter Historical Society, Scone, N.S.W., 1977.

Greaves, B., (ed.), *The story of Bathurst*, 3rd edition, Angus and Robertson, Sydney, 1976.

Green, D. and Cromwell, L., *Mutual aid or welfare state: Australia's friendly societies*, Allen and Unwin, Sydney, 1984.

Green, W., 'The old north: story of Hillgrove', *Northern Daily Leader*, press cuttings, vol.2, 1936, pp.28-9. [ML Q991.8N.]

Greenhalgh, A.J., *Time's sujects: the story of Goorangoola, a small community in the Hunter Valley of New South Wales, 1839-1939*, the author, Roseville, N.S.W., 1982.

Grocott, A.M., *Gleanings from Glen Innes*, the author, Glen Innes, N.S.W., 1985.

Halliday, F.E., *A history of Cornwall*, first published 1959, Duckworth, London, 1963.

Halstead, G., *The story of St Ives (N.S.W.) and some of its neighbours*, Nungurner Press, Turramurra, N.S.W., 1982.

Hamilton Jenkin, A.K., *The story of Cornwall*, Nelson, London, 1935.

Hamilton Jenkin, A.K., *Cornwall and its people*, first published 1945, paperback edition, David and Charles, Newton Abbott, 1988.

Hamilton Jenkin, A.K., *The Cornish miner: an account of his life above and underground from early times*, 2nd edition, Allen and Unwin, London, 1948.

Hampton, D.P., *Retail co-operatives in the lower Hunter Valley*, Newcastle history monograph no.12, Newcastle Public Library, Newcastle, N.S.W., 1986.

Hannan, N., *Travels and heartaches of a mining family*, the author, Romford, Essex, 1984.

Harper, L.F., *The Adelong goldfield*, Department of Mines, mineral resources no. 21, New South Wales Government Printer, Sydney, 1916.

Harris, K., *Hevva!: an account of the Cornish fishing industry in the days of sail*, Dyllansow Truran, Redruth, 1983.

Hassall, J.S., *In old Australia: records and reminiscences from 1794*, first published 1902, facsimile reprint, Library of Australian History, North Sydney, 1977.

Hawken, S., *A Hawken history: from St Tudy, Cornwall to the Fish River, New South Wales*, Development and Advisory Publications, Dubbo, N.S.W., 1988.

Hedley, K., *People and progress: Tumut Shire 1887-1987*, Tumut Shire Council, Tumut, N.S.W., 1987.

Henderson, C., *Cornish church guide and parochial history of Cornwall*, first published 1925, reprinted Barton, Truro, 1964.

Henderson, C., *Essays in Cornish history*, first published 1935, Barton, Truro, 1963.

Hendry, J., (ed.), *Darlinghurst Public School Centenary 1883-198<u>3</u>*, Darlinghurst Public School, Sydney, 1983. [NLA Npf+ 372.99441 D221.]

Hendy-Pooley, G., 'History of Maitland', in *Royal Australian Historical Society Journal and Proceedings*, vol.II, 1909, pp.283-96.

Hodge, B., *Valleys of gold*, Cambaroora Star Publications, Penshurst, N.S.W., 1976.

Hodge, B., *Touring Hill End*, Cambaroora Star Publications, Penshurst, N.S.W., 1988.

Hodge, H., *The Hill End story*, book 1, 3rd edition, Hill End Publications, Toorak, Victoria, 1986.

Hodge, H., *The Hill End story*, book 2, 3rd edition, Hill End Publications, St Ives, N.S.W., 1980.

Hodge, H., *The Hill End story*, book 3, 3rd edition, Hill End Publications, Toorak, Victoria, 1987.

Hohnen, P., *A history of the Lane, Tom and Dale families*, the author, Canberra, [n.d.].

Hopkins, R., *Where now Cousin Jack?*, Bendigo Bicentennial Community Committee, Bendigo, Victoria, 1988.

Hoskins, W.G., *Provincial England: essays in social and economic history*, Macmillan, London, 1964.

Hoskins, W.G., *The human geography of the South-West*, the George Johnstone Lecture, 1968, Seale-Hayne Agricultural College, Newton Abbot, 1968.

Hosking, R., *From Cornwall to the outback: a history of the Varcoe family and its activities*, Hosking Publishers, Hawthorn, South Australia, 1987.

'"In Memorium", ministers who have laboured in New South Wales and the mission fields', in *New South Wales Methodist Conference Minutes 1943-45*, Appendix E, 1944, pp.362-73. [UCA.]

*Inverell Week 1933: official souvenir*, Jones and Harvey, Brisbane, 1933. [NLA Npf 919.444 I62.]

Jervis, J., 'The Hunter Valley: a century of its history', *Royal Australian Historical Society Journal and Proceedings*, vol.XXXIX, 1953, pp.97-150, and pp.191-202.

Jervis, J. and Flack, L., *A jubilee history of the Municipality of Botany 1888-1938*, W.C. Penfold and Co., Sydney, 1938. [ML Q991.1/J.]

Jervis, J., 'The rise of Newcastle, eighty years of its history 1804-1884', in *Royal Australian Historical Society Journal and Proceedings*, vol.XXI, 1935, pp.143-96.

Johns, R.K., *Cornish mining heritage*, special publication no.6, Department of Mines and Energy South Australia, Adelaide, 1986.

Johnson, N., Rose, P., *Cornwall's archaeological heritage from prehistory to the Tudors: 8000BC-AD1540*, Twelve Heads Press, Truro, 1990.

Karlsen, C., *Return to Sunny Corner*, Mitchell College of Advanced Education, Bathurst, N.S.W., 1988.

Kay-Robinson, D., *Devon and Cornwall*, Bartholomew, London, 1977.

Keating, C., *Surry Hills: the city's backyard*, Hale and Iremonger, Sydney, 1991.

Kelly, G., (ed.), *The lacemakers of Calais*, Australian Society of the Lacemakers of Calais, Queanbeyan, N.S.W., 1990.

Kelly, M., (ed.), *Nineteenth-century Sydney: essays in urban history*, Sydney University Press in association with the Sydney History Group, Sydney, 1978.

Kelly, M., *Paddock full of houses: Paddington 1840-1890*, Doak Press, Paddington, N.S.W., 1978.

Kelly, M. and Crocker, R., *Sydney takes shape: a collection of contemporary maps from foundation to Federation*, Doak Press in association with the Macleay Museum, University of Sydney, Sydney, 1978.

Kelly, M., (ed.), *Sydney: city of suburbs*, New South Wales University Press in association with the Sydney History Group, Sydney, 1987.

*Kempsey Methodist Church Diamond Jubilee 1864-1924*, Epworth Press, Sydney, 1924. [UCA 287.944.3/KEM.]

Kennedy, B. and Kennedy, B., *Sydney and suburbs: a history and description*, Reed, Frenchs Forest, N.S.W., 1982.

Kenny, T., *The historic villages of Tempe and St Peters: the story of an original land grant of 470 acres made to provost Marshall Thomas Smyth by Governor John Hunter in 1799*, the author, Tempe, N.S.W., 1972. [ML 991.1/82 A1.]

Kerr, J., 'The first corporate investment in Queensland copper', in *Royal Australian Historical Society Journal and Proceedings*, vol.74 part 2, October 1988, pp.139-46.

Kittridge, A., *Cornwall's maritime heritage*, Twelve Heads Press, Truro, 1989.

Kneebone, D., *Fish, tin and copper*, Dyllansow Truran, Redruth, 1983.

Larcombe, F.A., *The history of Botany 1788-1963*, Council of the Municipality of Botany, Botany, N.S.W., 1963.

Lay, P., 'Not what they seemed? Cornish assisted immigrants in New South Wales 1837-1877', in *Cornish Studies Three*, University of Exeter Press, Exeter, 1995.

Leggat, P.O. and Leggat, D.V., *The healing wells: Cornish cults and customs*, Dyllansow Truran, Redruth, 1987.

Lobsey, I., *The Creek: a history of Emmaville and district 1872-1972*, 3rd edition, Emmaville Centenary Celebrations Committee, Emmaville, N.S.W., 1987.

Lowndes, J.G. *James Fletcher, the miners' advocate*, Newcastle history monographs no.10, Council of the City of Newcastle and Newcastle Region Public Library, Newcastle, N.S.W., 1982.

MacAlister, C., *Old pioneering days in the sunny South*, first published 1907, facsimile edition Library of Australian History, North Sydney, N.S.W., 1977.

McBurney, Y., *Road to Byng*, Educational Material Aid, Strathfield, N.S.W., 1982.

McBurney, Y., *Road to Cobar*, Educational Material Aid, Strathfield, N.S.W., 1984.

Mac. Smith, B., (ed.), *Quench not the spirit: merino heritage*, Hawthorn Press, Melbourne, 1972.

Madgwick, R.B., *Immigration into eastern Australia 1788-1851*, first published 1937, Sydney University Press, Sydney, 1969.

*Maitland 1863-1963*, the Council of the City of Maitland and Oswald Ziegler Publications, Sydney, 1963.

Maroney, R., 'Voices from the past', in *Central Western Daily*, 1983-1987.

Maroney, R. and Thompson, H., 'Orange: a history of the district', in *Locality: bulletin of the Community History Program*, University of New South Wales, Sydney, vol.5, no.1, June-July 1991, pp.3-8.

*Marrickville Council: souvenir to commemorate the 50th anniversary of the incorporation of the Municipality of Marrickville, 1861-1911*, McCarron Stewart and Co., Sydney, 1912. [ML Q981,1/M.],

Mawson, R., (ed.), *The Morpeth story 1821-1971: Illalaung, Green Hills, Morpeth: a chronicle of some of the events of Morpeth's story*, Morpeth Progress Association, Morpeth, N.S.W., 1971.

Maxwell, I.S., *The Domesday settlements of Cornwall*, the Cornwall Branch of the Historical Association, Redruth, 1986.

Mildren, J., *Saints of the south west*, Bossiney, Bodmin, 1989.

*Millthorpe Public School 1867-1967*, Committee of the Centenary Celebrations, Millthorpe, N.S.W., 1967. [NLA Np+ 372.99445 M657.]

'Mining', in *The Molong Historian*, vol.3, no.23, Molong Historical Society, Molong, N.S.W., February 1986, pp.91-4.

Morrison, T.A., *Cornwall's central mines: the northern district 1810-1895*, Alison Hodge, Penzance, 1980.

Muggleston, K., *William and Ann Webb: a family history: written for the 150th anniversary celebrations of the arrival of Ann and William in Australia 26.2.1840*, the author, [Tarana, N.S.W. ?], 1990.

Muir, L., *A history of Cooks River*, Cooks River Festival Committee, Belmore, N.S.W., 1978. [NLA Np+ 994.41 M953.]

Neil, M.H., *Valley of the Macleay: the history of Kempsey and the Macleay River district*, Wentworth Books, Sydney, 1972.

Nesbitt, M.K., *James Trevarthen: Cornwall and New South Wales*, the author, Bathurst, N.S.W., 1986. [NLA Npf 929.20994 T812N.]

Nesbitt, M.K., *Millthorpe: days gone by*, the author, Bathurst, N.S.W., 1988. [NLA Npf 994.45 N458.]

Newell, P. and White, U., *New England sketchbook*, Rigby, Adelaide, 1970.

*New South Wales Conference Minutes 1943-45*, Methodist Church of Australasia, Sydney, 1945. [UCA.]

Newton, J.A., *Methodism and the Puritans*, Friends of Dr Williams's Library, eighteenth lecture, Dr William's Trust, London, 1964.

Noall, C., *The story of Cornwall's ports and harbours*, Tor Mark Press, Truro, 1970.

Noall, C., *Tales of the Cornish fishermen*, Tor Mark Press, Truro, 1970.

Noall, C., *Smuggling in Cornwall*, Barton, Truro, 1971.

Noall, C., *Cornish seines and seiners: a history of the pilchard fishing industry*, Barton, Truro, 1972.

Noall, C., *The St Ives mining district*, vol.1, Dyllansow Truran, Redruth, 1982.

Noall, C., *Cornwall's early lifeboats 1803-1939*, Tor Mark Press, Penryn, 1989.

Norman, L.G., *Historical notes on the Glebe*, The Council of the City of Sydney, Sydney, 1960.

Oades, T., (comp.), *Two streams meet: the story of the Uniting Church Parish of Singleton 1835-1985*, Singleton Parish of the Uniting Church, Singleton, N.S.W., 1985. [NLA Np+ 287.93 T974.]

Oates, C.A., *A gathering of the Oates: to celebrate the centenary of 'Rosewick', Millthorpe, N.S.W.*, the author, Millthorpe, N.S.W., 1977. [NLA Np 929.20994 G259.]

*Orange and district illustrated: historical, statistical and descriptive*, first published 1928, facsimile reprint, Orange City Council, Orange, N.S.W., 1989.

Osborne, A., *Millthorpe in its heyday*, Millthorpe Historical Society, Millthorpe, N.S.W., 1989.

Padel, O.J., *A popular dictionary of Cornish place-names*, Alison Hodge, Penzance, 1988.

Palgrave-Moore, P., *Understanding the history and records of Nonconformity*, 2nd edition, Elvery Dowers, Norwich, Norfolk, 1988.

Parkes, W.S., Comerford, J. and Lake, M., *Mines, wines and people: a history of Greater Cessnock,* first published 1979, Council of the City of Greater Cessnock, Cessnock, N.S.W., 1989.

Payton, P.J., *The Cornish miner in Australia: Cousin Jack Down Under*, Dyllansow Truran, Redruth, 1984.

Payton, P.J., *The Cornish farmer in Australia or Australian adventure: Cornish colonists and the expansion of Adelaide and the South Australian agricultural frontier*, Dyllansow Truran, Redruth, 1987.

Payton, P.J., 'Cornish" in *The Australian people: an encyclopaedia of the nation, its people and their origins*, James Jupp, (ed.), Angus and Robertson, North Ryde, N.S.W., 1988.

Payton, P.J., *Cornwall*, Alexander Associates, Fowey, 1996.

Pearse, R., *The land beside the Celtic Sea: aspects of ancient, Medieval and Victorian Cornwall*, Dyllansow Truran, Redruth, [n.d.].

Pemberton, P.A., *Pure merinos and others: the 'shipping lists' of the Australian Agricultural Company*, Australian National University Archives of Business and Labour, Canberra, 1986.

Pickering, E.G., '"An old minute book": New South Wales District Minutes 1839-1845', *Australian Methodist Historical Society Journal*, vol.v, no.14, April 1937, pp.245-57.

Pitt, G.J., 'Wesley Church Chippendale 1844-1904', in *Australian Methodist Historical Society Journal*, July 1934, pp.107-115.

Plummer, J., *Australian mining notes*, 5 vols., 1904-1911. [ML Q338.2/P.]

Probert, J.C., *The sociology of Cornish Methodism*, occasional publication no.8, the Cornish Methodist Historical Association, [Redruth ?], 1964.

Prowse, Irwin, *From Cornwall to the colonies: a Prowse chronicle 1760-1990*, the author, Merimbula, 1992.

Pryor, O., *Cornish pasty:a selection of cartoons*, Rigby, Adelaide, 1976.

Ramsden, E., *Marsden and the missions:prelude to Waitangi*, Angus and Robertson, Sydney, 1936.

Ramsden, E., 'George Hawke of Pendarves: a pioneer of the Cornish Settlement', in *Royal Australian Historical Society Journal and Proceedings*, vol.XXIII 1937, pp.167-182.

Ravensdale, J., *Cornwall*, National Trust Histories, Willow Books, Collins, London, 1984.

Rawe, D., *Cornish villages*, Hale, London, 1978.

Rayner, E.O., 'Copper mining at Cobar', in *Australian Natural History*, No.14, June 1963, pp.188-192. [ML 507/A.]

Rees, T.L., *Historic Camperdown*, F.S. Pacey, Ryde, N.S.W., [n.d.]. [ML 991.1/58A1.]

Reeson, M., *Currency Lass*, 2nd edition, Albatross Books, Sutherland, N.S.W., 1988.

Reynolds, G., *The King's colonials: the story of Blayney and district*, the author, Millthorpe, N.S.W., 1982.

Reynolds P. and Irving R., *Balmain in time: a record of an historic suburb and some its buildings*, the Balmain Association, Balmain, N.S.W., 1971.

Richards, E., Reid, R. and Fitzpatrick, D., *Visible immigrants: neglected sources for the history of Australian immigration*, Department of History and Centre for Immigration and Multicultural Studies, Research School of Social Sciences, Australian National University, Canberra, 1989.

Richards, E., (ed.), *Poor Australian immigrants in the nineteenth century: visible immigrants: two*, Department of Historical Studies and Centre for Immigration and Multicultural Studies, Research School of Social Sciences, Australian National University, Canberra, 1991.

Richards, S., and Muller, P., *Morpeth: a brief history of Australia's oldest river port: where bishops and ships once rode tall*, Kookaburra Educational, Morpeth, N.S.W., 1989.

Ritchie, W. Roy, *Early Adelong and its gold: a tribute to the work of gold pioneers William Williams and William Ritchie in the discovery and development of Adelong's goldfield*, the author, Adelong, N.S.W., c.1987.

Robertson, R. and Gilbert, G., *Some aspects of the domestic archaeology of Cornwall*, special report no. 6., Institute of Cornish Studies and Cornwall Committee for Rescue Archaeology, Redruth, 1979.

Rolls, E., *A million wild acres*, Penguin, Ringwood, Victoria, 1981, reprinted 1985.

Rowe, J., *Cornwall in the age of the Industrial Revolution*, Liverpool University Press, Liverpool, 1953.

Rowe, J., *The hard-rock men: Cornish immigrants and the North American mining frontier*, Liverpool University Press, Liverpool, 1974.

Rowland, E.C., 'The life and times of Henry Dangar', in *Royal Australian Historical Society Journal and Proceedings*, vol.XXXIX, 1953, parts I and II, pp.1-23 and 49-76.

Rowley, C.D., 'Clarence River separatism in 1860: a problem of communications', in *Historical Studies: Australia and New Zealand,* Melbourne University Press, Melbourne, October 1941, pp.225-44. [ML 990.05/1.]

Rowse, A.L., *The Cornish in America,* Macmillan, London, 1969.

Rule, J., *The Cornish Settlement,* the author, Yagoona, N.S.W., 1978.

Rule, J., *The cradle of a nation: the truth about Ophir's gold discovery in 1851,* 2 vols., the author, Yagoona, N.S.W., 1979.

Russell, E., *Woollahra: a history in pictures,* John Ferguson in association with Woollahra Municipal Council, Sydney, 1980.

Rutherford, D.A., *Life and times of John Smith of Gamboola,* Molong and Llanarth, Bathurst 1811-1895, the author, Forster, N.S.W., 1990.

Scarborough, J., 'Early history of compressed-air rock drilling in New South Wales', *Royal Australian Historical Society Journal and Proceedings,* vol.60, June 1974, pp.124-31.

Scott, R., *The West Country's Australian links,* the author, Plymouth, 1988.

Sheridan, R.C., *Early Orange,* Orange and District Historical Society, Orange, N.S.W., 1971.

Sherington, G., *Australia's immigrants 1788-1988,* 2nd edition, Allen and Unwin, Sydney, 1990.

Sloggett, J., 'Locating Newcastle', in *Locality: bulletin of the Community History Program,* vol.3, no.5, University of New south Wales, Sydney, October-November 1989.

Sommerlad, E.C. and St Clair, E., *The Beardies heritage: a history of Glen Innes and district,* Glen Innes Municipal Council, Glen Innes, N.S.W., 1972.

Soulsby, I., *A history of Cornwall,* Phillimore, Chichester, 1986.

Spreadbury, I.D., *Famous men and women of Cornish birth,* Kingston, Mevagissey, 1972.

Stanier, P., *Cornwall's mining heritage,* Twelve Heads Press, Truro, 1988.

Stengelhofen, J., *Cornwall's railway heritage,* Twelve Heads Press, Truro, 1988.

Stevenson, R.L., *Across the plains: with other memories and essays,* Chatto & Windus, London, 1920. [NLA 824.8 S848.]

Swynny, F.R., 'Cornish Settlement', in *Sydney Morning Herald,* 14 October 1933, p.8, c.5.

Symonds, J.L., *Which Francis Symonds? Cornish oak or Australian eucalypt?* the author, Cronulla, 1993.

Tapp, E.J., ''he colonial origins of the New England New State movement', in *Royal Australian Historical Society Journal and Proceedings,* vol.49, part 3, November 1963, pp.205-21.

Tarrant, M., *Cornwall's lighthouse heritage,* Twelve Heads Press, Truro, 1990.

Taylor, M., 'House of Commons debate on the tin mines, 6th March 1991', in *An Baner Kernewek: the Cornish Banner,* no.64, May 1991, pp.6-9.

Thomas, B.W., *The Thomas family of Guyong 1849-1929: William Thomas (1805-1881) and the Thomas family of Guyong N.S.W.,* the author, Wahroonga, N.S.W., 1974.

Thomas, C., *Methodism and self-improvement in nineteenth century Cornwall,* occasional publication no.9, The Cornish Methodist Historical Society, [Redruth ?], 1965.

Thomas, C., *The importance of being Cornish,* University of Exeter, Exeter, 1973. [NLA p914.2370385 T455.]

Thomas, C., *The importance of being Cornish in Cornwall: an inaugural lecture delivered at Cornwall Technical College on April 10th, 1973,* Institute of Cornish Studies, Redruth, 1973. [NLA p309.14237085 T455.]

Thomas, C., *Celtic Britain,* Thames and Hudson, London, 1986.

Thorne, L.G., *North Shore, Sydney from 1788 to today,* L. Jillett, (ed.), Angus and Robertson, Sydney, 1968.

Thornton, R. and Sommerville, A.W., *Municipality of Balmain: retrospect,* J.B. Waldgrave, Balmain, N.S.W., 1935. [ML 991.1/T.]

Todd, A.C., *The Cornish miner in America: the contribution to the mining history of the United States by emigrant Cornish miners - the men called Cousin Jacks,* Barton, Truro, 1967.

Todd, A.C., *The search for silver: Cornish miners in Mexico 1824-1927,* Lodenek, Padstow, 1977.

Toole, K.F., *The annals of Burraga,* Burraga Public School, Burraga, N.S.W., 1982. [NLA Nq+ 372.99445 T671.]

*A town to be laid out: Maitland 1829-1979,* Maitland and District Historical Society, Maitland, N.S.W., 1979.

*Tumut Centenary Celebrations souvenir 1824-1924,* first published 1924, republished by Tumut Shire Bicentennial Committee and the Tumut Shire Council, Tumut, N.S.W., 1986.

Turner, J.W., *James and Alexander Brown 1843-1877,* Newcastle history monographs no.4, Newcastle Region Public Library in association with Newcastle and District Historical Society, Newcastle, N.S.W., 1968.

Turner, J.W., *Manufacturing in Newcastle 1801-1901,* Newcastle history monographs no.8, Newcastle Region Public Library, Newcastle, N.S.W., 1980.

Turner, J.W., *Coal mining in Newcastle 1801-1900,* Newcastle history monographs no.9, Newcastle Region Public Library, Newcastle, N.S.W., 1982.

Turner, J.W., (comp.), *Who was who in the Hunter Valley towns in 1888,* Hunter History Publications, Newcastle, N.S.W., 1984.

Turner, J. and Sullivan, J., *From Nobby's to Paterson: photos of old Newcastle,* Hunter History Consultants, Newcastle, N.S.W., 1987.

Upjohn, J., *They came to Thunderbolt country,* University of New England history series no.6, University of New England, Armidale, N.S.W., 1988.

Van Wienen, A., *History of Aberdeen N.S.W.,* part 2, the author, Aberdeen, N.S.W., 1987.

Van Wienen, A., *History of Aberdeen N.S.W.,* part 3, the author, Aberdeen, N.S.W., 1988.

Vine, G., *A branch of the vine: William Henry Vine 1851-1934: Helston, Cornwall to Boggabri NSW,* the author, Blacktown, 1998.

Wakelin, M.F., *Language and history in Cornwall,* Leicester University Press, Leicester, 1975.

Walker, R.B., 'New England tin 1871-1900', in *Royal Australian Historical Society Journal and Proceedings*, vol.50, part 5, November 1964, pp.395-410.

Walker, R.B., *Old New England: a history of the northern tablelands of New South Wales 1818-1900*, Sydney University Press, Sydney, 1966.

Watson, J.H., *Newspaper cuttings*, [ML Q991.1/W].

Watson, J.H., 'Kempsey: early settlement of the Macleay River', in *Royal Australian Historical Society Journal and Proceedings*, vol.VII, 1921, part 4, pp.199-212.

Wearne-Frost, V., *Wearne of Cornwall and Australia*, the author, Blackheath, N.S.W., 1981.

Webb, J. and Pile, S., *Bathurst sketchbook*, Rigby, Adelaide, 1975.

Webb, W.H., *The life of the late William Tom, Senr.*, A.K. Murray, Paddington, N.S.W., 1922. [Bathurst District Historical Society.]

Weingarth, J., 'The discovery and settlement of the Macleay River', in *Royal Australian Historical Society Journal and Proceedings*, vol.VII, 1921, pp.175-98.

Whitaker, R., *Sydneyside*, Gregory's, North Ryde, N.S.W., 1986.

Whitby, K. and Clancy, E.G., (eds.), *Great the heritage: the story of Methodism in N.S.W.: 1812-1975*, N.S.W. Methodist Conference, Sydney, 1975.

White, G.S., (comp.), *Back to Bathurst Week: official souvenir containing the history and progress of Bathurst and district 1813-1923*, Direct Publicity Co., for the Committee of the Back to Bathurst Week, Sydney, 1924. [NLA Np 994.45 WHI.]

White, G. Pawley, (comp.), *A handbook of Cornish surnames*, 2nd edition, Dyllansow Truran, Redruth, 1981.

Whitelaw, E., *A history of Singleton*, [Singleton Historical Society?], Singleton, N.S.W., [n.d.].

Whiteley, J.H., *Wesley's England: a survey of XVIIIth century social and cultural conditions*, Epworth Press, London, 1938, reprinted 1943.

Wiedemann, E., *World of its own: Inverell's early years 1827-1920*, Devill Publicity, Inverell, N.S.W., 1981.

Wilkinson, I., *Forgotten country: the story of the Upper Clarence goldfields*, the author, Lismore, N.S.W., 1980.

Williams, A., *Nankivell-a family affair*, the author, Miram Victoria, 1990.

Williams, D., *Festivals of Cornwall*, Bossiney, Bodmin, 1987.

Williams, H.V., *Cornwall's old mines*, Tor Mark Press, Truro, [n.d.].

Wilson, J.G., *Official history of the Municipal Jubilee of Bathurst 1812-1912*, [no publisher], Sydney, 1913. [ML Q991.6/W.]

Woodfin, R.J., *The Cornwall Railway to its centenary in 1959*, first published 1960, Barton, Truro, 1972.

Wyatt, R.T., *The history of Goulburn*, first published 1941, Landsowne Press, Sydney, 1972.

## C.) NEWSPAPERS AND PERIODICALS

*An Baner Kernewek: the Cornish Banner*, CNP Publications, St Austell.

*Australian Methodist Historical Society Journal*, Sydney.

*Australian Town and Country Journal*, Sydney.

*Bathurst Times*, Bathurst.

*Central Western Daily*, Orange.

*Church Heritage: Journal of the Church Records and Historical Society* (Uniting Church in Australia-N.S.W. Synod), Sydney.

*Cornish World*, Redruth.

*Goulburn Evening Post*, Goulburn.

*Journal of Hunter Valley History*, Hunter Valley Publications, Newcastle.

Journal of the Royal Institution of Cornwall, Truro.

*Locality: Bulletin of the Community History Program*, School of History, University of New South Wales, Sydney.

*The Molong Historian*, Molong Historical Society, Molong.

*Newcastle Morning Herald*, Newcastle, N.S.W.

*Royal Australian Historical Society Journal and Proceedings*, Sydney. [NLA 7DU 80.R62.]

*Singleton Argus*, Singleton.

*Sydney Morning Herald*, Sydney.

## D.) THESES

Burke, G.M., 'The Cornish miner and the Cornish mining industry 1870-1921', PhD., University of London, 1981.

Colman, A., 'Colonial Cornish: Cornish immigrants in Victoria, 1865-1880', M.A., University of Melbourne, 1985.

Crowley, F.K., 'British migration to Australia 1860-1914', D.Phil., Oxford, 1951.

Lay, P., 'Clotted cream and chapel: the Mullis family in Cornwall and New South Wales', Dip. FHS., Society of Australian Genealogists, Sydney, 1988.

McEwen, E., 'The Newcastle coalmining district of New South Wales, 1860-1900', PhD., University of Sydney, 1979.

Payton, P.J., 'The Cornish in South Australia: their influence and experience from immigration to assimilation 1836-1936', PhD., University of Adelaide, 1978.

Sloggett, J.M., 'Temperance and class: with particular reference to Newcastle and the South Maitland Coalfields, 1860-1928', M.A., University of Newcastle, 1989.

Tibbs, P., 'Illawarra Methodism in the nineteenth century: a comparative study of Wesleyan and Primitive Methodism in Wollongong, 1838-1902', B.A. (Hons.), University of Wollongong, 1981.

# III. FAMILY INFORMATION

## FAMILY NAMES and INFORMANTS

| | |
|---|---|
| Amy | Mrs Valma Murray. |
| Avery | Mrs Beryl Mason. |
| Ball | Mr Reg Ball. |
| Barfett | The Venerable T. Barfett. |
| Barrett | Mr Selwyn Hawken, Mrs Juanita Carroll. |
| Barton | S. Barton. |
| Bassett | Ms Marianne Eastgate. |
| Bawden | Miss Margaret Playford, Mrs Lesley Evans. |
| Baynard | Mr R.E. Nelder. |
| Bear | Mr Albert Bear. |
| Bellman | Mr David Hall. |
| Berriman | Mr Trevor Pascoe, Mrs Estelle Neilson. |
| Berryman | Mrs E. Pugsley. |
| Blamey | Mrs Marjorie Jesse. |
| Blewett | Mrs Helen Belcher. |
| Boase | Sally Shine. |
| Bosanko | Mrs Eveline Madden. |
| Boulden | Mrs Margaret Bauer. |
| Brabyn | Mrs Betty McGrath. |
| Bradley | Mr David Rutherford. |
| Bray | Ms Deidre Underwood, Mrs Chris Wright. |
| Bryant | Mrs R. Ambascheer, Mr Selwyn Hawken, Miss B. Bryant. |
| Bullock | Mrs Pauline Hartman. |
| Bulmore | Ms Marianne Eastgate. |
| Bunt | Mrs Vi Rose, C.L. Greig, Mrs Joy Hadfield. |
| Burnett | Mrs Peggy Richards, Mrs Shirley Richards. |
| Butson | The Rev John Butson. |
| Buttle | Mrs Roma Blackhall. |
| Button | Mr Philip Button. |
| Caddy | Mrs Dianne Minnican, Mrs Beth Robertson. |
| Cannon | Mrs Margaret Cannington. |
| Carbis | Mr Graham Gape. |
| Cardell | Ms Marianne Eastgate. |
| Carveth | Mr Daryl Lightfoot, Mrs J. Harvey. |
| Cavill | Mr Daryl Lightfoot, Mrs J. Harvey. |
| Chegwidden | Mr Rex Chegwidden, Mrs Phyllis Trevena. |
| Christian | Ms M. Eastgate. |
| Clarke | Mrs Loraine Cosgrove. |
| Clymo | Mr Steve Bartlett. |
| Coad | Mrs Heather Paul, Mr Allan Richards, Mr Peter Procter. |
| Cock | Mrs Phyllis Hohnen, Mr Grahame Thom, Mrs Gwen Griffin. |
| Colley | Mrs Sally Colley. |
| Collins | Mrs S.L. Adams. |
| Cooke | Mr W. Georgans. |
| Cornish | Mr A.T. Thomas, Ms. B. Cornish. |
| Couch | Mr David Rutherford. |
| Crago | Mrs Lesley Evans. Mr Richard Crago. Mrs Dot Clayworth. |
| Crapp | Mrs Pamela Sheldon. |
| Crispin | Mr Graham Gape. |
| Cronin | Miss Margaret Playford. Mrs Lesley Evans. |
| Crothers | Mrs Beryl McCooey, Mrs Jenny Evans. |
| Cundy | Sr Juliana Googe Mrs Enid Farnham. |
| Curgenven | Mrs Helen Boulden. |
| Dale | Mr Peter Hohnen. Mr Selwyn Hawken. |
| Dangar | Mr Peter Dangar, Mrs Nancy Gray, C.A. Cunningham. |
| Dawe | Mrs Ann Hodgens, Mrs Joan Dawe. |
| Deacon | Mrs Pat Stemp. |

| | |
|---|---|
| Dennis | Mr Bob Hay. |
| Doble | Ms Anne Carolan. |
| Dunstan | Mrs Joan Brown. |
| Dyer | Mrs Dorothy Fellowes. |
| Eade | Mrs Pat Eade. Mrs Marion Thompson. |
| Ellery | Mr Robert Sutton. |
| Eslick | Mrs Roma Blackhall. |
| Eva | Mrs Thelma Chippendale. |
| Evans | Mr A.J. Brown, Mrs Ann Hodgens, Mrs Jean Smith |
| Eveleigh | U.K. Eveleigh, E. Eveleigh, Mrs V. Eveleigh. |
| Frethey | Mr John Wilson. |
| Gale | Mrs Catherine Tizzard, Mrs Val Smith. |
| Geake | Mrs Jenny King, Mrs Beryl Pearse. |
| Gendall | Mr Bill Gendall. |
| Glasson | Mrs Helen Sullivan, Mr B.W. Thomas. |
| Goard | Mr Paul Goard. |
| Googe | Sr Juliana Googe, Mrs Enid Farnham. |
| Green | Mrs Pat McCormack. |
| Gribble | Mrs N. Trembath. |
| Grills | Mrs Joan Grills. |
| Grose | Ms Dorothy Heber. |
| Guard | Mrs Enid Wheeler. Mrs Pamela Sheldon. |
| Hambly | Mr H. Hambly, Miss Nell and Miss Grace Tremain, Mrs Beryl McCooey. |
| Hare | Mrs Carolyn Dunne. |
| Harris | Mr David Rutherford. |
| Harvey | Mrs Jean Saunders. Mrs Netta Stoneman, Bathurst, Mrs V. Harvey. |
| Hawke | Mr Will Hawke, Mrs Dot Clayworth, Mrs Allison Appleton. |
| Hawken | Mr Selwyn Hawken, Mrs Dorothy Heber, Mr Robert Jeremy, Mrs A. Lucas-Sullivan. |
| Hawkey | Mrs Dot Clayworth. |
| Hawkins | Ms Ann Shaunessy. |
| Hicks | Mrs J. Carter-Smith. |
| Hill | Mrs Thelma Weston. |
| Hocking | Mr Trevor Pascoe, Mrs Alison Stephen, Mr N. Hocking. |
| Hodge | Mrs Barbara Porteils. |
| Homan | Mrs Beth Williams. |
| Hosking | Mr Warwick Adams. |
| Jacka | Mrs Kathy Wills. Mrs Betty McLennan. |
| James | Mrs Lorna James, Mrs Mary Nesbitt, Mrs Lorna Spackman. |
| Jasper | Mr Stuart Batson. |
| Jeffery | Mrs Marie Lute. |
| Jeffree | Mr Harold Jeffree, Mrs Marlene Reed. |
| Jenkin | Mr Kevin Pollard. |
| Johns | Mrs Sharon Apthorpe. |
| Job | Mrs Jenny King. |
| Jonas | Mrs Jill Wilson. |
| Jory | Mr Victor Jory. |
| Jose | Mr Stuart Batson. |
| Juleff | Mrs Jean Juleff Roy. |
| Kendall | Mrs Peggy Richards. |
| Kerkin | Mr Norman Kerkin. |
| Kernick | Mrs Lorna Spackman. |
| Kissell/Kestall | Mrs Marnie Poulton. |
| Knight | Mr Ronald Knight, Mrs Bonnie Churchill. |
| Lane | M.H. McLelland, Ms Deidre Underwood, Mr Peter Hohnen, Mr Alan Lane, Mrs H.M. Lane. |
| Langsford | Mrs Peggy Richards, Dr D.H. Kirkham. |
| Lean | Mr David Lean Mrs Rosalie Hunter. |
| Leathan | Mr Kevin Pollard. |
| Lethlean | Mrs Jean Gibson. |
| Lightfoot | Mr Collin Brewer, Mr Daryl Lightfoot. |
| Lintern | Mrs Sue Lamrock. |
| Lobb | Major D.H.V. Lobb. |
| Lord | Mrs E.J. Lord. |
| Luxton | Mr David Rutherford. |
| Marshall | Mrs Gwen King. |

| | |
|---|---|
| **Martin** | Mrs D. Shuker, Mr Murray Martin, Mrs Heather Waddington, Mrs Marian Sullivan, Miss Jodi Goman. |
| **Michell** | Mrs Beryl Michell, Mrs Pat Ruffels. |
| **Mitchell** | Mrs Mary Devonshire Mrs Lyn Lyon. |
| **Morcom** | Mrs Doris Black. |
| **Mullis** | Mrs. B. McCooey, Mrs Loraine Cosgrove. |
| **Murrish** | Mrs Diana Crumpler. |
| **Mutton** | Mrs Netta Stoneman, Mrs Thelma Freeman, Mrs Joan Lynch, Mrs Joan Edgar. |
| **Nancarrow** | Mr Barry Nancarrow, Mrs Margaret Fisher, Mr Ian Nancarrow. |
| **Nankivell** | Mr James Nankivell. |
| **Nicholas** | Mrs Robyn Singh, Mr B.J. Ridge. |
| **Nicholls** | Mrs Merle Robinson, Mrs Pam Body, Mr Mark Gordon, Mrs Mary Thom. |
| **Noble** | Mrs Merle Bedwell, Mrs Dulcie Davies. |
| **Northcott** | Mrs Ann Hodgens. |
| **Northey** | Mr Robert Hay, Ms Maxine Gray, Mrs Val Swailes, Mrs Marjorie Jesse. |
| **Oates** | Mrs C.A. Oates, Mr B.W. Thomas, Mrs Phyllis Hohnen, Mrs Merna Kidgell. |
| **Odgers** | Mrs D. Martino. |
| **Osborne** | H.D. Osborne. |
| **Page** | Mr F. Page. |
| **Pankhurst** | Mrs Milred Pankhurst. |
| **Parker** | Mr Grahame Thom. |
| **Parkin** | Mrs Gwen Griffin. |
| **Pascoe** | Mr Trevor Pascoe, Mrs Linda Shepherd, Mr Leslie Thurling Mrs Pamala Tancred, Mr Jim Williams. |
| **Paul** | Mrs Heather Paul, Mr Allan Richards, Mr Peter Procter. |
| **Paull** | Mrs Eunice Traise. |
| **Pearce** | Mrs Maidee Smith, Mrs Jean Wright. |
| **Pearn** | Mrs Ann Hodgens. |
| **Penhall** | Mr Trevor Pascoe, Mrs Pam Body. |
| **Penney** | Mr Vic Wilkinson. |
| **Pinch** | Mrs Valda Pinch. |
| **Plummer** | Mrs Pat Sheriff. |
| **Poyner** | Mr Robert Sutton. |
| **Prisk** | Mrs Gwen Griffin, Mrs Anne Massey, Mrs Joy Prisk. |
| **Prowse** | Mr Irwin Prowse, Mr Ken Prowse,Mrs Pam Archer. |
| **Pryor** | Mrs Joan Brown. |
| **Rapson** | Mr Ronald Rapson. |
| **Reed** | L.B. Galbraith, Mrs Joan Northey. |
| **Richards** | Mr Kingsley Richards, Mrs Peggy Richards, Mrs Shirley Richards, Mrs Topsy Motton. |
| **Roberts** | Mrs Chris Wright, Mr Robert Sutton, H. Beckerley. |
| **Rogers** | V.L. Nicholson. |
| **Rowe** | Mr Dennis Rowe, Mrs L. Meeth, Mrs Marjorie Jesse, Mrs Pamela Sheldon. |
| **Ruddock** | M. Batley. |
| **Sandry/Saundry** | Mr Vic Wilkinson, Mrs Lorna Stephens. |
| **Sara** | Mrs Marnie Poulton. |
| **Searle** | Mrs C. Dunne. |
| **Sellwood** | Mrs Phyllis Trevena, Mr A. Selwood. |
| **Short** | Mr David Short, Mrs Bonnie Bush, Mrs Joan Edgar, Miss Grace Short, Mr B.W. Thomas. |
| **Sleeman** | Mr Oliver Sleeman. |
| **Sloggett** | Miss Jennifer Sloggett, Mrs P. Garnsey. |
| **Smith** | Mrs Phyllis Hohnen, Mr B.W. Thomas, Mrs Helen Sullivan, Mr David Rutherford. |
| **Snow** | Mr John Redman. |
| **Soper** | Mr Trevor Pascoe. |
| **Stanway** | Mrs Helen Dyson. |
| **Steer** | Mrs Judy Redden, Mrs H. Preston, Mrs Gail McQueen. |
| **Stephens** | Mrs Beryl McCooey, Mrs Phyllis Hohnen, Mrs Pat Nagle, Mrs Janice Thompson. |
| **Stick** | Mrs Jean Davies. |
| **Stocks** | Mrs E. Boyd. |
| **Stoneman** | Mrs Netta Stoneman. |
| **Sutton** | Mrs Merle Bedwell, Mrs Dulcie Davies. |
| **Sweetnam** | Mr B.W. Thomas. |
| **Taylor** | Ms Margaret Watts, Mrs Netta Stoneman, Mrs Aileen Roberson. |
| **Thomas** | Mr B.W. Thomas, Mr A.T. Thomas, Ms Juanita Carroll. |
| **Tippett** | Mrs Edna Townsend, Ms Juanita Carroll, Mrs Thelma Weston. |

| | |
|---|---|
| **Tom** | Mr Peter Hohnen, Mr Trevor Pascoe, Ms Deidre Underwood, Mrs P. Ruffels. |
| **Tonkin** | Mrs E. Pugsley. |
| **Towzey** | Mr Robert Jeremy. |
| **Travis** | Mr A.T. Thomas. |
| **Tredinnick** | Miss Margaret Playford, Mrs Elaine Bennett. |
| **Tremain** | Mrs Betty Bridges, Miss Grace and Miss Nell Tremain, Ms Carol Foster, Mrs Heather Green, Mrs Joyce Watt, Mrs Phyllis Hohnen, Mrs B. McCooey. |
| **Trembath** | Mrs Chris Wright, Mrs Narelle Trembath. |
| **Trenemon** | Mrs Marjorie Jesse. |
| **Treseder** | Mrs Mavis James, Mrs Doris Black, Mr and Mrs Paul Treseder. |
| **Tresidder** | Mrs Doris Black, Mr Russ Bell. |
| **Trestrail** | Mr Link Van Ummerson. |
| **Trewren** | Mr Garry Howard. |
| **Trevarthen** | Mrs Mary Nesbitt, Mrs N. Kingham. |
| **Trevaskis** | Dr K.G. Pont, Mrs Evelyn Conlin, Mrs A.V. Trevaskis. |
| **Trevena** | Miss Grace Short, Mrs Phyllis Trevena. |
| **Trevethan** | Mr Laurence Turtle, Mr Albie Willett. |
| **Trezise** | Mrs Jenni Trezise, Mrs B. McCooey. |
| **Trudgeon** | Mrs Olive Trudgeon, Mrs Helen Trudgian, Mr T.P.F. Trudgian. |
| **Verran** | Mrs Margaret Verran. |
| **Vine** | Mr George Vine. |
| **Walkom** | Mrs Liz Ayscough, Mr Harold Frape. |
| **Wearne** | Mrs V. Wearne-Frost. |
| **Weary** | Mrs Aileen Fisher. |
| **Webb** | Mrs Jenny King, Ms Deidre Underwood, Mrs Thelma Freeman. |
| **Williams** | Mrs Margaret Cannington, Mr Trevor Pascoe, Mr G.W.F. Williams, Mr A.T. Thomas, Mrs Helen Belcher, Mrs Jean Gibson, Miss Mearal Porter, Mrs Merle Walker, Mrs Rhonda Shallala, Mrs Joan Carty. |
| **Wills** | Miss Grace Thrush. |
| **Winsor** | Mrs Gwen Griffin. |
| **Woolcock** | Miss M. Playford, Mrs Lesley Evans. |
| **Worgan** | Mrs Thelma Freeman. |
| **Young** | Miss M. Playford. |

# INDEX